Our Children Live in a War Zone

Use the Power of Resilience to Improve Their Lives

Applied Positive Psychology 2.1

Also by ♥ Dr. Jeanine Joy

"*Trusting One's Emotional Guidance Builds Resilience*", Perspectives on Coping and Resilience. Ed. Venkat Pulla, Shane Warren, and Andrew Shatté. Laxmi Nagar: Authors Press, 2013. 254-279

True Prevention—Optimum Health: Remember Galileo

Prevent Suicide: The Smart Way

Is Punishment Ethical? The Fallacy of Good and Evil

Empowered Employees are Engaged Employees: Using Science to Solve the Employee Engagement Crisis, The Smart Way to Manage Emotions, Core Self-Evaluations, and Increase Psychological Flexibility, Emotional Intelligence, Motivation, Happiness, and Employee Engagement

More Books Coming Soon by ♥ Dr. Jeanine Joy

*Become **More** Resilient: The Smart Way*

Diversity Appreciation: A Leap beyond Tolerance To Joyful Inclusion: Using Science to Transform the Paradigm

BLOOM: Your Keys to Happiness

Emotional Agility: The Smarter Way

Success: The Smart Way

Thrive More Now Publishing

Our Children Live in a War Zone
Using the Power of Resilience to Improve Their Lives
Applied Positive Psychology 2.1

1ˢᵗ Edition

A Thrive More Now Book / 2016

Published by
Thrive More, Now Publishing
Charlotte, North Carolina

All rights reserved
Copyright © 2015-2016 Jeanine Joy

All rights reserved, including the right to reproduce this book or portions thereof in any form whatsoever. For information address: Thrive More Now Publishing, Rights Department, P.O. Box 6888, Concord NC 28078

For information about special discounts for bulk purchases, speaking engagements, training, or certification programs please contact Thrive More Now Publishing.

ISBN-13: 978-0692491416
ISBN-10: 0692491414

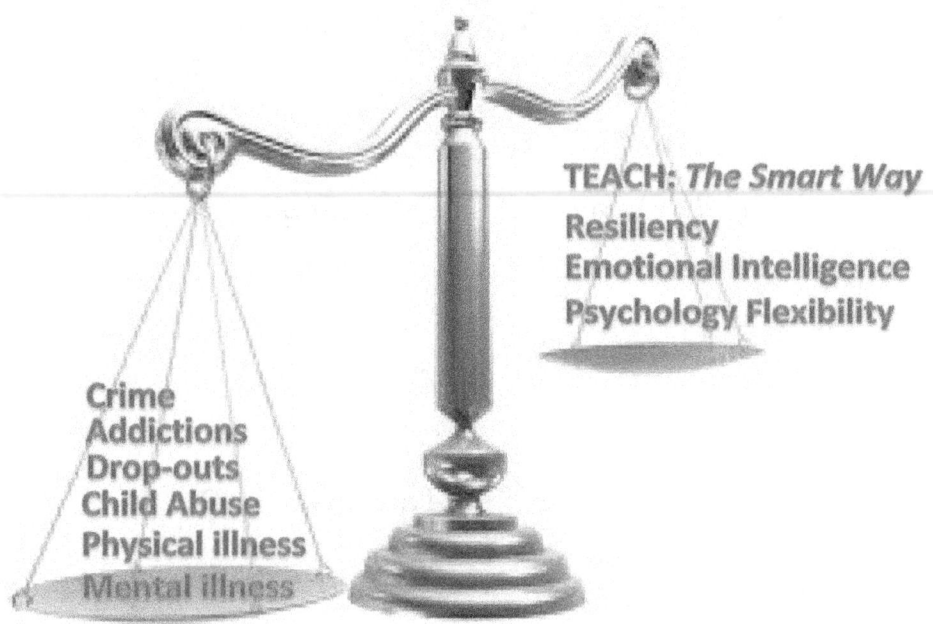

"The most important strength that the majority of people in society need to build is the capacity to self-regulate their emotions, attitudes, and behaviors."
Rollin McCraty, PhD, and Maria Zayas, EdD, The HeartMath Research Center[1]

Stress inoculation is a form of immunity against later stressors, much in the same way that vaccines induce immunity against disease.[2]

All of us need to begin to think in terms of our own inner strengths, our resilience and resourcefulness, our capacity to adapt and to rely upon ourselves and our families.
Steven Pressfield

In order to succeed, people need a sense of self-efficacy, to struggle together with resilience to meet the inevitable obstacles and inequities of life.
Albert Bandura

When we tackle obstacles, we find hidden reserves of courage and resilience we did not know we had. And it is only when we are faced with failure do we realise that these resources were always there within us. We only need to find them and move on with our lives.
A. P. J. Abdul Kalam

A good school teaches you resilience - that ability to bounce back.
Kate Reardon

It's one thing to show your love for someone when everything is going fine and life is smooth. But when the 'in sickness and in health' part kicks in and sickness does enter your lives, you're tested. Your resilience is tested.
Patti Davis

Entrepreneurship isn't for everyone, and not everyone is going to be an entrepreneur, but women who turn to business, turn to economics, because there are people depending on them, I think that their creativity, their resilience, their spirit, embody what's best about entrepreneurship.
Gayle Tzemach Lemmon

I am extremely interested in how people negotiate catastrophe, not because I'm morbidly interested in it but because I'm interested in the secret of resilience; that's what I'm always exploring in the stories and the novels.
Janette Turner Hospital, Australia

While positive mental states may be associated with less stress and more resilience to infection, positive well-being might also be accompanied by a healthy lifestyle.
Michael Greger, M.D.

Every quarterback can throw a ball; every running back can run; every receiver is fast; but that mental toughness that you talk about translates into competitiveness.
Tom Brady

Develop resilience and be brave. There are days when it is very discouraging. You have to develop personal resilience to environmental things that come along. If you let every single environmental challenge knock you off your game, it's going to be very, very hard.
Renee James

Military brats have this toughness: they're almost like orphans or foster children; they develop little mechanisms. It sets you up to look at things a little differently.
Padgett Powell

Above everything else I've done, I've always said I've had more guts than I've got talent.
Dolly Parton

The attempt to prevent our kids from struggling for fear it might scar their permanent records is, instead, scarring them for life.
Heather Choate Davis

The world breaks everyone, and afterward, some are strong at the broken places.
Ernest Hemingway

When we learn how to become resilient, we learn how to embrace the beautifully broad spectrum of the human experience.
Jaeda Dewalt

Dedication

To the millions represented by the sad stories that motivated me to write this book and to my husband for his faith in me.

Acknowledgements

Appreciation is a wonderful thing: It makes what is excellent in others belong to us as well.
Voltaire

I have far more than most to appreciate. First, I acknowledge my husband for his willingness and patience in supporting the time and effort I've devoted to acquiring this knowledge and pursuing credentials that demonstrate the level of my knowledge and of course, my appreciation of his unconditional love and of the love I feel for him..

I must also acknowledge those whose behavior toward me was less than desired for building my desire to understand the connection between behavior and emotional state. I gained valuable insights from each of them, for which I am grateful. I've gained just as many insights, of a different sort, from the daughters I've been blessed with—not because their behavior has been bad—but because they are so different from one another and from me. They helped me understand the uniqueness of all, which helped me become a person who deeply appreciates differences and sees the value of them.

I am truly blessed by a life that is perfect…and which keeps getting better.

Table of Contents
Contents

Our Children Live in a War Zone i

Copyright v

Dedication viii

Acknowledgements ix

Table of Contents xi

Forward 1

Part I – With a Broad Brush 6

Introduction and Overview 7

    The story begins with stress. 8

1: Everything is Connected 11

2: One Root Cause 21

3: The Smart Way 35

    Anxiety 40

    Depression 40

    Panic Disorders 41

    Bi-polar disorders 41

    Crime Reduction 41

    Improved High School Graduation Rates 41

    Treatment of and Reduction in Physical Pain 41

    Educational Success 41

    Bullying (Recovery from) 41

    Bullying Prevention 42

    Violence Reduction 42

    Prevent relapse of Mood Disorders 42

    Substance Use Disorders 42

    Smoking Cessation 42

    Problematic Gambling 42

    Schizophrenia and Other Psychotic Disorders 42

    Phobias 43

    Obsessive Compulsive Disorder (OCD) 43

    Posttraumatic Stress Disorder (PTSD) 43

Body dysmorphic disorder (BDD) 43

Hypochondria 43

Eating Disorders 43

Insomnia 43

Hypertension 43

Coronary Heart Disease (CHD) 44

Personality Disorders 44

Anger and Aggression 44

General Stress 44

Teacher (Trainee) Stress Levels 44

Type II Diabetes 44

Disease Management 44

Early Stage Breast Cancer 44

Distress Due to General Medical Conditions 44

Irritable Bowel Syndrome 45

Chronic Fatigue Syndrome 45

Rheumatoid Arthritis 45

Premenstrual Syndrome 45

4: Cognitive Behavioral Therapy vs. *The Smart Way* 47

5: Overview of Relationships: Happiness, Stress, Health, and Behavior 53

    Happiness - What is it? 54

    Why Happiness is Important 54

Part II: Core Knowledge 65

Self-Test 67

6: Perception 69

7: What We Cannot Yet Explain 77

8: Introduction to Emotional Guidance 91

9: Emotional Guidance Sensory Feedback System (EGS) 107

10: Personality 127

11: Filtered Consciousness 131

12: Beliefs and Expectations 143

    Influence of Expectation 150

13: Emotional Stance, and Focus 155

    Focus 162

14: Coherent Thought .... **Error! Bookmark not defined.**

Exercise	Error! Bookmark not defined.
15: Happiness Defined	177
Positivity	182
The Power of Hope	185
16: Permission to Self	189
Happiness Contracts	190
False Premises about Happiness	190
Bipolar Disorder	192
Freedom and Personal Liberty	193
Part III – Solvable Problems	195
17: Honoring our Father and Mother	197
18: Human Needs	199
19: Resilience	207
Resilience and Hope	213
Stress Inoculation	215
Internal Locus of Control	216
Optimism	216
Healthy Self-esteem	216
Meaning	217
Resilience Questionnaire	218
20: Crime Prevention	221
21: Poverty	235
Income Inequality	238
Homeless Populations	239
Hand-outs	240
Abundance	240
22: Overall Health	245
Disparate Impact	247
Early warning signs of stress	250
Exposure to Violence	252
Physical Health Contagious Stress	252
Diabetes	254
Obesity	255

- Pain 256
- Skin Disorders 256
  - Psoriasis 256
- Intersection: Physical and Mental Health 257
- 23: Mental Health 259
  - *Emotion Regulation Strategies* 260
  - *Stigma* 260
  - Depression 261
  - Suicide 264
  - Anxiety 264
  - Self-Esteem 265
  - Oppositional Defiant Disorder (ODD) 265
  - Perfectionism 265
  - Postpartum Depression 266
  - Trigger Warnings 266
- 24: Discrimination 267
  - Racism, Sexism and other isms 267
  - Microaggressions 275
  - Choices about microaggressions 277
  - A Given about microaggressions 278
  - Why it's important 279
- 25: Behavioral Health 287
  - Self-Control 288
  - At work: 290
  - At home: 290
  - While driving: 291
  - In Marriage: 291
  - Addictions 292
  - Alcohol, Drugs and Other Common Addictions 292
  - Eating disorders 293
  - Smoking 293
- 26: Violence 295
- 27: Victimization 299

Measures of Success 303

- 28: Relationship Success 305

Perception vs. Reality 306

Home 306

Dating 308

Rumination and Co-Rumination 308

Community 308

29: Educational Success 311

Why Mindset Should be a part of the Core Curriculum 313

Self-efficacy Beliefs 314

Positive Education 314

Contagious Stress 314

Fixed vs. Growth Mindset 315

Emotional Intelligence and Education 316

Appropriate Discipline 317

Labels 318

High School Dropout Rates 318

College 319

Degree Creep 321

30: Career Success 323

Unemployment 325

Employee Engagement 325

31: Parenting 327

Childhood abuse 333

When your child comes out 334

Transitions out of Foster Care 334

10 Things Your Child Must Know to Stay out of Jail 334

Myth: The Absent Black Father 335

32: World Peace 337

Part 4 – Toolkit 341

33 : Processes (How to Think Positive) 343

How to Think Positive (Root Cause Stress Relief) 344

Follow Your Guidance 347

Subtle Differences 354

Shift Your Focus 359

- Focus Shift—The List ... 362
- Make Happiness a Priority ... 363
- Deliberately Choose Happy Thoughts ... 363
- Positive Affirmations ... 365
- Think Positive ... 368
- Decisions ... 369
- Refute ... 370
- Setting Intentions ... 371
- Forgiving ... 372
- Mirror Work ... 379
- Changing the Past ... 379
- Specifically Negative to Generally Negative Shift ... 380
- See the Potential in Others and in Self ... 382
- Go General ... 384
- General to Specific Exercise ... 385
- Appreciation (not gratitude) ... 386
- Amplify Positive Emotions ... 391
- Find Joy ... 391
- Consider your Resources ... 391
- End Self-criticism ... 392
  - Being kind to yourself matters. Do it. ... 394
- Focus on Your Why ... 395
- Reframe Failure ... 396
- Improve Self-Esteem ... 398
- Find the Humor in Your Situation ... 401
- Beat Depression ... 401
- Use Role Models ... 404

34 : Betwixt and Between Processes and Techniques ... 407
- Massage Therapy ... 407
- Yoga ... 408
- Tai Chi ... 408
- Aromatherapy ... 408
- Energy Healing ... 408
- Relax ... 409
- Meditation ... 409

Traditional Therapy 409

Self-hypnosis 410

Bio-feedback 410

Optimism Exercise 410

Neuro Linguistic Programming (NLP) 411

Emotional Disclosure 411

EFT (Emotional Freedom Technique) 411

35 : Dose-dependent Stress Management Techniques 413

Exercise 415

Helping Others 415

Breathe 415

Pet Your Pet 416

Bathe 416

Pamper your body 416

Confide in a friend 416

Sleep 416

Knitting 417

Choosing Food 417

Journal 417

Be creative 417

18-second hug 417

Pause 417

Happy Place 417

Sing 418

Take Care of Your Body 418

Nature 418

36: Religious and Spiritual Views 419

Faith and Death 422

37: Recommendations and Running the Numbers 425

Conclusion 428

Imagine 428

38: PS 431

Appendix I 432

Copyright

Appendix II 432
Appendix III - Self-Test 434
Sources of More Information 435
Special Offer 436
Glossary I
Index II
Bibliography V
Citations XLIII

Forward

When a flower doesn't bloom, you fix the environment in which it grows, not the flower.
Alexander den Heijer

I am very excited about delivering this book to the world. Ever since I connected the dots between just about every major problem the world faces and the root cause of those problems I have been working tirelessly to explain my theories in a way that allows others to see what I see—a way to stop most of the suffering in our world. For anyone who sees the world as I did a decade ago, this claim seems too far-fetched to warrant further investigation. But those who read these pages where I explain step-by-step the link between one cause and poverty, crime, chronic illnesses and disease, divorce, and so much more will be able to see the connection and be empowered to help themselves and others.

According to the Institute of Medicine report, *Crossing the Quality Chasm: A New Health System for the 21st Century*, "the lag between discovering effective forms of treatment and incorporating them into routine patient care is unnecessarily long, lasting about 15 to 20 years."[3] The purpose of this book is to bring evidence-based methods of helping children thrive under any circumstances out of the halls of research journals and into the hands of parents, teachers, families, communities, and activists where they can benefit today's children instead of waiting decades to make their lives better.

- UNICEF, UNESCO, and WHO have identified core Life Skills. Techniques provided in these pages have a positive impact on each of the core Life Skills and the nature of the process creates intrinsic motivation to use it. The Life Skills are:

- Problem solving
- Critical thinking
- Effective communication skills
- Decision-making
- Interpersonal relationship skills
- Self-awareness building skills
- Creative thinking
- Empathy
- Coping with stress and emotions

The main focus of the techniques is on building resilience, happiness, emotional intelligence, healthy self-esteem, and cognitive skills in our children because doing those things leads to significant improvements in every other area of life. Resilience can make a person impervious to stress. A lack of resilience can make a person a victim of circumstances, unable to enjoy the life they prefer. Improvements in other Life Skills are a beneficial and automatic side effect of improvement in the core areas of focus.

I've named my solution *The Smart Way* because the primary focus is on preventing expected problems before they occur and prevention seems like a smarter way to go about helping people than waiting until problems occur when it is much more difficult to help them. *The Smart Way* solution includes practical step-by-step instructions supported by science and scalable in ways that make it affordable for widespread implementation. I offer training programs that teach *The Smart Way* to organizations and frequently speak about human thriving in one of its many forms. Everything you need to begin applying the principles of human thriving to your own life and to help children in your life thrive more is in these pages.

Forward

When it comes to improving psychological health, scientists approach interventions indirectly. For example, to increase resilience in families they may teach parenting skills that encourage establishing and maintaining routines. Yes, the research shows that routines create an environment that feels more stable (until routines are over emphasized and inflexible). But it is better to teach psychological flexibility directly.

People's own experiences show them fundamental truths. They don't have to be neurologists to understand that we all perceive reality differently and to grasp that filters below our level of conscious awareness are largely responsible for those varied perspectives.

People also understand their emotional state affects their behavior. It happens to them and is evident in every relationship they have and even in every relationship they see in movies or read about in books. It's time to stop using frameworks developed for experiments to teach what can be accomplished faster by being more direct. People are intelligent and should be treated as if they are.

A second problem is that science has become so specialized that most researchers struggle to keep up with changes in their own discipline and aren't aware of findings from other disciplines that relate to their work. Different disciplines use different terms with almost identical meanings. For example, work relating to resilience can be called resilience, hardiness, or grit. When I first began researching resilience I missed a lot of the scientific literature because I did not include hardiness and grit in my original search criteria. Language differences create a chasm

> *Why hasn't anyone brought this to the light of day before? There are a few reasons and they point to other problems.*

between disciplines, making it difficult to tie work together. The answers I've found are not from a single branch of science. Many branches intertwine to provide support for my theories. A quick glance at the bibliography at the back of this book reflects the many disciplines that relate to human thriving.

Scientists also study two ends of the same subject in separate disciplines. Research on stress and its debilitating effects on the physical, mental, and behavioral health of individuals essentially has the opposite of the effect of happiness, but the research on happiness is done by different scientists. Only when information from both disciplines is combined does the relationship between stress and happiness become not only visible, but highly apparent.

If you want to know how to make the world a better place, one that is kinder, more loving, peaceful, and an easier place to be for yourself or for everyone, read on. You will be glad you did. But don't just read; use the techniques in your own life. That is the fastest way to understand their power to change lives. You will get the greatest benefit from this book if you use it as a workbook and study manual—not just something to read.

The focus of the book is to help children whose circumstances are far from ideal, including children living in poverty and those with labels that lead to feelings of being marginalized. But it is not intended to stop there. The middle class straight *A* student may go home to a nightmare every afternoon. There is no way to know what a child's life is like; even parents can be in the dark. These resilience building skills will help every child thrive more.

Sometimes, even when their life seems almost perfect, a child's own perceptions can lead to problems. This is especially true for children who have formed beliefs that make them feel bad. For example, believing a parent loves a sibling more than them, or loves a sibling but doesn't love them can cause a child to want to escape the negative emotions, even though the negative thoughts aren't based on reality. The techniques provided in this book can help anyone that uses them thrive more.

This book is a combination of practical processes individuals can use to increase their ability to thrive and reduce their suffering and knowledge that overturns many false premises that hold people back from being their best self. The approach is unique for two reasons. The first is the solutions are designed to affect the root cause of the problems. Most solutions target symptoms, which makes them dose-dependent and leaves room for undesired side effects. This book represents over twenty years of research focused on one big question, "What enables humans so they can thrive?"

The second difference is that because I am not satisfied with helping some of the people (I want to help everyone) almost seven years have been devoted to finding practical ways to explain how to thrive in ways that individuals with any worldview (religious, spiritual, or scientific) find palatable. The most important component of *The Smart Way* is supported by science, six major religions, and many spiritual practices.

Just like with a tree or any living thing, when the root or core is healthy, the systems that compromise the living system flourish. The root of the answer to human thriving is mindset or beliefs combined with healthy metacognitive processes that depend on knowledge, not IQ. Because the solution begins at the root, it affects the entire being: physical, mental, emotional, spiritual, and behavioral health as well as relationships, and success in everything that is important to individuals and communities.

For our most vulnerable children:
- There is longitudinal research that shows how to significantly improve high school graduation rates. The same program significantly increases college enrollments and college graduation rates.
- There is research that demonstrates how to greatly reduce the school to jail pipeline.
- There is research that demonstrates resilience skills effectively and affordably lower drug and alcohol use and addictions.
- There is research that demonstrates we know how to effectively stop the cycle of violence in many families.

Implementing these recommendations can:
- Empty most of our prisons in a single generation by stopping the crimes that lead to incarceration
- Reduce poverty
- Reduce racism and discrimination
- Increase human thriving among those who seldom thrive
- Change our response to undesired behaviors in the early stages to one that creates better long-term outcomes for everyone

The same process that does all of the above can prevent:
- Mental illnesses including depression and anxiety.
- Stress
- Physical illnesses and diseases
- Pre-term births
- Adverse epigenetic changes
- Obesity, low physical activity, and smoking

One root cause solution solves many social and public health problems. The benefits of implementation extend far beyond greatly reducing crime.

Forward

This book is divided into four parts.

Part 1 – Provides a broad overview of the root cause of human thriving and a solution that is both scalable and affordable.

Part 2 - Provides detailed information that provides an evidence-based platform for the rest of the book. Many common beliefs about the world have never been examined—they've merely been accepted as truths by generation after generation because our parents believed the world worked that way. This often leads to dysfunctional thinking that increases physical and mental health problems because it makes life more stressful than it has to be.

Part 3 - Describes important areas of life that affect human thriving, research demonstrating that we are able to do better, and how people can improve their experiences by making changes to their mindset and using metacognitive processes The problems include crime, physical, mental, and behavioral health, relationships, employee engagement, high school dropout rates, disparate impact, race relations, peace, and more. If all you are interested in is learning about *The Smart Way*, Part III is optional reading because it shines the light on the research that indicates learning *The Smart Way* solves many problems, but Part II and IV provide the information and skills that constitute *The Smart Way*.

Part 4 –Includes a collection of practical processes that reduce stress and increase functional thinking and provide a deep understanding of why the process works and the emotional states at which each process will be most beneficial. They can be used to change neuropathways so that you can thrive more. Anyone can use *The Smart Way* to improve their life. They can be learned by school children, teachers, parents, prisoners, addicts, and anyone who wants to thrive more. I close with a call to action to those who wish to do their part to make Earth better for everyone by sharing this knowledge with others.

During my journey, many of my fundamental beliefs about life and the world were overturned. Much of the way I viewed the world, positions I staunchly defended not many years ago, were based on false premises that do not serve humanity. The only perspective I can take that feels good about what I used to believe is appreciation that I now know more than I once did. If I were willing to take a different perspective, I could feel guilty for how I used to view the world, or dumb, or incompetent, or ignorant, or any number of perspectives that would not serve me or anyone else.

I do not insist that others agree with me. I do ask that this work is approached with an open mind. My work builds on work the work of others and combines research from many areas into a cohesive whole. The individual who contributed the least, contributed greatly. Individuals who worked for years to attempt to find cures that did not work contributed greatly. Each person does the best he or she can in any given moment.

Many foundational premises on which our society is built must change in order to achieve the benefits of what science has shown us is true. When many people understand the big picture, I am confident there will be a groundswell insisting on these changes. The good news is that any individual, young or old, rich or poor, can benefit from the knowledge now. There is no need for anyone else to believe *The Smart Way* works before it can benefit you. Flawed but commonly believed principles prevent the masses from thriving. They do not impede any single individual. Anyone can accept more life-supporting premises about how life works at any time without waiting for a single other person to change. Every person who begins living according to the new principles helps all the others because when we feel better we are better. We also thrive more and become role models that others will look to for guidance about how they can also thrive more.

We all have an innate desire to share what helps us with others and it is especially strong when one's own life improves significantly. We want solutions to the social ills that plague our world to benefit everyone. We want good health throughout life, but many basic tenets accepted as truths today lead to the opposite of both. We are so close—we must move forward.

My job is to explain what I've learned well enough that others can benefit from the knowledge.

Part I — With a Broad Brush

This section provides a broad overview of the problem and solution. The charts in this section are designed to simplify the complex relationships that exist between mind and body and present a solution that can prevent many chronic diseases (both physical and mental) and reduce crime and violence.

The reason one solution is so powerful is because it was developed by finding the root of each problem and discovering they all share one root. When the roots are healthy, the person thrives. When the roots are damaged or weak, the person struggles.

Strengthening human roots requires both knowledge and skill. Both are provided in this book. The knowledge is critical because it overturns false premises that frequently hinder a person's ability to thrive.

The skills empower each person with skills they can use to gain control over their emotional state, allowing them to experience more frequent positive emotions.

This book is designed to be studied and for the reader to apply the ideas to their own life. The reader who applies the knowledge and skills in these pages will learn that he or she has far more control over whether or not to be happy than most people ever realize. The reader will find that happiness is achievable and that regardless of what life brings your way, you know the way back to happiness.

I wish for you a joyful journey.

Introduction and Overview

Your life should consist of more than commuting, working, eating, surfing the Internet, sleeping and watching TV. Your life should be filled with purpose-driven experiences and projects that bring excitement, passion, energy, and authentic meaning and joy into your life."
Richie Norton

This book is my "more." - JJ

My goals for this book include:
- Share information that is not commonly known that, when understood and applied, makes a significant difference in the physical, mental, and behavioral outcomes an individual experiences throughout life and also empowers the individual with the ability to develop stronger relationships and experience greater success.
- With the above knowledge, demonstrate that an individual or family can change their trajectory regardless of environment or obstacles in their path.
- Delve deeper into the reasons for many of today's biggest challenges (i.e. poverty, racism, divorces, violence, crime, and addictions) and draw a bright line solution that shares one root.
- Demonstrate a way to put peace in one's heart.
- Define the type of happiness that brings the greatest benefits.
- Provide information about new research on how beneficial happiness is.
- Demonstrate that stress can be lowered in a way that makes the automatic stress response less stressful, and therefore, the chronic stress load lower and happiness higher.
- Educate my readers about the negative impact of stress on every area of their life in an effort to help them decide to take steps to be happier (which is less stressful).
- Provide processes that individuals can use to feel better in any situation.
- Explain common barriers to happiness and how to overcome them.
- Share information about proven methods of helping at-risk children improve their chances of being able to rise above their early circumstances.
- Help individuals understand how stress and addictions are linked and how good stress management can prevent addiction and help a recovering addict prevent a re-lapse.
- How to have more peace in one's heart and home.
- How to have more peace in one's community.
- Explain the link between crime and stress.
- Share skills that prevent disparate outcomes
- Explain how our mind works from a practical point of view.
- Introduce and explain how to use Emotional Guidance.
- Explain how to develop an abundant mindset.
- Illustrate subtle differences that matter.

- Discuss how Employee Engagement fits in the big picture.
- Tie religious and spiritual worldviews into the scientific information so individuals with a religious worldview are also supported

In this book or any of my other work, I do not try to lead anyone to where *I think* they should be. I do not presume to know what is better for anyone. I recognize that each of us has different dreams and desires. I share what I've learned about what helps humans get what they want—their personally defined goals and dreams. I can help you find a straighter path toward achieving what you want. I don't know where you are because I have not lived what you have lived. You are fully capable of knowing what is best for you. I will give you everything I've got to help you achieve whatever it is you want to achieve. I have significant expertise in skills-based sustainable happiness, building confidence, resilience, psychological resilience, PsyCap, confidence, self-esteem and in perspectives that improve relationships of all types and with stress reduction methods that make life easier and more fun. If you want any of that, you'll find help in these pages.

This section will walk you through the connections that support the assertion that implementation of this plan will dramatically improve many of our most pressing social problems. In this section, no attempt is made to attach the science that supports these assertions, but the rest of the book is filled with that documentation. *Our Children Live In A War Zone* asserts that the current world our children inhabit, with its poverty and hunger, violence, racism, drugs, alcohol, chronic illnesses and diseases, abuse, bullying, disparate outcomes, pre-term births, and misdirection about how to best use the brain they were born with feels like a war zone even when they live in a country that is at peace.

We have the potential to alleviate these problems. Why am I shinning a spotlight on this solution and not someone from a fancy institution with important letters after their name? I think the very fact that I am not traditionally educated is why I could see the potential that is clear when information from many branches of science are viewed together, a perspective a traditionally trained individual is unlikely to take. I've been told by more than one scientist that my focus is too broad because you can't prove the answer to something like, "What empowers humans to thrive?"

They were wrong. Yes, I cannot do all the work in medical science, psychology, sociology, quantum physics, psychoneuroimmunology, epigenetics, bio-chemistry, motivation, education, criminology, addictions, organizational behavior, and more. But I can read research that has been done in those fields through a lens of what helps humans thrive more and put the pieces of the puzzle together in a new way. I can identify common false premises where the truth is evinced in the scientific literature but the truths have not been broadly disseminated—perhaps because their significance is not yet recognized.

I have often felt as if I stand where Daniel Goleman stood in 1990, but on a much broader scale because although Emotional Intelligence is part of the root, it is a small piece of the big picture.

In large part, psychology research ignored the individual and situational differences in emotions and the physical (physiological) manifestations that result from various experiences.[4] The research tends to be structured as if two people experiencing the same event will have the same response on a mental and physical level. Nothing could be further from the truth. How an individual's mind appraises the initial response to an experience, or if the person reappraises, makes a tremendous difference in the amount of stress experienced. This is not a matter of intelligence as much as it is a set of learnable skills that even children can understand and utilize.

The story begins with stress.
1. Science routinely reports that stress is the root cause of up to 95% of all illnesses. I agree. The research links everything from heart disease, cancer, Alzheimer's, and even the flu and common cold to stress.

2. Stress is strongly linked to mental health diagnoses from depression, anxiety, OCD, all the way up to psychosis.[5]
3. Behavior that is less than the best it could be, whether we are speaking of a preschooler, a spouse, a CEO, or a murderer is always rooted in stress.
4. Stress diminishes our ability to think, which compromises our ability to make the best decisions.
5. Relationships are negatively impacted by both the diminished mental capacity and the diminished pro-social behavior caused by stress.
6. Stress affects digestive function in a way that increases the risk of both obesity and diabetes—calories in and calories out does not tell the full story.
7. Stress and happiness have an inverse relationship. When you reduce stress, happiness increases. When you increase stress, happiness declines.
8. Addiction to both drugs and alcohol begin with an individual who is stressed that is seeking relief from the negative emotion and does not have the knowledge or skills to feel better in a way that exacts a lower price.
9. Behavior is decided by what will feel best. Even someone in a violent criminal situation who chooses to sacrifice his life to save another does so because he believes it will feel better to save the person than to let the other person (perhaps a woman or child) die and live with the guilt.

The purpose of emotions was incorrectly presented in the scientific literature for eighty years and I don't believe the importance of the truth is fully understood by some of the researchers who did the work to overturn the old paradigm, or they don't have the cross-disciplinary support that backs up the assertions I make.

For fifty years we've been being told to reduce stress. Early recommendations told us to give up activities we were not required to do—which generally meant giving up the things that we loved, the things that nourished us. That advice was not taken. Then we were told to *Think Positive*, but not told how to change our habits of thought. This book tells you *how* to develop and maintain a positive mental attitude, which has been the missing piece.

Mindset is at the root of stress. The mindset and metacognitive skills of an individual determines how much stress any given situation causes them to experience.

> *Longitudinal studies show that even children at the highest risk of poor outcomes due to poverty and environmental circumstances have much better than expected high school and college completion rates and lower crime, drug, and alcohol problems when they are taught skills that increase resilience.*

The healthiest mindset is a resilient one.

Longitudinal studies show that even children at the highest risk of poor outcomes due to poverty and environmental circumstances have much better than expected high school and college completion rates and lower crime, drug, and alcohol problems when they are taught skills that increase resilience. The tools those children have been provided are miniscule in comparison to the tools contained in this book. Accurate interpretation of emotions and understanding the new scientific perspectives about emotions builds strong resilience.

It also shines a light on a number of problems in our educational institutions. Teacher expectations are affecting outcomes and the majority of that effect is negative for the children who are most at risk. There are some teachers who use their power of influence the way I encourage it to be used in this book—to inspire self-confidence in the student that is required for success. Anyone can overcome the negative expectations of others if they know how, which you'll learn in these pages.

Risk Factors that decrease a child's chances of optimal outcomes include:

- Verbal abuse
- Neglect
- Learning disability
- Parental divorce
- Violent environment
- Low resilience
- Physical abuse
- Health problems
- Minority status
- Mentally ill parent
- Domestic violence
- Low life skills
- Sexual Abuse
- Low socioeconomic resources
- Dysfunctional Family environment
- Incarcerated parent
- Substance abuse by parent
- Low emotional intelligence

In a study that looked at **Adverse Childhood Experiences** (ACE's) of over 25,000 residents of America, the following obscenely high percentages were experienced:[6]

Verbal abuse	25.9%	Physical abuse	14.8%
Sexual abuse	12.2%	Family dysfunction	26.6%
Mentally ill family member	19.4%	Witnessed domestic violence	16.3%
Experienced at least one	59.4%	Experienced 5 or more ACE's	8.7%

Although society reacts to physical and sexual abuse with the greatest degree of outrage against the perpetrators and sympathy for the victims, verbal abuse is still openly practiced by many parents in public places. Think about your own experiences in the grocery store and other public places and ask yourself if you have heard a parent telling a child he is stupid, dumb, a dummy, bad, fat, ugly, or other negative remarks. Yes, that is abusive behavior. In fact, researchers have found that children who experience verbal abuse (with or without other abuses) have the worse outcomes. Verbal abuse is the more likely to create a memory that is replayed in the mind and contributes to the development of critical self-talk. When the hurtful words are remembered or replayed, the effect is as if it happens repeatedly. One interaction, positive or negative, can change the trajectory of a child's life. Using the skills presented herein, the repetitive negative voice can be silenced.

1: Everything is Connected

All things are connected like the blood that unites us. We do not weave the web of life; we are merely a strand in it. Whatever we do to the web, we do to ourselves.
Chief Seattle

Our Children Live in a War Zone refers to the many ways in which our children face adversity throughout their childhoods. Adversity comes in many forms: family, community, the larger environment, school, and from pervasive attitudes of the time. Long-term studies demonstrate that providing children with simple skills and knowledge at young ages effectively changes the trajectories of their lives in many positive ways.

"It seems naive to expect that young people can, at least to any significant degree, be shielded from the pressures and risk factors" of lower socioeconomic circumstances, ethnicity, or previous abuse history."[7] It is not only minority and low socioeconomic youth who face challenges. Education researchers found that, "While minority youth and those who experience family dissolution and transience are at greatest risk, a large proportion of adolescents eventually engage in some form of problem behavior, placing them at increased risk for school failure, involvement in the criminal justice system, and health problems."[8] This book is intended to help all children, not just those who society might expect to have problems. Studies repeatedly show that about 1/3 at-risk children significantly outperform expectations.[9] The factors that empower those children to succeed can benefit all children and help us stop losing two-thirds of the vulnerable children to death, drugs, suicide, mental illness, and prison.

By studying the children who overcame adverse circumstances like low socioeconomic status, discrimination, mentally ill parents, abuse, neglect, and chronic illnesses we know what skills and knowledge make a difference in the outcomes of vulnerable children. "The individual qualities and experience of disadvantaged young people who have coped successfully" include the following protective factors common in resilient children:[10]

- Possess characteristics that elicit positive emotional responses from family members and strangers
    - Are able to develop close bonds with adults at an early age
- Have a pro-active approach toward problem-solving
- Tend to perceive their experiences constructively
- Are able to elicit positive feedback from others
- Perceive life from a more positive perspective
- Possess flexible social skills
- Positive interactions with peers and adults
- High degree of social responsiveness and sensitivity (EQ)
- High Intelligence (IQ)
- Are empathetic
- Have a sense of humor
- High self-esteem
- An internal locus of control
- Critical problem-solving skills

- Easy temperament
- Optimism
- Determination and perseverance
- Family cohesion

Social connections have repeatedly been shown to provide some protection against negative mental and physical health outcomes. A study of 1379 students found that "positive emotion was positively associated with social acceptance and visibility."[11] In other words, when a child is happy, it is easier to make friends.

"Merely avoiding a stressful situation or negative event does not constitute resilience because no active process is involved."[12] Resilience is encountering a problem and returning to a psycho-socio-emotional state that is the same as or better than the state one was in before the situation is encountered.

According to Harvey and Delfabbro, good childhood outcomes have been approached from several directions including:[13]

- Removal of risks
    - Safe Sex campaigns
    - Head Start Programs (to enhance early cognitive functioning)
- Removal of factors that compound social disadvantage:
    - Enhance parenting skills
    - Decrease marital discord
    - Reduce substance abuse
        - Just Say No campaigns
    - Reduce delinquency
- Increasing the available resources:
    - Enhancing physical resources (i.e. parks, playgrounds, athletic compounds)
    - Increasing service infrastructure of an area
        - Better housing
        - Safer and healthier living environment
        - Greater access to services
        - Employment opportunities
        - Education
- Enhancement of protective resources
    - Strengthening of social networks
        - Mentoring
        - Role models

All of these approaches are indirect. We know an internal locus of control increases resilience, but many of these programs send a message that bigger and stronger people or organizations are in control. The focus on providing opportunities and services makes those who do not have them begin demanding them—from a stance that someone else has to provide them—a perspective that reinforces an external locus of control.

Many of the programs give the community the impression that they are not capable of success without outside help—increasing their sense of powerlessness and reliance on outside *others* for the things they want most in life.

Even mentoring programs are someone who must give of their time, someone outside themselves who has to do something, which can sometimes feel as if a role model is robbing them of autonomy or making them feel as if they are *less than* for needing help. None of the programs directly increase optimism, autonomy, internal locus of control, or self-esteem in a direct way. A few attempt to do so in order to achieve other goals (delay sexual activity, saying no to drugs, mentors and possibly parenting classes). *The Smart Way* Metacognitive Processes with Emotional Guidance directly addresses all factors that increase resilience—without reliance on anyone outside themselves once they learn how to use it.

Studies that followed children for a decade or more show they fare much better when they were taught skills that build resilience. Once we had scientific evidence that the training helped children avoid jail and drugs and rise above the poverty they were born into, I don't understand why the techniques used in those studies have not been implemented globally. The positive impact seen in children's lives and the adults they became warrant providing all children with the training. In my opinion, it is child neglect not to do so now that we know the effect it has on long-term outcomes. My efforts to introduce these methods at the local level ran into red tape so I decided to raise an army of motivated people who understand the benefits *The Smart Way* can provide. If it takes a grass roots effort from parents and activists demanding that we do what we can to help children before another generation suffers unnecessarily, a book is a good way to get the word out. It is also a good way to put the knowledge and skills that matter in the hands of parents and teachers so they can help the children in their sphere of influence now.

> *Are we afraid to have a society where nearly everyone thrives?*

The difference simple skills can make is evinced by a Robert Wood Johnson Study that followed 753 children from kindergarteners until age 25.[14] The children represented both genders and different races who lived in both rural and city environments.

A few highlights:

For every one-point increase on the 5-point scale in a child's social competence score in kindergarten, he/she was:
- Twice as likely to attain a college degree in early adulthood;
- 54% more likely to earn a high school diploma; and
- 46% more likely to have a full-time job at the age of 25.

For every one-point decrease in a child's social competence score in kindergarten, he/she had a:
- 67% higher chance of having been arrested by early adulthood;
- 82% higher rate of recent marijuana usage; and
- 82% higher chance of being in or on a waiting list for public housing.

There are interventions that work to improve social skills in children. In this book, you will also learn about the connection between emotional state and behavior. By the time you finish, you will see as clearly as I do how children's emotional states contribute to generational poverty and that we can end most of it in one generation. When the number of people affected by problems like poverty, the *cycle of violence*, drug abuse, premature ends to education, and incarceration is significantly reduced, the resources available to help those who still need will be more than adequate to accomplish the task.

By the end of this book, you will see as clearly as I do that we have to be willing to make a significant effort for one generation to help the millions who would otherwise suffer and be a financial and social strain on society. When we do whatever it takes to help that one generation, the generations that follow will never again have large numbers of people who need that level of help. You will learn how the emotional state of parents adversely impacts the children and methods children can be taught to be more resilient even if their parents are not helped. You will also see the wisdom of helping both parents and children because the parents are victims of their circumstances, whether those circumstances are generational poverty or other factors.

The social problems of our time are all symptoms of a society misguided and misinformed by false premises our society acts on as we raise our children and guide them to adulthood. When we believe certain things are true, our mind interprets reality as if they are true, irrespective of the truth. In many ways, our beliefs create our reality and each of us perceives a different reality.

This book is about helping all children and as many adults as possible who are suffering. It is not limited to helping minorities, but it feels important to mention some research done by Dr. Joy Degruy on something she has termed Post Traumatic Slave Syndrome (PTSS). What Dr. Degruy has found is that each generation passes social learning on to the offspring and that descendants of African-Americans whose ancestors were enslaved suffer from some of the largely non-verbal messages they receive from their parents.[15] By bringing this out into the light she is doing a great service because when we understand the root of the problem, we can heal it.

Although Dr Degruy's work is with descendants of African-American slaves, they may not be the only ones affected. There were White slaves in America and other countries. In many ways women were considered property and could not own property and were not entitled to their own earnings (if they were allowed to work outside the home) in most states until after the end of the Civil War. For example, the state of Georgia passed a law in 1868 allowing married women to own (but not control) property in their own name.

The concept can be expanded to other messages passed on from parents to children. In my own upbringing there was continual encouragement to know my place as the daughter of a blue collar worker—not someone who would become a Vice President in a large organization, not someone who would start her own company, not someone who would write books, and certainly not someone who would change the world. The early message was finish high school, get a job, get married and have babies. That was the expected role.

This book applies the latest science to pervasive beliefs that are not serving us or our children and which are being passed from one generation to the next. Until an intervention stops this damaging process, the problems will continue growing with each generation. There are a number of factors that lead to the best outcomes in life and other factors we can eliminate that lead to less than the best outcomes. In many cases, the beliefs that hinder us are based on false premises that keep us believing things that prevent us from achieving our heart's desire. Overall, what helps us thrive and what hinders us is not well known and it is certainly not taught in schools. It should be part of the mandatory curriculum at every school.

In this book you will learn the types of beliefs that hinder human thriving and how and why they sabotage your best efforts to thrive. Most of this boils down to our ability to effectively self-regulate our thinking, emotions, and behavior.[16] Emotion cannot be directly regulated and efforts to do so lead to unhealthy mental health. "It is clear that emotional responses to stressful events can be regulated via the use of cognitive coping strategies."[17] We can change our thoughts to change our emotions. Behaviors can be deliberate or impulsive. *The Smart Way* involves deliberate application of adaptive coping styles that are designed to develop supportive neuropathways in the brain which leads to automatic responses that support greater thriving.

The goal of emotion regulation is to feel better. When our thoughts move in directions that support our goals, we feel good (or better than we do when we move in opposition to our goals. Even if we are still in bad-feeling emotional states, if our thoughts become more supportive of our goals we feel a sense of relief (even if we have not yet moved far enough in the right direction to feel good).

The biggest conflict most people face is between feeling good and accomplishing their goals. The person who wants to maintain the ideal weight has a goal about weight management, but they may also love to eat a donut with their morning cup of coffee. When this person resists the donut, she can feel deprived of the donut, but at the same time she can feel proud that she is sticking to her weight management goal. She has a choice of what she focuses on and what she decides will determine her emotional state on that specific subject. If she chooses to appreciate her resolve to maintain her weight and the body she is able to enjoy as a result, she'll feel emotionally good because those thoughts support her goal and hold her in positive self-regard. If she chooses to focus on what she didn't get to enjoy—the donut—those thoughts will feel bad, she'll feel deprived, as if she can't have what she wants. The choice of what she thinks about is entirely up to her.

Most people don't make a conscious choice about what to think. They allow their existing habits of thought to dictate whether they think about sticking to the weight loss goals and feeling good or about the sacrifice made by not eating the donut. Your brain will decide for you, based on programming that has often been in place since age 6. Your habit of thought is a habit. Like any habit, it can be changed. But unlike many habits, such as whether you eat the donut with your morning coffee, how to change habits of thought is not always obvious.

Our brains, in fact, most of our body, has redundant systems. That is very good news because we don't have to think about everything we think, do, or say. We breathe whether we think about it or not. Our body will adjust our breathing to satisfy our needs. If we've decided we'll eat the donut and run five miles so we can have both the weight we want and the donut, our breathing will be deeper and probably faster when we're running than it is when we are drinking our coffee.

In the same way, our habits of thought continue on auto-pilot when we don't think about them. But, just as we can consciously adjust our breathing, we can consciously adjust our thought patterns by thinking about our thoughts. Thinking about what we're thinking is called meta-cognition. Some people rarely, if ever, use meta-cognition. Others frequently use meta-cognition to consciously evaluate the quality of their thoughts and whether their thoughts are moving them closer to their goals or in opposition to their goals.

The third thing we regulate is our progress toward our goals and avoidance of undesired impulsive actions. Just like with meta-cognition, whether we consciously establish our goals, or if they are simply the result of living our lives and determining what we like and do not like, we can operate on auto-pilot or more consciously choose which goals to move toward.

For example, we might have a goal of writing a book, but not have a set deadline. So every time we begin researching for the book we're distracted by interesting things that aren't related to our goal of writing a book. Distractions often prevent us from reaching our goals—especially when the goal is not well defined. Just like we can think on auto-pilot or more consciously, we can move in the general direction of our goals, allowing less desired short-term goals to distract us from more satisfying long-term goals, or we can be conscious about our goals. When we are highly conscious about our goals, we are more likely to achieve them.

Behavior regulation is driven by the desire to achieve a goal. The goal may be self-selected and intrinsically motivated or selected by someone else, but your acceptance of a goal selected by someone else supports other goals, which are ultimately supported by a personally selected goal.

For example, Andrew Carnegie was born to a poor family in Scotland and, not liking the poverty his mother endured, he vowed that when he grew up he would be rich and take good care of her. That goal drove him to become one of the richest men in the world through self-improvement and taking advantage of every opportunity he encountered to further his goal.

Peer pressure can result in your going along with a goal selected by others that you don't want to do, but your personally selected goal of being accepted, liked, or not ostracized makes you believe that going along with the peer pressure will support your own goal.

Someone may not want to work overtime and spend an evening away from their family, but if doing so supports keeping the job or getting a desired raise, she may do it.

Our individually selected goals are unique. Even if we have goals that sound like another's goals, our *why* may be different from theirs. The uniqueness increases our value to the world. We all have many goals. For example, most people want three meals a day. Everyone wants enough air to breathe. Most people want a good night's sleep. Most people have a goal of having at least one, and often more, good relationships with other people. Some people want to be the best in the world at something. Others may simply want to be left alone to enjoy solitude, a good book, or a Netflix marathon. We have different goals at different times. We can emphasize one goal more than another at different times.

Some people, like me, want to be on stage and inspire and/or educate other people. Others couldn't be dragged kicking and screaming onto a stage to speak in front of hundreds of people.

Measuring our progress helps us to achieve goals. Students who track their grades and the requirements to get good grades and the classes they have to take to achieve their goals are more successful than those who do not. Students who use the course syllabus to schedule time to complete assignments and study for exams do better than those who try to fit school work in between the stuff on their calendar.

Athletes who track their times, scores, achievements and practice with the goal of improving so their future performance is better than their past performance do the best.[18]

> *Notice that how much money a person's birth family has is not one of the factors that determine success—if the person develops the ability to self-regulate. What does that mean and why is that important? It's important because many people in our culture believe you have to have money before you can have any chance of success—especially if you have to overcome disadvantages.*

"People who are good at self-regulation do better than others in life... College students with high self-control get better grades, have better close relationships, manage their emotions better, have fewer problems with drugs and alcohol, are less prone to eating disorders, are better adjusted, and have higher self-esteem, and get along better with other people, as compared to people with low self-control... They are happier and have less stress and conflict... Longitudinal studies have found that children with good self-control go through life with fewer problems, are more successful, are less likely to be arrested or have a child out of wedlock, and enjoy other benefits. Criminologists have concluded that low self-control is a—if not the—key trait for understanding the criminal personality."[19]

The second is because self-regulatory skills can be developed at any time—they don't have to come from parents who have them. They can be learned in school. They can be learned from a book. They can be learned from mentors—and those mentors can live in books. *Exile's Honor* or *Joust* by Mercedes Lackey would be good for boys and *The Royal Diaries* series would be good for girls. My daughters both recommend *Harry Potter*. Since books don't have ratings I screened them by reading them first, which led to lively dinner table conversations about books we'd all read.

"Disadvantage could be seen as arising from poverty and high unemployment rates at a societal and community level, as well as from family conflict and unhealthy peer relations at the social level... factors such as poor mental health, lower IQ, as well as personality and motivational factors (e.g., high impulsivity, low delay of gratification) operating at the individual level."[20]

If successful people are people who are good at self-regulation and learning how to self-regulate can be learned from a book that means it is free. You can learn it at the library. You can spend a small amount of money and buy this book. It should be taught in schools. But even if it isn't, it can be taught in the home, and individual teachers can show students how to self-regulate. When you decide for yourself who you want to be and define yourself as what you want to be, it makes it much easier to regulate your behavior so that you are who you want to be.

One of the most important parts—one where many people are led astray—is the part where you define what your standards are. Who do you want to be in this world? Note: This is not who others think you should be or that you can be. No one else knows what you really want as well as you do. If they can't feel the energy that pours through you when you think about your true desires, they can't know that you can achieve them—even if your desires are as unlikely as a poor Scottish immigrant becoming one of the richest men in America and donating enough money to start 3,000 libraries and a University before his life was done the way Andrew Carnegie did.

What makes your energy flow? What excites you? Define who you want to be and then move toward becoming the person you define. The more you accomplish, the bigger your goals can become. The goal is not to achieve all your goals, the goal is steady progress because as soon as you achieve a goal, or are within sight of it, other goals and desires take root in your heart and mind. As long as you believe you can accomplish them and are moving toward them, you will feel good—unless you lament about how long it is taking you to get there.

Accomplishing a goal makes you feel good for a little while. Moving toward goals can make you feel good for a lifetime.

Sometimes you have to grow into a goal—it may seem too big for you the first time you think about a goal. When I realized that things I'd figured out could substantially improve life on Earth for a large percentage of people it was mind-boggling to me. But I kept moving toward explaining the path to better health, to emptying most of our prisons, to preventing suicide long before a crisis hits until one day a stranger sent me an email and began it with, "Hello World Changer." I'd known I wanted to change the world, but I had been unable to claim the title of *World Changer* because I know that everything we do changes the world, so everyone changes the world a little bit so I'm not special. But I want to change the world in big ways—ways that end suffering for millions of people—ways that change the fundamental principles our society is built upon.

When I accepted the mantle of *World Changer* everything changed. How I thought about my work changed. I was no longer thinking about getting an engagement with a client or a speaking gig. Now I was thinking about the preferred world I wanted to live in twenty years from now—what did that look like? How did it differ from today? What do I need today to move that vision forward?

No matter who you want to be, or what you want to do, in some ways your choices will change the world. I have other definitions of who I am and how I will show up in the world that have a direct impact on how I change the world. I have decided that I want to show up in the world as being kind, as being love, as loving, and as someone who inspires others. In order to be happy, anything I do to move the world closer to my preferred future must be consistent with those definitions of self.

I have not always been kind. In sixth grade, for a while, I teased a few of the other children. I was lucky. I was aware enough that it didn't feel good when I was not nice to others that I stopped doing it fairly quickly. Your emotions will guide you to who you really want to be, but you have to pay attention to their messages.

Take the time to set your own standards about who you want to be in this world. You don't need anyone else's approval of who you want to be and become. If the idea feels good to you, it is good for you. Now, let me clarify something here. When someone feels very disempowered, revenge may feel a lot better than the disempowered state. But revenge is not happiness or joy or love or appreciation. When I say *if it feels good for you, it is good for you*, I am referring to good-feeling emotional states—not just better-feeling than awful emotional states. In later chapters you'll learn how to feel better.

The emotional states, like revenge, that feel better than more disempowered states (like grief) are best moved through mentally without action. It is completely possible to move through anger and revenge and find better-feeling thoughts just by thinking about what you'd like to do, but not actually doing anything. Examples are detailed in the Processes section in the **Beat Depression** area.

One reason it is so important for a child or an adult to understand that who he will be and become can be defined by self is the default most people who do not decide consciously use to gauge their performance is others' expectations and comparison to others. Both methods can cause significant harm to our happiness. There are enough downfalls to comparing oneself to others that I could write an entire book about why it is not the best way to decide who you can become or how well you're doing. For example, adolescents who compare themselves to siblings and friends who drink are more willing to drink alcohol themselves.[21]

Much of the world approaches self-regulation with willpower. Willpower is the hard way. You'll learn more about this in the **Beliefs and Expectations** chapter.

Also, while most of the world still believes that personality traits are constant throughout life, *that one's personality is just who the person is*, modern researchers have successfully refuted that premise. Personality traits are closely connected with emotional state and since emotional state is largely due to habits of thought—something few people know how to change—stabile personality traits are common, but not because they cannot be changed. It was because people did not know how to change their habits of thought. You'll learn numerous ways to change your habits of thought in this book. Some personality traits lead to greater success. Self-control is a major aspect of the personality trait called Conscientiousness. People who are high in Conscientiousness have significantly better life outcomes in marriage, career, and health than people who are low in Conscientiousness.

Social Indicators Research Journal is the leading journal for quality of life and indicators measurements.[22] In 2015, they published *An Existential-Humanistic View of Personality Change: Co-Occurring Changes with Psychological Well-Being in a 10 Year Cohort Study*, where they shared, "Personality change was more strongly related to changes in Personal Well-Being than changes in other well-being indicators such as depression, hostility, and life satisfaction. Personality changed to a similar degree and explained greater variation in our well-being measures than changes in socioeconomic variables."

> "A human being is a part of the whole, called by us, Universe, a part limited in time and space. He experiences himself, his thoughts and feelings as something separated from the rest — a kind of optical delusion of his consciousness. This delusion is a kind of prison for us, restricting us to our personal desires and to affection for a few persons nearest to us. Our task must be to free ourselves from this prison by widening our circle of compassion to embrace all living creatures and the whole of nature in its beauty. Nobody is able to achieve this completely, but the striving for such achievement is in itself a part of the liberation and a foundation for inner security." Albert Einstein

The following chart contains beliefs that support thriving and beliefs that hinder thriving:

	Beliefs that feel like Struggle	Self-Control Beliefs that feel like Ease
School	I hate school	I am a good student
	School is hard for me	I can have fun while learning
	I don't like school.	I am good at learning
Work	My job sucks	I like _____ about my job
	My work is meaningless	My work is important
	My boss doesn't value me	My contributions have value to my boss
	I'm undervalued at work	I am respected at work
	I'm a F. U.	I am good at my job
	I don't understand how to get ahead	I learn more every day
	I'm in a no-where job	I make the most of myself
	I live for weekends	I can enjoy myself every day
Popular	No one wants to spend time with me	I am easy to get along with
	I'm afraid of what people think of me	Most people like me
	I don't want to show my true self	People are interesting
	Will they like me?	I like people
	The world has a lot of bad people	I have friends I can trust
Being Nice	No one can make me be nice	I am a nice person
	My teacher is mean	My teacher cares about me
	I won't do nothing for nobody	I feel good when I do nice things
	They'll let me down if I trust them	People will live up to my expectations
Drugs / Alcohol	Drugs make me feel better	I value my brain
	Alcohol makes me feel more social	I'm happy
	I don't know how to feel better	I can change my focus and feel better
	I can't stand this emotional pain	I can love and let go
	Drinking gets me through the day	I'm strong, I can make it
	Everyone I know does drugs	I can be whoever I want to be
Eating	Food comforts me	Food fuels my body
	I binge on junk food when I'm sad	I can eat what I want in moderation
	I eat when I'm lonely	I enjoy my own company
Crime	I can get away with this	I am a law-abiding person
	I only care about myself	I'm an ethical person
	I deserve this –they owe me	My life has lots of potential

There are a variety of habits or characteristics that hinder or support human thriving that you will learn about in this book. You'll learn what supports thriving, why it supports thriving, and how to develop characteristic that will help you thrive.

Hinders Thriving	Helps Thriving
Thinking on auto-pilot Exception: when you've rehearsed	Meta-cognitive thinking
Misinterpreting meaning of emotions	Understand emotions are guidance and correct interpretations & helpful response
Rigid psychological processes	Psychological Flexibility
Negative mindset	Positive mindset
High stress, especially chronic high stress	Low stress and positive stress
External locus of control	Internal locus of control
Fixed Mindset	Growth Mindset
Not resilient	Resilient
Beliefs and desires are not coherent	Beliefs and desires are coherent
Limiting beliefs	Supportive, expansive beliefs
Struggle with relationships	Healthy relationships
Struggle with health	Good health
Negative or Neutral self-regard	Positive self-regard
Problem focused	Solution focused
Competition	Cooperation (Competition is prior self)
Complete (finished product)	Ever-evolving
Look for faults in others	Look for best in others
Surround self with people who are there by happenstance or detractors	Surround self with positive influencers

2: One Root Cause

There are a thousand hacking at the branches of evil to one who is striking at the root.
Henry David Thoreau

This book provides solutions to some of the most pressing problems of our time. The solutions are evidence-based and cost effective. Most proposed solutions have two glaring problems:

1. They are designed using information from only one branch of science. Cross-disciplinary solutions are rare.
2. They address symptoms of the problem, not the root cause.

The solutions suggested herein incorporate information from a wide variety of scientific fields. Any information that I was able to locate that added to my understanding of the root cause of human thriving was considered. Research from fields as diverse as medical science, quantum physics, behavioral genetics, criminology, psychoneuroimmunology, psychology, organizational behavior, psychological health, neurology, motivation, and more was reviewed to identify pieces of the puzzle that answer the big question, "What makes humans thrive?"

If we look at the problems of our time, they are all essentially situations where individuals (or groups) have failed to thrive. Each of the following can be described as a failure to thrive:

Poverty	War
Crime and incarcerations	Poor mental health
Drug and Alcohol abuse	Suicide
Chronic illnesses and disease	Drop-outs
Divorce	Unemployment
Abuse	Hunger and poor nutrition
Disparate outcomes	

By studying the larger question, "What makes humans thrive?" instead of analyzing the symptoms (i.e. poverty, crime, etc.), the root cause was revealed. The root cause of all the problems is the same. This is the best possible news because efforts to solve just one of the symptoms at the root cause has a positive impact on all the symptoms that stem from the same root.

This is not something that a few sentences will bring into focus. The reason is that there are many commonly believed false premises that reinforce conditions that lead to a lack of thriving. But each of the false premises is easy to overturn with the right information.

Numerous false premises are widely accepted and lend stabilization to the lack of thriving that is so prevalent today. Providing accurate information that supports greater thriving makes a tremendous difference. Today, science publishes new information that demonstrates how widely believed information hinders thriving or new findings that show how taking another perspective increases thriving and the information sits unused while the world continues to suffer. These are practical solutions that are proven to work.

The Smart Way has been compared to a form of do-it-yourself Cognitive Behavioral Therapy. Several licensed therapists have shared with me that the mental processes I teach resemble Cognitive Behavior Therapy (CBT). I can see where this is true but the difference is that with CBT the therapist knows the techniques and gently guides you to the conclusions over time. When you learn processes that help you improve your emotional state, you have the ability to guide yourself to higher emotional states.

When you consider the fact that individuals have about 60,000 thoughts each day and are personally aware of them. Attempting to communicate even a fraction of those thoughts to a therapist could take years, the advantage of the individual recognizing the healthy response to each thought becomes apparent.

60,000 thoughts a day is far too many thoughts to regulate effectively. It is more efficient to pay attention to how thoughts make us feel and emphasize those that feel good and de-emphasize those that feel bad using a variety of metacognitive techniques (See Chapter 33).

Individuals who teach Neuro-Linguistic Programming (NLP) indicated *The Smart Way* sounded like NLP. I was intrigued enough to do some research on NLP and found that some aspects of *The Smart Way* are similar to NLP, but my techniques have one advantage that is lacking in the NLP methods I studied, which is incorporating Emotional Guidance.

Based on my own research, I would say that *The Smart Way* incorporate the best aspects of many techniques including some from motivation theory, self-regulation theory, life skills training, anger management, stress management, and more. But because my work is cross disciplinary, the methods have been fine tuned to maximize the benefit each individual receives. I often read of a method tested in one scientific discipline that demonstrates positive results that, with small tweaks, would generate more robust benefits.

In general, research does not delve below the surface in the mind. Individual differences are not considered in research design to the extent they should be. This is probably due to a combination of lack of understanding of the importance of thoughts and emotion and the cost of delving deeper. In essence, it is the result of inaccurate assumptions about the cost-benefit equation. If the value of the findings was understood, the cost would not be an obstacle. Because so much research stays at a superficial level, information is gained, but real solutions that will help the majority of humanity are identified slowly, if at all.

The Smart Way goes to the level of thoughts and even deeper, to mindsets. Each of us has about 60,000 thoughts in a day. Researching at that level would be impossible because we can't record all the thoughts we have. Moving deeper than thought is something we can measure and adjust—mindsets. When mindsets change, the results are evident in numerous areas that can be measured. Emotional state and outcomes in many areas of life change when mindsets change because we think different thoughts. The outcomes that change include physical, mental, behavioral health and motivation and success.

It sounds complicated when I attempt to explain it at a high level. Fortunately, I've spent almost a decade developing ways to explain each aspect in easy-to-understand ways that facilitate understanding. I've tested my explanations with individuals from many backgrounds, including teenagers, elderly individuals with low educational attainment, Ph.D.'s and physicians, waiters and sales clerks, young adults, teachers, and individuals who struggle with depression, PTSD, addictions, and other diagnosed mental health problems. I've had positive responses from every group.

One group I had difficulty with in the early days was individuals who have a religious worldview. They wanted an explanation of how my techniques fit with their specific worldview. Chapter 36 ties religious worldviews to *The Smart Way*. Because I was not satisfied only helping some people, I researched six major religions to identify how their texts support *The Smart Way*. Each of the six major religions I researched supported the key concepts, which has allowed me to help individuals of many faiths in ways that do not interfere with their worldview.

Science also supports all the key concepts I recommend, which makes them viable in secular environments. I have found that individuals in secular environments also want to know how their religion supports the key tenets, which makes sense when 86% of the world has a religious perspective. We are all beautifully unique and the explanations I've developed provide a path to understanding regardless of an individual's worldview.

Charts on the following pages show the relationships that are documented herein. The first set shows physical, mental and behavioral health problems that arise from mindsets that do not serve the individuals highest good. The second set turns the equation around and demonstrates findings about supportive mindsets.

Citations supporting each of the relationships in the diagrams are provided throughout this book. Not all the beneficial relationships are shown in the diagrams due to space constraints. Many of the relationships are circular ↷↶, with successes in one area increasing successes in others. Because positive outcomes feed other positive outcomes, upward spirals are easier to achieve than they seem. It is also the reason downward spirals can go out of control quickly when the basis of them is not known to the individual having the experience. It can feel as if life is out of control. When you know how the parts are intertwined, it is easier to put the brakes on a downward spiral and to increase the momentum of upward spirals.

Increasing Emotional Intelligence

Studies show that it is possible to increase a person's emotional intelligence by increasing their knowledge and understanding in this area.[23] Experiential learning models that provide mastery experiences give students an opportunity to internalize the information on a deeper level. Understanding information intellectually is not as productive as being able to use the information in one's day-to-day experiences. This book provides both knowledge about the basis—the why it works, and methods the reader can use to practice skills that increase Emotional Intelligence.

Relationships Between Beliefs (Mindset), Stress, and Important Areas of Life

The diagrams on the next pages illustrate many of the benefits a positive mindset provides and the detriments of a negative mindset. When research from positive psychology, social psychology, public health and other disciplines is combined the power of a positive mind becomes very clear. When you have this knowledge and look at the detrimental effect of a negative mindset in the neurological, psychoneuroimmunology, medical science and other literature it tells the opposite side of the story. A mirror image of the positive effects is revealed in the literature that looked at the effects of chronic stress. An evil twin analogy would fit the circumstances.

One of the most notable aspects is the effect of a positive mindset on lifespan in longitudinal studies. The net result is about 18 years of healthier life because debilitating illnesses arrive closer to death in the positively focused individuals, who live an average of 10.7 years longer and remain healthy until the last two years of life. The people with a pessimistic outlook tend to begin suffering from chronic illnesses about seven years prior to death. That's a difference worth talking about. If we could teach people how to reduce the number of years they spend chronically ill prior to death from seven to two, health care expenses would plummet. This is something we could do—we know how to develop more positive mindsets and can do it with children.

Our Children Live in a War Zone

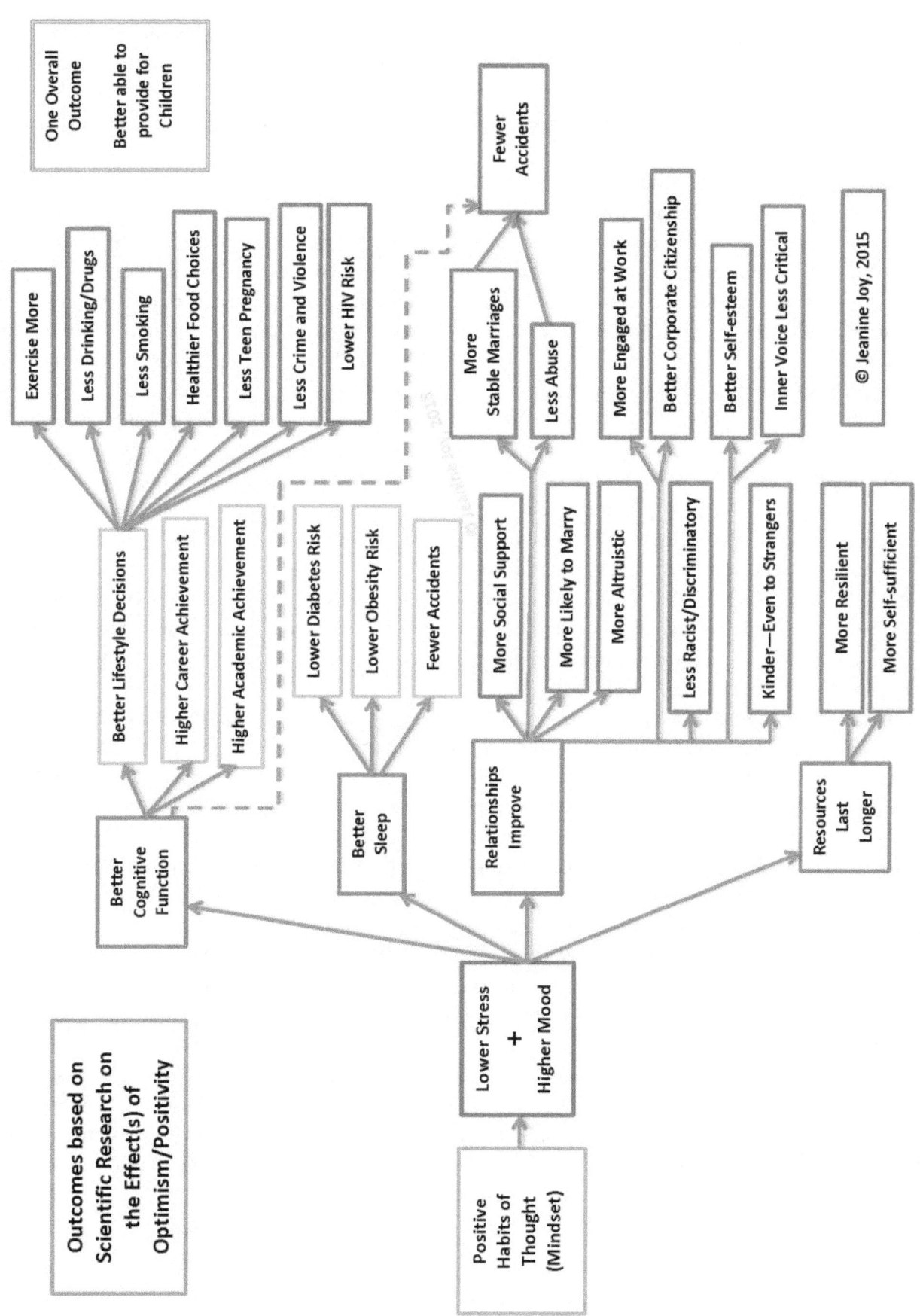

Mindsets are synonymous with beliefs. I am adamant about not telling anyone what they should believe. Instead, I focus on educating individuals about the outcome of various types of mindsets, thus allowing individuals to decide for themselves the types of mindset(s) they wish to cultivate in themselves. This respects individual differences while empowering them with knowledge that is critical to achieving a high likelihood of thriving.

Cognitive reappraisal is the basis of Cognitive Behavioral Therapy, where a trained counselor provides guidance to assist individuals in identifying and accepting more life-promoting perceptions. Cognitive Behavioral Therapy is effective in reducing stress for many people, but it is an expensive, one-on-one therapy. Cognitive appraisal is simply evaluating a thought in order to improve its impact. When an individual understands the techniques provided in this book, they become capable of moment-to-moment cognitive reappraisals to reduce their stress load, which is "a highly adaptive strategy for coping with stressful situations, not only in the short run, but also in the long run."[24] The techniques can be taught to large groups, which significantly reduces the cost of training.

Chronic stress is a significant contributor to serious physical, mental and behavioral health problems. A review of the scientific literature on the relationship between emotion regulation and depression supports my position that applying cognitive reappraisal reduces "stress-elicited emotions leading to physical disorders."[25] Unproductive thought patters such as "rumination and emotion suppression" lead to depression and physiological disease."[26] This research supports my position that teaching individuals to use positive emotional regulation techniques would prevent many instances of depression.

While therapy combined with learning these techniques is what I would encourage for individuals with diagnosed mental illnesses, everyone, especially individuals who are stressed but not yet severe enough to rate a diagnosis can benefit enormously from learning these techniques, which may prevent them from ever reaching the diagnosis stage.

Creating support groups where members can share what they learn as they apply the techniques is a beneficial and inexpensive way to reinforce the training. Epiphanies are common experiences in the support groups. As members share their experiences, it often deepens their understanding as they explain to others how they applied a specific process to their life and the effect it had. Others will listen or read what others share and assimilate the information to further their own understanding. Both those who share and those who observe gain valuable insights from the support group. After learning and applying what I learned to my own experience, I began teaching others about techniques that worked. As I taught, I gained a greater understanding of the processes.

Support groups can be informal. Something as simple as a private Facebook group works. More formal groups with regular meetings and presentations add value in a different way. Both are beneficial. The main point is that cost effective methods of providing large numbers of individuals with these skills are not difficult to create.

The flip side of the picture in the next diagram shows the debilitating impact of a negative mindset. A life lived with a negative mindset frequently feels as if you are being assaulted by bad luck on all fronts—health, relationships, and career. It often feels as if you no sooner survive one crisis and another one arrives. In many respects, a negative mindset leads to poor outcomes. Even among the most advantaged, a negative mindset results in more divorces, alcoholism, business failures, bankruptcies, and suicides.[27]

Our Children Live in a War Zone 27

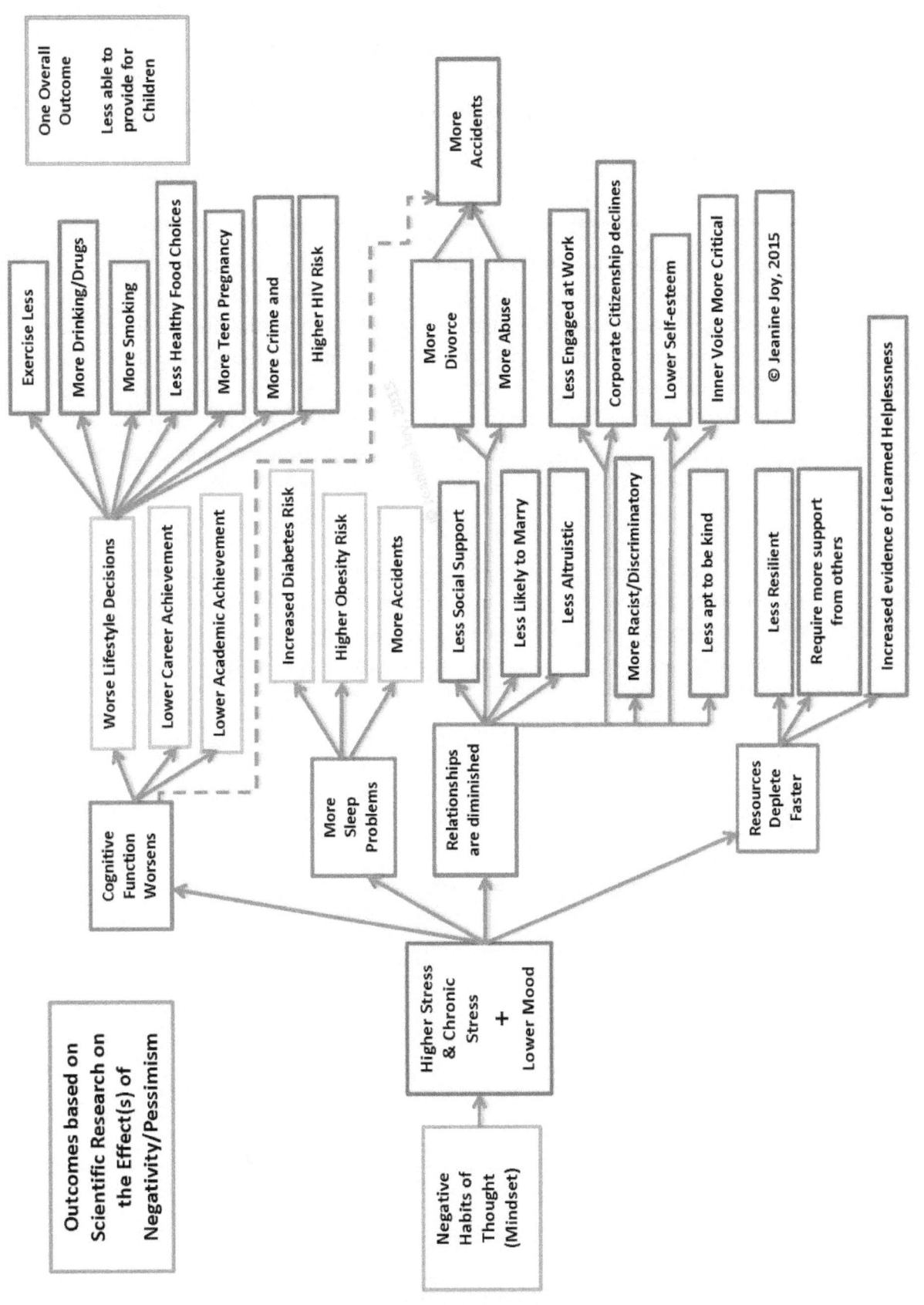

> *It is important to note that the absence of negative emotions is not the same as the presence of positive emotions. The significant benefits are caused by positive emotions, not the absence of negative emotions.*

The detriments of a negative mindset extend beyond undesired physical health outcomes. Mental and behavioral health suffers as well, often creating multigenerational problems. Two individuals in the same circumstances have decidedly different outcomes when one is optimistic and the other is pessimistic. It can lead to the difference between divorce and developing a deeper, more meaningful relationship. At its worse, it is the difference between life and death.

A negative mindset diminishes essential bodily processes. It's hard to understand how anyone can deny the mind-body connection. Anyone who was ever a teenager probably felt that connection strongly when the cute person they had a crush on caught them looking—the instant heat, the nervous perspiration, sweaty palms, and maybe a flushed face. Today, the science is clear. The immune system reacts immediately to stress.

Similar research shows the digestive function is adversely affected by stress. But we know that. We aren't surprised when the heroine in a story throws up when she learns the man she has been dating is her brother by blood. We know from experience that shocks disrupt the digestive system. Stress and anxiety can cause an upset stomach instantaneously. Most of us have experienced that at least once.

The negative impact of stress on digestive function is more insidious than we suspected.

As individuals, families, communities, nations, and humanity as a whole, we are all better off when the benefits of positivity are understood and the skills to develop positive habits of thought are known.

Our Children Live in a War Zone | 29

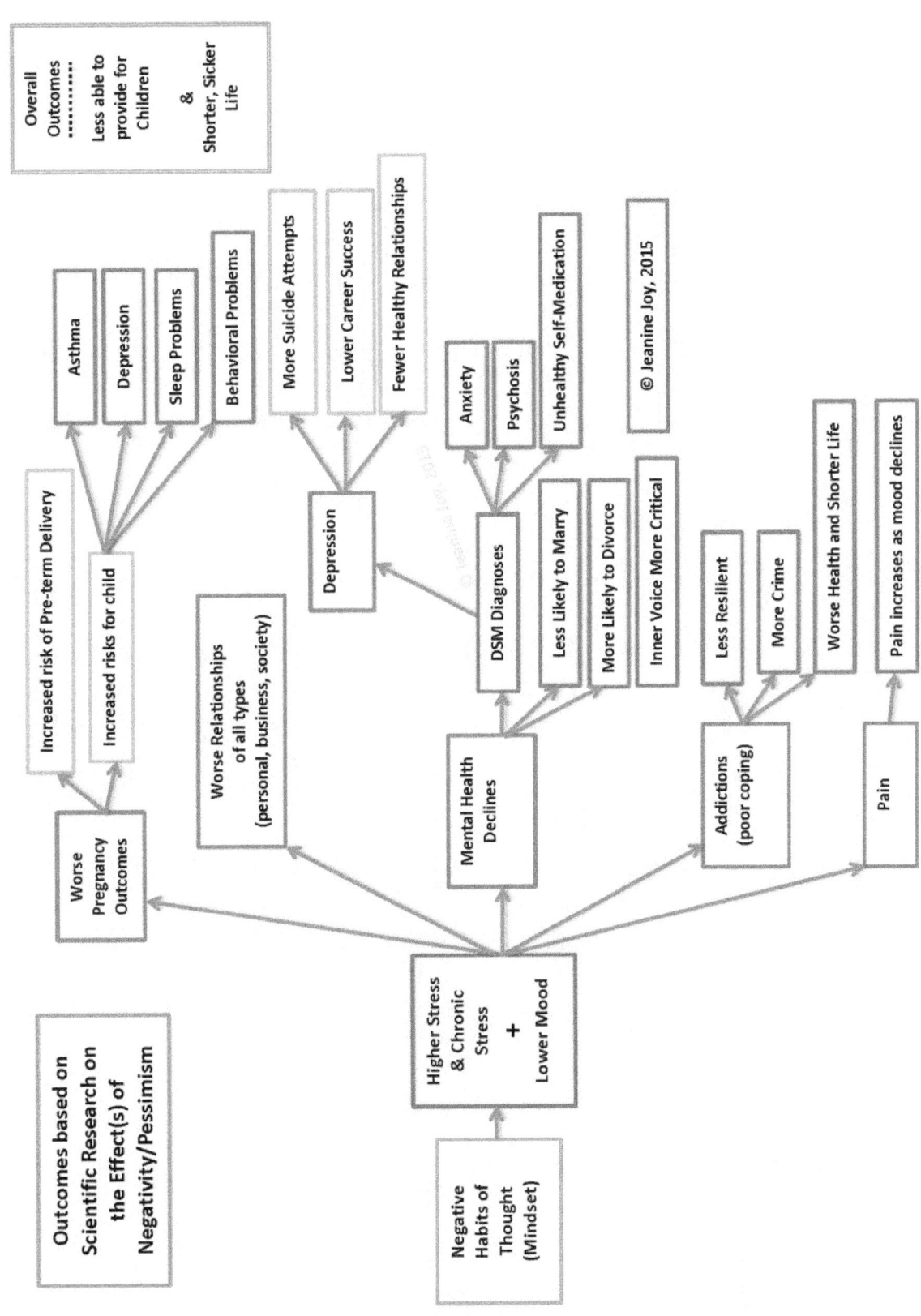

2: One Root Cause

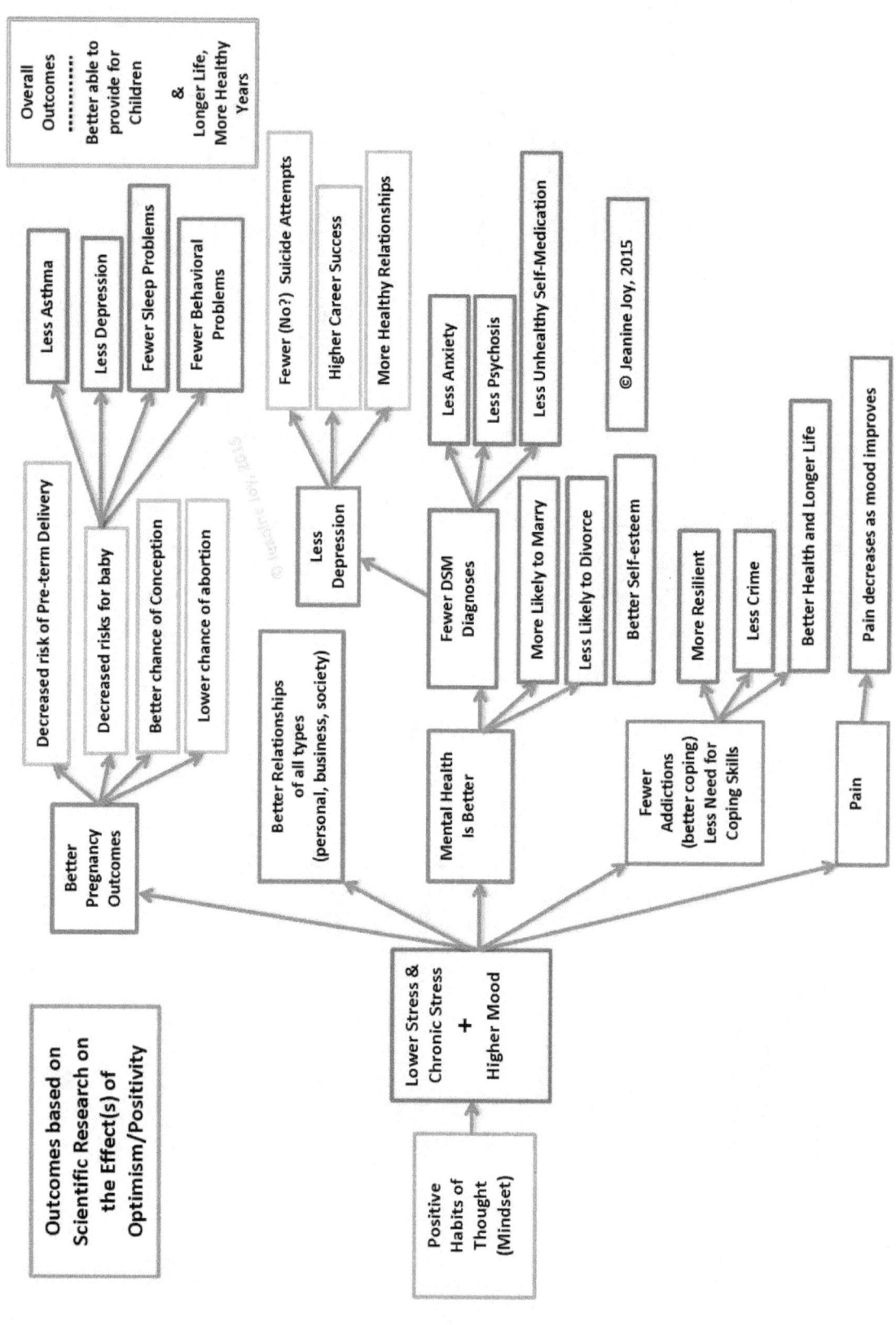

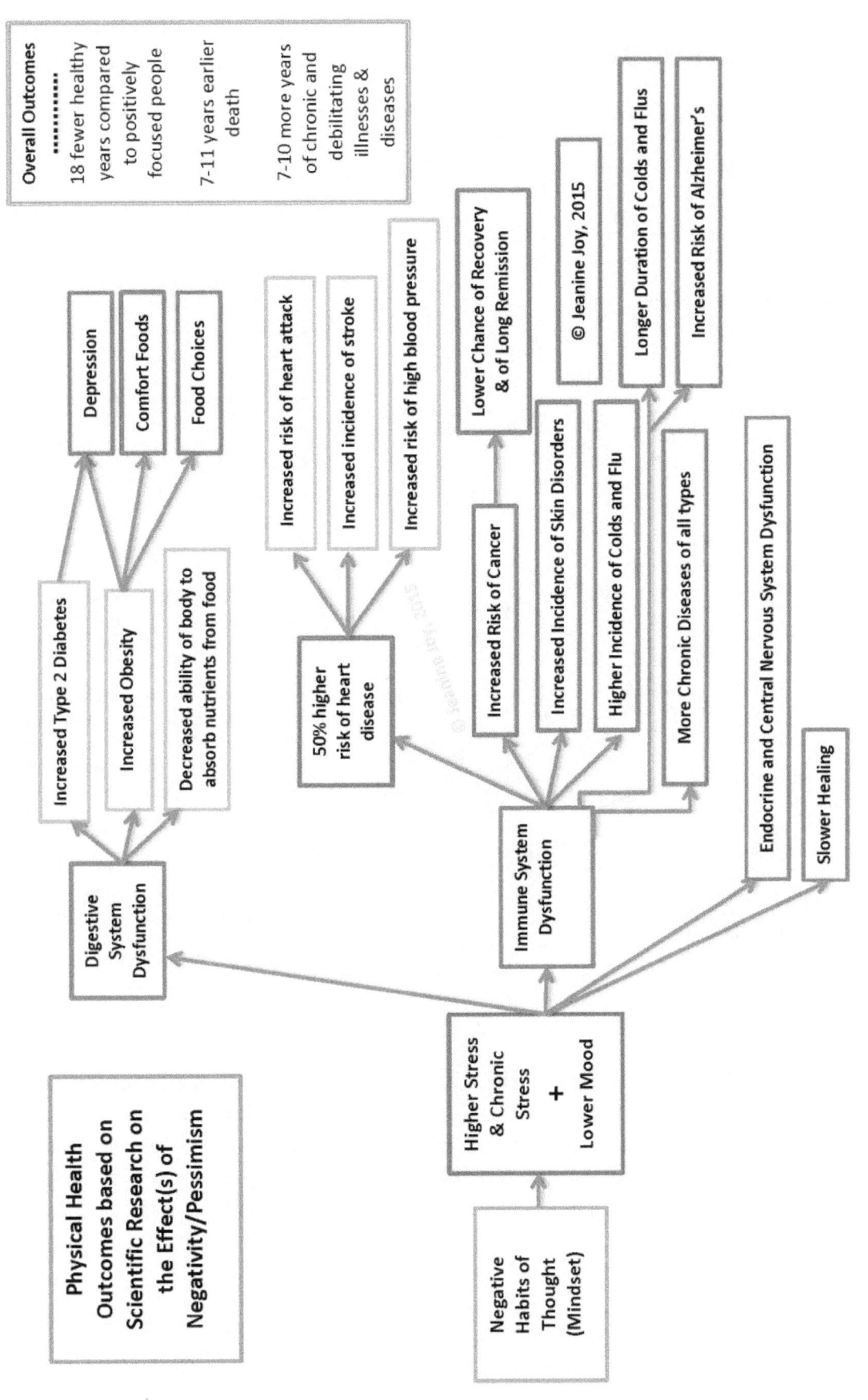

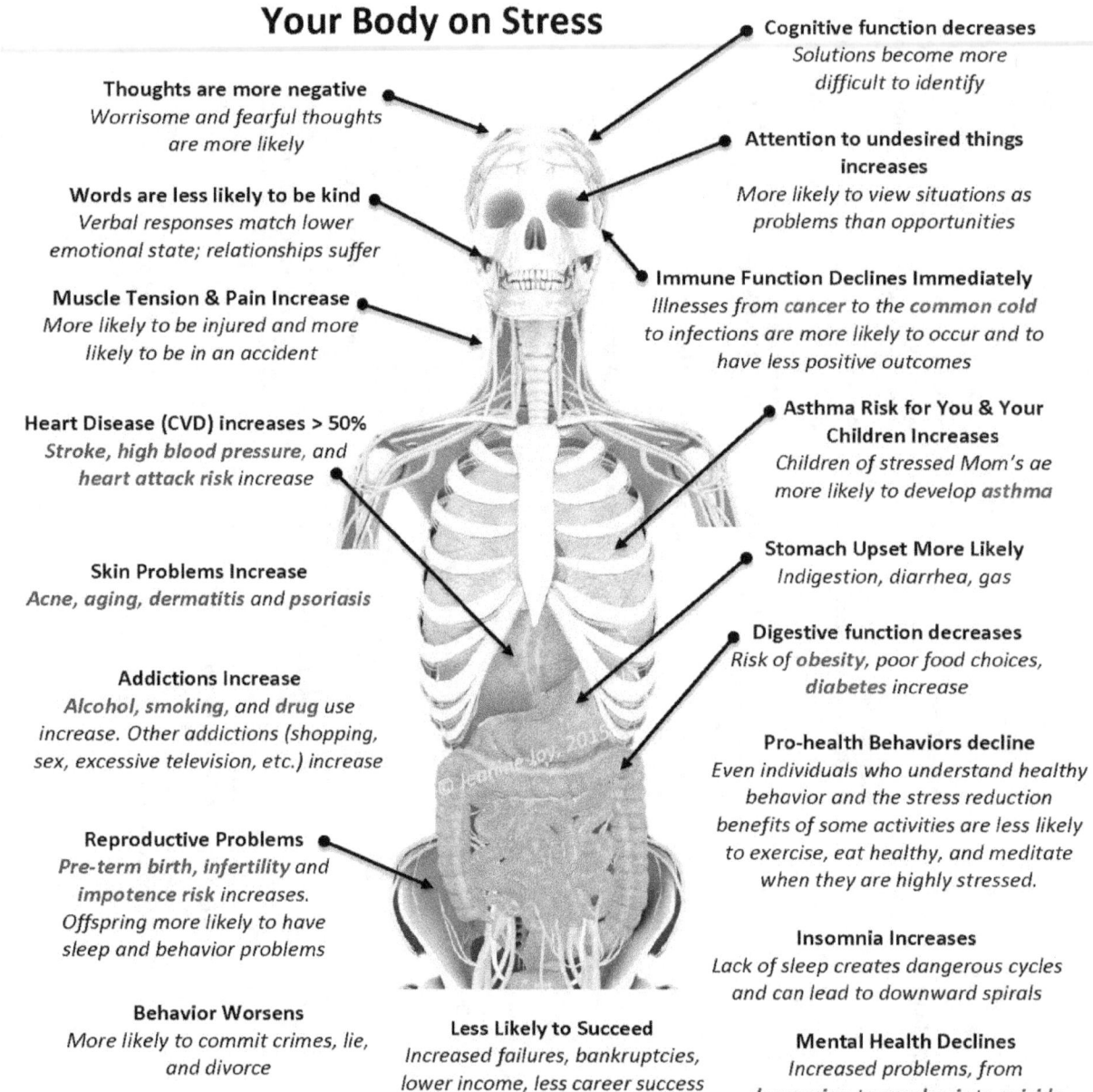

Most Americans are chronically stressed. We have become so accustomed to being stressed that it feels normal to us. But normal does not mean healthy. Many of us brag about how much stress we can experience and keep going, as if it is a badge of honor. Stress management does not work. Doctors treat stress symptoms, but are helpless against the root cause because the root is in the mind. Corporate wellness programs are designed to address symptoms, not the root cause. It's time for change. Many people believe they can ignore mild signs of stress such as headaches and stomach acid, but it's easier to fix before it becomes hypertension, obesity, diabetes, or heart disease.

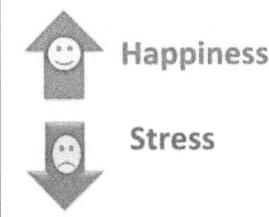

> *It is not possible to look at the negative aspects of a situation and be happy. A positive mindset can look at the same situation and feel happy because the positive mind focuses on the positive aspects of the situation.*

A negative mindset is not happy because it looks at the negative aspects of what it is focused on.

For example, a few years ago my husband and I took a Mediterranean cruise. The second day of the cruise my husband was under the weather and wanted to stay in our cabin all day. If I was negatively focused I could have railed against the fates for making him sick when we were on a cruise, which would have made the situation even worse. Instead, I had some work on a chapter for a peer reviewed textbook that I had not finished before we left for our trip. I considered the quiet day a boon that would allow me to finish the edits while my husband rested and recovered.

I would not have wished for him to be ill during our cruise, but it was easy to see the positive aspects of the situation because I have trained my mind to look for the positive in every situation. It has not always been an automatic process, but life is far better now that it is. Someone who has a negative mindset would have a difficult time perceiving anything good about becoming ill while on vacation.

In fact, it would not be unusual for a negatively focused individual to find a lot of negativity in such a situation. The actual mild illness could be seen as a pattern, "Nothing ever goes right for me." The negatively focused individual might lament, "Why does this always happen to me?" The situation could become a tragedy in the negatively focused individual's mind, "Why do I bother trying to have fun. Something always goes wrong." I've even seen individuals take a single day illness during vacation like this and use it to define the vacation. For the rest of the vacation they talk about how it was ruined by the day of illness. After they return home they continue telling the story about how the vacation was ruined by a day of illness. The other 20 days of the trip are barely remembered because the one day that did not go as planned is the primary focus.

Mindset matters more than most recognize.

Another point of clarification is that many individuals have been taught that optimism and pessimism are personality traits that cannot be changed. New research demonstrates that personality, including optimistic and pessimistic traits, is far more malleable than we have ever believed possible. I've seen many people make these changes in their lives and the happiness they've attained as a result.

There is one more point I want to clarify because I am seeing more and more people push back against the concept of happiness. Commonly they indicate that their life is such that they know they *should be happy*, and express feelings of guilt because they aren't happy. No one *should be happy*, but anyone could be. Believing you must pursue happiness or that you should be happy because the circumstances of your life are considered desirable by many others stem from believing false premises that will be explained later. Happiness is based on individual factors that are unique to each individual.

For starters, the definition of sustainable happiness includes feeling negative emotions on occasion. It is the way those emotions are perceived as temporary that leaves the door open for a quick return to better-feeling emotional states. While happiness includes emotional states that feel good,[a] True Happiness is a process defined as follows:

"The State of True Happiness does not require a constant state of bliss. It is a deep sense of inner stability, peace, well-being, and vitality that is consistent and sustainable. Awareness that one possesses the knowledge and skills to return to a happy state, even when not in that state, is a critical component of sustainable happiness. True Happiness is sustainable because the individual deliberately and consciously chooses perspectives that create positive emotions and has cultivated this habit of thought until the natural and habitual response focuses on the positive aspects of the current situation."

As you read, do your best to keep an open mind asking, "Could this be true?" If some aspect of what you read is not believable to you, skip it and come back to it later or try it yourself, in the privacy of your own mind. When I first learned what I am writing about here there were things that ran so counter to what I believed and had believed for most of my life, that I could not accept their truth. I skipped over them and came back later to find that what I had learned allowed me to see the fallacy of what I had been taught to believe and recognize the inherent truth of perspectives that were very different from my earlier beliefs.

Do not accept what I tell you as truth. Much of what is written can be evaluated against your own life experience, if your mind is open enough to consider the possibility. If your mind is completely closed to new ideas, don't bother turning the page—it will be of no benefit to you. Leave it to others to fix the problems that plague our world.

Einstein pointed to the need to think differently when solving problems when he said, *"We can't solve problems by using the same kind of thinking we used when we created them."*

If you are ready to be part of the solution, read on.

If you want a better life for yourself or your family, read on.

---

[a] See Appendix I

3: The Smart Way

In order to improve the mind, we ought less to learn, than to contemplate.
René Descartes

The Smart Way Metacognitive Processes used in conjunction with Emotional Guidance helps you optimize the way you use your mind and body.

Metacognitive simply means you think about what you're thinking. You're not thinking on auto-pilot. You think about what you're thinking and how it feels when you think what you think. It is actually natural. Some people naturally do it and thrive as a result. Like any skill, yours will get better with practice. Like any new skill, you won't be an expert the first time. But you can learn how to do it and the best part about it is that doing it feels good. Once you feel the empowerment the first time you are successful, you will want to do it again—because it feels good. The effort you exert toward self-empowerment empowerment today provides a stepping stool that provides empowerment for higher step you'll climb tomorrow.

"One particularly adaptive type of emotion regulation is reappraisal, which refers to changing how individuals appraise the situation they are in to alter its emotional significance."[28] Individuals who engage in reappraisal tend to:[29]

- Feel a higher sense of purpose in life
- Feel less depressed
- Have strengthened social bonds
- Higher well-being
- Greater social adjustment

In a sample of 222 individuals that recently faced stressful life events, those who habitually used cognitive reappraisal were experiencing higher levels of well-being, better social adjustment, and fewer depressive symptoms.[30] Several aspects of *The Smart Way*, which pre-dates the study, are designed to increase individual's motivation to use cognitive reappraisal techniques, both by overcoming common limiting beliefs and by educating participants about the benefit of maintaining better-feeling emotions. A meta-analysis of 51 independent studies with a total of 21,150 participants confirmed that cognitive reappraisal (a skill taught as part of *The Smart Way*) significantly contributes to positive mental health and protects against indicators of poor mental health.[31] Imagine how much more powerful cognitive reappraisal is when you add Emotional Guidance to the tool kit.

When you "accept thoughts and feelings without judgment and focus on the present moment,"[32] depression and anxiety decline. If therapies effectively treat mood and anxiety disorders because of individuals using cognitive reappraisal, wouldn't directly teaching individuals how to use Cognitive Reappraisal be more powerful because it would increase the conscious directing of the mind to use the technique, not rely on them making the connection between reappraisal and better emotional states? Wouldn't doing it before a diagnosis have the ability to prevent the illness from manifesting? Or the big question, is it really an illness or is it simply dysfunction thinking that we've labeled as a larger problem?

When it happens, it causes significant problems in people's lives. I'm not diminishing the realness of it when it is occurring. I'm diminishing the difficulty of the cure (or, preferably, prevention) when the right tools are used.

In the **One Root Cause** chapter you saw how the way we think is connected to everything else—mental and physical health issues as well as behavior and relationships.

Another area of research that points to the benefit of using *The Smart Way* in conjunction with Emotional Guidance demonstrates that self-compassion is important in recovery from stressful life events and can reduce or eliminate PTSD symptoms following "severe and repeated interpersonal trauma."[33] A study of women going through divorce found that women recovered faster when they were compassionate toward themselves.[34] Give yourself permission to be self-compassionate. The *Forgiveness* section in the **Processes Chapter** will help.

There is not just one of you. You are multiple people and you do not act the same way all the time nor do you think of yourself the same way all the time. We all have multiple selves that emerge in different situations.[35]

As a son or daughter, you have a certain perspective of yourself. You may view yourself as a good son or daughter, or you may view yourself as a disappointing son or daughter. You may view yourself as a duty-bound son or daughter. The number of ways you can view who you are as a son or daughter is endless.

> *The findings suggest that interventions may be beneficial that enhance positive implicit valuing of emotion regulation. Techniques that allow individuals to experience successful emotion regulation may positively influence the value they give such regulation. Training procedures that specifically enhance cognitive reappraisal would be promising as cognitive reappraisal abilities play a distinct and important role in successful psychotherapy.*
> *(Hopp et al., 2011)*

As an employee or student, you have another view of yourself. It may be more or less positive than your view of yourself as a son or daughter. You may be both a student and an employee. When I was in high school, the school treated us as if we were children, my parents treated me as if I was semi-adult and my employer treated me as a full blown adult. The more free I felt in the environment, the better I felt so I liked work better than home or school.

We also have ideas about who we are right now and who we will be in the future. For example, the last few years I've been very focused on my research and writing which has led to a more sedentary lifestyle than I prefer and weight gain. In my mind I am where I am, but I am also the person I'll be when the next two books are done and I can allow myself more time to care for my body. My future self is in better physical condition than my current self.

Who are you today?

Who do you see yourself being tomorrow?

I also see myself as reaching out to more people and doing more training than writing in the future so my future self will seldom stay home all day reviewing research and writing. My future self will spend a lot of time traveling to teach and speak.

Part of my vision of my future self includes changed relationships with people in my life. Right now my children, who are college educated adults, live at home. I have a large house and it seems to make more sense for them to share my space, but in the future I see them coming to visit—not living under my roof. My future self will have more time to play with my friends than I allow my current self.

What will your future self be able to do that you cannot or will not allow yourself to do today? Could you do them today?

The Smart Way Metacognitive Processes used in conjunction with Emotional Guidance provides a stable foundation for success throughout life. Evidence-based techniques address core skills that make the difference between choosing a path toward self-actualization and success or a less productive one.

The objectives of the curricula are:
- Foster skills and social competence through training that increases self-confidence.
- Increase participation and success by providing goal setting training that reinforces inherent desires for autonomy and competence.
- Reduce susceptibility to negative external pressures and stress.
- Increase growth mindset and intrinsic desire for continuous self-development.
- Develop skills that increase both happiness and resilience, which reduces stress.
- Develop a thorough understanding of how to accurately interpret emotions and respond to their signals in pro-health and pro-social ways (Emotional Intelligence Plus).
- Recognize the connection between emotional state and behaviors.
- Teach skills that lead to the development of habitual bias that allocates attention during new situations in ways that elicit positive emotions more often, essentially resulting in implicit emotion regulation.[36]

Skills that empower an individual to regulate their emotional response to the events occurring in their life (self-regulation) significantly reduce the risk of mental illnesses including depression, anxiety, panic disorders, bi-polar disorder and even psychosis. Individuals with the ability to self-induce desired emotional states "are happier in both positive and negative circumstances."[37] Regulating negative emotions downward reduces stress, which leads to improved physical health. "The existence of automatic, unconscious processes influencing human emotion, cognition, and behavior is widely accepted and confirmed by numerous studies."[38]

Although these processes provide regulation below our conscious awareness, the actual way they regulation emotion and whether they regulate emotion in ways that supports greater health or in ways that diminishes one's ability to achieve and maintain health varies between individuals. They are learned methods that can be adjusted to improve outcomes. When they are adjusted and begin automatically supporting healthy emotional states they are not dose-dependent. All other techniques and processes that are currently used (pharmacological, mindfulness, meditation, exercise, yoga, gratitude, helping others, journaling, and more) are dose-dependent. Research clearly shows that individuals do not give themselves the dose they need to maintain optimal emotional states when their stress levels rise.[39] In other words, frequent use of *The Smart Way* techniques for just a few months can improve the automatic stress and happiness regulation done by the brain. And, unlike most self-improvement techniques, *The Smart Way* feels good every step of the way so its use is intrinsically rewarded.

The Smart Way was designed by combining characteristics of individuals who thrive against the odds with the latest research in positive psychology, resilience, psychological flexibility, self-determination theory, and other research that points to the basis of human thriving.

Happiness and stress have an inverse relationship. Research on the presence of happiness and the presence of stress reveal the following benefits of higher levels of happiness and lower levels of stress:

Increased pro-social behaviors
- Reduced anti-social behavior
- Better citizenship
- Increased kindness (even to strangers)
- Intrinsically motivated diversity appreciation (a significant step-up from tolerance)
- Reduced (or no) criminal behavior
- Increased positive goal setting

Increased pro-health behaviors
- Reduced likelihood of alcohol, drug, and cigarette use
- Increased physical activity
- Better dietary choices
- Improved sleep habits and quality of sleep

Physical and Mental Benefits
- Improved immune function
- Improved cognitive function
- Improved digestive function
- Improved Central Nervous System Functioning
- Reduced risk of mental illness (including depression/anxiety)[40] and suicide,[41] which are all are strongly correlated to stress and poor emotion regulation skills

The Smart Way program is designed to build strengths associated with positive outcomes including:

- Autonomous Intrinsic Motivation
- Positivity/optimism
- Growth Mindset
- Emotional Intelligence
- Authenticity
- Positive goal-setting
- Internal Locus of Control
- Healthy self-esteem
- Metacognitive Skills
- Physical, Mental, Emotional, and Behavioral Health
- Positive self-image
- Acceptance of responsibility for actions and results

The Smart Way has been compared to Cognitive Behavioral Therapy in the following way:

Cognitive Behavioral Therapy (CBT) is done one-on-one and resembles having an expert marksman stand next to an amateur who is blindfolded while attempting to hit a target by obtaining instructions from the expert, who is the only one who knows the location of the target.

The Smart Way can be delivered in large group settings where hundreds can be taught at the same time because it removes the blindfold and makes the target fully visible to each individual, who is given skills that empower them to identify the right target and continually improve their aim. Intrinsic motivation occurs naturally because each step results in positive emotional feedback. Even when the overall emotional state is still negative, the student feels the relief of feeling better and the hope that comes from knowing one has the skills to shift to increasingly better feeling emotional states.

Cognitive Behavioral Therapy is further hampered by:
- Stigma associated with mental illness
- High cost of one-on-one therapy
- Recurrent need because CBT resolves current issues without necessarily developing skills to

address future issues
- ❖ Cognitive Behavioral and other types of therapies are reactive

Therapists have typically been trained to move people from a minus state to zero on the following scale:

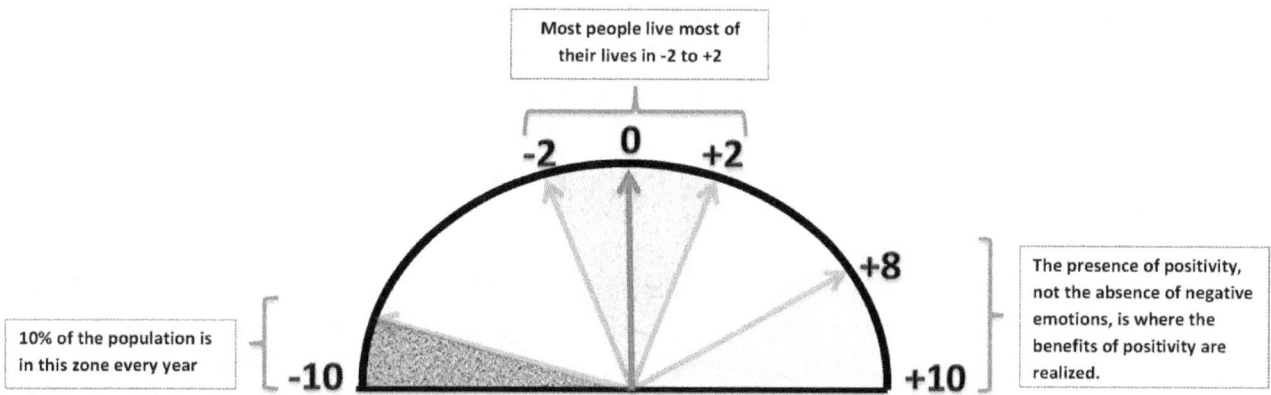

The Smart Way is proactive, low-cost, develops skills that improve results throughout life, and is designed to help individuals achieve and sustain emotions in the +8 range (from hope to joy). Because it is educational and structured to correct prevalent misconceptions, some due to prior errors in scientific hypotheses, there is no stigma. It is an evidence-based form of Primary Prevention. Training comes with added benefits, including improving morale, reducing burnout, enhancement of any existing wellness programs and reduction in any existing prejudices or biases.

"Cognitive behavioral therapies can be defined as those interventions with the core assumptions that what individuals think directly impacts how they feel and what they do."[42] Despite the fact that Cognitive Behavioral Therapy is used as a curative rather than a preventative method of improving mental (and in some cases, physical), health, "it is clear that the evidence-base of CBT is enormous." Hoffman, et al. conducted a review of meta-analyses of the use of CBT to address a wide variety of issues and concluded by recommending that countries adopt it as a first-line defense against mental disorders. I go a step further in my hypothesis.

My Hypothesis is that anything Cognitive Behavioral Therapy is effective at treating, The Smart Way can prevent from happening in the first place.

The Smart Way is not synonymous with Cognitive Behavioral Therapy provided before an individual develops a mental or physical health problem. It is **CBT Plus** delivered primarily to groups or provided as self-help using videos and books. It is significantly more cost effective because it does not require one-on-one therapy and because it prevents the problems before they happen, thus avoiding the costs associated with problems that have manifested. Also, it is more difficult to permanently cure a condition than to prevent its occurrence in the first place and there is no relapse because the illness did not manifest in the first place. Another major difference is that Cognitive Behavioral Therapy does not include Emotional Guidance, which overturns a prevalent but inaccurate interpretation of the purpose of emotions. *The Smart Way* also disabuses negative beliefs about the subconscious portions of personality that often include beliefs that the subconscious is secret, dark, and frightening as well as unreliable and dangerous to explore.

This is significant for reasons you will see throughout this book. The basic premise behind my hypothesis is supported by research that shows Cognitive Behavioral Therapy works by helping patients change the way they think to healthier thought patterns which significantly reduces the likelihood a person will relapse after treatment. Instead of waiting for someone to develop a mental health disorder, which may or may not receive treatment at some point, *The Smart Way* provides information and skills that empower individuals to develop healthy habits of thought before a problem develops.

Deci and Ryan point to another aspect of therapy that is designed to correct a manifested problem that makes waiting until the problem arises to adjust dysfunctional thinking a less beneficial alternative. The current treatment paradigm puts so much pressure on therapists to achieve results that therapists can become "controlling rather than autonomy supportive is often a function of the pressures they experience in the treatment . . . external pressures from clinic directors or insurers or internally controlling introjection and ego-involvements can lead therapists to make clients change."[43]

While there is a strong emphasis on prevention with *The Smart Way*, I have case studies demonstrating that *The Smart Way* is effective in restoring mental health to individuals who were suffering from severe long-term PTSD, severe chronic depression, and that is has been effective in preventing imminent suicides. It was those successes combined with the increased experience of positive emotions in those I taught that convinced me of the power *The Smart Way* has to help people even though the techniques are delivered to groups.

After Butler, Chapman, Forman, and Beck, conducted a meta-analysis to review the existing research relating to Cognitive Behavioral Therapy in 2006, they concluded, "The meta-analyses reviewed strongly suggest that across many disorders the effects of CBT are maintained for substantial periods beyond the cessation of treatment. More specifically,

> *Cognitive Behavior Therapy techniques produces vastly superior long-term improvements, with relapse rates half those of pharmacotherapy.*

significant evidence for long-term effectiveness was found for depression, generalized anxiety, panic, social phobia, OCD, sexual offending, schizophrenia, and childhood internalizing disorders. In the cases of depression and panic, there appears to be robust and convergent meta-analytic evidence that CBT produces vastly superior long-term persistence of effects, with relapse rates half those of pharmacotherapy."[44]

The robust support for persistence of Cognitive Behavioral Therapy suggests that learning metacognitive processes protects against the occurrence of many chronic problems our society would like to eliminate. The persistence of the results suggests (strongly, in my opinion) that prevention is possible.

Providing knowledge and skills that prevent the maladaptive cognitions Cognitive Behavioral Therapy is designed to correct will prevent the problems from manifesting in the first place, thus preventing a significant portion of the suffering that currently affects people around the world. There is evidence-based support that Cognitive Behavioral Therapy (CBT) is effective in reducing and/or healing the following issues.

Anxiety
18% of adults suffer from some form of anxiety,[45] which costs the US $148 billion (1/3 of the country's mental health expenditures).[46] Cognitive Behavioral Therapy is effective in treating anxiety[47,48] and was the preferred method for "children and adolescents, with effect sizes in the large range"[49]

Depression
Depression affects more than 16% of the population at some point during their lifetime and about 10% of the population each year. For individuals living in poverty, 31% have been diagnosed as depressed.[50] Because of stigma and the cost of care, it is likely that this number significantly understates the prevalence of depression in our nation's poor. The economic burden of depression in the United States in 2010 was $98.9 billion.[51]

Cognitive Behavioral Therapy is effective in treatment of depression, including severely depressed unipolar patients.[52] An article by Simona Bujoreanu, PhD., a Harvard Psychology instructor and an Assistant in Psychology at Children's Hospital Boston, and David Benhayon and Eva Szigethy about the Treatment of Depression in Children and Adolescents stated, "Cognitive Behavioral Therapy is widely recommended by professional groups for youth depression and has the most replicated success in clinical trials for youth depression."[53]

Panic Disorders

Cognitive Behavioral Therapy was found to:[54]
1. Be effective in reducing symptoms to levels "near or below those found in the general population by the end of treatment,"
2. Have lower attrition rates than pharmacological treatments (fewer people stopped treatment before completion),
3. The effect was stable with "virtually no slippage in effect" after one year.

Bi-polar disorders

Cognitive Behavioral Therapy is a useful adjunct therapy for bi-polar disorders[55] and appears to reduce relapses regardless of how many episodes of bi-polar disorder occurred prior to treatment.[56]

Crime Reduction

Chicago youths who were given Cognitive Behavioral Therapy committed 44% less crime than a control group.[57] Hoffman et al.'s review of meta-analyses indicated that ". . . behavioral therapy and CBT appeared to be the superior interventions in reducing recidivism rates, both with medium mean effect sizes."[58] Even the National Institute of Justice recognizes the value of Cognitive Behavioral Therapy, Patrick Clark commented, "One form of psychotherapy stands out in the criminal justice system. Cognitive behavioral therapy reduces recidivism in both juveniles and adults."[59]

Improved High School Graduation Rates

"Using cognitive-behavioral interventions can substantively lessen the kinds of problem behaviors that frequently result in school suspensions and/or expulsions that subsequently lead to school dropout."[60] The same study in Chicago that showed a 44% reduction in crime increased graduation rates from 13% to 23%.[61]

Treatment of and Reduction in Physical Pain

Cognitive Behavioral Therapy is an effective therapy for chronic pain in adults[62, 63] and improves the ability to cope with pain.[64]

Educational Success

Cognitive Behavioral Therapy combined with intensive tutoring profoundly improved academic achievements for children who were previously considered lost causes.[65]

Bullying (Recovery from)

"One of the most effective therapies in addressing the emotional distress caused by bullying is Cognitive Behavioral Therapy."[66]

Bullying Prevention

Recognize that if the bully was a happy child, he or she would not be a bully. "In 2007, 15.2 percent of U.S. children were identified as bullies by a parent or guardian. Overall, children with mental health disorders were three times more likely to bully other children . . . children with a diagnosis of depression were three times more likely to bully, while a diagnosis of Oppositional Defiant Disorder (ODD) was associated with a six fold increase in the odds of being identified as a bully."[67]

As noted earlier, Cognitive Behavioral Therapy is an effective treatment for depression. It is also used alone and in conjunction with other methodologies to treat ODD. If you look at the EGSc (See Appendix I), you'll see that ODD fits perfectly in the Red Zone. When the impact of emotional state on behavior is understood it is easy to see that the child who has been diagnosed with ODD needs help and the first place I would begin would be helping the child understand filters that impact the perception of reality and that ODD means they're set to increase his or her focus on things that result in angry emotions. See more about filters in Chapter 11.

Violence Reduction

Cognitive Behavioral Therapy has a small positive impact on domestic violence and . . . a medium to large positive effect on sexual offenders (although surgical and hormonal treatments were more effective for the later.[68] Butler et al found that Cognitive Behavioral Therapy was as effective as hormonal therapy and less likely to be refused and more likely to be completed.[69] Cognitive Behavioral Therapy combined with unusual sports reduced crime by 44% in a low-income minority neighborhood.[70]

Prevent relapse of Mood Disorders.

"CBT does appear to have an enduring effect that protects against subsequent relapse and recurrence following the end of active treatment, something that cannot be said for medications."[71]

Substance Use Disorders

"These disorders are highly common, with lifetime rates of substance abuse or dependence estimated at over 30% for alcohol and over 10% for other drugs, and past year point prevalence rates of 8.5% for alcohol and 2% for other drugs. . . Cognitive behavioral therapy (CBT) for substance use disorders has demonstrated efficacy as both a monotherapy and as part of combination treatment strategies."[72]

Smoking Cessation

"Treatments for smoking cessation found that coping skills, which were partially based on CBT techniques, were highly effective in reducing relapse in a community sample of nicotine quitters, and another meta-analysis noted superiority of CBT (either alone or in combination with nicotine replacement therapy) over [73] nicotine replacement therapy alone."[74]

Problematic Gambling

Pathological gambling affects 1 – 3% of the adult population and is a greater problem for adolescents . . . and the less severe problematic gambling affects an additional 1.3% to 3.6% of the population.[75] The societal cost of pathological gambling is estimated at 5 billion dollars annually.[76] Cognitive Behavioral Therapy is effective in the treatment of gambling problems.[77, 78]

Schizophrenia and Other Psychotic Disorders

Although Cognitive Behavioral Therapy does not cure Schizophrenia or other Psychotic disorders, it is effective in reducing symptoms.[79]

When other research is considered, the pathway to psychosis appears to be paved with chronic stress. For example, "The current literature provides some evidence that the onset of psychotic disorders may be associated with a higher rate of stress and changes to the hippocampus."[80]

Phobias

Cognitive Behavioral Therapy is effective in treating phobias and demonstrates the ability to provide long-term maintenance of improvements.[81]

Obsessive Compulsive Disorder (OCD)

A meta-analysis for OCD found Cognitive Behavioral Therapy provided substantial relief and that the improvements persisted over time.[82]

Posttraumatic Stress Disorder (PTSD)

Cognitive Behavioral Therapy is superior to supportive counseling and reprocessing for PTSD. I also have a case history where long-term (Vietnam era) PTSD was successfully alleviated for a veteran using *The Smart Way*. The veteran had received a variety of treatments over the years and was being treated using Mindfulness, counseling, and pharmacology at the time we met, but his level of functioning remained very limited. After learning *The Smart Way* he was able to participate in many activities he had previously been unable to enjoy and (under doctor supervision) stop taking medication for PTSD. The improvements included being able to attend an event where loud fireworks went off unexpectedly without triggering an anxiety attack and beginning to enjoy frequent travel, including international travel, with confidence. His improvements have been sustained for over six years at this writing.

Body dysmorphic disorder (BDD)

Cognitive Behavioral Therapy is more effective in treating this disorder than "psychoeducation, explanatory therapy, cognitive therapy, exposure and response prevention, and behavioral stress management."[83]

Hypochondria

Cognitive Behavioral Therapy is more effective in treating hypochondria than "psychoeducation, explanatory therapy, cognitive therapy, exposure and response prevention, and behavioral stress management."[84]

Eating Disorders

Cognitive Behavioral Therapy has a significant positive effect on eating disorders.[85] *The National Institute for Health and Clinical Excellence Review* "and two other recent systematic reviews is that cognitive behavioral therapy Cognitive Behavioral Therapy is the clear leading treatment for bulimia nervosa in adults."[86]

Insomnia

"Problems with falling asleep or daytime sleepiness affect approximately 35 to 40% of the U.S. adult population annually and are a significant cause of morbidity and mortality."[87] Cognitive Behavioral Therapy is well-established as an effective treatment for sleep disorders.[88]

Hypertension

Hypertension patients can be "easily upset by criticism or imperfection, possess pent-up anger and lack self-confidence."[89] Although I haven't found research to support my position yet, I expect the low self-confidence may (in some situations) appear as egotistical at times due to unstable self-esteem, not simply low self-esteem.

Coronary Heart Disease (CHD)

"There is strong evidence that psychological stress is a significant risk factor for CHD and CHD mortality."[90, also see 91]

Personality Disorders

Cognitive Behavioral Therapy was not the best therapy for personality disorders, but it did have a significant positive effect in a meta-analysis.[92]

Anger and Aggression

Beck and Fernandez found that, "the average CBT recipient was better off than 76% of untreated subjects in terms of anger reduction."[93] Cognitive Behavioral Therapy "is moderately effective at reducing anger problems."[94]

General Stress

My hypothesis is partially based on the pathway from chronic stress to physical, mental, and behavioral problems, highlighted in the charts in the prior chapter. Cognitive Behavioral Therapy has a large positive effect on occupational stress and is also effective (albeit with a smaller positive impact) on the stress of parenting a child with developmental disabilities.[95] "As a stress management intervention, CBT was more effective that other treatments, such as organization-focused therapies."[96]

Teacher (Trainee) Stress Levels

Teacher trainees experiencing high levels of occupational stress who received Cognitive Behavioral Therapy "had significant reductions in their levels of stress, depression, state and trait anxiety" compared to the control group following treatment.[97]

Type II Diabetes

Evidence that chronic stress and financial stress increases the risk of developing Type II diabetes is growing. To the extent Cognitive Behavioral Therapy can alleviate the chronic stress, it could be helpful in preventing development of Type II diabetes.[98]

Disease Management

Lansing and Berg recommend developing self-regulation skills to help adolescents improve self-management of chronic illnesses. In the conclusion of their article they stated, "effective emotion regulation through cognitive behavioral or stress-reduction interventions may have an effect on not only individual but also interpersonal outcomes."[99]

Early Stage Breast Cancer

Women with early stage breast cancer who underwent Cognitive Behavioral Therapy had increased immune function at the 3-month follow-up. They also reported more benefit finding than women in the comparison group.[100]

Distress Due to General Medical Conditions

Cognitive Behavioral Therapy had a small to medium beneficial effect on distress and also on secondary issues stemming from the primary medical condition.[101]

Irritable Bowel Syndrome

"Self-management programs that include cognitive behavioral strategies have been shown to improve gastrointestinal (GI) symptoms, psychological distress, and quality of life (QoL) in persons with irritable bowel syndrome (IBS)."[102]

Chronic Fatigue Syndrome

Cognitive Behavioral Therapy is moderately effective as a treatment for Chronic Fatigue Syndrome according to Malouff and his team of researchers.[103]

Rheumatoid Arthritis

Cognitive Behavioral Therapy of more than six weeks duration was consistently effective as an adjunct therapy for Rheumatoid Arthritis in the short-term but long-term efficacy was mixed.[104]

Premenstrual Syndrome

Premenstrual Syndrome depression and anxiety responded favorably in one study but further research is needed for the findings to be considered robust. [105]

4: Cognitive Behavioral Therapy vs. *The Smart Way*

A man has free choice to the extent that he is rational.
Thomas Aquinas

As you can see, the list of physical, mental, and behavioral health issues that Cognitive Behavioral Therapy techniques are effective at treating is lengthy. Since CBT is essentially teaching people to think in self-supporting ways, it makes sense that teaching them to do that before a problem manifests would effectively prevent many issues from ever arising. The benefits to individuals, employers, schools, and society in general of reducing the incidences of these problems should be obvious. Our children truly do live in a war zone. School hallways can erupt in violence at any moment. Threats, bullying, and pervasive tension are common aspects of our children's lives. We also live in a time where families are struggling and enduring many hardships, from job volatility and loss, foreclosures, to deployments, divorces, and random violence that strikes more frequently than ever at shopping malls, movie theaters, and other venues.

If we and our children have skills and habits of thought that make us resilient, we will fare much better than those who are not resilient if we find ourselves the survivor of such an event. We will also not experience the same level of chronic stress that leads to diminished physical and mental health in those who do not have skills. Our world has changed.

Add the improvement in employee engagement and happiness that result from learning *The Smart Way* and it begins to look like a miracle drug, except it's not a drug. I believe it is so effective because it corrects thinking that exists only because many common beliefs in our society are slightly off base. Metacognitive processes and Emotional Guidance correct those issues, helping people who learn them live up to their potential. One of the reasons so many suffer is because they know intuitively that life should be better for them, but without understanding their guidance or the false premises that are negatively affecting their life experience, they don't know why it isn't working out the way they feel it should. *The Smart Way* makes all the difference.

There is no need for a diagnosis before teaching *The Smart Way* because it is simply teaching individuals about how their brain works and how to think in ways that optimize outcomes. While learning *The Smart Way* may lead to recovery or better outcomes from manifested chronic illnesses, the main purpose is to prevent new manifestations of problems that can be prevented by using a skilled level of cognition that reduces experienced stress on a daily basis. Cognitive Behavioral Therapy teaches people how thoughts influence feelings and behaviors.[106] That is something everyone needs to know. To the average person, mental health care is shrouded in mystery, stigma, and secrecy. Just the thought of thinking about our innermost feelings can be enough to cause fear. But when one begins considering that Cognitive Behavioral Therapy is essentially about helping someone change the way they think to healthier thought patterns doesn't it make sense to teach people what healthy thought patterns are in the first place? When

> *Just the thought of thinking about our innermost feelings can be enough to cause fear. But when one begins considering that Cognitive Behavioral Therapy is essentially about helping someone change the way they think to healthier thought patterns doesn't it make sense to teach people what healthy thought patterns are in the first place?*

you delve more deeply and see how many mental health problems can be healed or at least improved with CBT, does it not point to the fact that information about how the mind works would be highly valuable to everyone?

The litany of mental, physical and behavioral health issues that CBT helps in the prior chapter is not exhaustive. How an individual uses her mind determines how much stress is felt in a given situation. Everyone who receives a lay-off notice does not feel the same degree of stress. Not even everyone with two children and a mortgage and no spouse feels the same degree of stress when a lay-off is announced. The amount of stress felt depends on the perspective the individual takes about the situation. When the individual understands *The Smart Way*, she has control over the stress.

How our brains, emotions, and thoughts are connected should not be information reserved for the elite. "CBT is a psychotherapeutic approach that focuses on the way in which people's thoughts influence their feelings and behaviors. CBT includes a number of different approaches that share the belief that it is not the event that causes our feelings and behaviors, but rather how we perceive or think about what happened . . . Socratic reasoning is a central technique."[107] The only aspects that really make CBT therapeutic is that it is done after-the-fact (once someone is already suffering from a diagnosis). CBT also has assessment procedures to measure progress toward healing. If done before an illness manifests there is no need for assessments to be done to determine when health is restored to a level where insurance will no longer pay and no need for a diagnosis because the point is to avoid ever having a diagnosable illness.

Albert Ellis developed a form of therapy in the 1940's that was much like CBT because the wisdom from philosophers such as Bertrand Russell, Marcus Aurelius, and Epictetus helped him with his own problems. His path is eerily similar to my own. I was teaching people to use early versions of *The Smart Way* techniques for years before my knowledge of CBT expanded and I realized that the techniques I'd developed independently were essentially a preventive form of CBT. Dr. Ellis and I even benefited from the wisdom of the same philosophers.

People are not disturbed by things, but by the view they take of them.
Epictetus

At about the same time Ellis developed his version, Aaron T. Beck was starting to lean toward a cognitive form of treatment. Both are considered founders of CBT although when Ellis's associates came to him upset that Beck was calling himself the Father of CBT, Ellis was undisturbed and simply referred to himself as the Grandfather of CBT. Now, that sounds like the way someone who has learned *The Smart Way* would respond to a situation many people would find highly distressing. It is a real reaction, not suppression of rage. The mind that uses skilled meta-cognition finds perspectives that feel good under almost any circumstances.

Ellis believed that "dysfunctional thinking came from cognitive errors including but not limited to overgeneralizations, un-validated assumptions, rigid or absolutistic ideas, and exaggeration."including:[108]

- Awfulizing that includes exaggerating negative consequences of what is happening. Later, Seligman would refer to this tendency as catastrophizing—a thought pattern associated with depression.
- Should, musts, or ought's which are connected to unrealistic demands on the world, self, or others
- Evaluating human worth, which includes self-worth and worth of others
- Need statements, which express requirements that have to be met for the individual to survive or be happy

- In 1991, Ellis added "goals to his model, hypothesizing that we are goal seeking and that goals are to:
  - To survive
  - Be relatively pain free
  - Be satisfied with our lives

Later, Ellis stated his use of rational referred to cognitions that "are effective and self-helping, not merely cognitions that are empirically and logically valid."[109] This is an important distinction and one I also make. In fact, I go further and under some situations, I encourage magical thinking. (See the **Beat Depression** and **Happy Place** processes.) As long as you understand on the meta-cognitive level that you're fantasizing even when you create something that feels real on the basic cognitive level, if it feels good when you do it, it's helpful. You can't spend all your time in a fantasy world, but you can do it often enough to improve your emotional state.

"Beck's system included different classifications of thoughts. Automatic thoughts are quick, evaluative thoughts that seem to come to mind immediately, without the person being aware of them and therefore without deliberation. People tend to accept their automatic thoughts as truths . . . Individuals use their core beliefs as a lens through which they interpret life situations."[110] That is what I refer to as *surface thinking*. Beck seemed to think that people consciously accept core beliefs as true. I disagree. Many core beliefs are not consciously understood—that is one of the reasons for dysfunctional thinking—accepted but erroneous core beliefs.

The difference between of Beck's "consciously accept core beliefs as true" and my hypothesis "the brain filters information using accepted core beliefs" is that Beck assumes the thinker is aware they have internalized the core beliefs and consciously and deliberately decided to view the world that way. Researchers have repeatedly found that many core beliefs are established by age 6. I don't think 6-year-olds are consciously and deliberately evaluating whether they should see the world as a good place or an evil one, or whether they should see the world as a competitive kill or be killed environment vs. one of mutual cooperation and co-existence.

My hypothesis is that the core beliefs develop based on the back stories our subconscious mind creates about our experiences. We could live in a mansion situated in a peaceful island paradise and have an older brother who resents us and physically harms (trips, punches, pushes, etc.) us every chance he gets and we could decide the world is a mean and violent place.

We could live in a slum where the sounds of knife and gun-fights ring out at all hours of the day and night, navigating past drug dealers and women reduced to selling their bodies to survive to get to the bus stop but have an older sibling who is protective and always there for us and feel protected and safe.

It is not our circumstances that lead to what we internalize about the world. It is what we are taught and the back stories we create about our experiences. The good thing is that our worldviews are not chiseled in marble. We can change them with a little bit of concentrated effort.

"Beck's theory also examines intermediate beliefs that the client may hold about self or others. Intermediate beliefs include rules, attitudes, and assumptions . . . the therapist who works with this model attends to relevant childhood information that may contribute to the client developing and maintaining the unworkable core belief."[111]

In Cognitive Behavioral Therapy: [112]	In *The Smart Way*:
Finding the client's irrational beliefs	Feeling the emotional discord and using meta-cognition to find thoughts that feel better
Automatic thoughts	When automatic thoughts don't feel good, question them and use meta-cognition to find better feeling thoughts
Assisting the client in changing them	Individual directs his or her own change. If a therapist is needed, Emotional Guidance will encourage assistance and help client overcome concerns about stigma
Verbally disputed by client and therapist	Mentally disputed by client. Individual may also verbalize (i.e. See Bogus Process)
Pragmatic: How is it working for you in your life?	Same: This question is used in *The Smart Way*
Empirical dispute: Prove to me that this belief is accurate by just giving me the facts	Individual uses emotions to gain greater clarity about the potential perspectives of a distressing situation, leading to a less emotional and more fact-based evaluation
Elegant dispute: Generate a new more effective belief to replace the old one for client to test in homework assignments to see how the new belief works in his actual life	Individual understands beliefs are thoughts you've thought repeatedly until you've created easy to follow neuropathways and changing neuropathways simply requires thinking new, better-feeling thoughts repeatedly until those neuropathways are easier to travel. Moment-to-moment adjustments in the new beliefs can be evaluated by how they feel—there is no need for the trial and error process to be applied in real life without knowing in advance (by how the idea feels) that it will bring improvements.
Shame-attacking	*The Smart Way* sees shame as an inescapable double-negative and refutes it directly. Sustained negative emotional states are inherently harmful to both body and mind, so shame is refuted as something based in unhealthy beliefs about self or others. *The Smart Way* sees beliefs that cause shame as dysfunctional.

In the above chart CBT is compared and contrasted with *The Smart Way* to demonstrate how much more efficient it is to give people information they can use to effectively use meta-cognition and other processes to adjust their thoughts in-the-moment. The time they would spend recording the frequency and events that co-occur with specific beliefs and how frequently those undesired behaviors occur so they can share the information with a therapist could be spent applying the processes and making progress toward better-feeling perspectives.[113]

Often, traditional methods address symptoms of the root cause, such as assertiveness training, anger management and social skills training.[114] The problem is that these programs do not address the root cause of the problem. They help, but not as much as using the same time to improve the root cause would help.

When it comes to ethnic minority populations, there are a number of problems:[115]
1. They are largely underserved by the mental health services community

2. They tend not to seek mental health care (stigma is an issue with every population, but ethnic minorities, on average, tend to perceive mental health care as even more stigmatized,)
3. When they do enter psychotherapy they often leave treatment after a single session
    a. Taking culture into consideration during therapy can be important because what would seem to be the dominant culture's prerogative might be seen as disrespectful of core beliefs held by other cultures, such as obeying one's parents about decisions the dominant culture would consider personal and not an area where the parent's preferences should be given much, if any, weight

I will point out that this not just a minority or cultural issue. There are wide individual variances. *The Smart Way* has a decided advantage for a number of reasons:
1. It can be delivered in a cost effective manner to large groups
2. It is prevention, not mental health treatment for a manifested illness so there is no stigma. The focus is on increasing happiness and resilience, which requires healthy cognition and self-esteem.
3. Because it is not a one-on-one therapeutic relationship, cultural differences are not a significant element. The student can use Emotional Guidance to decide what is personally meaningful and best. Classes should always include the instruction to follow one's own Emotional Guidance over and above the instructor's viewpoint. Instructors will disclose that they have their own core beliefs and that having different core beliefs is acceptable, and adds to the value and worth of each individual. Diversity is recognized as a form of collective strength that is to be appreciated.
4. It empowers the individual with skills and knowledge that leads to more functional thinking capabilities.

CBT focuses on client empowerment, positing that the client is capable of change by controlling her/his thoughts and emotions, conveying respect for the client's abilities and understanding.[116] *The Smart Way* does the same but reinforces it by putting the knowledge and power in the client's hands, helping to develop and reinforce a healthy internal locus of control. Despite its limitations, Cognitive Behavioral Therapy is highly effective, but I believe *The Smart Way* has greater potential because it can be delivered as a preventative measure and it overcomes some of the objections that our most vulnerable populations have about mental health services.

The Smart Way is **Cognitive Behavioral Therapy Plus** because it adds Emotional Guidance and a direct understanding of how the mind works, not just insights garnered by a guided tour led by a therapist.

I'm not suggesting mind-control—at least not by anyone other than the individual controlling his or her own mind. In fact, when individuals do not understand how the mind works or how what they expose themselves to affects their outcomes and the very thoughts they think, they make decisions that harm themselves without any awareness of what they are doing. We're careful about exposing ourselves to toxic chemicals, but most people do not realize that over a period of time, negative habits of thought are just as toxic as the chemicals they try so hard to avoid. Not understanding how the mind works is no different than giving someone the keys to a car without a map when some paths take them through hostile and even deadly territories.

Each technique described in the **Chapter 33** describes which emotional states they are most effective in and provides flexibility so students can choose techniques that feel comfortable to them. Even some of the most common techniques, such as positive affirmations, can have negative impacts when used by individuals in certain emotional states. Meta-cognitive processes are capable of effecting permanent improvements in emotional state on any subject.

We encourage providing *The Smart Way* training classes and materials to both employees and their families because it will provide consistent reinforcement and the techniques help families manage their own stressors, contributing to a more supportive and harmonious home environment. Improving the emotional state of any member of the family benefits every family member and the evidence suggests it can reduce family problems that eventually affect the quality of work and absenteeism.

In schools we encourage providing *The Smart Way* training classes and materials to students, teachers, parents and administrators for the same reason. We have not yet implemented a program in a jail or prison, but would encourage the program to teach both inmates and staff.

Almost 90 years ago, a theory about emotions and behavior became widely accepted and continued to be the paradigm through which researchers viewed the purpose of emotions until 2007 when it was debunked. In fact, many current teachers, practitioners, and researchers are not yet aware that the old paradigm relating to emotions has been reduced to a highly questionable hypothesis. *The Smart Way* is the only training program we are aware of that incorporates current scientific findings about the purpose and meaning of emotions, and overturns common false premises about the purpose of emotions that contribute to adverse outcomes.[117, 118, 119, 120, 121, 122, 123]

5: Overview of Relationships: Happiness, Stress, Health, and Behavior

Sincere appreciation is the powerful force which opens doors to unlimited abundance and happiness.
Anonymous

The most important contribution I can make is helping individuals understand the connection between Happiness, Stress, Health, and Behavior and how to achieve optimal outcomes. All of the following move in tandem along a continuum. If it helps, picture line dancers moving across the floor, each one moving together back and forth and side to side. In much the same way, the following aspects of our lives move in the same direction as one another.

- Stress
- Behavior
- Mental Health
- Relationship quality
- Intelligence
- Employee Engagement
- Immune system function
- Digestive Function
- Pain (Physical and Emotional)

- Emotional State (i.e. happy, sad, frustrated, fear)
- Physical Health
- Success
- Crime (both as victim and committing crime)
- Drug and alcohol abuse
- Racism
- Central Nervous System Function
- Cognitive Function

All of these things move in tandem along a continuum. Increase stress and mood declines. Lower mood and the risk of the person committing a crime increases. There are other factors that affect the outcomes, such as moral values, which might lead one person to commit suicide and another to commit murder/suicide. Factors such as self-esteem are accounted for because someone who has low self-esteem is generally not happy and when someone with low self-esteem is happy, it seldom lasts very long.

Understanding the purpose or meaning of your emotions is critical if one is to thrive in any area of life—much less all areas of life. Charts on the following pages reflect the continuum along which the above factors move. When you reduce stress, happiness increases. When you increase happiness, stress declines.

When you attempt to reduce crime, alcohol abuse, drug use, physical, mental, or behavioral health without addressing stress, you're focused on a symptom and not the root cause. It's an uphill battle when you work on symptoms. When you work on the root cause, problems are solvable. This book shows you how to shift your perceptions about existing and past problems you've experienced in order to help you develop metacognitive processes that, when used in conjunction with Emotional Guidance, reduce the amount of stress you experience. It is not intended as an intellectual exercise. You have to actually begin paying attention to how you feel and looking for alternate perspectives with the intention of finding other perspectives that feel better to you. When you begin actually using the techniques the processes will make sense to you and you will soon feel better and be able to help others do the same.

Happiness - What is it?

There are two main philosophical definitions of happiness with hedonic referring to feeling good and eudaimonic refers to self-actualization and being authentic (true to one's nature). *The Smart Way* Metacognitive Processes used in conjunction with Emotional Guidance combines both philosophies. Emotional Guidance provides information that lets us know the best thoughts, words, and actions for us to use in order to move toward self-actualization by providing positive emotion when our motion is toward fulfilling our potential. Emotional Guidance provides a stable relationship that is always there for you, always supportive, and always reliable when interpreted correctly. Appropriate use of Emotional Guidance allows individuals to develop stable Self-Esteem so relationships with others can be entered into without fear because your self-esteem is not dependent upon the success of the relationship. Relationships can be deeper when you're fearless. Emotional Guidance always leans toward love and forgiveness and away from hate and other negative emotions. *The Smart Way* makes it easy to find the healthiest perspective about the situations life brings to you. Before you finish this book, you will understand a clear path that will allow us to empty most of the prisons in a generation, greatly reduce the chronic disease burden around the world, improve race relationships, significantly reduce the disparate impact in physical and mental health and thriving between the socio-economic classes, and help more people thrive around the world.

Why Happiness is Important

The Smart Way empowers individuals to more directly achieve the benefits positive emotions confer. Much of positive psychology still behaves as if we are subjects that respond to buttons being pushed and if you push a particular button on a subject that has certain past experiences, the response of one speaks about the response of another. It comes from the concept of **Anthropic mechanism,** as if humans are machines.

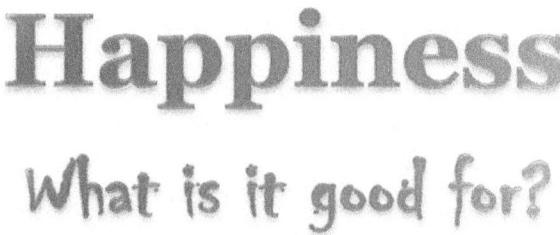

Notes:

5: Overview of Relationships: Happiness, Stress, Health, and Behavior

Sweet Zone

Joy	Free	Wonder
Appreciation	Love	Awe
Passion	Enthusiasm	Eagerness
Happy	Flow	Belief
Inspired	Trust	Faith
Optimistic	Serene	Satisfied
Fulfilled	Secure	At ease

Hopeful Zone

Hopeful	Gratitude	Upbeat

Blah Zone

Contentment	Boredom	Pessimism
Apathy	Dispirited	Empty

Drama Zone

Frustration	Irritation	Impatience
Overwhelmed	Indignant	Disappointment

Give Away Zone

Doubt	Worry	Blame
Discouragement	Guilt	Offended

Red (Hot) Zone

Anger	Revenge	Rage
Outraged	Provoked	Furious

Powerless Zone

Hatred	Bullied	Jealousy
Insecurity	Depression	Fear
Unworthiness	Despair	Grief
Unwanted	Guarded	Powerless
Hopeless	Suicidal	Learned Helplessness
Unimportant	Exploited	Melancholy

Lever

Psychological Problems, Growth, and Recovery

Characteristics following Psychological Growth/Problem Resolution
(Sweet Zone)
- Can creep up on you or come as an epiphany, insight, sudden 'Aha!'
- Feel you know yourself better than before
- Transformational. A sense of new self and old self
- Increased confidence and resilience, improved emotional state
- Awareness old perspective/thoughts/beliefs were inaccurate
- Able to see the silver lining
- See the problem in a new perspective: A Change of Perspective Changes Everything

Steps in the Direction of Recovery & Post Adversarial Growth
(Hopeful Zone)
- Believe you can find a way to solve the problem/to feel better
- Try to see source of pain from different perspectives (try on for size)
- Recognize something not previously considered is important

(Below Hopeful Zone)
Habits & Characteristics that Prolong Psychological Problems
- Denying that a problem exists; fixation on the problem
- Avoid dealing with the problem (understandable when you don't know how).
  - Common Avoidance Techniques: Playing video games, reading, watching TV, drugs, alcohol, surfing the internet

(Powerless Zone)
Characteristics of Transdiagnostic Psychological Problems
- Sense of disempowerment
- Hopelessness, lost, unsure how to resolve, stuck, trapped
- Feels permanent—no way out
- Feels as if your foundation is shaky—could move or losses could occur
- Don't feel understood and perspectives from others don't help—may be told your perspective is wrong
- You feel a lack of control
- Others may seem to want to exert control or to be in control of what you experience

Continuum

Emotional Guidance Scale

Sweet Zone

Joy	Free	Wonder
Appreciation	Love	Awe
Passion	Enthusiasm	Eagerness
Happy	Flow	Belief
Inspired	Trust	Faith
Optimistic	Serene	Satisfied
Fulfilled	Secure	At ease

Hopeful Zone

Hopeful	Gratitude	Upbeat

Blah Zone

Contentment	Boredom	Pessimism
Apathy	Dispirited	Empty

Drama Zone

Frustration	Irritation	Impatience
Overwhelmed	Indignant	Disappointment

Give Away Zone

Doubt	Worry	Blame
Discouragement	Guilt	Offended

Red (Hot) Zone

Anger	Revenge	Rage
Outraged	Provoked	Furious

Powerless Zone

Hatred	Bullied	Jealousy
Insecurity	Depression	Fear
Unworthiness	Despair	Grief
Unwanted	Guarded	Powerless
Hopeless	Suicidal	Learned Helplessness
Unimportant	Exploited	Melancholy

Characteristics that move in tandem, changing with stress

- Low stress
- Happiness
- Sense of empowerment
- Internal locus of control
- Healthy immune, digestive & central nervous system function
- Best possible cognitive function for the individual
- Best pro-health behaviors
- Best pro-social behaviors
- Resilience
- Healthy self-esteem

As emotional state changes, these factors change in tandem with emotional state.

- High stress
- Low emotional states
- Sense of disempowerment
- External locus of control
- Impaired immune, digestive and central nervous system function
- Declining cognitive function for the individual
- Declining pro-health behaviors
- Declining pro-social behaviors
- Low Resilience
- Low self-esteem

Sweet Zone

Joy	Free	Wonder
Appreciation	Love	Awe
Passion	Enthusiasm	Eagerness
Happy	Flow	Belief
Inspired	Trust	Faith
Optimistic	Serene	Satisfied
Fulfilled	Secure	At ease

Hopeful Zone

Hopeful	Gratitude	Upbeat

Blah Zone

Contentment	Boredom	Pessimism
Apathy	Dispirited	Empty

Drama Zone

Frustration	Irritation	Impatience
Overwhelmed	Indignant	Disappointment

Give Away Zone

Doubt	Worry	Blame
Discouragement	Guilt	Offended

Red (Hot) Zone

Anger	Revenge	Rage
Outraged	Provoked	Furious

Powerless Zone

Hatred	Bullied	Jealousy
Insecurity	Depression	Fear
Unworthiness	Despair	Grief
Unwanted	Guarded	Powerless
Hopeless	Suicidal	Learned Helplessness
Unimportant	Exploited	Melancholy

Childhood Outcomes

- Associated with better citizenship
- Associated with pro-health behaviors
- Associated with pro-social behaviors
- Associated with better relationships, less discord
- Associated with problem-solving
- Rarely associated with crime
- Low association with alcohol and drug abuse
- Associated with better life-long health
- Associated with better grades, graduation rates, and college attendance

Associated with undesired outcomes
- Increasing discord with classmates, teachers, and parents; fewer pro-social behaviors
- Potential for alcohol and drug abuse increases
- Less regard for established rules and procedures
- Increased risk of runaways and dropping out
- Increased risk of teen pregnancy
- Less likely to accept responsibility for errors and missed goals
- More likely to be violent
- More likely to join a gang
- Crimes of opportunity and retaliation for perceived wrongs become more likely
- Greater feelings of being lost, alone, insecure, victim, or worthless
- Increasing severity of crimes
- Increasing depression, risk of suicide
- Increasingly poor health and chronic illnesses; fewer pro-health behaviors
- Mental health impaired or at risk
- Less likely to use inherent strengths or to recognize them in oneself
- As emotional state declines, clarity of thinking declines

Sweet Zone

Joy	Free	Wonder
Appreciation	Love	Awe
Passion	Enthusiasm	Eagerness
Happy	Flow	Belief
Inspired	Trust	Faith
Optimistic	Serene	Satisfied
Fulfilled	Secure	At ease

Hopeful Zone

Hopeful	Gratitude	Upbeat

Blah Zone

Contentment	Boredom	Pessimism
Apathy	Dispirited	Empty

Drama Zone

Frustration	Irritation	Impatience
Overwhelmed	Indignant	Disappointment

Give Away Zone

Doubt	Worry	Blame
Discouragement	Guilt	Offended

Red (Hot) Zone

Anger	Revenge	Rage
Outraged	Provoked	Furious

Powerless Zone

Hatred	Bullied	Jealousy
Insecurity	Depression	Fear
Unworthiness	Despair	Grief
Unwanted	Guarded	Powerless
Hopeless	Suicidal	Learned Helplessness
Unimportant	Exploited	Melancholy

Behavior

- Associated with increased kindness
- Associated with better corporate citizenship
- Associated with pro-health behaviors
- Associated with pro-social behaviors
- Associated with better relationships, fewer divorces
- Associated with problem-solving
- Rarely associated with crime
- Low association with alcohol and drug abuse

Associated with increasing levels of crime
- Early signs = crimes of boredom
- Increasing levels of disruption (fighting, arguing, discord) in relationships
- Potential for alcohol and drugs
- Mid-level increasing violence, physical fights
- Crimes of opportunity
- Crimes of retaliation for perceived wrongs
- Increasing crimes due to financial needs and fear
- Increasing disregard for others life, limb, property
- Murders, rapes, cover-ups that escalate
- Horrific crimes that are perceived as ways to regain power or as retribution for withholding of power
- As emotional state declines, clarity of thinking declines
- In the Powerless Zone individuals may become more complacent, but they continue to want to move up and the longer they are held in the Powerless Zone the higher likelihood they will use violence against self or others

Part II: Core Knowledge

Throughout the years I've studied what causes human thriving I've had to discard many of the concepts about our world that I was taught as a child. I think many of us think that because information is printed in textbooks it means that at some point before it was put in a book experts agreed that it was true. That seems logical, doesn't it? But much of what was in the textbooks I learned from and the ones still being used today was accepted as fact without scientific verification.

If it was widely accepted, information had a good chance of getting into the textbooks, even if it led us to inaccurate assumptions about our world. We've never gone back and evaluated these accepted beliefs as new information has come to light. Common assumptions about the purpose and use of emotions, Maslow's Hierarchy of Needs, crime, physical and mental health, poverty, and other important areas of life have been accepted as truth but unverified for decades or longer.

Everyone experiences a different reality. Our senses show us a perceived reality—not an actual reality where there is one right interpretation. The reality we perceive is largely due to the back story we create. Now, most people will tell you they're not making up stories, but that is because back stories are created without our conscious awareness. Martin E. P. Seligman, the Father of Positive Psychology, examined how back stories affect our experiences in his work. Back stories should not be confused with the conscious creation of a story, white lies, or lies.

Burnette et al. describe it well, "Just as scientists develop theories to explain the phenomena they investigate, laypersons develop theories about human characteristics such as intelligence, personality, and athletic ability. Unlike scientists' theories, these lay theories are frequently implicit; that is, they are not explicitly articulated in the mind of the person holding them. Implicit theories . . . organize the way people ascribe meaning to events. This assumption—that personal beliefs are critical for understanding human behavior—has been influential in psychology for many decades. Piaget, for example, suggested that the development of meaning systems is just as important as logical thinking in shaping behavior. Similarly, Kelly suggested that, "man looks at his world through transparent templates which he creates and then attempts to fit over the realities of which the world is composed""[124]

It is important to remember that back stories aren't something you make up on purpose. Your mind seeks to make sense of the world and by creating a back story it makes your world make more sense to you. Back stories may not be true, but they are not lies in the sense that someone might lie to avoid telling someone a hurtful truth or avoid being scorned by others. Back stories are innocent of conscious wrong doing. A psychotic break is characterized by the creation of a back story that makes unthinkable actions seem to be rational choices. I'm not sure if all psychotic breaks involve unthinkable actions, but when someone thinks horrendous acts are a good choice, it's a pretty good guess that they've suffered a psychotic break.

Remember: Many of the hypotheses that form our back stories are well-established before our seventh birthday.

The next several chapters describe factors that have a major impact on the back story one creates.

> *The self-test on the next page is designed so that you can take it now and take it again after you've studied this book and applied the ideas to your life. You may copy it for your personal or family use. If you are a teacher, you may copy it for use in your classes. Teachers should be aware that different rules about psychological testing exist in different locations. If a student is seriously depressed, seek help locally with urgency.*

Self-Test[125]

```
  1     2     3     4     5     6     7     8     9    10
```

Mark the line below to indicate where you are now.
Example: Use a "B" to mark how you feel now (at the beginning of the book)
Tired frequently_____B_____Well-rested
The location of this B indicates you are in the middle of these two feelings
Sad frequently_____Rarely Sad
Fuzzy thinking_____Clear headed
Not sleeping well_____Sleeping well
Hopeless_____Hopeful
Exhausted_____Energized
Scattered_____Focused
Overwhelmed_____Capable
Stuck_____Letting go
Resentful_____Forgiving
Close-hearted_____Open-hearted
Frustrated_____Appreciative
Broken_____Whole
Depressed_____Happy
Anxious_____Calm
Unbalanced_____Balanced
Uncomfortable_____Comfortable
Defined by my illness/problem/or past _____Self-defined
Low self-esteem_____High self-esteem
Complete_____Evolving
No energy_____Vital and alive
Angry_____Accepting
Vengeful_____Understanding
Old_____Wise
My body does not recover quickly _____My body is strong
Isolated_____Connected
Bored_____Interested
Boring_____Fun
Life is hard_____Life is easy

6: Perception

We have to remember that what we observe is not nature in itself, but nature exposed to our method of questioning.
Werner Heisenberg

(Dukudraw, 2014)

The story of five blind men and the elephant is a parable that dates back almost a thousand years, with versions in Buddhist, Sufi, Hindu, and Jain lore. While their mistake may seem silly, you'd be surprised at how often disagreements in the modern world are based on the same type of problem—different perspectives. Research in large cities across the country with significant homicide problems indicates that many of the disagreements that turn deadly begin as mere arguments.[126] The life-ending outcomes are usually blamed on the easy availability of guns, but the truth is that only individuals who have habits of becoming excessively angry are involved in this outcome. Millions of people have readily accessible guns that do not resort to solving simple disagreements with deadly force.

Read the parable and think about an argument you've had recently. Consider whether the argument was about different perspectives, but seemed as if only one of you could be right and the other had to be wrong.

Once upon a time, there lived five blind men in a village. One day other villagers told them, "There is an elephant in the village today."

They had no idea what an elephant was. They decided, "Even though we will not be able to see it, let us go and feel it anyway." All of them went to the elephant and each touched part of the elephant. One man touched the leg, another touched the tail, a third touched the trunk, one touched an ear, and the final blind man touched the elephant's side.

"The elephant is a pillar," said the first man.

"No! It is like a rope," said the second man.

"No, it is like a thick branch of a tree," said the third man.

"It is like a big hand fan," said the fourth man.

"It is like a huge wall," said the fifth man.

The blind men began to argue about the elephant with each one insisting that he was right. The disagreement was becoming agitated. A wise man was passing by and saw them arguing. Hoping to help, he stopped and asked them, "What is the matter?"

The blind men said, "We cannot agree what the elephant is like." Each one of them told what he thought the elephant was like.

The wise man calmly explained to them, "All of you are right. The reason every one of you perceives it differently is because each one of you touched different parts of the elephant. The elephant has all those features."

There was no more arguing. The men proceeded to touch other parts of the elephant to better understand what their friends had felt.

This parable applies to everyday life more than most realize. Every aspect of what we perceive as reality—including what we see, smell, taste, touch, and hear—is not only subjective and unique to us, it is also filtered by our beliefs, expectations, emotional stance, experience, and focus. When this is understood disagreements disappear, especially heated ones. We learn to see that different conclusions are true from different perspectives. Once we understand, we can usually begin to see how they arrived at their conclusion. We can see that both are right—each from our own perspective.

Take a moment and consider how understanding this might influence heated disagreements over social issues, political issues, and religious issues. Consider that opposing sides simply interpret reality in different ways—not that one is right and one is wrong, but that they are just different. In many cases, the goal is the same but the method of achieving it becomes divisive. There are many ways to achieve any goal.

If the only thing dividing us is based on our personal interpretations of reality, how do we solve such issues? Are they solvable? My recommendation is that the discussions be taken to the deepest level, one where I believe we are all the same. There are only three goals at that level:

- To love
- To be loved, and
- To leave the world better than we found it. If we focus on the harmony at this level, we will be less insistent that others take the same path to the destination.

Even though this deepest level is not apparent when individuals are living in low emotional states, it is there. When their emotional state rises, it becomes visible.

One of the reasons so few people are thriving is that fundamental ways we are taught to look at the world are inaccurate. We now know that, to some degree, many premises we base our opinions and decisions upon are not absolutes, but we do not apply that knowledge to things our senses make us believe are real. It is important that the reader remember that our senses do not *report* reality to us—they *interpret* reality. For some of my readers, this may be an entirely new way of looking at the world. For others, it is a refresher course.

Failing to recognize that the reality we perceive is an interpretation and that there are numerous accurate ways to perceive the same situation, some more stressful and some less so, increases the level of stress in many lives. Recognizing that we can choose a perspective that creates less stress and remain accurate in our assessment of a situation allows us to reduce stress without requiring the circumstances to change. Chronic Stress is very detrimental to our physical, mental, and behavioral health and to our relationships and success in all areas of life.

This quote is from an early child psychology book published nearly 100 years ago, "If men define situations as real, they are real in their consequences. The total situation will always contain more and less subjective factors, and the behavior reaction can be studied only in connection with the whole context, i.e., the situation as it exists in verifiable, objective terms, and as it has seemed to exist in terms of the interested persons."[127]

Many people resist changing their perspective about something because doing so means they were wrong in the past. But when an understanding of the filters that work with our mind to create our unique and individual reality exists, changing perspectives begins to feel like the smart decision.

"Aronson et al. did a workshop with students and noticed how this led to an important change in how these students viewed school. Before the workshop, many students saw school as a place where you, as a student have to perform, and where the teacher judge you. After the workshop they saw school more as a place where you learn, with the help of the teachers, things that make you smarter. Also, they said that, while they were learning, they imagine how new connections in their brain were forming."[128]

> *Before arguing with someone, ask yourself if it is possible that each of you is right based on the way you interpret reality.*

There are myriad instances where most adults are aware that what their brains show them about reality is not accurate, but almost no one consciously extends that awareness to a deeper understanding. We often argue and fight with others when both parties are right—each from their own perspective.

Arguments about colors, tastes, sounds, and even intentions, actions, and words are not about the actual color, taste, sound, intentions, actions or words because we are not able to perceive any of those things in the exact way another person perceives them. For example, someone who believes the world is good interprets words and actions differently than someone who believes the world is full of evil. We believe we perceive actual reality, but we do not. What we perceive with our eyes, ears, nose, taste,[129] and touch are perceived using senses that are not identical to the sensors others' use. Once stimuli are sensed, it goes through a filtering process that distorts perception in significant ways.

For example, in Chicago there were 433 murders in 2011. An analysis by the police department[130] showed that more than 50% were the result of altercations (arguments) that escalated. About 5% were drug related. Individuals in low emotional states are more sensitive to disagreements and more likely to react with strong negative emotion. They are more likely to feel threatened by mere disagreements.

If those who engaged in life-ending arguments had understood the true nature of perception, would they have felt threatened enough to respond with violence? We cannot recreate the past but we can provide the education and measure future results. Someone who sees the world or a situation differently than you see it is not disrespecting you or your opinion. Often, both people are right, they're just looking at the subject from more than one perspective. If instead of arguing over who is right, they try to understand the perspective the other is using to reach the conclusion that differs with their own, they may find that from a different perspective, the other's viewpoint is understandable. Understanding a viewpoint from another angle does not make conclusions reached from the other's perspective wrong—just different.

The ability to perceive a single situation from multiple perspectives is psychological flexibility. Psychological flexibility leads to emotional flexibility, or, the ability to have greater control over one's emotional state. Psychological and emotional flexibility can be taught at young ages. Once a habit of thought that considers alternate scenarios of a situation is developed, it will be invaluable in reducing altercations during the more volatile teens and early 20's are reached. Psychological flexibility can be learned at any age—I began deliberately cultivating the skill in my 40's.

Perception is malleable. Our minds can make things up and we don't know if they are true or not. Sometimes the illusions are functional and helpful. At other times, they are highly dysfunctional. For example, a disorder named Capgras Delusion occurs when someone believes a friend or family member has been replaced by an identical looking imposter. The ability of the mind to *create* reality a unique reality is easy to see when your mind is open to the idea.

Teaching children psychological flexibility will help them manage their emotional state during their teens and beyond. Todd Kashdan and Jonathan Rottenberg stated in their conclusion about psychological flexibility, "In many forms of psychopathology, these flexibility processes are absent. If interventions to increase flexibility can be informed by strong basic science, we believe there is great untapped potential to aid people suffering from pathology, as well as help highly functioning people find greater efficacy and fulfillment in their daily lives."[131]

Without conscious awareness of different perspectives, we do things like attempt to get others to agree with our perspective on something—such as the color of a sofa—when the actual color is a perception that is subjective and greatly influenced not only by the physical apparatus we call a body, but also by our cultural indoctrination. In some cultures, the color wheel is defined differently. In those cultures, the perception of a color is viewed differently than it is in the USA. For example, another culture may consider what I call purple to be blue. When I look at a color, the actual shade I see may be different from the shade another sees because of physical differences in our eyes.

The structure of our eyes is not consistent. Some people have more cones than others. It is not possible for people with different numbers of cones in their eyes to perceive in an identical way. The way we learned to define colors as a child and different lighting also affects our perception of color. Even if we are both in the same room at the same time, it is not possible for both of us to have exactly the same angle looking at something. If we take a picture so we can look at something with the same angle and lighting, the lighting we have when we look at the picture will have the same limitation—we cannot both look at the photograph through identical eyes.

Our brains will see something one way, even when we know it can also be viewed another way; the brain is hard pressed to see it both ways at the same time. Life is a combination of events and experiences that pass through filters (which you can adjust). Your emotional experience is the result of the thoughts you have about what you perceive. When you change your perspective, your emotions change.

We tend to believe what I refer to as our *vivid senses*, sight, sound, touch, taste, and smell. We believe these senses because they seem distinct. Yet, they are also very fallible. Eyewitness testimony is notoriously inaccurate. It is now recognized as one of the least reliable forms of evidence in criminal trials.[132] Just this evening some neighbors shot off some fireworks and my ears perceived it as gun fire. My husband was outside and saw the fireworks.

Some people immediately see two faces when they look at the illustration. Others see a vase or goblet. Years ago, when I first saw this illustration, I saw only the vase. It took me a long time to figure out the two faces. Do you see the faces or the vase? Can you see the other perspective? When you see it from the other perspective, can you still see it from the a different perspective? For fun, try to see both at the same time.

Most of us accept that things referred to as optical illusions trick our minds into seeing something different from what is there, but expanding that concept to understanding what we see is not what is actually there can be a stretch. We have been translating sound waves and light waves our entire life—we're so good at it that we don't even realize we're doing it, much as we don't have to think "put one foot in front of the other" when we walk. We simply walk. We're good at it if our bodies are normal and healthy. Our mind is designed to make us believe what we sense is reality. Grasping the concept that what our *vivid senses* reveal to us is merely an interpretation is critical to the ability to increase thriving to optimum levels in every area of life. The more psychological flexibility we develop, the better our ability to find perspectives about situations that serve our highest good can develop.

Once you realize that your opinions, perspective, and beliefs about anything are merely one of many possible accurate interpretations of reality, different perceptions become interesting instead of points of contention.

For example, a recent discussion on Nextdoor.com discussed mud and pebbles in the road in front of a local business.

- Some of the neighbors blamed the business for the debris in the road.
- Some blamed a recent road crew that had worked on the sides of the road.
- Some thought the complaints were unjustified because the business was here before the neighborhood was built.
- Some thought complainers will always find something to complain about.
- Some blamed the business for being cheap and not paving their parking lot for the pebbles.
- Some thought they should stop complaining about the business because it was nicer to have a low density farm there than more housing on roads that are already overcrowded.

The thing is that all of them were right from the perspective they were taking about the issue. From one perspective, the others were wrong, but if anyone chose to adjust their perspective to understand what someone else felt, they could do so—if they chose to. The same thing is true of many arguments that lead to fatal shootings.

When the goal of conversations stops being to prove or determine who is right, and becomes an opportunity to understand the other person and their viewpoint, the risk of violence drops like a lead balloon. Both are right, each from the perspective from which they perceive the situation. In conversations where understanding is the goal there is an opportunity to discover other perceptions, to try them on for size and to accept or reject them without risk of ill feelings. Afterall, it's just a perspective, a viewpoint, an opinion. Remember, opinions are not facts. Opinions are based not only on what is known by an individual, but also what is believed by the individual—even if the belief is not factual. When we believe anything, our mind interprets the world as if our belief is true. It creates back stories to explain the events in our life as if what we believe is true. For all intents and purposes, the world is as we believe. **The world of someone who believes something else is not the same as our world.**

> *Opinions are based not only on what is known by an individual, but also what is believed by the individual—even if the belief is not factual. When we believe anything, our mind interprets the world as if our belief is true.*

As we open ourself to understanding one another more and stop demanding that others agree we are right, we can begin to appreciation our differences. If everyone had the same perspective the world would be in more trouble. One perspective is better at solving some problems while another perspective is better at solving other challenges. The differences are strengths and when we see them that way, they cannot be points of animosity.

Being the same would be a much greater problem. We want different things because we have different perspectives. If everyone wanted the same thing, there would be one individual who was the perfect spouse, one perfect job, one perfect physical location to live, and so on. If everyone wanted the same things, everyone except the one who had them would have to settle for less than he desired. We do not have a perfect world, but many people like their mates, jobs, and homes better than those that other people possess. Many people perceive their mate, career, and home as the best one, which it is—for them.

Just for a moment, imagine a world where every man thought that one single woman was the best mate. Every man on the planet desired that one woman above all others. Every woman on the planet except that one would know she was second best to her mate.

Now, just for a moment, imagine a world where every woman thought that one single man was the best mate. Every woman on the planet desired that one man above all others. Every man on the planet except that one would know he was second best to his mate.

How many people do you know who would be happy and have good relationships under those conditions?

Sameness is not what we really want. It's boring.

If all people wanted the same things, the creativity that is so abundant in our world would not have an outlet. Everyone would want the same picture on their walls, the same color houses and everyone would wear the same clothes. Are you bored yet? I don't even want to imagine such a world.

Our unique perspectives create unique desires. Our lack of understanding that others do not perceive reality in the same way we do creates unnecessary conflict. That conflict is completely avoidable when we make an effort to be more conscious that our perception of reality is as unique as we are.

Optical illusions may be only a cool phenomenon when viewed as something that tricks the mind. Considered from the perspective of "Is my mind showing me an actual reality?" the illusion gains greater meaning and provides insights that *surface thinking* does not begin to consider.

Surface thinking is thinking that does not look beneath the surface. It sees only what is perceived by the filters our brains use to determine what information is important to us. Surface thinking does not acknowledge that our perceptions are unique interpretations of reality. *Surface thinking* does not acknowledge that our very thoughts are the product of filters between our unconscious and conscious mind.

Have you ever wondered why civil court cases are so acrimonious? Usually both people believe they are telling the truth. From their perspective, most are being truthful. How many biter disputes could be avoided by looking for understanding of one another's perspectives? How many divorces could be prevented if couples sought understanding instead of defending the rightness of their perspective?

> *Most of our assumptions have outlived their uselessness.*
> — Marshall McLuhan

What we perceive is based on so many personal factors. In truth, no two individuals experience exactly the same reality. We are each creating our own version of reality from the information that exists.

For example, human sight is wavelengths in the perceptible range for humans interpreted by the physical apparatus we call eyes and then by the central nervous system and cognitive function of the individual's mind.

We are tricked into believing that reality is an absolute—but reality is an interpretation of wavelengths. Sight is interpretation of wavelengths and sound is also interpretation of wavelengths. Look at the spectrum of light visible to humans in the chart below. It's pretty easy to see that what we see is only a small (some would say miniscule) part of the light spectrum. Our bodies just aren't equipped with equipment that can interpret the other spectrums of light waves. It does not mean they don't exist.

When we go to the dentist and he takes an x-ray of our teeth, we can't see the x-rays but that doesn't mean they aren't there.

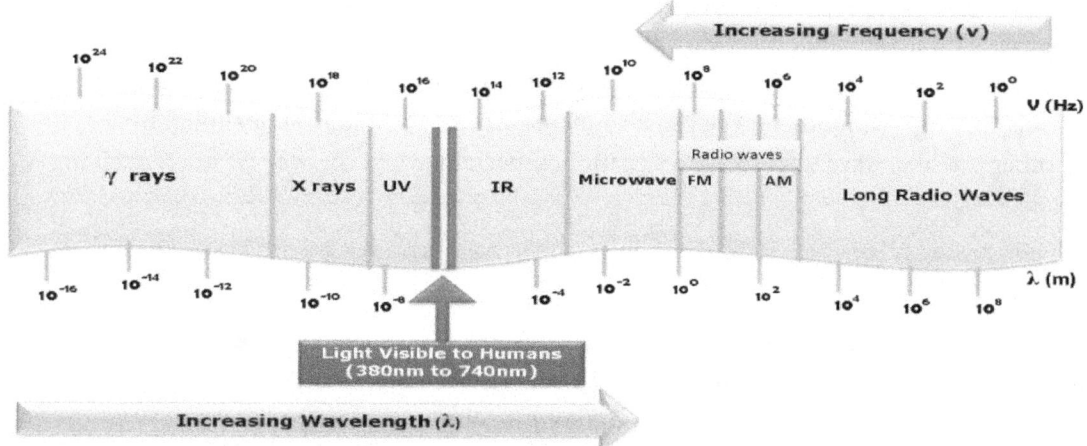

If you went through school a while ago, you may remember a map of the tongue depicting where we would taste sweet, salty, bitter, etc. I remember the map not making any sense to me because it did not match my personal experience. In recent years, research into taste has expanded our understanding of how taste is perceived. They have learned that our mood affects taste, what our mothers ate while we were in the womb affects what we like, as does the room we are eating in, and the plates our food is served on. Taste is a combination of input from our tongue, the back of our nose, and even our intestines.[133] The map of the tongue I had to learn about in school did not represent my reality, but someone thought it did. Perhaps it was his reality, but it was never mine.

Personal biases filter the taste experience in much the same way they filter the information our conscious mind receives. Even what we hear affects how our food tastes—such as crunchy. Our brain takes the inputs and revises it, sometimes beyond recognition.

How we define things affects how we perceive our world. My husbands' beliefs about how long food remains good in the refrigerator are different than mine. He will eat food that I can't even stomach the thought of eating. I've tried and a feeling of disgust overcomes me and I cannot put it in my mouth. He eats it with no ill effects. There is nothing visibly wrong with the foods he eats. It is my beliefs about how long food remains edible that make me interpret reality in a way that I feel disgust at the thought of eating old food. If I did not know how long the food had been in the refrigerator I could probably eat it with no ill effects.

Our brain combines the information from our senses and determines whether we like the taste. Our brain, not just our eyes, is where our visual perception occurs. An individual can experience a brain illness or injury and lose the ability to see in color while the eyes remain perfectly healthy.[134]

Machinery has enabled us to measure sounds that we cannot hear. We have known dogs could hear sounds we could not hear since the time dogs were domesticated. Most of us know dogs can hear things we cannot hear and smell things we cannot smell (thank goodness!). Birds are able to distinguish colors human cannot differentiate. We interpret colors we aren't equipped to distinguish as the same as one another, while birds can tell the difference between the two.

We refer to the wavelengths humans can see as the visual light region but it would be more appropriate to refer to it as the *visible by humans* light region.

Although humanity recognizes that our perception of reality is an interpretation, we easily forget this fact and behave as if our perception represents a fixed reality where there is one right way to perceive it that automatically rejects others perspectives as wrong or sees them as challenges. Be remembering more frequently that what we perceive as reality can be perceived in many ways and that other ways of perceiving reality do not make our perception wrong, we can move toward more harmonious relationships with others. We can also increase our psychological flexibility by considering other possible ways to perceive a situation, especially when the way we are perceiving it feels bad to us.

Important Concepts from this Chapter:
- Perception is individual. We all perceive a different reality.
- Most arguments are about what we perceive, not about reality.
- We can change how we view our reality by thinking of it as our perception.
- When it is simply different perspectives as seen by unique individuals, there is nothing to argue about or be upset by when someone else perceives it differently
    - Their physical apparatus may be different
    - Factors that affect how they interpret reality may be set on different settings than ours
- The thing that is perceived or viewed differently is not where the difference resides. We may want the same goals but simply see different ways to achieve them.
- Taking the conversation deeper, to what is desired, often leads to common goals.

7: What We Cannot Yet Explain

Miracles are not contrary to nature, but only contrary to what we know about nature.
Augustine of Hippo

Many things we know are not explicable using what we know. We know what happens, but not why or how. For example, the cuckoo bird is a brood predator. An avian brood predator lays its eggs in the nest of a host bird that cares for the hatchling. Cuckoo birds are not raised by Cuckoo birds, yet all the fledglings know to migrate and where to go when they migrate. The young birds leave after the adult birds. Their migration, from the UK to Africa, is 10,000 miles.[135]

Migration has been explained by *instinct*. What is instinct? How does the bird know when to go and where to go? Instinct appears to be a catch-all phrase used to explain otherwise inexplicable behavior in the animal world. The moth burning itself to death on the hot light seems to meet the definition of predetermined responses to stimuli. Complex behaviors do not fit as neatly.

The Parsimony Principle is a scientific principle that states the simplest explanation that fits the data is the one that should be used. As exceptions and inexplicable data accumulate, the Parsimony Principle tells us to discard a principle that is becoming complicated by the exceptions in favor of one with fewer exceptions and/or the one that explains the phenomena more fully. Is it time to reevaluate instinct based on the Parsimony Principle? The more we learn about non-human behavior, the further the concept of instinct is being stretched. Instinct is a concept that received a lot of air time in the 1800's. I submit that the evidence that has accumulated requires an overhaul of our understanding of instinctive behavior and perhaps an updated definition of much of the behavior that has been attributed to instinct.

Why do I care? Like almost everything that I care about, it has to do with human thriving. I believe that the same mechanism that leads to complex instinctive behavior is available to but seldom consciously used by humans and that using it more consciously would be of great benefit to humanity.

Instinct is one of many explanations about our world that is routinely accepted as true but largely unexamined in light of what we know now vs what we knew when the concept was introduced. There are quite a few theories that are accepted as fact by most of the world that have never been proved scientifically.

Instinctive behavior is not limited to the animal world. Every 4th generation of Monarch butterflies migrates to Mexico or California for the winter. Generations 1, 2, and 3 live much shorter lives. Since they cannot survive the climate in most of North America during the colder winter months, the 4th generation flies to warmer climates, ensuring the continuation of the species.[136] How does a butterfly, whose entire body weighs about 2 ounces, know to migrate to Mexico for the winter?

What exactly is instinct? Hundreds of species exhibit behavior we cannot explain with anything other than that catch-all phrase.

The dictionary defines instinct as "an innate, typically fixed pattern of behavior in animals in response to certain stimuli." Recently, researchers tracking Cuckoo birds noted that birds sometimes return to the last place they were able to forage successfully for food when drought or excessive wetness made food scarce on their usual migration pattern.[137] Clearly, the cuckoo bird and Monarch butterflies are not following a fixed pattern of behavior on their migrations.

If they are blindly following instinct, which is what it seems moths do when drawn to a hot light source, how do Cuckoo birds vary their behavior when conditions are not favorable for the usual route? Why does only the 4th generation of Monarch butterfly live longer and fly to California or Mexico?

Is it possible they receive some sort of communication or guidance that we cannot detect that directs their actions?

The explanation is not blind adherence to something predetermined. These two examples are not isolated. Entire books could be written about exceptions that do not neatly fit into the explanation of instinct yet we (modern?) people continue to use instinct to explain the inexplicable. Are we afraid to look deeper into these mysteries? Are our ego's too fragile to accept that we know less than we have believed we know?

When my children were younger they watched *Homeward Bound* dozens of times. It is the story of two dogs and a cat that make their way across the country to be reunited with their family. Although it's not a true story, it was probably inspired by the many miraculous tales of pets reunited with their families. All you have to do is Google, "stories of dogs that find their way home" to find 12 million articles about pets that find their way home. Scientists tend to explain animal navigation with either the magnetic fields or astronomy, both of which are still incredible feats for animals that aren't educated in astronomy or magnetic fields.

Each of us is essentially hypnotized about the nature of reality from infancy. Cultural anthropologists have thoroughly documented how people who grow up in different cultures perceive literally different realities.[138] Upon what premises is our *official* concept of reality based? How was that concept determined?

The *Physical Level* of reality is not a static fact. Humans behave, speak, and write as if only that which is perceptible by our *vivid senses* is real when we are well aware (intellectually) that many things we cannot perceive with the *vivid senses* exist. How long will we remain delusional?

In 1847, when Ignaz Semmelweis suggested that physicians should wash their hands between patients and between touching patients and cadavers, he was ridiculed and ignored. Why? The *physical world* was not yet defined in a way that included germs and viruses. Fifty years later, after the invention of the microscope the definition of our physical reality shifted to include germs, viruses, and other microorganisms that were unknown when the physical world was more narrowly defined. Despite considerable evidence that things we could not see were interacting with our bodies and health, humanity ignored the evidence and stubbornly refused to believe anything not revealed by our *vivid senses*. Scientists today, especially quantum physicists, would be quick to confirm the existence of matter and processes we cannot yet measure or define at a physical level. We know of their existence only because the affect they have on things we can measure has been detected and measured.

In 1847, Semmelweis demonstrated that the death rate from childbed fever could be reduced from 32% to 1% by introducing the process of hand washing between his patients. Because the world did not understand why hand washing mattered, despite results demonstrating a dramatic difference in the death rate of young women, his recommendation was ridiculed. This is not a human behavior pattern limited to the uneducated masses of earlier times. Most of humanity still refuses to accept things we cannot see or hear with our *vivid senses*, even when strong evidence exists pointing to its existence or we have developed an ability to measure them in some way. Exceptions are made for widely believed concepts, such as God. But when new evidence of something previously unknown is discovered, humans want to wait until it can be measured before they accept it as possible.

It is interesting to me that hand washing is now considered a form of Primary Prevention and that we continue to ignore other information pointing to beneficial methods of Primary Prevention because we cannot yet see all the links in the chain that show how they benefit humanity.

> *The notion of a separate organism is clearly an abstraction, as is also its boundary. Underlying all this is unbroken wholeness even though our civilization has developed in such a way as to strongly emphasize the separation into parts.*
>
> David Bohm and Basil J. Hiley, *The Undivided Universe*

Today, there are several areas where our ability to measure our environment has increased. As a result, our understanding of how things are connected is expanding, which is changing individual opinions about some previously controversial topics. For example, homeopathy was often ridiculed as a hoax, but thousands swear it helped heal them. Homeopathy involves diluting substances until there was no measurable evidence of the substance—at least measurable by current methods. People did not understand how it helped because, based on our ability to measure the presence of beneficial substances, no beneficial substances remained in the solution.

Last year, new research demonstrated that classically prepared homeopathic medicines contain measurable source nanoparticle and/or silica NP with absorbed source materials that are heterogeneously dispersed in colloidal solution and have biological properties that differ substantially from bulk forms of the same substance.[139] When our ability to measure nanoparticles expanded, we could physically measure something many previously said did not exist—because they lacked the ability to measure it. That view was based on an interpretation of reality, not reality itself.

> *Until you make the unconscious conscious, it will direct your life and you will call it fate.*
> C. G. Jung

The nanoparticles in the homeopathic solutions were always there. Humans just had not figured out how to measure them. Remember, there are many microscopic things that impact the quality of our lives.

This is another instance where society's views on a subject have been limited by our ability to take physical measurements. If we can't measure it, we proceed as if it does not exist. Now that the nanoparticles are measurable, it will be interesting to observe the shifts in public opinion about the homeopathy. I suspect it may begin moving into the mainstream with other Complementary and Alternative Medicines (CAM).

I am not arguing for homeopathy (or against it). I am arguing for minds open enough to consider the possibility that something we do not fully understand can exist even when we cannot measure it. If the evidence indicates something exists, our inability to measure it should not be a valid reason to dismiss its existence. When there is evidence of a beneficial effect the idea should not be dismissed merely because we have not yet learned how or why it works.

Many have argued that the beneficial effect of homeopathy is the placebo effect. I wonder if in some of the clinical trials conducted, if the nocebo effect might have affected the results. If the clinician conducting the trial did not believe homeopathy was beneficial, her belief could have created a nocebo effect that negated the benefits. I am not stating this is the case, but until it is ruled out, I question the validity of the trials that did not control for this potential. I often see this in comments disparaging techniques that are based on the *energy meridian* (i.e. acupuncture, acupressure, some forms of yoga, and other healing techniques). Measurable evidence of those subtle energies is being published more frequently in scientific journals, especially at The Institute of Noetic Science and The HeartMath Institute.

Mainstream science has yet to explain the rapid communication between the cells of our body despite full awareness that the communication regularly occurs. We ignore this and disparage other things we cannot explain. We need more awareness of when biases and blinders may be supporting arguments that hinder advances.

In numerous areas of medicine, many relevant factors are considered when we conduct clinical trials, but the mind-body connection is often ignored. The evidence that our immune system functions better when we are positively focused has been demonstrated biologically and in overall health results countless times. Ignoring emotional stance in clinical trials negates the value of the results.

As recently as 2008, Marinier and Laird pointed out that, "we traditionally think of the external world as being the total environment in which the agent [person] must behave" before going on to explain that when it comes to emotions, the internal perceptions must also be considered.[140]

Today we have strong evidence that positivity and optimism reduce the risk of developing heart disease by 50%.[141] Heart disease is the number one cause of death in the world—yet advice to increase positivity continues to be mocked and ignored. This is a failure to educate humanity about new research that makes a significant difference in their lives. I have termed the tendency to cling to what we already believe regardless of how convoluted our explanations have to become as new information that contradicts the original hypothesis accumulates The Galileo Effect.

I could just as easily call it the Closed Mind Syndrome. It is meant to point out that once we are convinced an idea is accurate, it becomes a truism regardless of the soundness of the idea. We like a solid platform and we tend to believe ideas others believe with unquestioning faith. We cling to those ideas even after overwhelming evidence that they are inaccurate exists. This is not a deliberate action on our part. It is not stubbornness or a lack of intelligence. It is what I have named The Galileo Effect. In the chapter on filters, the reason for this is explained.

Even when we move beyond The Galileo Effect and open our minds enough to consider whether something is true rather than rejecting it out of hand, a second obstacle to thriving can appear to block our way. We have ignored the Placebo and Nocebo effect for decades despite the Placebo effect often demonstrating an efficacy rate equal to that of drugs. We have ignored the stunning results from some of the Nocebo trials.[142, 143, 144] It is common practice for physicians to warn patients about the health problems they are *likely* to experience now that they are X old, with no consideration given to the potential Nocebo Effect from an authority figure advising them they are at risk of experiencing a specific malady. My requests to more than one physician to refrain from providing these warnings have been met with the response that his E & O insurance requires him to provide the warnings. If that is true, the insurers should re-evaluate their policies. There is already enough evidence to support legal complaints that a physician suggesting someone will develop a malady due to attained age could increase the risk of the patient developing the malady. There is very interesting research by Ellen Langer demonstrating how our expectations about aging affect our personal aging process.

The reality we can ascertain with our physical sensory feedback systems reflects one reality (and not the same one to each of us). The reality we can ascertain with our current technology and measuring capabilities reflects different information than our physical senses communicate to us. I find it impossible to believe that we have reached a stage where we are able to identify and measure everything that exists. There is significant evidence that points to more information we cannot yet measure yet we persist in defining reality as what our *vivid senses* and current measuring devices perceive as reality.

For example, when I was reading about the Cuckoo birds, it stated that the males and females of one subspecies were identical in appearance. Many birds are able to distinguish colors that humans cannot perceive with our eyes. Would it not be more accurate to say that Cuckoo's color differentiation, if it exists, is not perceivable by the human eye? Given the amazing and colorful foliage in the animal kingdom, I find it far more plausible that we simply are unable to see the differences, not that they do not exist. The Cuckoos may be able to easily discern the difference because their eyes do not have the same specifications as human eyes.

Color is created by our perceptual system, the experience of what we call color is an arbitrary one. Color, pitch, smell, hearing, and taste[145] are all created internally—which explains why some people like a particular smell and others do not.[146] If humanity would make an effort to recognize that what we perceive with our *vivid senses* is unique to each individual, it would be easier to realize the same about the most common reason for altercations—our emotions. Emotions are also feedback from a sensory system and how we perceive a situation impacts how we feel about the situation.

It can be helpful to think of your body as separate from yourself, sort of like a vehicle you operate, limited by the installed equipment in what and how it perceives. If back-up sensors are installed, there is one experience. If a back-up camera is standard equipment, there is another experience. If it has gauges, the experience is different from the experience in a vehicle that only has warning lights. Add a moon roof and the experiences changes even more. A Ford Taurus and a Cadillac Escalade do not get the same gas mileage, the view out the windows is not identical, and the sounds perceived within their confines differ from one another.

Our eyes are designed to see between 380 – 740 nanometers, not higher or lower. They interpret the environment within the confines of those specifications. Humans come with a variety of specifications. We are not all identical in our ability to perceive. Some of us have three cones in our optical system and others have four cones. Our ears also hear within the limited frequency range they are designed to perceive. Bats and dogs hear sounds we do not hear—we do not doubt the existence of the sounds bats and dogs hear. We do not tell them they are crazy, making things up, or hearing voices. Following the vehicle analogy, we understand that the vehicles they are utilizing have different specifications than ours.

We also have an onboard computer that checks incoming data against several factors, providing us with only the data it believes is relevant based on its programming. This onboard computer can help us thrive if it is programmed correctly. If the programming produces unsupportive data—it can make life much more difficult.

New cars will stop automatically to avoid an accident. Older models are not designed to do this. In some instances it is not that our equipment can't do something, it is that it is not programmed to do it properly. If we do not believe something is possible, our brains will not pass on data demonstrating a way to accomplish it. It will file the information in an irrelevant file—meaning the information is not passed from the subconscious mind to conscious awareness. The input of information our subconscious mind receives each second is about 10 million bits of information compared to the 50 bits our conscious mind is aware of. Our conscious awareness is like the tip of the iceberg. If we later decide to believe something different, we can retrieve data from the irrelevant file and evaluate it from a new perspective. An example of this is someone whose spouse cheats but they did not believe the person was capable of doing so. After the fact, the person will often beat themselves up for *not seeing the signs*. It was not lack of intelligence that prevented them from seeing the signs—it was faith in their partner. Understanding that their own brain filed the signs of infidelity in the irrelevant file because they did not believe their spouse capable of cheating might help them stop unproductive self-criticism.

An individual who does not believe their spouse capable of infidelity has programmed their filters to ignore the warning signs—signs that might be seen if the spouse was considered capable of infidelity. But that does not mean you should assume your spouse is capable of cheating because expectation can have an effect on outcome. When someone believes their spouse will cheat or is fearful about the potential, they are communicating that they do not trust their spouse on a level that is perceptible even though it does not meet our regular standards of measurable communication. When you feel distrusted it is difficult to feel loved. When someone doesn't feel loved, temptations become more tempting because everyone wants to feel loved and trusted.

In *The Happiness Hypothesis,* Jonathan Haidt described research done with patients whose brains had been separated (to help them with epileptic seizures). Researchers discovered that both sides of the brain continued to function but only one side had access to language. Each eye communicated with only one side of the brain. When researchers showed the eye on the side of the brain that did not have language a picture, the patient could be made to take an action. These actions were things like choosing a specific picture out of a group of photographs or getting up and walking away. When researchers asked the patient to explain the reason for choosing the picture or for walking away the patient would immediately provide a reason, but the reason had no relationship to the stimulus.[147]

> *Until you program your brain in ways that support thriving, you will not even be able to guess at your full potential— much less hope to achieve it.*

For example, someone shown a photograph of a house covered with snow chose a picture of a shovel but when asked why they chose the shovel; his answer had nothing to do with snow. When asked why they were walking away, one patient answered that he was going to get a cola. Researchers termed this *confabulation*. This interpreter part of our brains makes up explanations but does not even realize it has done so. This is not limited to split-brain patients. All of our brains do this. Martin Seligman referred to the stories we make up to make our world make sense as back stories.[148] Then, because we don't realize we've essentially made up the reason, we believe it is true. The back-stories we create are what give our life meaning. If we create back-stories that feel good, we feel good. If we create back-stories that feel bad, we feel bad.

An article that looked at cognition and emotion from a neuro-evolutionary perspective found, "there cannot be cognition without emotion."[149]

When someone says something that *hurts our feelings*, in most cases the truth is that our back-story is what makes their words feel bad—not their words. Consider a situation in which the Mother of a grown-up woman is aware the daughter's marriage is experiencing difficulties. The Mother loves her daughter and does not want her daughter to experience the pain and heartache she did when she went through a divorce when her own children were young. The situation agitates the Mom because she is associating her own experience to what her daughter is experiencing.

Although the Mother is not living in the daughter's household and is not aware of all the nuances of the situation, she provides advice to the daughter. She expects the daughter to take her advice. After all, she is older and wiser and she has been divorced so she has experience. She loves her daughter and wants the best for her but when she gives the advice; the daughter becomes agitated by her interference.

The daughter becomes upset, feeling that her Mother is treating her like a child by telling her what to do in her marriage. At a time when both would be best served by strengthening their relationship, they have a fight and stop speaking to one another. If the daughter had a different back story, she would not feel threatened by her Mother's advice. She could see that her Mom is giving her advice out of love and from wanting the best for her and appreciate that she has a Mom who loves her. She is under no obligation to act on the advice she is given. Likewise, the Mom could see her daughter is different than she was when she divorced. Perhaps the daughter has more education and is therefore more capable of taking care of herself and her children if a divorce does occur. The very fact that the Mom is in the picture and willing to help with the grandchildren may be a very different scenario than what the Mom experienced when she divorced.

But in order to find these better-feeling perspectives, to create back stories that feel better, we must be consciously aware we are creating back stories that give our lives meaning. The back stories that we create are not completely random. Our current and chronic emotional states influence the back story our minds create.

In the mother/daughter scenario above, if we broaden our scope and look at the marital trouble we find that one of the main areas of discontent within the marriage is the wife feels her husband does not respect her opinion and often treats her like a child. Notice how the back story she created around her Mother's advice feels like the same story.

Likewise, the Mother's agitation about her daughter's troubled marriage stems from her own experience—one that actually bears little resemblance to her daughter's situation. She did not have a supportive parent to help her if she needed it and she had not finished high school. Her daughter has her support, education, and training that make her able to support herself and her children if the marriage should end. The Mother's back story about the situation is not recognizing the reality of the situation. The back story she has created reflects her own experience.

We do not create our initial back story consciously. We simply explain our experiences in our own mind to ourself as if the back story is true and react based on the story we've created. What most people do not realize is:

1. We have the ability to change back stories that do not feel good to us.
2. We can change our chronic emotional state, which changes the automatically created back story created by our subconscious mind.
3. Back stories are not reality—they create the meaning we use to make sense of our interpretation of reality.

4. We can change back stories we made up in the past and reduce emotional pain we still feel from those experiences.

In the example of the Mediterranean cruise, my initial back story to my husband's illness was that he'd been working very hard before our trip and he needed a day of rest. It was a sea day so we weren't missing a port, but even if it had been a port I would have simply created a back story that said we could come back and see it another time. I perceive reality in ways that feel good automatically because I have trained myself to do so. Your back story determines your behavior.

For example, a co-worker of my husband's was on the same cruise. It was not planned that way. We learned that we would both be on the cruise a few days before we flew to Spain. We only saw his co-worker once. Speaking with him briefly we learned he was signed up for long shore excursions in every port. On a Mediterranean cruise you're in a different port almost every day. Shore excursions often have to meet around 7 or 7:30 a.m. and return to the ship twelve hours later. For example, in Civitavecchia, the port for Rome it is a 2-hour bus ride to reach Rome, four hours round trip. Shore excursions are good for being able to say you saw something, but not for really experiencing it. Back-to-back excursions for two weeks would exhaust most people.

The one time we saw the co-worker, he made the comment that the cruise was a once-in-a-lifetime event. That was part of his back story about the cruise. I told him it did not have to be a once-in-a-lifetime trip, that I had taken an almost identical trip four years before when I took my daughters. I could tell my words shocked him. The idea of doing it more than once was foreign to his way of thinking. Our approach to the trip was to enjoy the ports at a leisurely pace and if we wanted to see more, we could plan a non-cruise trip to explore it.

We opted not to take the grueling trip into Rome. We knew we could not see everything we would want to see in a day. Instead, we enjoyed a leisurely breakfast with excellent service and then explored Civitavecchia. It turns out there is quite a bit to see there. Then we found a wonderful little restaurant on the water and had an adventure because the staff did not speak English and our translation device was not working (or we could not figure out how to make it work). We had no idea what we ordered but it was delicious. It is one of our best memories from the trip. I am horribly inept with foreign languages. I took an Italian class before my first trip to Italy, but my ability to pronounce unfamiliar words is non-existent.

The back stories we create are truly creations and not reality. If we expect to have a frustrating encounter, we will interpret the encounter in that way. Have you ever seen someone who is upset attempt to solve a problem—perhaps with a front desk person at a hotel? The front desk person can be doing an excellent job, understanding the issue and attempting to provide what most would consider a reasonable remedy, but the person who expected to be frustrated does not understand the solution being offered—not because it is complicated, but because their brain is interpreting the situation as expected—frustrating.

If you find yourself frequently frustrated, it is your back story more than reality that is causing the frustration. If you are angry often, your back story is causing the anger—not the people or situations that you blame for your anger. At any time you can decide to re-write your back stories. You can re-write them as they occur and you can also go back and re-write them for your past. If you worry often, you create back stories about undesired potential futures and then think about them with fearful or worrisome thoughts.

There were about 13,716 murders in 2013. If the national trend matches Chicago in terms of motive, almost seven thousand of those murders began with an argument—arguments caused by back stories that made the situation escalate into senseless violence. What difference could be made if we taught children about back stories and how to create ones that feel good and support their wellbeing? I'll add more pieces to the puzzle that make teaching children about back stories even more compelling in later chapters. For now, just imagine how much difference it could make. What are we losing every year by not doing it?

What could those people have contributed to the world if they had lived? What would those who are incarcerated have contributed if they knew more about how their minds worked and it kept them from committing the crime? How much are the families of both the victims and the offenders suffering and how much of that could have been avoided?

If we are chronically appreciative, we will find something to appreciate in even unpleasant circumstances. Our minds evaluate how we feel the majority of the time and create back stories that feel much like our chronic emotional state. This is one of the main reasons there are so many individual and unique responses to stimuli.

Daniel Kahneman, a 2002 Nobel Prize winner in Economic Sciences explains it this way, "If you ask peple their opinions about ObamaCare, their views usually have nothing to do with the policy itself, it's their political predispositons you'll hear. . . The emotion comes first, and the rationale second. We think we do things for a reason, but the retrofit reason comes later."[150] It's no wonder politics is so divisive—we're really defending our emotions, not talking about the real issues. Greater awareness of how the mind works can lead to deeper discussions that are civil and productive.

If you are focused on something, orange cars for example, your mind will make you more conscious of orange cars. It is not that there are more orange cars; it is that once you program your mind to focus on them, the information is passed to your conscious mind. This filter can be a tremendous tool when it is understood. Just reading this paragraph is enough attention to orange cars that you may find yourself suddenly noticing orange cars over the next few days.

If you focus on making sure others do not offend you and watch every word said to you for any sign that the individual means offense, you will feel offended frequently. Sometimes you will interpret compliments as offensive in some way. You will miss playful opportunities by misreading the cues as being potentially offensive or disrespectful to you.

Our vehicles (bodies) are equipped with sensory systems that provide feedback to guide us toward self-realization. We are not equipped to see the whole of reality. We cannot see x-rays, we cannot see gamma rays, and we cannot see radio waves or Wi-Fi. Our vehicles are not equipped with sensors to detect those. That does not mean those things do not exist—it simply means we cannot perceive them with our onboard systems.

The next few chapters will provide background information about a newly discovered sensory feedback system. (Sensory feedback system is a scientific term that refers to how we see, hear, smell, taste and touch.) This newly recognized system is called our Emotional Guidance Sensory Feedback System (EGS). One of the reasons our EGS was overlooked in the past is because it is such an innate part of us that we don't think about it. Like the air that we breathe, we don't give it much thought.

Unfortunately, almost everyone has been taught to misinterpret the feedback from the EGS. The system provides the feedback, but when we misinterpret the meaning of our emotions and don't know the best way to respond to the feedback, we do not derive the intended benefit. We have Emotional Guidance in response to every thought we think and we've had this since birth (or before). It feels natural. A filter I do not often speak about often is the shift or change filter. This filter highlights new information. It is the reason someone will notice that someone had their hair cut, nails done, lost weight, gained weight, or any number of other changes. The Change/shift filter highlights information that is different. Because our EGS has always been present, we don't notice it. We have to consciously notice it in order to thrive. Once we understand how it works and make an effort to notice the feedback and respond in supportive ways, it is unmistakable.

A change of perception changes everything. Each mind interprets the world according to factors specific to the individual.[151] These factors create a filtering system in the brain that determines the sensory input that is communicated to the conscious mind. The filtering process uses the programming of the filters to determine how we will interpret what we see and experience in the world. When we change our thoughts, our world changes. People give thoughts power when they accept them as true. Everyone has a choice about whether to accept the back story their mind creates or not—even if they do not know they have this ability.

Humanity being taught to misinterpret sensory feedback that is so critical to human thriving was not a deliberate act or intended to cause harm. At least not by those who taught us—when it began is unknown. Misinterpretation has been going on throughout recorded history and was supported by misguided science 90 years ago.

The amount of stress we feel in any given situation is the direct result of how we perceive that situation.[152] Do we think it is more than we can handle? Do we think we're capable of handling it? Do we see it as specific to this situation or as part of a widespread problem? Have we successfully dealt with this type of situation in the past? Has someone we know or heard about successfully (or unsuccessfully) dealt with the same problem? The answers we give to these questions and more determine how we experience the moment—including how our bodies respond.

Right now, the course of human history is going to change. We, and future generations, will enjoy a kinder[153] and more harmonious world, one where each individual has greater resources than ever before to fulfill his or her own potential. It does not matter who the person is, rich or poor, blue, green, purple, or fuchsia, none of the arbitrary labels that we have used to disempower ourselves, or that others have invoked and convinced us could hold us back, will hold anyone back unless the individual allows them to do so. The truth is, it has always been this way, but without understanding our guidance, few people could find the path to the life they desire. Now it is a bright line for anyone who takes the time to learn the skills described in these pages.

Your brain has many abilities or functions.

Cognitive Abilities and Functions:

Awareness	Perception	Reasoning
Judgment	Intuition	Attention
Memory	Motor	Language processing
Auditory processing	Smell processing	Visual and Spatial processing

Executive Functions which include: [154]

- Meta-cognition
- Setting and Focusing on goals
- Insight
- Pattern recognition
- Decision-making
- Emotional self-regulation
- Perception of our emotions
- Behavior Self-Regulation

- Planning
- Flexibility
- Anticipation
- Problem-solving
- Working memory
- Perception of other's emotions
- Breaking tasks into parts

Most of our activities require multiple functions. For example, when someone knocks on your door you have to perceive the knock, decide to respond or not, take physical action to respond (walk, turn handle), and you must use language skills including talking and understanding what is said. The decision to answer may be made multiple times. You may automatically go to the door but when you see strangers at the door, you may decide not to open the door—after evaluating whether or not you should—using both your emotional and rational response to their appearance. Then come social skills (interpreting tone of voice, responding properly, using the right language if you are multi-lingual, using the right language (age-level) for example if a child is selling cookies vs. a neighbor who has arrived to join you to watch rival football teams.

It is a commonly believed myth that you can't teach an old dog new tricks. This has been considered true of humans for a long time but new research has shown that it is not true.[155] Our brains can change throughout life. New neuron connections form when we learn new information. New neuron connections also form when we re-write the back story that explains events in our life. A painful memory can be transformed into a less painful (or even a good) memory by changing our back story. It does not matter how old the story is—changing the back story can remove the pain.

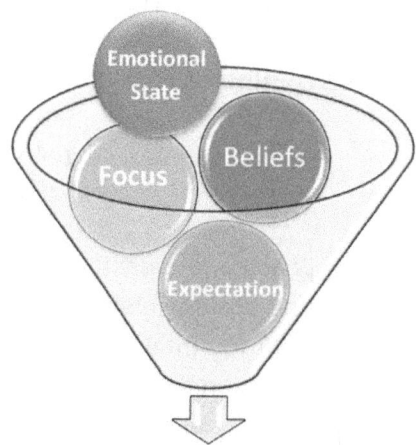

Personal Perception

I'll give you an example. One of my clients always felt a degree of pain inside because his father was seldom there during his childhood. His father never went to any of his games or school events and was usually not home for dinner. When I met him many years later he still felt resentment against his father for not having been there for him when he was growing up. At a deep level, he equated being loved and lovable with whether his father paid attention to him.

When his father died he went to the funeral and learned a lot about the work his father was doing during his childhood that he had not known until then. It became obvious that his father's absence from the home on so many evenings was because he was actively working to make the world a better place—a better place for his son to live. The father was in Detroit, Michigan in the 1960's. When he passed away more than 50 years later, the work he did during those tumultuous times was recognized.

With the new information the man was able to reframe his memories, giving them the back story that his father was so intent on helping to create a better world for him to live in that he sacrificed time with his family for the greater good. His memories are less painful today. He feels less abandoned. He can see that his father knew he had married a woman who was a wonderful mom, who could be there for his son while he worked to make the world a better place. Eventually, his automatic response when he thinks of his father will be pride about what his Dad accomplished, work that was decades ahead of its time in race relations.

How fast the change takes place is completely up to him. In the beginning, the old neural connections took him to the same emotional state but as he repeatedly redirects his thoughts to his new back story, the new neural connections become the easier path for his thoughts to follow. Based on my experience with motivated clients, the painful perspective about past memories that have been thought about often can be fully replaced in just three months. The more an individual goes through this process for different memories, and the more deliberately new back stories are chosen for current events, the faster the reframing of old memories becomes the person's new normal.

Einstein said, "I have no special talent. I am only passionately curious."

New science adds truth to this statement. When we learn about a subject, the part of our brain that deals with the subject grows. Research on the brains of London taxi cab drivers was instrumental in revealing how our brains grow as we learn new information.[156]

> *Our perception of reality is about whom we are, not what reality is. When we believe something is possible, our brain will show us information that helps us achieve our goal. If we believe the goal is impossible, our brain will not pass information that would be helpful to our conscious mind and will create assertions that explain why we are right about the impossibility of the goal.*

The ability of something to be shaped or molded is called plasticity. It is where plastic got its name. Brains have plasticity. I believe the root of the myth that old dogs cannot learn new tricks stems not from an inability, but from a lack of knowledge that we create our back stories. When we perceive reality with the same back stories for too long, we believe our back story is the only accurate back story. This can manifest in stubbornly clinging to ideas and concepts even when there is more than enough evidence to overturn the old belief, revealing The Galileo Effect in action.

As we will see in subsequent chapters, our brains interpret reality in ways that support our beliefs. Our brains continually change as we experience life. In *Happiness*, Matthieu Ricard[157] writes:

> *As influential as external conditions may be, suffering, like well-being, is essentially an interior state.*

Often people will claim their pessimism is realistic or objective. Those claims demonstrate that they do not understand how the brain works. No one can come to purely objective observations. Objectivity requires us not to be influenced by personal opinions or desires. We interpret reality through filters that show us information that supports our beliefs and do not show us information that contradicts our beliefs. Our perception of reality is about whom we are, not what reality is. When we believe something is possible, our brain will show us information that helps us achieve our goal. If we believe the goal is impossible, our brain will not pass information that would be helpful to our conscious mind and will create assertions that explain why we are right about the impossibility of the goal. This is one reason why negative self-talk and pessimism have such a detrimental impact on the outcome of lives.

For example, when I first began talking to a wider audience about how understanding the brain's filtering system and Emotional Guidance could solve many of the world's social problems it was common for people to tell me that you could not teach happiness to people with significant problems, such as homeless people and drug addicts. They used many arguments including that such people had bigger problems than being unhappy. I always maintained that anyone could be learn how to use this information in their life and that anyone who had the opportunity to learn would welcome it.

They called me naïve and an idealist. They told me I was living in la-la land and that I did not understand reality. They didn't hurt my feelings. I knew I could help such people learn to be happier, to understand that their past did not have to dictate their future. The fact that they did not know what I knew did not have the power to hurt my feelings.

For the past seven months I've had the privilege of teaching a group of adults that include a large percentage of recovering addicts, some who are still using, many who were once homeless and some who are still homeless, and some with significant health challenges. While I knew I could help them and that I had higher expectations of their potential than the general public has, I severely underestimated the wisdom and talent I would discover in their ranks. Several of them write poetry I believe is worthy of being published.

Life has taught them wisdom in many areas. Many are talented artists. All are capable of love and all want to love more and to feel peaceful in their hearts. Are they happier? Yes. They're also more hopeful and hope is very near happiness on the Emotional Guidance Scale and hope is a long way from despair. Hopeful represents a state of empowerment from which someone can get anywhere. Increasing happiness improves cognitive abilities which will aids decision-making.

Many of them lack basic skills in reading and writing, but I don't despair. I remember stories of people who were completely illiterate who were able to be successful. I believe this group can begin where they are and go anywhere they chose to go. The lives they've led have taught them a great deal that is valuable to the rest of humanity.

Ralph Waldo Emerson observed, "Nothing great has ever been achieved without enthusiasm."

Important Concepts from Chapter 7:
- The purpose of our emotions is to guide us toward self-actualization is the most important concept of this chapter and of this book.
- One of the most important concepts from this chapter is that humanity does not yet have all the answers nor can we explain how some basic aspects of our world actually work.
- We have guesses supported by research that support hypothesis about animal navigation, but they don't begin to explain how it works—only that astronomy or the Earth's magnetic field is involved.
- Keep an open mind and avoid The Galileo Effect
- Age does not prevent us from learning new information. That's an old myth.
- Rational thought is far less rational than most people believe it to be
- Emotions help us make good decisions if we know how to accurately interpret their meanings

8: Introduction to Emotional Guidance

No man can reveal to you aught but that which already lies half-asleep in the dawning of your knowledge.
The teacher who walks in the shadow of the temple, among his followers, gives not of his wisdom but rather of his faith and his lovingness.
If he is indeed wise he does not bid you enter the house of his wisdom, but rather leads you to the threshold of your own mind.
Kahlil Gibran

When you know how to interpret your Emotional Guidance System (EGS) accurately you will become aware of more and more subtleties, the awareness of which makes your life feel easier. Beneficial synchronicities will begin to show up in your experiences. You will have an internal lie detector and GPS system that directs not only your actions, but your thought.

What does your Emotional Guidance System direct you to? Its purpose is to direct you toward your personal goals and desires. What you want is part of the programming. In fact, it's such a big part of the programming that it may seem you've been given faulty guidance if you look at too small of a picture.

Charles S. Carver is one of the most respected names in psychology. He is the editor of the *Personality Processes and Individual Differences* section of the *Journal of Personality and Social Psychology*. I have read many of his research papers on optimism vs pessimism, self-regulation theory, coping, and more. His work as a professor at the University of Miami has helped shape my positions and I was delighted when he recently published a paper supporting my position that the purpose of emotions is to provide moment-by-moment guidance to us about our behavior.[158]

My stance goes deeper as I believe that emotions provide moment-by-moment guidance to let us know whether our very thoughts are helping us move toward our self-defined goals or away from them. It is still satisfying to see that he has reached the conclusion that emotions are part of a feedback loop, "managing rate of progress at goal attainment or threat avoidance" and that he went on to say that "given multiple simultaneous goals, these functions assist in moment-to-moment priority management, facilitating attainment of all."[159]

I'll give you an example you may have experienced or know of someone who has. Someone is in a relationship that isn't serving their highest good but they are clinging to the unhealthy relationship. It could be a relationship with another person, with a job, or even with a place to live. Then something happens that increases their motivation to move. A woman in a relationship with the wrong man may find that an old flame shows up on the scene and she is strongly drawn back to him. But after she has left the unhealthy relationship the heat from the new flame quickly dies.

What often happens in this situation is the woman begins questioning her judgment, or her decision to leave the unhealthy relationship. But if she understood her Emotional Guidance she would quickly realize that the desire to reunite with the old flame was simply what I'll call the *path of least resistance* to what she really wants. Your guidance seems to know the best possible path to get you on the road to what you want.

When she was in the unhealthy relationship she needed a stronger emotional pull to motivate her to leave the relationship. Once she was clear of that relationship, the new relationship, which was only needed to motivate her to leave the relationship she was clinging to, is no longer serving her and it is no longer on the path toward what she really wants so the energy supporting it subsides.

I'll give you an example of how my guidance helped me find a book. I don't have a library in my home, but I have bookcases in every room. As a result I sometimes have to search when I want to find a particular book. I knew this one book had a passage I wanted to quote and I looked all over the house for it, scanning every bookcase without success. When I passed the dining room after looking upstairs I noticed that a case of Malbec my husband ordered from Argentina was on the table. It had been delivered the day before. I felt a sudden urge to put it in the wine rack. There is a small bookcase next to one of the wine racks in the dining room. I'd already looked for the book there. It wasn't until I bent over to put a bottle in the bottom of the rack that I spotted the book. It was in a horizontal stack and the book above it was slightly larger so it was not visible from above.

I immediately recognized that the urge I'd felt to stop and put the wine away during the workday, was my guidance knowing the *path of least resistance* to get my head in the right position to see the book I was searching for. When you become aware of your guidance you begin noticing synchronicities like this every day. The source of my guidance knew where the book was and the easiest way to get me to find it.

When you begin using your guidance you feel the emotion and urges in a stronger way. Before I understood my guidance I would have felt the urge and ignored it because it was the workday. I wanted that book enough that I might have ordered a new copy, perhaps assuming a friend had borrowed it and not returned it. I would probably not have found it because I usually leave my husband's wine for him to take care of as he's something of a connoisseur.

The woman whose guidance encourages her to leave the relationship that isn't serving her who understands her guidance can view her actions and emotions from a larger perspective. She is far more likely to reach the conclusion that she is on her way to the relationship she wants than to mourn the one she left. She can even learn from the situation by paying attention to how she felt in the relationship she left (not the new one) and realize that if she ever feels that way in the future it might be best if she did not cling to a relationship that was obviously not serving her highest good. When the energy and emotion that pulled her toward the new one stops calling her in that direction she can quickly recognize that it was merely the *path of least resistance* and move on.

The woman who does not know she has guidance has all sorts of pitfalls and traps in this scenario. When the energy supporting the new relationship drops she may think she made a mistake and attempt to return to the relationship she left. Or she may cling to the new relationship because she gave up the old relationship so she could be in the new one. Not understanding that you have guidance and how it works can make life seem as if you are in a rudderless boat being tossed on stormy seas.

The same basic scenario can play out when a job is not serving your highest good. Your guidance can begin making some aspect of the job distasteful. It can be the work itself, a co-worker, the commute or any other aspect of the job. It can direct your attention with encouraging emotions toward other jobs, locations, or industries. It can give you an urge to click on a link that takes you to information about a better job even before you've consciously decided to look around.

The person whose guidance is encouraging him to relocate to a new home can either begin highlighting aspects of the current home that aren't as he'd like them to be in order to decrease his dissatisfaction with the current home or increasing his awareness of aspects of other homes that his doesn't have, increasing his desire for a new home in that way. Guidance can even lead him into a conversation where he learns something that helps him decide he can or should move.

At one point in the past one of my friend's credit was destroyed while she was in the process of getting a divorce. She was very unhappy with her landlord because he was not doing repairs that needed to be done for her to be able to enjoy the home she was renting. She felt stuck and frustrated, but she did not believe she had done enough to repair her credit to be able to buy a home of her own. Because she had the belief that she could not get a mortgage, she had not taken any steps to try to find out if she could. She already believed she couldn't do it yet.

When we talked I disrupted her inertia by simply asking her what the worst that could happen would be if she did try—they could say no and she'd be right where she was now—not any worse off. I didn't know if she could buy a house, but I thought she might be able to. As a result, my cognitive process gave me thoughts hers did not have access to. She tried to buy a house as the result of that conversation and was successful. She thought her credit score was standing in her way, but it was her belief about her credit score, not her credit score that was stopping her from doing what she wanted.

For a woman in my generation, buying a house on your own for the first time is a very empowering event. I remember the first time I did it. I watched my friend's confidence in herself surge after she bought the house. That surge in her confidence extended to other areas of her life and her career began advancing faster than it had in the past. When you feel empowered others perceive you differently.

"Meta-cognition refers to awareness of one's own knowledge—what one does and doesn't know—and one's ability to understand, control, and manipulate one's cognitive processes. It includes knowing when and where to use particular strategies for learning and problem solving as well as how and why to use specific strategies." – Teacher Excellence in Adult Education (TEAL)

Metacognitive is defined in a variety of ways in the scientific literature. The way I mean it involves the conscious overseeing and regulation of cognitive processes. Instead of just letting thoughts come and go without thinking about why you're thinking the thoughts you're thinking, or about alternative thoughts you could think, or how the thoughts you're thinking are affecting your experience, meta-cognition involves conscious awareness and exertion of some control over the process. It does not mean you have to control every thought. Using a combination of meta-cognition and Emotional Guidance is the best way to improve your life experience. Your Emotional Guidance provides you with information that helps you know which thoughts you may want to adjust, which it would serve you to give more air time (in your mind), and which aren't serving your highest good.

Thoughts you might want to adjust would be ones where you can find a better feeling perspective using one of the processes in the **How to Think Positively Process Chapter 33.**

Thoughts you want to give more air time in your mind (or by talking and/or writing about them) are the thoughts that feel good when you think them.

How your emotional sense feels when you think the thought lets you know if it is serving your highest good (feels good or better than prior thought) or not serving your highest good (feels worse than your prior thought, or, if the prior thought felt bad, it feels the same).

If you're aware you have Emotional Guidance and how to accurately interpret its meanings, you can think about what you're thinking in a more intelligent way.

Our emotions are a sensory feedback system designed to guide us toward self-realization. Self-realization, as intended here, refers to movement toward the full development of one's abilities and talents. It is toward, rather than the fulfillment of, because as we achieve more, our ability to achieve expands—there is no end to what can be accomplished by an individual who continually moves in the direction of self-realization. The goals our guidance guides us toward are what we want—not what another person or what God wants. But if our goal includes doing what we believe God wants us to do, our guidance will help us do that. But that help is not because it is what God wants, it's because we have decided that we want to do what we believe God wants.

Let me break it down.

We make decisions about our behavior based on what we believe will make us feel the best. This can be doing something we believe will make us feel better or not doing something that we believe would make us feel worse.

We have information about how we believe it will feel because emotions respond to our thoughts about doing (or not doing) the subject we're thinking about doing.

How we believe we will feel regulates our actions.

For example, let's say your boss is being an arrogant jerk and really pushes your buttons. You want to lash out at him verbally; you may even want to punch him. But you take a moment to consider the consequences of your actions and you decide it's better to have a steady paycheck than to face your wife after being fired for insubordination or jailed for assault. It feels better not to act on the impulses that would lead to those outcomes.

What you've done is had a thought that felt better. It feels better to stand your ground and attack (verbally or physically) someone who is being as mean-spirited as your boss is being. But it feels better not to have to explain to your wife why you were fired than it does to lash out at your boss. So restraint wins. You self-regulate your behavior. Now, you still have anger at your boss. If you're the common man, you'll take it out on someone else or dim the emotions using alcohol or drugs. You may go to the gym and spend some time pretending the punching bag is your boss. You may go golfing and imagine the ball is your boss's head (this can result in a good round of golf). You may go home and pick a fight with your spouse or child.

But what you could do is soothe the anger using your mind. You can remember that your boss has a lot of demands on his time that make him more thoughtless when he interacts with others. You may remember calmer times when your boss showed you a different, kinder and gentler, side of himself. You may remember that you're going to finish obtaining a degree or a professional certification soon that will open up new job or promotional opportunities for you. You can remember that you've seen other bosses like this who enjoy their power for a brief time and then are responsible for their own downfall—that the company does not want that type of boss. You can refocus your commitment to continuous self-improvement to prepare yourself to step into your bosses shoes after he self-destructs and enjoy the thought that he is making it easy for the person who follows him into that position to shine.

Those are just a few ideas of thoughts that would make you feel better without requiring you to take any action. When you begin perceiving the situation from a more general or broader viewpoint instead of focusing on today's specific incident, your emotion changes. You're in charge of your thoughts and the perspective you take about the situation—your boss has no control over that.

You could also have a boss you feel great respect for and when a co-worker does something that feels wrong to you, something that could potentially harm the boss you respect, your desire to protect your boss is greater because you hold her in high esteem. It feels worse to have someone you respect have something harm them than it does if your boss is someone you despise. Who you have decided to be can impact this. For some people, it would always feel wrong, even if they despise the boss because they've decided to be someone who does the right thing under all conditions. Someone else who hasn't given much thought to who she wants to be might not notice an ethical issue in allowing her boss to be harmed.

Both scientific circles and laypeople commonly believe emotions tend to be unreliable and that emotions directly cause behavior. In 2007, Roy F. Baumeister et al. presented a new theory of *How Emotion Shapes Behavior: Feedback, Anticipation, and Reflection, Rather Than Direct Causation* in which they conclude "the direct causation theory should be converted from a standard assumption to a questionable hypothesis." Their thorough analysis of current research lends support to the theory that the purpose of emotion is to guide behavior. This series of quotes from their extensive work reflects a small portion of the support it contains for the concept that emotions are guidance:

Anticipation of emotional outcomes is an important aspect of the feedback theory. As people learn to anticipate feedback, they may alter their behavior (constructively) to pursue the feedback that they like. Emotion is ideally suited for this because of its hedonic power: Behavioral choices could well be swayed by the anticipation of feeling good or bad thereafter.

The resistance of emotion to direct control is, in short, a puzzle to self-regulation researchers. Why did the human self-regulatory capacity evolve so as to be able to exert direct control over actions and thoughts but not emotions? The answer, we think, is that **you cannot control your emotions because the purpose of emotions is to control you.** *Emotions are a feedback system for facilitating behavioral learning and control. If they were themselves controllable, they would lose that crucial function.*

In sum, the human emotional apparatus may shape behavior by providing a feedback system that may be useful for sophisticated goal pursuit and learning to behave effectively in complex social and cultural situations. Conscious emotions provide feedback about behavior, stimulate cognitive analysis, and promote revisions of the programming on which people react to events. Conscious emotions can also be anticipated and so people behave in ways that will pursue desired emotional outcomes.

. . . the reality is that behavior pursues emotional outcomes. . .

. . .much prosocial behavior turns out to be informed by anticipation of possible mood changes. Other research supports the notion that whether people give mood-congruent or mood-incongruent responses depends on their beliefs about the power of the stimulus to enhance their mood.

. . . one could entertain a view of human behavior as fundamentally and pervasively guided by the quest to regulate one's emotions. A person could certainly do far worse, and arguably not much better, than to go through life making all decisions so as to maximize positive emotions (especially in a long-term perspective) and minimize negative ones.

. . . there is a fair amount of evidence that anticipated emotion does lead to adaptive, beneficial, socially and personally desirable behaviors, especially insofar as these take the form of choosing a safe, readily defensible option.

Modern science is catching up with ancient philosophers and supporting what Aristotle said so long ago:

Happiness is the meaning and the purpose of life, the whole aim and end of human existence. Aristotle

Before Baumeister et al.'s paper, the former belief about emotions had been the central accepted belief in the scientific world for eighty years. The belief that we act at the whim of our emotions, without conscious cognition between feeling the emotion and action, has created a society filled with mental health problems. Between 20 – 25% of the population suffers from a form of mental health illness every year. Diagnoses from depression, anxiety, bulimia, anorexia, OCD, and more can be prevented through an understanding of one's Emotional Guidance. Some of the people I worked with when I first began teaching had suffered chronic bouts of depression for decades and have now been free of depression for seven years. I can't guarantee that everyone will achieve these results, but I believe that anyone who really understands their guidance has a very low risk of depression and has the ability to recover if something should cause them to become depressed.

I used to suffer from periodic bouts of depression with suicide ideation and have been completely free of such episodes for a decade because of the tools and knowledge in these pages. I no longer worry that something will upset me and throw me back into a depressed state. The person I was when I was suffering in that way is so different from who I've become that the memories seem to be of another person or another life. I am no longer who I was when I had those problems. I am stronger, more resilient, more confident, more sure that I can handle whatever life brings me.

And it's not a strength born of willpower. I used that type of strength in the past... to keep going when I wanted to stop... to put an acceptable face on at work and pretend everything was okay. Using willpower drains you so that when you are finally where you can stop pretending everything is alright you have nothing left to give to your family, yourself, your community, or your world.

The strength understanding your Emotional Guidance gives you comes from your core and does not require willpower. It is who you have become. It's unshakable and deep.

Emotions are literally guidance from one of our senses. Katherine Peil demonstrates that our emotions are a sensory feedback system in *Emotion: A Self-regulatory Sense*.[160] Her position is that emotion is our oldest sense, and she uses molecular biology and the biophysical processes of living systems to lead us on a step-by-step exploration of this idea. In her work and our discussions, Peil has explained that the function of the basic negative emotions is to provide information that helps us keep our bodies safe. The function of positive emotions is to point us toward self-development and well-being. Peil states we derive no benefits from ignoring the output from our emotional system and that our guidance provides information that will improve our lives if we act upon it appropriately.

Humans tend to override the feedback from their emotional sense with rational thought. Yet, filters (biases) in our minds distort our perception of life. Our emotional feedback by-passes the filters and provides feedback that contains greater clarity and accuracy.

Only a small amount of the information gathered by our senses comes to our conscious awareness. The information that we do become aware of is not reality, it is filtered based on our emotional state, expectations, beliefs and focus. Psychologists call these filters biases. Our emotions do not lead us astray—a common and false belief. Faulty thinking stemming from emotional distress can lead to self-defeating behavior, but the behavior is the result of the desire to feel better by someone who lacks skills that empower him/her to feel better in the circumstances being perceived. It can be exacerbated by misinterpreting the meaning and best response to negative emotions.

Inaccurately interpreting what our emotions mean is what leads us to actions that do not support our highest good.

While science misunderstood emotions for eighty years, leading us even further from *trusting our instincts* and *gut reactions*, it's no wonder so many are suffering so much. Dr. Dan Siegel shares, "We now know that the intestines, our gut, has a set of neural net processors that function like sophisticated computers. The computers we have at home are linear processors, and they can do all sorts of fancy things quickly, but the really sophisticated computers are those that are in a spider web like network called parallel distributed processing. We have these parallel processors in our intestines and also around our heart. So the heartfelt feelings that we have are not just poetic metaphors of the *gut instinct* and *heartfelt feelings* but instead are really sophisticated processors. Now, it's not rational—meaning it's not a logical thing where you could say, 'A went to B went to C.' But it is a very important way in which our whole being is processing information, and often this source of bodily wisdom is very useful when contemplating an organization's direction."[161]

We live in the best time ever to solve society's most pressing problems—poverty, crime, racism, war, disparate outcomes, addictions, and chronic mental and physical diseases can all be significantly reduced using *The Smart Way*. This book is designed to demonstrate not only why Emotional Guidance is the best weapon we have, but also how to empower all people with its benefits.

Before delving into the science and some of the very practical applications of Emotional Guidance, a foundation of the basics of how to use the guidance is needed. When fully understood, the guidance our emotions provide is simple enough for anyone, even children, to use to enhance their life experiences. Within the snippet of a story I'm going to share with you is a brief story about when I learned I had an innate *creep alert*.

I hope you find this chapter fun. I use a different method to introduce the basics of our Emotional Guidance system. Because using one's Emotional Guidance is largely a mental process, a topic that can be quite boring to describe in a non-fiction book, I wrote a fiction book in which the main character teaches this process. An excerpt from that book follows to introduce you to the basic premise.

You need some background on the characters to understand the scene. The main character, Maia, teaches human thriving in our time. She has been transported to the future, a world divided into a Utopian society filled with individuals who understand their Emotional Guidance, and a dystopian society filled with violence, shorter life spans, and other undesirable traits. The geo-political map in this future time bears little resemblance to what we know today. The dystopian society is divided into territories led by violent, dictator-like warlords.

The Utopian society (Solis) brought Maia to the future, but she has now been kidnapped by Marcello, the leader of the largest dystopian territory. I hope you enjoy this excerpt from *Shades of Joy*:[162]

Marcello led Maia to a cozy library, "Will this be an acceptable classroom?"

Maia's eyes took in the rich cherry cabinets climbing high up tall ceilings; a ladder was needed to reach the top shelves. She was delighted to see some classics and her heart was gladdened to know the book burning had not been as thorough as she had been led to believe. A fireplace flanked by large windows looked out onto Puget Sound. Two comfortable chairs were situated in front of the unlit fireplace and Turkish rugs graced the hardwood floors.

"Yes, this will do. Do you have a White board?"

"A White board?"

"Yes, a board where I can sketch out concepts to make them easier to understand."

"I don't have one. I will have one of my men check on it. Couldn't we just use paper?"

"Paper will do for now." Maia stated, "But a White board would be helpful as we move along."

Maia sat in the chair to the left and waited for Marcello to sit in the other.

"The first thing you have to understand is the path to where you want to go is the path to happiness. I will speak often of happiness. I don't know how happiness is viewed here. It would help if you shared that with me."

"Happiness?" Marcello laughed harshly, "Happiness is a myth."

Maia took a deep breath. "I assure you, happiness is not a myth. It is a reality for many people and attainable by all. It is the primary motivation for everything you have ever done."

"Bah! You don't know anything about why I do what I do."

"I know far more than you believe I know and I know more than you do about your motivations. Of this, I am sure. By the end of our time together, you will understand how that is true. However, you have a decision to make. One I thought we covered this morning. Do you want to learn my secrets, or do you want to argue with me?"

"How could you know more about my life than I do?" Marcello visibly bristled at Maia's words.

Maia could tell it was all bluster. Marcello had been behaving that way so long; he no longer even realized it was not the way he wanted to behave. Should she kowtow to him or stay in her power? That was a silly question. She was an indomitable force when she stayed in her power. He would not harm her as long as she had the secrets to what he wanted. Once he had the secrets, he would no longer want to harm her.

"Do you want to remain ignorant of the truth? Right now, you know so little about the truth that you cannot understand or comprehend it when you hear it. I know the secrets to a life that is as good as one can be. I know that is something you could have. But, more importantly, all the people in your territory could have better lives."

She paused and felt greatly rewarded when she saw a spark of interest in Marcello's eyes following her last statement. "I am happy to teach you what I know, but you have to be the student. In time, we will learn from one another. However, your only job right now is to let me know whether you understand what I say. You must keep an open mind, or you will not hear or understand."

Marcello sighed while visibly relaxing. "I want to learn, but you make no sense."

"The reason I make no sense is because you have been lied to your entire life; this entire society is full of lies—lies and false premises that lead everyone astray."

"My father did not lie to me."

"I am not saying he lied intentionally." Maia sighed, realized the beginning would be a slow start. "He was lied to, and his Father before him, and so on back through time."

Brushing a stray hair away from her face Maia said, "Let me begin again."

"There are things about your brain that few people understand. Let me explain those things. We may be able to move more quickly once that understanding exists. What do you believe the function of your brain is?"

"It is for rational, unemotional thought. It is to give me information to make good decisions, for remembering, and on an unconscious level, it beats my heart, keeps me breathing when I sleep, and more."

"Those are pretty common beliefs, but they are not accurate. Before we are done you will see that what you considered *rational thought* is actually the most irrational thoughts you have access to." Seeing Marcello about to protest once again, Maia stated, "Don't interrupt."

Maia calmly watched his face; rage was his first response to her insolent comment. She bit her tongue to keep the smile from her face, knowing it would just enrage him more—and maybe too much. Marcello soon gained control of the rage and overrode it with his desire to understand what she knew. Maia waited until his face showed he was receptive to her words before continuing. "Your brain's primary job is to prove your own beliefs to you. It filters out information that contradicts your beliefs, and perceives information in a way that is consistent with your existing beliefs. It does not care if your beliefs are true, or if they serve you. It only cares if the information is presented in a way that is consistent with your established beliefs."

Pausing to allow Marcello time to absorb the enormity of her comment, Maia continued. "It is easier to see it in others than in ourselves. Think for a minute about people you know—maybe someone who believes they are not treated fairly, but you believe they are. How do they perceive life? Do they perceive it as if life is unfair to them?"

Maia could see Marcello considering her words. She decided she needed to move slowly through this initial stage until he trusted her.

"Think about it for a few minutes. Look for examples of people who believe life is a certain way and make excuses for why others' lives are different from their own."

Maia rose and went to a bookshelf where she had spotted a book of quotes. Unsure of what she might find within its pages, but hopeful, she returned to her seat with the heavy book. Paging through she found the category "Expectation" and scanned the quotes. Grinning when she found the one she sought, she said, "I like to share the wisdom of the ages with my students. This wisdom has been known throughout history. What makes me different is just that I have just put all the pieces together in a way that provides answers and helps humans thrive. That is what is unique about my methods—I have connected more dots than others." Looking back at the book, she read, 'Whether you believe you can, or you believe you can't, either" Marcello joined her as she said the last words, "way you're right. Which are you? Henry Ford.'"

"How did you know I love that quote?"

"I didn't. It is a favorite of mine as well. Without my usual resources available, I have to improvise with what is available. I will tell you something else you will not yet understand: I was guided to use it."

"Don't lie to me! There is no one else here. You were not guided. Don't give me your superstitious mumbo jumbo. I want clear answers."

"Marcello," Maia said with a calm voice while reaching out and touching his arm, knowing the Reiki energy would help calm not only his temper, but also his wounded spirit. "No one is alone in this life. We can choose to feel alone. We can choose to act alone. Nevertheless, all of us have guidance that is available to us in every moment. At any time, we are free to tune in to it and use its power to aid us. Have you never known to do, or not do, something but not known why? Known it so strongly that nothing could convince you otherwise? When you know that strongly, aren't you always right?"

Maia saw the recognition of unexplained knowledge in his eyes.

"It's not there all the time." He said. "Usually, I don't know. But sometimes, yes, there have been times when I knew without knowing how I knew. Bringing you here was one of those times."

"Then do not waste the opportunity by arguing with everything I say. Clearly, your guidance is telling you I have something you want very badly. When someone is not usually tuned to their guidance they still notice it when the urges are powerful. They don't recognize it is guidance, but the sense that they must act is too strong to ignore. Once again, may I have your agreement—this time I want your word on it—that you will stop arguing with me?"

Maia thrust her right hand toward Marcello. She was not sure if a handshake still had the meaning attributed to it in her time but she was willing to hope.

Marcello eyed her warily, dismayed by her offer. She waited, leaving her hand outstretched while he decided. She could see the resignation in his eyes as he clasped hers and shook.

"Good. Now that that's out of the way, do you see how Henry Ford's quote is saying much of what I said? Our belief, or expectation, impacts the outcome."

"Yes, and I've seen it in my men as well."

"Thank you, a straight-forward answer." Maia smiled sweetly. "Did you understand that their brains actually filter out solutions, when they don't believe they can accomplish something, and help them find solutions, when they believe they can?"

"No, I did not make that correlation. So, if I believe something, my brain provides evidence to prove it to me? It interprets reality differently than it would if my beliefs were different?"

"Exactly! You've got it. That is step one. The next step is to begin recognizing when it happens, to you and others. A couple of keys are to recognize, in yourself, when you believe something is true for you but not for others. Remember, beliefs are able to help or hinder. They are not all good or all bad. Most importantly, the brain does not differentiate between those that serve our higher good, and those that thwart it. It *irrationally* attempts to support whatever we have decided to believe."

"Actually, "*irrationally* attempts to support" what we have decided to believe is probably too harsh. I believe the brain is designed as if we understand the impact our beliefs have on our experience, so when we have a belief it acts as if we have deliberately chosen that belief and understand the ramifications of it. Unfortunately, most people have no idea how their beliefs affect their thinking and their experiences."

"A couple of things may help you identify beliefs that are not serving you. If you find yourself saying, 'I want to but,' you are pointing out a belief that limits you. The second is when you believe that another has it better than you, and have an excuse or explanation for why that is. Think about that for a bit while I think about the best next step in your lesson."

Marcello looked steadily into Maia's eyes after a few minutes of looking out the window with his eyes brows furrowed, he said, "Do you realize you have already shattered a paradigm I have lived with my entire life?"

"Yes, I do." Maia laughed. "Get used to it. I am going to do it again, but first, there is something you need to know. You can't go back. What I teach, you cannot unlearn. Your worldview will change. We are not so far down the path now that you cannot stop, but soon much of what you have believed will lie in shreds on the floor. I can lead you in a way where you feel good about that, instead of bad that you lived so long with misleading beliefs, but you have to trust me if we are to move forward."

"If I can't trust my brain, what may I trust?"

"Your Emotional Guidance System, I'll call it your EGS for short."

"Trust a woman to tell me to trust my emotions!"

"Marcello, emotions are far more valuable and accurate than you understand. It is not the inaccuracy of emotions, but humanity's lack of understanding of the language they use and their meaning that makes them seem irrational. I will teach you to understand them. Once you do that, they will never again seem irrational. Let me give you an example. Did your men relay to you anything about my behavior after they kidnapped me, anything that seemed unusual or unexpected to you?"

"Yes, they wondered if you were crazy. You did not seem docile, yet you came with them almost willingly after the initial confrontation. Yet, you also did not seem afraid to speak up or let them know that something was unacceptable to you."

"Do you have any idea why that might be? How could a woman grabbed in the middle of the night by two men, one of them as big as a mountain with a deformed face that helped to hide the kindness in his heart, not be deathly afraid?"

Marcello shook his head. He had wondered about it. He even, briefly, considered if this was all a set-up, if Maia was a spy. However, Brazil was too far away to impact his territory so that hadn't made sense and he'd dismissed the thought.

"Tell me."

"After the initial shock, I checked in with my EGS. I understand its language. I know that at low emotional states, my thinking is impaired, and the better my current emotional state is, the better my cognitive abilities will be. At first, I wanted to assuage my fears so that I could think of a way to escape. I am not accustomed to feeling bad-feeling emotions. I have mastered techniques that allow me to self-manage myself into consistently good-feeling emotional states most of the time and to, at a minimum, know I am able to return to feeling good in short order if something goes poorly."

"What is 'emotional state'?"

"There are two ways I will use the term. One is the emotional stance or state in any given moment—how an individual feels in that single space in time. The other is their chronic emotional stance. Both impact behavior and how the world is perceived. I will tell you more about that later."

"Right now I want to make a different point." Maia gently led him back to discussing her reaction to being kidnapped, feeling they were on the brink of his understanding an important concept more fully.

"One way to feel better when something feels bad is to go more general. I could not come up with a specific plan for escape, especially the further they took me from Solis. Racking my brain for the specifics felt worse. But, I could go general and find thoughts that soothed my fears. I thought things like, "I don't have to figure this out right now" and "I will find a way. " Since I understand how accurate my EGS is, because I habitually use it, when I felt better not only did I feel better, but I knew those statements were true."

"The only way to know with certainty that things that feel better are true is to use your EGS frequently, beginning with small things that are easy to verify. As your trust in your guidance builds, you will begin using it on bigger things. I am considered very rational and analytical. At first, I used both my Emotional Guidance and my *rational brain* to make decisions. In time, I came to rely less on my *rational brain* and far more on my EGS. My life has gotten continually better as a result."

Marcello laughed, "You want me to believe your life has gotten continually better yet here you sit, kidnapped, at my mercy." His laugh grew in volume until his entire body shook with his amusement.

Maia sat serenely in her chair, not bothered at all by his finding humor in her statement, a mysterious small smile on her face. "Au contraire, I began this day taking a boat ride, on a dazzling sunny day, across Puget Sound in the most luxurious yacht I have had the pleasure of boarding. My ride was enhanced by a spectacular view of Mt. Rainier. I was given a delicious meal that I did not have to purchase or prepare, ate it at a table with a resplendent view of the sound and of a very attractive man. Then I enjoyed a period of rest where I bathed in luxury and saw a bathtub that I will be able to enjoy later. I am savoring the anticipation of it now. My biggest passion in life is helping others thrive more. Even though you are one of the most powerful men in the world, you are not, and have not been, thriving. Your life is killing you inside. You brought me here to heal that. The potential for good to come from this situation, good that is in alignment with my ultimate desires, is tremendous. Now I sit with an intelligent man who wants to learn what I know in one of the most magnificent libraries that I have ever had the pleasure of enjoying. The Biltmore is more impressive, but this is lovely and I will not diminish it by wishing myself elsewhere. My guidance assures me I am not in danger."

With fiery conviction in her eyes, Maia met Marcello's gaze, defying him to see her reality in a less favorable light. They locked gazes, her conviction firm until Marcello gave her the point, "Touché."

Then he looked down and shook his head. "I see I have a powerful adversary."

"No, you do not. I am not your adversary." Maia deliberately projected appreciation of the opportunity Marcello provided through her eyes. "You're not my adversary. You want to learn what I know. I want you to understand what I know. I know what will happen when you know it. That is the only advantage I have."

"How are you so sure you're not in danger?"

"I have been using my guidance for years. It tells me, loudly, when there is danger and helps me avert or avoid it. When an obstacle in the road ahead while I am driving necessitates a change of lanes, I know before I see the danger. If someone comes to my door that I should not allow inside, it lets me know before I open the door. It works. It knows far more than I have the ability to know through any other means. I trust it implicitly, without exception."

"How can you have such a positive outlook on your situation?"

"I can't have a bad outlook on my situation. Beliefs are just the first filter that distorts the information our rational brain transmits to us. Our habitual emotional stance creates another filter. Because I manage my emotional stance to a place that feels good on a consistent basis, my filter highlights information that feels good to me. It also dims negative aspects."

"But, like I said before, it will tell me of danger. In fact, one of the first ways I learned to trust my EGS was because of what I termed my *creep alert*. Back then, I was like most of humanity, trained away from my guidance by parents and a society that did not understand anything about emotions. I was taught to trust my *rational mind*. Someone came into my experience and I had a strong and immediate negative reaction to him. I talked myself out of it. Even though I am not a racist person, I told myself that I was being racist. I did not understand the wisdom of one's guidance and thought the only basis for the distrust I felt toward this person had to be because he was a different race than I am. I ignored the fact that his first cousin, who was almost twice his size and should have seemed more dangerous if his race was the reason for my reaction, was someone I was drawn to. In fact, I was enjoying his first cousin's company and developing a friendly, fun relationship that included easy bantering with him."

"My *rational mind* discarded this evidence and highlighted the fact that I was having this reaction to someone of a different race for no known reason. My rational mind deduced the reason must be racism. At that time, I did not know I had guidance. Since I did not have an established belief that I had reliable guidance, my rational mind could not attribute my appropriate response to guidance. It had to supply some other reason for my reaction. It was aware of racist individuals in the world and I believed there were racist people in the world. So, my so-called rational mind irrationally attributed that trait to me to explain what it was unable to explain within my existing belief system in another, more accurate way. Not only did my *rational mind* discount the first cousin, it discounted countless other experiences in my life that clearly demonstrated I'm not racist—events involving the same race that this man was. The man I had the intense negative reaction to robbed us that same night. Conversing with a friend who was also there, and also not a racist individual based on many experiences we had previously shared, I learned he had the same reaction and had talked himself out of the feelings for the same reasons I had."

"From that experience, I learned that my *creep alert* as I termed it was an accurate predictor of undesired behaviors. I did not know why, but I began listening to it. Later, when I learned more about the EGS, I understood it was just strong Emotional Guidance. I am able to maintain a positive outlook because I have developed that habit of looking at life. It does not mean I will not know about danger, or take appropriate action. In fact, I have had experiences where my *creep alert* has let me know about danger and I have been able to take evasive actions. My focus in those situations is far more on appreciation for having my guidance than in seeing the world as an evil place full of trouble."

"Why did it not warn you away from harm last night?"

"I have not been harmed. In fact, as I said a minute ago, this may be the path of least resistance to goals that are important to me. What made me get up in the middle of the night and take a run? It was the first time I had done that, ever. Perhaps my guidance was leading me to a situation that left the least probability that others would be harmed when I was taken. Had you considered that? I have. In fact, I believe that is why I was inspired to go for a run. Do not try to tell me your men would not have harmed anyone who stood in their way. I know they would have done whatever was necessary to follow your order to bring me to you."

"You have that much faith in your guidance?"

"That and more, but I do not expect you to have faith in yours until you practice. You must begin using your guidance to check things, even as you continue to make decisions the same way you always have. It won't be long until you begin seeing how trustworthy your guidance is. Only you can build your own trust in your guidance. It is a three-pronged approach. First, you have to pay attention to it and begin trusting it. As it proves its value to you, you have two jobs. The first is to listen for and check in with the guidance. It has always been there, but how often have you actually listened? Since you did not know you had guidance, you have really only listened when it was screaming at you. The guidance will guide you in every moment, if you listen carefully."

"I don't want something else telling me what to do." Marcello protested.

"What is it guiding you to?" Maia patiently inquired.

"I don't know. But, I am in charge of my life. I make my own decisions about what I want."

Maia relaxed back in the comfortable chair, allowing Marcello to absorb what he had just stated before asking, again, "What does your guidance guide you to?"

"How should I know? I am not even sure I have this guidance. It sounds impossible."

Enjoying herself greatly, but hiding most of her mirth, Maia repeated the question again, "What does your guidance guide you to?"

"Why do you keep asking me that?"

"Because you told me you do not want your guidance telling you where to go. If you do not know what it guides you to, how do you know?"

Deflated, Marcello finally understood he had been making a decision without knowing what he did not know. "What does my guidance want me to do?"

Giving Marcello an encouraging smile, Maia began the explanation, "It guides you to the dreams, goals, and desires that you have decided you want."

"It guides me to my goals? How does it know what my goals are? I don't tell anyone what all my plans are." Marcello protested.

"I can't tell you the mechanics of how it knows. But, you can show yourself that is what it does—in many ways it seems magical. It will take into account goals that seem to conflict and actually guide you to a path where both may be accomplished—but you are able to get there only if you trust it and only if you believe it is possible to satisfy two goals that seem to conflict with one another. As long as you believe you must make a choice between the two, it will not show you the path to achieve both. However, your EGS will. The clearer you are about your goals, the clearer the guidance you receive will be. You do not have to even know or remember your goals or desires for your guidance to include them. I have been led to outcomes I had forgotten I wanted; only remembering having that desire when it showed up in my life."

"Then how do you know your guidance led you there?"

"It really is much easier to understand as you experience it. I know there is a level of energy below what we can measure, on the level of Quantum Physics. We feel things from that level. The more we pay attention to how things feel, the more sensitive we become to our own guidance. In many ways, guidance is like our other senses. Our eyes interpret light waves that are translated into what we see. Our ears interpret sound waves that we cannot see. We do not doubt our ears—even though we cannot see the sound waves. Our taste buds translate molecules into specific tastes. Our nose translates the vibration of scents we cannot see, enabling us to smell. Do we ask our nose if the smell we enjoy is real? We were trained to trust those senses, so we do not question them. Our emotions are also sensory feedback. We question them only because we were trained to disregard them. We were trained to believe emotions are unreliable and irrational. We were trained to believe that our *rational minds* are the source of intelligent decisions. Most people still believe that. They do not know the real function of the *rational mind* is to prove our own beliefs to us."

"Just like the artist or the musician, using the sense increases its abilities. The artist does not paint his best picture the first time he holds a brush. As he practices seeing from an artist's perspective, his ability to create the image he sees increases. The musician does not have perfect pitch the first time he picks up a guitar. Practice enhances the ability of his mind to translate what his ears hear and fine tune sounds in ways he could not have done before he practiced for many hours. As you use your Emotional Guidance it will become easier for you to do so."

Marcello was listening intently. Maia believed much of what she said was resonating with him on a deep level.

"Our *rational mind* does not consider what is best for us. It trusts that we have established beliefs that serve us. Unfortunately, society did not train us to do that. Society trained us to establish beliefs that were similar to those around us. For the most part, beliefs are passed from parent to child with little change. Teachers pass on their beliefs, not realizing that many of the beliefs they share have the opposite effect of what they truly desire—which is helping students live a better life."

"I will give you some practice exercises to help you begin understanding. Sometimes it will seem to be leading you in the wrong direction. I have learned that if I trust my guidance is taking me the right way, it actually knows the quickest path to my goals. Only in hindsight does the route make sense to me. With enough practice, full faith that you are on the path you want to be on is possible—just by paying attention to how you feel. When you get to that point, life becomes incredibly awesome."

"I can't imagine ever trusting it that much." Marcello's doubts were evident.

"Don't worry about it. Trust will come in time. You will be ready when you are ready. But first, you have to understand its language. Let me see if I am able to be succinct in this explanation."

Maia shut her eyes for a moment, concentrating on allowing the best words to flow through her. Laughing, she jumped up and grabbed what looked like a solid gold pen from Marcello's hand. "Go stand in the corner with your eyes closed."

He looked like he was going to refuse, but the determined look in Maia's eyes seemed to persuade him to do as she requested.

She looked around the room for a place to hide the pen. There was a very large book on a shelf midway through the room. She lifted it up and slid the pen under it. She was glad the room did not need dusting because disturbed dust would have given the hiding spot away. She then continued walking to the far end of the room, slowly, and then back to where Marcello stood in the corner. She wanted him to hear her steps throughout the room so he would not know by the sound of her steps where the pen was hidden.

She touched him on the shoulder and told him, "You may open your eyes and turn around now."

She returned to the chair she had been using. "Your guidance guides you away from danger and toward thriving. I have hidden your pen. I am going to use clues to help you find it. I will tell you, 'You're getting warmer' when you move toward your pen and I will say, 'You're getting colder' when you are moving away from your pen. Got it?"

"Warmer is toward and colder is away?"

"Yes, much like positive emotions are toward your goals and emotions that feel worse indicate you're moving away from what you want."

"If Emotional Guidance is that simple, how could we be so confused?"

Standing back up, Maia explained, "Well, for one thing, most people will interpret fear as meaning that the thought they just thought is true. When in reality, it means that the thought is moving away from their dreams, desires, and goals if the fearful thought felt worse than the thought before it. Someone could be in such an awful place that a fearful thought actually feels better, but that is a lesson for another day."

Widening her stance, Maia playfully put her hands on her hips and ordered, "Stop stalling and find your pen."

Gaping at her before deciding to join in her playfulness, Marcello took a step toward the far end of the library and Maia said, "You're getting warmer."

He moved slowly and deliberately toward the other end of the library with Maia giving a clue after each step. When he had passed the hiding place far enough that it was behind him she said, "You're getting colder."

Marcello turned toward the books lining the wall opposite where the pen was hidden, taking a step toward them. "You're getting colder." Maia said with a giggle, knowing he would soon have his pen back and gain a rudimentary understanding of how Emotional Guidance works.

Marcello turned with more assurance toward the opposite wall.

Maia said, "You're getting warmer."

He moved to the wall and she said, "You're getting quite warm."

He had a smile on his face now as he studied the books before him. He reached out and opened a drawer that was hidden, built to look like it was part of the shelf, but there was no pen inside. Maia remained silent. He looked at her and she laughingly said, "Your guidance will be more specific than I am."

His eyes returned to the books in front of him. He removed a book close to the one his pen was hidden under and Maia said, "You're getting hot."

Marcello seemed to think she had hidden it behind the books as he drew out another one, looking behind. Maia said, "Hot, hot, hot! That would equate to interest or passion if it were your guidance letting you know how close to the right path you are on."

Marcello drew out the book the pen was hidden under by sliding it along the shelf and the pen fell, landing on top of his shinny patent leather shoe.

Marcello picked up the pen and said, "What is my prize?"

"Your prize is a greater understanding of your Emotional Guidance. Most people think when they feel an emotional response to a thought that feels worse, the emotion is a warning, telling them the thought is something to fear, worry, fret about, or feel concern about. That interpretation is off the mark. Just like, 'You're getting colder' means you are moving away from your goal, those emotions are communicating that you are off-track."

Sitting back down, Maia continued, "Each thought you think elicits an emotional response. If the thought is much like the prior thought, there will not be much emotional variance in response to the thought. However, if someone is thinking about a loved one and feeling love but then they think about something that could be of concern, they feel an emotional response that feels worse. For example, let's say your daughter is out with friends. You think about her and feel the love you have for her. Then you think about young people driving and you feel fearful for her safety. The emotional response is _not_ saying, 'Yes, that is a valid worry.' The emotional response is saying, 'You're getting colder,' moving away from what you desire. Energy flow follows your attention. Attention to the unwanted increases the probability of the unwanted."

"The layers in that single scenario are deep and complex. You do not create what will happen in your daughter's life, but you have the power of influence. The first thing that happens is within your own body. When you feel positive emotions, your body thrives; it functions at its optimum level. Your immune system works best when you feel positive emotions and much of one's health flows from that. The life expectancy in Solis is far longer than in the dark zones. Cognitive abilities are at their best when one feels positive emotions and decrease as negative emotions increase. So moving from feeling love for your daughter, to worry or fear, decreases your ability to think clearly."

"An individual who is feeling love treats others well. An individual who is worried or fearful is far more likely to snap at another person, be grumpy, or even say hurtful things to a loved one. Relationships are diminished when the parties in the relationship have chronic thoughts that elicit a bad-feeling emotional response."

"There are other repercussions. Racism increases with negative emotion, the ability to negotiate increases with positive emotions. Access to insights and inspirations increases as habitual positive emotions increase."

"Is this beginning to make sense to you?" Maia checked in to see whether Marcello was keeping up.

"It makes sense when you say it. But when I compare it to what I think I know, the differences make it confusing again." He admitted.

"Relax. You will learn better if you relax into this. You have a lifetime of false premises to overcome. You are not going to grasp it all in one day. I didn't understand it all at once. In fact, there were things that were so contrary to what I believed that I skipped them for a while. I just told myself, the rest of this makes so much sense; I am going to learn all I am able to and come back to that idea when I have a better understanding. Now I know that the areas I had the most difficult time with were because I had very strong practiced beliefs that contradicted the truth. Once I experimented with the rest of it and began trusting my guidance, I was able to come back to those areas and understand them. I am a very different person than I was before I understood my EGS. I am far wiser, but also kinder, gentler, more serene, confident, and so much more. Who I used to be is a mere shadow compared to who I have become."

Maia's eyes were shining as she spoke of how far she had come on her own journey. "The old me would be fighting like a cornered tigress with cubs at being kidnapped. Some people might think that was the right response. But I know, based on the feedback from my guidance that this is on a path of least resistance to the accomplishment of my goals. If I was fighting, I would not be moving toward my goals. At the same time, my unproductive emotional stance, panic, fear, hatred, would be growing."

"That response would not serve me or my goals. It would have been merely the trained response of a mind conditioned to resist what it did not understand. I achieve more when I pay attention to the subtler clues guidance provides. Does that give you a glimpse of the type of difference understanding ones guidance could make?"

"I think so. I need to think about it."

"Yes, you do. You'll be able to do that soon."

"Before we break, you need to know a little more. To use your EGS, all you have to do is think of a thought, think it, and pay attention to how it feels. Does it feel warmer or colder? In other words, does the emotional response to the thought feel better emotionally or worse emotionally? I try not to refer to emotions as positive or negative, although I do not always succeed. All emotions are good. They are guidance. Our job is to find thoughts that lead to better-feeling emotions."

To emphasize this important point, Maia said, "A road sign that says, 'Danger Ahead' is not a bad sign. In many ways, the sign is good because it gives warning that a different route might serve you better."

Marcello nodded.

"I want you to practice paying attention to your thoughts, and your emotional response to those thoughts until tomorrow afternoon. That is enough for today. It is a lot to absorb. I want to be able to sleep in tomorrow without worrying about what time I need to get up. What's for dinner?"

I hope you enjoyed the excerpt from *Shades of Joy* and that it helped you understand how Emotional Guidance works. In the next chapter, the subject of Emotional Guidance will be covered from a scientific perspective.

9: Emotional Guidance Sensory Feedback System (EGS)

Just as your car runs more smoothly and requires less energy to go faster and farther when the wheels are in perfect alignment, you perform better when your thoughts, feelings, emotions, goals, and values are in balance.

Brian Tracy

Emotions are the sensory feedback from our oldest sensory system. There is scientific evidence that demonstrates even one-celled organisms have an Emotional Guidance System (EGS). Researchers say humans are the only animal that disregards the feedback in favor of the *rational mind*. Emotional feedback, when understood, provides far better guidance than the rational mind.

The EGS appears to consider information available on the quantum level of physicality. There was a movie or a TV show that I saw part of when I was at someone else's house. In the show, a man could predict the probability of future events with precision. That is what our EGS does. It knows what we want and the fastest way for us to get there from where we are. It's much like a GPS in your car can tell you how to get where you tell it you want to go from where you are. But our EGS is much more sophisticated. We don't have to tell it what we want—it's been collecting that information our entire lives, including every tweak and amendment we make to our desires. It knows where we are and the shortest path to get us where we want to go.

Our EGS is very creative and it understands us. It knows what will help us move toward something and will use that something as a detour if it is the easiest way to move us toward our goals. It doesn't use only emotions—it uses our likes and dislikes and our preferences to guide us. For example, when my EGS guided me to find the book I was looking for described earlier.

The EGS also appears to bypass filters that distort information our conscious mind receives from our other senses. **The only reason humanity is not thriving is because we have been taught to misinterpret the feedback from our guidance.** I do mean the *only* reason. Everything else anyone might point to as a reason is a symptom of this root cause.

I'm going to use an example of racism. For this example, I'm going to invent a new race—pink polka dotted people. I don't want to use a real race because that causes too many people to pick sides and brings up existing beliefs about how that race is treated and/or about their worth. Humanity has made race conversation so convoluted it's easier to make up a new race than to discuss the problem using reality.

So, this pink polka dotted race (called Pinky's) was at one time highly prized and people collected them. It was possible to own pink polka dotted people. The people who owned them treated them like beloved pets, restrained but pampered—sort of like a Maltese. Then the Pinky's began developing a disease, but they were usually carriers who spread the disease to their collectors who would sicken and die. Those who recovered were often left with deformities or crippling injuries.

Collecting Pinky's went out of vogue. Some people thought all the Pinky's should be killed. Others thought they should just be kept away from those they could infect. They moved all Pinky's to small separate communities, restricted them from working among the rest of the races so they could not spread the disease and the conversation about extermination stopped only when a cure was found for the disease.

Once the cure was discovered the Pinky's no longer posed a threat to other races. Some of the people who collected them wanted to do so again, but there was a fear that they could develop a new strain of the illness that there was no cure for. So they were left in their small communities. No one was making an effort to remove the restrictive laws on the books that limited their ability to mingle with the other races.

Pinky's who tried to get jobs outside their community were treated poorly and usually not given an opportunity to show that a race that was once considered a pampered pet could be anything else. Many people who had lost a family member to a disease carried by Pinky's blamed them for the death. Most of the Pinky's remained in their separate communities for several generations. The stories about how awful outsiders treated them were told to each new generation, emphasizing how they were abandoned.

The other races distrusted the Pinky's, as if the Pinky's had deliberately developed the illness that killed so many collectors. Pinky's who attempted to get jobs outside their own communities continued to be treated poorly.

Then, many years after Collector's had stopped collecting Pinky's, a Woman of God came and began preaching love and peace among all peoples. She was a powerful orator who inspired people to see the world through new eyes. She spoke to all the races at different times about how wonderful the world would be if they all lived in harmony. Some people from every race embraced her words and friendships between the Pinky's and others started developing. The braver Pinky's began seeking jobs outside their own communities and finding success. Pinky's began moving into other communities where their ancestors had once been pampered pets.

In time, the majority of the people of all races were getting along well. But there were still people who resented or feared the Pinky's for their role in carrying the disease that killed so many. There were Pinky's who resented that their families had been made to live in small communities with little opportunity for generations. Pinky elders in those communities warned their children and grandchildren to expect the other races to discriminate against them and that they should not trust other races or the Pinky's who had moved out of the Pinky communities.

There were some people among the other races who did not want the Pinky's to have access to job opportunities and houses outside their small communities. While most of the Pinky's and most of the people of other races had learned to get along and even to appreciate one another, a subgroup of each was still angry at the other. They were vocal and would complain loudly to anyone who would listen about how badly the other group treated them.

The other races saw the Pinky's that complained about having to live in their small communities where they had limited opportunities and did not understand why they were complaining when they knew Pinky's who lived in their own neighborhood and other Pinky's who worked beside them. The Pinky's that remained in the small communities saw some of the other races who treated them poorly and believed that everyone in the other races was the same as those who weren't good to them.

Both the unhappy groups taught their children not to trust the other group. The Pinky's who remained in their small communities blamed the vocal ones from the other races for their inability to thrive. The vocal ones in the other races blamed the Pinky's who were beginning to thrive for their inability to thrive.

The only reason either group was not thriving was because they thought they couldn't because of what others were doing. They did not notice that others in their own race were thriving. Their own beliefs held them back. It was bewildering to them that others thrived so their minds made-up back stories about why they thrived and why the ones who weren't thriving couldn't thrive.

The actual job of the rational mind, as you'll learn in the next chapter, is to prove our personal beliefs to us and create meaning from our experiences. This would be fine if the beliefs were deliberately crafted in a society that understands the impact of beliefs and nurtures beliefs that lead to thriving. We have not had that luxury. Many common beliefs diminish thriving yet our rational minds trap us into lives that repeatedly prove those realities to us.

This chapter provides some of the science behind the emotional sensory feedback system as the scientists refer to it.

Baumeister et al explain that "Anticipation of emotional outcomes is an important aspect of the feedback theory. As people learn to anticipate feedback, they may alter their behavior (constructively) to pursue the feedback that they like. Emotion is ideally suited for this because of its hedonic power: Behavioral choices could well be swayed by the anticipation of feeling good or bad thereafter. The affective residue of prior emotional outcomes is likely to contribute to this process... A twinge of anticipatory guilt may be enough to steer the person away from doing something.

Anticipation of emotional outcomes can also be important when the person is currently already experiencing emotion. In particular, an unpleasant emotion may motivate the person to act in ways that hold the promise of mood repair (i.e., feeling better).

The output of emotion-stimulated cognitive processing can then guide future behavior, and it can even have input into current responses when there is sufficient time for the sequence to be completed: An action or event leads to a full-fledged conscious emotional reaction, which stimulates cognitive reflection, which in turn produces some conclusion in the form of a (new or revised) prescription for action."

In a sense, then, the anticipation of emotion is more important than the actual emotion, particularly with regard to the duration of each... When considering how to act, anticipating emotional outcomes can help the person make a better decision ... the ideal system might be for the person to anticipate emotions as strong (so that they exert a beneficial, guiding effect on decisions) but for actual emotions to wear off rather fast (so they don't impair further decision making)... research on affective forecasting suggests that this is precisely the pattern in human emotion."

Acting on the basis of current, intense emotion is generally not a good idea—and we deliberately chose that colloquial phrase because it expresses the point that cognition (ideas) rather than emotion should be the proximal influence on behavior. At least, that is how we think the system is designed. To be sure, emotion may occasionally bypass rational analysis to influence behavior directly, sometimes with dire consequences. Still, the fact that the heat of emotion may cause irrational behaviors is not a problem for this view because the benefits of emotion depend on their long-term benefits, and occasional short-term costs might be outweighed.[163]

When you consider emotions as guidance, buffered by reappraisals that find perspectives that lead to the most self-supportive perspective (the one leading toward the greatest self-actualization), the benefit of emotional guidance becomes evident.

As discussed in earlier chapters, the common explanations of ill health and social problems are complex. That complexity is largely because we have too long held onto a concept that is not true about the origin of both ill health and social ills. Excessive stress was suggested as a cause of all major disease in 1978. A strong link between stress and cancer was reported in research.[164] A similar relationship between stress and heart disease was suggested in 1981.[165]

At the time, recommendations were made to avoid excessive stress, monitor stress, and remove stressors when possible. For all practical purposes, this advice was useless to most of humanity. Life in the 20th and 21st centuries is stressful for almost everyone. There is so much stress, we have begun building language around the concept: time stress, financial stress, relationship stress, definition of self-stress, socioeconomic stress, and stress from wars, fluctuating economies, discrimination, and much more. There is stress from the frequent (and often conflicting) information about what is healthy to eat.

At a time when there were more divorces, blended families, re-evaluation of social and professional roles, redefining of social values, and much more rapid change the level of stress continually increased for most individuals. Stress is much like the old analogy of the boiled frog. The metaphor that if you put a frog in a pot of water and heat it very gradually, the frog will not jump out and will remain until boiled to death. Whereas, a frog put in hot water will jump out immediately.

Whether a frog will actually remain in the pot long enough to die is subject to debate. I am not going to try, so we'll leave it as an analogy—a very valid analogy about human behavior.

One of the most common situations where we see this play out is in the area of abusive relationships. This is true of both abused women and men. If the abuser began the relationship with abuse, the abused partner would have left immediately. The abuse would not have been tolerated beyond the first incidence. Abusers tend to introduce abuse gradually, increasing the reign of terror as their victims' tolerance increases. Those watching from the outside have difficulty understanding why the behavior is tolerated.

Abuse is a form of stress. The boiled frog analogy works with employees, too. If the employer had asked for what is demanded a few years into the arrangement on the first day of work, the employee would have immediately looked for a better job. Because demands increase gradually, we do not respond to the increasing levels of stress the same way. We are used to suffering with the level of stress and we continue to accept more until the proverbial straw that breaks the camel's back—which may be in the form of depression, heart disease, divorce (from taking the stress home), cancer[166] or other illness.

It is not all the employer's fault. Employees need to communicate when the demands on them are stretching their ability to deliver. Bosses often forget all an employee's current tasks when more is requested. A long time ago, I worked for one of the big box banks. My schedule was four ten-hour days. One of my peers once remarked, "You don't work 4/10's. You work 7/14's." Unfortunately, she was right. However, the fault was not all on my management. I did not push back. I worked remotely and most of my interaction was across department lines and with other people around the country—not with my boss. My boss probably had no idea how many hours I was putting in.

It is easy to believe that if you push back it will reflect poorly on your performance evaluation. The truth is, the reason you are overloaded is probably because you are reliable. The boss knows that work sent your way is done right the first time. The boss is not overloading you with work because he dislikes you, although you may perceive it that way.

The recommendation to avoid stress is also not a valid way to reduce stress if one wants to live a full life. Even after decades of research demonstrating that recommending people cut back on activities to reduce stress levels is not practical, the advice is still given. Michigan State University Extension published an article suggesting that the way to deal with stress was to plan by "setting priorities and working on simple problems first, solving them and then going on to more complex difficulties." The article went on to say, "When stress is mismanaged, it's difficult to prioritize."[167] First, this method of stress reduction might work if you're doing math homework. It's useless if you're attempting to manage one child with a school play she's been practicing every day for two months and another child who is running a 102° fever and you're a single parent with limited financial resources—a far more common scenario for adults.

Only by adjusting our mental perspective about the situation can we actually avoid the stress in a healthy manner. Which brings me to second part of the article that states stress is difficult to prioritize if it's mismanaged, which could easily make someone who is struggling to manage stress feel less competent because it implies that failing to manage stress means you're mismanaging it. I'd agree with that summation if everyone had equal knowledge of *The Smart Way* metacognitive processes and Emotional Guidance—but we aren't living in that world yet.

When I see someone having difficulty with stressful events in their life I feel compassion, knowing that not only are they in a difficult situation, they don't have the knowledge or tools they could have if this knowledge were widespread. When someone is in the middle of a panic or anxiety attack is not the time to educate them about this information.

Worry Warts

Learning to use our minds effectively is important. Worry is one of the mental processes that diminish well-being. I had a friend tell her daughter that as long as she lived she would worry "because she loved her daughter." She believes that if you love someone, you will worry about them. Worry makes now feel worse than it could out of fear that someday something bad will happen—something that usually never happens. She could just as easily practice seeing her daughter as competent and capable and enjoy now. But like anyone with an ingrained belief, if she is not asking for help with it, telling her that her belief is misguided just makes her defend her current stance. We can only help individuals who want help and wish the others well.

Continual worrying keeps the body in a state of stress that increases inflammation and reduces immune function. It increases the risk of chronic illnesses.

If you are a worrier, understand that the emotion of worry means, "There is a better-feeling thought you could be having about this exact same subject right now." Worry does not mean your worrisome thoughts are being validated as something you should spend time worrying about. If the worry is only coming from your mind, it is not being validated. If the hair on the back of your neck is standing up, or your gut is churning with fear, it may be a valid concern. But purely mental worry is a waste of your mental capacity.

That is not to say you should not look at and evaluate problems—but perceive them as solvable—not as insurmountable. Just believing there is a solution, even before you know the solution, eases worries. "I will find a way to solve this problem" is a far healthier outlook than, "I'm not capable of solving this problem." Even if you need help, gathering the resources you need to solve it is a form of problem-solving.

The recommendation to monitor stress may have back-fired as monitoring stress without the ability to change the situation (or perception of the situation) has the potential to increase stress. The awareness of high levels of stress, and the potential negative health effects of that stress, without a release valve increased stress by creating stress about being stressed.

Some individuals give up activities they enjoy because of time stress. Our pleasurable pursuits contribute to our health and resilience by providing a stress relief valve that helps us maintain stasis.

The recommendations provided in the 1970's were about as helpful to the typical individual as telling a pessimist to *think positively*. Pessimism is a habit, not an inborn personality trait. However, it is an insidious habit that is difficult to break without the right knowledge and skills. With the knowledge and skills, anyone determined to become more optimistic is able to do so. Without the knowledge and skills, it seems impossible.

Additional research has been done and some of the recommendations being made today are more helpful. Some help reduce stress for brief periods and one (meditation) is effective both immediately and long-term (but long-term results occur only if the individual is persistent with their practice). But most of today's advice still falls short of best practices. For the most part, it addresses symptoms rather than the root cause of stress.

The concept of positive thinking has become a common refrain. Sadly, the *how* is usually absent when the advice is given. Imagine giving someone who was raised by wolves a book and telling him to read it—without teaching him to read. Telling a pessimist to think positively is not much different. Teach the individual how—in either situation—and the goal becomes attainable.

Although some individuals evolve optimistically, or learn it from a positively focused parent or grandparent, once pessimistic habits are developed, the opportunity to be optimistic without conscious knowledge is greatly diminished. Even today, many simply refer to the benefits of positivity and optimism and encourage people to think positively, but fail to provide knowledge and skills to help the person achieve the goal.

This often increases the level of stress because the person is now aware that being pessimistic is not in their best interest, but they do not have the skills and knowledge to change the pessimism. They've been practicing being pessimistic for a lifetime. No mention was made, at that time, of the human ability to adjust ones mindset to reduce stress—the easiest response—also often the only one an individual has any control over.[168]

The absence of the answer to the how question is what motivated me to create Happiness 1st Institute—because life is better when you are happy first. The techniques being taught—from gratitude, affirmations, meditation, exercise, helping others, being in nature, and others—all have some benefit. But real change, changes in the default responses in your mind, requires a deeper level of knowledge—a level where the student understands why these things work. Chapter 11 on **Filtered Consciousness** explains the impact. Chapter 33, the **How to think Positive** processes provides the how. Together, the knowledge and skills provided are sufficient for individuals to significantly reduce their stress. First, we provide information about cutting edge science that demonstrates that each of us has guidance that leads us away from harm and toward self-actualization.

The first question most people ask when they hear we have guidance is why the world is not thriving if we have this guidance. The answer is that society habitually teaches us to misinterpret the guidance we receive and put other information ahead of our guidance. What the guidance means, the correct way to interpret it, and the healthiest way to respond to its messages is our next topic.

This path is simple enough to teach to children. In fact, they are born understanding the path and parents, teachers, church leaders, and society—who are well meaning, but ill-informed—teach them to ignore the simple path.

EGS refers to our **Emotional Guidance System**.[169] EGSc refers to the *Emotional Guidance Scale*. The scale is included in the Appendix. It is helpful to keep a copy of the scale handy. The desire to feel happy or joyful is strong, but when we are at the lower end of the scale attempting to reach those emotions will typically result in failure—if we attempt to get there in one step. The most successful method is to simply reach for a better feeling thought, which will give you a sense of relief from the tension (stress) you are feeling.

The scale is very beneficial because it is easiest to move up one emotional level at a time—and certainly not more than one zone at a time. That does not mean we have to remain in a lower emotional state for a long time. Generally, an individual who has some experience shifting perspectives to feel better can move up fairly rapidly—one step at a time. The definition of rapidly varies depending on the circumstances and level of experience. It can mean as little as less than a minute to a day or two or three.

That may not sound fast but compared to the typical situation, where movement only occurs when circumstances change and some people remain in lower emotional states for years, even a week is fast. Early in my own journey, I went from feeling so devastated by the end of a relationship that I could not talk about it without choking sobs to feeling ready to move on with my life in one weekend. A few years later, at the end of another relationship, I did not suffer the feelings of emotional devastation. The difference was that by then I knew there was a silver lining, so within minutes I was reaching for the better-feeling thoughts that come with knowing there was an upside.

The same is true of a lay-off. It is possible to feel excited anticipation about what is coming when you're in the middle of being laid off. It is also possible to hold onto anger about a lay-off for years and allow it to diminish your enjoyment of life the entire time.

"Things turn out best for people who make the best of the way things turn out." John Wooden

Humans, on the other hand, often ignore or suppress their emotions and suffer the negative consequences of doing so by living lives that are less robust than they could be.[170] Ignoring negative emotional output is no different from ignoring pain from one's sense of touch. Emotional pain should be responded to in much the same way physical pain is managed. When emotional pain is ignored or suppressed, it can be as harmful to our well-being as leaving a burning hand on a hot stove.

Learning to follow the guidance from our EGS may conflict with instructions received throughout life. For example, the opinions, expectations, and desires of others. In a world that does not currently understand the EGS, it is common for others to want you to behave in ways that make them happy. On the surface, it sounds very selfish to follow one's own guidance over what others may desire from you. But turn it around, why do others want you to do what they want you to do instead of doing what you want to do? Is it not their selfishness that leads to a perspective where you are called selfish for not seeing the world through their perspective?

This misinterpretation of selfishness has led to inaccurate conclusions. Donald Campbell, president of the American Psychological Association in the mid-1970's argued for the notion of a genetic predisposition of selfishness in humans which leads to a "social personality of self-serving opportunism," and that "socialization and culture … are necessary to counter this disposition."[171]

> *Emotions are information designed to guide us.*

Perhaps socialization and culture aid the process, but not when they convict selfishness of being misguided. When socialization and culture point each person to their own Emotional Guidance, where feeling good causes us to do good, we will be on the right track.

Consider, too, that when we are happy uplifting others feels good to us. By setting goals that include being loving, respectful to others, or to have good relationships, the EGS will provide guidance that considers these goals. Emotional Guidance opens the door to a path to resilience that is simple and sure.

By heeding the guidance emotions provide, one increases their level of resilience.[172] Emotions provide information about whether we are moving toward or away from our best interests. While people have labeled emotions that feel bad as *negative* and those that feel good as *positive*, all emotions are good because they are providing guidance, whether the receiver understands the message or the appropriate response to the message, or not. Emotions that do not feel good indicate action should be taken to feel better; action can be actual physical action or may consist of changing the perception that is leading to the emotion that does not feel good.

The research is clear that we have more to give to others when we are happy. Our EGS guides us to happier states. The increased resilience we gain from following our guidance can greatly benefit our families, employers, and communities.

In Peil's groundbreaking paper, *Emotion: A Self-regulatory Sense*, she clearly demonstrates the importance of heeding the messages from the emotional sensory system. The paper also points to the true nature of humans and of the simplicity of following the Emotional Guidance System. Humans are good at the core of who they really are. However, it is only when they follow their Emotional Guidance that this is demonstrated consistently. When they do not follow their Emotional Guidance, behaviors that society does not favor can be the result.

Peil's theory expands the responses to negative emotion from Fight or Flight to include Right Responses. Right Responses (RRs) should be the first response to most negative emotion experienced in modern life. There are different types of Right Responses, one is:

"...*to affect the internal environment in the personal mindscape, in conscious knowledge acquisition, in an act of deliberate learning and personal mental tactic to invoke optimal belief structures to reappraise.*"[173]

In other words, reach for a different perspective about the situation, one that feels better, and adopt that perspective because it serves your highest good to do so. Peil elaborates and clarifies the difference between a RR and suppressing emotions,

"*There is a vast difference between a RR and suppressive emotion regulation, as the corrective action itself is informed by the specific emotional message, is consciously undertaken and it self-preserves through open, approach behavior, adaptive development and social cooperation. In short, the RR is a self-developmental response more indicative of the neurally well-endowed, culturally creative human being.*"

The knowledge and skills necessary to become adept at utilizing Right Responses are easily learned. The skills increase the level of positive emotions experienced by individuals—daily and over time—thus reducing stress and increasing their level of resilience.[174] The main direct impact of emotion is to stimulate cognitive processing, not behavior.[175]

Teaching someone, even a child, to follow her own Emotional Guidance is simple. As Maia demonstrated to Marcello, the method resembles a simple children's game. There are myriad variations in the situations it can improve. It takes practice to respond consciously using RRs in the midst of a situation. However, in time it can become the default response.

If you have ever had a *Hell Yes* experience, it was your guidance shouting encouragement. I have had several. Yes, your guidance could have told you that someone you are now divorced from was a *Hell Yes* to marry. I know that from our perspective that seems wrong but sometimes the shortest path to where you really want to go involves what appears to be a wrong turn. The key is to take the good, the silver lining, and leave the unpleasant parts out. If you felt the *Hell Yes*, it was on your best path to what you wanted.

Sometimes you can see what that was—or at least make a guess that feels right (which to me is the same thing). Sometimes you will never know. I was on an Alaskan cruise a few years ago. After the cruise, I planned to spend a few extra days in Seattle. Mid-way through the cruise I began having a strong urge to go home as soon as the cruise was over. I changed my flight and went home early. I have never learned why my guidance encouraged the change of plans, but I trust that it was the right path at that time.

Other times, I have known why. For instance, a few years later my fiancée and I were booked for a cruise and months before the trip we both began feeling we should not take the trip. We cancelled and my

Fiancée's father died when we would have been on the trip. I enjoy several vacations each year and that is the only one I have ever cancelled after it was booked.

Truly, the best way to understand how strong one's faith can be is to consider how strong our belief is when another sense has convinced us of its truth. If we see something, we tend to believe it. If we hear something, we tend to believe we heard it. If we touch something, we tend to believe what our sense of touch tells us about it. If we smell something, we believe it smells the way our nose interprets it. Oh, sometimes we ask for a second opinion. "I think this milk smells bad, do you think it's okay?" is something I've heard more than once from my daughters. I notice that sort of double-checking behavior most when someone expects something to be good and is disappointed.

Emotions are sensory feedback from our oldest sense. The only reason we do not trust them as much as our eyes, ears, nose and touch is that we have been trained not to trust them. Yet, when interpreted accurately, emotional feedback is the most accurate sense.

The myth that negative emotion means something outside ourselves is bad is commonly believed. It is responsible for significant amounts of unnecessary stress every day. Negative emotion means we are looking at something from a perspective that is less than ideal, or that we should focus elsewhere.

Let's look at a difficult situation for an example of alternative ways to perceive an event. Imagine a law enforcement officer working a murder investigation. If the job required the officer to focus on the loss felt by loved ones, the experiences the victim will miss in the future, and other aspects that feel awful, the negative emotion would quickly prostrate the officer. I am not saying officers do not think about these things, I am saying their job does not require them to focus on these aspects.

The job requires a problem-solving attitude. When gruesome details are the focus, the perspective is in relationship to answering the question, "What will this tell me that will help solve this case?" The focus on future action feels better in comparison to focusing on an unchangeable past event. The focus on solving the mystery feels better than a focus on a life ended too soon. The focus on providing answers to the family feels better than thinking about all the times the family will miss their loved one in the future.

The negative emotion is not saying the situation is bad. Nor is it saying it is good. The negative emotion is communicating that there is a way to perceive the situation that is more in alignment with our personal goals. A law enforcement officer choosing to focus on the aspects of a case that feel the worse will not be able to achieve the goal of solving the case. Her cognitive function will be impaired. Her immune system will be depressed. Choosing the worse feeling perception will not advance the goal of solving the case. A mental stance of hopefulness that a case will be solved supports the cognitive function required to accomplish the task—and is accompanied by better feeling emotional responses.

Any law enforcement officer or combat veteran will already know that sometimes he or she just knew. They may not have the language to describe how they knew, but they did. You probably do, too—in some situations. Think about a time when you knew something but you didn't know how you knew it. It could be as simple as knowing who did it in a mystery book or television show or knowing that two friends would hit it off if they met. It could be KNOWing that something was going on between two people with no reason to believe it was true. It could be the instinct that led you to go into your child's room and find something you needed to know about. It could be when you picked up the phone to call a friend who needed you or you know who was calling before you looked at your phone, even when the call was unexpected.

It's the tension you feel in the air when you walk in a room. It's the sureness you have with no reason. It's KNOWing that you'll find the parking space if you turn left. It's catching the thing that falls out of the cupboard that you anticipated falling without knowing why. Sometimes I write KNOWing in all caps to differentiate it from rational knowing.

Now that you've read about this you'll be more aware of such incidents over the next few days. As that happens, celebrate recognizing the times when you just KNOW and pay attention to the subtle energy you can feel that is associated with KNOWing. The more you tune your Focus filter (See Chapter 13) to pay attention, the more often you'll recognize that you just KNOW.

We have the ability to choose the way we perceive any event. Our EGS guides us to the one that gives us the best chance of achieving our goal.

With practice we can learn to trust our Emotional Guidance as much as, or more than, our other senses. Once that level of trust develops, life improves immeasurably. This is because our emotions take into consideration information available on the quantum level that our other senses cannot consider.

Biofield science is an emerging field of research that is exploring "the idea that living systems generate and respond to energy fields as integral aspects of physiological regulation . . ." It is based on a foundation formed from "advances in biophysics, biology, psychology, and the developing fields of mind-body research such as psychoneuroimmunology and psychosocial genomics . . . which have been combined to form a foundation for this expanded integrative medical model."[176] A growing body of scientific literature suggests "the existence of a more subtle level of bioinformation transduction operating at extremely low energies . . . contemporary biophotons research and cell to cell communication via coherent biophotons emissions has been demonstrated in several studies . . . suggesting a new paradigm wherein the concept of regulation via a biofield of dynamic information transfer may become central to biology."[177]

For example, our EGS considers others' intentions. While our eyes might catch a glimmer of intent through body language, accurately interpreting body language is a science that few have mastered. Likewise, our ears might sense something in the tone of voice, but unless we are experts, we may not trust our interpretation. If we were experts at determining truth from lies in the spoken word, we would not need a machine to detect lies. Interpreting and trusting our EGS is far easier than becoming an expert in body language and the nuances contained in various tones of voice.

Without an understanding of one's guidance, it would be extremely hard to have enough faith in things that do not make sense and that one cannot see clearly from lower emotional levels. With an understanding of one's guidance, faith can be strong and sure, unshakable, and certainly not in need of validation by someone else.

For example, this morning a young couple had an interaction during which it sounded as if Fern was upset at Bob when he asked if she would join him in an activity they both enjoy. Bob interpreted it as if Fern was upset with him for asking and his feelings were somewhat hurt. He had no idea why she was being prickly. Fern declined his invitation because she had responsibilities to take care of. She was not upset with Bob, but with the fact that her duties made it necessary to forgo the desired activity with him. Her reason was almost polar opposite to the reason he perceived (upset with him) whereas she was upset she could not accept his invitation.

Utilizing my guidance to interpret what was really going on, I was able to know, with certainty, that there had been a miscommunication. I let them know how it was misinterpreted and clarified the intent of the female. I then asked each of them to correct me if I was in any way wrong. "Nope, you nailed it," was the reply.

How many times a day do misunderstandings like this interfere with the smooth functioning of an office environment? How much more productive would it be if the employees could use their guidance to check on the others' intent. Even better, if the employees understood that even if someone intended to be rude, their behavior has far more to do with their own emotional state than it does with anyone they are interacting with they would not take it personally. After all, it is not personal. If the co-worker were happy, he would not be rude.

The lack of knowledge of the EGS and thus society's failure to use it leads to many problems, from simple misunderstandings to wars between nations. In more traditional relationships and lifestyles, the desire to have ones choices validated by others is evidenced by disagreements that often become divisive.

Regardless of the choices a person makes, there are usually people who disagree with the choice. We are surrounded by examples, including single Mom, working Mom, stay-at-home Dad, public school, private school, structured activities or free play, make your bed every day, don't make your bed every day, mow your grass to 2" or mow it to 4", eat meat, don't eat meat, and more. Having choices is good, but expecting everyone else to make the same choice we make creates conflict.

At the root of it all is a defensiveness born of insecurity. Because they do not use their guidance, people feel an unsatisfied desire to have their decisions validated. The desire for validation is natural. We are born with guidance that provides validation. When we have a *Hell Yes* experience, we are receiving validation from our EGS loud and clear. When we do not receive the validation, we can become quite upset—because we inherently feel that our choices should be validated. We have been looking in the wrong place for validation. Our guidance is where that need should be satisfied. Our guidance is validating our choices when they are correct for us and letting us know when they differ from our best path. But if we do not recognize our guidance for what it is we do not gain the satisfaction of feeling validated.

There's no such thing as insecurity......it's only thought.
Unknown

This discord is seen in every area of life. It is common in religion, politics, and even music. A great deal of time, effort, and stress results from attempting to demand conformity.

Actions that someone with a belief that the world is a good place would interpret one way, someone who believes they live in an evil world will interpret extremely differently.

This points to another reason there are so many conflicts, and why it could be so hard to convince people of something that others could see clearly. People are taught that their minds are rational. They are encouraged to trust their mind over their emotions.

With most people, unbelief in one thing....is founded upon blind belief in another.
Georg Christoph Lichtenberg

Emotional Guidance is not filtered by ones beliefs. It is often difficult to understand its messages once one has been trained to believe the rational mind is the better source of decision-making. But, it is not hard to straighten out with a little bit of effort and practice.

Using a dual system for decision-making, using both the rational brain and Emotional Guidance for the same decisions and giving their EGS more weight in areas that do not seem important develops confidence. By beginning in this way, it soon becomes clear that guidance from the EGS leads to better outcomes. Many students quickly begin giving greater weight to the EGS.

Our society does not give emotions the credit they deserve. We are taught to give our *rational minds* and thought processes the credit for our intelligence. This is another false premise. Researchers have worked with individuals who have lost part of their brains, the part that recognizes emotions, to disease or injury. Many people would assume that not having emotions would create a person who was very good at decision making, they might even envision someone like Spock from Star Trek. If you get an opportunity to take that bet, bet the farm.

What the researchers found is that rationality depends critically on sophisticated emotionality. Our emotional process works so well that we do not even know much of what it is doing. It provides instant and automatic appraisals of tremendous amounts of data that we never have to consider consciously. Robbed of this function in their brains, individuals find it almost impossible to make even simple decisions.[178] Even choosing what to eat becomes almost impossible for individuals who cannot feel their emotions.

What are some of the ways we are taught to misinterpret our guidance? From young ages, many of us are taught to ignore or suppress our guidance. When we were two and our brother took our toy away, Mom did not show us how to feel better using our guidance. She distracted us by giving us another toy. Or she told us, "Don't cry. You're alright." While those may not be considered bad ways to parent, and they are certainly superior to the angry parent who smacks her child for crying, they ignore the guidance the child was born with. The first technique teaches the child the parent will make him feel better when he is upset. The lesson the child learns is: *"Finding a way to feel better is not your job. Mom will do it for you."* In the second example, the message is: *"Expressing your emotions is not good behavior. Suppress them."* Emotions become bothersome things that we have to deal with instead of the valuable tool they are.

Emotions are our friend. We should understand them as messages letting us know if we are moving in the direction we want to go. We should understand our power to change our emotional stance by changing our perception of any situation. When I say "any situation," many people want to argue that some situations are just so awful that there is no way to find a better feeling perception. As long as someone has that belief, they won't find it. In his book *Infinite Love and Gratitude*, Dr. Darrell Weismann writes about how he found a better perspective about his daughter's death and how doing so helped the wound heal.

No one would wish for that situation but many live through it. A book I found especially helpful after my first miscarriage was, *Ho for California!: Pioneer Women and Their Quilts* by Jean Ray Laury and the California Heritage Quilt Project. The book chronicles quilts that came to California, by wagon train, around the horn and, if memory serves, by train. The great value I found in it was the strength of the women, some of whom birthed a dozen children and lost over half of them before they reached adulthood. That these women could suffer losses like that and still function, much less leave a lasting legacy in the form of a quilt, helped me see the potential for resilience in each of us.

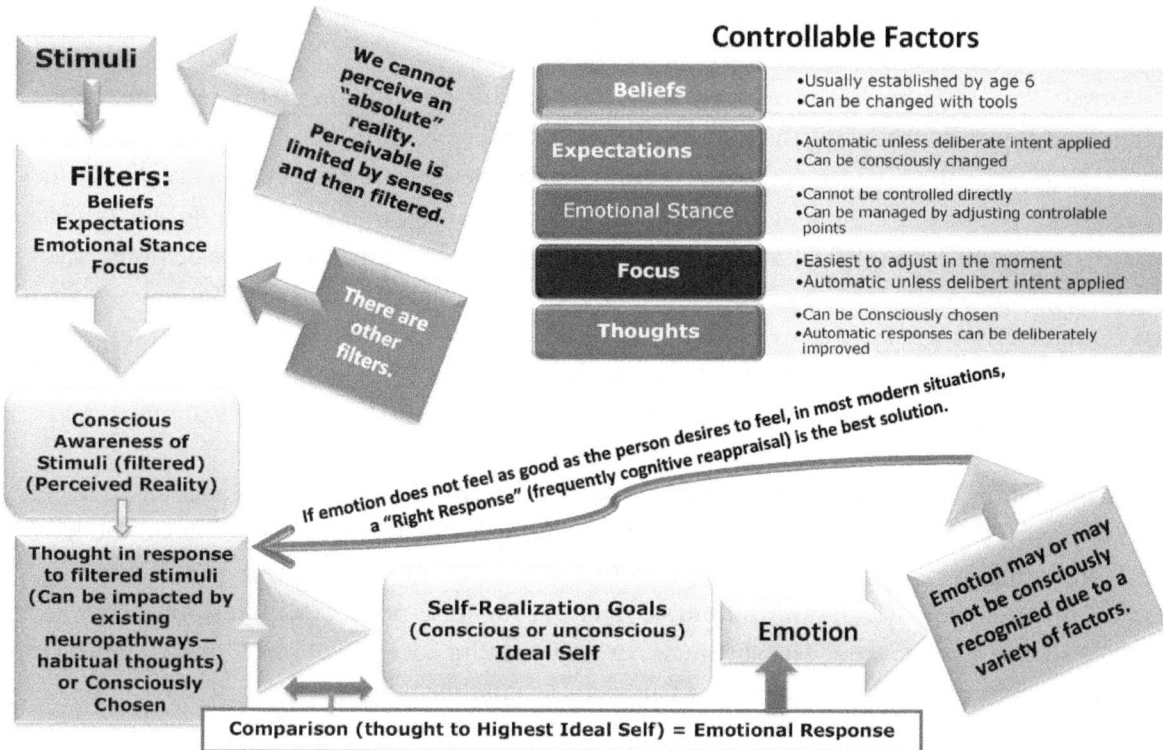

> *I do not think stress is a legitimate topic of conversation, in public anyway. No one ever wants to hear how stressed anyone else is, because most of the time everyone is stressed out. Going on and on in detail about how stressed I am isn't conversation. It'll never lead anywhere.*
> Mindy Kaling
>
> This quote reflects how many people feel about stress. But I think it goes deeper—there is an inner urge to help the stressed person but they're so stressed themselves they feel they don't have time to help—and they don't really know how to help. When society understands that **help means helping the individuals find a better-feeling thought** and they know the EGSc, they know the path to a better thought, helping will be easy. I do it all the time and it brings me great joy to uplift others as I move through my days.
>
> The not knowing how to help is what brings the discomfort. We can change that.

Once something happens that must be lived through, there is a choice. Live through it and celebrate your life, perhaps giving greater meaning to your child's life, or choose a path of suffering. Another example of a parent who brought meaning to her daughter's death is the founder of MADD, Cindy Lightner. Although I am sure no parent would ever choose to sacrifice their child, the fact that MADD has been instrumental in decreasing DUI fatalities by about 50%, saving 12,000 lives each year must bring some solace and meaning to her loss.

There is a way for anyone, in any circumstances, to move forward. If you are currently suffering, I do not know your path forward—but your EGS does know. It is with you 24/7 providing feedback in response to your every thought. Find the one that feels better. Soak it in until you feel stable in holding that thought and then reach for one that feels even better.

I've met many people in my life who are actually afraid of what they will find if they explore too much of their inner world. Somewhere along the way they have been convinced the possibility evil could be hiding inside them. Peil's paper suggests the true nature of humans: they are good at the core of who they really are. Seligman echoes this argument in *Flourish* and Dacher Keltner reinforces it in *Born to be Good*.

However, only when Emotional Guidance is followed consistently is our true nature demonstrated. Frequent positive emotions lead to pro-social behaviors. Prolonged negative emotions that result when the Emotional Guidance system is ignored can lead to undesirable behaviors. We feel emotions in response to thoughts. Even when our body communicates, for example, the physical hair standing up on the back of the neck in response to danger, it is not until we consciously recognize that we feel the hair standing up, a thought about the physical manifestation, that fear is felt.

I see a distinct difference between the fear that makes the hair on the back of your neck stand up and the fear you feel when someone tells you a story about something awful happening to someone you have never met. Fight or flight is an appropriate response when the hair on the back of your neck is standing up, unless it's a mountain lion, in which case you should freeze. A Right Response is a more appropriate response to the second type of stress. This distinction is important in a world with 24/7 news scouring the planet and looking for every awful thing that has happened around the world.[179]

Stress does not come from doing too much;
it comes from doing too little of what makes us come alive.
Alexander den Heijer

Far more goes right in the world, every day, than goes wrong. If we put the worlds' troubles in the perspective of our body with the bad things in proportion to the good, the world has a hangnail. I am not saying awful things aren't happening. I am saying that filing your head with them as you begin your evening and/or as you head to bed is not healthy for you. It does not solve the problem. In almost every situation, there is nothing you can do. But what do most people do? They feel fear. Look at where fear is on the EGSc. The fear is increased when loved ones, especially teenagers and young adults are out or away at college.

The 24/7 negative news has primed most of us to be afraid of this beautiful world we live in. Many will argue that they have to be realistic. Viewing a minute percentage of the things happening on the planet is not at all realistic—it is a view with a major negative bias. If the 24/7 news channels reported good news and bad news in proportion to their occurrence, the bad news would last less than a minute each day.

If you are feeling you live in a bad world, I encourage you to shift your focus to one that is more realistic. Start with the big picture and get as specific as you can while still feeling good. The sun came up today. Even if it was on the other side of clouds, the sun rose today. The atmosphere is filled with air I can breathe. Wow! Two huge, necessary hurdles done! Are the birds singing? Are the plants growing? Is the sun feeding the plants? Are the clouds watering the plants? Did people fall in love today? Did people hold hands today? Were any babies born today? I have two eyes that see, two ears that hear, one nose, two arms, two legs complete with feet. I have family I love, who love me. I have friends I love, who love me. I have a bed and a kitchen and windows. I have guidance that responds to every thought I think. I could go on like this for an entire book so I'll stop now. You get the idea. The amount of wonderful going on, every day, is enormous. So be realistic, think positive.

*Life has a bright side and a dark side, for the world of relativity is composed of light and shadows.
If you permit your thoughts to dwell on evil, you yourself will become ugly.
Look only for the good in everything so you absorb the quality of beauty.*
Paramahansa Yogananda

One more point about the news. Have you considered what the job of the news stations is? Follow the money. They are paid for ratings. Researchers figured out a long time ago that if you make people fearful they watch the news more often. How do you get ratings higher? More viewers equals higher ratings!

Don't take my word for it. Use your own guidance to make your decision.

Emotions are responses to thoughts.[180] Each thought elicits an emotional response.[181, 182 & 183] Emotional Guidance is unique to the individual thinking the thought. Unique goals, beliefs, expectations, emotional stances, and focuses cause differences in the emotional responses individuals receive. When we move away from our goals, our emotions feel worse. By deliberately choosing a different perspective, our thoughts change and better-feeling emotions can be deliberately cultivated.[184] Thoughts actually create meaning for events in life.[185] For example, if someone cancels an appointment the individual who is told the meeting will not occur is free to assign meaning to the event. Even when a reason is given, the reason may or may not be accepted by the receiver. If the reason is not accepted, the individual will create a reason to explain the event to himself. That explanation may be one that feels good or one that feels bad. Whichever is chosen, the event will be experienced (felt emotionally) by the individual as if the assigned reason is true.

> *I can't make you believe any of this, but you can prove every bit of it to yourself simply by experimenting with the ideas and processes in this book.*

For example, someone who is living in the Drama Zone whose meeting is cancelled may assign a far greater meaning to the cancellation than someone who is in a state of appreciation. The person in the Drama Zone may decide the cancellation means the person who cancelled does not care about them, if it was a personal situation. In a business situation the person living in the Drama Zone may feel disrespected and unappreciated regardless of the reason for the cancellation.

It is really as simple as understanding that better feeling thoughts are guiding us toward our desires and thoughts that feel worse are advising us that we are moving away from our desires. Some clarity regarding desires is required. There is a difference between short-term and long-term desires. Although all desires contain the characteristic that we believe we will feel better in the attaining of them, some desires relate to immediate gratification; a response to current conditions without consideration for the long-term. Desires for some foods, drugs, alcohol, and other addictions are fueled by these types of desires. Short-term desires are often accompanied by conflicting emotions caused by conflicts with longer term desires. For example, a desire to feel better right now may be satisfied by enjoyment of a piece of chocolate cake but the desire to maintain a comfortable weight in the long-term may be in direct conflict with that desire.

There is an inherent desire to feel better. Many *desires* are not beneficial in the long-term. Without knowledge of techniques to change thoughts, endless loops can result—sugary foods, alcohol, drugs, shopping and more can temporarily improve mood, but do not build long-term resilience. To build long-term resilience one must reach for better feeling thoughts. The more attention that is given to long-term goals, the more they will be considered in the emotional response you receive when a short-term goal conflicts with the long-term goals.

For example, in an upsetting situation it is not uncommon for individuals to reach for alcohol to provide relief from their negative emotions. Unfortunately, alcohol provides only a temporary dulling of the pain (or lessening of the focus on the painful thoughts) and can lead to even greater problems.

A more permanent method of approaching an upsetting situation is to reframe ones perception of the event in a way that feels better.[186] With practice, finding better feeling thoughts becomes the easier choice.

No beating yourself up. That's not allowed. Be patient with yourself. It took you years to form the bad habits of thought that you no longer want. It will take a little time to form new and better ones. I promise you this: Even a slight move in this direction will bring you some peace. The more effort you apply to it, the faster you'll find your bliss, but you'll experience rewards immediately.
Holly Mosier

It is possible to maintain a positive bias about life when circumstances are not ideal. This has been proven by many in very adverse circumstances. There are many accounts; one of the direst is the story of Viktor Frankl, documented in his book, *Man's Search for Meaning*, about his experiences in a Nazi concentration camp. In the worst of circumstances he discovered the importance of finding meaning in all forms of existence, which made his current circumstances, even though unchanged and reprehensible, feel better and provided a reason to continue living. This is an example of a RR, where the individual found better-feeling thoughts. Although the thoughts he found were philosophical in nature, any thoughts that felt better and thus made the situation more tolerable would be considered RRs.

Science has tended to study various aspects of humanity in isolation (Psychology, biochemistry, medical, neurological, consciousness, behavioral, sociology, criminology, genetics, physics, etc.). These areas of science are often subdivided into specialties, such as addiction, immunology, cardiovascular disease, beliefs, epigenetics, and more.

It is all interrelated. Root cause solutions require an understanding of the larger picture. Thoughts create the emotional feedback. The emotional stance affects body chemistry, bodily processes, behaviors/actions, and ultimate outcomes.

Circumstances do not create the emotion. There is evidence from individuals who live in far less advantageous circumstances who are happy with their lives and receive the benefits of positivity. Research into disparate outcomes in situations with homogenous incomes vs. situations with greater differences reflects that it is not actual circumstances, but perception thereof that matters.[187]

Likewise, there are many stories of cancer survivors who claim that being diagnosed with cancer was the best thing that ever happened to them. The reasons vary, but most of the individuals learned to live more consciously instead of being content with an *autopilot* life,[188] where they merely react to their circumstances without any knowledge that they can control how they respond to events. "With the cancer diagnosis, my priorities changed in an instant. The list of what was truly important got real short, real quick. Decision-making became easier. I became more motivated to do things I had been putting off. The old phrase about not sweating the small stuff became crystal clear."[189]

Human societies train people to "keep a stiff upper lip" and to "be strong" by which they mean endure negative emotions instead of finding better feeling thoughts.

A change of perception changes everything. Each mind interprets the world according to factors specific to the individual,[190] including beliefs, expectations, emotional stance, and focus. These factors create a filtering system in the brain that determines the sensory input that is communicated to the conscious mind. People project their thoughts onto what they see and experience in

> *Science, spiritual, and religious worldviews are more in agreement about our guidance than almost any other topic.*

the world. When you change your thoughts, your world changes. You give thoughts power when you accept them as true. Everyone has a choice. Right Responses involve deliberately changing perspectives, beliefs, expectations, and focus.

In a recent study of individuals experiencing divorce, self-compassion, which would translate into less negative self-talk—was cited as the factor that uniquely predicts good outcomes.[191] "Negative self-statements, also known as negative self-referent cognitions, have been linked with levels of social anxiety."[192]

Marketers are skilled at changing consumers' perspectives. It really isn't difficult to do with people who aren't mindful about what is happening. In a study that looked at the importance of perspective the participants were all told that a teacher had scored 70% on a teacher competency exam while half were told that the passing grade was 65% and half were told the passing grade was 75%. The group that were told passing was 75% and therefore thought the teacher failed the test judged the teacher as less competent than those who thought the teacher passed the test, even though the score was still only 70%.[193]

Several branches of science have been studying human thriving. The results, when compiled, point to the fact that people thrive when they feel emotionally good and suffer when they do not.[194]

When individuals know they have guidance, and have practiced using it, they also know that no matter how bad their current circumstances may seem, they can find ways to feel better. Hope, a belief that a positive or desired outcome is possible, is a key emotional state for resilience. Just knowing guidance exists builds a firm foundation for hopefulness.[195] Without this knowledge, it is easier to feel hopeless, which can lead to inertia or giving up.[196]

I am often asked to explain the source of the guidance. Realistically—it does not matter. Our guidance guides us toward our individual goals and toward our highest good. Experimenting with your guidance makes it clear it guides us around obstacles and toward goals. Sometimes faith is required because the path the mind wants us to take seems more logical but when our guidance is followed we usually, eventually, learn why the straightest path is where our guidance feels best. Our guidance helps us be more of who we want to be. Conforming to society instead of our EGS confuses us.

Where it comes from is another matter. Quantum physics provided many of the answers. The research into biophotons and cellular communication using light are illuminating. "Experiments are showing that biophotons can be captured and stored inside of cells and can even travel through our nervous system; suggesting that biophotons might provide a way for cells to transfer energy and communicate information."[197] Light carries information through our brain, nervous system, and even our DNA."[198] We have the ability to affect light with our thoughts. Study participants in a dark room who visualized a bright light increased their levels of biophotons emissions significantly, revealing that our intentions influenced light.[199] There is much that is not known yet. I strongly encourage readers to experiment with their own EGS because experience is the only way to know for sure that the guidance is beneficial, accurate, and always present.

In a peer-reviewed textbook I contributed to, *Perspectives on Coping and Resilience*, I detail my research into whether common religions including Buddhist, Christianity, Islam, Hindu, and Confucius support guidance. More than 90% of humanity has a worldview that is influenced by religious and/or spiritual beliefs. It is important to understand if those views support the science and if the science supports them. In every religion I researched, I found passages that support the existence of guidance that dovetail with what science now understands about the purpose of our emotions. Chapter 36 provides more information if you want to understand how six major religions support the concept of Emotional Guidance.

The chart on the following page was developed to point out that individuals who developed certain behaviors were more resilient. In many ways, the resilient statements feel less stressful despite describing the same circumstances.

Positive emotions are immensely beneficial for us—increasing our resilience, reducing the risks from negative life events, decreasing the risk of all types of major illnesses and improving relationships. We have an EGS that helps us enjoy better-feeling emotions. It makes sense to understand and use the guidance available to us.

Negative emotional states are harmful to our bodies, minds, relationships, and choices. Depressed individuals will participate in riskier behaviors than individuals at higher emotional states.[200]

The chart on the next page indicates some mindsets that diminish your ability to thrive and ways you can reprogram the mindset in ways that will allow you to achieve more success in any area of your life. In the column on the far right specific processes that will help you adjust your mindset are indicated. The processes are described in Chapter 33, **How to Think Positive**.

Write down a problem that bothers you fairly often. Then use the chart to find a different perspective about the problem that feels better to you.

Chart of emotions to reach for:

When Feeling	Reach for	Process(es)
Disempowered	→ A more Empowered perspective	See EGSc
Problems are unsolvable	→ More general thoughts	Go General
Victim Mindset	→ What steps can you take	Too many to list, see Chapter 11
Blames	→ Take responsibility	See EGSc, Forgiving, etc.
Feels fearful	→ Belief in self	Refute
Feels helpless	→ What steps can you take	Role Models, Refute, Go General, See the potential, etc.
Emotionally out of control	→ Any thought that feel better, long-term goals, more general thoughts	Go General, Forgiving, Set Intentions
Rigid Thinking	→ Ask self if there is another valid perspective	Remember how your brain works
Clinging to anger	→ Remember that anger hurts you	Forgiving, Reframe
Resistance to new ideas	→ Confidence that you can learn, remember that your brain is trying to prove your existing beliefs to you—even if they do not serve your highest good	Humor, Use Big Picture
Negative emotional bias	→ Begin leaning more positive	See Positive Affirmations
Hopeless	→ Remember you have skills to feel better and/or perceive differently	Go General—you'll have better ideas
The worse will happen	→ Ca sera sera (What will be, will be)	Refute, Stop Catastrophizing
Tendency to attack oneself	→ Refute the negative voice	End self-criticism
Holds onto guilt	→ Realize you've learned	Forgiving
Feelings of shame	→ Why were you taught to feel that way about the subject? Who benefited? Let it go.	Refute (shame is a construct of man)
Long-term worry and anxiety	→ Set an intention to change	Think Positive, Focus Shift
Being "right" is highest goal	→ You have nothing to prove, develop growth mindset	Stop self-criticism
Feels life "just happens"	→ Use control over perspective	Set Intentions
Seeing obstacles as enemies	→ See obstacles as challenges (opportunities)	See the potential

9: Emotional Guidance Sensory Feedback System (EGS)

10: Personality

Man is most nearly himself when he achieves the seriousness of a child at play.
Heraclitus

While working on this book, I read a great synopsis of many of the personality models by Carver. What was most obvious to me, however, was the lack of consideration given to emotional state and chronic emotional state in 2005. Last year he published a new paper supporting the hypothesis that emotions provide guidance.

The researchers describe personality as if it is fixed and unchangeable, without regard to the emotional state of the individual. But we all know that is ridiculous. Our behavior changes with our mood. In better-feeling moods, we are nicer, kinder and even more likely to help strangers. In bad moods, we are not as nice, even to those we love. Sustained low emotional states can lead to the most egregious behaviors.

I believe better accuracy and completeness of personality models can be obtained by including mood/emotional state in the data collected when research is done.

Can greater accuracy and completeness of personality models be obtained using emotional state data? I believe it can.

Existing personality models seem to explain behavior because most individuals maintain a relatively consistent chronic emotional state throughout life.

Emotional State (ES) is a way of referring to the emotion someone is feeling in-the-moment. (i.e. happy, sad, depressed, hopeful, hopeless, frustrated, angry, anxious, eager, etc.)

Chronic Emotional State (CES) is the set point, or emotional state a specific individual tends to return to repeatedly in the absence a significant reason to feel otherwise.

The behavior individuals exhibits is tied most closely with the current Emotional State. The personality model research I've reviewed looks at behavior, but not emotional state at the time the behavior is observed. Self-reports of behavior also do not gather data on emotional state at the time of the behavior.

An individual whose Chronic Emotional State is happy exhibits behaviors consistent with that Emotional State. There will be variances due to occasional lower Emotional States and during times of resource depletion (i.e. illness and sleep deprivation). High stress will cause temporary changes in Emotional State.

The consistency of Emotional State is well documented in the scientific literature. Lottery winners, newlyweds, and newly disabled individuals typically return to their Chronic Emotional State within two years after these significant life changes. The reason for the stability of Chronic Emotional States is not because it is genetic or a fixed human trait.

Chronic Emotional State is the result of habits of thought.

Why isn't this commonly recognized? The first reason is because researchers do not tend to explore individual difference at the level of thought. The work would be extremely time-consuming and would lack consistency because at the level of thought the uniqueness of each one of us becomes very apparent. Even two people who make identical choices can follow very different thought processes to reach the decision.

Secondly, because habits of thought are habits--but not recognized as such and we are taught our personalities are who we are, few people change their thought patterns. Many people have a fear that if they change their personality they will no longer be the same person. Some fear they will no longer know their self. The truth is, those who deliberately change their habits of thought know their self better than they ever did before they experienced the liberating power of changing habits of thought that weren't serving them well.

Like any habit, changing habits of thought takes commitment and does not happen overnight.

Patience with oneself is required, but the knowledge and establishment of realistic expectations about how long it takes to create new habits of thought is not readily available. While we can think, and can even believe, new thoughts immediately. But even when we believe something that opposes our former habits of thought, the old habitual thoughts will continue coming to mind until the thought-paths that supported the beliefs are allowed to diminish and new thought-paths that support the new belief are developed. Until this process is completed, you may find yourself thinking (and in the early stages) even speaking things you no longer believe. It's just old programming that is still stronger than the new programming you're creating. It's natural and it does not mean you can't change the habit of thought, just that the process is not yet complete.

What we do and why

We do what we believe will feel better, vis-a-vis approach or avoidance.

Long-term vs. Short-term Goals

Whether we're looking long-term or short-term when we make decisions about what will feel best depends on a variety of factors, but mostly on which ones we've focused on more. If long-term goals aren't given a lot of airtime in our mind, short-term goals will steer our decision-making because we have not created thought-paths to thoughts about the potential consequences of our actions as they related to our long-term goals.

Focusing on long-term goals increases the consideration we give the consequences of our words and actions. However, it is important that the goals be tied to our own--not goals others impose upon us. (See Chapter 18 for more about motivation.)

Recommended Research Direction

If personality trait researchers would begin collecting data about mood (Emotional State), they would see more clearly why inconsistencies between their models and research findings continue to appear. The connection between Chronic Emotional State and behavior would become more apparent.

If personality trait researchers did a study where they collected the usual data and mood and then put the study group through my 40-hour program where they are taught the effect habits of thought may have on their lives and how to develop new habits of thought that support their ability to thrive more in all areas of life, they would be amazed at the results. By collecting the usual data and mood before and after (at the end of the course, 3-months post course and 1-year post-course), they would see clearly why there are so many inconsistencies.

An additional step that would be labor intensive but provide very valuable insights would be to collect and analyze answers to brief essay questions before the course and again one year later. Using questions that pertain to common life events would provide significant insights to the value to individuals and to society of empowering individuals with the knowledge and skills that allow them to deliberately change their habits of thought.

As a starting point, I suggest the following questions:

Instructions: Read each question and imagine yourself in the situation described. Write the first thoughts that come to your mind. There are no wrong answers. When it asks "What do you do," your answer can reflect what you think because thinking is doing something. Biological functions (i.e. go to the bathroom) should not be reported unless they are related to the emotional state you're imagining. Please limit your answers to 300 words, but be sure to answer each element of every question. Thank you.

- You are in a restaurant. Your spouse/date/significant other is late meeting you and has not called or texted. What do you do? A) When s/he is late (immediate response)? B) How do you feel (emotion)? C) If you wait, what do you do while you wait?, and D) When you see him/her, what do you do?
- Your boss gives an assignment you wanted to someone else. What do you do and how do you feel?
- You're in a bad mood. A) What do you do and how do you feel? B) Define bad mood as it personally applies to you.
- You're given an opportunity that requires you to do something that makes you anxious, but doing this could lead to something you want but don't know how to achieve/get otherwise. The thing that makes you uncomfortable is legal, ethical and moral. What do you do and why?
- You want two things that seem to conflict. You don't see how you can have both. What do you do and why?
- Someone is rude to you. A) Describe the situation B) What do you do? C) Why?
- You disagree with someone close to you (i.e. parent/sibling/spouse/child/sibling/long-term best friend). How do you feel and what do you do?
- You find someone's wallet and there is cash in it. What do you do and why?
- Someone who hurt you a long time ago asks for forgiveness. What do you do and how do you feel?
- You decide you want something you have no idea how to get or achieve. What do you do and how do you feel?
- You have company over and the dog eats dinner before it is served. What do you do and how do you feel?
- You're on your way home from somewhere that you go frequently and you miss your turn. What do you do and how do you feel?
- Before you go to sleep at night, how do you usually feel and what do you usually do?
- When you wake-up in the morning, how do you usually feel and what do you usually do first?

I would be happy to participate in research with any interested researcher.

Readers who want to answer one or more questions now and after using the techniques in the book will find it interesting. I'd love to see your results.

10: Personality

11: Filtered Consciousness

Reality is merely an illusion, albeit a very persistent one.
Albert Einstein

Our consciousness does not perceive an actual reality.[201] The reality our minds perceive is filtered.[202] This chapter will explain the main filters that impact our perception of reality.

When I have written about a topic in a way that feels just right, it is better to use it than attempt to reinvent the wheel. I begin this chapter by sharing part of a speech I wrote for a peace rally. Imagine yourself in a large, crowded auditorium as you read the next few pages.

The first thing I will speak of is the function of our minds.
We are taught to believe our minds. Let me ask you some questions.
Until this moment, when I mention it, did you feel your clothing?
Unless you are experiencing a binding or itchy clothes day, the answer was no.
Yet, I do not see anyone who is naked in the audience.
Do you think your skin was not feeling your clothing? Or do you think your brain said something like, "If I continually send reminders about what the skin is feeling, it will take up too much capacity. That capacity is needed for things that are currently being focused on" Our brains are expert resource managers—they filter the information our sense of touch receives so irrelevant data is not transferred to our conscious mind.
Yes, or yes?
If any of you are holding hands with a loved one, how much are you noticing that you are holding hands?
Isn't it when the hands move, when they caress, that you feel the touch?
Right now, turn to your neighbor. Touch one another's hands.
Do you feel the sense of touch?
But if you remain there, after a while, when you are comfortable, you will not feel it unless you focus on it.
Right, or right?
It's a cold day. On days like this, I love to put dinner in the crock-pot and let it cook all day. When I do, I do not notice the wonderful aroma of my dinner cooking.
But when I go outside to bring in the mail and return, the aroma is strong when I enter the house.
Yet after I am back inside for a minute or so, I no longer smell them. Do you think my nose stops working?
Does your nose work the same way?
Sometimes that is a good thing, yes?
If I continually smelled the delicious aroma while I am working, would it interfere with my productivity?
Maybe.
Probably.
Let me ask you another question. When I am working at home with a fine roast in the crockpot, what is my reality? In reality, does my home smell delicious? If a visitor walks in, will they not smell the aroma? Yet,

in my personal reality, I do not smell it. Is my nose broken? Or, is there a filter between my conscious mind and the information my senses receive?

Whether I am not feeling my clothing, not smelling dinner, or not feeling the chair I am sitting on—reality has not changed. My senses are aware of these things and more. My conscious perception of reality is being filtered. What causes my mind to filter these things? When dinner is in the crockpot and I have been in the house a while, can I inhale and smell the aroma if I think about it? Yes, I can. My nose still smells the aroma. It is just being filtered from what my conscious mind receives.

Our brain uses filters to decide which information is passed to our conscious mind. The four main filters are beliefs, expectations, emotional stance, and focus. These filters are important. They are tools we can use to make our lives better. They are very powerful.

In the chapter on perception, you began understanding that the reality you experience is based on how you, personally, interpret reality. Before you become consciously aware of anything in your life, the data you receive is filtered by filters in your brain.

Before big data (all the information from your senses) reaches your conscious mind it is mined for what is relevant—the programming of your filters determines what is important. Imagine a miner looking for sapphires but he has no idea what a diamond is. This miner is in your mind, scanning the big data, finding sapphires, and sending the information to your conscious mind. When the miner sees a diamond, it goes in the irrelevant file—because the miner is not programmed to find diamonds.

Your beliefs are established by around age 6 and in the typical human, they do not change much after they are established.[203] Some adjustments might be made, but most are the result of experiences lived—which are interpreted after the data is filtered by the programming your brain is using. We perceive reality in a way that supports our established beliefs.

Your filters are of enormous value to you. Millions of bits of information are received by your senses every second. You do not have the capability to pay attention to all the input so the information is filtered. The programming regarding what information is passed to your conscious mind is, in most individuals, an unconscious action that is programmed at a young age. However, at any time, we can choose to reprogram our filters in ways that serve us better.

For example, someone who has decided they are unlovable will attribute ulterior motives to the actions of others. The person cannot perceive love even when it is given freely, because it contradicts their belief that they are unlovable. Unless and until this individual changes the belief, he will not experience being loved. This will be true even with his wife and children. If he is successful, he may interpret the wife as being with him for financial reasons. He might have accepted this arrangement because he wanted to have companionship, children, sex, or give a public perception of normalcy. (This may have absolutely nothing to do with why she married him.) His wife may love him dearly but he will interpret her actions as if they are due to another motivation if he does not believe he is lovable. His children will receive the same treatment. He might, seemingly out of the blue, complain that all the child wants him for is his financial support—with no basis in reality. In fact, even strong evidence will not counter information that conflicts with his belief that he is not lovable.

Someone who believes they are unlovable will never be able to feel loved unless and until they change their belief about being lovable. If this man were to shift his belief so that he truly believed he was lovable, he would then interpret the actions of his wife and children through that filter and see them in an entirely different light.

Because he does not believe he is lovable, the back stories his mind creates to explain his experiences will not give love credit for peoples actions toward him. The world he perceives and experiences will be less than it could be—not because the world is harsh and cruel—because his beliefs about the world interpret it that way.

Let's take this into the workplace and use an employee who believes she is not appreciated. It won't matter if you give her more appreciation than any two other employees combined, she will not feel appreciated. As long as she has a filter programmed with the belief "I am not appreciated" she will attribute the employer's appreciation to another motivation. Feeling a lack of appreciation is often associated with the emotion of resentment so her back story is likely to create the emotional response of resentment.

Likewise, if someone believes they are the best, no matter how much information (big data) exists indicating otherwise, the person will interpret reality as if he is the best. If someone whose performance is actually better is promoted ahead of him, he will not attribute the promotion to the other's superior performance. In fact, he will not be able to perceive the others' performance as superior—often giving himself excuses (creating back stories) to explain why his performance did not match the others' combined with a strong belief that if the playing field were equal, he would be better. For example, in sales, he might use the excuse that his territory did not have as much opportunity as the one who had better sales numbers. He will not attribute the others' promotion to higher skills because that would conflict with his belief that he is the best.

> *You are not capable of perceiving a reality you believe is impossible.*

The same thing happens with appearance. If a beautiful woman does not believe she is beautiful, it will not matter how many times she is told she is beautiful. Each time, she will make up a reason, (a back story other than her beauty) to explain why the person said she was beautiful. She will not experience compliments emotionally the same way she would if she believed she was beautiful.

If she someday changes her perception of self and begins believing she is beautiful, the first time someone tells her she is beautiful after she believes it, she will experience the moment as if it is the first time she has ever heard the words. In many ways, it is the first time she has heard them. The other times were accompanied by negation from the voice in her head. "He's just saying that because he wants something" or "He's just saying that to make me feel good." The actual experience of being told she is beautiful and believing the words is a very different experience.

If you have ever wondered how or why some highly successful people are not happy, why they sometimes ruin their careers and even their lives with drugs and alcohol, the root problem may be that they have underlying beliefs that are hindering their ability to enjoy their success. If you believe you are a failure, all the success in the world will not make you feel successful. You may feel increased fear that you will be found out—that others will realize what a fraud you are.

This is a very common issue with highly successful people. If you don't believe you are good enough for your achievements, self-sabotage often occurs and insecurity builds as success increases. I often hear it expressed in relationships when one person doesn't think they are good enough and fears their partner will find out and leave. These insecurities usually have little basis in reality but they are very real to the individuals who feel them because their back stories support their view of reality. It *feels* real to them.

There is a difference between striving to improve oneself because of a desire to be the best one can be and striving to improve because of a belief that one is not good enough. Michael Jordan reminds me of the individual who strives to improve himself because he has a desire to be his personal best. There is nothing wrong with striving to be our personal best. In fact, when we do that with a belief that we can achieve our goals, it is healthy and fulfilling. But when the striving is done from a position of lack, of not being good enough, the individual will never feel that he's reached the goal—no matter how good he becomes.

11: Filtered Consciousness

You know the saying "Statistics can be used to prove anything." Well, the same is true of the filters in our minds. They will prove whatever we believe to us.

Let's return to the speech:

Of the four main filters, focus is the easiest to adjust in any given moment. Adjusting your focus can change your emotional stance. Continually and deliberately adjusting your focus over time changes your chronic emotional stance.

Your brain does not care if the filters it uses serve you or not. In fact, I believe that we are expected to understand how to set our filters to maximize our life experience and to help us attain our highest good. The filters are designed as if we understand how they work. The filters literally hide information that is inconsistent with how they are set—whether it is in our best interest or not. They are not malicious, vindictive, or determining our deservability or worthiness. Our belief about our worthiness creates a filter, which then determines how the filters process information. The judgment of anyone outside yourself about your worth does not change your filters. If you allow another's judgments to affect your beliefs about yourself, your filters adjust. The filters just carry out their programming—whether they help or hinder your ability to thrive.

I do not believe our minds would deliberately harm us yet they do when the filters are set to unhealthy or unproductive settings. I choose to believe that we were meant to understand how to set our filters to serve our highest good.

When I mention beliefs, many people think I am speaking of their religious beliefs. While religious beliefs are beliefs, I am speaking of more than religious beliefs. I have no intention or desire to change any beliefs that are serving you.

I will not tell you what to think. Nor will I tell you what to believe. You have guidance that will do that. My guidance is for my goals. Your goals and my goals are not going to be the same. Most of this room has no desire to stand up here on the stage. It is one of my biggest desires because it fulfills another, stronger desire— that of being able to help as many people as I can to thrive more in every area of their lives.

My guidance leads me to my goals. Yours leads you to yours.

If you have not consciously set goals, your guidance is muted. There are many factors that mute the guidance, but consciously setting goals increases the volume enough for some people that they begin thriving. That is why goal setting has remained an important business tool for decades. It works because it makes our guidance about our goals louder. By louder, I do not mean you will hear voices in your mind. I mean your thoughts will consider the goal. Your choices will consider the goal. The very thoughts you think are affected by goal setting. There are other ways to increase the volume even more than goal setting.

What is a belief?

A belief is just a thought you have thought repeatedly until a filter is established making it part of your reality. Just as I cannot smell the pot roast when I am in the house, belief filters filter out information that contradicts our beliefs about our reality. That is why you can see something so clearly and someone else, with different beliefs, cannot see it no matter how clear your arguments may be.

You could have a burning question, maybe a solution to a health or employment crisis and have the answer on a piece of paper in your hand, but if you believe an answer does not exist, your brain will not make the connection between the solution in your hand and what you are seeking.

Yet, shift your belief to one that believes a solution is possible to find and you will see the solution.

Think about that. Think about looking for a job in an economy you believe makes it impossible to find a job if you're over 50, under 30, or whatever other criteria you've used to decide you can't find a job. It is true, for you. You can't find a job. But it is not the economy. There are those who thrive and those who suffer in every type of economy.

The reason some thrive is they believe they can.

The reason some suffer is they believe they cannot thrive.

The reasons they hold those beliefs does not matter The truth or falsity of the beliefs does not matter. Only the belief matters to the filtering system. The filters support our beliefs. The filters do not decide what is best for you, they just follow instructions.

If you believe something is true for yourself and not for others, that thing is a filter you established. You may not have done it deliberately, but you did do it. This is actually good news. We can adjust and control our filters. Just like driving a vehicle, when we know how to do it we can keep it on the road we want to take.

Most of us do not understand the filters, so we never consciously adjust them. We just suffer from poorly programmed filters based on what we believed when we were about six-years-old. Because our brain's job is to prove our beliefs to us, the longer we live the more sure we are we are right. Our filters ensure we repeatedly interpret reality in a way that is consistent with our beliefs about reality.

Yet, if the belief is not true for everyone, it is merely that—a belief.

I want you to think to yourself—do not say it aloud about—the amount of annual salary you believe you are worth. The number I want you to think is not what you are paid, it is what you believe you are worth.

Now, think for a moment, to yourself, about why you make what you make. Pay attention to the first thought you have about why this number is more or less than what you think your work is worth.

Did you think you make your current salary because you are too much something or too little something?

Now, let me ask you some questions.

Do all people who make more than you have more education than you?

Are all people who make more than you smarter than you are?

Are all of the people who make more than you better than you do in terms of morals and ethics?

Are all the people who make more than you older than you are?

Are all the people who make more than you younger than you are?

Are all the people who make more than you born into wealthier families?

Are all the people who make more than you a different gender than you are?

Are all the people who make more than you a different race than you are?

Are all the people who make more than you prettier or more handsome?

Those are common excuses people use to explain why they can't make the income they believe they should.

Your excuses point to beliefs that are limiting your ability to succeed.

Life is much better when we look for the reasons we can. We find what we look for.

A long time ago, I believed only people who knew secrets I did not know made six figure incomes. Making that kind of money seemed mysterious to me. My mind did not dwell on the topic because it did not feel good to do so. But I remember thinking about it and feeling as if those who made that kind of income were somehow different than I was. It was not based on a label, to me it was more of a mysterious something I believed I lacked.

When I deliberately changed my belief and began believing I could make six figures my income increased 64% in a year, taking me well over six figures. The only thing that changed was my belief. As a result of the belief change, I was able to recognize opportunities to achieve that goal. Before my belief changed, I would have self-selected myself out of the running, telling myself I was not ready or was not good enough. I would not have even tried. Once I believed I could do it, I tried and succeeded.

If the reason you believe you make less than you believe you are worth is one where you answered "no" to one of the above questions, you have identified a limiting belief. Sometimes individuals who learn they have a limiting belief, or about limiting beliefs, decide to go on a search and destroy mission to find and eliminate beliefs that are hindering their ability to thrive. Don't do that. It can take years and tends to have unsatisfactory results. Take the shortcut. What is the shortcut?

The shortcut is to decide which beliefs would serve you and develop those beliefs. Read about individuals you admire and wish to emulate. Pay attention to the way they think. Quotes can be very helpful. Using your Emotional Guidance System(EGS) when you read a quote makes identifying ideas that make your heart sing and your pulse race easy. Your EGS will also identify beliefs that will not serve you by giving you negative emotion when you read it. When you find beliefs that you want the world to reflect back to you, take steps to believe them. Processes for this are in the Processes section of this book. Remember, a belief is simply a thought you have thought repeatedly until it becomes a habit of thought.

Your filters, if not set to maximize your thriving, will filter out opportunities that are available to you. If your beliefs do not make those opportunities part of your reality, you won't see them, you won't hear about them, and you won't benefit from them.

Right about now many of you are thinking "there's no way it was right in front of me I'd know about it and see it." But think about your clothes, the crockpot, and the chair you are sitting in. The evidence that filters in your brain have the ability to filter aspects of reality from your conscious experience is clear.

If believing this is too much of a shift, don't believe it. Just ask for more clarity. Ask yourself, could it be true? What sort of evidence might I see that will help me know? Where do I feel limited by limits that don't seem to apply to everyone? Can I shift those beliefs a little bit and just see what happens? Would that hurt anything? It would make me wrong. Will I chose to hold onto an old belief so that I am not wrong in the past when adopting a new belief would serve me so much better? I don't have to believe this to play with the idea—to experiment a little bit. I can try the new belief out in the privacy of my own mind to see how I feel if I believe it.

That's not too much to ask, is it? It does not cost anything. No one even has to know. You can do every bit of it in the privacy of your own mind.

I can't prove any of this to you. But you can easily prove it to yourself; slight shifts in our beliefs literally change our world because our experience of reality is a personal interpretation. When you change a belief, the meaning you give to events shifts.

You may also be able to find examples in the life you've already lived.

Think about someone you know, or knew, who was struggling, perhaps with an addiction of some sort. We've all heard the stories. Think about them being offered a program that would help them move on—a program where the benefits seem tremendous to you—yet they did not jump on the opportunity. In fact, they did not see the opportunity that was so clear to you.

They were in a state of hopelessness. They were filtering help out because they did not believe it would or could come to them.

Now you understand it better? Don't you?

Every thought you think receives an emotional response. Interpreted accurately, they will lead you directly to your dreams and goals.

The feeling we can reach for, no matter how we feel, is a feeling of relief.

Now, let's talk about guidance for a minute.

Our guidance is there for us all the time.

But how do we know?

I cannot prove it to you but you can easily prove it to yourself.

I can also show you science that shows that we and all living things, have guidance.[204, 205]

If you are frustrated, you are likely to notice something frustrating about your spouse, child, commute, boss, job, or world. Your filters essentially say, "Oh, she is feeling frustrated. She must want to feel that way. I will highlight this aspect of this situation because it will make her feel frustrated. I will highlight this aspect of this person because it will make her feel frustrated."

> Few are those who see with their own eyes and feel with their own hearts
> Albert Einstein
>
> I believe Einstein was referencing that we tend to believe what others think about us (and other things), even when it is not true.

Your filter is not being mean when it does this. I am convinced it believes that if you are focusing in a way that makes you feel frustration that you want to feel frustrated.

I believe this because when you shift your perspective it does not continue showing you frustrating things. It begins showing you things that match your new emotional stance.

If you are in a state of appreciation, you will notice things you appreciate. I have managed myself into this state and maintain it on a fairly consistent basis. One huge difference I notice is my awareness of things I appreciate. For example, sitting on my deck, I will feel an impulse to look up just as the bright red Cardinal flies toward a tree. Once the bird is in the branches he is not visible but I looked up at the exact moment that allowed me to appreciate his plumage. It has become characteristic of me to interrupt conversations to say, "Look" as I point out something appreciable that has caught my attention. Yesterday, a yellow finch landed on my trellis. The bird was not there more than about 20 seconds, but I saw him land and take off. I was in the middle of a conversation with my husband as I was preparing to leave. I usually maintain eye contact when I am conversing but I glanced over to the other side of the driveway at exactly the right moment to be delighted by the bright yellow finch.

Imagine how your relationships would change if what you notice first about your spouse, child, commute, boss, job, or world is something you personally find pleasing.

Your emotional stance does more than affect what you notice. It affects what you say. If you are in a state of appreciation, you are far more likely to offer compliments than criticism. What does that say about hurtful words someone may say to us?

Is it us? Or is it their current emotional stance?

Their emotional stance determines what aspects of you they focus on. Someone who is frustrated will notice something about you she finds frustrating. Someone who is angry will notice something about you that fuels their anger. Someone in a state of appreciation will notice something about you to appreciate.

Our emotional stance and awareness of the effect of emotional state on communication determines how we respond. When you fully understand that someone who is lashing out verbally at you is coming from a low emotional state and that their words reflect far more about their emotional state than anything about who you are, you can feel compassion instead of anger. When you recognize that their words would be appreciative of you if the person was in a state of appreciation, the derogatory words lose their bite. You do not take the words to heart or use them as reasons to question your own worth or value. You recognize they do not reflect your worth—they reflect the low emotional state of the person speaking the words.

But if you don't consciously recognize the connection between thoughts and words and current emotional state, you will take it personally when someone says hurtful things to you. More than likely, your emotional state will sync with theirs and depending on the social norms you've internalized this can lead to anything from severed friendships, divorce, fisticuffs, or even homicide.

One of the most heart wrenching things I experience when I do work in high schools is the question from students who ask if it is possible for someone to live in those lower emotional states for decades. The answer is yes and it provides tremendous relief. When you teach this to a teenager you can see the relief in their face and in the release of tension in their body. If a child has been attempting to please an unhappy parent her entire life, she often develops a belief about herself that does not serve her. She may be thinking she can't do anything right. But that is not true. The truth is her angry parent cannot perceive anything she does as right through a filter that is programmed to look for things that make the parent angry. It is heart wrenching because while the answer provides relief to the children I am able to reach, I know there are many more that are not yet getting the information and there are many adults whose lives are far more painful than they have to be because they grew up with an unpleasable parent.

In every one of these situations, the child has been living in a chronically stressful environment.

Sometimes a parent will perceive one child as good and another in negative light. Even in this situation, it is not the child's fault. Every child is lovable and if the parent does not feel the love, it is a problem in the parent, not the child. There are so many different reasons a parent might favor one child over another but they are all because of the parents' beliefs and filters—not anything that is inherently wrong with the child. The parent does usually does not realize this because the parent does not understand that the back stories are merely interpretations of reality.

Do you want to see how absolutely wonderful your children are? You can't, not unless you program your filters to look for beauty in others. If you are looking at the world and calling it evil, you will not see the beauty in yourself or others. The way your filters are programmed affects your life in profound ways. There is nothing that is more important anyone can do than become consciously aware of how the filtering process affects their experience and begin adjusting the programming to serve their highest good.

Recognizing that if another person felt good he would find something nicer about you to focus on takes the sting from angry and bitter words.

Make up your own opinion about yourself. Do not accept what others tell you about yourself as true unless your guidance agrees. That means your heart sings when you hear the words. If you feel bad, that is your internal lie detector telling you the words are not truth—not your truth. From the other person's perspective, they may believe they are true. Arguing serves no purpose. Just know, in your heart and mind, that when the words sting it is your guidance telling you there is a perspective that will feel better to you. Then look for it or simply let it go as an untruth that does not have to distract you from whatever it is you are about. Do not give others the power to hurt you. Their words only have the power you give them. Howard Thurman explained the danger of allowing another's opinion or words to disrupt your equilibrium well:

> If a man knows precisely what he can do to you or what epithet he can hurl against you in order to make you lose your temper, your equilibrium, then he can always keep you under subjection.
> Howard Thurman, Jesus and the Disinherited

Sometimes the nasty words come from a nasty person living in your mind. Someone who continually tells you what is wrong with you. If that person lives in your head, kick him or her out. You can develop a kinder and gentler voice in your head by refuting the nasty voice and reinforcing more positive attributes about yourself, to yourself, in the privacy of your own mind.[B]

You do not need to feel bad to be motivated.

You can be motivated at the high ends by interest, passion, joy and feelings so good they are ineffable.

[B] More information about how to evict the critic from your mind is provided in subsequent chapters.

To summarize, more information than we can consciously manage is picked up by our senses in every moment (about 10 million bits of data). The filtering process between the raw data and information the conscious mind perceives uses our programming to decide what data reaches our conscious mind (about 50 bits of data). In essence, our brain interprets reality in a way that proves our beliefs to us. The filtering process does not take into consideration whether the information that is filtered out would benefit our highest good. It does not care if we want the information. This is not about punishment—it is merely how it is programmed. I believe this is because the design is such that we are expected to understand how the filters work—that we are supposed to deliberately program the filters to serve our highest good.

I can tell you that for myself and thousands of others who have learned the techniques to re-program these filters, their lives have improved significantly. The improvements begin immediately and continue coming.

Happiness is also a way of interpreting the world, since while it may be difficult to change the world, it is always possible to change the way we look at it.
Matthieu Ricard

Our beliefs create a powerful filter and once a belief is established it appears to be true from our perspective. Our filters pass information that supports our beliefs to our conscious minds. Information that contradicts our beliefs is either not passed to our conscious minds or is interpreted to mean something consistent with our current beliefs.

Think about Semmelweis's hand washing recommendation. Before microscopes, the idea that we were surrounded by and covered with things too small for us to see would have gone against our beliefs and would have been frightening to contemplate. Even with his research showing significant benefits, the general population and even other physicians dismissed the idea. They weren't stupid. The filters in their minds did not pass information that conflicted with their beliefs to their minds or misinterpreted the information in a manner that was consistent with their beliefs.

I remember learning about Galileo when I was a child and wondering how people could have been so stupid and being glad that I lived in a time when people were smarter. Today I am not so sure that conclusion was accurate. Yes, we recognize that Earth revolves around the sun. But there is a lot of evidence that we frequently ignore information that contradicts what we have been taught to believe. In many cases, the information we are ignoring could be of great benefit to us.

I've made a conscious effort to be open to information that conflicts with what I was taught for about a decade and the result is that my brain is able to make connections between research and desired solutions that it would not have made when I clung more tightly to believing what I was taught. It seems there is an adjustment to the filters our brain uses that allows us to loosen or tighten our insistence that what we believe we know is accurate. This makes sense. Most of us have known someone who stubbornly insists something is true when it clearly isn't. Those individuals have that filter locked down tight. This is not about being gullible—it's about being open to new information and risking having been wrong in the past.

It can be humbling to discover a long-held and righteously defended belief was based on a false premise. I've had that experience. But releasing that old belief led to a world that makes far more sense than it ever did while I clung to a false premise. I can appreciate my capacity to assimilate new information instead of focusing on the years when I held tightly to a belief that was not true.

I don't have to beat myself up for having been wrong in the past. I can appreciate that I now know better so who I am and what I know today is more than who I used to be. I now see life as a process of becoming more. I don't know everything and I never will, but I can continually learn more about subjects that are interesting to me. Learning more today does not negate the value of who I was yesterday. Sometimes what I learn changes beliefs I've held in the past and sometimes what I learn supports what I believe I know. I've made the biggest leaps when I've let go of long held beliefs that are not supported by the evidence. I don't know what I'll believe tomorrow; only that it will be an expanded version of what I believe today.

Once a microscope was invented, revealing the presence of viruses, germs, bacteria and other microorganisms, hand washing became a common form of primary prevention that is often mandated. They reference this shift in human ability to measure reality as if we *discovered* the organisms. In fact, the word discovered is telling. The microorganisms existed before the microscope but humans speak as if things do not exist until we perceive them, or discover them. In most instances, there is evidence that something exists before we measure it. The discovery is usually credited to the person who figures out how to measure it. The individual who knew there was something and recommended ways to benefit from it before it was measurable is often lost to history. We delay humanity's benefits by waiting until the ability to measure something is developed. I think we can be smarter than that. What do you think?

In the speech, I talked about goals and differences in our goals. Philosophers from Aristotle to modern day researchers have disagreed on how to define *the good life*.[206] The reason they cannot agree is they are searching for a single definition. If they would view happiness as a journey instead of a goal, as movement toward myriad goals that are unique to each individual, they would learn more about the basis of human thriving. Every individual has unique goals wherein they will find satisfaction in positive motion forward and dissatisfaction from movement away from the goals. A goal that inspires and energizes one person may feel dull and of little or no interest to another person.

In 2001, Ryan and Deci[207] described a few theories of happiness including one that "…suggests well-being is a function of expecting to attain (and ultimately attaining) the outcomes one values, whatever those might be…" and another by Chris Peterson, that states "…the goals through which well-being is enhanced can be highly idiosyncratic and culturally specific." However, the "and ultimately attaining" should be changed to "the movement toward" and it should include something about the fact that one never reaches the point where all goals have been achieved. Humans will always find something new to desire because who they become as they achieve a goal is not the same person they were when the original goal was conceived. Some, those who have not been successful in the pursuit of their goals, may deny the new goals or resist them but only because the idea of wanting more they do not believe they can have is painful. It is the perspective, not the goal, which causes their discomfort.

For example, I have no desire or interest in winning the Indy 500. I would be bored hearing about who has won in the past, how fast they travel, what the cost of the cars is, or other such details. But if I'm seated at a dinner party next to an Indy 500 winner or sponsor our unique perspectives needn't put us at odds. There is common ground if we look for it. It is when we believe others should want what we want and object when they don't that discord arises. The fact that I have no interest in winning the Indy 500 says nothing about the worthiness of that goal. It says only that my interests are different—not better—not worse—just different.

I could find common ground with someone with that goal if he or she were willing to talk about how they feel when they move toward their goal and what they're thinking when they doubt themselves. I could find common ground talking about how the person prepared his or her mind to believe winning the Indy 500 was personally possible and how they felt when they did their best.

As a parent, this was one of the more difficult concepts to accept. I like the way my career unfolded and felt I had learned a lot during my journey that could help my children. Neither of them had any interest in following in my career footsteps. I had to realize that my disappointment was in a feeling that I could not be as much help to them as I would like to be. At least, this was my initial belief. I've found that life experience allows me to be helpful in supporting the goals that are right for them—goals they choose.

11: Filtered Consciousness

12: Beliefs and Expectations

Success or failure depends more upon attitude than upon capacity successful men act as though they have accomplished or are enjoying something. Soon it becomes a reality. Act, look, feel successful, conduct yourself accordingly, and you will be amazed at the positive results.
William James

Beliefs are just thoughts an individual keeps thinking. In a global sense, some are valid and others are not. However, when an individual believes the thought, his life will demonstrate the truth of his belief to him. Our minds will show us evidence of our beliefs and will not show us evidence of things outside our beliefs. Many researchers have agreed that, "people often resist information that conflicts with their personal views. Though new information may improve understanding, people seem motivated to discount both the source and the content of a challenging message in an effort to protect their existing beliefs."[208] In my first book, *True Prevention—Optimum Health: Remember Galileo*, I refer to this tendency as the Galileo Effect because most educated people are aware of the persecution Galileo suffered as the result of his views. Most people believe his contemporaries responded that way because they were ignorant and lived in a time when we didn't have modern science. That is certainly the impression I had until I realized that the tendency to reject new information that is more accurate than the information we believe is true is alive and flourishing today. It takes conscious effort to overcome this tendency. It takes a willingness to step outside our comfort zone to ask ourself, "What if this is true?" even when it might change our worldview.

Trust me, a major shift in worldview is not something to fear unless you are going to beat yourself up for not knowing before you knew. If you will focus on appreciating that now you know it is not a painful process. If you're going to criticize yourself, you may have a fixed mindset and not see yourself as a person who will continue learning throughout life. If that is the case, keep reading. You'll find a more comfortable self-concept in these pages that will make the rest of your life better than the life you've already lived.

Some of our beliefs support our highest good while others limit our ability to thrive. What we believe is important. I do not tell people what to believe, I inform them about how beliefs impact their ability to achieve their personal goals. Carol Dweck, a well-known researcher focused on the different outcomes achieved by people who believe intelligence if fixed vs. those who believe we are able to expand who we are found, "that acquired beliefs play a critical role in how well people function."

In the 1980's movie *Rainman*, Raymond (played by Dustin Hoffman) could accurately count the number of toothpicks dropped in a millisecond. The number was around two hundred and forty-three. This is an example of the information your brain receives in every moment. Most of our filters would not pass the count (243) to our conscious minds. This could be due to a belief that we cannot know the number without the physical act of counting. It could be due to a lack of focus in the way that would be required to pass the information on to our conscious mind.

The reason you can hear someone say your name in a loud room is because your filters are programmed to pay attention to your name. As a Mom, my filters are programmed to hear the word Mom, but only if the voice sounds like one of my daughters. If the voice is significantly different from my children's voices, I do not notice someone calling for their Mom when I am focused on something else.

12: Beliefs and Expectations

Believing that our brain shows us reality leads us to believe the information it passes to our conscious mind is an accurate reflection of reality.

Beliefs do not just hold people back. Those who developed empowering beliefs soar. Studying the beliefs of those who are thriving and compare theirs to your own can help you identify beliefs you might like to adopt. *The Magic of Thinking Big,* by David Schwartz is highly useful for this process. [209]

Our beliefs form our back stories or *implicit theories* about how the world works. A thorough meta-analyses of implicit theories and self-regulation concluded, "Implicit theories are consequential for self-regulatory processes and goal achievement."[210]

What we believe determines part of our emotional response. Even scientific researchers are not immune from accepting conclusions that fit their belief patterns without evaluating them as fully as they should. In a critical review of unconscious influences on decision making, Newel and Shanks found, "a tendency to uncritically accept conclusions that fit with our intuitions have all contributed to unconscious influences being ascribed inflated and erroneous explanatory power in theories of decision making."[211]

If we see someone who has attained something we want our emotional response can be extremely different because of what we believe. If we believe their attainment of it means it is something that is attainable for us, we will be pleased by their achievement. It will increase our belief in our ability to attain something we desire.

However, if our belief is that we cannot have what they have attained (for any reason) our emotional response will be quite different. We will feel jealousy or envy. Those emotions are basically the result of seeing someone else having something we want but believe we cannot have.

Even jealousy in relationships has this basis. It is not so much the person we want (even when we think that we want the specific person). It is the emotional experience we believe we will have with that person that we really desire. It is how we believe it would feel to have the relationship we imagine with that person. Our ideas about how it would feel were created by the back story our mind created about how it would feel. We have bundled that specific person with the ability to have the emotional experience we desire.

> *The vision that you glorify in your mind, the ideal that you enthrone in your heart, this you will build your life by, and this you will become.*
>
> James Allen

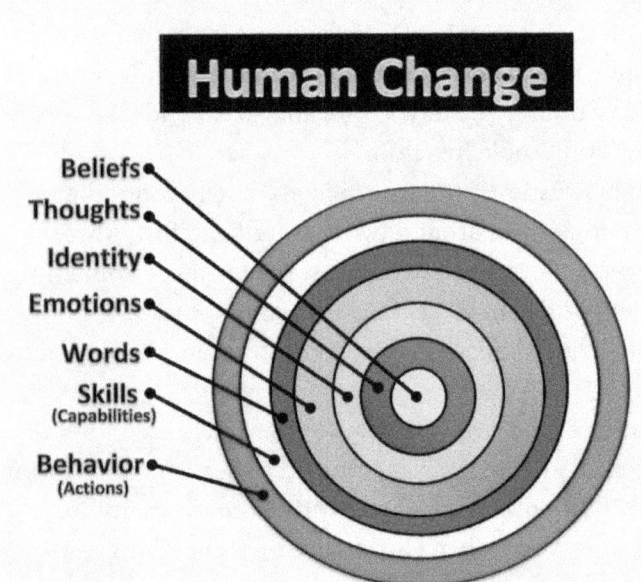

Carol Dweck's research and book lay out two separate mindsets about intelligence and learning. In the growth mindset, people perceive themselves as capable of learning and increasing their knowledge. In the fixed mindset, people tend to perceive academic tests as evaluating their worth and intelligence. They are less likely to work hard to improve because they believe people either have it or they don't. Individuals with fixed mindsets have a much more difficult time with failures because it tends to make them question their value and worth. Students who believe that intelligence is fixed tend to feel more negative emotions (shame, hopelessness, boredom, anger, and anxiety).[212] The concept of fixed intelligence is not supported by the research so helping such people understand how malleable our minds are can help them significantly.

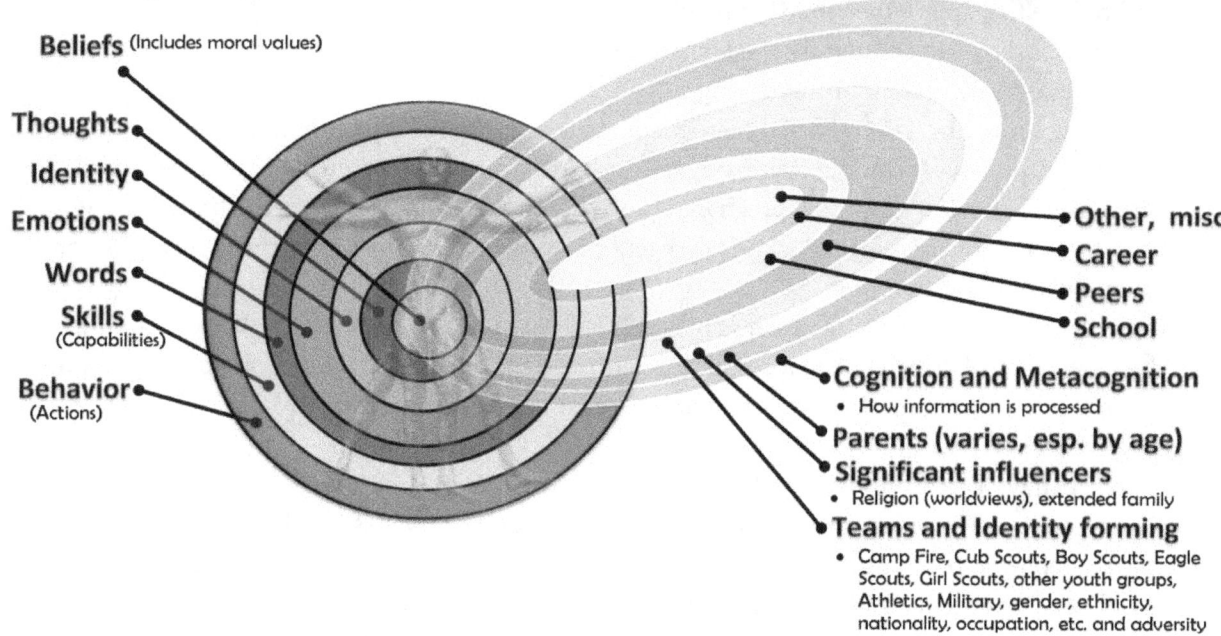

Influencers that can change an individual's beliefs or self-concept about identity will have the greatest impact on outcome, regardless of circumstances.

If influencers reinforce autonomy, an internal locus of control, optimism, and healthy self-esteem, they will contribute to resilience and improve outcomes.

If influencers reinforce neediness, external locus of control, diminish autonomy, create or reinforce an external locus of control, or negative expectations, they will diminish resilience and outcomes.

Our beliefs have a significant effect on our behavior. Our subconscious mind creates backstories to explain our experiences and observations that are consistent with our beliefs. If we have a belief that we cannot do something, or that we aren't good at something, the back story our mind creates supports our belief. If we succeed at something that we don't think we can do or be good at, our back story will reflect that—perhaps crediting luck for the success.

If we believe we are the best at something but someone else wins, our mind will create a back story that explains the other person's win without shattering our belief. The back story might give credit to something that seems unfair or dishonest in order to protect our belief that we are the best—even without evidence to support the conclusion. The mere fact that someone beat us when *we're the best* is sufficient evidence for the subconscious mind to create such a back story.

Changes at inner levels affect every larger layer

Changes at larger layers can have an impact on inner layers, but it is the more difficult path to change

Changing the outer levels without changing the inner layers creates conflict that the inner layer will eventually win (if it does not change)

Changes made at outer layers that are assimilated into the inner layer can become permanent (i.e. using willpower to force daily exercise can lead to an identity change regarding exercise but most people fail before they achieve an identity change). Defining oneself as an exerciser uses less willpower and does not result in resource depletion along the way. A study that looked at the development of an identity that supported their new role as a Mother helped teen mothers form healthy attachment relationships with their infants and reduce the stress experienced in their new role.[213]

"Willpower is the most commonly cited barrier to making lifestyle changes. 32% of Americans say a lack of willpower prevented them from making a change."[214]

Baumeister, Vohs, and Tice reported that "Inadequate self-control has been linked to behavioral and impulse-control problems, including overeating, alcohol and drug abuse, crime and violence, overspending, sexually impulsive behavior, unwanted pregnancy, and smoking . . . and it may also be linked to emotional problems, school underachievement, lack of persistence, various failures at task performance, relationship problems, and dissolution and more."[215]

When the action is consistent with one's beliefs it feels natural and does not deplete the energy required for self-control. When the action conflicts with one's beliefs about the self or world, self-control is required and the energy required for self-control can become depleted, leading to a decreased ability to control one's own behavior.

Adaptive behavior refers to using an ability to access one's environment and adjust behavior in order to, at a minimum, survive and at maximum, excel in the environment one is in. I'll use a rather unusual example of someone who is being held as a hostage. Adaptive behavior at its minimum might be trying to figure out what makes the captor violent and avoiding that behavior so the person can maintain his health and well-being longer. At a maximum might include finding a way to escape captivity. In the television show 24, Jack frequently exhibited adaptive behaviors by escaping from captors against high odds (i.e. when he was handcuffed and his captors outnumbered him). If you watched the show or any show where such events are depicted, you'll see that the person who escapes believes he or she can escape. Maladaptive behavior would be behavior that hastens adverse actions by the captor.

Individuals adapt their behavior to their surroundings. If you're attending a family holiday dinner at the home of your girlfriend's parents, someone who is adaptive will display good manners even if he does not do so when he is home alone eating a pizza while watching television. There are some people who hold themselves to high standards as far as manners that they use the same manners when they are alone as they do when they are being observed. That can be adaptive or maladaptive. If it is because of self-respect and enjoyment of good manners, it is adaptive and stems from core beliefs. If it is because of an inability to relax under any circumstances it is maladaptive. Such a person might have stiff and shallow relationships with others. They might be perfectionistic or lack sufficient flexibility to allow their self to *go with the flow*. Or, it could be as simple as they have never considered that they could relax a little bit and are carrying over patterns they learned as children.

"A match between implicit (beliefs) and explicit (conscious desire) in goal achievement is associated with adaptive outcomes."[216] When our beliefs and our desired behaviors conflict, beliefs win. For example, many years ago I was a 2-pack-a-day Marlboro girl, but I wanted to quit smoking. Society was becoming increasing difficult for smokers, the expense of cigarettes was increasing, and I was aware of the potential for adverse long-term health consequences from smoking. I tried a number of different methods to quit smoking, but none of them were successful and I did not manage to quit for more than a day, until I changed my tactics and changed my belief first.

There were two beliefs standing in my way. The first was due to early indoctrination to *finish what I have begun*—a motto I memorized when I was a Blue Bird (a very young Camp Fire Girl). To me, finishing what I began translated to not being a quitter. I'd already recognized the genesis of this stick–to–itiveness.

The second belief standing in my way was the belief, "I'm a smoker" or "I smoke." Smoking had become part of my self-defined identity.

So, what is a girl to do when she wants to stop smoking but she is not a quitter? She can become something new instead of quitting. I decided to become a non-smoker and determined a date six-weeks out when I would become a non-smoker. Then I mentally began elaborating all the reasons I wanted to be a non-smoker and did not want to be a smoker every time I lighted a cigarette. Within four weeks I had to force myself to light-up. I'm not sure if that step was necessary, but when I found myself no longer wanting to light-up I reinforced that I was still a smoker until the date I became a non-smoker and kept smoking until midnight of my last day as a smoker. I was concerned that if I stopped smoking before I became a non-smoker I would begin smoking again.

On my first day as a non-smoker, I stayed in bed until 1 p.m. crying because I wanted a cigarette so badly but I wasn't a smoker so I couldn't have one. The first three days were difficult, but after the third day it was remarkably easy not to smoke, regardless of opportunity or stress level. It's been twenty-six years and I have rarely had an urge to light-up and when they did occur they were not compelling. Simply reminding myself that I am a non-smoker and non-smokers don't smoke was enough to quell any random urges.

Beliefs are simply neuropathways created by repeatedly thinking a thought. You can create new beliefs by reinforcing thoughts you want to believe. Please look at the Affirmation Process for guidance—not all affirmations are productive and some are counterproductive.

You can choose to define yourself and that by doing so, it affects your thoughts. Your definition of self equates to your beliefs about yourself. I've learned that when you define yourself with deliberation in how you want to show up in the world, that when you start to stumble into something that would be contrary to your definition of self, you feel the discord and in-the-moment course corrections can be done in the early stages while they are still easy.

Your beliefs become your thoughts,
Your thoughts become your words,
Your words become your actions,
Your actions become your habits,
Your habits become your values,
Your values become your destiny.
Mahatma Gandhi

When you change your beliefs to align with your goals and desires, you do not need willpower to force yourself to comply because doing the things that you need to do to support your motion forward feels good. The same is true of actions you refrain from doing because not doing them is consistent with your new definition of self—as in my example of becoming a non-smoker.

When willpower is the primary method, people "have to resist many desires and impulses and must control themselves in other ways, and so over the course of a typical day many people gradually become ego depleted. The result is that they become increasingly likely to give in to impulses and desires that they would have resisted successfully earlier in the day... During the state of ego depletion, people become less helpful and more aggressive, prone to overeat, misbehave sexually, express more prejudice, and in other ways do things that they may later regret."[217]

12: Beliefs and Expectations

You have to expect things of yourself before you can do them.
Michael Jordan -- GQ, March, 1989

The expectation filter plays a massive role in success. If an individual expects exceptional opportunities, he is far more likely to spot them. If he does not expect much, the opportunity could be right in front of him, and he will not recognize it. The brain will not pass information, which contradicts or exceeds expectations, to the conscious mind, even when the information is right in front of the person.

Jerry Rice is a veteran of twenty seasons in the NFL and "widely considered to be the greatest wide receiver in NFL history and among the greatest NFL players overall."[218] He won three Super Bowl rings playing for the San Francisco 49ers. The day before Super Bowl 2016 a news report showed a man who had hired a Uber driver to take him somewhere and, from a hidden camera, recorded the driver asking the passenger (who was in the front seat) which team he supported. The passenger said he was a life-long 49ers fan because he was born and raised in San Francisco. A lifelong 49er fan was being driven by Jerry Rice and did not recognize his driver until Rice introduced himself. If you watch football on television, you know that the most popular players are interviewed frequently. This man would have seen Jerry Rice without his helmet hundreds of time and still didn't recognize his face or voice—because he did not expect Jerry Rice to be his Uber driver.

In my own career, I remember some of the deciding moments when I realized I could expand my goals. I remember giving a speech when I was just 21. There were two speakers that day; we were both being honored for obtaining a highly respected designation. The other speaker, a Vice President where I worked began fulfilling the requirements for achievement of the designation before my birth. I gave a 7-minute speech with no notes to over 400 people, including all the executives of the company where I worked. The Vice President read his in a monotone voice. I clearly remember realizing that if a Vice President could take more than 20 years to earn a designation I had earned in 23 months, and do such a poor job on the speech in comparison to my performance, I could be a Vice President. It did not mean it would happen that day, but my personal perspective of my potential changed in that minute. My expectations for my life changed. When the opportunity came, I saw it clearly.

I also remember a time when I did not recognize an opportunity. We were looking for a lake house. We were aware there was a lot that was larger than what we wanted being offered for not much more than we were willing to pay for a lot. We never considered buying the lot, subdividing it and selling part of it and keeping what we wanted. When someone else did exactly that a few months later we felt pretty stupid for not having thought of the idea. At the time our filters were not set to see such opportunities. I am pretty sure I did not think I was *lucky* enough to find an opportunity to get the lot for almost nothing, which is what the buyers who sold half of it did. Now I realize such opportunities exist and I would be more likely to recognize the opportunity if I became aware of it.

Our expectation also plays a huge role in how we age.[219] If we see a certain age as being old or anticipate ill health at that age, we are far more likely to experience that age in that way. When we change our perception of that age, our personal experience of it changes.[220]

Regarding expectation, think of the children who do not thrive no matter the resources sent their way. Ask yourself, what is the expectation? Then, do all you can to increase the expectation if you are around any of those children. The potential of someone who lives without what is desired is even greater than that of someone who lives a mild life—once it is unleashed.

Sometimes we are told to beware of behaviors by those who love us because they want to protect us, but their warnings cause us to interpret reality as if the thing they're warning us about is happening even when it isn't. This can significantly increase our chronic stress level and diminish our happiness.

Two areas where I've seen this playing out is in expectation of racism and expectation of sexism. I elaborate on this in Chapter 24.

The mind-body connection is clear. What we think about our body affects our body.[221] This is true about our health. Placebo and Nocebo Effects are just the tip of the iceberg. When we are mentally stressed, our physical health is directly affected in a negative way. Stress in our mind leads to the body creating a chemical cocktail that negatively impacts its function. Even aging is affected by mindset.

In one study, Dr. Ellen Langley experimented on a group of 75-year old men.[222] She took photographs of them, had health examinations and then put them together for a week and asked them to pretend they were 55, to wear clothes like what they wore two decades before, to speak as it was two decades earlier, as if the President was the one who was in office twenty years previously. At the end of the week, on every test, they had aged in reverse during the week they pretended to be 55-years old.

What types of beliefs are limiting you? Do you find yourself telling yourself you can't do what you want because:

You don't have the right education

The Wright Brothers weren't educated and they built an airplane.

You tried and you couldn't do it

Failures are a form of education. Dust yourself off and try again—you know more now than you did when you failed. Check out Milton Hershey's life story.

You haven't earned it yet

What you achieve is not about what you earn. It is about what you believe you can do. Look around. How many people who haven't seemed to earn what they have get what they believe they can obtain?

You aren't worthy of having your desire

This is a flat out bogus belief. Use your Emotional Guidance to overcome this limiting belief.

You're not smart enough

Intelligence is not a precursor to success. I don't want to be mean so I won't mention untelligent people who have been very successful by name, but look around and you'll see that not being smart enough is not what matters the most. You'll also see that there are many very smart people who struggle to be successful.

All the good ones are already taken

I had this belief about men and until I changed my belief, good men were not coming into my life. Once I changed the belief they showed up. I did not shift it overnight. First I began acknowledging that sometimes good men became widows and sometimes women had a mid-life crisis that resulted in them leaving a good man who would then be available for a brief period of time.

I've seen people hold this belief about jobs. But the truth is that what is a good job to one person is not a good job to another. Jobs are stepping stones where we learn and grow, eventually outgrowing most jobs, making what once was a good job for us into not the ideal, which causes us to move on and someone who perceives it as a good job to move into the vacancy.

I've also seen this (even experienced it a bit in my own life) belief associated with locations for homes. It wasn't true—it just seemed true because I was being too narrow and specific in my determination to have a specific one. When I relaxed my insistence on a specific outcome, the solution that arrived was better than the one I had previously been insisting upon.

You are afraid you'll fail

Failing is learning. If you hold yourself back because you're afraid to fail, you'll never achieve much. Trust that you have the resources to pick yourself back up and keep going if you to fail—smarter and wiser for the experience. See the Reframe Failure tool.

You don't have the money or connections needed to succeed

Daymond John began his billion dollar empire with $20. T. Harv Eker began his success journey by using $2,000 charged to his credit card.

It's selfish for you to have more than others have

This is a viewpoint that sees financial resources as limited—as if it is one pie being divided up by everyone. Nothing could be further from the truth. What others are able to achieve is based on their beliefs and efforts—not limitations of resources.

I don't stick to things long enough, I lack willpower

Not sticking to things stems from either pursuing the wrong things or attempting to change behavior before you've changed beliefs.

You're not the right race, religion, gender, age

Unless absolutely no one with similar circumstances has ever managed to accomplish it (and possibly even then), these are just limiting beliefs that get in your way.

Influence of Expectation

Expectations greatly impact accomplishments. Learning how to use the power of expectation in your life and in the lives of others leads to significant improvements. Researchers have repeatedly shown that expectations create a sort of self-fulfilling prophesy. The prophesy can be about our own accomplishments or about another's accomplishments. Expectations influence outcomes bi-directionally. High expectations improve outcomes. Low expectations decrease outcomes.

A bias toward optimism or pessimism influences assumptions individuals make about the future, as do people's past experiences. An experience in the past that resembles a current situation may cause the brain to interpret it as the same even when there are significant differences. One way to ensure one's expectations are serving the highest good is to think more deeply about why we view things the way we do. Emotional Guidance is of great value in helping discern better ways to perceive our environment; the EGS contains more wisdom than the brain.[223]

> *What are you expecting:*
> *From life?*
> *From others?*
> *From your body?*

> *The greatest wisdom is in simplicity... Love, respect, tolerance, sharing, appreciation, forgiveness. It's not complex or elaborate. The real knowledge is free.*
> Carlos Barrios, Mayan Elder

There are also many examples of the way humans do not do things considered impossible but once one person accomplishes it, whether it is learning to walk again after a spinal cord injury or running the first 4-minute mile, others who hear of it become able to do the same.

Our belief or lack of belief in our ability to accomplish something plays an important role in whether or not we succeed.

When we use what others have accomplished to decide what is possible, we limit ourselves to the successes of our predecessors. It is possible to use our EGS to determine what is possible for us. If you're dreaming of an accomplishment that no one else has done before, use your Emotional Guidance to reinforce your belief that you can achieve your goal.

Individuals who are ill can use the process to increase their belief and hope that they will get better. Think the thought, "There is a way for me to get better" and compare the emotional response to that statement to the emotional response to the thought "I am going to die." The thought that there is a way for me to get better will feel better to anyone who has not decided they actually want to die (which does happen). Individuals who have practiced using their guidance and trust it, will know that hope is not misplaced and there is a way. That belief opens up possibilities that do not exist when one believes it is hopeless. The emotion of hope is also a much higher emotion, which translates into less stress and an immune system that functions better than it does when you feel hopeless.

Developing familiarity with one's own guidance system to the point where trust is developed can provide as much advantage as knowing someone else has accomplished your goal. It opens the possibility of not needing anyone else to do it first before we believe it is possible. Stories about walking after spinal cord injuries are a good example. When it was believed hopeless, it was unheard of for someone to recover the ability to walk. Today there are frequent stories. Some are the result of new techniques but one has to ask, would anyone have developed those techniques if they believed it was hopeless, or did having hope stimulate new research? How much of what we *can't* do is the result of a belief that we can't?

We want to control others, often because we have low expectations of them. Research has shown that our expectations influence the outcome.[224] My favorite study is one where an elementary teacher was told that two of her incoming students were exceptionally bright. The person who advised her of this did not have firsthand knowledge—he was merely the messenger. The two students were actually performing very poorly.[225]

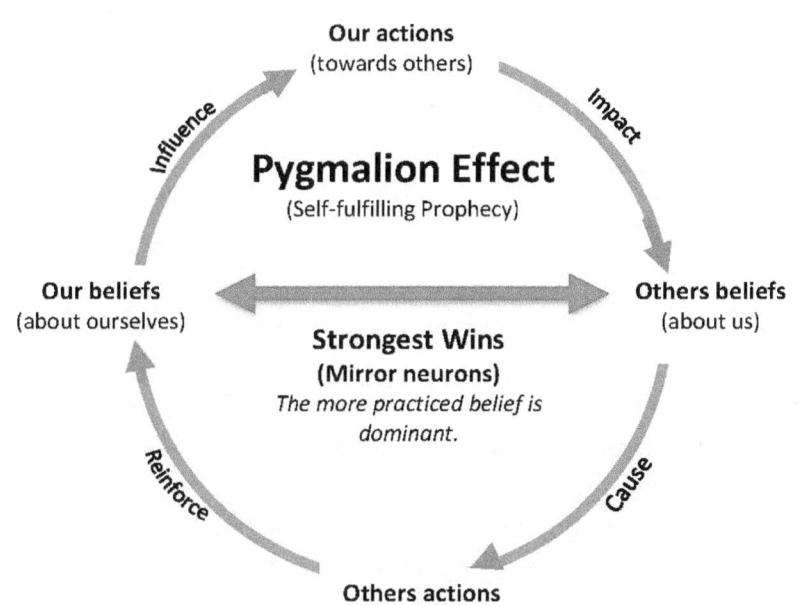

At the end of the year, the two previously poorly performing students were performing exceptionally well. The study was one of the ones that said, "We observed this but we do not understand it so we need to do more research." However, in quantum physics they have discovered the mirror neurons,[226] which explain how others' high or low expectations influence another's' behavior.

Students who could do better in the existing educational system are sometimes impeded by the strong and practiced low expectations of the teachers. Most teachers do not understand the impact of their own expectations on a student's performance. They are not taught how to cultivate positive expectations or why they are beneficial. Instead, prior outcomes for students from lower socioeconomic groups are used to establish the expectation—without realizing low expectations negatively impacted the outcome of the earlier students.

One of the best (and sadly somewhat common) examples of low expectations negatively impacting the outcome is in a family where one person has been battling an addiction. The individual successfully completes rehabilitation and feels very confident about his future. Then he is back out in the world, amidst a family that is just waiting for him to backslide. The family did not go through the program with him so they anticipate another failure. If his intention and belief in his ability not to relapse is not greater than his family's expectation, the family's expectation will win.

Who wins when the expectations conflict? The one with the strongest belief wins. How do you counteract another's low expectations about you? Develop a stronger belief about who you are and where you're going than the ones held by those who see you as less successful.

Individuals in our society repeatedly define themselves based on how others perceive them. They allow others' low opinions to influence who they believe they are. Another's opinion reflects who *they* are—not *who* you are.

Making conscious decisions about whom you are and what you can accomplish is the best way to fulfill more of your personal potential.

Mirror neurons[227] do not require conversation or even body language. The mirror neurons sync to the stronger belief when we interact with one another. Have you ever ridden in an elevator with a complete stranger who seemed to think he was superior to you? Did you feel diminished as a result of the encounter? Was your self-esteem bruised?

If your answer is yes, strengthening your cohesion about who you are would benefit you. If your belief about your value and worth is more established than the person with whom you share the elevator, his beliefs won't be able to make you feel diminished—no matter how superior he feels to you.

Your core beliefs about yourself matter. No matter who you are, where you are, and who you've been it is important to develop positive expectations about your future. Even if you're serving consecutive life sentences for murders you did commit, you don't have to continue being the type of person who would do those actions. Just because you were someone in the past does not mean you are destined to remain that person forever.

You have the ability to transform yourself. It may not mean you'll be released (if you're incarcerated murderer) but your life won't be as miserable. It is possible to be locked up and utterly miserable and it is possible to be locked up and find meaning and purpose in your existence. You are the only one who can decide which you'll do. There are techniques in the processes section that will help you form a healthy self-image.

We have the equipment to measure the syncing of the brains described by the term mirror neurons—but do not yet understand the mechanics behind the actual process. There have been a number of replicated studies reporting phenomena that cannot be explained by what we know we know.

Research into biophotons is a promising area of research. Early work indicates biophotons are responsible for cellular communication in our own bodies—something earlier theories could not explain because the instantaneous speed of the communication is faster than physical processes can account for.

Our bodies quickly respond to stimuli, such as nervous perspiration the moment we are in a situation that causes us to be anxious or salivating the moment we see or smell something delicious. Chemical reactions in one cell triggering chemical reactions in adjacent cells do not explain the speed of our responses.

We should not wait until researchers reveal all the nuances of how mirror neurons work before we begin using what we do know to benefit one another. Seeing others for their potential rather than their current state would help them achieve more of their potential. This is true whether we ever speak a word about it to them.

The best way to help others is to create strong positive impressions of their potential is in the privacy of your mind when you are not with them. This practice works with family and with students, employees and even bosses.

Treat a man as he is and he will remain as he is.
Treat a man as he can and should be and he will become as he can and should be.
E. E. Cummings 1894–1962

The Pygmalion Effect (or Rosenthal as it is sometimes called) is well-documented.[228, 229] High or low teacher expectations of students affect the outcome of the students.[230] There is significant evidence that low teacher expectations negatively impact the outcome of many Black children and on Maori children in New Zealand.[231] Surprisingly, even rats respond to experimenter expectations. Students were told that some lab rats were bred to be smart and would run the maze faster than other rats that were not as intelligent. The rats were actually no different in terms of breeding. The rats the students believed would learn faster did learn faster.

Educating teachers about the Pygmalion Effect is not enough. A district level employee relayed to me that her teachers understand it intellectually, but still (unfairly) perceive students from poor families as having less potential. New research adds another piece to the puzzle of chronic poverty. Various realities of poverty require the use of resources that can deplete cognitive resources on the same magnitude that people experience when they miss an entire night of sleep.[232] *The Smart Way* would help to alleviate the Pygmalion Effect because a teacher who understands Emotional Guidance and pays attention to how thoughts feel would be aware the negative emotion that accompanies thoughts of poor children having low potential is evidence that the perspective is moving away from the teacher's goals.

12: Beliefs and Expectations

13: Emotional Stance, and Focus

To know that we know what we know, and to know that we do not know what we do not know, that is true knowledge.
Nicolaus Copernicus

What is *emotional stance*?

I have mentioned Emotional Stance (ES) before so let me clarify exactly what it is. I refer to ES in two distinct ways. One is the emotional stance in any given moment—how an individual feels in that moment in time. The other is their chronic emotional stance, a practiced emotional stance that an individual chronically returns to over time. It may be practiced deliberately or unconsciously, but everyone develops chronic emotional states. Individuals can change their chronic emotional state with deliberate effort, which is made easier by the use of their EGS. Both types of stances impact behavior and how the world is perceived.

Emotional state has a significant impact on both our behavior and our interpretation of others behavior. Thoughts, words, actions our interpretation of them are all affected by our current emotional state. "Research with college students has found that the perception of others' actions were intentional and controllable were significant determinants of anger rather than just frustration."[233] Understanding that our interpretation of others behavior is subjective and that their behavior is far more dependent upon their emotional state and emotion regulation abilities than on their opinion of us, it is easier to give them the benefit of the doubt and feel frustration instead of anger. Researchers have also found that the emotional state an individual is currently in can affect his judgement of risks, which would then impact behavioral choices.[234]

In an article in Psychological Reviews, R. S. Lazarus wrote, "Aristotle wrote in Rhetoric, 'Anger may be defined as a belief that we, or our friends, have been unfairly slighted, which causes in us both painful feelings and a desire or impulse for revenge . . . and then asks us to consider:

What the state of mind of angry people is,

Who the people are with whom they usually get angry, and

On what grounds they get angry with them

It is not enough to know one or even two of these points; unless we know all three, we shall be unable to arouse anger in anyone. The same is true of the other emotions'"[235]

In the chart in Appendix I, emotional states are divided into seven zones:

- ❖ Sweet Zone
- ❖ Hopeful Zone
- ❖ Blah Zone
- ❖ Drama Zone
- ❖ Give Away Zone
- ❖ Hot Zone
- ❖ Powerless Zone

- The Sweet Zone is where we would all like to spend most of our time. From the Hopeful Zone it is easy to move into the Sweet Zone.
- The Blah Zone is pretty self-explanatory.
- The Drama Zone is where emotions become more heated but don't reach the level of anger. There is a lot of drama in this zone. Comments like, "You won't believe what he did" or "You won't believe what she said" are common in this Zone.
- The Give Away Zone is where you've given your power away by making someone else responsible for your emotional state or your circumstances. If you're not responsible, you have no power to change what you don't like and there is a lot you don't like in this Zone.
- The Hot Zone contains anger and rage.
- The Powerless Zone is depressed, living in despair, feeling hopeless. It is the least empowered zone. The chart in Appendix I has more details about the emotions in each Zone.

The higher the Zone you're in, the happier you are and the less stress you experience. Immune function, cognitive function, creativity, digestive function, and the central nervous system work better the higher you are on the scale. Good relationships are easier to establish and maintain in the higher Zones and worsen as Emotional State moves to lower Zones. Success at work and in school improves in the higher Zones and declines in the lower Zones. A combination of factors lead to the relationships between emotional state, behavior, success, physical and mental health, and relationships.

For example, the decreased immune function in the lower Zones negatively impacts health, which leads to more absences from school or work, which reduces performance. The bad moods associated with the lower Zones make maintaining good relationships more difficult, which leads to less social support, which is associated with worse health outcomes. Social relationships impact both physical and mental health and social isolation is associated with a higher risk of mortality. Poor quality relationships are also associated with poor health. It is important to associate with people who help you feel good, not pull you down.

That does not imply you should only associate with people who don't have problems—that would lead to social isolation because everyone has problems. It is the way your social network deals with problems that determines the quality of the relationships. If the attitude of your network reflects a victim mentality it is not as healthy as a network that speaks and acts as if they have power over the outcome of their lives. The challenge of successfully facing problems can be exhilarating. Problems aren't the problem. It is our attitude when we face problems (challenge vs. fear) that determines whether they induce harmful and lasting stress cocktails into our bloodstream.

Both positive moods and negative moods have a tendency to feed on themselves with positive moods increasing well-being in multiple areas of life and negative moods decreasing well-being in multiple areas of life. It is 100% possible to be in circumstances that are far from ideal and find perspectives that put you emotionally in the higher Zones. It takes practice, but the practice has immediate rewards in feeling better and the long-term pay-off could be a change of circumstances that makes it easier to sustain the more positive emotional states.

For example, positively focused individuals are more likely to be hired than negatively focused individuals. Some headhunters won't even work with negatively focused individuals both because they find doing so personally draining and because they are much harder to place. Learning how to achieve an authentic and higher emotional state could make a significant difference in career potential. Once hired, positively focused individuals are more successful in almost every job classification.

Positively focused individuals are more likely to marry. They are also more likely to remain married. Being married to a good partner provides social support that can improve your life.

Positively focused individuals are more likely to make beneficial decisions about their health including obtaining adequate sleep, exercising and making healthier eating decisions.[236]

The same individual has better thinking skills when he is happy than when he is not happy (i.e. stressed).[237] This can make significant differences in every area of life. Making a good decision about a home purchase, a career move, whom to marry, and investments can alter the course of one's life.

Happiness causes success.[238] It is worthwhile to learn skills that increase happiness and then pursue your goals.

Both our habitual and current emotional stance creates a filter our brains use to determine what information to pass to our conscious minds and how to explain the information via the back story. I manage my emotional stance to a place that feels good on a consistent basis, so my filter highlights information that feels good to me. It also dims negative aspects.

By dimming, I don't mean I don't see bad things when they happen. It means I don't dwell on them. I don't focus on them or allow them to become dominant in my thoughts. It means I turn more quickly to solutions when a problem arises.

I found a tragic example of emotional state impacting one's interpretation of events in an article in the Times of Israel. A woman who was apparently not White believed she was being discriminated against and sought the help of the manager who was already assisting someone else. Based on the article, she interpreted his instruction to "get back in line" to mean "get back in the long line—not the one for Mothers with young children." But by her own account, what he said was "get back in line." There is no evidence that this clerk knew which line she was standing in before she came to the front to complain about the treatment of her being racist.

Her potential misinterpretation caused her to view his request as racist, which she then proceeded to complain about, taking it to a higher ranking official. His explanation of the event,

"Two days ago a woman came to the office to get service," he recounted. "At the time I was assisting other people. She demanded the service immediately and instantly began shouting that not receiving it was racism." . . .

"And here this woman was accusing me of racism. I told her to stop right there. I would not have her take that route. Not in my office. There is a queue for mothers with small children and she must stand in that queue like all the other mothers. Not everything you want but don't get is racism," he said.[239]

From my perspective, the woman who later (after the official who told her to leave his office and get in line committed suicide after her story received considerable attention on Facebook) indicated that she has been discriminated against in Israel for years, had developed a belief that she was frequently discriminated against. Because her mind filters information using that belief, when he told her to get in line, he meant the line for Mothers with small children and she assumed he meant the longer line. I believe she unconsciously perceived the discriminatory meaning because she has a belief she is discriminated against frequently.

A similar miscommunication happened between my daughter and her boyfriend (but thankfully, without the horrendous consequences). They were cooking breakfast and my daughter asked her boyfriend a question. She seemed upset by the answer and he perceived it as she did not want to go with him to an event. I perceived it as her being upset because her business required her attention and she was upset that she was not free to go with him if she was going to meet her obligations. Her boyfriend was feeling hurt that she did not want to go (his perception—not reality) when I stepped in and asked if they would mind if I shared an observation.

I proceeded to tell each how the other perceived the conversation and both affirmed that I had accurately perceived their thoughts about what was being communicated. Her boyfriend was relieved to know that her upset was because she wanted to go but did not feel she could and not what he thought—that she did not want to go.

Communication is imperfect. The best response when your emotional response to communication feels bad is to see if there is a better-feeling way to perceive the words and actions. In my daughter's case, her boyfriend felt negative emotion when he perceived she did not want to go with him (an inaccurate assumption he believed to be true—because he believes his emotional response validates the thought that brought forth the emotion). If he had understood that his emotions were encouraging him to find a different (better-feeling) perspective about the exchange, he might have thought about how well her business was doing and thought that maybe she wants to come but doesn't feel she can (which would have elicited a far better emotional-response).

In the situation with the strangers, if the woman understood her Emotional Guidance, the outrage and offense she felt when she believed he was directing her to the longer line would have given her a clue that her interpretation of his words might not be the best. She might have been able to calm down and ask for clarification of what he was saying. Or, she could have assumed the Universe works in wonderful and mysterious ways and that maybe the person she'd be standing next to her in the longer line was someone she should meet and trust the process to unfold perfectly.

In any event, she would not have made the Facebook post about the event that had a result she did not want—even if her perception of the situation reflected reality. I think many people would have a difficult time living with the thought that something they posted on Facebook contributed to another person's decision to take his life in a substantial way. If the post was in America, there would even be a possibility of criminal or civil charges against her for bullying or something similar, perhaps defamation of character. The man who died "had always espoused treating all people equally, regardless of religion or origin . . . even publishing a book on the subject and forming an organization dedicated to "equality between all citizens, especially minorities, and their integration into a homogenous Israeli society."

I am not blaming the woman. Based on her beliefs and knowledge at the time she posted on Facebook, she was portraying what she believed was an accurate depiction of reality. If she understood how filters in our minds work and how to use her Emotional Guidance, the outcome would have been different. I am advocating for the importance of people having this knowledge.

Self-schema refers one's beliefs, experiences and generalizations about the self, in specific behavioral domains. For example, we will generally have a self-schema as it related to our profession and it may be further divided into a self-schema for interactions with our boss, one for interactions with customers, and another for subordinates. We might have a different self-schema during time when we are with our family. Research demonstrating that our self-schemata is mood-congruent shows that our mood affects our self-schema.[240] When we are in a good mood our self-schema is more likely to include pro-social behaviors. When we are in a bad mood our self-schema is more likely to include worse behaviors.

Emotional stance has more effect on behavior than the other filters. Emotional stance is tied directly to how empowered or disempowered we feel. Joy is a reflection of feeling very empowered. Depression reflects feeling very disempowered. Many undesired behaviors help an individual feel temporarily more empowered. If the individual understands how to use his or her EGS, they will have more socially approved methods of regaining a sense of empowerment. When individuals do not have that information, less desirable ways of feeling more empowered are chosen.

We automatically chose the method that costs the least. If we don't know a better way, or our attempts to use more accepted ways of feeling better have been thwarted, we will turn to violence, crime, alcohol, drugs and other panacea's for disempowered emotional states. If we know techniques that will help us feel better that don't run the risk of arrest, hangovers, and other negative consequences, we will chose those methods. People who have turned to those methods of regaining a sense of empowerment (or drowning the lack thereof) tried other ways before they went down the dark path. Those efforts did not work so they turned to other options.

The techniques in this book work. Many of them are not dose-dependent, which means they literally help you reprogram your brain to be more optimistic. The techniques also indicate which emotional states they work best with. Techniques that work well when you're in the Drama Zone won't necessarily be the best choice when you're depressed. It is important to choose techniques that work well with your current emotional state.

We all strive to feel better. The first response to being in a lower emotional state than we are comfortable with is not usually crime. However, over time, especially if all the ways of increasing ones sense of empowerment that are *perceptible to the individual* have been exhausted without success, crime becomes an acceptable method of regaining power (in the individual's mind).

In Baumeister and Beck's book, *Evil: Inside Human Violence and Cruelty* they reported that criminals always felt their crimes were justified.[241] A combination of factors leads to their conclusion. The low negative emotional state narrowed their thought-action repertoire so they literally could not conceive of solutions that someone in a better emotional state could see. They may have already tried to feel better through other means and failed, leading them to believe the more socially acceptable option would not work.

We naturally want greater degrees of empowerment. But we can become comfortable in levels that are not ideal. Many people live in an uncomfortable comfort zone. They are accustomed to feeling the way they do in that Zone and their back story begins telling them that attempts to feel better will feel just like the Zone they have been chronically living in.

An individual who has been depressed for a long time and unsuccessful in his attempts to regain power may eventually commit suicide or a murder/suicide or just murder. Suicide can feel better to someone who feels trapped in despair. It is because suicide is something he or she can control so it feels more empowered than feeling trapped. It is a more empowered feeling the individual is seeking—not death. An alternative method to increase empowerment will bring someone back from the brink. In *Prevent Suicide: The Smart Way* I detail a situation where this exact method was used to prevent an imminent suicide.

One of the reasons our society is so unsuccessful in helping individuals beat depression is we reject aspects of the path from depression to more empowered states. Anger and revenge are more empowered than depression. We view those emotional states as more dangerous and discourage them. If it were generally understood that anger and revenge are no different than cities you have to drive through when they are along the route from Point A to the destination, Point B, we would do better. If people generally understood that how they feel is within their control they would not blame others.

> *Emotion and sense of power are linked.*

I am primarily speaking of suicides that result from emotional pain, but I would be remiss if I did not mention the research that demonstrates physical pain is worse when the mood is down and improves when the mood is better.[242] So, even someone who is contemplating suicide to escape intolerable pain could find some relief by working on her emotional state.

Sometimes an individual who is enraged and cannot find a thought that will provide relief from their intense pain will commit murder and then kill himself. This is an indication he is blaming someone else for his being trapped in the low emotional state. Because he is holding someone else responsible for how he feels, just committing suicide feels like he is letting the one who is to blame off the hook. Encouraging this person to anger is not the right path. Helping the person realize he has some control over how he feels and to accept responsibility for his own emotional state is the most productive tactic. This stance indicates an external locus of control. If he can see how a slight change in perspective changes how he feels and that he has control over his perspective, a tragedy can be prevented.

You might have to stop for lunch but you do not have to buy a house in anger or revenge or take up residence indefinitely. When the path from depression to higher states is understood, assisting an individual quickly through the Hot Zone is not difficult. Someone who has practiced the techniques can usually do it without assistance if something disrupts their emotional equilibrium.

Our society tends to see individuals who are moving into anger and revenge from depression as more troublesome (in those states) so we push them back down to depression where they are easier to manage. We discourage anger, rather than guide the individual through anger to more empowered emotional states. This makes the path of anger appear blocked to the depressed individual, increasing the likelihood of criminal behavior or suicide being the next choice.

Chronic bad-feeling emotional stances are not cured through punishment. We cannot punish or guilt someone into better behavior. Individuals must be given the knowledge and skills to master their own emotional stance. Our guidance always points us toward better-feeling emotions. More importantly, it eliminates the sense that the only path to feeling better is one society abhors. In fact, after some experience, reaching the Hopeful Zone is easy because once you understand a tool that works, finding the feeling of hope is easier.

White-collar crime increases during economic declines. Underneath, it is often someone who was more afraid than they were in a better economy who commits the crime. Selling corporate secrets or client lists to competitors is not just a lack of ethics—it is fueled by fear. The fear comes from a mindset (belief) that the person has no control over her financial future and that her financial security is in peril.

The employee who feels confident about his future will not commit the crime. If you feel confident about your future and then you commit a crime, you would begin feeling fear that you would be caught. Humans have the capacity to anticipate the fear they'll feel if they commit a crime and it is usually enough to prevent the choice of crime. Committing the crime would make the person feel less empowered. We act in the direction that will increase our sense of empowerment. This is true even when it does not appear to be the case to observers. If you could know, thought by thought, the way the individual perceives the decision; it would become clear that the words or actions were chosen because they felt more empowering.

> *We (wrongly) assume others' thought processes are the same as our own.*

Many theorists attempt to use economic theory to explain and anticipate human behavior, but money is one aspect of things we think about when we consider how we will feel. It is ultimately how we believe we will feel that guides our decisions.

When we are in lower emotional states, the contrast between our thoughts and our goals creates stress. When we change our thoughts in a direction that supports our dreams and goals, the stress decreases.

Follow your dreams.......they know the way.
Julie Veitch

If you practice paying attention to the emotional feedback from your thoughts for a while—the length of time required depends on how attuned you are when you begin paying more attention—you can literally think a thought and feel the stress go up or down in your body, depending on which direction the thought takes you.

Emotional stance affects every relationship in our lives, from strangers on the road to our most intimate relationships in our homes. While the higher emotional states support close and loving relationships, the lower emotional states contribute to frequent friction and problems.

Each Zone has a myriad of emotions within it. The separation is by the degree of empowerment felt while those emotions are being experienced.

Emotions are responses to thoughts and each thought elicits a new emotion. The emotion is the sensory guidance feedback systems response to the thought. Two consecutive thoughts may generate the same emotion or emotions so close to one another they cannot be differentiated, but the emotion changes in response to each thought. This can be easily shown using a guided meditation designed to move the emotions around. Changes in emotions are quickly recognized.

Another thing to understand is that you have an emotional stance on every topic. When you hold an infant in your arms, you may immediately move to the Sweet Zone with feelings of love. When you hear of violence on the news you may immediately move to anger or fear. Even specific people you have not talked to or seen in years will have an emotional set point wherever it was when you last left it or in your chronic emotional stance. I've noticed that someone I cared about who was once in my life with whom I parted on less than amicable terms tends to be where I chronically was with them—not the last emotional stance. However, I see people who ruminate about partings from their past whose emotional stance stays angry and some with whom it even worsens over time. It really depends on how you remember the person or situation.

Find your set point on the EGS and then reach for the next higher emotion on that subject. You will not be able to move up more than 1 or 2 levels at one time, but you don't have to remain at a level any longer than it takes to become stable there before you can begin successfully moving up another level.

Topic must be very narrowly defined. You have a different emotional stance for every topic. Your relationship with your mother can be different from your relationship with your father. Your relationship with your mother on a specific subject, say money, can be different from your relationship with her on other topics such as gifts, food, shopping, clothes, career, marriage, or travel. The way you generally feel about your mother will have more to do with which topic you focus on when you think of her. If your mind automatically goes to the one troubled topic between you, you will experience the relationship as if you do not have a good relationship, even if there are dozens of other topics on which your relationship with her is good. If your mind tends to ignore the topic(s) where there is disagreement and focuses on those where harmony exists, you will feel you have a good relationship with her, even if one or more of the topics where there is dissention are areas of significant discord.

This example clearly demonstrates that our relationships with our mothers (and really anyone) are under our control as far as how we view it. If you decide to wait until your mother changes on the point(s) of discontent before you can be happy, you may wait forever. If you change your focus away from the areas where you disagree to the areas where there is harmony, you can feel better about your relationship right away.

At first, it requires a conscious effort to focus on different aspects of your relationship. This is only because your previous habit of thought created neural pathways in your mind that are easier for the neurons to travel than the new, more desired paths. The refocusing of your attention requires patience with yourself. If it is a topic you think about often, it will take about three months to shift your neural pathways.

When you find the old perspective coming to your mind, recognize it is merely an old habit that has not yet been fully replaced with the new habit. Do not criticize yourself for the old habit not yet being gone. As soon as you recognize the thoughts, deliberately think about the thoughts you would rather focus on. This reinforces the new path. You can make it even firmer by writing or speaking about the new path.

When I listen to stories from people whose prior efforts to change their habits of thought failed to achieve the desired changes, this is where the failure most often occurred. It was not because the attempt to change was not working, it was because their expectation and interpretation of how long it would take to change the habits of thought did not match their experience. They could not see how close they were getting to the goal and gave up, often within sight of the finish line. One of the main factors that contributed to giving up was the tendency to berate themselves for not yet achieving the goal.

Changing our thought processes requires kindness to oneself. Just making a conscious decision to change is a big deal. Give yourself credit for doing that and then allow time to assist you. I have deliberately made many changes to my thought processes. One in particular was extremely ingrained. I was much like Pavlov's dog when the subject came up. It was as if I carried a soapbox on my back and as soon as the subject came up, I would set the box down, jump on it, and begin spouting my beliefs about the topic to all who would listen. I had strong convictions that my beliefs were right. (They weren't.)

After my research convinced me that those beliefs were based on false premises, I decided to change them. I no longer believed them to be true. I would still find myself a few minutes into my tirade before my mind would engage. I remember the first time I realized what I was doing. I was back on my soapbox, spouting things I no longer believed, about five minutes into my typical spiel. I stopped talking, took a deep breath, and ended the conversation. Then I spent some time mentally reviewing the new beliefs about the subject. I felt appreciation that I now knew more and understood the truth.

The next time, I was only about five sentences into the old habit before I stopped myself. Soon, I would realize that I was going where I did not want to go in the first sentence. My EGS was helping because I had also been working on being more sensitive to the onset of negative emotions so I would feel my emotional state decline, which gave me a clue that I was doing something I did not want to do. I celebrated when I stopped myself at just the thought, before I uttered words I no longer believed. The next time I thought about it, the thought was that it had been a few months since I had traveled that neuropathway. Now it has been years.

It took a long time to develop the neuropathways you want to change. You won't change them overnight, but you can begin clearing the new paths you want your thoughts to travel. Nothing will change until you take action and three months is not a long time when you compare it to how long you've lived with habits of thought that do not serve your highest good. You won't change all your habits of thought in three months, but you can be well on your way to more supportive automatic thoughts.

The aspect that makes it easy is this is the only change where there is no pain from the gain. Even deciding to think more empowered thoughts feels better than not taking action. The process of changing your thoughts also feels good. The only way it wouldn't feel good is if you beat yourself up about what you used to think about, or how long it is taking. Neither of those steps are productive and they are not recommended. Be kind to yourself.

Focus

Focus is the easiest significant filter to consciously direct, but it, too, has default modes. When one's focus is not responding to deliberate intentions, it uses its default settings, which differ because of many other factors. Researchers have found that attentional bias toward negative information may have a significant role in depression susceptibility.[243]

Most people focus on whatever their *vivid senses* are most aware of in the moment. It can be the news channel where the negative emotions elicited are not recognized as a sign that watching is not serving their highest good. It can be the latest fad or the hot new television show. You have the ability to choose what you focus on. You can choose to give things that feel bad air time in your mind and feel worse or you can choose to give things that feel good air time and feel good. It may help to think of what you give time to like programming a radio station. You are the audience. If you are not going to be in the present about what you are thinking, choose to re-play favorite hits that help your mood. If you want to think about the future, think about things you are looking forward to, not things that make you worry or feel dread.

My husband loves the St. Patrick's Day milk shakes at McDonalds. They're only available for a few weeks of the year, but at any point of the year he can look forward to his next one. He can be frustrated that he can't have it right now, or he can remember how good they are and savor the desire that will be fulfilled the following March. He could even be thankful that they are only available in March because if he could buy them anytime 1) he might not appreciate them as much, and 2) he might need new (larger) clothes.

There are exceptions. Passionate interest in a topic will guide ones focus. Although the default mode of focus is largely due to what the *vivid senses* are making you aware of, focus is the easiest and fastest filter to redirect. It is the go to filter when you're in a negative thought pattern that you can't seem to escape. In the process section there is a process designed for just that scenario. Read it and be prepared in advance, especially if you've ever experienced depression. If you're young and have not experienced many heartaches (or any), read it and prepare in advance even if you've never been depressed. You may never need it but if you do, you'll be glad you did.

Unconsciously focusing on what we do not want ruins many relationships. Let's say a man went golfing with the guys on Saturday afternoon and had a five some in front of them, so they were unusually slow. He had told his wife he would be home at a certain time. Maybe they were going to see a movie, going to dinner, or she was cooking for him. He

> *By placing the blame for her irritation on him, she gives all her power to change her emotional state away, leaving her with no power to fix it.*

did not call her to let her know he would be late. She was looking forward to an activity that did not work out because he was delayed on the golf course so she feels upset. She is thinking about what she lost, the opportunity to see the movie, go to dinner, or that she took the time to fix dinner for him, and it was overcooked because he arrived late—it does not matter what it is. We are not talking about a big deal here. We are talking about something that could be perceived in many ways, but she is upset, so she focuses on his action rather than something that feels better to think about. Maybe she calls her best friend and tells her about it. She really gets a head of steam up about the perceived problem.

It is bad enough that she spent time feeling less emotionally good when she could have focused elsewhere and felt good the entire time. Doing so depresses her immune system during the time she is upset and increases the stress she experiences. She also spread the lack of joy by telling her girlfriend about her irritation. She probably said, "How irritated he made me," but the truth is that her perspective caused the irritation.

She can be upset all she wants but if she is going to allow his lateness to upset her, she does not have control over how she feels. That is a disempowered perspective. It is the reason blaming someone else is considered a maladaptive way of coping with stress.

It can get worse. After the couple is all made up and happy with one another again, the friend, in a misguided attempt to be supportive, will say, "Has he done anything else that is irritating?" That just refocuses the unhappy wife's attention on the issue again. The focus filter will begin highlighting irritating things, instead of for reasons to love.

Your mind will point out what you focus on and ignore information you are not focused on. Once a member of a relationship begins looking for the unwanted, they can't see desired behaviors, even when they are present. They have changed their perspective. They are no longer giving their partner the benefit of the doubt. The *back story* they begin assigning to the other's actions changes. The same actions that were once interpreted as loving may now be interpreted in a less pleasing way.

I often hear comments such as "I don't even know who he is any more" or "She's changed so much I am not sure she was ever the woman I thought I knew" and other similar remarks. Most people have no clue that their perception changed far more than the other person did. More importantly, they do not understand their own power to adjust their focus to a better-feeling place to put the relationship back on track. If they knew how simple it could be to get back on track, the divorce rate would plummet.

> *The greatest discovery of my generation is*
> *that a human being can alter his life by altering his attitudes of mind.*
> William James

What could she have thought instead of being frustrated by his tardiness after his golf outing? She could have focused on being happy that he is able to go spend time with his friends. Leisure activities he enjoys make him happier, which makes him a better husband because happier people are easier to love. She could use the time to do something she enjoys. Even while she waited for him, she could:

Edit pictures	Meditate
Paint her nails	Watch a movie
Learn something new	Garden
Call a friend	Listen to music
Read	Do something creative

Can you think of other activities she could have chosen instead of becoming upset? Would she feel more empowered or less empowered if she chose to use the unexpected time to do something she enjoys? In the long run, is she letting him off the hook or will repeatedly choosing to do things that feel good make her life better?

Another example is the perspective you take about what you are doing. For example, you can want to be successful at something (getting a new job or a promotion, or winning a game, etc.). One individual may perceive their desire to win as not wanting to loose, while another person sees it as pursuit of wining—not the avoidance of failure. Always focus on what you want, not what you do not want. Pursue success instead of attempting to avoid failure. You will be more successful when you focus on what you want.

The processes described in Chapter 36 enable you to shift the filters that create your reality.

14: Coherent Thought

Quantum theory provides us with a striking illustration of the fact that we can fully understand a connection though we can only speak of it in images and parables.
Werner Heisenberg

In quantum physics, quantum coherence means that subatomic particles are able to cooperate. Subatomic waves, or particles, can communicate with each other because they are highly interlinked by bands of common electromagnetic fields.

If you've never heard of quantum physics, don't be intimidated. When I was in school I was taught that an atom was the smallest building block of humans and other things. Now we know there are smaller building blocks than atoms. We can measure some of these smaller things, much like we can see cells through a microscope. There are other things we can't see yet, but scientists are aware they exist because of the effect they have on other things. Atomic merely means at the level where matter (i.e. cells) are built. Subatomic is smaller than atoms.

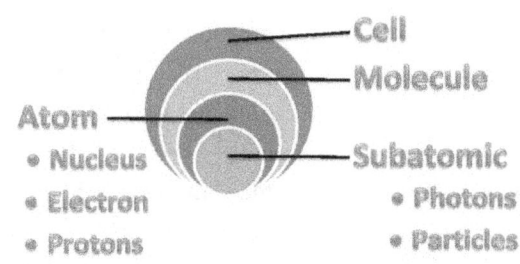

All physical matter (atoms and larger) are said to behave in ways described in Classic Physics. But unlike atoms and large physical objects, subatomic particles don't behave the same way. They can have patterns, either waves or streams. There is evidence that observation of subatomic particles can change the particle.

There is more that we just don't know because we have not discovered all there is to discover and do not yet have the ability to measure things that are even smaller. To think any other way is to risk slowing progress.

Physics dealing with the subatomic level is called Quantum Physics. They needed a different name because rules that work with Classic Physics don't explain what has been observed with subatomic particles.

The following information is provided to help you understand why *what we think* is important by shedding light on the relationship between your thoughts and the outcomes you experience every day. If thinking that small, invisible things can have a significant effect on your life feels like a stretch of the imagination, consider the power of viruses, germs, and bacteria.

Think about how much damage something that tiny can do to your body or mind. Also think about how beneficial tiny things are for you. If you're squeamish about the fact that your body is actually an entire ecosystem and not just you, skip the next two paragraphs.

Microorganisms inhabit our body, live on our skin, and in our intestines. Although no one has actually counted how many cells exist in our bodies or how many microbiotas[c] inhabit our bodies and live on our skin, the general consensus of the Human Microbiome Project is that what we think of as our bodies are composed of 10 times more microbiota than human cells. The microbiota cells are much smaller than human cells, so even though there are more of them, in size/weight current researchers estimate human cells still make up about 97% of our mass. In healthy individuals, the relationship between our bodies and

---
[c] Formerly called normal flora

microbiota is symbiotic, a harmonious and mutually beneficial partnership. Neither humans, nor the microbiotas that live on and in us, could survive without the other. Microbiotas aid the digestive process and may even help to remove dead skin from our faces.

It is clear that humans cannot live without the healthy relationship with microbiota. Microbiotas help us digest carbohydrates and extract nutrients from our food so our blood can deliver it to our cells. The Microbiota work with and may even train our immune system to recognize intruders.

A sense of coherence between one's life and personal values has a positive influence on health because there are more waves with Constructive Interference arising from their thoughts. Generally, individuals who have significant adverse events during their lives have negative health impacts, but developing a positive mental attitude can offset the negative impact of adverse life events. For example, researchers who followed Israeli women who stayed healthy despite experiences in concentration camps during WWII referred to this sense of coherence as salutogenesis.[244]

The way I think of the quantum level of reality, including subatomic particles, is that they respond to subtler energy than atoms. Fritz-Albert Popp researched both healthy and unhealthy subjects and eventually concluded good health was a state of perfect subatomic communication (coherence) and ill health was a state where communication breaks down. We are ill when our waves are out of sync. Our emotions let us know whether our waves are in sync. When we have Constructive Interference toward something we desire, we're feeling joyful. When we have Destructive interference, we're feeling stressed and our emotions are in lower Zones on the EGSc.

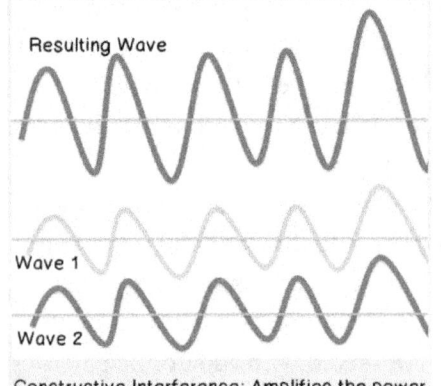

When the waves are in sync, they begin acting like one giant wave and one giant subatomic particle. Coherence creates the ability to communicate, like a highly sophisticated computer system.

In Quantum Physics, waves are encoders and carriers of information. When two waves are in phase (sync), and overlap each other (technically referred to as *interference*) the combined amplitude of the waves is greater than the combined amplitude of the separate waves; there is a compounding effect.

Now, think of thoughts as a pattern of energy with the ability to affect subatomic particles. Imagine that a thought is wave 1 and a desire is wave 2. In this case, the waves are in sync (thoughts and desires are in sync). The individual in this situation would not be stressed about this subject—waves in sync do not create tension. The resulting outcome is positive. Popp found that individuals whose waves were in-sync were healthy.

This is consistent with research indicating that positive and optimistic individuals enjoy significantly better health[245] and greater success.[246] A pilot study by The HeartMath Institute achieved a 36% reduction in pain ratings by increasing heart coherence in a group that had moderate to severe perceived pain. The same technique reduced negative emotions by 49% and perceived stress by 16% while physical limitations decreased by 42%. The control group was unchanged.[247] This successful intervention included instructions to be more aware of their feelings and emotions and use self-regulatory techniques to shift into a more coherent state of mind to achieve heart coherence.[248]

Constructive Interference could be represented by the desire "I want a job where I make enough to take good care of my family" amplified by the belief "I am well prepared to find a good job." The math we are taught in elementary school relates to Classic Physics. The same math does not work in Quantum Physics.

When what you want and what you believe you can achieve don't conflict your thoughts are in-sync (Constructive Interference) and energy on the quantum level is working in your favor. Everything from the function of your cells (immune, digestive, cognitive, and central nervous system), to the thoughts you think and the words you speak are supportive of achieving your desire. There is power in Constructive Interference as illustrated by the compounding effect seen in the amplification of the wave in the diagram.

The amount of energy it takes to shift thought into alignment with desires is far less than the energy required to make an equal change in the world of Classic Physics where:

Work = Force x Distance
Force = Mass X Acceleration

I'm not Einstein, but I've come up with a way to attempt to explain Interference mathematically. Constructive Interference acts as a multiplier because it increases power and Destructive Interference acts as a divider because it decreases power. Begin with the following equation:

Interference = Desire x Belief = Power (multiplier/strength/energy)

With a belief that one can accomplish a desire, Constructive Interference increases the power the individual has to achieve the desired goal.

Constructive Interference = Desire x 100 (belief = "I can")

With an "I want it but I believe it is possible" belief, Destructive Interference decreases the power the individual has to achieve the desired goal.

Destructive Interference = Desire x 0 (belief = "I can't")

I created the following chart to illustrate a few of the mindsets and how they would affect the power or energy to achieve the desired goal. Fractions or percentages would be used as the multiplier between 0 and 1.

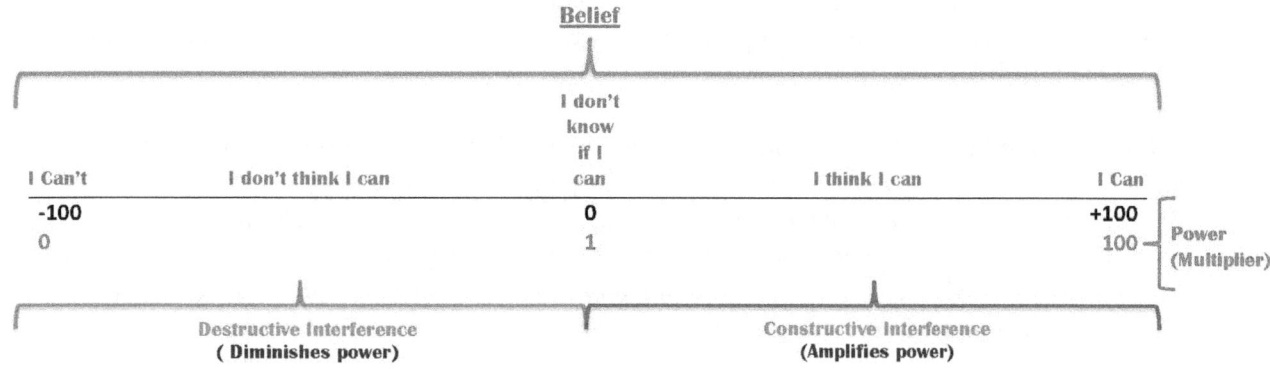

This next example is not yet explainable using modern science, but anyone who has deliberately attained and sustained a positive mental attitude will tell you they've observed this effect. It is also documented in Carl Jung's work in synchronicity.

Published research reports about (currently) inexplicable things are common. Experiments in quantum entanglement and quantum coherence in biological molecules is considered proved at experimental levels.[249] In replicated experiments, researchers have been able to measure changes in the brains of individuals who are separated by distance where changes to one affected the other while at a distance.[250] Also currently unexplainable but documented are incidents where a loved one experiences symptoms of physical distress at the same time a loved on suffers an actual injury. In one instance, a nurse who did not regularly experience headaches was suddenly in severe pain from a headache centered in the back of her head.[251] After going home and taking pain pills to help her headache she learned her brother had been shot in the back of the head at the same time she developed the headache.

Some people are reticent to share examples of such events in their own lives. I'd love to have your stories. Because we cannot yet explain how they happen, old superstitious ideas and stigmas can be associated with anyone who claims such experiences. But in groups where folks are more open-minded and less concerned with being adversely judged, it is my experience that almost everyone has stories of synchronicities that, while fortunately not as tragic as the nurse's story, are nonetheless compelling. It is often difficult to verify such stories. I've had numerous times in my life that made me a believer. Or, perhaps it would be more accurate to say, events that kept me believing. The earliest incident I remember was when I was under 10-years old and I woke up and told my Mom that her brother and his wife and their three children were going to come for a visit the following summer. Mom and I were in the midst of arguing about how many children my uncle had, with her maintaining that he only had two and my insisting he had three, when the phone rang and it was my uncle who rarely called. He was calling to tell us that he and his wife were expecting and that they wanted to come from Michigan to California to visit us the following summer.

I still remember my mom questioning me after the call. She was convinced that my uncle had called the day before and spoken with me because there was no way she could conceive of for me to know they had a baby on the way. I had dreamed it and was sure the dream gave me accurate information. I was too young to *know* we shouldn't **know** things in that way. I have continued to experience synchronicities throughout my life. What sort of synchronicities have you experienced?

The writings of many of the greatest business minds tell stories about synchronicities that occurred after they believed they could succeed and decided they would find a way to do so but did not know what that way would be. Soon after they made the decision they'd go somewhere and be introduced to or meet (by happenstance) exactly the right person to move their goal forward. If you read biographies of men like Henry Ford, Napoleon Hill, and Joseph Murphy they are filled with such stories. This is not luck. Decisions have power.

Two of my favorite quotes are from philosophers who wrote about the power of decisions. The German philosopher Johann von Goethe wrote:

Until one is committed, there is hesitancy, the chance to draw back; always ineffectiveness. Concerning all acts of initiative and creation there is one elementary truth, the ignorance of which kills countless ideas and splendid plans; that the moment one definitely commits oneself, then Providence moves too. All sorts of things occur to help one that would never otherwise have occurred. A whole stream of events issues from the decision raising in one's favor all manner of unforeseen incidents and meetings and material assistance which no one could have dreamed would come his way.

Once you make a decision, the universe conspires to make it happen.
Ralph Waldo Emerson

Remember: Not making a decision is a decision. **Make Decisions** that feel good for long-term goals. Short-term goals can de-rail your long-term goals (i.e. drugs and alcohol). Drug and alcohol problems begin because a person wants to feel better and does not have skills to do feel better in a healthier way.

We may not know exactly how it occurs, although it is not a difficult jump to see the link between the compounding effect of Coherent Interference and the synchronicities that are commonly reported. The Harvard Men's Study, (formally the Grant Study) began in the 1930's followed 268 Harvard men for the rest of their lives. Individuals who were positively focused, which includes positive self-regard and belief in one's abilities, were far more successful than those who were not positively focused, despite all of them having the advantage of a Harvard education.

Individual positivity or negativity had a great impact on success in all areas of life including business, marriage, and health. The correlation between a positive attitude and Coherent Interference is obvious. You must believe you can (have positive expectations) before you can achieve Coherent Interference.

> *The absence of negative emotions is not the same as the presence of positive emotions.*

Herbert Fröhlich, of the University of Liverpool, was one of the first to introduce the idea that some sort of collective vibration is responsible for getting proteins to cooperate with each other (in our bodies) and carry out instructions of DNA and cellular proteins. Waves (at the quantum level) synchronize activities for the living system. Positive thinking creates Constructive Interference, allowing clear communication between the cells of the body.

Negative thinking creates Destructive Interference that interferes with communication between the cells of the body. Desires are always about positive emotion and positive motion forward. Negative thinking, by definition, is in opposition to goals and positive motion forward. Anything less than positive thinking loses the beneficial impact of Coherent Interference.

Researchers at Harvard found that positive emotions reduce the risk of developing heart disease by 50%.[252] Heart disease is the number one cause of death, responsible for about 33% of all deaths. Boehm's research report clearly stated that the absence of negative emotions was not the same as the presence of positive emotions. Positive emotions are required to obtain the health benefits. This fits the theory that positive emotions create clear communication between our cells, evinced by (or supported by) Coherent Interference while neutral emotions and negative emotions do not create Coherent Interference.

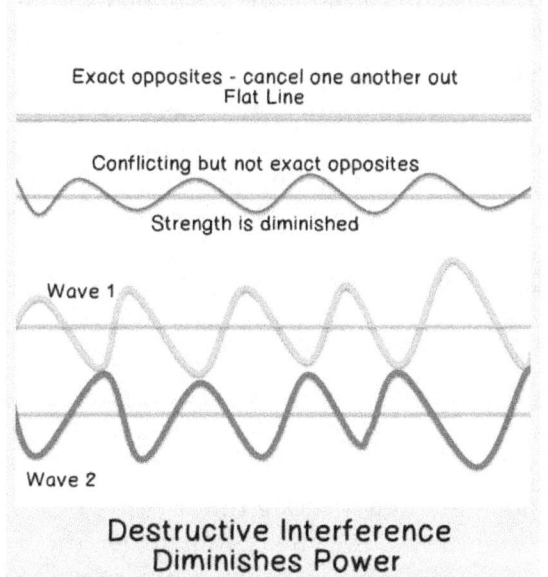

Negative emotions create Destructive Interference. The flat line at the top of the chart is indicative of someone who wants something but whose belief is opposite the desire. For example, the desire "I want a job where I make enough to take good care of my family" contrasted with the belief "It is impossible to find a good job in this economy" would be a flat line.

The lower power wave (conflicting thought) indicate the same desire combined with a less pessimistic (but still not positive) belief "It will take a long time to find a good job in this economy."

Mathematically, $1 \times .5 = 50\%$ *power*

Can you feel how conflict between the belief and the desire create tension or stress? This stress exists at the quantum level, which is why it is the root cause of ill health. When our thoughts and beliefs are in sync, tension (stress) is lower.

Although many people try, I have not found evidence of a way to pull back our desires and maintain positive emotions. I have found ways to shift our beliefs to be more coherent with our desires. Increasing Constructive Interference on the quantum level magnifies our success and our health. Better cellular communication could explain the greater cognitive abilities that are documented when people are in positive emotional states. Improved immune and digestive function could have similar explanations.

Imagine that our thoughts are waves. A healthy, positively focused individual will have more coherent and positive thoughts. In other words, their thoughts will be consistently looking for solutions and believing they exist, their thoughts will reflect a belief that they will get through whatever hardship or turmoil they are surrounded by and be able to move forward. Or, if their life is going well, that it will continue to do so. Their waves are in sync, combining and amplifying one another. Communication with the body is consistent and clear. The level of stress is low.

On the other hand, someone who is experiencing illness will want the same things, they will want to get through it and move on, and they will want to believe things will turn out all right, but their negative bias will create Destructive Interference with the desires, thereby leaving the positive desires without enough power to manifest. Someone whose life is going well but who believes that it will not continue to do so creates Destructive Interference with continued wellbeing which eventually manifests in their reality.

When we think a thought, an "electrical charge occurs in our brain that causes the synapses to grow closer together in order to decrease the distance the electrical charge has to cross . . . the brain is rewiring its own circuitry, physically changing itself, to make it easier and more likely that the proper synapses will spark together—in essence, making it easier for the thought to be triggered."[253] In essence, once you think a thought it is easier for you to think the thought again. If you repeatedly think the thought it begins acting like a belief. A belief is a thought you've thought repeatedly, which your brain then uses as a filter to interpret reality.

During my life time, we've shifted from a view of cellular communication that was the equivalent of a key being able to find its own keyhole to one that involves biophotons that move at the speed of light and vibration.[254] Science does not have all the answers yet, but this new direction answers more questions. It is clear that a lot is going on that we have been unaware of because it occurs on a subtler level than our *vivid senses* allow us to observe. We can deliberately cultivate awareness of the subtler sensory feedback. We have sensory feedback that informs us about our state of coherence but most humans are taught not to trust it or to trust it less than their *vivid senses*.

Imagine holding a meeting with hundreds of people in a room. You cannot hear the hum of the air conditioner. When you sit quietly in the same room when it is empty, you are able to discern the hum of the air conditioner.

In our normal state, input from our *five vivid senses* is much like the meeting room with hundreds of people. The input from those senses is so clear and strong, the ability to perceive the subtler aspects of our environment is muted. We have far more than five senses. They are more accurately categorized as the five *vivid senses*. We know that when one of the five *vivid senses* is muted, as in someone who is deaf or blind, the perceptual ability of the remaining senses increases.

Three examples of thoughts and their coherence (or lack thereof) are shown below. The first example is of someone who lacks resilience and is in a low emotional state. Their thoughts oppose their desires leading to Destructive Coherence because of the negative thought patterns, which can cause a downward spiral. Notice the negative self-criticism. In each example, Emotional Guidance would let the person know when thoughts were not productive.

Thoughts	Power Multiplier	Direction
I can't believe this is falling apart. Nothing ever works out for me.	0	↓
Every time I think something is finally working out it crashes.	0	↓
If I wasn't stupid I might be able to find someone who loves me.	0	↓
No one is going to hire someone my age.	0	↓
I can't remember the last time something worked out really well for me.	0	↓
I might as well stop trying. It never works out for me.	0	↓
I must be cursed. What is the point?	0	↓
I don't know what to do. I can't do anything well.	0	↓
Life is awful and then you die.	0	↓
I'm a loser.	0	↓

In the next example, the random and unfocused thoughts of someone whose thoughts are inconsistent cancel one another out. The person has some positive thoughts, but not enough to cause thriving. If the thoughts continue to be more negative than positive, a downward spiral is a possibility.

Thoughts	Power Multiplier	Direction
I really hope this will turn out OK (without any real feeling of hope)	0	↓
Sometimes things turn out OK	100	↑
Maybe my brother will help me out (hopeful but no real faith)	.79	↗
Bad things happen in three's; what is next?	0	↓
At least I have people in my life who will always love me no matter what	100	↑
I hope Joe never hears about this; he will never let me live it down	.25	↙
Every time I think things are going well something bad happens	0	↓
I've been in worse situations. I can probably find my way out of this	.75	↗

Deliberately choosing to focus on better feeling thoughts could turn the situation around and create the far more desirable upward spiral. Most people's thought patterns are a lot like the second example. If they understood the importance of focusing on what they want with positive expectation, they would make a greater effort to think more thoughts that would benefit them.

Each one of the thoughts that has a multiplier of less than 100 could be improved using metacognition and reappraisal. For example, worrying Joe will hear you've had a hard time is giving Joe's opinion of us power. That thought could be reappraised by focusing on the fact that if Joe is in a state of appreciation he will probably feel compassion toward our situation and that if Joe ridicules our situation it would be a reflection of Joe's own low emotional state.

The concern about Joe finding out could also be reappraised with the concept that by the time Joe finds out the situation will be solved and Joe (if we insist on making his opinion important) will be impressed at our resilience while we dealt with a tough situation. Research shows that we typically underestimate other people's opinions of us and this is especially true when our own self-esteem is low.

Constructive Interference is at the root of why businesses have taught goal setting and other techniques that have proven successful, even if they didn't know about Constructive Interference. Setting goals creates greater coherence and amplifies the ability to achieve them. In the third example, of thoughts from a positively focused and optimistic mindset, the coherence of thoughts that support the individual's underlying desires increase wellbeing in all areas of life where this thought pattern is present.

Thoughts	*Power Multiplier*	*Direction*
Every time I think something bad has happened to me it turns out to be good when I get a clearer view of it	*100*	↑
I wonder what the silver lining will be here?	*100*	↑
I know there is a solution. There always is. I wonder what it is.	*100*	↑
Things always work out well for me. I don't have to know the ending to know this will work out well, too.	*100*	↑
I wonder what new things I will learn because of this?	*100*	↑
It is fun to solve problems.	*75*	↗
I have lots of people who will help me if I need help.	*100*	↑
I am really blessed. My life is going well.	*100*	↑

When comparing the above examples of thoughts, the scattered, powerless nature of the middle example, the destructive power in the first, and the amplifying power in the third example can be felt. On the quantum level, we understand that as coherent thoughts and desires overlay one another, the combined strength is amplified. The last example is indicative of individuals whose situations are changing because the Constructive Interference of their thoughts have amplified power.

The middle example is a more common thought-pattern, characteristic of a person who seems to be moving in circles or chasing his own tail, so to speak. He moves around a little bit but often ends up back where he began.

He may change jobs only to find that six months later he has an equal number of similar problems in the new position as those he was experiencing in the role he left. Until he changes something about himself he will continue thinking in ways that lead to the same outcomes.

Sometimes an event in one's life causes a temporary decrease in one's perception of worthiness. This results in a decrease in wellbeing in areas that may have previously evinced a strong coherent pattern of thought toward their desires.

In essence, the emotional stance decreases. For individuals who live in the public eye, such as Donald Trump and Tiger Woods, it is possible to see the dip in their financial success while the emotional stance is lower. In the case of both of these men, it was trouble in their marriages that led to the lower emotional state which then impacted their financial success. Eventually, they return to their original chronic emotional stance and their finances improve. It is possible to shorten the duration of the downturns using the techniques outlined in this book. The same dips occur in the lives of people who do not live under the microscope of public opinion. If you think about your own life, you will see evidence of this. People who are more deliberate about their thoughts and use metacognitive processes are able to reduce the volatility even when some areas of their lives aren't as desired. Everyone has that power.

Someone can have cohesive positive thoughts about one area of life and destructive interference in another area of life. Some factors create spillover into many areas of life. Self-esteem, or worthiness, is one of the areas that will have an effect across the board. Other factors may only affect one aspect of life or an even narrower topic, such as a single relationship or goal.

Once you desire something, you won't be in-sync with your desire unless and until your thoughts are consistent with your ability to have the desire.

Want it + Don't believe you can have it = stress/discord/Destructive Interference

Want it + Believe you can have it now = Constructive Interference/harmony/low stress

Once you want something you cannot stop wanting it. But to fully understand what that means you have to understand that what you want is not the specific thing that you think it is. If you fall in love with someone, you can stop wanting that particular person because what you really want is the way that person makes you feel when you're in love. If you want a new sofa, it is the way you believe you will feel when you have that new sofa that is the real desire—the sofa is just the excuse you're using to feel that the way you want to feel.

Thoughts are a pattern of energy with the ability to affect subatomic particles. Your EGS will guide you toward greater positive (Constructive) coherence. Your heart is always in a positive, loving, appreciating, hopeful state. When you attempt to be other than that you can feel heartache. The more you bring your mind into alignment with your heart, the better you will feel and the better your life will become.

The HeartMath Institute has been studying Heart Rate Variability for a couple of decades. They define coherence as, "Coherence is the state when the heart, mind, and emotions are in energetic alignment and cooperation . . . it is a state that builds resiliency—personal energy is accumulated, not wasted—leaving more energy to manifest intentions and harmonious outcomes . . . When the physiological coherence mode is driven by a positive emotional state, we call it psychophysiological coherence. This state is associated with sustained positive emotion and a high degree of mental and emotional stability."[255] They could just as easily be discussing the results of using *The Smart Way*. I remember my former boss asking how I could display so much equanimity while being laid-off about six years ago. Our potential for equanimity is so great; it can remain stable in the midst of a lay-off that occurs during a bad economy.

Write one of your goals or desires at the top of the blank chart. Use the chart to record your own thoughts. Add arrows to indicate the whether your thought patterns are consistent or inconsistent with your goal. Nuances do matter. "I can" is not equal to "I think I can," use your EGS to feel for the difference between the two thoughts.

If your thoughts do not currently support your goals, use the metacognitive processes described in this book to shift your thoughts to ones that support your goals. A separate chart for each topic can be beneficial. However, the goal is not to complete a lot of charts. The goal is to pay attention and recognize how the emotional discord feels and then adjust your perception to one that feels better.

Do you need some help coming up with ideas for your topics? Do you have a co-worker who tends to be irritating to you? Are you happy with the current political climate? Are all your relationships as good as you want them to be? Do you have a health condition that is not as good as what you would like it to be? See if your thoughts are in alignment on these topics.

If you enjoy good health, you can use the way you feel when you are ill—such as when it feels like a cold is starting. Another alternative is to think about how you think about an illness someone you care about is experiencing. Remember mirror neurons and the influence of expectation.

Thoughts Worksheet	*Power Multiplier*	*Direction*

Another way to use the chart is to ask your friends about things you say on a regular basis. One example is "I can gain weight just from smelling the cakes in the bakery."

Because our society currently operates as if the quantum level does not exist or matter many common beliefs and phrases that do not serve our highest good are in common usage. I used to think such thoughts could not really matter. However, after consistently feeling for how different thoughts felt, I began to feel the discord of unsupportive thoughts in a stronger way. When that happened, I shifted my mindset away from unsupportive thoughts and my results changed.

Here are some more examples of common unproductive expressions:

- *A good man is hard to find.*
- *I always choose the slowest line at the checkout counter.*
- *I can never (fill in the blank). i.e. find my keys*
- *I always (fill in the blank). i.e. anything you don't want*
- *Nothing good lasts forever.*
- *I am always a day late and a dollar short.*
- *He does not respect me.*
- *I can't (fill in the blank). i.e. anything you want to do*
- *(fill in the blank) is too expensive for me to do.*
- *It's a once in a lifetime experience. (unless you only want to do it once)*

Just realizing you have more ability to exert control over how you feel by changing your perspective (and therefore your thoughts) about a subject reduces stress significantly.

Exercise

Create revised statements that are more empowering than the ones listed above. Can you think of expressions you think or say that may be creating Destructive Interference with your ability to achieve your goals?

Don't be afraid of your thoughts. Occasional negative thoughts won't kill you. The accumulation of your thoughts creates momentum. You just want your momentum to be more positive than negative. The more positive outweighs the negative, the better life feels, but any step in the direction of feeling better is good. This is not something you should, must, or ought to do. This is something you do because it feels better to do than not do. The benefits of doing it are secondary.

15: Happiness Defined

When I was 5 years old, my mother always told me that happiness was the key to life. When I went to school, they asked me what I wanted to be when I grew up. I wrote down 'happy'. They told me I didn't understand the assignment, and I told them they didn't understand life.
John Lennon

Ed Diener and his son, Robert Biswas-Diener teamed up to write, *Happiness: Unlocking the Mysteries of Psychological Wealth*. In the introduction they summed it up this way, "Flaubert was dead wrong in his assertion that happiness is stupid and selfish. Happiness, as it turns out, not only feels good, but is often good for you and for society."[256] They went on to cite specific benefits stating, "Research shows that happy people live longer, succumb to fewer illnesses, stay married longer, commit fewer crimes, produce more creative ideas, work harder and smarter on the job, make more money, and help others more."

In *The Happiness Advantage*, Shawn Achor mentioned the results of over 200 studies reflecting, "that happiness leads to success in nearly every domain, including work, health, friendship, sociability, creativity, and energy."[257] When Tal Ben-Shahar taught the first Happiness class it was the most popular class ever taught at Harvard University with about 800 students.[258] In his book, *Happier*, Ben-Shahar reflected on the relationship between happiness and success, describing it as one where happiness feeds success and success feeds happiness. He said, "All else being equal happy people have better relationships, are more likely to thrive at work, and also live better and longer. Happiness is a worthwhile pursuit, whether as an end in itself or as a means toward other ends."[259] The Academy of Management Perspectives published a paper in 2011 that stated, "A key conclusion is that happiness and the processes associated with happiness depend on perspective, especially level of analyses."[260] *The Smart Way* was developed as a practical and understandable method of teaching groups how the mind works in order to create intrinsic motivation to learn how to use Meta-cognitive Processes and Emotional Guidance, taking advantage of the human focus on self, knowing it leads to outcomes that improve life for everyone. In other words, *The Smart Way* teaches individuals how to consciously choose perspectives that increase happiness.

Sonja Lyubomirsky and Matthew D. Della Porta provide a good summary of known benefits of happiness in *Boosting Happiness and Buttressing Resilience: Results from Cognitive and Behavioral Interventions*,[261] which included:

Superior work outcomes
More activity, energy, and flow
To live longer
Higher levels of resilience
More likely to show good coping abilities
To have bolstered immune systems
Less likely to display symptoms of psychopathology
More likely to act cooperatively and pro-socially
Associated with relatively stronger social relationships

Other researchers have also identified:
Better digestive system function
Lower stress
Lower risk of heart disease[262]
More pro-health behaviors[263]
Less likely to commit crimes[264]
Lower risk of obesity and diabetes
Lower risk of depression and anxiety

As the research about happiness has grown, the pursuit of happiness has received some criticism in research that, on the surface, seemed to indicate contra-findings. I reviewed much of that research and found the reason for their results in their details. For example, researching individuals who are focused on *finding happiness* does not provide insight into the benefits of happiness. The study participants were unaware of their Emotional Guidance and did not have knowledge or tools to facilitate being happy. They were less happy than they would have been without a focus on a goal they did not know how to attain. The cure is not giving up the goal of being happy—the cure is knowledge of how to be happier.

This research does not speak to any contra-indications about happiness. It speaks to the great need humanity has for tools and knowledge that allow individuals to experience positive emotions quickly and easily. The search, combined with their lack of knowledge and skills about how to attain happiness, led to a diminishing belief in their ability to achieve happiness. As a result, they felt less empowered. Anyone who understands the information shared in these pages would be able to predict the outcome of their study. Happiness does not require pursuit. It does not require a search, it requires knowledge and skills. Fortunately, you have in your hands (or on your e-reader) knowledge and skills that facilitate happiness. The skills that help you create happiness are simple to understand—when the false premises believed by much of the world are eliminated. Happiness is within your reach.

The findings that individuals who were focused on the goal of happiness but did not know how to achieve it and therefore were more stressed and not as happy would be anticipated based on the EGS. The lack of knowledge about how to be happy would cause a lower emotional state and higher stress—thus decreasing happiness.

> *Happiness does not depend on outward things...but on the way we see them.*
> Leo Tolstoy

A more helpful study would gather data about an individual's current level of positivity, provide the knowledge and skills to increase happiness, and then take new measurements about the level of positivity. A study that followed the participants over time, looking at not only increased positivity but also health and relationship status would be of the greatest benefit to humanity.

When I introduced the idea that happiness and chronic stress are two ends of the same continuum, I mentioned that stress and happiness being opposites is not my definition of happiness. To me, this is a trait, but not the definition of stress and happiness. Many situations cause individuals to temporarily feel positive emotions. There is nothing wrong with enjoying things that make us happy, but using them as the basis for being happy sets us up for failure.

Basing happiness on outer conditions is the way most of the world currently approaches the subject. Some common, conditional happiness delaying techniques include:

I'll be happy when I find the person I want to marry.
I'll be happy when I get that promotion.
I'll be happy when I get to go _____ on vacation.
I'll be happy when I have a baby.
I'll be happy when I retire.
I'll be happy when my children are grown.
I'll be happy when I lose weight.
I'll be happy when I graduate.

Learning the skills that lead to sustainable happiness leads to a life that fulfills more of its potential. Unfortunately, outer focused criteria for happiness do not contribute to long-term sustainable happiness. Most outer focused paths lead to temporary happiness and often include undesirable side effects. In addition, individuals who delay happiness using excuses like the above criteria do not know how to be happy so when the stated goal is achieved, another reason to delay happiness is typically substituted.

Here are some facts that negate the above delaying tactics:
- Happy people are more likely to marry and stay married.
- Happiness increases the ability to attract a desirable mate.
- Happiness is a precursor to success. Individuals who are more positively focused enjoy more careers that are successful.[265, 266]
- Many people go on vacation and bring their unhappy selves with them; forgoing much of the joy they could have on their journey.
- Stress (lack of happiness) poses several risk factors for individuals who want to have a baby.[267, 268, 269] A stressed woman has more difficulty conceiving. Once conception occurs, a stressed woman's child has a higher risk of behavioral and sleep problems, asthma, and if she is depressed, the child's risk of depression increases. Even a depressed Father is linked to higher incidence of depression in the child.[270] The marriage of a happy couple provides the child with a more stable environment.
- By the time some people retire, they have been practicing unhappiness for a great many years. The habit of unhappiness is entrenched. While someone who really did not enjoy their profession will feel better than they did while working, there is a difference between feeling better and being happy. Also, the benefits of happiness (better health, lower risk of every disease studied, better immune system functioning, increased cognitive abilities, better relationships, more successful careers, and more) are so significant, why would anyone wait until the last quarter of their life to enjoy the benefits?
- Waiting until the children are grown to be happier results in your teaching your children that happiness is not a priority. It also means you will not be as good of a parent as you could be. My children would tell you there is a significant difference in my parenting once I learned how to be happy in a sustainable way. It is a positive improvement. In many ways I wish I had known what I now know throughout their childhoods because I know I would have been a better parent.
- Being happy facilitates healthy weight management.[271] The old paradigm of calories in equaling calories out has been overturned. Stress (which is essentially lack of happiness) disturbs the digestive system, causing the body to fight against your efforts to eat nutritiously and maintain the ideal body weight.

Basing our happiness on anything outside of ourselves brings the potential for adverse side effects. There is always the possibility that someone or something we cannot control will disappoint us. True Happiness requires greater stability and less reliance on outer, uncontrollable factors. The definition of True Happiness in Chapter 2 is the basis of my work because it is the only one in which the individual is empowered to choose happiness.

With outer, uncontrollable factors, results are inconsistent. What made an individual feel joy at one time could have no impact, or even a negative one, at another point in time.

For example, when I was 18, a Monday – Friday job paying $400 a month made me feel great joy. That same job today would be terribly upsetting. Even if the wages were adjusted for inflation, it would still be far below my expectations.

Our goals are ever changing. Movement from wherever we are in the direction we wish to go—whether that movement is in thought or deed—feels good. Movement away from our goals—whether in thought or deed—feels bad.

One more thing humanity does on a widespread scale is judge whether another's circumstances are good based on their personal desires. Each of us has a different perspective and desires that are uniquely our own. Our guidance considers our unique desires. The individual who wants to be a teacher is guided toward being a teacher, and the individual who wants to be an accountant is guided toward his goal. We feel good when we are moving toward our own goals.

If, when I was hired for the Monday-Friday job when I was 18, someone had begun pointing out to me how much less than many others I was making, or other aspects of my achievement they viewed as less than wonderful (based on their goals) it would have diminished my joy. Diminishing an achievement can diminish the motivation to be successful in the future, especially if the individual cares too much about what others think about their achievements. Lower intrinsic motivation results in lower success. Less success equates to less positive feedback. This creates a circle of repetitive negative outcomes.

> *True happiness comes from positive movement towards our goals.*

Some of us have family members who are experts at making us unhappy with our situation. We might be excited about movement in the direction we want to go and they immediately look for flaws in what we have achieved and point them out to us. They are comparing our achievement to their goals. We feel deflated by those encounters. If you have someone like that in your family or at work, it is often best not to share your excitement with him or her—so they do not go into their deflation routine. Give them the facts and share your excitement only with those who are supportive.

The International Journal of Wellbeing published a paper by Mark Walker promoting the idea of developing a happy pill to gain the advantages of positive emotions. A happy pill is not a good idea for a variety of reasons, including:

- Developing meta-cognitve skills that empower you to change your mood by changing your perspective is empowering and increases the internal locus of control. Internal locus of control is correlated with life-promoting behaviors including resilience.
- Reliance on a pill for happiness would increase the external locus of control, which is associated with poorer outcomes and mental health.
- Emotions serve a purpose. Their purpose is to guide us toward self-actualization and away from danger.
- A happy pill would be like going on vacation to Lake Tahoe by covering the inside of your windows with pictures of Lake Tahoe so it just looks like you're in Lake Tahoe.
- Drugs have adverse side effects. Authentic happiness has beneficial side effects.
- True happiness is not difficult to achieve or sustain when you learn *The Smart Way* and there are proven positive benefits of authentic happiness. Authentic happiness is also free.

One of the arguments in favor of the happiness pill is genetic differences in happiness levels which researchers generally put at 50%. I disagree with their findings for a variety of reasons. They're based on twin studies, but there are tendencies passed on in utero that affect thought processes. Since the twins studied were separated at birth, their shared pre-birth experiences still bind them. Quantum physics has demonstrated that twins separated at birth retain a connection. We don't know what we don't know about that and to conclude without knowing more that genetics accounts for 50% of happiness levels is jumping to a conclusion for which there is no basis. Other research demonstrates that a Mother's depression during pregnancy affects the child's risk of depression through age 16. They've also found there is a correlation to the Dad's depression during pregnancy, but they can't explain how the connection works.

The premise that happiness is 50% genetic ties back to "following increases (or even decreases) in their well-being, people tend to return to their baseline levels of happiness over time."[272] Habits of thought are habits. Very few people understand how to change one's habits of thought, which is what causes the return to baseline. The unique circumstances that change the emotional state cause individuals to focus on something that feels better (or worse) for a while, which changes their happiness level. But as the novelty wears off, they return to their prior habits of thought. The research also points to the stability of personality traits, which for a long time was considered stable throughout life. A study that evaluated 3,990 found that personality changes can improve health outcomes.[273]

Newer research demonstrates that personality traits are not stable and can be changed.[274, 275, 276, 277, 278,] Personality is based on habits of thought and is strongly tied to one's emotional state. When someone feels better, their personality tends to be more outgoing than when the same person feels upset. They're essentially pointing to two effects and naming them as evidence that the genetic predisposition is accurate. I welcome a challenge from Sonja Lyubomirsky. Give me a group of test subjects to teach *The Smart Way*, and they will be able to demonstrate that they are able to change their happiness level, their habits of thought, and personality traits in positive directions.

Finally, hedonic adaptation is cited as a final reason why happiness cannot be increased. Hedonic adaptation is the human tendency to take what one has for granted after one has had it for a while. But just because our society takes things we have for granted does not mean we cannot change our habits of thought and begin appreciating what is available to us. I teach appreciation and use appreciation as a regular practice in my life. I can make myself emotionally high just by doing an appreciation exercise where I appreciate things that have always been freely available to me—the air I breathe, enough food to eat, plates to eat it from a table to set the plate upon, a mouth capable of tasting the food, a body brilliant enough to digest the food and deliver appropriate nutrients to about 70 million cells and separate out the waste and dispose of it properly.

Yes, hedonic adaptation is the norm. But if one is okay being considered weirdly happy, there are many natural ways to increase and sustain happier emotional states. Savoring past and future events is another way to amp up the happiness quota. One can plan their life so there is always something to look forward to. It can be a chance to have a meal with a friend or something larger—it is not as much about what is being savored or looked forward to, as it is feeling the emotion. Most of the 1st world has plenty of things they can savor. I like to plan vacations well in advance because it allows me to enjoy them for months even before I go as I savor the anticipation. Right now one of my girlfriends from the UK is planning a visit that is four months off and every day I savor the fun we will have together while she is here. I am already enjoying her visit.

A tendency not to adapt fully to negative life events is also cited as something that can prevent one from achieving increasing levels of happiness. Yes, some people cling to what was and never find the silver lining in what has become. But there is also a great deal of evidence about Posttraumatic Growth, something I am a beneficiary of, that shows we can become more following adverse life circumstances. The key is in looking for the silver lining. You can come to know that it will be there so well that you are looking for and finding it even before you've fully processes a negative event. Joseph and Hefferon reported that "between 30 – 70% of people tend to report some benefit following an adverse experience."[279] For the most part, they're finding that silver lining organically—without being trained to look for it. With a little training those percentages can increase significantly. Yes, this takes practice, but I know it is possible because I've done it.

Just like the Losada ration that was introduced a number of years ago, when I first heard the assertions that 50% of happiness was genetically determined, it felt off. Since I trust my guidance, feeling off is off in my book. Dr. Robert Holden has been teaching happiness for nearly 25 years. Five years ago I asked him his opinion about the 50% genetic and he concurred with me based on what he has seen in his students.

In the article, Mr. Walker argues that a happy pill for everyone is no different than using depression medicine. Depressed people are suffering from a mental illness and I strongly encourage them to learn *The Smart Way* while following their physician's instructions regarding treatment and medications. I've seen enough people use *The Smart Way* to overcome chronic depression after decades of suffering from chronic depression that pills and therapy could not resolve that I would never recommend a pharmacy only therapy.

You would not say to your young child, "Don't bother learning to walk. I can put you in this wheelchair and you can just roll around—no need to use the legs you were born with." Attempting to substitute a Happy Pill for skills that utilize innate sensory feedback systems is just as unhealthy and wrong-guided. I'm not saying that when someone is ill not to use pharmacology, but if someone doesn't know how to use his mind-body, teach him.

Positivity

As scientists study the subject of positivity, they also attempt to define it. In some instances, happiness is measured by a small action that creates a better emotion temporarily. This research demonstrates that the more positive emotion is good for the individual feeling it and also for those she interacts with, including strangers.

Researchers are using numerous terms to describe happiness including positivity, optimism, and General Well-Being (GWB).

It does feel great to experience something that causes a temporary lifting of one's mood. The difference between a mood temporarily uplifted by something outside of ourselves over which we have no real control and deliberately adjusting our perspective to feel better is like the difference between a baby who has learned to crawl and a world-class Olympic decathlon gold medalist.

The recent focus on happiness has received some backlash from some researchers. One common criticism of positivity is the belief that negative emotions are being repressed. This is not based on empirical evidence. In fact, in *Positivity*, Barbara L. Fredrickson, Ph. D. states, "On the contrary, resilience is marked by exquisite emotional agility."[280]

There have been publications arguing that anxiety is good for us. They are right that we should feel anxiety—anxiety, like any other emotion—is communication. We should feel anxiety for 60 seconds or less, just long enough to assure ourselves that a solution is possible. We don't have to solve the problem—just the knowledge (which our EGS will affirm) that the problem is solvable—reduces anxiety. Reducing anxiety increases our cognitive abilities. Believing a solution is available primes our mind to be ready when information that leads to a solution comes into our awareness. I'm serious about the sixty seconds. In fact, for someone who has been utilizing her guidance consistently for a few years, sixty seconds may be longer than necessary. Solutions and the belief that solutions exist creates intrinsic motivation. You cannot believe a solution is possible and remain anxious (unless you doubt you'll be able to accomplish the solution). In anxiety, you do not have cognitive access to the best path to the solution.

Some arguments have been put forth that positive emotions are not always good because anxiety can be a call to action. The goal is not to remain always joyful and carefree. The goal is to know that no matter what happens an individual knows how to return to being joyful. The accomplishment of a goal is not necessary to feel happy. Just progress toward the goal will bring emotional relief. When we feel anxiety, we should recognize it for what it is, Emotional Guidance, and then take appropriate action. Once appropriate actions begin, we can feel immeasurably better knowing that we are moving in the right direction. Their emotional response will give us this feedback.

The "call to action" resulting from anxiety pales in comparison to the "call to action" from passionate interest. The anxious individual does not dream the big dream. The anxious call is much further down on Maslow's Hierarchy of Needs. Typically, anxiety involves moving away from something undesired. Essentially, retreat. Passionate interest, on the other hand, is a movement toward something bigger than oneself that increases energy and motivation.

Optimists and pessimists are both often adamant about the correctness of their stance. Looking deeper, we find that they are both right because of the impact of expectation on outcome.

Examined more deeply, it becomes clear that positive expectation results in more desirable outcomes:

"People who regard themselves as highly efficacious act, think, and feel differently from those who perceive themselves as inefficacious. They produce their own future, rather than simple foretell it."[281]

15: Happiness Defined

The Power of Hope
Optimism and hope are entwined. Without optimism, it is difficult to be hopeful. With optimism, hope is ever present. The Regional Research Institute (RRI) for Human Services at Portland State University conducts research focused on the goal of improving the lives of under-served children, adults, and families. RRI published a paper on the importance of hope that supports many of the points the reader needs to understand about how the presence of (or absence of) hope leads to desirable (or undesirable) outcomes.

A child in an untenable situation, one most people cannot imagine enduring, can endure and even do well in some areas, if hope is present. A young woman whose childhood included frequent violence and daily sexual abuse maintained good grades and an outward appearance that did not arouse suspicion. She attributes her ability to maintain outwardly calm to a belief that a relative would take her away on her 16th birthday. That promise kept her from giving up hope, shortening the time she thought she would have to endure the situation. Basically, she always had hope that the future would be better than the present.

Her belief that the better future would be hers helped motivate her to do well in school because she recognized that if she failed school, getting out of the violent environment would be temporary—she knew success in school could lead to a safer future. RII said "... building and maintaining hope may be particularly important for young people with emotional and behavioral challenges, because hope is a key part of both resilience and recovery. People who work with adolescents can benefit from understanding the role that hope can play, and how hopefulness can be increased, during this crucial time of transition to adulthood.

Hope as we define it[282] is a future-oriented pattern of thinking that involves the abilities to:
(a) set clear and challenging "stretch goals,"
(b) develop the strategies or pathways to those goals, and
(c) muster the necessary motivation to use those pathways to pursue objectives.

All three hope components are necessary in order to successfully attain goals. Success in this context does not simply mean "getting what one wants," but rather ***getting what one wants in such a way that mental health benefits are maximized*** [emphasis added].

When each of the hope components is present in sufficient magnitude, people will **expect** to succeed. Even when they do not succeed, however, high- as compared to low-hope people are better able to cope with their failure experiences.

When low-hope people fail to achieve goals, they typically cannot create alternate pathways to go around obstacles. Accordingly, these individuals with low hope are prone to:
- Give up,
- To criticize their own abilities,
- And to experience strong negative emotions.

On the other hand, when individuals with high hope fail to attain goals, they:
- Simply acknowledge that they did not try hard enough,
- Or that they did not have access to the most useful pathways.

Instead of becoming stuck in criticizing themselves, the high hopers get busy in finding solutions. As a result, any negative emotions experienced by high-hope people are not likely to incapacitate them. On this point, we have found that high- relative to low-hope people **try harder and persevere longer after failure experiences precisely because of their abilities to retain their positive emotions.**"[283]

The Regional Research Institute for Human Services at Portland State University suggests *"that having hope is vital for the successful transition from adolescence to satisfying adult roles . . . and [they] proposed that **intentionally instilling hope in young people should be a societal priority**".*[284]

I completely agree with their findings regarding hope. I disagree, however, on the method they recommend to solve this problem for at-risk children, but not because their method doesn't work. It will often work. I do not believe their recommendation is the best practice for a variety of reasons:

1. From a practical point of view, it is expensive and therefore, unattainable for the vast majority of children in need,
2. Not all **children in need** are easily identifiable. Children may come from two parent households with adequate (or more than adequate income) and still be in need of hope for a variety of reasons, including, but not limited to:
    - Authoritarian Parenting Styles
    - Permissive Parenting Styles
    - Rejecting Parenting Styles
    - Abuse
    - Child's Self-Worth judgments
3. Relying on the Emotional Guidance System is more reliable because it is always available and not subject to personal biases a mentor may introduce into the equation

The Regional Research Institute use what we know about attachment and the way attachment to caregivers provides a sense of security or safety that children return to when they are stretching their limits and begin to feel insecure or uncomfortable. This sense of having a safety net allows children to feel secure enough to venture out into the world because they know they have a safe place to return to if they become frightened. "Over time, children with secure bases will internalize beliefs in the availability of other people, in themselves as being lovable, and in the world as being a safe and predictable place. If negative life events interrupt the development of the beliefs that support a hopeful outlook, the beliefs may shift to less hopeful ones."[285]

Negative Life Events defined:

Death of a parent, life-threatening illness in a parent or the child, or parental psychological disorders, economic patterns necessitating parents working long hours and thereby being less available and/or less responsive, divorce, war, military deployment of a parent, eviction.

Researchers find that insecure attachment styles can cause different reactions.[286]
- Refusal to develop relationships with others out of fear of rejection,
- Self-sabotaging attempts to cultivate favor with others (allowing oneself to be used), or
- Attempts to dull emotional pain with drugs and alcohol

If left unchecked, the sense of being adrift without a safe harbor can lead to increasing problems with anxiety, depression, self-sabotaging behaviors, and restricted cognitive abilities from the lower emotional states experienced by such individuals. Together, these factors can lead to downward spirals of both emotion and behavior, which ultimately move them further from hopefulness.

Maslow's Hierarchy of Needs stood the test of time for many years before it began to lose favor. Although it is no longer considered 100% accurate, it is still instructive in helping to demonstrate that as a downward spiral gains momentum, self-actualization needs such as good grades, admission to an esteemed school, and a good job begin to lose significance as long as the greater needs of love, belonging, and safety are unmet. During adolescence, the love and belonging needs are not usually sought in the home. Some common ways immature individuals seek to fulfil these needs include:

- Romantic relationships
- Gangs
- Having a baby
- Sports
- Military service affiliation

Because more significance than youthful relationships can usually handle is put upon the meaning of and continuation of the romantic relationship, the power dynamic in the relationship is off kilter. This leaves the individual who needs the relationship the most at the mercy of the partner. This can lead to many undesirable outcomes including, but not limited to:

1. Willingness to engage in undesired activities in order to please the partner and maintain the relationship—sometimes at steep costs to personal safety and self-esteem,
2. Promiscuousness in the misguided belief that sex will lead to a steady relationship,
3. Lowering of standards in order to have a relationship at any cost,
4. Good relationships ending due to too much pressure from an insecure partner

I think the problem with gangs goes without saying.

I can't count the number of girls I've known who believed that having a baby would provide them with someone who would love them. The disconnect between this and the Mother's these same girls say they hated was obvious to someone whose mental abilities was not impaired by a low emotional state and its constricted ability to think clearly.

Sports can provide a healthy outlet, unless and until the child is let down by being kicked off (or not selected for) the team. Just as in relationships where too much pressure is present, the emotional suffering of a child who relies on sports to satisfy unmet emotional needs for safety and security and be tremendous and lead to undesired outcomes.

Military service often helps a teen experiencing unmet emotional needs turn his or her life around. The sense of belonging to a group (i.e. Semper fi) can be a powerful force and fulfil the need to belong and to serve a greater purpose. While it works for many teenagers, military service is not without its drawbacks and is not a panacea for everyone who does not have a safe harbor.

Understanding how to use one's emotional guidance is a better solution because it is consistent and always present.

Adults would help those they wish to help more if they are aware of the relationship between emotional state and behavior as well as between emotional state and the ability to focus on higher goals (self-realization vs. more fundamental goals). Adults who preach about attaining the higher goals to teenagers whose basic needs are not met will be ineffective.

"Research has indicated that the key characteristic of resilient children is that they find their own mentors in the community."[287]

Although I am not aware of any research on using one's emotional guidance as an ever-present mentor, I and many of my students have done this and felt profound differences in anxiety, depression, confidence, and overall success in every important area of life. During childhood, my mentors were historical figures and fictional characters in books and movies (i.e. Daniel Boone, Jim Bowie, John Wayne, and more). I was not taught to use characters in books as mentors; it was more that I followed a desire to emulate my heroes. In addition to following one's emotional guidance, a child can be taught to deliberately seek mentors in books and movies.

In order of value, I rank mentors as follows:
1. Emotional Guidance (when understood)
2. Psychologically mature mentor with high availability and low personal agenda
3. Fictional characters and historical figures in books and movies

Not only do I believe that the purpose of emotions is to guide us away from danger and toward self-actualization, they are the best mentor because they are always present and seem to possess other-worldly knowledge of how to best proceed in order to meet our goals. Just because we can't explain how they work does not negate their value. Emotional Guidance always sees our best potential and will never agree with negative self-doubts that creep into our mind. Emotions are the quintessential ever-present coach.

Emotional guidance will always lead to a hopeful perspective. "Among college-aged students, for example, the hope of achieving social goals (relating to friends, family, or romance) had a direct impact on positive mental health, whereas hope for achieving performance-oriented goals (relating to work or academics) did not."[288]

". . . Children will be willing to try new strategies and behaviors to the extent that they have secure bases to retreat to for comfort, support, and guidance when they stumble or encounter impediments."

Open-ended goals are not measurable and do not have specific time frames within which they can be reached. The pursuer cannot know when the objective has been reached, nor can he or she experience the positive emotions associated with successful goal attainment.[289] Goals should be:
1. Measurable,
2. Have specific time frames
3. Are described in a singular fashion,
4. Are consistent with long-term goals
5. Cause no harm to self or others and (ideally) uplift self and others

The first goal should be to feel as good as one can feel under the circumstances, day-in and day-out. This breaks down into being psychologically flexible in perception of one's situation and using skills to shift perspectives to ones that feel better as needed. As the emotional state improves, cognitive abilities will improve, bringing to mind solutions to current challenges.

16: Permission to Self

All enlightened men wish for the good of others.
Neville Goddard

    The Oxford Handbook of Happiness "outlines the function of positive emotions as broadening attention, cognition, and social cognition, all of which contribute to building well-being and resilience."[290]
    Research is very clear that individuals who are positively focused are more successful.[291, 292, 293, 294] How does understanding and using your EGS create greater success? It naturally makes you more optimistic, which is a key component of success in every area of life. Some of the common road blocks to success are:

Feelings of unworthiness	Fear
Lack of self-confidence	Lack of forgiveness (of self and others)
Negative thoughts	Negative beliefs (especially about money)
Worrying	Self-criticism

Success requires the right attitude, a positive mindset, about:

Happiness	Failure (it's a stepping stone)
Open mindedness	Sense of control (autonomy)
Your reason why	Faith/Trust
Your potential	The small voice within
Growth and Learning	The goodness of self and others

    Match your talents and interests with the line of work you do. When something others find hard is easy for you, it may be where your best path is. When the work is so rewarding it is not work to you and you enjoy going to work—those are signs you're matched well with your role. If you're not, you've two choices. One is to move elsewhere but remember, you take yourself with you. The other is using your Emotional Guidance to find your purpose and deliberately aligning your current role with your purpose in order to find more meaning in what you are doing by changing your perception about it.

Everyone enjoys doing the kind of work for which he is best suited.
Napoleon Hill

    See yourself as your vehicle to success—not others, not your employer. This does not mean you do not align with employers who have the same goals. But it means you do not align with those whose goals or values differ from yours.

Happiness Contracts

Each individual has developed beliefs about happiness. In *Be Happy*, Dr. Robert Holden wrote, "Your Happiness Contract asserts every condition, rule, and law that you absolutely must abide by in order to be eligible for any amount of happiness. Any happiness that you experience without first fulfilling these conditions is strictly 'illegal' and may result in personal penalties of guilty feelings, inner discomfort, and moral foreboding."[295]

Your personal happiness contract is the result of the way you perceive the life experiences you have lived. If you had to be good for Santa Claus to bring you the much desired toy, you probably have a requirement to *be good* in your happiness contract.

The truth is that happiness is your right. Happiness is free. There are no dues, no conditions, and no way to earn happiness.[296]

The **Happiness Defined** chapter provides examples of limits many people place on their ability to be happy. Use your Emotional Guidance to test the validity of any clauses in your personal happiness contract. You'll realize that any condition that puts your happiness off until another day or after you complete a goal is a belief that limits your ability to be happy, but it is not one that applies to everyone. By shifting your beliefs, you can stop its effect on your happiness.

I suggest adopting the following **happiness contract**:

I deserve to be happy. When I am happy, I am at my best. I am in the best health. I am in the best mood. I am able to think with greater clarity. I am able to see solutions to problems far more readily. I need less from others (pumping up, assistance of all types, etc.). I contribute more by being happy so being happy is a priority for me. When I am happy, I contribute to others by inspiring them to happiness. I contribute to others because when I feel great I want to help others feel just as wonderful. Sometimes when someone feels rotten, it makes her feel better to see someone else who feels rotten, or see someone who is even worse off than she is. When I am happy, it lifts me even higher to help others up and I gain no happiness or relief from their not being in a good place. When I am happy, seeing others succeed reminds me that I am capable and if they can do it, it is possible for me. Minding my happiness is minding my health because when I am happy I am inclined to make good decisions about my diet, exercise, and other habits. Happiness reduces stress on my body and enables it to maintain its health with ease. My happiness is good for me and good for the world.

Use your Emotional Guidance to decide for yourself whether you believe any of the false premises about happiness listed below. If you do, I encourage you to use the processes to develop new beliefs about happiness that will serve your highest good.

> *Your emotions affect your behavior. Your job is to feel good so you will be good.*

False Premises about Happiness

#1: *I have to be perfect before I deserve happiness.*
#2: *I must sacrifice good things for happiness.*
#3: *Happiness must be earned.*
#4: *You cannot know happiness unless you have suffered and sacrificed.*
#5: *Happiness will be punished.*
#6: *I must be enlightened to know real happiness.*
#7: *Everyone must agree that I deserve happiness before it is okay for me to be happy.*
#8: *I must have control of my circumstances before I can be happy.*
#9: *I have to be completely independent in order to be happy.*
#10: *I must be good before I can be happy.*
#11: *Too much happiness will change me and that makes me afraid.*
#12: *Happiness is about materialism.*
#13: *It is more important to be right (and never be shown to have been wrong) than to be happy.*

Although I recommended you adopt a personal happiness contract that will serve you well, you get to choose what is right for you. My hope is that your choice will help you be all that you dream of becoming. Remember:

In your state of happiness, you have sereneness about you that others find pleasurable, comforting, and calming to be around. Often, once you choose happiness and become stable in that zone, others will ask you how you have done it. From a position of happiness you can encourage and inspire others to happiness, not because you are saying "I need you to be happy in order for me to be happy," but because they see how you are doing and want to come to have what you have achieved. You can't push others to happy when you are trying from a state of unhappiness in order to get them happy so it will be "okay" for you to be happy but once you are happy you can inspire them to come to where you are because you suddenly seem wiser when you are happy. In their desire to be happy, people will seek "pearls of wisdom" from you. Everyone wants to be happy, even if they have buried the desire so deeply that they are not aware of it.

Happiness indicates a low level of stress. Either way you view it, increasing happiness or reducing stress, the result is improved health, relationships, success, and well-being. That may be the most important reason your happiness is good for the world; your unhappiness is not.

Researchers and others, including the media, who don't understand the psychology underlying True Happiness are sending a false message that is making some people less happy. The July-August edition of *Harvard Business Review* had an article by Alison Beard[297] that began with "Nothing depresses me more than research about happiness." The reason the research depresses her is she has developed the false belief that it is telling her she should be happy. I responded to her article by telling her that "the premise that you should be happy is false, "The huge and growing body of happiness literature promises to lift me out of these feelings. But the effect is more like kicking me when I'm down. I know I should be happy."

The reason the "Social scientists tell us that even the simplest of tricks—counting our blessings, meditating for 10 minutes a day, forcing smiles—can push us into a happier state of mind." are not effective at increasing long-term happiness is that they address symptoms of unpleasant feeling moods, not the root cause.

Your emotional state is not dependent upon your life circumstances and is especially not dependent upon a comparison of your life and those of others. Comparing yourself to others can lead to lower levels of happiness. Don't worry if what you're doing is not the same as what others are doing. They may not want what you want. We are all beautifully unique and life is more fun when we don't think we have to embrace things others are embracing that don't appeal to us.

Your emotional state is the function of two major things and some less important things that affect it. The first is whether you're moving toward your unique personal goals. It does not matter what those goals are. They could be to become the richest person on the planet or to become a stay-at-home Mom who has time for bubble baths each day or simply someone who has time to get enough sleep or the ability to get enough food for one day, or any other goals that are meaningful to you. If you're moving in the direction of your goals, you feel much better than if you're moving away from them. If you're staying equal distance (not toward or away) your emotion varies by how long you've been there and how far you are and whether you believe you'll ever get there. That brings us to the second major factor--mindset.

Mindset is, to me, the habitual pattern of thoughts that an individual usually uses. Because they are habits, they are the default mode of that individual. Like all habits, they can be changed, but not by simple tricks in a few minutes. Habits of thought include many things, but one that is important to this topic is whether a person tends to react to situations with appreciation, irritation, frustration, anger, envy, despair, etc. Our chronic emotional state is the product of our habits of thought. Two people can have the exact same meal with the exact same waiter at the same table and one can thoroughly enjoy it while the other is frustrated because he finds it lacking in many ways. Both are right, from their personal perspective. We can choose the perspective from which we view any situation. It's a function of psychological flexibility and a key element of resilience, both of which strongly support good mental health (even following trauma), good relationships, and greater success in all areas of life.

The ability to perceive or think differently is more important than the knowledge gained.
David Bohm

Other factors come into play. The level of your personal resources such as adequate sleep, nutrition, hydration and whether your body is in pain or ill affects the best you can be in this moment.

There are no *shoulds* in happiness. You are where you are. *Should-ing* yourself will usually make you feel worse. You can choose what to do from where you are and if being happier is not important to you, leave it to those who want to be happy. It's not difficult to be happy while pursuing goals that are important to us personally if our habits of thought aren't sabotaging us.

Bipolar Disorder

Other recent research demonstrated that individuals who place a high value on happiness tend to have worse psychological health and, in fact, that the high value on happiness is a risk factor for bipolar disorder.[298] Unfortunately, the researchers did not use subjects who possessed skills that enabled them to attain and sustain high levels of happiness. The subjects only had common knowledge. I believe they missed the root reason such individuals develop bipolar disorder. The high desire without happiness skills leads them to extremes because when they manage to be happy, they are very happy both because of the circumstances that led to the happiness and because their strong desire for happiness is satisfied in that moment. Without skills, most of the world relies on circumstances that are *just right* to fuel their happiness, much like Goldilocks. When their circumstances do not feel just right, the lowered emotions are more intense because they have two sources—the actual circumstances and the thwarted desire for happiness.

I would love to revisit the research but teach the participants skills that decrease their reliance on external events and increase their ability to change their thoughts to attain desired emotional states. I believe the conclusion would be that the lack of skills, not the desire for happiness, is at the root of bipolar disorder.

Another article reported by Karen Kaplan relayed information on a very ridiculous study with a very misleading title, *Happiness? Totally overrated, study finds*. The researchers in this study clearly did not know the first thing about the importance of authenticity or that we can sense whether someone is being authentic or not. They also do not know how much we want those we care about to be happy. In the study they began with the very sexist premise that husbands would rather be happy than right and wives would rather be right than happy. Yes, I know sometimes it feels this way—but when you understand *The Smart Way* by using it in your own life, you'll understand why it seems like their premise is true but you'll know as fully as I do that it is not.

To test their hypothesis, researchers instructed the husbands to agree with everything their wife said, even if he believed she was wrong. The wives knew they were involved in an experiment, but not what or how it was being conducted. Participants rated their quality of life at the beginning, day 6 and they were going to rate it again at the end. Wives began at an average score of 8, went to 8.5 by day 6, but by day 12 when the experiment was abruptly terminated, they refused to provide their score. The women had become increasingly critical of everything the husband did. I suspect they knew on some level that he was not being honest with them. You can't be honest and agree with everything someone says, even if you believe they are wrong. This deception made their minds look for other signs of deception (Focus Filter), which made them more critical. The criticism reflected growing distrust. The men's quality of life plummeted from a starting score of 7 down to 3.

If the title of the article, which seems to have originated in The Los Angeles Times and then been picked up by my local paper, The Charlotte Observer, would have been appropriately titled, *Uninformed Researchers Conduct Worthless Study.*

Freedom and Personal Liberty

> *That some achieve great success...is proof to all...that others can achieve it as well.*
> Abraham Lincoln

Most of the world has the ability for individuals to pursue their dreams and be as successful as they make up their minds to be.

> *Fantasy is hardly an escape from reality.*
> *It's a way of understanding it.*
> Lloyd Alexander

I would say that since we can be mobile, if where we are does not provide that freedom, we are still free because we can find our way to somewhere where we can. Before you argue for any limitations, you may perceive about your ability to do so ask yourself whether anyone has managed to do it. If someone has done it, then you can find a way.

An example of this is a beautiful friend of mine, Nomanono Isaacs. She was born in South Africa eleven years before Apartheid. Her family was well-to-do in her village—not by standards in America perhaps but by the standards where and when she was born. Nomanono's rich uncle had land and animals. Her childhood was good until Apartheid came and her family was moved to a place where there was no way to earn a living, a place where there was hunger and illness. She was 11 when Apartheid came to South Africa. When she was twenty, she walked out of the country on bleeding feet toward her future. She has written a book, *Escaping Apartheid, A Letter to My Mother*. I encourage you to read it. Nomanono has a beautiful soul. She lived through that yet she is a Being of Love. She now works in the UK and abroad to increase peace and love in the world. They say we are like those we surround ourselves with and reading her book will show many that forgiveness of others is a gift we give to our self. You will also probably be as amazed as I am that someone who lived through what she endured could become such a Being of Love. See the **Forgiving** section of Chapter 33 for help with the how of forgiving. She demonstrates that when you're determined, you can find a way to enjoy personal freedom.

> *Rightful liberty is unobstructed action according to our will within limits drawn around us by the equal rights of others. I do not add 'within the limits of the law' because law is often but the tyrant's will, and always so when it violates the rights of the individual.*
> Thomas Jefferson

16: Permission to Self

Part III — Solvable Problems

This section describes the problems *The Smart Way* can solve and discusses the science indicating that the outcome of applying it will have a significant positive impact on the problems. The problems include crime, physical, mental, and behavioral health, relationships, employee engagement, high school dropout rates, disparate impact, relationships of all types (including in the home, community, and world), peace, and more.

Humanity has been living with so many problems for centuries that most people don't believe we can solve them. They're right—as long as all we do is try to fix the symptoms.

But now, for the first time, we understand the root cause and can put our efforts toward solving these problems that make life on Earth such a struggle for so many people.

In each chapter in this section I'll share the results of research that demonstrates that stress and resilience are at the root of the problem and that when we reduce stress and increase resilience, people enjoy better lives. If you just want to get right to using the processes, you can safely skip ahead to Part IV.

My goal is to establish a firm foundation–a foundation that allows humanity to move confidently forward in healthier, happy, more loving, and peaceful ways. There are two obstacles in our path. One is what I have termed *The Galileo Effect*. I use Galileo because most educated individuals are aware that Galileo proposed a new idea that was accurate and provided a better understanding of our world but his findings met with criticism, ridicule, and worse. Most of humanity seems to believe the reception his findings about the Earth revolving around the sun was a product of less educated, church controlled times and that the people of today are too intelligent and too educated to treat the truth with disdain. I used to believe this, too. Now, I can demonstrate that we have repeated the same behavior throughout history and that it continues today. I've even seen it cloaked in the guise of scientific skepticism but accompanies by an unwillingness to learn about something because it seems to contradict what the person believes they know.

While beneficial progress always wins—eventually—a lot of suffering happens between awareness by some and adoption of new paradigms by the masses. My passion is fueled by my desire to avoid as much suffering as possible.

What is seen cannot be un-seen.
Folk saying

I include the folk saying here because it reflects how I feel. I have seen the evidence that makes it clear to me that solutions to our most pressing problems are far closer than most imagine. The Galileo Effect keeps many from seeing them. But having seen them, I cannot ignore their existence. I cannot stop being aware that every social problem our world is experiencing could be made better through far less effort than most believe. Recognizing new wisdom sooner is the easiest way to avoid unnecessary suffering. *The Smart Way* helps humanity become comfortable with new ideas faster.

Pause for a moment and ask yourself what might have been different if humanity had accepted the following ideas more quickly?

Ignaz Semmelweis suggested doctors wash their hands between patients and between working with patients and cadavers.

Delay: 50 years. Initial response was ridicule.

Reason for acceptance: Microscopes were invented that could see germs.

Evidence that was available before microscopes were invented: 33% reduction in deaths from childbed fever for women giving birth in hospitals when physicians washed their hands between patients.

The concept that all people are created equal
Delay: ongoing
Reason for acceptance: Personal transformation
Evidence: I have to point to Emotional Guidance because that is where I believe it flows from, even if it was not recognized as such—it as an inner knowing.

The concept that the mind and body are connected, with each affecting the other
Delay: ongoing
Reason for acceptance: Many have accepted this, but Western Medicine is still focused on episodic care, where symptoms are treated instead of the root cause, which is often stress. Wellness programs aren't about wellness, they're about early detection and early treatment—not actual prevention
Evidence:
- Measurable changes in HPA axis when psychological stress occurs.
- Nervous perspiration
- Stress pain (i.e. headache)
- Too many more to list

The concept that happiness is justification enough to take specific actions
Delay: ongoing
Reason for acceptance: Usually a combination of learning new information and trying methods that increase happiness and experiencing the difference it makes in one's life.
Evidence: Longitudinal studies that show positivity and optimism increases success in every area of life.

Room must also be made for wonder and for love. As Dr. Larry Dossey recently noted, scientists that see humans in a materialistic way will not find the healing power of love or connection. He referenced a comment by David Lindley,

> We humans are just crumbs of organic matter clinging to the surface of one tiny rock. Cosmically, we are no more significant than mold on a shower curtain.

That sort of thinking will never create a back story that can solve the problems of our world. I encourage you to use your Emotional Guidance to refute his comment and any other comment you encounter that minimizes your value and worth—even if it comes from someone who is highly educated. Your guidance knows the truth.

17: Honoring our Father and Mother

I come from a Scots-Irish family. I mean really, really dark. I remember my Grandfather saying that if something good happens; there must be something wrong with it.
Robert Redford

Much of the world teaches us to honor our Father and Mother—it is taught by both tradition and religious perspectives. The concept is good but the execution is often flawed. We believe honoring our parents' means believing as they did, acting as they did, and making choices like they did. But that is surface thinking.

- Why did your parents believe as they did?
- Why did your parents act as they did?
- Why did your parents make the choices they made?
- And most important of all, what did your parents really want?

I'll start with the last question. They wanted you to thrive. They wanted you to be happy and healthy. and some cultures place a high value on honor to the family. That's it. That is what they wanted. It is what parents want for their children.

How your parents went about it was based on their beliefs. For the most part, they learned their beliefs from their parents who learned them from their parents and so on back through time. But now you know that those beliefs may have been based on flawed premises. Premises accepted as fact so far back in history that finding the source is no longer possible. Those flawed premises kept your parents from having lives that were happier and more fulfilling. Your parents did the best they could with what they knew, or believed they knew. Most simply lived with whatever emotional state they found themselves in or self-medicated if their emotional state was more than they could endure.

Repeating their mistakes is not honoring them. Looking at their real intention and desire for you—for you to be happy and healthy—is the way to honor them.

Your parents wanted you to be happy and healthy. They may have shown that by spoiling you, making you work hard, or even by spanking you. But, in the end, their behavior was based on their belief that it was the best way to achieve the goal of your being happy and healthy.

Do you see how different beliefs about the world result in different behaviors even though the goal is the same one?

Your parents' beliefs determined how they went about attempting to achieve their goal of molding you into a happy and healthy person. They did not know you had inborn guidance leading you to your highest potential. In most instances, they worked very hard to substitute their beliefs and approval for your guidance. It works better with some children than others but most parents try. A predominant beliefs held by most people is that the parents are responsible for molding their children into the adults they wanted them to be.

The beliefs they had about how the world worked are largely formed by age 6. If they understood that their beliefs were based on decisions they made about life when they were still young children they would not be so eager for you to adopt those same beliefs. They would not define honoring them as adopting their beliefs.

To truly honor your parents it is best to look at their real goal—your health and happiness. When you honor that goal, all of you are in alignment. If they are still living they may not see your adopting beliefs about the world that differ from theirs as honoring them but that will be due to surface thinking. It may or may not be possible for you to gently help them understand that at the deeper level you are in sync.

It is not necessary for your parents to be in agreement with you on this topic. It is your choice. If you subjugate yourself to their beliefs, beliefs that your guidance tells you are not serving your highest good, you are going to be very much like them—surface thinkers. Then your children will someday face the same decision you are facing about what it really means to honor your Father and Mother.

Today, our society tends to believe what our parents believed. Our minds are designed to develop the beliefs of those around us and incorporate them into our lives. But if our great, great, great, great, great grandfather was misled into believing something that did not serve his wellbeing and he taught it to his child who taught it to her child who taught it to his child and so on for generations, the misleading information continues to harm your family. We behave as if there is honor in believing what our parents believed and shame in believing differently than they did. I am not speaking of religion, per se, but of all areas of life.

My interpretation of honoring them is different. It is attributing to them the best of intentions—regardless of whether their outcome was the best possible one. Even if it was awful, I give them the benefit of the doubt that they did the best they could at each moment in time. In this way, I am free to determine for myself those beliefs that serve my highest good. This perspective eliminates any guilt I might feel at reaching different conclusions from those held by my ancestors.

We all want what is best for our children, but sometimes children know better than we do what is best for them. This subject will be expanded on as we move forward.

Our guidance works on the quantum level and more physical proof of it is being discovered all the time. If someone is an atheist or believes in the clockmaker version of evolution, the science (especially when combined with practical experience) is sufficient to show guidance is there, as much as the urge we receive to attend to biological needs such as elimination of waste, hunger, and thirst.

If you have a religious point of view, many religions tell us to put God first in our life. If we consider the guidance as communication from God then our guidance has priority over our parent's preferences. The chapter on **Religious and Spiritual Views** provides details from a variety of religious texts that reference guidance from God.

Those on the spiritual path are often already looking for and listening to inner wisdom. Understanding your Emotional Guidance provides more direct access to the guidance than many have achieved on other spiritual paths.

18: Human Needs

Your vision will become clear only when you look into your heart . . .
Who looks outside, dreams. Who looks inside, awakens.
Carl Jung

There are multiple theories that attempt to conceptualize human needs. Self-Determination Theory (SDT) is one of my favorites. SDT indicates three basic needs:

- Autonomy
- Competence
- Relatedness (social connection)

Core Self-Evaluations are another way to perceive human needs for thriving. Core self-evaluations including self-esteem, generalized self-efficacy, internal locus of control, and emotional stability "independently and when combined into one higher order construct, have been shown to be significant positive predictors of goal setting, motivation, performance, job and life satisfaction, and other desirable outcomes."[299]

For example, a core self-belief that states, "I am good but not better than others" or "I am wonderful but so is everyone else" holds a positive self-view without diminishing others in the process. You can use your Emotional Guidance to find a statement that feels good. When I think about myself being wonderful and others not as wonderful I feel negative emotion that tells me that perspective is not the best one I can hold. When I think about myself being wonderful and everyone else being wonderful as well a sense of calm contentment comes over me and since I like the way it feels, that is my stance. It represents a positive self-concept and a positive concept about others.

I do not look to others to validate my self-concept (self-esteem). The emotional response I receive from my guidance is enough to satisfy me. That makes my self-esteem very stable because it does not depend on others validation or agreement. Narcissism, "preoccupation with one's status compared to, and in the eyes of others . . . is associated with delinquency and aggression."[300]

Family resilience researcher Ann Masten said, "Interventions and policies that promote healthy development have the potential for spreading positive effects over levels and time. The observation that 'competence begets competence' in human development may wall apply to family units as well as individuals."[301]

When human needs are not met, the outcomes are less than ideal. Non-Suicidal Self-Injury (NSSI) is a growing problem among adolescents and young adults. Researchers found that individuals who engage in NSSI have lower levels of personal satisfaction with the core human needs identified in Self-Determination Theory and experience, "more difficulties with all aspects of emotion regulation."[302]

Compared to students who had never engaged in self-injury, University students who had engaged in self-injury: [303]
- Did not accept their own emotional responses
- Experienced difficulty engaging in goal directed behavior
- Experienced impulse control problems
- Lack of emotional awareness
- Lack of knowledge about healthy emotion regulation strategies

Movement toward ever-expanding goals significantly contributes to life satisfaction, which contributes to improved health and behavior across the lifespan. Individuals, who lack the characteristics that improve outcomes struggle more, experience higher levels of chronic psychosocial stress, and poorer health and behavior outcomes.

Also, "evidence shows that self-efficacy influences the goal level chosen on experimental tasks. Those high in initial self-efficacy tend to set higher goals than individuals who are low in self-efficacy. This finding has been validated in the training context. Goals, in turn, are widely known to influence performance. During self-regulation, goals direct attention and effort toward the task through a process that involves self-monitoring with respect to the goals and adjustment of effort to achieve desired outcome."[304] So, essentially, higher self-efficacy leads to higher objectives to which one manages oneself.

"Teachers and students with high mathematics anxiety, irrespective of ability, perceive they are less competent than individuals with lower mathematics anxiety . . . the uncomfortable feelings and worry associated with mathematics anxiety facilitates an intellectual paralysis, usurping precious working memory resources, and diverting attention which might otherwise be directed to task processing."[305]

Emotion regulation strategies that increase children's skills at emotion regulation can be taught.[306] A study of South African children in child and youth care centers, poverty-stricken communities and schools in middle-class suburbs found that "the sites with the highest levels of resilience invest significant effort in the psychosocial development of the children in their care."[307]

The Smart Way metacognitive processes plus Emotional Guidance help individuals develop the characteristics that lead to greater success and well-being in all areas of life.

Possessing self-chosen goals and progressing toward them turns out to be a key source of happiness.
Christian Schubert

Maslow's Hierarchy of Needs Theory was introduced without supporting empirical evidence and quickly became accepted as truth. Despite successful empirical challenges, Maslow's Hierarchy of Needs has remained popular with businesses and educators.

I believe where the theory makes its first mistake is isolating self-actualization from other needs. In truth, our entire life is the pursuit of self-actualizing experiences. When you're young and just learning to support yourself, your self-actualized self is that of someone who can provide adequate food, water, and shelter. The potential person the typical person imagines becoming is nothing compared to who the person can (and often will) become. But the shift from depending on others to satisfy basic needs and becoming independent and capable of providing those needs for oneself is part of the self-actualizing process.

There are always four of us:
- Who we are
- Who we used to be
- Who we believe we can become
- Our fully self-actualized self

Within the "who we were" exist a multitude of people we were at one time or another in our lives (i.e. infant, toddler, preschooler, 1st grader, someone who is learning the alphabet, someone who has learned to read, someone who has their first crush, someone who experiences their first major loss, etc.). In each of these situations and many more, we were expressing as someone different than we are in this very moment. We cannot go back and be who we were, we can only be who we are now and move toward who we are becoming.

As we become more, our fully self-actualized self becomes more so we never become our fully self-actualized self. The child who is learning to read does not see herself as a future novelist. The administrative assistant usually does not see himself as a future executive until he is further along in his career. Even though I've achieved considerable career success, I still have more that I am becoming. Someday I'll be a grandma. My speaking career is still expanding and I'm looking forward to an Australian tour and an Egyptian one may be on its way.

Yes, our priorities focus on our more immediate needs, but self-realization is a continuous process. If we're hungry, we focus on satisfying our hunger before we worry about other needs, usually. But we can also continue working when we've made achieving a work-related goal a high priority even when we're hungry. We can remain at the bedside of a loved one who is ill, offering comfort, even when we are hungry or have other urgent biological needs.

I believe safety needs are misunderstood. It is the expected levels compared to existing safety levels that matters the most. For example, an officer worker does not expect to be exposed to hazardous working conditions and will not react well to safety threats at work. A soldier, on the other hand, expects danger at work and has a very different reaction to safety threats. Part of that is the result of training, but a bigger part is expectation vs. actuality. Someone who served as a soldier but is now an officer worker will respond differently to unexpected violence than someone who has never had training, but their reaction (emotionally/psychologically) will be different than it would be if the violence had occurred in an environment where it was expected.

Observers who are not directly at risk also respond differently. When we watch a movie where someone is living a life we would expect to be safe and they meet a tragic end it affects us more than it does when we watch a war movie and a soldier dies. The outrage is greater when a civilian life is lost than when it is a military or law enforcement life. It is not that we value military or law enforcement lives less—we don't. It's that we don't see civilian lives as at risk. We simply don't expect civilians to be lost as the result of violence. If we pay attention, even when a soldier or law enforcement officer is lost when not on active duty, the sense of injustice about the loss is greater than if the same loss had occurred while on duty.

If you've ever wondered how people have lived through awful times and retain their sanity—wars, plagues, etc.—it was by adjusting expectations of possible norms. Martin Luther King Jr. refused to accept a norm of his time and led the civil rights movement. I'm no longer willing to accept the norm of everyone not knowing about their Emotional Guidance the suffering that so many endure as a result. It is wrong to fail to provide life-saving information to millions of people. It is wrong to keep the characteristics of functional and live-supporting thought shrouded in mystery and stigma, only providing the information in the confines of therapy after a problem has manifested and caused damage.

It serves no one. Humans are too good to accept the status quo. They deserve so much better.

There are men and woman who put their lives on the line every day for decades to serve and protect others. The safety first concept does not explain that type of behavior. For these individuals, self-actualization requires risking life and limb in service to others.

The third level of Maslow's Hierarchy of Needs is social needs. This, too, varies by individual. Some people enjoy their own company and have solo pursuits they find very satisfying. They don't pursue socialization and are happy in their solitary existence. Others have solo existences because they don't know how to develop the type of relationships required to satisfy their social desires.

Recent research shows that our sense of belonging is more important than social time.[308] Many people have felt intense loneliness while surrounded by other people.

Esteem needs, self-respect, and the approval of others are another misguided need. If one's confidence in themselves is truly healthy and without doubts, the approval of others is not a necessity. It is only when someone doubts their own value or worth or feels unstable in their belief about their value that others' opinions become important. I'm not referring to someone who is egotistical, because braggadocio is usually hiding insecurities. The truly confident person can move through life quietly sure that they, like everyone else, have value—assured that their opinions and actions matter.

A strong human need is for autonomy, the sense that one is in charge of one's own life and decisions. Edward Deci and Richard Ryan have done extensive research on the self-determination theory of motivation. When an individual autonomously makes decisions about goals, they are intrinsically motivated to self-actualize toward those goals. When goals are externally imposed motivation is not as strong. Self-determination theory attempts to explain the "needs necessary for psychological growth, integrity, and well-being."[309] In their paper on the *"What" and "Why" of Goal Pursuits*, they explain that "Social contexts and individual differences that support satisfaction of the basic needs facilitate natural growth processes including intrinsically motivated behavior and integration of extrinsic motivations, whereas those that forestall autonomy, competence or relatedness are associated with poorer motivation, performance, and well-being."[310]

Autonomy is also important for pro-health behaviors and good health outcomes. Attempting to control the pro-health behaviors of our partner can backfire. Individual perception of control has an effect on coronary function.[311]

Intentional Motivation

| Amotivation (helplessness) | External Motivation | Introjected Motivation | Identified Motivation | Integrated Motivation | Intrinsic Motivation |

| Controlled Motivations | Autonomous Motivations |

Extrinsic Motivations

Least Self-Determined → Most Self-Determined

Based on Deci & Ryan SDT, 2000

Intrinsic Motivation is:
- More autonomous
- More Stable
- Done with greater care and quality
- Accompanied by more positive experiences
- Higher persistence
- Lower anxiety
- Higher adherence

> *Because I want to vs. because the doctor told me I have to*

Integrated Regulation the person identifies with regulation and has coordinated that identification with other core values and beliefs
- Stable and persistent
- Fully self-endorsed basis for action
- Behavior is willing with no sense of coercion
- Fully self-determined
- Medical outcomes are better (when it is a patient)
- Work outcomes are better (engaged)

> *Self-identity: I help people I will do this task in a timely manner because that helps the customers.*

Identified Regulation involves the conscious acceptance of behavior as important to achieve personally valued outcomes. Strong incentives can overcome difficulties in maintaining behavior.
- Stable and Persistent effort
- Commitment
- Positive experiences

> *Doing this moves me toward accomplishment of my personal goals*

Introjected Regulation, one's self-esteem is at risk. Tasks are considered self-esteem contingent. There is pressure on the self, which may lead to self-disparagement or shame at failure. Pride and self-approval may occur with success
- Individual may feel ambivalent
- Unstable maintenance
- Can include negative emotion
- Tension
- Inner conflict

> *I have to finish this task on time or Harry will think Bob is better than me.*

External Motivation involves externally regulated behaviors, rewards, punishments, and mandates that exude pressure to comply on the individual
- Regulatory efforts are temporary (only when controls are in place)
- Only when rewards are meaningful
- Compliance only when controls are operating
- Minimal effort
- Poor quality
- Individual is not invested and does not care

> *I can take it easy today because the boss is on vacation.*

When you want to increase someone else's motivation, how can you do it without decreasing any intrinsic motivation that may already be in place?

Physicians who use open-ended questions have better relationships with their patient's and the patients are more likely to adhere to the treatment plan.

Can you tell me more about what brings you here today?   vs.

~~Can you~~ Tell me more about what brings you here today?

Researchers have found that highly restrictive goals "are likely to create a sense of restricted personal freedom."[312] Restrictive goals feel disempowering, which activates the natural desire to feel empowered leading to resistance. In teenagers, we refer to this resistance as rebellion. Highly restrictive goals also makes it more difficult to integrate the goals with personal motivators because once the urge to resist is born, the individual is not looking for ways to cooperate and comply—she's looking for ways to resist. Now, someone who is has developed metacognitive skills by paying attention to her own thoughts and motivators for those thoughts could recognize what is happening and decide to consciously look for ways to align with highly restrictive goals.

For example, someone who has been diagnosed with diabetes who is told they can no longer indulge in some of their favorite sweets, not even chocolate peppermint cake, may feel rebellious despite the fact that he does not want his illness to worsen. The restrictions activate rebellion because freedoms are being threatened. If he decides to consciously align with the restrictions he might think of his 4-year-old granddaughter and how he enjoys dancing with her. She puts her tiny little feet on top of his shoes and leans back, allowing him to hold her weight up as they move to the music. He dreams of dancing with her at her wedding. He could decide that he wants to comply with the dietary restrictions because he wants to be healthy to dance at her wedding many years in the future. By focusing on his personal desire he can align with the event and become a cooperative patient who does not feel the desire to rebel.

Before he goes to the grocery store or to a party where he might feel tempted, he can prime his mind by imagining dancing with his granddaughter at her wedding someday. By keeping that desire active in his mind, his compliance with the restricted diet becomes something he does to achieve a self-inspired goal—not one that is being forced upon him by his doctor.

Where do we most often see highly restrictive goals?

Authoritarian parenting	Schools
Incarceration facilities	Military
Nursing homes	Some employers and some types of jobs

It is not the difficulty of the goals that make them authoritarian. It is the lack of flexibility in how the goal is achieved that makes them feel as if they are limiting one's freedom. There is significant research demonstrating that "highly difficult goals increase performance on more than 100 different experimental tasks, including behavioral measures of self-control, like persistence."[313] Lack of ability and/or commitment can lead to reduced success on difficult goals.[314]

Buzinski and Price's paper also discussed ego-depletion that occurs from complying with highly restrictive goals and how the need to comply can deplete the ability to exert self-control on subsequent tasks. I think any parent who has picked up a 3 or 4-year-old from a day-long pre-school program can relate to how frequently the child seems to have a melt-down after a *good* day at pre-school. The theory about this that I heard when my children were young was that the child was on their best behavior all day while they were at pre-school, but when they return to an environment where they feel safe and secure, they have to let the tension out. At the time, we were told it was a process the child had to go through to learn how to behave in a classroom so she would be ready for school. I am not so confident now that the advice we received was wise.

If you view the child's behavior while considering the continuum associated with the Emotional Guidance Scale (EGSc), you see that the restrictive environment is not just a process of learning, but also one of disempowerment that is associated with many undesirable outcomes. What if the reason young children in pre-school are ill so often is not just exposure to new germs, but declines in immune function as the result of feeling disempowered? It's worth considering.

The integration of external motivations is a key concept for socially desirable behaviors in the home, at work, and in the community. The ability to take external goals and perceive them in alignment with intrinsic goals is a key factor in success in every area of life. The worker whose employer has high demands may resist those demands or slack off if the only motivation force is coming from external demands. If that same worker perceives successful fulfillment of the employer's demands as supporting self-determined intrinsic goals, the worker will be self-motivated to complete them.

The student that perceives the purpose of homework assignments as "making the teacher happy" or "following some dumb rules set by the school" will not be motivated to complete the work. If the student sets his own goals about obtaining an education and can perceive the homework assignments as one aspect of successful completion of the self-determined goal, the student will be motivated to complete the work.

When a person aligns externally created goals with self-determined goals, life feels easier. Progress seems like less work and more like doing what you want to do. Stress levels are lower, even when the same actions are being taken. There is a greater sense of freedom (autonomy and/or empowerment), which equates to a higher level of happiness. We should all retain an open-minded willingness to learn and transform throughout life. We are never a finished product. We are ever-evolving individuals with increasing potential to know, understand, learn, share, and create.

The ability to integrate external motivators with intrinsic motivators is a metacognitive process which can be learned. Although some seem to accomplish this merging intuitively, once the skill is learned, there should be no difference between those who intuitively do it and those who learn how to do it. In fact, those who learn how to do it as a skill may be better off than those who intuitively merge the two motivators because in situations where it is more difficult to do, the one with the skills will be more aware and will more consciously pursue finding alignment between the two. The one who intuitively found this balance may not consciously realize what led to the success.

I was an intuitive merger and did not realize what I had been doing until I was preparing to teach some of my students how to align their purpose with their roles. Once I consciously recognized that I had been doing it intuitively for many years I could see how important it had been to my long-term success.

Individuals from all walks of life would be well served if they learned how to deliberately do this by the time they enter 6th grade because they will benefit from intrinsic motivation during school and throughout their career. The same process can be used to enhance important relationships including marriage and parenting. Setting goals for marriage, such as maintaining a close emotionally and physically satisfying and supportive relationship can help keep the relationship on track. Parenting goals that specify the outcome you want most can help you do all the tiring responsibilities that come with being a parent. In my case, I knew I would always love my children, but liking them was another matter. My goal was to raise productive citizens who I liked. That simple goal guided many of the best decisions I made as we moved through the years from birth to college graduation. It kept me centered on my ultimate goal. It gave me a barometer to measure my decisions with when the right answer seemed elusive. Best of all, it worked, the goal was successfully achieved.

The goal must be autonomous. I'm not telling you to use the goal I set when raising my children. I'm merely sharing an example of a goal that worked. If my goal resonates with you, feel free to use it. If it doesn't, find an overriding goal that resonates with you and use it.

19: Resilience

There is no problem that doesn't have some underlying need for more optimism, stamina, resilience and collaboration.
Jane McGonigal

What is it?

Resilience is the ability to bounce back following adversity or stress and return to one's prior state or better. By definition, resilience involves flexibility because adverse situations humans encounter vary in great degree. Sometimes there is a single event and at other times individuals experience a series of adverse events. Some individuals can be resilient enough to handle a single adverse event, but crumble under a series of misfortunes while others seem to take them all in stride. Resilience is "not related merely to the availability of resources in the social environment, but also to the agency shown by young people as they identify these resources, recognize them as opportunities and mobilize or activate them towards helpful engagement."[315]

A group of researchers from the Netherlands used a definition I like. Resilience is "Reflective of the capacity of an individual to avoid negative social, psychological and biological consequences, and cognitive impacts of extreme stress that would otherwise compromise their psychological or physical well-being."[316] I would add avoiding damage to one's relationships as well. Stress can be damaging to one's relationships and marriages frequently end because of heightened stress caused by a variety of factors including the loss of a child or building a new home.

Six years before the twin towers fell, a review of the lifetime prevalence of exposure to severe traumatic events in the United States indicated ranges between 51.2 to 60.7% of the population experienced such an event during their lifetime.[317] I have not found a new review that provides updated numbers, but the events being reported in the news media, from school shootings, the war, and terrorist attacks on American soil indicate that number may have increased. Exposure to traumatic events leads some people to develop mental illnesses such as anxiety, PTSD, and depression while others experience posttraumatic growth, becoming more than they might have become if they had not had the traumatic experience.

When stress happens, resilience makes a tremendous difference in how an individual responds. Even the most vulnerable members of our society, children from economically disadvantaged environments, are able to avoid the poor outcomes so many of their less resilient neighbor's experience. In a study of 2024 low-income inner-city men and women higher resilience was associated with lower lifetime hazardous alcohol and illicit drug use. Resilience protected children whose lives were impacted by poverty, child abuse, and other forms of trauma from the ravages of substance abuse.[318] "Consequences of having high resilience include positive factors such as decreased mental health symptoms and career and personal success, especially when placed in stressful situations . . . Conversely, consequences of having low resilience include increased risk for mental illness, such as anxiety, depression, PTSD, and suicidal ideations."[319]

Over the course of one's life, resilient characteristics are like a steady friend who protects against illicit drug use across the lifetime, mitigate risks of PTSD, major depression, and suicidality, even if the individual's early life experiences increased those risks.[320]

In our current world, many children live in less than ideal circumstances. Resilience helps the pattern not carry on to the next generation. In a study that looked at pre-school children of alcoholic parents and non-alcoholic parents, the presence of resilience (psychological flexibility) led to less alcohol use as adolescents.[321]

As much as we might want to cure poverty and suboptimal parenting, I don't believe it is an achievable goal in this decade. But I think teaching children how to be more resilient and therefore less likely to perpetuate problems for another generation is a goal we could easily achieve if we made it a priority. The long-term benefits are certainly worth the effort.

Individual resilience plays out on a large scale following adverse events such as prolonged war. "Public resilience seems to be linked with more beneficial postwar responses, which contribute toward returning to normal life after experiencing the distress of war."[322] Public resilience increases "belief in a better future, and belief in its ability to overcome hardship and to strive for improvement despite current anxiety and distressing conditions."[323] Worldwide this has very relevant impacts. While many would say that this is not true in the United States, I would argue that for many children being raised in urban poverty, the circumstances of their surroundings are no better than those of children living in war torn countries and in some cases, worse.

Interventions that increase positive emotions can increase resilience.[324] A panel of resilience experts at International Society for Traumatic Stress Studies concluded that although "interventions to enhance resilience can be administered before, during or after stressful/traumatic situations . . . Ideally, interventions/training will occur prior to stressful events so that the individual is better prepared to deal with adversity."[325] I completely concur because when resilience is high, the amount of time someone spends suffering in negative emotional states following a stressful or traumatic event is minimized. "One study that looked at 230 outpatients suffering from depression and anxiety disorders found, "cognitive emotion regulation strategies of refocus on planning, positive reappraisal, and less rumination contribute to resilience in patients with depression and anxiety disorders."[326]

> *Ideally, interventions/training will occur prior to stressful events so that the individual is better prepared to deal with adversity.*

Endurance can be increased by changing how we look at what we have to endure. Smaller increments of time can make the unbearable, bearable. I only have to stay here five more minutes is easier to endure mentally than thinking you have to be there ten hours. Calculating the days until you can leave an abusive situation on your terms can make it easier to endure. You can also increase your trust in others and leave now by calling for help from those who help people escape abusive environments.

The Smart Way meta-cognitive processes and Emotional Guidance support all the factors commonly associated with resilience including healthy self-esteem, optimism, and an internal locus of control. Learning to be conscious about reappraising one's emotional state lowers negative rumination.

Wingo, Ressler, and Bradley, "theorize that resilience characteristics mitigate risks for substance use disorders in individuals exposed to childhood abuse or other traumatic experiences via a combination of factors including emotional and cognitive control under pressure, tolerance of negative affect, utilization of cognitive reappraisal, goal orientation, spiritual coping, nurturing role models, or strong social support."[327] A study published in *International Journal of Environmental Research and Public Health* found that resilience made teens "less likely to engage in risky behaviors" including smoking, drugs, and alcohol and they were better able to resist peer pressure.[328]

There is broad agreement that a lack of resilience leads to a wide variety of problems including, "unsafe sex, poor educational performance and completion, bullying, crime, employment, job productivity and the likelihood of poverty."[329]

The factors that increase resilience can be learned. In fact, the research that made me decide to write this book found, "Resilient beliefs predicted positive developmental outcomes, especially among children facing adverse life circumstances."[330] I already believed, based on prior research, observations, and personal experience, that adversity can lead to desirable . When I see the research supporting my hypothesis but no evidence of widespread implementation to help the most vulnerable among us, it feels like criminal negligence. My goal with this book is to create momentum and a resource that can be utilized to implement training programs to help vulnerable children.

Another study, this one in Australia, introduced a resilience intervention to ten primary schools in low socioeconomic areas in Brisbane, Queensland Australia. Both the ten intervention and ten control schools were tested to establish baseline levels of resilience. Eighteen months after the resilience intervention began the schools were tested again and the intervention school had significantly higher scores in several areas including "family connection, community connection, peer support, and their overall resilience."[331]

I also strongly disagree with the suggestions I've seen to only provide the training in areas where we know children are living in adversity. We do not know what happens in homes that look as if they are normal and supportive. We also do not know what sort of adversities life might bring. Socioeconomic benefits do not protect children from tragedies and other negative life events where resilience is necessary. In fact, some researchers believe that resilience is like a muscle that must be exercised, something children raised in higher socioeconomic situations are less likely to do as frequently as children in impoverished families do.

We must stop dividing people by their current status. The Smart Way speaks to a basic human need—knowing how to optimize one's personal use of his or her own mind.

Resilience is derived from a combination of internal and external resources although some of the external resources are perceptually based (i.e. support from friends), which I would argue is internal because one might have highly supportive friends but not perceive them as supportive so their willingness to offer support is ignored. In other situations, individuals might perceive their friends as supportive and as providing a back-up plan to fall back on when their friends would not actually be willing to provide the support. As long as the back-up plan is not needed, the individual will benefit from perceiving that it is available.

Frontiers in behavioral science published *Understanding Stress Resilience* in 2013, which said in part:

"Adverse events can impact brain structure and function and are considered primary sources of risk for depression, anxiety, and other psychiatric disorders. However, the majority of individuals who encounter adverse or stressful life events do not develop untoward outcomes, and so an understanding of the factors that promote resistance to the deleterious effects of stress is of clinical importance. At the level of basic research, there has been considerable effort directed at identifying experimental parameters that blunt/augment outcomes from an adverse event, but even when parameters are held constant, there is inter-subject heterogeneity in behavior. This has shifted the focus to understanding how genetic and experiential factors can shape an organism's resistance to future adversity. The articles in the present Research Topic provide an overview of recent efforts directed at elucidating the neural mechanisms underlying resilience, and utilizing such information to mitigate vulnerability."[332]

This work is being done as if we are mechanistic beings, where when a button or switch is pushed or pulled, the reaction of the organism will be based on the physical apparatus in terms of its genetic make-up and neurological construction.

Another article in the *International Journal of Hospitality Management* reads as if it comes from the same mechanistic viewpoint, "this study reveals the role played by age and work experience in individual coping efforts and a high possibility of female workers as a task-oriented coper in hospitality work settings."[333] This sort of comment leaves no space for the very real potential for coping methods to be learned and incorporated in one's psychological responses. Since we know the quality of one's coping skills affect whether stressful life events lead to "anxiety, depression, psychological distress, and somatic complaints" it makes sense to teach the best possible coping skills to everyone.

Their assumptions could not be further from the truth. Neurology is created by the thoughts that an individual thinks which then affects the chemical composition of the body. We have free will to choose our thoughts. Many individuals may feel their thoughts choose them, but that is only because they have not yet learned how to use their minds. Our education system teaches us to memorize, not to think in ways that support our highest good.

Humans possess the ability to think about what they are thinking about. This is called meta-cognition. An individual who has experienced a rape can find herself repeatedly re-playing the event in her own mind, which neurologically, is like repeating the actual event. An individual experiencing this can react emotionally and physically to the re-play or she can take a step back and observe herself replaying the event in her mind and deliberately intervene to stop the re-play. In such a situation, the best way for someone who has not practiced meta-cognition to stop the re-play is to deliberately re-focus. Even if all she does during the first event when she uses meta-cognition is decide she will come up with a focus-shifting strategy for the next time, significant progress has been made.

Then, when she is not in the middle of a re-play she can come up with a strategy about something to focus on instead of the re-play. The first time she implements the strategy she may be five minutes into the re-play before she remembers she has a plan and implements it. But in the moment she does it, she will feel more empowered than she has in a while. Taking control of one's own thought processes and deliberately shifting focus to something that feels better is a liberating experience. The next time she finds herself in the re-play, she will remember she has a strategy sooner, so she'll experience less of it than she did the time before. Each time recognition that she can use a strategy to stop the re-play will come faster and the time between re-plays will be longer until the re-plays become rare. When you realize it has been years since you thought about something that used to bother you frequently, your power to exert control over your emotional state feels strong and sure.

An individual who has learned to use metacognitive practices and practices them to reduce stress in their daily life before a traumatic event can use meta-cognition during the actual event. It can be used to help escape the reality of what is happening or to increase one's chances of escape by reducing fear, which improves one's ability to think clearly and identify opportunities for escape.

Nothing can stop the man with the right mental attitude from achieving his goal; nothing on earth can help the man with the wrong mental attitude.
Thomas Jefferson

When scientists begin looking at habits of thought to evaluate individual differences in outcomes they will discover that a positive mental attitude greatly increases the chance of Posttraumatic Growth—the best possible outcome following an adverse life event. They will also discover that a negative mindset is common among those who suffer the worst outcomes including PTSD, psychosis, and suicide. Update: Research published in 2015 is beginning to reflect what I suggested they would find, "These findings suggest that difficulties with using cognitive reappraisal, specifically to decrease negative affect, might be linked to suicide risk."[334]

Beliefs about self and the world have an effect on the thoughts the person thinks.

Existing habits of thought determine what new beliefs and self-image arises as the result of an adverse life event. The habits of thought also determine the actions that follow.

- A belief that one just has to live with the debilitating emotional pain of loss following a trauma makes it unlikely that the person will reach out to a professional for help or even search the self-help aisles of the local bookstore or library.
- A believe that a professional can help but that the help would adversely impact one's career makes it unlikely the person will reach out to a professional for help, although this person might try to find a book that will help him deal with the situation.
- A belief that a professional can help but that society might ridicule her for obtaining counseling makes it unlikely the person will reach out to a professional for help.
- A belief that a professional will be of benefit and that it is worth the price (financially, career-wise, or stigma-risk) would be present in an individual who reaches out to a professional for help.

There are thousands of variations of beliefs individuals can hold on just this one topic. All of them affect the outcome. Individuals who are thinking the first three thoughts will feel negative emotion. That negative emotion is telling them there is a different thought they could find and believe about the same subject that would serve their highest good better than the thought they are thinking.

Negative emotion is telling you that the thought you're thinking is not the best thought you could have about that subject. Yes, from the perspective you're viewing it, the emotion you feel is valid. But in most cases, negative emotion means: "Find another perspective; there is one that would help you feel better right now."

> *Negative emotion does not validate the thought that brings it forth!*

The event itself has an impact. A violent rape, car accident, domestic violence, or repeated exposure to violence and death in a war zone or as a first responder can all lead to adverse outcomes. But in each type of situation there are those whose suffering continues endlessly and those who seem to recover and live lives that they enjoy. If scientists would study the connection between the mindset and habits of thought as I did, they would discover that it is mindset more than the event itself that leads to the outcome.

A negative mental attitude is a self-imposed handicap. It makes a person more susceptible to adverse outcomes from traumatic events.

In Zimmer-Gembeck and Skinner's 2014 research, *The Development of Coping: Implications for Psychopathology and Resilience*, the prevalence of "major life stressors, including the death of a loved one, witnessing a traumatic event or experiencing abuse by family members or others, are common experiences among children and adolescents, occurring for about 25%."[335] By the time they've lived as adults for a while, the prevalence of exposure to traumatic events soared to 89.7% and exposure to multiple traumatic events was more common than a single exposure.[336]

> *A negative mental attitude is a self-imposed handicap. It makes a person more susceptible to adverse outcomes from traumatic events.*

Roughly half the participants in the study had experienced a disaster, accident, fire, physical or sexual assault, or the death of family or a close friend due to violence, accident or disaster and only 7.8% was combat exposure. Out of this group of 2,953 individuals, 9.4% had experienced PTSD as defined by DSM-V during their lifetime and 5.3% had experienced PTSD during the past year.[337]

Clearly, there is a high likelihood that an individual will experience a traumatic event during his or her lifetime. Developing a mindset that will lead to the best possible outcome before the event is much like wearing your seatbelt when you're in a car or an airplane. It's a preventative measure. Your risk of exposure to a traumatic event is greater than your risk of being in a plane crash.

Developing a resilient mindset, unlike wearing a seatbelt, comes with many other advantages. A resilient mindset is a positive mental attitude, which improves physical and mental health (even if you don't experience a traumatic event), because you experience less stress in everyday situations when you have a positive mental attitude. Success in all areas of life and relationship health is also better when you've developed a resilient mindset.

Potentially traumatic events are events that can lead to the dysfunction the media so often reports, such as PTSD. But the same type of situation can have a minimal impact or even lead to posttraumatic growth in others.[338]

It is good to have an end to journey toward.....but it is the journey that matters in the end.
Ernest Hemingway

Resilience and Hope

> *"... are we not now duty bound to speak up as scientists, not about a new rocket or a new fuel or a new bomb or a new gas, but about this ancient but rediscovered truth, the validity of Hope in human development -- Hope, alongside of its immortal sisters, Faith and Love?"*
> *Karl Menninger (1959)*

In her research and in *Positivity*, Barbara L. Fredrickson shares three factors that are critical to resilience:

1) Internal locus of control
2) Optimism
3) Healthy self-esteem[339]

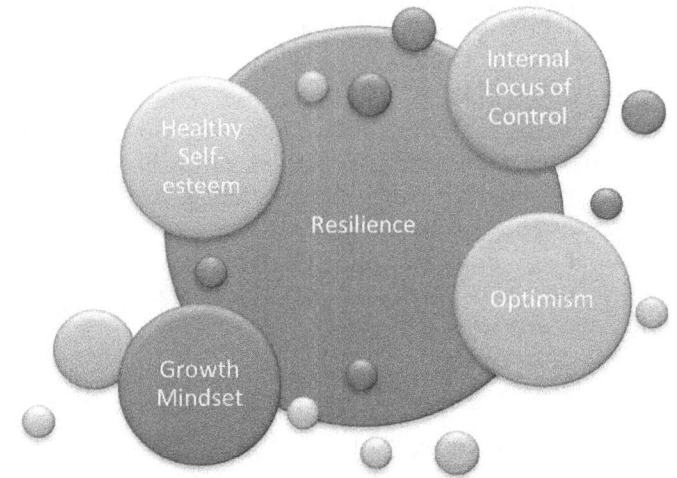

What is an internal locus of control? It is the belief that your words and actions matter—that what you do can change the outcome of your life. The thought, "If I go to college and get a degree, I'll be able to make more money" represents an internal locus of control. An external locus of control, often associated with a victim mentality that blames others for what happens, believes someone or something outside of oneself determines the outcome. The thought, "Even if I go to college and get a degree, no one will pay me well because _____" is indicative of an external locus of control. A severe form of external locus of control is *Learned Helplessness*, where an animal or individual won't take an action that others can clearly see would be beneficial and possible. In a *Learned Helplessness* state, the person does not believe his or her actions will matter.

"People who believe life events are a product of their own effort, rather than fate, experience better outcomes in multiple domains . . . students with low socioeconomic status feel less control over their lives."[340]

The plan in this book puts the premise of "It takes a village" on its head. It does not say that children don't need others—they do. But it says that a child that seems to have everything going against him or her can, if given the knowledge and skills in this book, thrive in spite of those circumstances.

Understanding and following our Emotional Guidance increases all three of the factors that are critical to resilience. In *Resilience as a Positive Youth Development Construct: A Conceptual Review*, Lee, Cheung, and Kwong noted that:

> "Studies have shown that the main difference between individuals who adapt very well despite facing risks and individuals who end up in maladaptation is the existence of protective factors. Thus, enhancing both internal and external protective factors of adolescents may help them adapt to stressful and risky life situations. For internal protective factors . . . optimism, perceptions of control, self-efficacy, and active coping are associated with better health. Grotberg cited longitudinal studies to show that about half to two-thirds of children with resilience could overcome their initial traumatic life experiences, such as growing up in families with a mentally ill member, being abused, or having criminally involved parents."[341]

Additional factors including emotional flexibility, social problem solving skills, and cognitive skills have been cited as elements that contribute to individual resilience.[342] Although conscious awareness of our Emotional Guidance is not required to develop resilience, conscious awareness strengthens the benefits of our Emotional Guidance because we become more attuned to the subtle energies of our guidance and are able to resolve negative emotion much more quickly. Emotional Guidance continually reinforces the three critical elements of resilience (internal locus of control, optimism, and healthy self-esteem) when it is interpreted accurately.

Resilience is sometimes recommended as a way to cope with the ravages of chronic diseases and while it is useful in that way, the greatest power of resilience is in reducing chronic stress, which reduces the risk of developing the chronic disease that one would then have to deal with.

> "It is important to note that although research has outlined numerous ways in which developmental environment can negatively impact a person, resilience is in fact a common trait, following even the most severe adversities. Between 50 and 60% of the general population experience a severe trauma during their life time, yet the prevalence of PTSD is estimated at 7.8%. Other studies have found that neural circuits involved in resilience can be modified for many years after adversity. For instance, the majority of adolescents whose development was stunted in childhood due to trauma were able to developmentally "catch-up" when relocated to a supportive, loving environment."[343]

Despite the known benefits of resilience and longitudinal studies showing it is possible to increase resilience and that doing so improves long-term outcomes for children who are at high-risk for suboptimal outcomes, the enormous data collection machine that is part of the Federal government reports:

> "**Social connections and engagement.** *The formation of close attachments to family, peers, school, and community have been linked to healthy youth development in numerous research studies. Additional research needs to be conducted to strengthen our understanding of how these relationships promote healthy development and protect youth from risks that, in turn, affect later life success. We currently lack regular indicators on aspects of healthy development, such as relationships with parents and peers, connections to teachers and school engagement, resilience when confronted with difficulties and civic or community involvement.*"[344]

Although this 2015 report from the Federal Interagency forum on Child and Family statistics indicates they do not have indicators of healthy development, an earlier report from the Regional Research Institute for Human Services at Portland State University found that the ability to maintain hope is an indicator. According to that paper, published in *Research, Policy, and Practice in Children's Mental Health*,

> "When low-hope people fail to achieve goals, they typically cannot create alternate pathways to go around obstacles. Accordingly, these individuals with low hope are prone to give up, to criticize their own abilities, and to experience strong negative emotions. On the other hand, when individuals with high hope fail to attain goals, they simply acknowledge that they did not try hard enough or that they did not have access to the more useful pathways. Instead of becoming stuck in criticizing

themselves, the high hopers get busy in finding solutions. As a result, any negative emotions experienced by high-hope people are not likely to incapacitate them. On this point, we have found that high- relative to low-hope people try harder and persevere longer after failure experiences precisely because of their abilities to retain their positive emotions."[345]

What the researchers describe as high-hopers could easily be described as optimists although there is a difference. Hope is the belief that the future will be better than the present and that you have some power to make it so.

Stress Inoculation

If a parent keeps his child isolated at home, the child is not exposed to common viruses and will not develop immunity to them, which leads to a weaker immune system. Vaccines are based on this premise. Give a small dose of a harmful virus and the body develops antibodies that will prevent a full-blown manifestation of the illness. One of the first things I did when after becoming a single Mom was get a chicken pox vaccine. I never had chicken pox as a child and adult chicken pox can be debilitating. My greatest concern was how I'd care for my children if I was that sick. A few years later they both contracted chicken pox within a week of one another. I had a mild case that did not interfere with my ability to care for them.

A similar theory exists for resilience that is supported by "research in rodents" suggests the protection "may be due to neuroplasticity induced by stress inoculation."[346] There may be some neural basis for higher levels of resilience, but I think it can be described more simply. When you experience adversity, recover, and find the silver lining in the experience you're more likely to do so the next time because humans are creatures of habit and repeat our patterns. When something works well for us, habitual patterns are very good for us. When things don't work out, they do not serve us and we would be better off disrupting the pattern.

Monkeys that experienced brief separations from their mothers periodically over ten weeks "were less anxious and . . . showed higher cognitive control, higher curiosity when they were older."[347] That sounds like self-confidence. I don't think we need to create artificial stressors to inoculate our children but neither do we need to artificially remove stressors. We need to provide them support and guidance about how to deal with stressors, provide a firm platform of healthy self-esteem, an internal locus of control, and optimism.

Researchers are leaning toward a stance that, "resilience develops in response to challenges, not in their absence, and the person (or system) can become stronger than before."[348] I disagree. My stance is that resilience is *displayed* following adversity, when it is present. But it is the way a person thinks and how she approaches problems (or avoids them) that leads to resilience. If the thinking patterns do not support thriving, repeated adversity will simply wear a person down and in extreme cases, lead to psychosis. I do agree that adversity helps build confidence, but the adversities can be slight. A child being picked last for the team, not making the team, rejection by a desired person, a college rejection letter, and other common events can help a young person realize that they can be fine following something undesired. Those experiences will help them when they are faced with more severe adversities, but only if they find a way to think about the small ones that allows them to move on.

If the person who is not picked for the team makes it into a personal and global rejection of self, which would stem from dysfunctional habits of thought (catastrophizing), no resilience would be built. If the person who is rejected by a desired other decides that means no one will ever love him, he will not build resilience as the result of the experience. Healthy thinking must come first and that is what *The Smart Way* is designed to provide.

Internal Locus of Control

An Internal Locus of Control is the belief that one's actions make a difference. It is essential to believe one's actions matter because when they don't believe they do, they are unlikely to take beneficial actions that would help them. At the lowest extreme, an External Locus of Control can lead to Learned Helplessness (a concept discussed elsewhere in this text).

Anxious children with an external locus of control whose parents give them lots of autonomy had greater difficulty dealing with negative events.[349] The importance of autonomy is also discussed elsewhere in this book.

Optimism

"Optimism is correlated with many positive life outcomes including increased life expectancy, general health, better mental health, increased success in sports and work, greater recovery rates from heart operations and better coping strategies when faced with adversity."[350] A historic view of optimism popularized by both Voltaire and Freud is still believed by many individuals today, but the evidence soundly refutes those historic views. These people are still easy to find and education is the only way to change their mind about optimism.

Seligman developed a program to teach children optimism that protected them from depression for two years, but without boosters the protective factor faded. When you add Emotional Guidance to the equation there is continuous positive reinforcement that acts to provide boosters at no cost and with intrinsic benefits.[351]

Healthy Self-esteem

Emotional Guidance supports the development and maintenance of healthy self-esteem. The processes section includes processes that use guidance to refute negative self-concepts. Self-concept is simply one's beliefs about oneself and the thoughts that they think because of those beliefs. When beliefs change, the thoughts change. Once someone has used their Emotional Guidance for a month or two, they develop a high degree of trust in its guidance that can help them feel confident refuting life-long negative perceptions of self. The ability to use Emotional Guidance to call *Bogus* on thoughts that may have formed as the result of verbal abuse or bullying during childhood is of great value.

Who we perceive ourself to be is part of our self-concept. If we see ourselves as someone who messes up, it leads to more mistakes. If we see ourself as capable, we will display greater levels of confidence. 291 9th graders in a predominantly Latino high school participated in a study about the relationship between behavioral self-concept and alcohol use. Students with low versus high self-concept had a predicted probability of 31% versus 20% for drinking, 20% vs. 8% for binge drinking, and 14% vs. 4% for drinking at school.[352] Considering the personal health and potential school expulsion risks being taken and given the significant difference in the behaviors, teaching children how to establish positive behavioral self-concepts seems to be a worthwhile goal. I want to point out that the students with the better self-concept may still have had a self-concept far below their potential self-concept. Despite the better behavior displayed, it was not necessarily the best possible outcome. All the 9th graders could benefit from the training—not just those with the lowest levels of behavioral self-concept.

Negative life events do not automatically translate into bad outcomes for children. The reasons the child attributes to the negative event have a significant impact on long-term outcomes. Children who blame themselves or who believe that things happened because they *were bad* or *not good enough*, have worse outcomes. Children who have similar negative life events who do not use negative self-attributions to explain the event fare better.[353] Children can be taught to use their Emotional Guidance to identify perspectives about any negative life event that support good outcomes.

There are some core beliefs that lead to healthy self-esteem:

❖ At my core, the person I really am, is good. This is true of others as well. Departures from my essential goodness are a form of illness. When I feel happy it is a sign that I am being more of my potential, good self. When I am not feeling happy, I have skills I can use to feel better before I take actions I may later regret.

❖ I can use my guidance to feel the positive feedback when I think well about myself and others.

❖ Others' opinions represent their emotional state and not anything about my true value or worth.

❖ I, just like everyone else, provide value and worth to this world by my presence.

❖ I, and everyone else, does the best they can in any given moment. My best in the moment is not necessarily my potential best. My emotional state, sleep, nutrition, health, stress, meta-cognitive skills, and hydration can negatively or positively affect my best performance in any given moment.

❖ When I make a mistake I will learn from it and appreciate that I now know more than before and then I will move on.

Meaning
Friedrich Nietzsche said, "If you know the why, you can live any how."

Although the common thoughts on human competence at work focus on knowledge and skills, Sandberg's alternate viewpoint focuses on the "meaning work takes on for workers in their experience of it, rather than a specific set of attributes, constitutes competence."[354]

You may copy the Resilience Questionnaire on the next page for your personal or classroom use.

19: Resilience

Resilience Questionnaire

Mark the answer that best describes how you or your child feels:

	Not at all	Seldom	Occasionally	About half the time	often	Most of the time	Always
I am pretty good at figuring things out.							
Things never work out well for me.							
I trust a higher power (God) to help me.							
I understand why I do what I do.							
I am pretty good at a lot of things.							
I enjoy being with other people my age.							
I like myself.							
I have goals and plans for my future.							
I get mad at myself for making mistakes a lot.							
I can work out my problems.							
I like my school (job).							
I have a friend I am comfortable talking to.							
I don't like to try new things.							
I enjoy surprises.							
I know that at least one person loves me.							
Someone tells me I do a good job.							
Someone listens to me when I talk.							
I think the future will be good.							
By working hard I can improve my future.							
I know how to feel better when I get upset.							
I am good.							
There is someone else who thinks I am good.							
My friends help me do the right thing.							
My friends do the right thing.							
When I feel bad I don't know how to feel better.							
Somehow I always get what I need.							
There is a purpose for my life.							
When I want something it never works out.							

Score all but 2, 9, 13, 25 and 28 using this scale	1	2	3	4	5	6	7
Score questions 2, 9, 13, 25 and 28 using this scale	7	6	5	4	3	2	1

Not resilient	0 - 28
Low resilience	29 – 56
Somewhat resilient	57 - 84
Resilient under many circumstances	85- 112
Good resilience	113 - 141
Strong resilience	142 - 158
Highly resilient	168 – 196

An individual who answers with 7's on many of the questions, but has very low scores about optimism or internal locus of control would not be resilient when under high stress. The good news is that it is simple to teach skills that increase resilience, optimism, and to develop an internal locus of control. The best use of the scale is to identify areas to work on to increase resilience. All the necessary skills will increase when the knowledge and skills provided in this book are applied to one's life.

> *It takes great learning to understand that all things, events, encounters and circumstances are helpful.*
> *A Course in Miracles*

When you practice using meta-cognitive processes and your Emotional Guidance on a regular basis, it becomes possible to find equanimity in the middle of a crisis or other event that would have previously derailed your emotions. Do not wait until you're in the middle of a problem to begin—that would be like trying to stop a freight train with broken brakes. When you practice on a regular basis, it keeps the brakes in good repair.

Resilience can build upon prior success at navigating life's obstacles. However, someone with high optimism, internal locus of control, and self-esteem who has led a relatively mild life can be resilient in the face of adversity. Someone who lacks one of those three factors is not likely to fare as well in the face of their first real adversity.

19: Resilience

20: Crime Prevention

There's no such thing as a bad boy
Father Flanagan (Boy's Town)

Two things are clear throughout recorded history. The first is that societies have been concerned with and attempted to control the behavior of citizens without much success. The ever-increasing punishments, rules, and enforcement efforts demonstrate that this battle is not being won. The second aspect of behavior that is evident in the research, but not yet consciously recognized by society, is that happy people are not behaving in ways society finds undesirable.

By teaching children how to manage stress and emotional state to a good feeling level, we can greatly increase the likelihood they will fulfill their potential and not become criminals. For the first time in history, a way to stop multi-generational poverty and the childhood to delinquency to prison pipeline is evident and is a method that even fiscal conservatives deem affordable.

Faulty thinking stemming from emotional distress can lead to self-defeating behavior, but the behavior is the result of the desire to feel better by someone who lacks skills that empower him/her to feel better in the circumstances being perceived. Leith and Baumeister found that "high-arousal negative emotions (but not other states) caused a shift toward favoring high-risk, high-payoff choices, even if these were objectively poor choices."[355] It seems high intensity negative emotions create a sense of urgency to feel better that leads people to focus on feeling better, to the exclusion of information that might lead to better decisions. In one of Leith and Baumeister's studies, participants made better decisions after they were instructed to pause and list the pros and cons of their options for 30 seconds, demonstrating that simple skills can lead to better outcomes.

Ignoring a negative emotion is just as unhealthy as repeatedly rubbing your hand across sand paper while attempting to ignore the pain. Pain is information that tells us to take some action. Likewise, emotions are guidance designed to help us recognize unhealthy thoughts or circumstances. Our emotions provide guidance, but we teach children (who are born knowing how to be joyful) to pay attention to pleasing others instead of following their natural guidance. Parents, teachers, ministers, and peers say, "Do this so I will feel better," not realizing they are steering the children away from their innate guidance.

Society has developed a belief that without external guidance, such as rules, human behavior would be unacceptable. This is evinced by the plethora of rules we are expected to comply with in every area of life. Many recent findings in positive psychology including those by Lyumborisky, Diener, and Fredrickson, refute the premise that our behavior is uncivilized without rules.[356, 357] When individuals are in a positive state, they exhibit behaviors that are better than those society requires; altruism and cooperation increase substantially when higher levels of positive emotion are present. Negative emotion is associated with crimes and behaviors that often lead to crime, such as addiction.

An article published in *Criminal Justice and Behavior* reported that both rapists and child molesters have more negative emotions than non-offenders.[358] The same article reported that college students who were sexually violent against women, rapists and child molesters all had low impulse control. The famous Marshmallow experiments conducted by Stanford found that impulse control improves long-term outcomes based on results the grown children from the experiments had in SAT scores, educational attainment, health and other measurements of positive life outcomes.[359] Huntjens et al. reported that impulsiveness is associated with poor cognitive control.[360] In other words, individuals who don't think about what they're thinking (meta-cognition) are more likely to act impulsively. This tendency leads to worse decisions that add up over time to worse lifetime outcomes.

Baumeister et al also discounts the need for pervasive rules, citing research that individuals don't actually consider moral rules when determining their own behavior.[361] *The European Journal of Criminology* reported "results suggest that deterrence perceptions are largely irrelevant for those who lack a propensity to commit acts of crime."[362] Instead, decisions are made based on what they believe will feel better to them. However, moral values will be used in attempts to impose the behaviors they prefer on others and to justify decisions made. Helping children understand that listening to their own Emotional Guidance is important and reliable will change our world.

Most individuals do not understand how to respond or interpret to their emotions to obtain optimal outcomes. It was not until 2007 that Baumeister et al challenged the prevailing belief that emotions directly caused behavior, a well-accepted but unsupported theory that has endured and been accepted as fact for nearly eighty years. It's difficult for people operating on a false premise to adopt best practices that are effective when the basis they are working from is flawed.

Emotions are not difficult to interpret accurately once one understands the language of emotions and the best way to gain greater understanding is to practice feeling emotional responses and being aware of how the emotion changes in response to deliberate changes of thoughts. Understanding Emotional Guidance is all anyone needs to make sense of their life, to find deeper meaning, and to cultivate and nurture positive emotions and relationships.

> *Understanding Emotional Guidance is all anyone needs to make sense of their life, to find deeper meaning, and to cultivate and nurture positive emotions and relationships.*

Emotion regulation is a common human reaction to negative emotions. In fact, when Dan-Glauser and Gross attempted to study strategy-specific effects of emotion regulation, they found, ". . . the natural disposition of our participants while confronted with emotional stimulations could well have been to accept their emotion, even when they were asked to refrain from modifying their emotion in any way."[363] If you think about it, everyone breathes but if you speak to experts on breathing, most of us do it imperfectly and some would say we do it poorly. Healthy breathing involves the diaphragm, but most people do not take deep breaths all the way into the bottom of their lungs. They take shallow breaths that send a signal to the body that they're stressed. If we hold consciously hold our stomachs in to make it appear smaller we can't breathe properly while we do that. Good breathing draws the breath in through the nose and exhales on a slow 5-count expelling all the air from the lungs. The key to begin breathing well is to think about how you're breathing and consciously draw in deep breaths and expel them slowly.

In much the same way as most people don't breathe well; most people do not use meta-cognition to evaluate the quality of their thinking so they can think well. Like good breathing, good meta-cognition requires conscious awareness of what you're thinking and a conscious decision to do the best you can to minimize stress and increase joy with the perspectives you chose. When they say Happiness is a Choice, what they mean is you can chose a perspective that increases happiness or one that diminishes it and you are the only one who can decide what you're going to do.

In *Intuitive Intelligence, Self-regulation, and Lifting Consciousness*, McCraty and Zayas tell us that "If one's capacity for intelligent, self-directed regulation is powerful enough, then regardless of inclinations, past experiences, or personality traits, people can usually do the adaptive or right thing in most situations they encounter."[364] In their paper, *Self-Regulation and Personality: How Interventions Increase Regulatory Success, and How Depletion Moderates the Effects of Traits on Behavior*, Roy F. Baumeister et al. state,

It has been shown that the practice of making efforts to self-regulate can produce broad improvements in self-regulatory capacity similar to strengthening a muscle, making people less vulnerable to depletion of internal reserves. When internal reserves are depleted, normal inner restraints are weakened and intelligent decision-making can become compromised through inappropriate behavior, lost opportunities, stress, and damaged relationships. Despite the importance of self-directed control to optimal function, self-regulatory capacity for many people is often far less than many would consider ideal. In fact, failures of self-regulation, especially of emotions and attitudes, are central to the vast majority of personal and social problems that plague modern societies.[365]

On the surface, factors that contribute to criminal behavior are as distinct as the individuals involved. When one looks deeper, it becomes apparent that emotional state is a significant contributing factor to behavior. Digging further still, one sees that stress, specifically unmanaged stress, is a systemic issue that leads to low emotional states. In 2010, Ou and Reynolds undertook a study for The Institute of Child Development at the University of Minnesota that found common predictors of future crime by adult males was directly related to childhood stressors.[366] When positive effect (happiness) increases, stress declines. Using Emotional Guidance increases happiness (positive effect).

In *As a Man Thinketh*, James Allen refers to the power our thoughts have to affect our emotional state:
Man is made or unmade by himself; in the armoury of thought he forges the weapons by which he destroys himself; he also fashions the tools with which he builds for himself heavenly mansions of joy and strength and peace. By the right choice and true application of thought, man ascends to the Divine Perfection; by the abuse and these two extremes are all the grades of character, and man is their maker and master.[367]

The belief that some people are good and others are evil is so prevalent in our society it is accepted unquestioned by most despite copious evidence to the contrary. To dispel this belief we have to look at the effect of emotional state on behavior. That mood affects behavior is evident in the research already cited. Most people easily recognize that when someone apologizes for an unkind remark with the excuse "I was in a bad mood" that the mood did impact the behavior. It is the degree of conscious awareness of this relationship that needs to expand in order to fully comprehend that good moods are a protective factor against crime. Global Advances in Health and Medicine reported, "emotions . . . can significantly bias or color the cognitive process and its output or decision."[368]

David Winter looked at the profiling information for criminals. In every instance, the worst criminals are assumed to have horrid events in their past.[369] However, not everyone with horrid events in their past becomes a criminal. The back story an individual creates has a direct influence on the effects of the experience on future emotional states, which in turn have an effect on future behavior. A child who is repeatedly abused may become abusive or even a serial killer. Another child who was repeatedly abused may work tirelessly to help others recover and thrive. The difference is not that one is good and the other evil. The difference is the perspective the child and later, the adult, takes regarding the experiences. Emotional Guidance is an invaluable tool in guiding individuals to create back stories that are adaptive and that lead to optimal outcomes.

Lyubomirsky, King, and Diener cite strong research that individuals who are more positively focused are kinder to others,

> *It is not that people who do not help lack compassion or that they don't care, it is that the way their mind processes the data may not reveal the person's need for compassion to them.*

including strangers.[370] In one of Darley and Batson's studies, a man of God walked over someone who needed help after researchers primed him with a negative mood and time constraint for his task.[371] They concluded that negative emotional states restrict our thought-action repertoire making us overlook opportunities to help that we would respond to when in a more positive mindset. Researchers repeatedly find that positively focused individuals are more likely to offer help and provide more assistance than negatively focused individuals. McCarthy reported that happy individuals are less likely to commit crimes.[372]

It is not that people who do not help lack compassion or that they don't care, it is that the way their mind processes the data may not reveal the person's need for compassion to them.

When Wu, Feder, Cohen, et al explored childhood trauma, they became one of many research teams that found undesirable behaviors, such as drinking to excess and drug abuse, are usually the result of unmanaged stress.[373] An understanding of one's Emotional Guidance greatly reduces stress and increases resilience. The pathway from alcohol and drug abuse to crime has been well documented.[374, 375] When stress is reduced the results include: reduced drug and alcohol abuse, increases life satisfaction, and reduced crime. The stress may be the result of low self-esteem, financial worries, relationship worries, peer pressure, high demands, poverty, environment, abuse, perceived discrimination, experiences, or any other cause. The cause of the stress does not matter. Using *The Smart Way* can reduce stress in all areas of life.

In every situation, if sufficient information is obtained, there are valid and scientifically explainable reasons why an individual exhibited even the most horrendous undesirable behavior. There are no inherently evil people. There are simply people who have experienced situations that made them feel bad, or disempowered, which led to their maintaining perspectives that did not serve their highest good.

Fredrickson and Branigan found that disempowered perspectives create negative emotional states, which exacerbate situations by constricting cognitive processes while positive emotional states broaden and build thought-action repertoires. "This research demonstrates that stress, anxiety, and other kinds of emotion can profoundly influence key elements of cognition, including selective attention, working memory, and cognitive control."[376] Swanston, et al report overwhelming research demonstrating that early life experiences such as abuse, maternal depression, maltreatment, poverty, family adversity, violence, and other stressors are linked with physical, mental, and behavioral health problems in children and the adults they become.[377]

While it is not yet commonly recognized as such, crime, acts that are contrary to the love that we are at our essence, are a form of illness, a separation from our eternal nature, with the same root as physical illnesses. That root is stress.

There is great evidence in the scientific research, and in each of our individual lives, that behavior is largely based on chronic and current mood with better moods eliciting better behavior. Yet society responds to bad behavior in ways that further reduce the mood of transgressors. We ignore that the reason for the transgressions is the existence of a low mood or low chronic emotional state. It is no wonder that crime has been steadily increasing decade after decade. It is no wonder that crime increases when the economy plummets as reported by Hill and Lapsley.[378] The relationship between behavior and mood is evident, but the belief that some nebulous evil aspect of personality, genetics, the devil, or fate is responsible keeps our eyes averted from the truth—and the solutions that are available to us when we recognize the truth. We blind ourselves to the solutions and the root cause by pointing at a non-existent figment of imagination—a person who is inherently evil. This is not a truth that requires extensive new research. There is already sufficient research linking happiness to lower crime and unhappiness to crime to satisfy the most discerning analyst.

A review of some of the most notorious murders of all time including Jeffrey Dahmer, Stacey Lannert, and Charles Manson reflects horrendous abuses. In *Construing The Construction Processes of Serial Killers*

And Other Violent Offenders, David Winter wrote about Stacey Lannert, "Violence may seem to be the only option to remove the threat."[379]

Childhood trauma does not excuse bad behavior, but it does create it—in some individuals. Not every child who is neglected, raped, abandoned, or abused becomes a criminal. What is the difference between those who do and those who do not? It is not an inherent goodness or evil. It is how resilient the child is. If the child can find and maintain emotional states that don't feel awful, the child is more likely to lead a productive and possibly even a happy life.

Cathy Spatz Widom researches the *cycle of violence*.[380] Children who were maltreated were "almost twice as likely to be arrested as a young offender for a violent crime than children of the same gender, age, and race who grew up in the same neighborhood or were born in the same hospital at the same time... Overall, childhood victimization significantly increases a person's risk of arrest by 59% as a juvenile, by 27% as an adult, and by 29% for a violent crime."[381] Maltreated youth were also more likely to be convicted after arrest, which I suspect is for the same reason individuals are re-victimized, some as yet undiscovered communication that we respond to on unconscious levels.

Victimization can also result is dysregulation of the *HPA axis* as evinced by a study of 242 low-income urban adolescents who had experienced victimization. The youths whose caregivers reported they used emotional regulation skills (i.e. reappraisal) experienced less dysregulation of the *HPA axis*.[382] (See the Glossary for an explanation of the HPA axis.

Strains such as unemployment, school exclusion, length of time in care and instability of placement were significant predictors of involvement in criminal activity among foster youth. Conditioning factors, namely self-esteem and life skills acquired prior to leaving care, tend to mediate the relationship between these strains and criminal involvement... Providing children with skills that enable them to reduce the amount of stress they experience in response to life events beyond their control reduces the cumulative effect of stress, thus reducing the likelihood of developing aggressive tendencies.[383]

Pietrzak and Southwick found that individuals who are more resilient going into combat have fewer problems following traumatic experiences and are more likely to experience posttraumatic growth.[384]

We have far more control over how we perceive any given situation than most realize. We could feel fearful about a situation, which would result in a pessimistic outlook (and a more disempowered perspective than other possible perspectives). Lerner and Keltner reported that if we felt angry about the same situation, we would feel more optimistic and empowered.[385] Voss found that our perspective about any given situation is usually based upon habits of thought rather than thoughtful consideration of the current situation.[386]

Baumeister may be the world's leading social science researcher in the field of good and evil. In *Human Evil: The Myth of Pure Evil and the True Causes of Violence*, he wrote, "Most people whose acts are condemned as evil do not see their own actions as evil. For example, they may recognize that they harm or exploit someone but believe that the action is justified or that the victim deserved to be treated that way."[387]

Haidt quotes from Baumeister and Beck's earlier examination of evil from the perspective of both victim and perpetrator in *Evil: Inside Human Cruelty and Aggression*, "When taking the perpetrator's perspective, they found that people who do things we see as evil, from spousal abuse all the way to genocide, rarely think they are doing anything wrong. They almost always see themselves as responding to attacks and provocations in ways that are justified."[388] This reflects the narrowing of the thought-action repertoire reported in research cited previously. When they can no longer see a socially acceptable path from which to respond to their perceived situation, the only path(s) they can perceive then feel justified.

There is a consistent message in the way misbehavior is dealt with that creates an, "I was punished so others should be as well." sense of fair play. This will never end without conscious decisions to end it. Whether a child is made to sit in the corner or spanked for transgressions, a belief develops that punishment is the appropriate response to misbehavior. The argument that the punishment is for the child's own good does not stand up to the known facts today. Punishing a child decreases the child's immune, cognitive, digestive, and central nervous system functions if it decreases the child's emotional state. Punishment usually decreases mood, which also means that the likelihood of undesired behavior increases as the result of punishment.

It feels counter-intuitive to help criminals feel better, but only because we have developed a belief that the proper response to undesired behavior is punishment. Gang research shows disturbing information that, if it were fully understood by the public, would show how irrational it is to respond with punishment to someone who commits even violent crimes. Criminals are victims as much as their victims are victims. Wood's survey of 4,664 men from lower socioeconomic and high minority residents revealed the following statistics for gang members: [389]

- 85.8% had an antisocial personality disorder
- 66.6% were alcoholics
- 25.1% screened positive for psychosis
- 57.4% were drug dependent
- 34.2% had attempted suicide
- 58.9% had an anxiety disorder

I believe anyone who understands this type of background information would perceive this population as needing help. The scientific evidence would predict that without help many of these adolescents and young adults would commit crimes. Given their mental/emotional state, it is to be expected. Who is responsible for their not receiving the help they need earlier?

I can't speak for the past, but as of now, when the research so clearly demonstrates what will happen without help, it is not right to hold them wholly responsible and let the greater society that ignores their needs and desperate situations remain unaccountable. If we did not know how to prevent the problems, then fine, society can hardly be held accountable for not preventing something it does not know how to prevent.

But that excuse is no longer valid. We know how. We just aren't doing it. That is child neglect on a national scale.

There is nothing that motivates people more than the well-being of children. There is no reason we cannot come together as a nation and as a world and share this knowledge and these skills with as many children and adults as possible. With modern technology, we have no more excuses. It's on us now. It is no longer an unsolvable problem. It is a problems society is currently refusing to solve—to the detriment of all.

"Prisons and jails have become America's "new asylums": The number of individuals with serious mental illness in prisons and jails now exceeds the number in state psychiatric hospitals tenfold."[390]

The same study that reported such high mental illness in gang members indicated that gang members who had themselves been victims of violence, had high levels of fear about further victimization, and that many suffer from PTSD. The most common scenario leading to incarceration is a series of circumstances where life seems to punish an individual that results in low emotional states which leads to retaliation through crime, or to drugs and alcohol use, which then leads to crime. Research shows a clear correlation between life skills and lower crime rates.

Barn and Tan describe General Strain Theory (GST),

The core assertion of this theory is that the presence of strains in the life of an individual can lead to feelings of fear, depression, anger, and frustration. Such negative emotions can generate pressure for corrective action, resulting in risky behaviours that may be deviant or criminal, including internalizing behaviors such as substance misuse, and externalizing behaviours such as violence and theft.[391]

Agnew addressed the correlation between anger and delinquent behavior,

"Anger increases the chances of delinquency by increasing the level of perceived injury, creating a desire for retaliation, energizing the individual for corrective action, and lowering inhibitions."[392]

Stressful life events are associated with higher aggression in children. Garland explains,

Positive emotions are not mere epiphenomena. They broaden thought and action repertoires, increase mental flexibility, augment meaning-based coping, and motivate engagement in novel activities and social relationships. Importantly, positive emotions . . . have lasting consequences; they build durable personal resources whose accrual triggers further positive emotions, leading to self-sustaining upward spirals of well-being. Conversely, when negative emotions accrete into downward spirals of defensive behavior, focus on threat, and feelings of inefficacy, these self-destructive, vicious cycles can lead to impoverished life experiences, and potentially, devastating psychopathology.[393]

Punishments tend to keep people at low emotional states so progress toward better-feeling emotional states is very slow, if it happens at all. Helping someone with undesirable behavior feel better goes against what almost everyone has been taught from a young age. On the other hand, when we look at how things really unfold, we understand that this is the only path to permanent improvement and perhaps eventually, eradication of many socially unacceptable behaviors. What do we really want: to punish criminals or to prevent individuals from becoming criminals in the first place? Right now, the resources flow to punishing criminals and attempts to prevent crime. There is a plethora of growing evidence suggesting that social ills including crime, teen pregnancy, drug and alcohol abuse, and more are casually related to long-term emotional pain. There is also mounting evidence that indicates improved desirable behaviors are linked to increased positive emotion including better corporate citizenship, altruism, kindness to strangers without expectation of reward, better relationships of all types, and much more. Garland supports this argument,

Reckenwald, Mancini, and Beauregard recently provided a review of research supporting the view that abused children are far more likely to become violent themselves; a view that has been well-documented and accepted fact in scientific circles termed the *cycle of violence*.[394] None of their theories adequately explain why one child continues the abuse while another overcomes it. Emotional Guidance fits neatly into that gap by introducing the connection between emotional state and behavior. This position is supported by Shahba and Allahvirdiyani who reported that increasing emotional intelligence, resilience, and coping skills reduces aggression.[395] Increased resilience equates to lower stress, which equates to a better-feeling emotional state. Research clearly demonstrates that the outcome can be improved via "…efficient self-regulation, active coping styles, optimism, and secure attachment…"[396]

> *It is the difference in our cognitive response to our experiences, not a difference in our goodness that separates us.*

Using one's Emotional Guidance is an active coping style that leads to efficient self-regulation, optimism, and it supports forming secure attachments by reinforcing positive perspectives about those with whom one has relationships. The truth is that many of us would be capable of atrocities if we shared the history and perspectives of those who commit them. It is the difference in our experiences, or response to our experiences, not a difference in our goodness that separates us. Not all individuals who suffer abuse become abusers. The saving grace is the mental processes the individual uses to cope and make sense of the world. Providing information about our Emotional Guidance system and how to accurately interpret its messages supports the psychological flexibility needed to adjust to changing and unique circumstances. With all that I am, I believe goodness resides in the heart of everyone. This belief is not one I was taught. It is based on years of studying what makes humans thrive and it is supported by scientific evidence.

Given a path that allows one to simultaneously feel better (more empowered) and be nicer, I believe it will always be chosen over a path that provides the same feeling of empowerment but requires one to be less kind. Only those who do not understand the kinder path is open to them will choose the one that is more harmful to self and others. What we've been trying (criminalization) has not worked. The problem worsens on a daily basis. It is time to move in a new direction. This is not a call to stop the current methods, but to add to them. Teach children (all children—because we have no real idea who is suffering abuse) as well as the abusers, self-mastery skills and about their Emotional Guidance System and metacognitive skills that increase psychological flexibility. The results will point the way for the future—a vastly improved future.

Effective Training Works

Mastering our perceptions and enjoying the journey leads to greater life satisfaction and, ultimately, greater accomplishment. One might ask why these ideas have not been implemented previously. Assagioli explains that the study of psychology focused almost exclusively on:

…this pathology approach (which) has. . . an exaggerated emphasis on the morbid manifestations and on the lower aspects of human nature and the consequent unwarranted generalized applications of the many findings of psychopathology to the psychology of normal human beings. This has produced a rather dreary and pessimistic picture of human nature and the tendency to consider its higher values and achievements as derived only from the lower drives, through processes of reaction formation, transformation, and sublimation. Moreover, many important realities and functions have been neglected or ignored: intuition, creativity, the will, and the very core of the human psyche—the Self.[397]

Although the research pertains to a work environment, researchers have found that positivity is reinforced by the benefits it confers:

Positivity is potentially self-sustainable as the employees positive experiences generate a desire for maintaining and sustaining positive workplace climate, which establishes an ongoing cycle of reproduction of positive workplace perceptions, emotions and behaviors that eventually become incorporated and internalized in the workplace environment.[398]

The chronic stress pathway to undesired behaviors that increase the likelihood of criminal activity and the protective aspects of learning good stress management have been demonstrated repeatedly.

This knowledge has been with us throughout recorded history, albeit without as much support from so many scientific disciplines. In the past, it has been suggested that modeling positive behavior was the solution. It is important to model positive behavior and emotional states using Emotional Guidance, but modeling alone is not sufficient.

People demonstrate many wonderful behaviors and most people think, "I couldn't do that or be like that". They don't know how to go from where they are (truthfully, where society trained them to be) to the kinder, gentler, happier person they were born to be. Their back stories and beliefs separate them from those who are able to successfully achieve the positive behaviors being modeled. Anyone can learn positive behaviors, but they need step-by-step instructions or a lighted path and encouragement that they have the potential to be that good. Historically, the individuals who achieved this state were put on pedestals, which separated them from the average person and increased the belief that only special people could achieve such states.

In The Happiness Hypothesis, Jonathan Haidt describes "The myth of pure evil is the ultimate self-serving bias, the ultimate form of naïve realism." He speaks of it as a way to protect the ego. While it may have begun in this way, it was perpetuated by religious teachings from many worldviews, and I believe this was motivated by a desire to control others' actions and, sometimes, to provide a rallying cry that motivated followers to fight for a common cause. Of course, it is a chicken and egg sort of thing; at this point there is no way to know which came first.

"…man must evolve for all human conflict a method which rejects revenge, aggression and retaliation. The foundation of such a method is love." The goal Dr. Martin Luther King Jr. so eloquently spoke of in his acceptance speech for the Nobel Peace Prize in 1964 can be achieved. This is it.

Culturally, almost everyone is imbued with the belief that some people are good and others are evil.

It is only from the vantage point of competition, winners, losers, and good and evil that harming another finds fertile ground in the minds of men. Harm of another comes only from a lack mindset (perspective) that believes it is the only way. An empowered individual will not see any advantage in harming another person—financially, emotionally, spiritually, or physically. Understanding of and trust in Emotional Guidance allows individuals to feel hopeful even when their intellect cannot find a path to what they desire. "Promotion of beliefs in the future for positive youth development deserves greater attention since there is growing research evidence demonstrating its positive effects on adolescent well-being. Hope and optimism are the two core components of beliefs in the future."[399]

Lack of understanding or belief in Emotional Guidance can lead an individual to believe the only paths available to them are the ones they can see with their limited intellectual abilities. The only way to learn to trust Emotional Guidance fully is to experiment with it in one's own life and experience how beneficial it is.

When we feel more empowered we see many paths to our goals, which is why science has found that individuals are more creative and intelligent when they are happier—their happiness reflects a greater belief in their abilities. In fact, the ability to see that we have choices adds to our sense of empowerment. When someone is held down, either by society or his or her own limiting beliefs, the pull to regain some power and to move up the scale gets stronger. When the only path(s) that are visible to the individual are ones that society abhors, they will take those paths if and when the pull to feel better becomes stronger than any resistance they have to taking those actions. Understanding this relationship is the key to seeing the importance of changing the way we commonly respond to undesired behaviors.

In general, one can assume that someone behaving in undesirable ways has negative emotions that have not been responded to in one of the three constructive methods. Violent criminals sometimes appear happy at their own actions, but what is being witnessed is a sense of relief from moving up the Emotional Guidance Scale to a more empowered Emotional State. Moving from the vicinity of despair (which feels totally powerless) to revenge, where some of their power has been taken back, feels emotionally good. Their seemingly positive emotions are not joy, appreciation, or love. They are just reflecting a feeling of relief—which is always present when we move up the EGSc. It is not necessary to commit violent acts in order to move up through the Hot (red) Zone (See Appendix I) and stabilize at higher emotional set points. Violence does not usually happen until a person has tried to move up and been repeatedly thwarted in their more socially acceptable attempts to feel better, such as a child who tries to tell her mom about abuse who is not believed. It is possible to move up from despair and hopelessness through anger, rage, and revenge just using thoughts. Actions are not necessary to move up the scale.

We were not designed to suffer negative emotions on a long-term basis and, when we endure them, we do suffer—physical, mental, and behavioral health and emotional pain. We were never designed to tolerate negative emotions for longer than it takes to complete our corrective action, which is usually a Right Response, a change of perception. That is why the many benefits of positivity are coming to light as we study positive emotions. We were designed to feel good. We were also designed to be good, which we are—when we feel good.

Societal systems designed to make us feel bad and maintain negative emotional states are fighting against our very nature. These systems literally create the undesired behaviors we want to avoid. Right Responses can be an individual's default response in most stressful situations. Stress can be defined as not moving in the direction of our Higher or Ideal Self. When we move away from our Higher or Ideal Self, the stress level is even higher. Think of it like a tug of war. If everyone holding onto the rope is moving in the same direction, there is no stress. If one person is holding the rope so the other side cannot back up, there is tension (stress) in the rope. If one person is pulling on the rope so that it moves in opposition to the direction the others are pulling, there is increasing stress.

Understanding how to interpret guidance accurately gives the best chance of finding thoughts that will lead to optimum outcomes. If our Emotional Guidance leads us to thoughts that create strength, peace and joy, can we not avoid the destruction of self brought about by unhealthy habits of thought? Could this not be true regardless of circumstances? When society begins consciously recognizing that mood affects behavior and teaching skills that empower individuals to improve their mood and maintain *True Happiness*, crime rates will decline rapidly. The research is very clear that happy individuals are kinder and exhibit a greater willingness to help others—even complete strangers. The behaviors idealized in a Utopian society are present in happy individuals. At the lower levels of the Emotional Guidance Scale (EGSc), the only path visible that will allow the individual to regain some of their personal power is often a path that would never be chosen if they perceived a more desirable path. This answers the question of why most people cannot conceive of the actions some people take—because most people can see other potential paths. We will often second guess why a person did not seek help before he committed an abhorrent act. From the perspective they held at the time the act was committed, they did not perceive a less destructive path that he believed would work. If the individual had been taught skills and an understanding of how to feel emotionally better they would not be so low on the EGSc that they can no longer see better paths. A society that understands the relationship between emotion and behavior will change their public policies, education system, and public service announcements to ensure that citizens understand and use their Emotional Guidance to achieve and sustain a healthy emotional state.

We cling to the idea that there are good people and evil people because it helps us believe that if we do our best to be good, we won't be evil. The truth is that it is a sustained low emotional state (which may be because of environment or because of learned thought-processes) that leads to evil behavior—not an inherent attribute of the individual. Emotional state can be managed with skills even children can learn. If everyone learned those skills very few people would live in low emotional states long enough to become a problem for society. We have an inherent, natural desire to feel good.

Emotional Guidance will support a positive self-image with positive emotions in response to positive thoughts about self. Once trust in one's Emotional Guidance has been developed, the positive response facilitates developing healthy self-worth and resilience.

In the first century A.D., Seneca exhorted his fellow Greeks, "He who does not prevent a crime when he can, encourages it," and Cicero added, "Every evil in the bud is easily crushed." "Since Seneca and Cicero, the cloak of prevention has been wrapped around a large body of interventions."[400] When Emotional Guidance is correctly interpreted, it guides each person to personal satisfaction and happiness which brings us right around to reducing crime.

In the same way that illnesses such as cancer and heart disease are considered something bad that happens to the body of an individual, the inclination and willingness to harm others—physically, emotionally, financially, or spiritually—can also be seen to be a form of illness—something other than a healthy, thriving human. Humans, in their optimum state, are good to one another. Any departure from that is an illness—of the mind, body, or spirit. We would not seek to punish individuals who develop physical illnesses like cancer and heart disease. Punishment of those who harm others is no more a cure than it would be to punish someone who has become ill with something we recognize and acknowledge as an illness. The entire concept of crime as something other than illness is because of the classification system and labels mankind has applied to it. These labels were applied in the past when we did not have a clear understanding of the fact that a thriving human treats others well. The mistaken thinking that some people are inherently good and others are inherently evil brought humanity to this erroneous conclusion and it is time to reject that premise in light of overwhelming scientific evidence demonstrating that humans who are happy treat others well. Illness, whether it is in the form of a recognized medical problem or in the form of recognized crimes, is a departure from our optimal nature and wellbeing. The root cause is the same in all cases. We were designed to function at our best when we feel good. Our functioning in all areas, not just behavior, declines as our emotional state declines. Emotions are guidance to show us our path of least resistance toward our highest potential. When we are moving toward that potential, we feel great. The degree to which we are moving in opposition to our highest potential determines how bad we feel.

The more we pay attention to the subtlest guidance, the clearer the presence of guidance becomes. The effect is self-sustaining because there are intrinsic rewards for using Emotional Guidance that are felt immediately and increase over time.

I believe with all that I am that we can come close to eliminating future criminals by teaching Emotional Guidance to the world's children and, to the extent possible, to their parents and teachers. Science has clearly demonstrated that happy individuals do not commit crimes yet our current system strives to make those who commit crimes feel worse—something we know will lead to continuing and increased criminal activity. It is clear that the current system is not working and is on a trajectory where it will eventually fall under its own weight. Gabbidon and Boisvert reported there were 14 million arrests in 2010.[401]

It is time for brave individuals to step up and point out that the current system is fatally flawed. It is not achieving society's desires. In fact, it is not achieving the purpose for which societies were formed—making living together safer than living outside society. Reforms will not fix the problem. We have to be smart enough and bold enough to look at the situation in an entirely new way, apply cutting edge science to the problem of crime, and then move forward with a solution that solves the problem at its root.

It is time for a paradigm shift.

The system is not working because it is rotten at its roots—the belief that man is sinful in nature and will behave poorly if the threat of punishment is not severe enough to control behavior is bogus. This is not working well for society as a whole or for the many millions whose lives are directly affected, whether as a victim, perpetrator, or families torn apart by harm to, or incarceration of, a loved one. The solution requires a global change of perception about man's nature and a new approach to undesired behavior that has its roots in a clear understanding that humanity behaves in life promoting ways when individuals are happy and in life diminishing ways when individuals are unhappy. It also requires an understanding of the skills that lead to individual happiness including accurate interpretation of one's Emotional Guidance. The global potential for improvement in lives and reduction of costs associated with crime is enormous.

Using your own Emotional Guidance is the only way to really understand how it works and how valuable it is. Almost all of us are accustomed to some level of struggle—so familiar that we only notice it by its absence. Rich or poor, this tension exists when we ignore or misinterpret our guidance.

Success requires that we set our intentions on the lofty goal of creating a better world and cling less to the need to have been right in our opinions and judgments in the past.

I do not advocate opening the doors of the prisons and emptying their contents back into society, rather I am advocating that we provide knowledge and skills to every member of society (incarcerated or not) that enables individuals to manage his or her own Emotional State to a high level, thus greatly reducing their likelihood of committing crime.

The tide of humanity that is heading to prison can be redirected into productive paths where they can thrive.

My conclusion was based on research from many esteemed institutions demonstrating that emotional state (happiness vs. unhappiness), or stated differently (calm vs. stressed) or (empowered vs. disempowered), is the largest factor determining behavior and not an innate *goodness* or *evil*.

When you put the *good* person under extreme stress, especially if the stress lasts a long time, or seems as if it will continue indefinitely, that person's behavior will typically become worse and may even become criminal. Individual who live where they experience chronic stress, especially stress that threatens their physical well-being (including food and shelter fears), are far more likely to commit criminal acts. Chronic stress and resultant low emotional state leads to undesired behavior—not an innate *evilness* or other flaw in the individual.

This may sound as if I am attempting to remove responsibility for actions away from wrongdoers. That is not the intent. The intent is to point out that without skills to self-regulate one's emotional state to good-feeling levels, crime will continue to be a significant problem. The criminal justice system should focus on helping individuals develop these skills. The skills should be taught to all children. First offenses after a system to teach these skills is in place should be given training in developing the skills.

By first offenses, I am not just referring to first-offenders. Most of our population is handicapped by the lack of these skills. It does not surface as much when someone lives in a low crime neighborhood and is able to make a decent living. But increase the stress on that person and the behavior will deteriorate. We see it in the increase in White collar crime every time the economy goes south. Children raised in poverty, in areas where violence and drugs are commonplace and schools are substandard (not to mention housing) have had little chance to develop positive mental attitudes that are so critical to success. *The Smart Way* can change that.

This is good news because while we may not be able to solve poverty and hunger today, we can teach those afflicted metacognitive processes that help them feel better. Remember, feeling better is helping. When you feel emotionally better it also means your stress level is lower. A lower level of stress means your cognitive function, digestive function, immune function, and central nervous system processes are working better. When cognitive function improves, solutions that could not be conceived of from the low emotional state become apparent, leading to actions that help individuals change their environment.

For years I wondered why people who could qualify for need-based scholarships did not use them to get out of the ghetto in much larger numbers. It wasn't until I understood the link between emotional state, locus of control, and the necessity to have hope that I realized they don't do it because they don't feel hopeful, they tend to have an external locus of control, and the low emotional states prevent them from the clarity of thought available to observers.

Powerful people with an internal locus of control design programs to help the needy but don't consider the psychological perspectives that must be present before they can benefit from the programs. From their personal perspective, the powerful policymakers don't see why the programs they design don't work—they believe if they were in their shoes, they would use the program to lift themselves out of poverty. It hasn't worked because there are more fundamental needs that aren't being met that must be met before the helping-hand will be seen as a viable option.

It is the same reason they don't help themselves. Trust is an essential element if people are to work together, but individuals living in high crime and drug infested areas are less likely to trust one another. Understanding their Emotional Guidance will help people know who they can trust and foster community cohesion and partnerships that can help change occur from the inside out.

For years people have been telling me you can't teach people who are struggling with poverty, crime ridden environments, and food and shelter fears to be happy. They've gone so far as to tell me such people won't care about happiness because they have greater needs. I maintained all along that they were wrong, but I only had my theory to stand upon until recently.

I was given the opportunity to teach a group of individuals largely composed of people recovering from addiction including a large homeless and formerly homeless subgroup. Just like Tal Ben-Shahar's Happiness class at Harvard was the most popular class; my Journey to Joy class is the most popular one at the non-profit where I'm teaching it. I see the difference it is making in the lives of those I'm serving. For example, after using an example I developed to explain how to stop frequent angry outbursts, one gentleman in the audience commented, "I think what you said is what my therapist has been trying to tell me, but when you said it, it made sense."

Consider a man from the lower echelons of society who has lived a hard life and developed a hair-trigger for his temper. Now imagine this same man makes a decision that he wants to do better so he gets yet another job, but he brings his hair-trigger with him, so the first or second time someone is rude to him, it sets his temper off and he loses the job that was his pathway to a better life and adds one more short-term job to his employment history. How valuable is training that allows him to get rid of the hair-trigger?

Now, take that same hair-trigger out on a Saturday night in that rough neighborhood. How likely is it that this same man will become involved in a fight, or even a shooting (as shooter or shootee), if he takes his hair-trigger out with him?

The same metacognitive process training that will help him be less likely to become angry will increase happiness, reduce stress, and make him feel more empowered. One process accomplishes all those goals. Just the other day my mom asked me, "Wouldn't it be better to give them housing?" I used an example from our own family of a woman who inherited a home from a relative that was free and clear to explain that smart thinking processes are an important aspect of keeping that home. The woman who inherited the house with no mortgage lost it within a few years. I don't know if she borrowed against it and couldn't pay the mortgage, or if she just didn't pay the taxes, but whichever one it was, it was not the best thinking she was capable of using. She tended to be negative, which led to her chronic emotional state being low, where cognitive abilities are at their lowest. I can't afford to give every homeless person housing, but I can help them in other ways that will improve their chances of getting and keeping housing. It's all interlinked. The sooner we realize it, the sooner we can solve social problems using the best possible methods.

21: Poverty

Rich people believe "I create my life." Poor people believe "Life happens to me."
Rich people play the money game to win. Poor people play the money game to not lose.
Rich people are committed to being rich. Poor people want to be rich.
Rich people think big. Poor people think small.
Rich people focus on opportunities. Poor people focus on obstacles.
Rich people admire other rich and successful people. Poor people resent rich and successful people.
Rich people associate with positive, successful people. Poor people associate with negative or unsuccessful people.
Rich people are willing to promote themselves and their value. Poor people think negatively about selling and promotion.
Rich people are bigger than their problems. Poor people are smaller than their problems.
Rich people are excellent receivers. Poor people are poor receivers.
Rich people choose to get paid based on results. Poor people choose to get paid based on time.
Rich people think "both". Poor people think "either/or".
Rich people focus on their net worth. Poor people focus on their working income.
Rich people manage their money well. Poor people mismanage their money well.
Rich people have their money work hard for them. Poor people work hard for their money.
Rich people act in spite of fear. Poor people let fear stop them.
Rich people constantly learn and grow. Poor people think they already know.
T. Harv Eker, *Secrets of the Millionaire Mind: Mastering the Inner Game of Wealth*

If you talk to anyone who began with nothing and became wealthy and they will tell you that the secret was changing their thoughts or mindset. Read the biographies of people who grew up poor and became wealthy and you see the same pattern.

For example, while Will Smith did not grow up in abject poverty, he was close to bankruptcy when he signed to do the Fresh Prince of Bel Air in 1990. He set a goal to become "the biggest movie star in the world." Forbes ranked to him as the world's most bankable star.

"You got a dream, you gotta protect it. People can't do something themselves, they wanna tell you, you can't do it. If you want something, go get it. Period."
Will Smith

Les Brown is an inspirational speaker with an equally inspirational story. He was born in an abandoned building and given up for adoption, but his adopted family was not the rich one orphans hope for in terms of material wealth. But in the wealth that matters, he had all he needed. His adoptive Mom encouraged him despite the fact he was declared "educable mentally retarded" as a child. He inspires me.

Life has no limitations, except the ones you make.
Les Brown

Talk to anyone who grew up poor, became wealthy and then lost their wealth and you'll notice that they think the way Harv Eker's quote says poor people think.

In the abundance section of this chapter I share my personal story, The Story of Three Ladies. Mindset played a significant role in the outcome.

Poverty alone is a significant burden, but poverty does not travel alone. It comes with increased violence in one's neighborhood, less community infrastructure and opportunities, health disparities that can be tied to lack of nearby resources and increased stress, and living conditions and occupations that have more environmental risks. When the neighborhood is unsafe people are more likely to be sedentary, which increases health risks even more. Poor women are at greater risk of intimate partner violence.

"Child maltreatment affects proportionately more African American, American Indian, Alaska Native, and multicultural children than White children."[402] Maltreatment during childhood often has adverse life-long physical and psychological consequences.

Researchers who looked at wages found, "similar individuals receive quite different earnings: a person's age, years of schooling, years of labor market experience, parents' level of schooling, occupation, and income tell us surprisingly little about the individual' earnings. In standard earnings equations for individuals of the same race and sex in the United States, between two-thirds and four-fifths of the variance of earnings is unexplained."[403]

So, for example, you could look at two Black women with bachelor's degrees who both have the same job title and find that one makes $50,000 each year while the other makes $90,000 for essentially the same job. Or, you could look at two Latino men with GED's and find that one makes $30,000 each year while the other makes only $20,000 even though they have jobs that are highly similar. If you then looked at the individuals and compared them, the ones who make less would have lower self-esteem. I am convinced that when self-esteem increases, wages can increase significantly if the person is qualified for a position that warrants higher wages. Elsewhere in this book I share *The Story of Three Ladies* who essentially changed their beliefs about what they were worth and experienced salary increases that brought their wages up to the new amount they believed they should be paid, even though the salary increases required to achieve the new amount was about a 60% increase.

Research indicates that in the United States low- compared to high-wage workers are more likely to:[404]
- Be exposed to occupational hazards
    - Dust
    - Chemicals
    - Ergonomic strain
    - Fumes
    - Noise
    - Job Strain
- Have less job autonomy
- Have less or no coverage for health insurance
- Possess fewer resources to live a healthy life
- Experience more social hazards
    - Racial discrimination
    - Workplace abuse
    - Sexual harassment
- Are more likely to be minorities or women

Although the article did not mention environmental stress relative to higher crime rates in poorer areas, other research provides adequate documentation of that environmental factor. Additionally, schools in lower socio-economic areas have fewer resources and have a more difficult time retaining the best teachers, leading to what could be deemed a second-class education for the children, which can lead to even fewer resources to help them leave poverty behind.

All of these factors lead to increased stress, which leads to reduced cognitive capabilities, which can trap them in the environment.

Diana Baumrind used the *Goldilocks and the Three Bears* analogy to describe three parenting styles, finding the Authoritarian style *too hard*. "Authoritarian parenting attempts to shape, control, and evaluate the behavior and attitudes of the child in accordance with a set standard of conduct, usually an absolute standard, theologically motivated and formulated by a higher authority. She values obedience as a virtue and favors punitive, forceful measures to curb self-will at points where the child's actions or beliefs conflict with what she thinks is right conduct. She believes in keeping the child in his place, in restricting his autonomy, and in assigning household responsibilities in order to inculcate respect for work. She regards the preservation of order and traditional structure as a highly valued end in itself. She does not encourage verbal give and take, believing that the child should accept her word for what is right."[405] "Researchers reported that, "paternal authoritarian behavior appeared to reduce young people's happiness through weakening their self-esteem."[406]

Ms. Baumrind found the Authoritative style *just right*. "The authoritative parent attempts to direct the child's activities in a rational, issue-oriented manner. She encourages verbal give and take, shares with the child the reasoning behind her policy, and solicits his objections when he refuses to conform. Both autonomous self-will and disciplined conformity are valued by the authoritative parent. Therefore, she exerts firm control at points of parent-child divergence, but does not hem the child in with restrictions. She enforces her own perspective as an adult, but recognizes the child's individual interests and special ways. The authoritative parent affirms the child's present qualities, but also sets standards for future conduct. She uses reason, power, and shaping by regime and reinforcement to achieve her objectives and does not base her decisions on group consensus or the individual child's desires." [407]

Permissiveness was considered *too soft*. "The permissive parent attempts to behave in a non-punitive, acceptant, and affirmative manner toward the child's impulses, desires, and actions. She consults with him about policy decisions and gives explanations for family rules.. She makes few demands for household responsibility and orderly behavior. She presents herself to the child as a resource for him to use as he wishes, not as an ideal for him to emulate, nor as an active agent responsible for shaping or altering his ongoing or future behavior. She allows the child to regulate his own activities as much as possible, avoids the exercise of control, and does not encourage him to obey externally defined standards, She attempts to use reason and manipulation, but not overt power, to accomplish her ends."[408]

Authoritarian parenting is associated with poor outcomes for a variety of reasons and is more common in low socioeconomic homes. One reason authoritarian parenting is worse is that it violates the basic human need of autonomy detailed in Chapter 18.

The lessening of self-esteem that is associated with authoritarian parenting may be a significant reason for generational poverty. Research that looked at the effect of self-esteem on wages found that 80% of wages earned are tied to the self-esteem of the employee.[409] Using *The Smart Way* with Emotional Guidance is an effective and affordable method of increasing self-esteem that could help end generational poverty.

The real tragedy of the poor is the poverty of their aspirations.
Adam Smith

Self-esteem also effects people's decision about whether or not to pursue additional education, which is another pathway on which self-esteem can affect the ability to rise above poverty. Some say that self-esteem is the result of the higher wages or higher educational attainment, but research shows my personal experience that higher self-esteem comes first is not an anomaly. Much the same way we know happiness increases success, self-esteem increases success. It makes sense that self-esteem would also come before the higher income because healthy self-esteem is a component of True Happiness.

For the poor this is really good news. It means you don't have to figure out how to make more money, how to leave the slums, how to pay off debts, or how to get more education as your first step. The first step out of poverty is to believe that you can achieve your dreams. That's all. That's it. The first step is to believe in yourself. Don't let anyone convince you that you can't, and if they have already convinced you, convince yourself that you can. Believe you are worthy and that you have what it takes. If you don't have it, you'll get it—you'll find a way.

An image is coming into my mind that shows someone with low self-esteem walking along a gravel path, being careful where he puts his feet so he does not bruise them further on the small and sometimes sharp rocks on the path. The same person walking on the same path after self-esteem is increased walks with more confidence because he now has a pair of sturdy shoes or hiking boots between his feet and the gravel. It's a lot easier to move along when you don't have to worry about each step you take.

Other work indicates that an internal locus of control accounts for some of the higher wages.[410] An internal locus of control is a key component of resilience and is also required for True Happiness.

When someone learns to interpret and respond to emotional signals in optimal ways, they thrive. The process is empowering and creates upward spirals that increase intrinsic motivation. The process is self-fueling.

Income Inequality

Researchers will sometimes put forth the idea that all incomes should be equal because research shows that people are not as happy when others around them make more. The researchers are approaching the issue from the wrong perspective.

They're using a model of economics that has a limited pie that must be shared by everyone. This is a flawed premise.

Wealth is not a limited commodity. If that were true, we'd still be trading pemmican for furs and beads. People who are becoming wealthy today are doing new things that create new demand for products and services. You have to get rid of the idea that someone else has yours or is getting your share. They're getting theirs. Yours is there waiting for you to find the right path for you to get it. Create value and the money and resources will come to you.

The Universe is Infinite and bountiful,
and there is enough for all to create the dream in their heart and live within it.
Story Waters

1. Comparing yourself to others is never a wise idea. Two people could live next door to one another in identical homes and make exactly the same amount of money doing exactly the same job and one could be happy and the other unhappy. If one is living her dream, she'll be happy. If the other one is far from living her dream and does not believe she is on the path to live her dream, she'll be unhappy. She may even resent that her neighbor is happy if she is in the habit of comparing herself to others.

There is nothing noble in being superior to your fellow man; true nobility is being superior to your former self.
Ernest Hemingway (or Hindu Proverb)

2. When you look at what another has and feel envy or jealousy you are telling yourself, "Someone else has been able to be, do, or attain something I can't do."
   Take such thoughts to the Coherence chart in Chapter 14. You'll find that thoughts of envy or jealousy are not coherent. Now take the attitude of, "If that person can be, do, or have something that I want to be, do, or have, that is proof that it is possible It means I can do it, too. I just have to believe and then I'll be able to find a way to be, do, or have what I am desiring."

It is not a situation that can be cured by giving everyone the same because not everyone will be satisfied by being the same. The Pilgrims tried that in the 1600's. Most people don't know that socialism was the way the colony was first structured. The fruit of everyone's efforts were shared. It didn't last long because disagreements about who was working hard enough quickly erupted and led to discord. Some aspects of socialism continue to this day. For example, in some parts of the country they have barn raisings, when someone needs a new barn the community comes together and helps them build the barn. But unlike when socialism is for everything, if a neighbor does not help other neighbors when it is time for their barn raising, they won't show up when he or she needs one.

Homeless Populations
Beds with some privacy would be better than rooms where many people sleep together even if the room is tiny. An environment filled with homeless people is almost by definition an environment full of people in low emotional states, which means people who may be capable of undesirable behavior.

There is a link between sleep and stress, health, and cognitive processes. Some of the homeless people I've spoken with get very little sleep because they do not feel safe when they're sleeping—even in a shelter. Providing small rooms for sleeping—even if they aren't much larger than a handicapped bathroom stall and shared bathroom facilities—would, I believe, help individuals more than shared sleeping quarters. They should have the ability to lock the door and feel safe and secure while they sleep.

Money alone is not the answer. There are enough rags to riches and back again stories to show that just providing money is not going to solve the problem. That's because the lack of money is a symptom—not the root cause. Many people think poor people are lazy. I don't. I think many impoverished people have developed (or been trained into) Learned Helplessness relative to money. Developing an internal locus of control overcomes Learned Helplessness. *The Smart Way* helps people change their beliefs and provides clear feedback showing they have control.

I don't have all the answers to poverty, but there is enough evidence indicating the way someone thinks has a significant role that we should do what we can now and as we can do more, do it. Children who are taught *The Smart Way* won't develop Learned Helplessness.

It is important to point out some of the ways government policies hinder efforts to help everyone thrive. It may have been unintentional, but the result was counterproductive. It would serve us all better if solid psychology instead of politics was used to determine how to structure needed government programs.

Hand-outs

If someone was instructed to design a system that would decrease motivation and build resentment, they could model it after today's welfare system. The invasive checks into the lives, the lack of autonomy recipients feel and the punishments incurred when people begin to make progress could have been deliberately designed to keep people down—they are that good at it.

Consider the research communicated in these pages about the importance of autonomy to intrinsic motivation and compare it to the current system.

Consider the research communicated in these pages about the importance of self-determination and empowered thinking and compare it to a system that makes people jump through so many hoops it requires a Master's Degree in street knowledge to understand how to conduct oneself. When you live in public housing someone else can decide who it is okay for you to have visit your home and if you allow people on the not approved list you may lose your home.

There is little room for self-esteem for welfare recipients if they maintain a worldview where independence and self-sufficiency are valued. Only by changing to a worldview that values taking advantage of the system can they exist and feel better than awful. It's no wonder that the focus is often not in improving one's situation, but on gaming the system. It is predictable that people would find that perspective when you understand what makes people happy and what disempowers them.

The system needs to be reviewed by experts in psychology who can find a way to provide a safety net and empower those who need the net in ways that help them not only survive, but thrive. It can be done, but it requires a different perspective. Done right, dignity could be maintained during the time someone needs the safety net and long-term progress can be far greater than what is normally seen today.

It is possible for someone who was once on welfare to thrive. If one can do it, so can many. If you're hard pressed for an example of one, look no further than your local bookstore and pick up one of J.K. Rowling's or Eckhart Tolle's books. Look for what is possible and make more of it happen.

Abundance

Today there is a lot of backlash against the wealthy. It is as if people believe there are a limited number of resources available and we have to all share them. But if you step back and take a broader viewpoint it becomes clear that the most valuable asset anyone can have is a good idea and no one can prevent you from having an idea. Only you control your mindset.

The concept of a pie that we all split, which is currently split very unevenly is flawed at its basis. It probably originated with an economist attempting to illustrate the distribution of wealth using a pie chart and someone decided the pie represented all the wealth.

Not long ago, in this country, feathers, beads, and furs were currency. Then money was represented by paper and coins. Now there is frequent talk of moving toward an economy with electronic money. But a barter economy also exists in this same time—an economy of trading X for Y, with no currency changing hands. Money is a convenience, but it does not represent all the assets in the world. It does not represent all the potential assets in this world.

Many of the wealthiest individuals of our time became wealthy selling products that no one had ever conceived of before I was born. Ideas made them wealthy. They did not steal wealth from others. People wanted what they created and were happy to give them money in exchange for their product. Others created wealth by selling the opportunity for others to earn dividends and capital gains by owning pieces of their company called stocks.

We don't complain that John has been healthy all year while we've had both the flu and bronchitis. We don't say that John is using all of our health. It is the same way with money—someone else does not have your share. You have to have the right mindset to get what you want—you don't have to take it from someone else. If you don't think mindset has anything to do with money there are some things you should look at with an open mind.

The National Endowment for Financial Education, a Denver-based nonprofit estimates that as many as 70 percent of people who land sudden windfalls lose that money within several years. If people who are handed millions of dollars can't remain wealthy it means there is something going on beyond the ability to get the money.

I, and many others, believe that *something else* is one's mindset about money.

One problem is that the Biblical admonishment that "The love of money is the root of all evil" has been converted to a belief that money is evil. It was never money that was evil—it is loving money for money's sake. You can love money for the freedom it gives you, for the access to healthcare or travel, for the education it can provide or the safety and security it affords and none of that is evil. You can even love money for the ability it gives you to do things for others.

If you think money is evil and that you're good you've created cognitive conflict between your desire to have money and having money that will be even stronger on the quantum level where one cancels out the other in Destructive Coherence.

Others believe they have to earn the right to wealth, but when asked they don't have a way to determine when they've done enough to earn the right to be wealthy.

If your mindset is anything other than one that believes you deserve to have the money you need to do the things you want to do, Destructive Coherence exists. You're self-sabotaging yourself on the quantum level.

Pay attention to how people speak about money and the money that comes into their lives. I had a friend who was retired and had a nice five-figure monthly. He would often say as he splurged on some small or large luxury that the *Pension God* was sending him more next month, so why not? He had an expensive car he seldom drove and another nice vehicle he used most of the time. After telling this story for about a year, he unexpectedly inherited a rather large sum from an uncle who he had not expected to inherit anything from. The uncle was no longer around to ask him why he'd changed his will, but it is consistent with my theory about Constructive Coherence. My friend developed beliefs that money came easily to him and money began coming very easily to him.

If you know two people who have worked side-by-side for a long period of time and made roughly the same amount of money and had the same size of family take extra care to see how each speaks about money. You'll find that the one who has a more positive attitude about money has a better financial situation.

One occupation I find where a lack mindset is common is teachers. I know many teachers who struggle every month and only a few who seem to do just fine on similar incomes.

I tell a story about my own finances when I was buying my house. I needed to come up with $80,000 in five months, which was more than I made in a year at that time. I had no idea where the money would come from but I was absolutely determined to buy the house. If someone had asked me how I would get the money in March when I first signed the contract to buy the house none of the sources of the funds would have been on my list. I got $86,000 in five months—legally. I made up my mind that I was going to buy the house, which meant I would get the money somehow, and I made it happen. The bulk of the money came from a 9-year old debt that was partially repaid to me, after not being successful in collecting a penny of it in the preceding 9 years.

Collecting that debt felt a lot like a pickle jar lid that was too tight for me to open for 9 years and then someone loosened the jar so opening it was easy. The 9 preceding years had been a struggle, but actually collecting the money was not.

Our own beliefs about what we are worth affect what we receive. I love using the story of the three ladies to illustrate this point.

Three ladies who had just turned 40 and saw many men around them making much more than they did and not working as hard. (This is not male bashing; it was just the environment they were in.) One of the ladies said "I want to make six figures. I am worth it." Another said "I want to make more than six figures. I am worth it." The third lady made a presentation for a new division at her work and included in the proposal a salary of $120,000 for herself. She also excitedly shared the proposal with her family and waxed poetic over what life would be like when she made that much money.

Although they did not understand at the time what exactly they were doing these ladies were re programming their belief that they were worth that much money so their filter would allow them to see opportunities for this type of income. Prior to believing they could make that sort of money their filters would have filtered out information about such opportunities.

What happened after they set their filters? In less than three years lady #1 went from +/- $57,000 to $100,000. Lady #2 went from +/- $37,000 to over $100,000 a number that varied with bonuses, etc. but was always over $100,000 and sometimes exceeded $250,000. Lady #3 lost her $72,000 a year job. Then phone rang because her former boss had recommended her to a neighbor who offered her a job and the negotiated salary was $120,000 to the penny. She also received a raise in less than six months.

What you believe you are worth matters. What you believe yourself capable of matters. If you say "I can't" you can't.

The mind is the limit. As long as the mind can envision the fact that you can do something, you can do it, as long as you really believe 100 percent.
Arnold Schwarzenegger

Now, let's do some fine tuning. The more general "I want to make over six figures" did the best financially. The one who did the proposal did the best as far as a job that she loved – Her filter showed her the absolutely perfect match of a job for her that continued to grow and be what she desired. The one who said she wanted to make $100,000 was still making that amount five years after she began making it.

The more general belief in worth "I am worth over $100,000" was less limiting than the other two. The one who did the proposal for $120,000 had included bonuses and a budget of expected growth in the department with increases so her receiving a quick raise was consistent with what she had decided she was worth.

Let's review. The Three Ladies felt they were underpaid. They looked at men in their work environments and decided that they were just as smart as the men and that they worked harder (all three had a very limiting belief that hard work was what caused high pay) but they overcame it by comparing how hard they worked with how hard others who made more worked and decided they worked harder than the men who made the larger salaries therefore they were worth the larger salaries. Through this process, which was just an empowering gripping session, they increased their own belief in their worth which re-set their filters. From another perspective, you could say they increased their self-esteem by beginning to believe they were worth six figure salaries. Self-esteem has a significant impact on earnings.

If they had just complained about how much more the men made it would not have re-set their filters but they used the situation to empower themselves by believing that if the men who did not work as hard as they did made six figure incomes then they should too. Each was supportive and they did not worry about how. The conversation was left at "we are worth more, much more". If they had went on to lament how they could possibly make that much more they would have set their filters to "I am worth this but it won't happen" so the belief that they were worth that much would have been overridden by the contrary belief that it was not possible for them to get there.

The *how* is not the concern when you change beliefs. When you are changing the belief you won't be able to see the *how* because the filter has been filtering out the *how's* that would have been available because of the earlier belief. Getting the new belief firmly in your mind is the work.

You do things when the opportunities come along. I've had periods in my life when I've had a bundle of ideas come along, and I've had long dry spells. If I get an idea next week, I'll do something. If not, I won't do a damn thing.
Warren Buffett

To succeed, jump as quickly at opportunities as you do at conclusions.
Benjamin Franklin

Once your belief is established, you can turn your attention to the *how* but it is not a matter of trying to figure it out so much as watch the new information coming through your filters for the opportunities that arrive. When the opportunity that feels exciting or of high interest makes its way through your newly re-set filter you will know, you will feel the emotion of excitement or passion or interest or feel very optimistic about it. That is the time to take action.

You can help those opportunities arrive but only do as much as feels good. If you begin doing things that cause you to feel discouraged then your filter will get the message that it is not likely that it will happen (a new belief) and begin filtering based on that belief. It becomes a self-fulfilling prophesy, so to speak.

Also, this is important. If there are those in your life who would doubt your ability to have what your new belief says is possible do not speak to them of it or of your hopes. Their doubt can influence your belief(s) in a negative way. Speak to them of other pleasant topics. Do not allow them to rain on your parade. Trust your own belief. If the other person holds the old belief they will not believe it and their negativity will impact your newly formed belief. If you can't be quiet just stay away from them for a while. Only tell them when it has happened or when it is sure.

Or, if it is something that is hard but you could communicate part of it as "I am going to do this" without generating questions about the details you can do that. Just don't tell them the obstacles you need to overcome in order to achieve it.

The key is to keep company only with people who uplift you, whose presence calls forth your best.
Epictetus

If you have someone who believes in you then telling them is usually okay. Personally, I prefer to hold things close to my vest until it is a sure thing.

Sometimes others try to add ideas to what I am planning and the ideas do not sync with what I want and that muddies the waters. I begin thinking "I want it my way not the way they described" and the filters get confused a bit.

Don't get too detailed. Remember the example of the woman who said "I want to make more than $100,000". She fared better than the other two although all three improved their financial situations dramatically by shifting their beliefs.

No society can surely be flourishing and happy, of which the far greater part of the members are poor and miserable.
Adam Smith

22: Overall Health

Health is a state of optimal physical, mental and social well-being, and not merely the absence of disease and infirmity.
World Health Organization (WHO)

My approach to health is that physical, mental, psychological, social, and spiritual aspects of life are interconnected with health and well-being beginning with the invisible and unmeasurable and expanding outward. This means that our thoughts, stress, and emotions affect our genetics, cells, and organs. The scientific evidence that supports a holistic view of physical, mental, and behavioral wellbeing grows daily and is already compelling. Yet, despite the evidence, our current medical system is designed as if thoughts, stress, and emotions are irrelevant. This is the primary reason it treats symptoms, but does not cure illnesses.

I am not going to expand greatly on the connection between physical health and stress in this book because that was the subject of my first book (*True Prevention—Optimum Health: Remember Galileo*) and an updated version that extends the health benefits of happiness and low stress to many other illnesses and diseases is in the works. *The Smart Way* provides all you need to optimize your health.

If the tree in front of your house is ill at the roots, cutting off the dead branches will not correct the problem. The illness in the roots must be healed. When it comes to humans, our thoughts are our roots and the first symptom that our thoughts are unhealthy is negative emotion. We must pay attention to how we feel and respond with skill when we feel negative emotion lest it festers and becomes a symptom that requires a physician.

We recognize that the body has innate healing power. We don't freak out when we cut our finger while preparing dinner because we know our body can easily heal a small cut. But when bigger things go wrong and we consult a physician, we tend to forget that the body has the ability to heal. In chapter 14 on **Coherent Thought** you learned about biophotons and coherence. When our thoughts are at cross purposes with our goals, it interferes with the cell-to-cell communication via biophotons, which can lead to illness. The lack of Coherence also creates stress, which we know on the biological level causes a chemical cocktail of stress hormones that in turn decrease the body's innate immune function.

But physicians are trained to look at the manifested illness, name it, and then treat it as if it arrived in isolation. They don't explore what was causing stress prior to the manifestation of the illness nor do they advise you to evaluate what is going on in your life. It's not their fault. They aren't trained to look beyond the treatable diagnoses.

"There is growing literature to support a reciprocal relationship between physical and mental illnesses: chronic medical conditions can have an adverse effect on psychological well-being, and psychopathology and stress can have a negative effect on physical health . . . a wide array of pathophysiologic mechanisms seem to converge in different illnesses, resulting in common symptoms such as anxiety, depression, and pain. Promising psychosocial treatments for psychopathology can be tailored to target physical symptom relief, medical adherence, and quality of life (QoL) among individuals vulnerable to psychological and medical stress caused by their experience of chronic medical illness. One of the most promising and empirically researched therapies for medical comorbidity is cognitive-behavioral therapy."[411]

Stress and Chronic Stress

Psychosocial stress, especially chronic stress, impacts health and relationships across the lifespan and beyond. Daily stressors such as traffic jams, feeling overwhelmed by work duties, caring for a family, marital disagreements, and financial concerns can cause chronic stress.[412] It is important to have a method of relieving stress that works for you and that you will use on a regular basis, or if it is a method that will become automatic when it is a habit, that you take the time to develop the habit. "Research shows that almost every system in the body can be influenced by chronic stress . . . and it suppresses the body's immune system and ultimately manifests as illness."[413]

"Reviews of the general stress and coping literature have widely shown the role of stress as a contributor to important aspects of physical, cognitive and emotional maladjustment . . . when stress is not handled appropriately, it may have considerable influence on the development of negative emotional responses that can lead to reduced levels of wellbeing."[414]

Stress can be in the form of negative life events or a series of minor stressors or daily hassles "such as disagreements with teachers, academic difficulties, disappointments by friends, conflicts with parents, and problems with mastering the school-to-work transition."[415] Additional stressors include "victimization, grief and loss, divorce or separation, violence, child abuse or neglect, substance abuse, natural disasters, school crises, military deployments, familial mental illness and poverty."[416]

The following three concepts are used relatively interchangeably in this book:
- Happiness
- Low Stress
- Heart Coherence

I use them interchangeably because happiness is marked by the absence of negative stressors. Low stress is marked by the presence of happiness. Researchers at The HeartMath Institute have consistently found that greater heart coherence is associated with increased positive emotions and low stress.

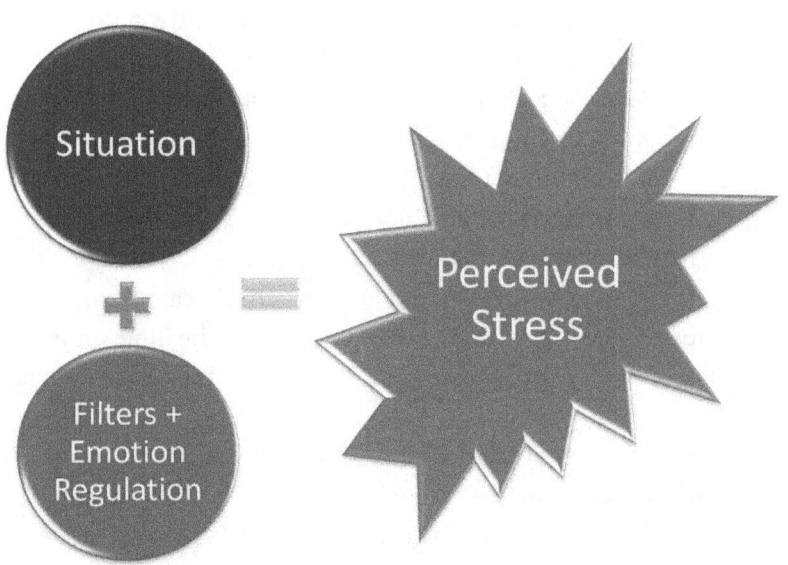

Communicating these interrelationships between emotions, stress, and overall health is critical to gain support for interventions that will make a significant and lasting difference. The charts in Chapters 2 and 5 demonstrate the interrelationships. Teachers and students should be taught skills that help them proactively manage stressors. My work focuses on using one's mind and emotions in a harmonious concert that allows people to feel good which leads to better physical and emotional well-being. This is made easier by the fact that stress is about perception. We all know that two people facing the same circumstances do not experience the same level of stress. We've seen people remain calm under conditions that would make us tremble. Or, maybe, you're the strong one who has wondered why those around you are acting so panicked when you are not afraid. There are multiple factors that work together that lead to the level of stress an individual feels. First you have the actual circumstances. But perceptually, a solvable problem may appear to be unsolvable. An opportunity may appear to be a problem. A friendly overture may be interpreted as an undesirable or even hostile overture. The filters discussed in Chapters 11-14 explain how they impact individual perception below the conscious level of thought.

The Smart Way is designed to assist in shifting those filters so they benefit the individual and reduce the perceived stress. Emotion regulation can occur unconsciously or consciously. Self-regulation of emotion means you do not simply accept that your first impression of the situation is the only one or even the best one for you to have. Emotion regulation seeks to decrease the level of stress you feel when you are experiencing emotions outside the Sweet and Hopeful Zones. Emotion Regulation can also be used to maintain or even increase positive emotions when you are in the Sweet and Hopeful Zones. It may be helpful to think of emotion regulation as a mode of transportation between Zones on the Emotional Guidance Scale.

Individuals skilled in emotion regulation experience less stress and depression and more positive well-being (happiness).[417] When you use *The Smart Way* strategies to reduce stress over a period of time, they become implicit responses and reduce the stress response to situations before (or simultaneously with) your perception of the situation. When this is in place, situations you may have once found upsetting or that would have led to anger can be responded to calmly because your mind immediately sees that they are solvable and you know that you are capable of solving them. In some cases, what you may have perceived as a problem at one time will seem to be an opportunity. While you will not lose awareness that it could still be perceived as a problem, the opportunity inherent in the situation will be more vivid to you. Your emotional response will be to the perspective that you chose to accept.

Stress has an immediate impact on how you feel in the moment, but because stress changes your body's chemistry, it also has long-term effects on your mental and physical health. When emotion regulation skills are low, the lifetime accumulation of stressors is "associated with incrementally worse health outcomes, including increased prevalence of psychiatric symptoms and increased vulnerability to psychiatric disorders. The effects are not limited to mental illnesses. Individuals who have experienced higher levels of lifetime stress (due to low socioeconomic status, poor emotion regulation skills, minority status, or other factors) experience more chronic illnesses and are far more likely to die prematurely. This is so common that it has been given a label, disparate health outcomes. There is evidence that "stress accumulation may accelerate biological aging processes."[418]

Disparate Impact
While most studies about disparate health outcomes point to lower availability of health care or the higher distrust of the healthcare system, both of which are factors that increase stress, the stress pathway to illness and disease is not generally part of the conversation. This is unfortunate and one of the reasons I am writing this book. I don't know how to solve poverty or the lingering racism that poisons our country and the world, but I do know how to reduce perceived stress. The research is clear that reducing the stress load will improve disparate outcomes. It is something that can be done today and provide immediate benefit to millions of people.

But the likelihood is that the majority of the disparate impact is due to chronic stress from a variety of sources including lower socioeconomic status, perceived lower social status, lower education levels, racism, perceived microaggressions, and socially, a tendency not to seek treatment for mental health issues. I would love to see a study of minority participants that does a very deep dive into the mindsets of the participants and follows them over time. By deep dive, measure not only income, education and marital status, but also feelings about whether they are empowered or disempowered, whether they are optimistic or pessimistic, etc. I've spoken with college educated Blacks who said they could not get ahead because of their race, I've met others who have told me they don't think their race is relevant, and others who feel it affects their experiences but that they don't let it bother them because that would diminish their experience. The stress levels experienced by individuals with these three attitudes would vary significantly. Knowing what we know about the myriad ways stress harms health and well-being, the more stress an attitude creates, the worse long-term health such individuals would experience.

The HeartMath Institute defines coherence as "a state in which the heart, mind and emotions are balanced and operating in sync and the immune, hormonal and nervous systems function in energetic coordination."[419] Heart Coherence is essentially the same as experiencing low levels of stress and positive emotion. The HeartMath Institute cites numerous benefits of achieving coherence and detriments of not achieving it including:

Benefits of Coherence	**Effects of Negative Emotion**
Significant improvement in brain function	Reduced muscle mass
40% improvement in long-term memory	Brain cell death
24% improvement in short-term memory	Impaired memory
Increased ability to focus	Accelerated aging
Increased ability to process information	Impaired mental function
Improved ability to learn	Depleted energy reserves
Increased ability to self-regulate	
Higher test scores	

The HeartMath method combines breathing techniques with simple emotion regulation strategies to achieve coherence but does not incorporate Emotional Guidance which should improve the results even more. The mind is your most powerful path to feeling good and learning to find perspectives that serve your highest good is the most stable and sustainable way to reduce stress. The mind and body are connected, combining conscious emotion regulation strategies with breathing can enhance the effects.

A study conducted via collaboration between the Centers for Disease Control and prevention and Kaiser Permanente's Health Appraisal Clinic in San Diego included more than 17,000 members of Kaiser's Health Maintenance Organization (HMO). They concluded that "some of the worst health and social problems in our nation can arise as a consequence of adverse childhood experiences." I completely agree with their conclusion and this book is an effort to raise awareness of the root cause of many undesired outcomes and propose a solution. I have modified the ACE Pyramid created as the result of the CDC and Kaiser's collaborative effort to reflect the multi-generational nature of negative outcomes stemming from chronic psychosocial stress.[420]

There are numerous paths that lead to the adverse results. The psychosocial stress of poverty, racism, and abuse all negatively impact parenting and numerous mind and body functions. Child abuse, witnessing domestic violence, and neighborhood violence add further to the psychosocial burden of many children living in poor neighborhoods. But throwing money at the problem to eliminate the poverty is not enough. In fact, beyond meeting basic needs, it may be counterproductive unless and until meta-cognitve capabilities are increased. An individual who feels like a victim reaches different conclusions than one who feels empowered. An individual who is afraid reaches different conclusions than one who is fearless.

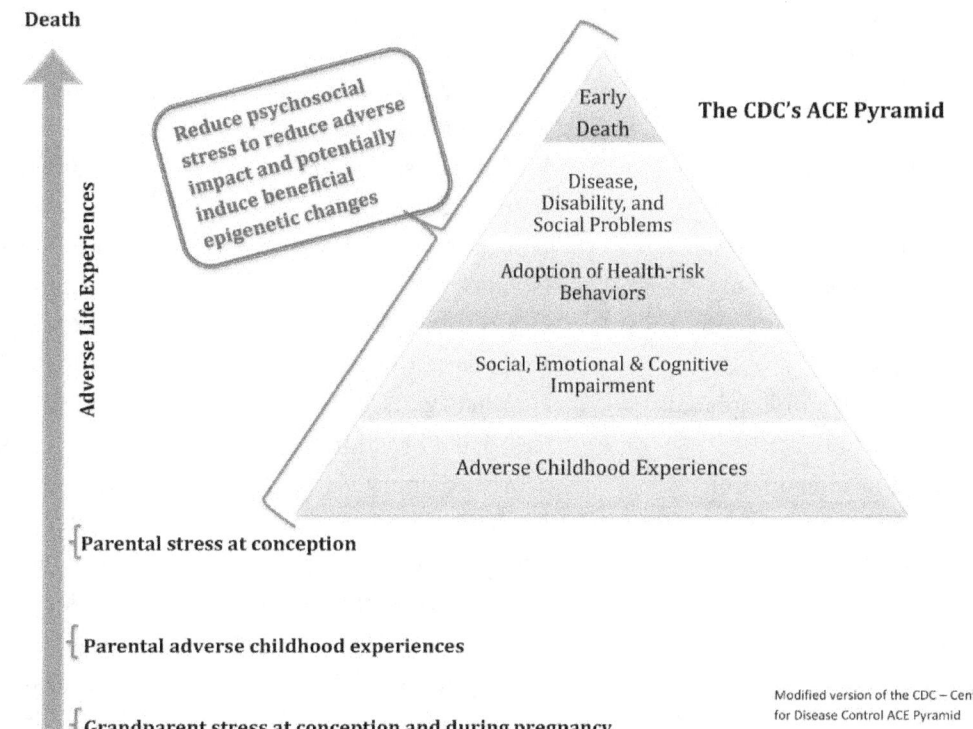

Even in improved financial circumstances, habitual lack and fear thoughts will perpetuate chronic psychosocial stress. Only by empowering the mind will the stress burden be alleviated.

Our society does not recognize stress as a problem that should be addressed early enough. Many people take pride in how much stress they can handle and still keep going. When we change our attitude toward stress, our outcomes will improve. For some people who do understand the negative consequences of chronic stress even the word stress can induce greater levels of stress. Increasing awareness without simultaneously providing relief will make matters worse. Individuals who use *The Smart Way* will not experience greater stress when they learn about the negative consequences of stress because they will feel in control of their response to the stressors in their life.

Common causes of stress all stem from perceiving experiences in suboptimal ways. Whether it is congested traffic, an argument with a family member, feeling overwhelmed, a micromanaging boss, a body that is not functioning at 100%, financial stress, time stress, relationship stress, work stress, or some other situation that is causing a perspective that leads to negative emotion.

22: Overall Health

Early warning signs of stress

Early warning signs of stress can come in the form of physical, mental, cognitive, and/or behavioral symptoms including:[421, 422]

Physical	Behavioral	Psychological
Muscle tension	Hurrying	Irritability
Headaches	Increased accidents	Less emotional control
Exhaustion/fatigue	Decreased productivity	Often worried
Weight changes	Increased use of drugs	Feeling overwhelmed
Sleep disturbances	Increased use of alcohol	Easily frustrated
Teeth grinding	Unhealthy eating patterns	Poor concentration
Frequent illnesses	Isolation	Thoughts of running away
Stomach aches	Cigarette smoking	Loss of sense of humor
Hypertension	Procrastination	Difficulty making decisions
Sweating or trembling hands	Conflicts with others	Crying spells
Sexual dysfunction	Restricted breathing	Intense bouts of anger
Diarrhea or constipation	More sedentary	Attitude critical of others
Back pain	Bossiness	Restlessness
Restlessness	Compulsive gum chewing	Nervousness
Indigestion	Inability to get things done	Anxiety
Increased pain		Boredom, no meaning
Indigestion	**Cognitive**	Edginess, ready to explode
Dizziness	Trouble thinking clearly	Feeling powerless
Racing heart	Lack of creativity	Loneliness
Ringing in the ears	Forgetfulness	Unhappy for no reason
	Memory Loss	Easily upset
	Inability to make decisions	

Given the long-term consequences of chronic stress, the government should be educating its citizens about prevention and early symptom recognition, but it is not. The earliest symptom of stress is the emotional response to your thought that feels worse than the prior thought, or that simply feels bad. If it feels bad, you're experiencing stress. If it feels worse than the prior thought, you've turned in the direction of stress, even if your thought still feels good.

The United States Department of Health and Human Services has a website with a fact sheet about stress and women. It was last updated in 2010 and was obviously written by someone who did not fully understand stress (i.e. they list negative life events as "the most common causes of stress"). Poverty and being a minority aren't mentioned as sources of stress.

The same article lists numerous methods of "handling the stress" including:

Government Advice: Develop a new attitude

Problem: It does not tell you *how* to change your attitude

Government Advice: Become a problem solver.

Problem: This lists action steps to take but does not consider the fact that someone who is highly stressed has impaired cognitive function. The first step in most situations should be to use a meta-cognitve process to feel better (unless one is in immediate danger).

Government Advice: Be flexible.

Problem: Beyond stating that sometimes it is not worth the stress to argue, it does not give anyone the *how* to help them be more flexible in their interactions with others.

Government Advice: Set limits.

Problem: Many people have significant issues with saying "No" to additional demands and just telling them to do it does not empower them with skills that allow them to actually do it.

Government Advice: Relax

Problem: This is so vague as to be worthless. If an individual does not understand Emotional Guidance, they could go get a massage to relax but think about their problems the entire time, perhaps even ruminating in such a way that they feel worse afterwards.

Government Advice: Take deep breaths.

Problem: Deep breathing is a good dose-dependent method of stress reduction, but it is dose-dependent. It would be fine to mention as a technique, but without techniques that provide long-term solutions it can give individuals the impression that there are no better ways to manage stress, which is misleading.

Government Advice: Stretch.

Problem: This is addressing muscle tension, which is not the cause of the stress—it's a symptom.

Government Advice: Get enough sleep.

Problem: Stress can interfere with one's ability to sleep. Using meta-cognitve processes to reduce stress improves the ability to fall asleep and to rest well.

Government Advice: Eat right.

Problem: The research is clear that even individuals who have committed to a good diet do not do as well when they are stressed. This can be an impossible goal for a comfort eater who is stressed. It can be even worse for someone who has an eating disorder.

Government Advice: Get moving.

Problem: Much like eating well, people who know exercise reduces their level of stress frequently report they don't do it when they feel *too stressed*.

Government Advice: Don't deal with stress in unhealthy ways.

Problem: People will seek stress relief in the lowest risk way they know, but drugs, alcohol and other unhealthy ways to feel better are often the least risky way the individual knows to feel better. Unless and until the person is empowered with skills that reduce the stress, telling them to *just say no* is not effective.

Government Advice: Connect with others

Problem: Stressed people experience worse moods and interpret others' words and actions in ways that match their mood. Being with someone when you're in a bad mood can lead to worsening relationships with that person.

Government Advice: Get help from a professional if you need it.

Problem: While I have no problem with recommending someone consult a professional for help managing stress, many

> Also, most people will wait to get professional advice after they manifest an illness. It is far easier to prevent the illness by educating the public about how to deal with stress in the early stages.

recommendations (even from their trusted family care physicians) are not acted upon. This is partially due to the lingering stigma associated with mental health services and it is also due to cost considerations, which can be a significant factor for individuals experiencing high levels of stress. Providing information about meta-cognitve processes that would be helpful in reducing psychological stress is likely to help more people. It is not as if this website is a written document with size limitations due to printing costs or other restrictions. They can include more detail about helpful information. If there is a concern about overwhelming someone with too much information, they can manage it with links to more detailed information.

Government Advice: Help others.

Problem: This is a commonly suggested method of feeling better. It can also induce guilt in individuals who are time-stressed and don't feel they have time to help others and in individuals who are physically limited and don't feel they can be of benefit to others. An individual with low self-esteem whose perception is that he has nothing to offer others may feel even worse as he contemplates that other people who feel bad can find a way to feel better by helping others, but because he perceives he has nothing worthwhile he can offer others, he might feel even lower self-worth.

Prevention, Health Promotion

Evidence that supports my position that a combination of knowledge and abilities that help individuals optimize their personal perspectives to reduce chronic stress would be a significant factor in preventing a wide range of undesirable outcomes including behavior, physical and mental health as well as success in career and marriage. The evidence is overwhelming to anyone who delves deeply into the results of cross disciplinary research. Because "Research suggests normal brain development may be particularly vulnerable to stress during adolescence and puberty making adolescents vulnerable to developing depression and bipolar spectrum disorder"[423] prevention and health promotion is strongly advised. *The Smart Way* solution is very affordable when all the potential benefits are considered. In fact, it should reduce future costs by far more than the cost of widespread implementation.

A review in *Psychiatric Investigations* "suggested that preventive intervention for adolescents needs focus on the common determinates of health as a whole in conjunction with education rather than one specific or problems."[424]

The Smart Way more than satisfies this recommendation and it is far more cost effective than the recommendation alluded to in the article because it can be delivered via large groups and via the internet.

Exposure to Violence

Exposure to violence, even if injuries do not occur, can lead to both adverse mental and physical health outcomes. From PTSD to depression on the mental health side and increased risk of "asthma, significant alteration of healthy eating and activity, heart disease and hypertension, ulcers and gastrointestinal disorders, diabetes, neurological and musculoskeletal diseases, and lung disease" are all associated with violence.[425]

Physical Health Contagious Stress

> *There is also emerging evidence that there is a direct pathway between positive affect [happiness] and health, involving reduced psychobiological activation of neuroendocrine, autonomic, immune and inflammatory pathways.*
> Samantha Dockray and Andrew Steptoe

Scientific research literature is full of findings that attribute between 65 - 95% of physical health problems to stress and the biochemical reaction of the body when the mind is stressed. Riva, Wirth, and Williams stated, "Our findings add to Engel's claim that the ultimate criteria for the patients' well-being are psychosocial, even when the complaint is physical in origin (i.e. pain)."[426] In 2008, the Center for Disease Control (CDC) estimated that 75% of all doctor visits were due to stress.[427]

". . . real or perceived challenges requires activation of a complex range of responses involving the endocrine, nervous, and immune systems, collectively known as the stress response. Inappropriate regulation of the stress response has been linked to a wide array of pathologies including autoimmune disease, hypertension, affective disorders, and major depression."[428]

"This new formulation emphasizes the cascading relationships, beginning early in life, between environmental factors and genetic predispositions that lead to large individual differences in susceptibility to stress and, in some cases, to disease. There are now empirical studies based on this formulation, as well as new insights into mechanisms involving specific changes in neural, neuroendocrine, and immune systems."[429]

"Chronic, unmanageable social and psychological stress, and maltreatment, especially early in life, are also linked to shorter telomeres, which have been associated with increased risk of developing somatic diseases such as cancer, diabetes and heart diseases, and psychiatric disorders, particularly depression."[430]

With those definitions of stress in mind, The following premises, supported by science, support all my work:

Mindset determines thoughts > Thoughts lead to an emotional response > Emotional response guides thoughts, words, and actions.

True Happiness is associated with low stress and a high state of empowerment.

Meta-cognitve processes can be used to reduce stress (increase happiness and one's sense of empowerment) without requiring circumstances to change.

Stress, especially chronic stress, has been linked with poor outcomes in all areas of life in scientific literature, so reducing stress has a beneficial impact on physical, mental, and behavioral health, relationships and general success in life.

Cardiovascular (Heart) Disease

Most wellness programs approach cardiovascular risk by addressing obesity, physical activity, diabetes and blood pressure. The evidence strongly suggests that those are efforts are not true prevention; they are early symptom detection and management. The evidence strongly suggests that the real root cause

is chronic psychosocial stress. "The higher the aggregate levels of positive effect [happiness], the lower the Heart Rate over the day."[431] The pathway from chronic stress to obesity, heart disease and diabetes is clear. In 2007, a journal article by Kim Innes et al. at University of Virginia details the pathway and states, "A growing body of research suggests that chronic psychosocial stress and related factors significantly contribute to the pathogenesis of . . . insulin-resistant states(IRS), and cardiovascular disease(CVD), in part by promoting dysregulation of the sympathoadrenal system and hypothalamic-pituitary-adrenal axis . . .

chronic or recurrent psychosocial stress may lead to a destructive cascade of neuroendocrine, metabolic, inflammatory, and neuropsychological changes that fosters the development of IRS and, ultimately, CVD."

This stance was later strongly supported by a 2012 meta-analysis completed at Harvard that found that optimism reduces the risk of developing cardiovascular disease by 50%. Optimists feel less stress than their non-optimistic and pessimistic counterparts. The Harvard meta-analysis was very clear that it is positive emotions and not just the absence of negative emotions that afforded protection against the development of heart disease.[432]

"Currently in both Brazil and the United States, approximately 32% of deaths are caused by CVD, disproportionately affecting the elderly and individuals with both low income and education."[433] "A 3.5-fold increase in death due to CVD is expected over the next 30 years worldwide."[434] The study, from 2014, makes no mention of the fact that a meta-analysis from Harvard found both a 50% reduction of the risk of developing heart disease when optimism was present and that the presence of positive emotions improved pro-health behaviors such as sleep and exercise.[435] According to the World Health Organization (WHO), 80% of CVD cases can be avoided by adopting a healthier lifestyle, including a healthy diet, regular physical activity (PA) and smoking cessation."[436]

Although it is mentioned elsewhere, the connection between positivity and health bears repeating:
- Better pro-health decisions are made when an individual is positively focused (experiencing positive emotions of hope or better)[437]
- The absence of negative emotion is not the same as the presence of positive emotions[438]
- 71% of dieters eat foods they do not want to eat when they are stressed and 44% eat foods they usually avoid for health reasons when they are stressed
- 43% of people who usually engage in physical activity and know exercise helps their stress level do not exercise when they are stressed
- 69% of those who still smoke suffer from anxiety

The bottom line is that effective stress management improves every behavior targeted for improvement and the lack of stress management skills impedes the ability to achieve desired outcomes. In a recent study, self-affirmations used to maintain a positive view of oneself when self-confidence was threatened predicted "changes in sedentary behavior consistent with successful affirmation in response to a separate physical activity intervention."[439] Instead of submissively expecting a 3.5 fold worldwide increase in cardiovascular disease over the next 30 years, I'd propose we aggressively teach skills that reduce psychosocial stress and reduce the incidence of cardiovascular disease by 50% over the next twenty years. *The Smart Way* is designed to do that at the lowest possible cost.

One target area begins with self-esteem. A study published in the *Journal of the National Black Nurses Association* found that African-American women with higher self-esteem were more likely to participate in behavior's that reduced the risk of dying from cardiovascular disease, such as diet and exercise.[440] Low self-esteem increases stress. See the **Improve Self-Esteem** process for how *The Smart Way* can help increase self-esteem, which would improve pro-active risk reduction behaviors and lower psychosocial stress.

Diabetes

In a systematic review of the science on the mind-body connection between diabetes and mind-body approaches, Anderson and Taylor stated, "There is mounting evidence that chronic psychological stress and negative mood states are strongly associated, in a bidirectional manner, with insulin resistance, glucose intolerance, central obesity, dyslipidemia, hypertension, and other components of the metabolic syndrome."[441] They went on to recommend that physicians consider recommending mind-body therapies for metabolic syndrome, indicating that the only current recommendation was physical activity and dietary controls, which are often not followed by patients for a variety of reasons.

Another journal article concluded, "Stress may play a role in the onset of diabetes, it can have a deleterious effect on glycemic control and can affect lifestyle. Emerging evidence strongly suggests, however, that interventions that help individuals prevent or cope with stress can have an important positive effect on quality of life and glycemic control. The clinical implications of this research illustrate the need for greater understanding of the effects of stress, as well as a serious acceptance of the need for psychosocial support for people in this predicament."[442]

A study that followed 321 African American women over a 10-year period found that chronic financial stress increased inflammatory factors that can lead to type II diabetes.[443] The study recommended teaching effective coping strategies and interventions that boost economic security.

Stress that reduces one's sense of autonomy (i.e. work stress caused by low decision latitude) significantly increased the risk for Type II diabetes.[444] Even when someone does not have the ability to make decisions at work, they can reframe their position by focusing on the fact that they could change jobs, thus increasing the personal sense of autonomy. Even if the person is incarcerated and does not have the ability to change jobs, they can focus on their ability to focus on different aspects of the job and the fact that they have control over what they think about.

Obesity

In 2002, 32.2% of American adults were considered obese—two times as many as there were in 1980.[445] In 2008, 66% of Americans were either overweight or obese.[446] Obesity and depression frequently occur together with one feeding the other in many situations with current or prior diagnosis of depression increasing the likelihood of obesity by 60%. Negative body image and the stigmatization of obesity can reflect and/or lead to low self-esteem and psychological distress.[447] Increased food intake, which is associated with depression and anxiety, can contribute to obesity. The use of comfort foods to regulate emotions is common. High levels of stress reduce physical activity, even with people who know exercise will help them deal with stress.[448] Low levels of physical activity contribute to obesity. In a group of 187 extremely obese individuals who were evaluated for bariatric (weight-loss) surgery, "61% reported a history of childhood abuse, 30.5% reported adult interpersonal abuse, and 15% reported clinically significant depressive symptoms."[449]

Childhood abuse (sexual, physical, verbal, and neglect) create neuropathways (patterns of thought) that increase the risk of depression, emotional eating, and obesity. Part of this is a lower emotional state sustained by both the presence of adverse memories and the lack of connections that lead to positive emotional states. Lower emotional states indicate higher stress levels, which has a negative impact on the endocrine system (digestion). Childhood adversity can lead to elevated BMI (body mass index) as early as age 7.[450]

A 2010 meta-analysis that looked at studies including over 200,000 people found a significant association between depression and obesity.[451] Although this study suggested the common link was unknown, other studies link both depression and obesity back to stress. Obesity makes individuals more susceptible to depression and depression makes individuals more susceptible to obesity.

One factor known to contribute to obesity is emotional eating, or eating in response to (as a way of coping with) stress. When a similar frequency of stressors occurs, those that have more confidence in their ability to cope were better able to maintain weight loss than those with low confidence in their ability to cope with stress.[452] A longitudinal study of 2,359 men and 2,791 women found that emotional eaters had the highest body mass index at 31 years of age. The study concluded, "Programs aimed at preventing and treating obesity should cover the way in which people deal with emotions, ways of achieving greater emotional support, and strategies for handling stress caused by unemployment or work."[453] Unless psychological issues related to weight loss maintenance are addressed, the problem will continue or return (i.e. after bariatric surgery).[454] *The Smart Way* is an affordable and effective method of increasing stress management skills so psychological eating is easier to control.

Pain

Pain is one of the health issues where a disparate impact exists for minorities. When you understand the moving parts, it is easy to understand why this is so. Pain increases as stress increases and decreases as stress declines. Said in another way, pain increases as mood declines and decreases as mood improves. If you have pain that comes and goes, pay attention to your mood when it comes and goes and you'll see the connection. A few other factors can affect pain, such as the weather and whether or not you have adequate rest (both sleep and periods where the body can relax).

Minorities, on average experience more stress. Many experience significant amounts of stress from racism—some of it real and some of it perceptual. Minorities also tend to have more financial stress. These factors would cause one to expect a higher incidence of pain from low socioeconomic minorities and minorities who experience high levels of racism or who feel disempowered or held back or held down. The more empowered one feels the less pain and less cumulative and chronic stress the person would experience.

"The experience of racism is highly stressful, ranking in significance with other major stressful life events such as job loss, divorce, and the death of a loved one . . . Researchers found empirical associations between perceived discrimination and impaired psychological well-being, depression, and self-esteem."[455] If they look, they will also find links between perceived self-esteem and all the physical illnesses and undesirable behavioral outcomes tied to stress.

Friborg et al. found that subjects scores on standardized resilience questionnaires predicted their reported levels of pain and stress in laboratory tests a few days later.[456] The higher the stress the participants were exposed to, the greater protection resilience provided against pain. Resilient traits are correlated with lower levels of physical pain.

Researchers, who encouraged parents to play with their children while they were in the hospital following surgery, experienced less pain by three different measurement techniques than children in a control group in the same hospital.[457]

The research indicates pain can originate with psychological pain and manifest as physical pain and physical pain in the body can cause psychological pain in the mind. Addressing psychological pain lessens physical pain and addressing physical pain can lessen psychological pain.

Skin Disorders

Psoriasis

Research suggests that a biopsychosocial approach to managing psoriasis may be the most effective strategy.[458]

"I have moderate plaque psoriasis all over my body for nearly 30 years. I've tried everything under the sun to manage it. Sunlight has been by far the #1 treatment for me. Falling in love is also a very effective treatment. I cleared from the worst case ever to totally clear in 30 days when I feel in love last summer. –poster on Inspire.com"

Intersection: Physical and Mental Health

Anyone is capable of anything (will plus belief is ability) if they themselves create the opportune moment and incentive. Heaven gives no genius to disbelievers and no vengeance worse than the body denied.
Austin Osman Spare

The mind and body are connected. Mental health can both predict and exacerbate physical health problems. It is one reason the stigma surrounding mental health problems are such a problem. For example, depression can both predict and exacerbate cardiovascular disease. This can happen through various pathways such as increased blood pressure, interference with social life (healthy relationships are preventative for heart disease), and individuals suffering from anxiety and/or depression are less likely to adhere to instructions about lifestyle and healthy behaviors.[459]

Researchers evaluating the effectiveness of meditation on stress reduction, positive affect, and plasma catecholamines concluded that, "mind-body training may influence stress, positive affect and the sympathetic nervous system."[460]

I first saw the correlation between negative affect and accidents when I read Dr. Seligman's *Learned Optimism* and he stated that individuals experience more accidents after a negative life event, but they could not yet explain why. In Lisa Kalynchuk's 2010 preface to *Progress in Neuro-Psychopharmacology & Biological Psychiatry* she mentioned that stress can affect the spatial memory/navigation and hippocampal-dependent object recognition tasks in rodents.[461] Although the research she referenced was done with rodents, that's a necessity because stressing a human out and waiting to see if they experienced more accidents would not meet today's ethical research standards.

Having been aware of the correlation between stress and accidents for about a decade now, I've been doing my own primary research within my circle of family and friends. I've observed that there are more accidents (from paper cuts, broken dishes, to totaled vehicles) when stress levels are higher and fewer when stress is lower. Even stubbed toes seem to coincide with higher stress levels. I haven't found any conclusive evidence with humans but you can pay attention in your own life and see if you don't observe the same outcomes I've seen amongst my friends and family.

Interestingly, researchers found that "Blacks exposed to chronic stress who lead the most healthy lives have the highest estimated probability of depression."[462] Blacks who engaged in some negative health behaviors that are used as stress relief (i.e. comfort food and alcohol), had a lower level of depression. This is not mentioned to encourage negative health behaviors, but to point out that people naturally seek stress relief. Given better alternatives (i.e. *The Smart Way*), almost everyone will choose the least risky method of stress reduction that is effective.

Intersection: Physical and Mental Health

23: Mental Health

Isn't consciousness awesome?
It does such an amazing job of making our thinking seem real.
Anonymous

According to the American Academy of Pediatrics:

Mental health encompasses behavioral, emotional, neuro-developmental, psychiatric, psychological, and substance abuse issues, as well as family and community issues that contribute to this condition and the somatic manifestations of mental health issues. An imbalance between one or more of these factors can interfere with the child's ability to successfully develop into a healthy, productive adult.

According to the National Alliance for Mental Health (NAMI), "Approximately 20 percent of youth ages 13 to 18 experience severe mental disorders in a given year. For ages 8 to 15, the estimate is 13 percent."[463] "Roughly half of all lifetime mental health disorders start by the mid-teens."[464] "And, between 40 – 60% of families who access mental health care end therapy prematurely."[465]

Poor mental health (psychopathology) is strongly associated with maladaptive emotion regulation strategies and chronic stress (an outcome of poor emotion regulation skills).[466] In other words, weak or absent abilities to handle stressors with cognitive skills causes accumulated stressors to manifest as mental illness. Good mental health is strongly associated with adaptive and flexible emotion regulation skills, which reduce the stress experienced by the individual. The purpose of *The Smart Way* is to help individuals develop skills that empower them to successfully manage emotion.

There are a number of pathways to good mental health. The absence of emotion regulation skills that help an individual self-motivate or relax contribute significantly to the formation of ill-being and symptoms of mental disorders.[467] Chapter 33 is filled with easy and practical emotion regulation techniques that allow individuals to become experts in regulating their own emotional state. Developing emotion regulation skills reduces chronic stress and the negative consequences thereof, affording protection against the development of depression, anxiety, and other mental illnesses.

The Primary Care Training Task Force stated, "seasoned clinicians have consistently known that the distinction between medical and psychological care has always been **arbitrary**, having more to do with the focus and socialization of practitioner training than the reality of patient care."[468] [Emphasis added] In other words, our medical system that separates care of the body from care of the mind is based on an artificial separation, essentially, a made-up differentiation that is not supported by the evidence. The body affects the mind and the mind affects the body.

Emotion Regulation Strategies

Adaptive		Maladaptive (Dysfunctional)	
Covert	Overt	Covert	Overt
Cognitive reappraisal	Seeking Advice	Suppression	Drinking alcohol
Problem-solving	Re-appraisal	Rumination (brooding)	Co-rumination
Acceptance	Self-soothe	Avoidance	Escape
Distraction	Refocus on planning	Passive-Aggressive	Substance use:
Labeling			Enhance
			Blunt
Humor	Positive refocusing	Forgetting	Expressive suppression
	Meaning-making	Self-harm	Co-rumination
		Self-medication	Complaining
		Withdrawal	Self-blame
		Suicide ideation	Self-devaluation
Active-constructive responding to others' good fortune[469]			Defensiveness
			Comfort Food
			Fighting
			Other risky behaviors

Depending on use can be adaptive or maladaptive:
- Distraction
- Affect labeling (i.e. challenging vs. stressful)

Stigma

Many people view mental health issues as something an individual can control and thus view depression, anxiety, and worse as the individual's own fault. In one regard, I agree, and that is from this perspective:

If we lived in a world where everyone understood The Smart Way, *they would have control over many of their cognitive processes, understand the true purpose of their emotions, and be equipped to make pro-health decisions about the perspectives they accept as their own about the events in their life.*

Since we are nowhere near living in that word (my preferred future), then, in our current environment, most individuals do not have the knowledge required to completely avoid common mental health problems. It does not matter how hard they work or how much they want to succeed at achieving and maintaining good mental health—in our current environment the resources are inadequate. Few psychologists or psychiatrists understand the true purpose of emotions or how to respond in the most appropriate (Right Response) way. Many do not fully understand the Emotional Guidance Scale. The system is set-up so that an expert guides the individual instead of empowering the individual to guide his or her own thoughts to optimal results.

Beyond the fact that current treatments are incomplete (lacking Emotional Guidance and do not empower clients as much as possible), there are serious lacks in availability of mental health care from two perspectives. There are over 3,000 counties in the United States that have inadequate resources to handle the mental health needs of their residents. Even where resources are present, the cost of care can prevent many of those who would benefit from assistance from being able to obtain it. Add to the last piece the interrelatedness of poverty and mental health issues (i.e. depression, anxiety, low self-esteem, Learned Helplessness, substance use disorder, and more) and you have a society that lacks the resources to help its citizens achieve the best possible outcomes.

One way to reduce stigma is exposure to individuals who have mental health needs. Just understanding that almost two people out of every ten suffer from anxiety and one out of ten suffer from depression at some point each year lets us know that we probably know people who would benefit from care. There are many people who suffered from severe mental health issues that we may be familiar with. In modern times, Robin Williams is the first example that comes to mind. Historically, Abraham Lincoln, whose depression was often severe, reportedly said that he could not have a knife when he was alone for fear he would harm himself. Terry Bradshaw, successful quarterback in four Super Bowls suffered from clinical depression.[470]

A quick search of the internet shows more than three hundred famous people who suffer (or suffered) from one or more forms of mental illness:

Who	Famous for:	Illness
Earl Campbell[471]	Football pro & businessman	Panic disorder
Winston Churchill[472]	Leader – United Kingdom	Bipolar disorder
Princess Diana[473]	Princess of Wales	Bulimia and depression
Catherine Zeta Jones[474]	Actress	Bipolar II disorder
Greg Louganis[475]	Olympic Medal Winner	Depression/suicidal
Michelangelo[476]	Artistic Genius	Mental illness
Isaac Newton[477]	Scientist	Manic Depression
J.K. Rowling[478]	Author Harry Potter series	Depression
Ricky Williams[479]	Heisman trophy winner	Social Anxiety Disorder
Thelonious Monk[480]	Jazz Great	
Theodore Roosevelt[481]	President of United States	Bi-polar disorder
Ruth Graham[482]	Daughter of Billy Graham	Depression
Dr. Kay Redfield Jamison	Professor of psychiatry at Johns Hopkins University	[483]

This list is a small sample of famous individuals who have suffered from mental illness. Clearly work ethic and worthiness have nothing to do with mental illness, based on the long list of accomplishments attributable to this brief list of individuals.

Depression

Commentary by Benjamin I. Goldstein, MD, PhD, at the beginning of the February 2015 issue of the *Journal of Clinical Psychiatry* concluded, "In summary, it is not entirely clear why we have yet to curtail the costs of MDD (Major Depressive Disorder), but focusing on prevention, early intervention, and integration of physical health considerations may yield much-needed traction."[484] I am delighted to see the focus shifting to prevention—it is what I've been encouraging. This past July yet another article was published speaking to the inadequate level of care our children are receiving, "Despite national recommendations, screening for adolescent depression is generally uncommon and is typically characterized by regional and racial/ethnic disparities. This variability in practice may leave some adolescents disproportionately vulnerable to untreated depression."[485]

More recently, research indicates that some adolescent depression can be explained by emotion dysregulation and psychological inflexibility.[486] An article published in the *Journal of Psychiatric Research* in 2010 stated, "In the coming decades, unipolar depression is projected to be the second leading cause of disability worldwide and the leading cause of disability in high-income nations, including the United States." My response to reading that was, "Not if I can help it."

An article published in February, 2015 found, "Our results emphasize the importance of **stress reduction** and **emotion regulation skills** as simultaneous targets for interventions that seek treat or reduce the prevalence of depressive vulnerability and pathology."[487] As early as 1992, Martin E. P. Seligman, the Father of Positive Psychology, stated, "Explanatory style predicts depression . . . [elaborating by saying] . . . Depressed people blame themselves if the event is bad, but they credit other if the event is good."[488]

In unipolar depression, which is what most people think of when they hear depression, there is the single episode, usually occurring during or following a period of high stress. Then there is chronic depression, which is recurring episodes of depression. Traditional psychology and pharmaceutical methods, or even just the natural tendency to lean toward feeling better or returning to one's baseline means that a single episode of depression can be treated and individuals usually recover.

Chronic depression on the other hand is a much greater problem. It will disappear for a while but then reappear, often multiple times over decades, leaving the individual who suffers from chronic depression always on edge waiting for the next episode. Depending on the severity, episodes of depression interfere with marriage, career aspirations, physical health, and can lead to or exacerbate drug and alcohol abuse problems.

I am intimately familiar with chronic depression because beginning in my teen years, I suffered from recurrent bouts of depression that sometimes led to suicide ideation and even plans that I fortunately never acted upon. Since I began applying the techniques presented in this book to my life a decade ago, I have been depression free. One of my earliest students also suffered from chronic depression that was worsened by his use of drugs to escape from the empty feelings. He was a survivor of severe childhood sexual abuse. He has now been depression free for seven years from learning these techniques and applying them in his life.

If you are under a physician's care for depression do not stop your treatment, but do learn the techniques described herein and begin applying them in your life. Depression is a disempowered emotional state that seems permanent and pervasive. Learning to accurately interpret your Emotional Guidance will lead you to question the perspectives that hold you and help to alleviate depressive thoughts.

Over the years I've had many people argue that depression is the result of a chemical imbalance in the brain. It's true that sometimes a chemical imbalance is present in the brain of a depressed person. It is also true that chronic stress, a frequent precursor to chronic depression, causes changes to the chemical composition of your body. By learning techniques that effectively reduce stress your body will benefit from healthier biochemistry. The unhealthy biochemistry came after the chronic stress. Fix the chronic stress and your chances of recovering from chronic depression will increase.

Depression and poverty walk hand-in-hand more often than not. 31% of Americans in poverty have been diagnosed with depression at some point, compared to 15.8% of those who are not in poverty.[489] US born Whites suffer from less depression than other US born races and are more likely to seek treatment, which may prevent long term problems with depression. US born African Americans experience depression 1.66 times more frequently than Whites and US born Mexican Americans experience depression 1.54 times more frequently than Whites.[490]

For anyone who has ever experienced poverty, you know that the stress associated with financial concerns and other worries associated with lack of resources, can feel like an ever-present weight. Many people will describe high stress as heavy and low stress as lighter and free. The pathway to depression is paved with chronic stress.

Depression also strikes young adults at exceedingly high rates, even those considered socially advantaged because they are in college. A meta-analysis of 24 separate studies of depression in college students reflected that over 30% suffered from depression. The fact that medical students were the subject of 12 studies may have impacted the data, which ranged from 10% to 85% depression rates. Non-poverty and non-college depression averages affect 10% of the global population.[491]

"Depression in this early life stage can lead to an accumulation of negative consequences through adult life through its impact on career prospects and social relationships. Depression has been linked to poorer academic achievements, relationship instability, and poorer work performance."[492] Depressed individuals are twice as likely to have inactive lifestyles as people who are not depressed, which contributes to other illnesses [493]

One habit of thought that is highly correlated with depression is rumination. "Rumination is considered an emotion-regulation strategy in which an individual focuses repetitively on the causes, consequences, and meanings of negative mood states."[494] Co-rumination is the same behavior by two or more people in conversation or correspondence. While ruminators may insist they are attempting to solve their problems by focusing on them, rumination, especially depressive brooding, is maladaptive and is associated with impaired problem solving, reduced task performance, and establishing and sustaining negative emotional states. [495] Self-blame and catastrophizing are also consistently associated with depressive symptoms.[496] Children who experience, "domestic violence, abuse, or maternal depression . . . who understand or explain them" without self-blame "are not as vulnerable" to later depression.[497]

The Smart Way Meta-cognitve Processes are effective in helping ruminators change their habits of thought to more adaptive ones that lead to increased levels of positive emotion. It incorporates adaptive coping techniques that increase mental flexibility and wellness.

A review of a variety of studies that looked at how diet, sleep, and exercise affected development of and continuation of depression concluded, "Mental health intervention, taking into account the bidirectional relationship between these lifestyle factors and major depression are also likely to enhance the efficacy of interventions associated with this disorder."[498] This conclusion is acknowledging that stress and emotional state affect sleep, dietary choices, exercise activity, and other lifestyle choices that may influence recovery.

Depression is at epidemic levels around the world, and direct annual costs for treatment of major depression averages about $5,988 per person, not including costs for co-morbid illnesses. Nationally, the cost in 2010 was $98.9 billion.[499] "Depression increases the risk of decreased workplace productivity and absenteeism resulting in lowered income or unemployment. In a study of 539 workers in the United States, the monthly cost of absenteeism was $199 for the severely depressed and $188 for the moderately depressed.[500] Absenteeism and presenteeism (being physically present at work but functioning suboptimally) have been estimated to result in a loss of $36.6 billion per year in the US. Worldwide projections by the World Health Organization for the year 2030 identify unipolar major depression as the leading cause of disease burden."[501] For example, a study that evaluated seven conditions (allergies, arthritis, back pain, headaches, high blood pressure, asthma, and major depression), only Major depression was strongly related to significant decreases in both task focus and productivity. The effect of major depression on productivity of employees whose primary responsibility involved customer contact via the telephone equated "to approximately 2.3 days absent because of sickness per depressed worker per month of being depressed."[502] In other words, even if the employee was not absent, productivity was as if the depressed employee missed 2.3 days each month.

A study that looked at 12,866 men found depressive symptoms were associated with higher levels of mortality from all causes including cardiovascular disease.[503] Over 16% of the population experiences depression during their lifetime. It makes sense to teach individuals skills that increase emotional intelligence, resilience, and reduce the risk of depression.

Several illnesses are often blamed on chemical imbalances in the brain but the chemical imbalances could be symptoms, not the cause. This is an area where more research should be done because when depression is blamed on a chemical imbalance in the brain, it is treated with drugs but the thoughts that lead to the low emotional state are not corrected. Treating symptoms without fixing the root cause leads to both undesired side effects and relapses.

Suicide

I'm not going to spend much time on suicide, primarily because I wrote a book on it, *Prevent Suicide: The Smart Way*, which was published in 2014. Children (and adults) who use *The Smart Way* are unlikely to have suicidal thoughts and if they do, they have processes they can use to feel better. Using *The Smart Way* as it is described in this book will have the same benefits as reading my earlier book. The main missing aspects are details about warning signs and risk factors. If you or someone you are with is feeling suicidal call for help immediately. In the United States, call 911 or the suicide hotline. In other countries, call your emergency number or go to an emergency room.

Suicide Prevention Lifeline now at 1-800-273-TALK (1-800-273-8255); TTY: 1-800-799-4TTY (4889) to talk to a trained counselor.
Or, **call your doctor**
Dial 911
or go to an emergency room
For a free detailed booklet on depression and its treatment, go to:
http://www.nimh.nih.gov/health/publications/depression/complete-index.shtml

International Emergency Numbers

Australia	000	Switzerland	112	UAE	112
New Zealand	111	India	102	Brazil	192
Fiji	000 or 911	Hong Kong	999	Costa Rica	911
United Kingdom	112 or 999	Israel	101 or 112	S. Africa	112, 10 177
Ireland	112 or 999	Japan	119	China	120
Turkey	112	Nepal	102	Philippines	117 or 112

Anxiety

Researchers from the public health sector and universities estimate that 18% of adults in the United States have an anxiety disorder,[504] affecting 40 million adults in the U.S. according to the National Institute of Mental Health.

"Anxiety disorders are highly treatable, yet only about one-third of those suffering receive treatment . . . According to a 2007 ADAA survey, 36% of [the 15 million] people with Social Anxiety Disorder (SAD) report experiencing symptoms for 10 or more years before seeking help."[505] Anxiety disorders cost the U.S. more than $42 billion a year, almost one-third of the country's $148 billion total mental health bill, according to *The Economic Burden of Anxiety Disorders*, a study commissioned by ADAA.[506]

Research published in the *Current Psychiatry Reports*[507] reported that Cognitive Behavioral Therapy (CBT) is effective in treating *Social Anxiety Disorders*, specifically citing improving emotion regulation strategies and "fear extinction," both of which can be achieved as a preventative measure using *The Smart Way*.

Negative self-images contribute significantly to chronic depression and anxiety. "Relatively strong negative self-cognitions may make people vulnerable for developing unfaourable course trajectories of depressive and anxiety disorders."[508] Individuals who use their guidance for a while develop trust in the truth of the correctly interpreted emotional responses, with some trusting their Emotional Guidance in as little as a week and most taking no more than three months. Once a level of trust is established, the person can use their guidance to help them accept the truth of more favorable views of self. **The Bogus Process** in Chapter 33 is a fun way to increase positive self-worth. **Refuting** is also helpful.

Merrifield, Balk, and Moscovitch found that childhood teasing can result in social anxiety because the person "develops negative self-beliefs" and then fears others will learn those secrets.[509] As long as someone has a negative perspective of self, they will not only be susceptible to recurrent bouts of depression and/or anxiety, they will not receive positive reinforcement from others. Their mind will create back stories that negate the attempts at positive reinforcement in order to protect the established beliefs. This is one reason children who experience verbal abuse experience the worse outcomes—they internalize the negative perspective of self that is projected at them.

Self-Esteem

Research conducted at Wake Forest University over twenty years ago highlighted some of the problems associated with low self-esteem, "Low self-esteem ranks among the strongest predictors of emotional and behavioral problems. Compared to people with high self-esteem, people with low self-esteem tend to be more anxious, depressed, lonely, jealous, shy, and generally unhappy. They are also less assertive, less likely to enjoy close friendships, and more likely to drop out of school. Furthermore, they are more inclined to behave in ways that pose a danger to themselves or others: low self-esteem is associated with unsafe sex, teenage pregnancy, aggression, criminal behavior, the abuse of alcohol and other drugs, and membership in deviant groups."[510] Shawn Achor said, "One of the greatest buffers against picking up others' stress is stable and strong self-esteem."[511]

Work by Murray and colleagues showed that low self-esteem people substantially underestimate how positively they are regarded by relationship partners.[512]

"The pursuit of self-esteem can encourage a wide range of prosocial behaviors and creative accomplishments. However, because self-esteem is predicated on the beliefs and values of the meaning-providing worldview to which the individual subscribes, it can also contribute to horrible antisocial behavior, such as prejudice and aggression, as the horrific efforts to achieve heroic martyrdom by the terrorists who attacked the World Trade Center on September 11, 2001, made all too vividly clear. The pursuit of self-esteem is thus neither a good thing nor a bad thing but rather, a part of the system that human beings use to both regulate their behavior and cope with their existential situation."[513]

Oppositional Defiant Disorder (ODD)

When you understand *The Smart Way*, the suggestions that ODD may have a genetic component loses much of its valence because frequent reports of family members with mental illnesses like mood, anxiety and personality disorders can explain the cognitive dysfunction and aggression. Commonly noted environmental factors add to that viewpoint because a dysfunctional family life, parents with substance use disorders, and the subsequent low quality parenting would all predict problems in many children who face such situations without the advantages of conscious metacognition and Emotional Guidance.

Perfectionism

Perfectionism typically includes putting unrealistic demands and expectations on yourself and accepting unrealistic demands from others, which leads to self-criticism and harsh judgments of self when you are unable to meet the expectations.

Perfectionism is a risk-factor for suicide.

Many people believe perfectionism is a positive trait. Doing your best is a positive attribute. Perfectionism is holding oneself to goals that are unattainable in the set of circumstances and self-blame instead of realistic evaluations of the situation.

Seeing yourself as perfect as is, a human with room for improvement who is on a journey toward becoming more is one way to lessen the harsh judgments that rob most perfectionists of happiness. Understand that no matter how wonderful anyone is, individuals will always want to strive for more. No one is happy just Being as they are—we all want to become more. Life would be terribly boring if we could achieve a state where we were not striving for more. We might as well have been a rock instead of a human.

Researchers have found that enjoying the journey is the key to a happy life because we "discover new valuable things along the way," which means we never *arrive*. We are always traveling through time toward desired outcomes.[514]

Postpartum Depression

In a study of 1319 women, 16% reported exposure to childhood maltreatment. The study found that childhood maltreatment increased depression in the postpartum period and was associated with low parenting morale.[515] A Mother's anxiety and stress when her child is a newborn can negatively impact her ability to bond with the child, contributing to the cycle of violence and poor outcomes across generations.

Trigger Warnings

Trigger warnings are warnings before potentially emotionally disturbing information is shared. A desire or demand for trigger warnings is actually a symptom indicating that the person does not have adequate stress management skills to process and move past a past trauma or to address the stress from hearing about traumatic events that happen to others. Going through life worried about what someone might inadvertently disclose or say in your presence is very limiting and decreases one's sense of control.

Using *The Smart Way* to increase resilience will reduce the need to be vigilant against things that might make a person uncomfortable.

24: Discrimination

Good people do not need laws to tell them to act responsibly, while bad people will find a way around the laws.
Plato

The word discrimination can describe a wide variety of behaviors including "being treated with less courtesy or respect, receiving poorer service than others, being threatened or harassed, being unfairly denied rights or benefits, and other disempowering behaviors." Google's dictionary defines discrimination as "the unjust or prejudicial treatment of different categories of people."

A recent report from the American Psychological Association reported that "nearly seven in 10 adults in the United States (69%) report having experienced any discrimination with 61% reporting experiencing day-to-day discrimination . . . adults identified by subgroups including age, race or ethnicity, disability, gender, sexual orientation and gender identity reported on their experiences . . . adults with a disability are twice as likely as adults without a disability to say that discrimination has interfered with them being able to live a full and productive life."[516]

Racism, Sexism and other isms
I have a different viewpoint regarding *ism's* than many do. In my last book, one of my conclusions was that someone who commits a crime has actually departed from their true state of mental health. Much the same way cancer or heart disease is a departure from your natural state of physical health; beliefs and attitudes that harm others are a departure from your core state of mental health, which is a loving being. In the same line of thought, I view *ism's* as an illness of the ones who hold those views—an illness in them that can be responded to with compassion—not a flaw in the persons they are discriminatory toward.

That being said, I can't cure all of them today but I can help reduce or alleviate the stress and negative emotion the experiences they inflict have on you. That is the focus of this chapter.

The American Academy of Public Health held a webinar on the impact of racism on children's health. It's a grim story. Basically, the impact of racism (and racist perceptions) on children creates psychological stress, which is quickly transmitted to their bodies. Stress is harmful:

Stress reduces cognitive abilities. It literally makes it more difficult to solve problems, to learn, and to think clearly.

While most of us would like to end racism today, it does not seem likely that we will do so. But there is something we can do besides wait for it to die like the dinosaur it is.

There are skills we can teach children that help them reduce the impact of stress on their bodies and minds. We can make children more resilient and far less dependent upon other's opinions for their emotional well-being. It's like giving them a vaccine against racism's toxic effects.

Also, we have to stop teaching children to expect racism, genderism, and other disempowering experiences. Why? The negative expectation harms the child.

I'll say it again, setting children you love up to expect negative experiences, especially pervasive ones they cannot control, harms them psychologically, which leads directly to physical harm and may manifest in physical and/or mental illness. It does the opposite of what you want, which is to protect children from harm.

24: Discrimination

You already know we do not experience a fixed reality. The reality we experience is based on back stories our brain creates to explain what we see and hear. If we believe people don't like us (for any reason) we create back stories that are stressful and disempowering about the situation. If we believe people will like us (for any reason) we create back stories that are less stressful and more empowering about the same situation. Our perception, not reality, determines our level of stress. The extent to which we feel disempowered reflects the amount of stress we feel. When we feel empowered, we aren't stressed.

The chart on the next page illustrates different realities that can be experienced about the same situation with the variable being whether the perceiver believes racism is common and expected or not.

Here are some examples to explain what I mean.

Situation	Person Who Believes People Will Discriminate Against him or her	Person Who Does not expect People to Discriminate Against him or her
Person receives slow service at a restaurant.	Feels frustrated or angry. Believes slow service is because of discrimination. Less likely to believe that going elsewhere will be a better experience. Feels disempowered.	May feel frustrated, not likely to feel angry unless already stressed about something else. Attributes slow service to incompetence or inadequate staffing. Likely to believe going elsewhere will provide a better experience. Not disempowered by experience.
Teacher calls on another student more when both hands are raised	Feels disempowered, attributes situation to discrimination. Upsetting. Reinforces hopeless view of life. Unlikely to make an effort to change by taking issue to parent, teacher, or administration because viewpoint is that it is a fact of life. Simmering anger may build.	Feels frustrated with teacher, but has hope that other teachers will not be unfair. May feel asking parent to talk to teacher or administration would be beneficial. May feel disempowered, but it is not pervasive because the assumption that it will be everywhere is not part of the back story. May view the student who is called on more as a teacher's pet. Not hard to maintain hope that future will be better.
In a store, security pays attention to the person	Assumes it is because of his race or ethnicity. Feels discriminated against, distrusted. Feels disempowered.	May assume it is because of age (i.e. teenager), or because of the way he was dressed. May find it humorous that security wasted time following him around the store.
Someone walking toward you on the sidewalk switches to the other side of the street.	Feels the behavior reflects a distrust of his/her race/ethnicity. Feels disrespected and disempowered.	May not even notice and if s/he does notice, may assume they crossed because they needed to do so. Does not have an emotional impact.
A job representing a promotion the person would like is posted at work.	I've literally had other women who were qualified tell me they wanted a job, but they weren't going to apply because there was no point because "they wouldn't hire a woman for that role." In one specific case when a friend said this, the successful candidate was a woman.	They will pursue opportunities they are interested in. They won't stand in their own way, counting themselves out of the running before they're even in the race.

The other aspect of this is that the world the parent (or grandparent) experienced that trained them what to expect of their world is not the world the child (or grandchild) actually lives in. Since our brains interpret reality based on our beliefs about the world, the parent or grandparent who believes discrimination will occur interpres situations that may not be discriminatory as if they are.[517] This reaffirms their view of the world.

The truth is that discriminatory attitudes have been greatly reduced during the past 50 years. The likelihood that bad service is simply bad service is much more likely than it was in the past. The likelihood that a teacher's favoritism is not based on race or gender is better than it was in the past. The likelihood that a person's gender or race will be a determining factor in selection for employment is far lower than it used to be.

> *Your child or grandchild will experience a better world sooner if you refrain from priming them to expect a bad world.*

Your child or grandchild will experience a better world sooner if you refrain from priming them to expect a bad world. That lowers his/her stress level, which improves cognitive function. That means they'll do better in school, make better decisions, and be better prepared to deal with overt discrimination if they do encounter it.

We have not eradicated racism, genderism or other types of discrimination yet. But much more of it is created in the minds of the perceiver today and far less is actual. Research has also demonstrated that stereotypes can lead to automatic prejudice, but this can be reduced by consciously affirming intentions to treat others equally and also by interpersonal contact with individuals from other races. This is effective even when an individual was deliberately taught to hold prejudice stereotypes.[518]

It is possible to perceive a person treating you in a discriminatory manner when they have no desire to do so and even when they have the opposite intent.

One example, that went viral last year referred to a young woman who is 16% Native American and 34% Caucasian as White while accusing her of discriminating against Native Americans when the actual intent of her actions (which she and I had discussed BEFORE the event that made national headlines) was to honor a culture she (and I) hold in high regard.

All of the racism of that event was perceptual. 100%. Yet, many Native Americans felt as if the event was a disempowering blow against Native Americans. They were highly stressed about it. That was bad for them—for their psychological health, as well as disruptive to their immune, cognitive, digestive, and central nervous system function. Not to mention how upsetting it was to the young woman who was unjustly accused. All based on a false perception of reality. This is not an isolated incident. It happens all across our land on a daily basis.

When I look at the findings from the American Psychological Association's report on *Stress in America* this year, a report focused on discrimination, there is one finding that stands out and confirms to me in strong terms that a lot of the discrimination experienced today is more perceptual than actual. The report indicates that younger adults are the most likely to say they have experienced any discrimination:

- 75% of Millennials
- 72% of Gen Xers
- 67% of Boomers
- 56% of Matures

The world I grew up in was far more likely to discriminate than the world of today. These statistics reflect perception more than reality. Yes, people should treat one another well. A large basis of my motivation for my work stems from knowing that happy people treat others better. They treat strangers better and they treat loved ones better. But when your experience is not pleasant, you have to make a choice. The choice is whether to allow someone else's problem to harm you. If you see the world as being against you, your choice is to allow them to harm you. If your choice is to see the person as a dinosaur with antiquated beliefs that will soon die away you keep your power.

If you change the way you look at things......the things you look at change.
Wayne Dyer

People who treat others poorly don't feel good. If they felt better they'd treat you better. When you allow their words and actions to bring you down to their emotional state, you're allowing them to win. When you retain your dignity and stay above the fray—even if it seems like a life altering problem—not just an inconvenience, you win.

Some will argue that it is better to expect the bad treatment and be prepared, but that is not supported by reality. The reality is that just expecting bad treatment increases stress, which leads to self-inflicted harm, even if no discrimination ever occurs. The reality is that someone who does not expect discrimination will have more resources with which to deal with it if it does occur.

I was one of the lucky ones. My parents did not prime me to expect discrimination. My level of success has been greater as a result of expecting that I could be successful and that the deck was not stacked against me. Don't stack your child's deck against them.

If your child believes she can be successful it is far more likely that she will be successful If your child does not believe he can be successful, the odds are 100% that your child will not be successful (unless the belief changes).

Stress impairs digestive function, which adds to the chronic disease burden from obesity and diabetes as well as lesser maladies such as upset tummies.[519]

Stress impairs immune function. Researchers have shown that stress has an immediate negative impact on immune function. This increases the incidence of mild illnesses, such as colds and flu, and also diseases that a healthy immune system manages, but an impaired one can't handle, like cancer.

Chronic stress is linked to mental illnesses including depression, which is at epidemic levels. Other forms of mental illness, including psychosis, are also linked to chronic stress.

Chronic stress is linked to pre-term delivery, a significant problem for minority women. The internal clock that determines when to go into labor speeds up when the Mother is experiencing chronic stress. The higher the lifetime stress load, the greater the likelihood of pre-term birth seems to be.

Chronic Stress impairs the Central Nervous System Function.

Douglas Fields, PhD, a senior investigator at the National Institutes of Health and editor in chief of *Neuron Glia Biology* adds another reason to avoid chronic stress, that Chronic stress places the triggers of rage on edge. His new book, *Why We Snap: Understanding the Rage Circuit in Your Brain* tell us chronic stress makes the triggers of rage more likely to misfire at inopportune times.

Early positive psychology research revealed that positive emotions reduce feelings of racism because they expand our sense of who is *like us*. The writings of African American college students asked to write about Barack Obama near the time of the 2008 Presidential election revealed "more plural self-references, fewer other-references, and more social references . . . and increased positive emotions, which in turn increased the likelihood that people thought in terms of more inclusive categories (we and us rather than they and them)."[520]

The American Public Health Association recently hosted a webinar titled *Racism and Its Impact on Children's Health*.[521]

They spoke about and ranked three approaches to socializing children about race:

Best: Promotion of racial pride
Okay: Preparation for bias together with coping strategies
Bad: Promotions of mistrust without coping strategies

Quite frankly, I was gravely disappointed by the options because there was no mention of what is a much better option for the child and society.

Better: Promotion of self-worth and self-pride based on the concept that everyone has value and worth and everyone has unique gifts combined with a perspective of the *in-group* not as a narrow race defined group, but as humanity as a whole.

I found it interesting that encouraging racial pride was a solution. Encouraging self-pride, regardless of race, and defining self as part of the human family would be more effective. I'd love to see research on this approach. A *Human Pride* approach would solve (or at least reduce) another problem. In bystander situations, bystanders are more likely to come to the aid of someone that they perceive as being affiliated with the same group as the bystander. There have been situations where no one came to the aid of a victim that had tragic results.[522] If we consider ourselves part of the Human group, we would be more likely to come to the aid of another human, regardless of their race, gender, ethnicity, religion, and sexual orientation or other *label*.

A focus on racial pride can ostracize bi-racial children who may feel as if they do not belong anywhere. Encouraging human pride might also soften culturally imposed restrictions on success that are prevalent in some Black communities. Focusing on racial pride is limiting. I hear people who have strong racial pride express sentiments that people of their race can't (or aren't allowed to) do things that others can and do accomplish. A bi-racial student of mine disclosed that she hated her race in her teens because friends told her she shouldn't be interested in things she liked because it wasn't *Black* to like those things and if she liked those things, she wasn't really *Black*. By restricting oneself to what others in your race have accomplished, you limit your ability to achieve. These are false limits. If anyone has done something, your race does not restrict you from doing it, too.

Black examples of success are available. You could read, *Why Should White Guys Have All the Fun? How Reginald Lewis Created a Billion-Dollar Business Empire* for an example of a middle class Black man who became very wealthy. You could read, *Gifted Hands: The Ben Carson Story*, for an example of a Black man who was raised in poverty by an uneducated woman who became a world renowned neurosurgeon and a candidate for the GOP Presidential nomination. For an inspirational story about a Black woman who faced significant adversity in her early years, you could read, *Oprah Winfrey - The Inspirational Life Story of Oprah Winfrey: From The Little Speaker To The Queen Of Talk (Inspirational Life Stories By Gregory Watson Book)*. And, of course, you can read about President Obama, but that brings me to another reason building racial pride instead of human pride can be problematic.

When President Obama was nominated for the Democratic Presidential candidate in 2008, researchers wondered how it would affect racial self-perceptions in the Black community so they did some research and

> *A sense of belonging is more important to health and to lower depression and increased life satisfaction following an adverse event than actual contact. How we feel is the most important criteria.*

found that President Obama's election resulted in increased scores on standardized tests. But the thing is, the people whose scores improved because their opinion of their own race improved were always capable of those better results. They limited their own ability by limiting their beliefs about their personal potential with race-based stereotypes.

As long as some dinosaurs that still ignorantly see Blacks as less intelligent are around to influence attitudes and Black children, tying self-esteem to race could hinder a child's ability to thrive. A child who sees herself as human first will see the highest of human accomplishments as possibilities. Some of the smartest and wisest (they're not the same thing in my book) people I've known happen to be Black.

In my classes I often use a friend of mine as an example. Charles Beauford was born in the southeastern United States in 1936. He was short, overweight and by the time I met him, mostly bald. Because skin color is associated with the ability to succeed with some darker Blacks believing they're at a disadvantage I'll mention that his skin was on the dark side of medium. I've known darker Black men, but he was not on the light-skinned side of the equation. Charles went to college before affirmative action was implemented. Charles became a psychiatrist and eventually opened his own clinic. He raised one daughter of whom he was very proud who also went to college. If Charles could do what he did during that era (get through medical school), and Reginald Lewis could do what he did, and Ben Carson could do what he did, you can do what you want to do. Your race won't stop you, but if you believe your race limits your potential, it will.

The same is true of your gender, your height, your weight, your religion, your socioeconomic beginnings, your sexual orientation, and anything else you can think of as an excuse as to why you can't achieve your dreams. Research is clear that we treat insiders better than outsiders. If everyone learned to consider themselves human first, then religion (if any), then country or race, then etc. etc. but with human first, we could all feel closer to one another.

I've personally made this transition from feeling very American to shifting my perspective to one where I see myself as part of the human family. Shifting that inner belief shifted a lot of other things, all toward greater positive feelings towards others around the world.

Also, along with the concept of self-pride, appreciation for our differences can be built. My unique perspectives, talents and abilities would not be nearly as valuable if everyone had the same perspectives, talents, and abilities. My uniqueness adds value to the world, so does yours.

Researchers who looked at 1,824, patients found that "the greater the number of social groups with which one identifies, the healthier one's behavior on any of the four (physical exercise, smoking, drinking, and diet) health dimensions considered."[523] The study also evaluated whether it was feeling a sense of belonging and affiliation that led to the health benefits or actual contact and found that the sense of belonging was what led to the improved health behaviors and also to lower depression and greater life satisfaction following an adverse health event.

Broadening your definition of your in-group can have other benefits. Being offered comfort when you're experiencing pain lessens pain more when support is "from a member of a group with which the participant identified."[524] Hospitals would not be very accommodating if, during childbirth a woman requested they provide someone who was from a narrowly defined in-group because it would lessen her discomfort. Such a request might even result in backlash. Social identity researchers found group identification:[525]

- Provides a sense of meaning, permanence, and stability, which protects against existential anxiety.

- Affords a sense of structure and meaning
- Constitutes a precondition for positive social relationships based on trust, support, and respect, which paves the way for positive mental states and mental health.

"An implication of our findings is that in order to understand how in-groups may improve our mental health we must take into account the fact that they are experienced as 'we' and 'us', thereby defining who is either similar (and therefore to be trusted) or different (and therefore to be seen with some suspicion) to self. Without acknowledging this, it is hard to explain how and under which circumstances contact with others and social support received from others is going to be beneficial."[526]

Having personally transitioned from a Nationalistic/Patriotic American viewpoint to one that embraces humanity as a whole, I can tell you that it makes a significant difference in my comfort level when I interact with people from different cultures and backgrounds and different belief systems.

The best way for any individual to know is to broaden your personal definition of your in-group and see how, or if, your feelings towards former out-group members change. Having already done this and felt first-hand how it changed my perceptions, I strongly encourage you to try it in the privacy of your own mind. Early research on racism demonstrated that automatic responses to other races could be changed by changing conscious aspects, leading the researchers to conclude "these experiments are optimistic in terms of the ability of even overlearned automatic attitudes to shift in response to positive interpersonal contact."[527]

Fewer children in the USA are *purely* a single race than those who are multi-racial, especially if you exclude children from families that immigrated in the last few generations. I mention excluding recent immigrants not because they aren't important, but because many of the issues that the Black community feels regarding race and heritage aren't issues with more recent immigrants.

Blacks whose heritage involved being captured in Africa and sold as slaves in the New World sometimes feel they don't know their roots and some express not knowing who they should be as a result of this lack of knowledge. Recognize that this is a process whereby they focus on something they can't change and make it a problem today. There are many families who don't really know their roots. My own mom always told us we were German on her side of the family and we told others we were German when we were growing up. Then, after Mom retired she was bit by the genealogy bug and she learned that we weren't German. There was a German step-father in her line that made the family think they were German and that belief was passed down.

On my father's side of the family I have Native American roots but I don't know which tribe because my family chose to pass as White during a time when being Native American meant you were denied some of your rights. I feel closer to my Native American heritage than I do my Caucasian heritage both because of my personal spiritual beliefs and because of my love of the great outdoors, the land, and animals. I feel more comfortable in a forest than I do in New York City. I don't have to know which tribe my ancestors come from to know what resonates with me today. Would I like to know? Sure. Am I going to allow not knowing to diminish my life and emotional state or to dim my self-worth? No.

Americans with a Black heritage can chose to look back and find lack; they are certainly free to do so. However, if they make that choice they can't escape the negative impact it has on their emotional state and self-confidence. Understanding that it is a choice, not a mandate, is important. Researchers have shown that developing emotion regulation skills can reduce the negative impact of experienced racism.[528] As to my own heritage my usual response is that I had ancestors on the Mayflower and some who were already here when the Mayflower arrived. I don't know much about them or any of the generations in between. I would submit we don't even know our parents that well.

I often use an exercise with my trainees where I tell them to think of something they do that their parent also does and then ask their parent why they do it. I learned this from a quilting instructor I had in the early 90's. She would tell a story about her Mom visiting her during the holidays some years after she had married and asking her why she was cutting the ham bone out of the ham she was preparing for dinner. She responded, "Because you always did, Mom." To which her Mom responded, "That's because I don't have a pan big enough to bake the ham with the bone-in, but when you got married I gave you a pan big enough to roast a ham with the bone-in."

Here you have a Mom and daughter who have a good relationship, who do the exact same action, but for different reasons. If you're looking for answers as to who you should be by looking at those who came before you, you're looking in the wrong direction.

Who you are is who you are. It is not who your ancestors were that matters.

There is a tremendous propensity in our world to compare ourselves to others and it serves us not.

If you make being better today than you were yesterday your goal there is no limit to how far you can go. If you make being better than some other person, you'll stop when you have bested the person, you'll feel competitive, and you are not likely to fulfill as much of your personal potential. Comparing yourself to others to decide what you are capable of limits you—even if you compare yourself to the best of humanity.

Your guidance can help you know what you can do by what feels good and right to you.

Associating with a small in-group can lead to adverse consequences. Pool et al. found that learning your in-group supports an attitude that contrasts with one's own led to decreased self-esteem.[529] Likewise, disassociating from a group who one learns supports attitudes that are consistent with the participants own caused self-esteem to decrease. Those participants who were indifferent to these group identifications, however, evidenced no such effects.[530]

In the real world, this could be seen in someone claiming to be a dedicated member of the Democratic or Republican party only to learn that the party they support values something they disagree with or that the party they do not support promotes something they value. A viewpoint that one is human and will find agreement about some things with everyone and disagreement about some things with everyone, rather than identifying oneself with a more limited subset of humanity, which then requires adherence to attitudes and beliefs determined by the group instead of those which are self-determined as right, can lead to Cognitive Dissonance.

Looking outside oneself for validation of what is right for oneself can cause many negative outcomes. Whereas looking inside, toward ones Emotional Guidance presents no such risks. Even if one's Emotional Guidance leads to perspectives that are significantly different than the norm of one's time, as experienced by Galileo, Semmelweis, and countless others who were early adopters of new paradigms, reliance on Emotional Guidance as the basis of self-worth protects the avant-garde from experiencing damaging emotional blows to self-worth or self-esteem.

Microaggressions

As you read this section, remember the filters between your subconscious and conscious mind that highlight things that you focus upon. The more you focus on things you do not want in your life, the more those things will reach your conscious mind. It is not that microaggressions are *just* in the mind of the perceiver; it is that the perceiver has trained his or her mind to be hypervigilant for perceived threats in a way that may not be serving his or her highest good. It is up to each individual to decide how to move forward.

"One of the most important concepts is that of microaggressions . . . defined as 'brief and commonplace daily verbal, behavioral, or environmental indignities, whether intentional or unintentional, that communicate hostile, derogatory, or negative racial slights and insults toward people of color' . . . Those who engage in microaggressions are often not aware of them when interacting with individuals who are members of racial or ethnic minority groups. It is likely that some psychotherapists also perpetrate microaggressions. These slights can torpedo the therapy relationship during the first session, and the therapist who considers her/himself culturally competent probably will not be able to understand why the client did not return to therapy." [531]

Microaggressions against Blacks may include: [532]
- Covert messages that Blacks are unintelligent (clearly misguided)
- We are all human beings is sometimes viewed as negation of person as a racial cultural being (I have more to say about this later = JJ)
- Trust issues
- Homogenizations (i.e. "You are all the same")

Microaggressions against Asians may include: [533]
- Those of being an alien (i.e. Where were you born?)
- Being seen as intelligent (i.e. You're so good in science and math)
- Invisibility
- Pathologizing cultural communications and styles

A note about "Where are you from?" I am not Asian. Most people assume I am Caucasian although some do recognize my Native American heritage. Since moving to the Southeast area of the United States I have been asked, "Where are you from?" by at least half the people I meet. Perhaps it is the absence of a Southern accent, but I don't take it as meaning that I do not belong here. People have a natural curiosity about other places and people and they are merely interested in where I lived before I came to North Carolina. I've even asked others this question, including some Asians. I used to ask it of Asians a lot, but it wasn't to aggress. It was because my first husband thought he was half Korean when we married, but when his Dad died we learned his Mom was his step-Mom and he was actually half Japanese. I was trying to learn how to distinguish between various Asians. One reason for this was I could inadvertently insult someone I thought was from one country who was from another. One of my good friends was Japanese but she married a Chinese man—something their families were not happy about and I had no idea until I asked her about the tension I'd sensed at her wedding reception. (I'm happy to report that they're still married 30+ years later.)

Sometimes people ask questions because they are interested in you as a person, because they do not want to insult you, or simply because they want to learn more about the people they share the world with. If you interpret questions as microaggressions, they diminish you. When you do this when that is not the intent, you're actually creating the racism you're experiencing in your own mind via the interpretation you're giving the experience. It's a form of self-harm, albeit unintentional.

I know what it is like to be asked personal questions frequently. Strangers frequently stop me as I am walking past to ask me personal questions. Many of them even ask if they can take my picture and some just take photo's without permission. They're just curious. Women with floor-length hair are not common.

If you give people the benefit of the doubt as far as their intentions, you're helping yourself. You get to choose whether you want to live in a world where every person's motives are suspect and probably bad or in a world where most people are simply curious and the answer is to a question such as, "Where are you from?" is not going to elicit an emotional reaction from them. Before my Mom became ill, my parents were planning to take a trip to China and I know they would ask people they encountered whom they thought might be from China where they were from. They certainly didn't want to start asking someone from Japan or Singapore where they should go when they visited China.

I do the same thing when I meet people who are from, or who I learn have spent time in, a place I'm planning to visit. I ask what I should do and see when I am there and I'll often ask them what they would do if they only had a single day there. "Where are you from?" is just one of the questions, but if you think about it, many of the identified microaggressions may not be aggressions at all. Earlier today I learned that using the term "gyped" is considered a microaggression against Romanians. Until I read that I had no association between Romanians and the term gyped or between gypsies and gyped.

Microaggressions can happen against anyone, for example, obese people, women, LBGTQ, Native Americans, and others. Bi-racial individuals often face both overt and microaggressions from both sides. Microaggressions also occur in our homes and between family members.

Microaggressions are subtle forms of discrimination that may or may not be conscious by the individual considered the aggressor. They may be real and intentional. They may also be perceptions by the victim that reflect the personal beliefs about a world or groups that oppose them for a variety of reasons that do not reflect the thoughts, feelings, or intentions of the perceived aggressors.

This is actually good news because if the microaggression is the result of perception, the victim has complete control over the disempowering perspective and the ability to change to a more empowered perspective. Unlike overt, deliberate discrimination and aggression against subgroups of the human population that require changes in widely accepted thoughts and beliefs about various groups, the psychosocial damage inflicted by microaggressions is largely within the power of the victim to control.

Microaggressions can be as the result of a wide variety of *labels* that serve to divide humanity and include race, religion, nationality, gender, sexual orientation,[534] body type, and more.

Choices about microaggressions
From my perspective there are two choices about microaggressions. We can choose to let them disempower us or we can choose to learn how to be stronger and negate their impact on our lives. Researchers have demonstrated that emotion regulation skills help individuals cope with anxiety and stress related to racist experiences.[535] Emotion regulation skills achieved using *The Smart Way* are more powerful than common skills. I am confident the skills you're learning here will afford you even greater protection against adverse effects.

With the prevalence of discrimination, from my perspective there is only one choice—chose to define yourself and not allow others' opinions to sway your opinion of yourself.

Another choice you have is to lock microaggressions out of your home when they arrive over the airwaves. I turned off my television in 1995 and kept it off for nearly twenty years because the shows that were being aired in 1995 portrayed family relationships that were disrespectful and demeaning to one another. If they had been in my home in person and acted that way I would have asked them to leave. So I turned it off. Today with the ability to watch selected shows commercial free I am once again watching selected shows. I still avoid shows where I would not welcome the main characters into my home.

I don't have the citations at hand, but I've read research that showed some of the worst behavior that demeaned overweight people came from their own family in their homes. Decide what sort of family environment you want to live in and then discuss it with your family. Be emotionally intelligent about hurting feelings of your family members because verbal knives in the hands of those we love cut deepest.

A Given about microaggressions

Even with my positively focused view of our world and our potential to make it better, I cannot conceive of a way to stop all microaggressions today. If there is a way, I don't know what it is.

Discrimination is decreasing over time as attitudes change. I also believe that there are ways to reduce it further by increasing awareness. However, the best path to this is with little focus on attempting to define every potential microaggression and much emphasis on understanding our Emotional Guidance and defining the type of person we want to show up as in the world. My life has also shown me that when someone who picks on me stops getting a reaction from me, they lose the motivation to pick on me.

There is a "statistically significant positive relationship between racial ethnic microaggressions and depression, and racial microaggression and self-esteem."[536] "Microaggressions seem relatively harmless, and are, in fact, routinely left out of reports of bias and harassment by school psychologists. They can, however, be quite harmful to stigmatized groups. They are often characterized as constant, continuing experiences, and the weight of these summed experiences can be considerable . . . microaggressive experiences were linked with posttraumatic symptoms in LGB participants, indicating that the strong sense of helplessness created by systemic discrimination may be categorized as trauma"[537]

The attitude behind microaggressions may be adverse to the individual and represent beliefs that are held by the aggressor. In some cases, these beliefs may simply be what they were taught to believe by a prior generation and they have not evaluated the beliefs they've adopted. In other cases, the beliefs could be deeply held religious convictions. If you flip it over and demand that someone change deeply held religious beliefs to accommodate someone else's needs, that is an aggression toward them and there is no peaceful way to settle the matter. We can't ask for others to approve of our choices. We can ignore their opinion about our choices. If we wait for the world to approve our choices we'll never be happy. By now, you know how much being happy matters.

The only way I know to address the issue is to encourage people to use their Emotional Guidance and set their intentions to feel as good as they can. When we look at someone else and find fault with them, regardless of whether we perceive their religion, sexual orientation, race, or some other factor as undesirable, we don't feel good in that moment. If we turn to our Emotional Guidance, we find that being more accepting of differences feels better. We also find that we can accept that others are different but that does not require us to be like them. Just because someone gets divorced does not mean we have to divorce. Although I haven't seen it mentioned in the microaggression literature, divorcees are sometimes discriminated against. I've personally experienced that on more than one occasion. Attempting to convince someone else that my choices are right for me is a fruitless effort that typically accomplishes nothing other than frustrating me. I long ago gave up the effort.

Someone who defines themselves as wanting to be kind who also understands their Emotional Guidance will feel the discord between thoughts and feelings that contradict the desire to be kind and whenever possible, refrain from words or actions that would be perceived as microaggressions.

With that being said, we may not always be able to predict what might be perceived as a microaggression. Last week my husband and I were driving to another city and he noted that the driver of another vehicle was texting. I looked over toward the driver with what I'm sure was an unfriendly expression on my face. At about the same time my mind processed the fact that the driver was a minority I saw reflected in the driver's eyes recognition of my negative emotion (which was about someone endangering others by texting while driving), but which I could sense he perceived as a racially based microaggression. The individual's filters led to that perception based on an inaccurate view of the world. He assumed that any negative perception of him by someone who appears to be of another race is racially-based. That assumption does not serve him well.

If using your Emotional Guidance is not enough to give you relief from negative feelings (whether you are being aggressed against or you are the aggressor) I encourage you to seek counseling with an understanding therapist. Negative emotion is not something I encourage anyone to tolerate longer than it takes to do a Right Response. Use your power to do what is within your control.

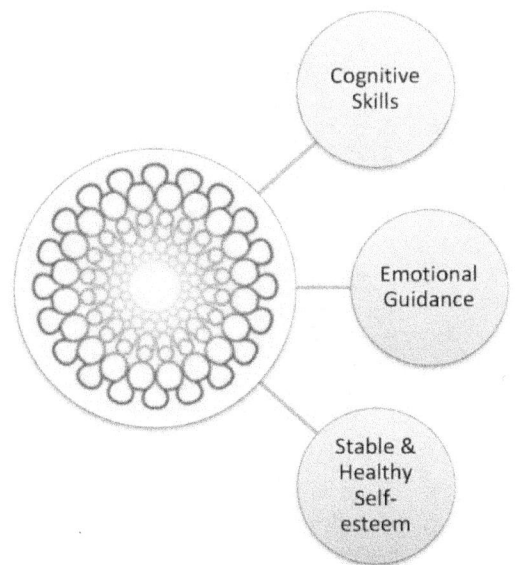

Why it's important

What may seem to be harmless microaggressions can, when the receiver is not resilient, lead to suicide ideation.[538] "Even supposedly innocuous forms of discrimination are associated with elevated levels of anxiety, anger, and stress."[539] We cannot end racism in the next five minutes. At least, if someone has found a way, they aren't sharing it. I agree that ending racism is a better alternative. But given what we can control and what we cannot control, and the harm that can be alleviated by improving what we can control, I strongly advocate improving everything that is within our immediate control, while continuing to do what we can about aspects that we can't change in this moment. The consequences of not doing what we can are too great to ignore.

Now, some people may say that my point that microaggressions can lead to suicide ideation in individuals who are not resilient is itself a microaggression against people who are not resilient. There must be a way to discuss an issue without the discussion being an aggression. The truth is that if someone is resilient enough they will not become depressed and engage in suicide ideation as the result of microaggressions. Since we know resilience can be increased, the negative harm of microaggressions can be reduced by increasing resilience.

That is not a damning of an individual for not being resilient. It is a simple fact. It is pointing out a significant reason to develop resilience; something the skills provided in this book can increase.

Also, it is important to point out that when an individual learns skills that allow her to be happy and understand her Emotional Guidance she will quickly realize that her guidance lets her know (by how it feels) when she is doing or saying something that is harming another. Emotional Guidance may be the best method of increasing awareness of implicit microaggressions by unintentional users. It may also reduce the desire, intention, and actual use of microaggressions by those who deliberately use them to inflict harm.

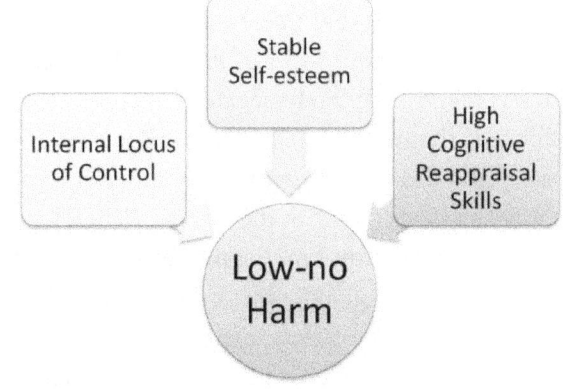

Researchers found that rumination (repeated thoughts about negative experiences) increases emotional distress and aggression from perceived ethnic discrimination.[540] *The Smart Way* helps ruminators stop ruminating about stressors in their lives, which would include microaggressions and even overt discrimination.

Researchers found that individuals who use a process of Values Clarification following the experience of racism were able to buffer the negative psychological impact of the experience of racism.[541] The experiment was with a small group, but it did have a control group and additional research is planned. Fortunately, with *The Smart Way* you don't need someone else to tell you if it is helpful to you. You can try it and if you feel better, you know it is your guidance letting you know the practice is beneficial to you. If it doesn't feel good to you, stop doing it.

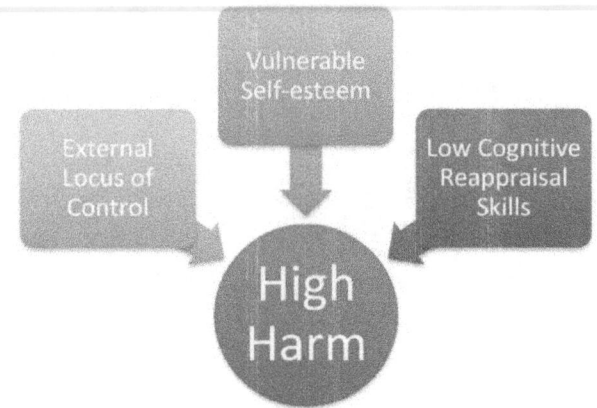

Values Clarification means thinking about what you have decided is important to you in your life—who you want to be, how you want to live and how you want to show up in the world.

"Sue et al. described three forms of racial microaggression that seem readily adaptable for understanding microaggression based on several aspects of the target persons' identities. The three forms are:

Microassaults: Explicit racial derogation characterized primarily by verbal, nonverbal or environmental attack meant to hurt the intended victim through name calling, avoidant behavior, or purposeful discriminatory actions

Microinsults: Characterized by communications that convey rudeness and insensitivity and demean a person's racial heritage or identity; and

Microinvalidations: Which are characterized by communications that exclude, negate, or nullify the psychological thoughts, feelings, or experiential reality of a person.

Let's evaluate how much of each type of microaggression could be characterized as perceptual vs. actual. In other words, those which have the potential to be perceived as microaggressions when they are not and/or when there is no intent to diminish another person. In the LGBTQA community they recognize what they refer to as Allies, defined as straight but supportive. In the world of race relations, the concept of an Ally is frequently negated by the radical fringe indicating that White people can't be supportive of black people because of White privilege.

I've been told that referring to people as Black instead of African-American is a form of microaggression, but I've had African-American friends who have told me using Black is fine. That using Black is racist completely negates my childhood experiences where I was culturally indoctrinated by billboards that proclaimed "Black is Beautiful"—a perception I internalized. The African-American description did not show up in my experience until later and I don't have any culturally indoctrinated positive associations with the phrase. When I say or think the term Black it feels positive. When I think or say the term African-American it feels inauthentic—as if I am attempting to mold myself into something I am not. It makes me uncomfortable. So, according to the definition of a microinvalidation, when someone tells me that using Black, a term that has a positive connotation to me (i.e. Black is Beautiful), is racist, it is a microinvalidation against my lived experience.

I read quite about quite a few different viewpoints and talked to dozens of people while writing this chapter to try to gain greater clarity surrounding the issues. I finally realized that I was trying to gain clarity by seeing all the varying perspectives as representative of the whole and then felt really dumb, but it helped me see the larger view—not just about race, but about religion and other *labels*. Radicals stand out and if you're not part of the in-group, it is easy to ascribe radical traits to the whole. I created an illustration to attempt to convey how outsiders view other groups—through the lens of the radical element. This seems true regardless of whether you're looking at a religious, ethnic, LBGT, racial or other group. I think it is as true of non-whites looking at Whites as it is of non-Blacks looking at Blacks or non-Hispanics looking at Hispanics and non-Christians looking at Christians and non-Muslims looking at Muslims, and so on.

The small circle in the lower right part of the larger circle represents the radical elements of the label. is the lens through which outsiders view the whole group—not because the radical fringe represents the whole group, but because they are the vocal part of the group that is most visible. The vocal minority create the public impression of the group. The larger circle can represent the majority of any *label*.

For example, KKK activities and words may be perceived by outsiders as representing views held by everyone who is White. When you're not part of the group, it is not as easy to see which sub-groups hold radical views and which represent the views of the majority. It was my struggle to assimilate all the perspectives I was reading about the Black viewpoint about racism that at first confused me (because I was attempting to reconcile radical ideas with the mainstream (Silent Majority) views within the Black community. By talking with a variety of people about what I was trying to assimilate and reconcile with my own experiences, I finally realized that I was looking through the lens of the Vocal Minority attempting to perceive what the Silent Majority think and feel about the issues.

I created another illustration that represents my hypothesis that the vast majority of people in any group are more alike the vast majority of people in other groups and that they have more in common with the silent majority in other groups than they do with the radical fringe that is considered part of their *label*. So in the second diagram, the *all silent majorities* represent the majority of people in each group (Asian, Black, Hispanic, Native American, White, Christian, Muslim, Hindu, Buddhist, etc.). The little egg-shaped lesions on the outside represent the various radical elements of the combined *labels*.

Out groups view the Majority through the lens of The Radical Minority, thus believing the Silent Majority agree with the divisive views of the Radical Minority. As the book goes to print I'm gathering a group of people interested in reducing racism in this country in order to expand on the idea of the silent majority and radical and vocal minority. Keep an eye on my Twitter, Linkedin, or website for updates or if you'd like to get involved. My contact information is in the back of the book.

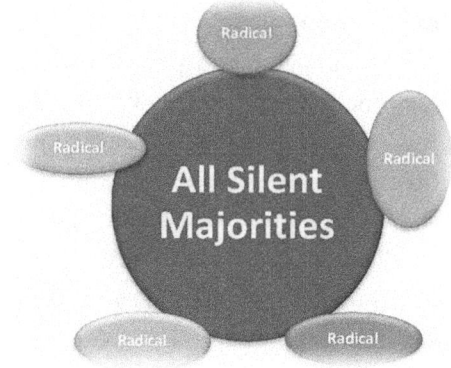

In the examples of the microaggression insults I've seen in the literature, many of them are based on an expectation that other people understand your perspective. That just isn't possible. Your siblings, parents, and children don't fully understand your perspective on everything. The more time you've shared, the more you may have come to similar conclusions—but not always. There are often significant divides in the way families view the world, despite shared experiences. Every thought we think, every back story our mind creates leads to a unique and valuable perception of the world, but to expect anyone else to understand your perception as intimately as you do is folly. *No one does and no one will.* If you take conversations below the surface level it is easy to uncover disparate beliefs and perspectives in your inner circle. When you widen that, you will find even wider variations in worldview and occasionally someone who seems nothing like you who seems to share many of your worldviews.

In one example, an article in The Atlantic by Conor Friedersdorf, several Hispanic college students were sent an email inviting them to play fútbol if they chose not to attend a talk that was part of Latino Heritage Month that was scheduled at the same time. One Hispanic college woman was upset because she felt the email was a microaggression on numerous fronts—an email that could have easily been perceived as an invitation that attempted to invite the students to play if they weren't going to the talk that was being held at the same time. She could have even considered the fact that the other possible activity was acknowledged as supportive of their cultural heritage.

The escalation of the simple, polite email to the harsh commentary it led to on a website at Oberlin College was an amazing Oscar-winning level of victimhood. Every word in the original email was analyzed for any sign of affront and each one that could, by some stretch of the imagination, be perceived as one was publically lambasted as if the negative connotation was the accurate connotation. The author and I reached the same conclusion—a victim culture characterized by perceived microaggressions is a one-way road to nowhere.

Microinvalidations is the category that seems most prone to perception errors, although the others aren't immune. Someone with low self-esteem or self-worth is far more likely to perceive themselves as being invalidated. Someone who is confident will not perceive it that way. Having had low self-esteem as a young woman and then developing into a confident woman I am intimately familiar with how self-esteem affects one's perceptions of others words and actions. When I had low self-esteem I often perceived that I was being deliberately ignored by those I wished would pay attention to me. Later I realized they simply had not been aware of me. If I had possessed the confidence to approach the people I wanted to notice me it is doubtful I would have been rebuffed.

Later in my career, I had employees who expressed their perception that a higher level boss was unapproachable, but the boss was quite approachable and would have been happy to converse with them. There were other employees at the same level who were more confident with whom the bosses conversed. Frankly, if an employee is uncomfortable in your presence you don't generally seek them out for conversation.

We all perceive separate worlds. The individual who has always been confident may have no idea how someone else might feel. Even if they're told, they still can't relate. I can't relate to the comradery athletes develop with teammates because I have never been one. Not understanding their relationships and unique communications does not mean I am invalidating their experiences. It simply means I don't have a basis to fully understand their relationship.

Perceiving microaggressions against oneself is a clue that the person's psychological processes will contribute to poor physical and mental health outcomes. Stances such as, "This bigger, more powerful person did something that made me feel bad and all I can do is complain about it. It is upsetting to me and I'm going to make a fuss so others will solve this problem for me" reflect an external locus of control

While college campuses may coddle young adults who haven't developed the psychological flexibility to change their perception to a better-feeling one, the workplace is not going to tolerate the discord that will exist between employees if they bring their high sensitivity to microaggressions into the workplace. For one thing, there are some cultural things that one culture finds offensive that other cultures demand one do. Burping is one that comes to mind. There are almost 200 countries on Earth today and even within a country there are cultural differences. More than 100 languages are spoken in the Los Angeles area.[542] The diversity is too great for any single person to be culturally competent with everyone they might encounter.

Colleges are allowing those who feels harmed to direct the dialogue when they should be taking a broader view and asking why some people seem to be harmed by perceived microaggressions while others don't even perceive them and then help those who scan their environment for aggression to develop healthier perspectives about the world. They should recognize that the view that every word that might be interpreted as aggressive and meant in the worst possible way will lead to unhappiness, depression, and possibly worse as well as an inability to connect and develop relationships that could help them understand that most people have no ulterior motive or hidden aggressive agenda. Quite frankly, most people just aren't paying that much attention to the needs and desires of others—doing so contradicts our innate selfishness.

This world has a lot of significant issues to solve, if everyone is expected to become an expert in 200+ cultures so as not to offend anyone, we won't have any time left to solve more pressing problems—especially when it is a problem each individual can easily solve herself via meta-cognitve processes. Also, how many assumptions would one have to make about others cultural and racial heritage to avoid microaggressions?

We must each be responsible for our own happiness and the best way to be happy is to find perspectives that feel good. People who perceive microaggressions are doing the opposite. They are expecting the rest of the world to perceive the world the same way they do. It will never happen. It is a battle that could endure forever without a true win. Oh, someone might feel vindicated in their opinion if they gather enough others who support their position and vilify the *aggressor* enough. If they're aggressive enough in their vilification of an aggressor he or she may even commit suicide, but that is not a win for anyone.

I'm almost finished with this book and I've just today come across a paper, *Worse Than Blatant Racism: A Phenomenological Investigation of Microaggressions among Black Women* and it has me very excited.[543] I'm excited because if I've ever heard of Myers' theory of Optimal Psychology, I haven't seen it depicted in exactly this way. The researchers describe Myers' theory as Afrocentric where an optimal worldview is one where reality is both spiritual and material. In this worldview, "self-worth stems from intrinsic value and validation. People are worthy because they uniquely reflect spiritual energy with the highest value given to positive interpersonal relationships. Within the optimal conceptual system, the self is multidimensional, encompasses the ancestors, the unborn, nature, and community."[544] I'm excited because the framework they describe reflects a worldview close to my own and close to the one I am attempting to convey in these pages, albeit with far more words than this beautifully succinct description. The paper, which I encourage you to get (it's available online), goes on to describe and compare forms of optimal resistance to microaggressions to suboptimal resistance. I'll share some of the forms of optimal resistance and you'll see that they support my commentary in this chapter and elsewhere in this text.

Umoja—*Unity with others across race, gender, class, and age.* This is what I'm referring to when I encourage everyone to consider themselves human first instead of narrower labels.

Kujichagalia—*Incorporation of a healthy identity.* This is what I'm referring to when I talk about the importance of self-esteem and in the process section, using Emotional Guidance to call Bogus on negative and critical self-concepts.

Ujima—*Healthy reliance on self and others.* This relates to developing an internal locus of control.

Kuumba—*Actively creating new and empowering ways of being in the world.* This is what the reappraisal process is all about—creating more powerful perspectives and deciding to be who you want to be—not who others might perceive you to be.

Imani—*Trusting that life gets better and the universe is benevolent and responsive.* This is essentially optimism plus trusting your Emotional Guidance.

In the chart in Chapter 5, you can see that an external locus of control reduces immune, digestive, cognitive, and central nervous system function. Over time this leads to higher incidences of chronic health problems and earlier mortality. Taking the same line of reasoning that someone should know every nuance of another's culture, I could insist that everyone understand the relationship their psychological functioning has on their physical and mental health and raise a ruckus because their insistence on being offended when they could easily adjust their perception to one that is more empowered and reduce their risk of developing chronic illnesses has the potential to increase the health care load on an already overtaxed system.

If we want to find a perspective that offends us, we can. But doing so does not serve our highest good.

But I would prefer not to take on the mantle of "do it for the good of all" and keep it where selfishness will lead to more productive perspectives. Each individual's health, relationships, and even success in life is more dependent upon where their mind is on the Emotional Guidance Scale than their race, national origins, religion, gender, sexual orientation, or any other *label* they have agreed to wear.

Anyone and everyone can choose to attach an *Empowered* label to themselves. Empowered is a mindset more than anything else. When you have an empowered mindset, others respond to it and give you the power.

Second of all, there is this thing called "giving others the benefit of the doubt."

I have friends who live on four different continents and in a dozen different countries who are not US natives. I am. I do not attempt to learn all the cultural nuances that might offend them. I did learn what fanny means in Australia and refrain from using it when I'm there. But for the most part, I simply don't concern myself with it and I don't try to get my friends to learn my culture. We all simply assume that any misunderstandings are lack of knowledge and that the intention is good—which is all that matters. We are able to have wonderful relationships that feel free and easy and full of fun and love. No one is on edge or watching every word we utter. We simply enjoy one another.

If you're anxiously watching for signs that someone is being aggressive toward you via microaggressions you'll never have that sort of free and easy relationship with anyone outside your immediate group. Good relationships are strongly linked to good physical and mental health and lower mortality. In fact, constantly looking for microaggressions in your environment is likely to make your close relationships with in-group members less satisfying because your brain will be looking for words and actions that make you feel diminished. People we love say and do things that can be interpreted that way—one of many possible interpretations—but a mind that is vigilant about watching for microaggressions will find them. Looking for them creates a filter in the subconscious that results in the brain creating back stories that interpret innocent words and actions as microaggressions. Unless and until the underlying belief that people are out to victimize you is changed, a person will interpret the world as hostile. That does not serve them or anyone. It will lead to diminished success in life, which will be interpreted as someone else holding them back because of their *label*. Because they interpret the world through that lens, they will experience the world as if that is reality and they will teach their children that harsh, cruel version of reality. Others with the same *label* with better psychological flexibility will begin thriving, but the one who focuses on microaggressions will continue to experience a world that holds them down or back.

My remarks may seem harsh, but in reality I hate to see anyone suffer unnecessarily. There is enough suffering that cannot be easily alleviated in this world. The negative effect of a microaggression on a person' experience is really up to the person perceiving the microaggression—not the one who is perceived as microaggressive.

Using meta-cognitve processes together with Emotional Guidance will minimize any negative effects. Attempting to control the behavior of everyone in the world is an impossible task that will increase stress and deprive you of happiness. The far easier solution is to control your response using your mind and emotions.

- Decide to commit to your strength—not your vulnerability.
- Decide to see yourself as empowered—not dependent on the power of others.
- Decide to give others the benefit of the doubt—it's surprising how trustworthy trusted people become.
- Decide to discard any perceived advantages of wearing the victim hat—that you've outgrown it.
- Decide that you are a thriver—not merely a survivor.

There is an old song that always makes me feel empowered, *I am Woman* by Helen Reddy. If you don't know the song, check it out on YouTube.

I am strong.
I am invincible.
I am Woman.

Substitute any word you prefer for Woman and feel your power.

I am statements have power. Be selective about what you lay claim to. It will change your life.

If you can perceive who you are as human first, your perspective about everyone changes and the world becomes friendlier overnight. It stops the us vs. them attitude and becomes one of a large family. Have you ever attended a family reunion or funeral where you met distant relatives you'd never met before? Did you have a level of comfort with them just because they were family? Well, everyone is family.

Affirming membership in the human race and warmth and closeness with other humans is supported by my Emotional Guidance. While Emotional Guidance is unique to each individual, supporting individual goals and desires, this concept has been presented to others whose guidance has supported the *human as my in-group concept*. Use of one's Emotional Guidance makes it very difficult to feel alone or detached because the guidance is ever-present, ever-helpful, and ever-supportive of a positive self-image.

24: Discrimination

25: Behavioral Health

Live your life as though your every act were to become a universal law.
Immanuel Kant

As discussed in Chapter 13, an individual's emotional state has a significant effect on behavior. It is a rare person who behaves the same when he is angry as he does when he is happy. In general, desirable behaviors are associated with good-feeling emotional states and undesirable behaviors are associated with bad-feeling emotional states. Risky behaviors are common amongst adolescents. *Global Advances in Health and Medicine* compiled information from the US Centers for Disease Control and *Prevention Youth Risk Behavior Surveillance System* which demonstrates how risky the behaviors of our young have become. A study of 890 Texas children in grades 9 – 12 reported the follow prevalence of risky behaviors:[545]

Behavior	**Females**	**Males**
Riding with a drinking driver in the past 30 days	30%	30.3%
Driving while drinking during past 30 days	11.2%	16%
Texting while driving during past 30 days	33.7%	33.8%
Smoking cigarettes/cigarillos during past 30 days	21.7%	23.4%
Drinking alcohol during the past 30 days	46.6%	43.2%
Drinking 5 (or more) drinks in a row in the past 30 days	31.5%	28.6%
Using marijuana during the past 30 days	30.1%	35.5%
Using hashish during the past 30 days	4.8%	11.8%
Using any form of cocaine during lifetime	6.2%	11.3%
Sniffing/inhaling glue, paints or spray during lifetime	7.9%	10.2%
Having more than four sexual partners during lifetime	15.4%	29.7%
Not using a condom during last sexual intercourse	58.6%	55.2%

Many parents believe their children do not engage in risky behaviors because they have educated them about the risks or because they have told them the behavior(s) are forbidden. Research is clear that education and restrictions from parents or law-makers do not prevent risky behaviors. Most of the above behaviors are not legal, yet the number of children who engaged in them is high. The best protection against risky behaviors is high self-esteem and good stress management. Research has shown repeatedly that drug and alcohol abuse begins with unmanaged psychological stress. The

> *Research is clear that education and restrictions from parents or law-makers do not prevent risky behaviors.*

following diagram illustrates the minimum risk of not using a condom with a sex partner when both partners have had four past sexual partners. The diagram does look complicated, but that is because it is complicated. Multiple sexual partners, especially without a condom, significantly increases the risk of sexually transmitted diseases. Some youth think that they are protected because they are young and their partners are young and translate youth to protection because they don't see how they or their partners would have contracted a sexually transmitted disease.

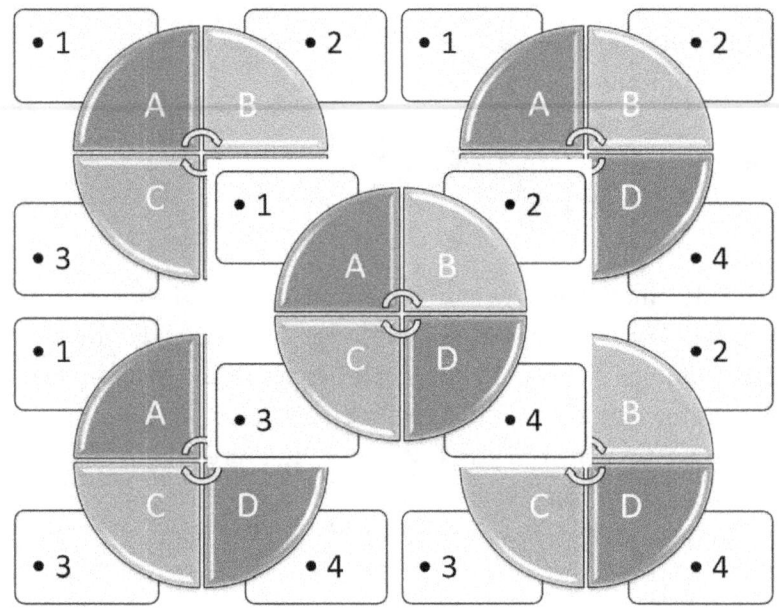

If each teenager has sex with four partners, the last couple to have sexual intercourse with one another is effectively having sex with 32 people from a risk management standpoint. Both partners would have had sex with 4 people; each of those people would have had sex with four other people.

The four partners of each prior partner (4 x 4) = 16

If each partner has had four prior partners, that equals 32 potential sources of sexually transmitted diseases, including HIV. If one of the prior partners or current partners has had more than four partners, this number increases by the total number of partners their prior partners have had.

Unfortunately, some adults seek young sexual partners because they have the same thought process. If one of the teenage sexual partners (of either partner) had a sexual relationship with an adult who may have had many more sexual partners than a teenager, the potential risk increases significantly. Furthermore, the reported number of children who suffer through child sexual abuse is consistently above 10%, and frequently much higher. Sixteen percent may be a more accurate number. Child sexual abuse increases the risk that a child will engage in both unsafe sexual behavior and promiscuous behaviors. By its very nature, child sexual abuse cross contaminates a pool of adolescents with the sexual partners of an older person who, in most cases, has been active with more partners. Assuming youth of oneself and one's partners affords protection against sexually transmitted diseases can be a costly mistake.

Risky choices are generally aimed at alleviating emotional distress. The choices made by participants in experiments are the best perceivable way to alleviate a stressor, even if the chances of success were so low that the choice was irrational.[546] If they had skills they could use to feel better without the risk, it is highly likely they would use them to feel better.

Self-Control

In many areas of life, the approach to better behavior targets educating people about the risks of unhealthy and undesired behaviors. It is the most common approach to preventing drug and alcohol use, smoking, unsafe sex, obesity, low physical activity, and other behaviors that contribute to poor outcomes. The rising rates of chronic diseases as well as numerous specific research studies demonstrate that education alone has little impact on behavior—even when one's life depends on making the changes. Patient adherence to physician prescribed treatment plans is one of the most common reasons diabetic patients are admitted to the hospital. Depression and anxiety are associated with poor self-care even when individuals have been educated about the importance of self-care. Improving depression "was significantly associated with better self-care behaviors throughout a 6-month" study.[547]

"Self-control can be broadly defined as the regulation of thoughts, emotions, impulses, task performances, and attentional processes. Low self-control ability is the culprit of many problems in daily life. It is manifested in spontaneous, usually troublesome behavior that is often experienced as difficult to prevent and hard to be stopped. Low self-control constitutes a core criterion in various psychiatric disorders."[548]

> *The rising rates of chronic diseases as well as numerous specific research studies demonstrate that education alone has little impact on behavior—even when one's life depends on making the changes.*

"We want to emphasize that poor cognitive control is associated with a stronger influence of automatic processes on behavior, in other words, relatively less impact of the reflective system and relatively more of the associative, impulse system."[549]

Just three years after this was written, the main contributor participated in another paper[550] where it was concluded that emotions cannot be controlled directly—only by changing thoughts can emotions be controlled in a healthy manner. The conclusions in that paper support the foundations on which *The Smart Way* is built. By learning meta-cognitve methods of changing thoughts with deliberate intention, self-control increases. Practicing the meta-cognitve processes builds mental muscles and neuropathways that increase the likelihood reflection will occur between stimulus and reaction. With practice, equanimity in almost any circumstance can be achieved and even if it is temporarily absent, the skills enable the individual to quickly return to desirable emotional states.

The presence of self-control is a significant contributor to success in all areas of life and to avoidance of trouble. As discussed in the **Beliefs and Expectations Chapter**, self-control requires an energetic resource that research shows becomes depleted with use. The more you can align your definition of self with required actions and create intrinsic motivation within yourself, the less you will be affected by this energy depletion. Baumeister, Vohs and Tice report that desired goals (and/or requirements of some environments) which cause some degree of depletion of self-control include:[551]

- Politically correct speech
- Controlling thoughts[d]
- Managing emotions[e]
- Fixing attention
- Guiding behavior
- Making many choices
- Meeting poor behavior with kindness[f]
- Interracial interactions (for some people)[g]

---

[d]

[d and e] Your skill and experience with managing emotions makes a tremendous difference. When you're learning to be positively focused being around negatively focused people is draining. After you are skilled in managing your own emotional state, being around negative people is easier.

[f] But if you have defined yourself as *a kind person* the depletion is less because your kind behavior is consistent with your belief about who you are and who you want to be, you're intrinsically motivated to be kind.

- Self-presentation and presentation management[h]

Later, Kathleen Vohs wrote a paper, *The Poor's Poor Mental Power*, describing explorations into the way the requirement that poor people make trade-off decisions, because their resources aren't adequate to provide all their desires and how the self-control required to live with chronic pain can also deplete this limited resource.[552] The findings equated poverty to operating with the loss of one night's sleep.[553] Imagine attempting to function and improve your life with the level of cognitive capacity available to you after you've been without sleep for an entire night. The researchers defined poverty broadly as, "the gap between one's needs and the resources available to fulfill them."[554] They used this definition to be able to evaluate the effect of poverty across nations and include individuals who experience a sudden loss of income, such as that caused by job loss, divorce, or the death or disability of an income source when plans to replace the income are inadequate.

I haven't seen any research on it, but observing my parents dealing with health issues and the self-control required to manage multiple medications and restrictions on how long they can safely be away from home as well as the extra care needed to navigate from the house to the vehicle or into a business, it appears as if the same depletion of self-control may be happening to them. Fortunately, the severity of their current status appears temporary, but for many it is not.

Important areas where self-control can become impaired include:
- Food intake goals (i.e. dieting and nutrition)
- Spending limits
- Controlling aggressive responses when provoked
- Sexual impulses
- Intelligent and logical decision-making

How does this play out in real life?

At work:

When we were 17, my (then) future sister-in-law was very happy when she moved from working at Taco Bell, a job that led to her always smelling like a taco, to working at a retail store that has long since disappeared, Gold Circle. She lost the job because she whispered B&#%h under her breath about a very irritating customer, but her whisper was not quiet enough because the customer heard her and demanded she be fired. It all happened very quickly. The accurateness of her comment did not prevent termination of her employment. That is an example of lack of self-control.

At home:

Years later, still not having developed self-control, I witnessed my older but still immature sister-in-law shoving my 9-year-old nephew so hard he flew about six feet through the air, after which she proceeded to threaten to push me down a flight of stairs when I protested. Needless to say, Child Protective Services

---

[g] Defining self as human instead of by a more narrow label would reduce the energy required to feel comfortable interacting with others because the perception of others as a threat increases when they are considered *other*.

[h] I haven't seen documentation, but based on my own journey and response to giving speeches at 21 vs. today, confidence and self-esteem play a tremendous role in the energy depletion in this type of task with greater confidence and self-esteem lessening the amount of energy expended

was called and, based on what I heard, supervised the parenting for a period of time thereafter. I lived 2,000 miles away and we were both in my parents' house visiting when the event occurred.

I like to think that no parent would want to treat their child the way she treated my nephew. But when one does not have self-control or know how to develop it, bursts of anger often have undesired consequences. That was nearly twenty years ago and I did not know what I do now about how to empower someone with skills that give them greater self-control. She grew up in an authoritarian and sometimes violent household, which the literature indicates is more likely to lead to such outcomes. Strictly controlling children deprives them of opportunities to develop self-control.

While driving:
I've witnessed numerous events as a passenger that were the result of lack of self-control.

On one occasion, the driver became angry at another driver, reached for a pistol he had in a pocket in his door, rolled down the window and began pointing it at the other driver. I don't even remember what set him off—all I remember is wishing I could ask Scotty to beam me out of there. Fortunately something, perhaps my screaming, got his attention enough to prevent further escalation of the encounter.

Another time, the driver had a terse phone conversation while driving that angered him and he began speeding more than twenty miles per hour more than the speed limit. He was taking his anger out by speeding. According to research I've seen, this is not uncommon.

In Marriage:
There are so many ways a lack of self-control can sabotage a marriage. It can happen as quickly as allowing an unkind remark pass your lips that you never intended to say, but which is unforgivable to your spouse. It can also result from giving into an impulse that leads to infidelity, which then leads to increasing efforts to cover it up or to bringing home a sexually transmitted disease. Sometimes, marriages occur because the person lacked self-control. I remember breaking up with a nice young man when I turned 18 because he kept asking me to run away to Lake Tahoe and marry him. Once I turned 18, I was worried he would catch me in a weak moment and I'd say yes. I was aware enough to know I did not want to marry him, but did not trust my self-control enough at that age to be steadfast in my refusal.

My instincts were good. He wanted to be married. I don't know why. Within a month of my breaking up with him he asked a co-worker to marry him. I hope they are happy. He was a really nice guy, but was obsessed with the idea of getting married far more than he was with the idea of finding the right partner first. His obsession is also an indicator that he lacked control. The idea of getting married took over and put aside practical considerations so much that it was no longer about the person as it was about being married.

How has self-control helped or its lack hindered your life? Can you think of times when you would have acted differently if you'd taken a moment to think before you acted?

Another way poor cognitive self-control manifests is "Reduced cognitive control seems to be an important cognitive process that underlies the role of rumination in exacerbating and maintaining psychological distress. Thus, there now is evidence for a reciprocal relation between rumination and cognitive control: Cognitive control influences rumination and rumination influences cognitive control. It seems likely that in real life this reciprocal relationship can hamper emotion regulation severely."[555] As discussed in the mental health chapter, rumination tendencies are predictive of depression. Developing the ability to focus on solutions instead of problems, and following Emotional Guidance to better-feeling thoughts can prevent depression.

"Cognitive Problem Solving is a competence-building model of primary prevention"[556] but it does not go as far as the meta-cognitve processes included in *The Smart Way*. Cognitive Problem Solving seeks to "improve interpersonal relationships and impulse control, promote self-protecting and mutually beneficial solutions among peers, and reduce or prevent negative *health-compromising* behaviors" . . . and develop "the ability to think ahead to the consequences of different behaviors or solutions can help children make positive choices."[557]

While a child might learn many of the consequences of behaviors that are not pro-social, the potential consequences of low emotional states are not available to the child unless the child understands how to develop positive habits of thought. Without that, the risk of developing habits of thought that lead to undesirable health outcomes (i.e. rumination, catastrophizing, and pessimism) are left to chance. Understanding Emotional Guidance will help the child control words, actions, and habits of thought.

Addictions

When people hear the word addiction, most people think of alcohol or drugs. Some may extend their concept of addiction to shopping, sex, or gambling. Addictions can be many different things. If the behavior is difficult for the person to stop and interferes with their life, it might qualify as an addiction. Being aware of where you give your time and how you would feel if you could not do something can help you control your own behavior before it gets out of control. Some less common addictions include tanning and texting.[558]

Alcohol, Drugs and Other Common Addictions

Resilience provides both children and combat veterans protection against developing addictions.[559] A study that looked at 1421 students at a large rural state university and 452 students at a historically Black college/university found an "association between daily stress drinking to cope behaviors."[560] If the young adults had skills that helped them deal with daily stressors, the need/desire to drink as a coping method would be diminished. A study that looked at 995 multi-ethic youth from an urban sample found that "affective self-regulation skills during secondary school and young adult substance use . . . suggest that interventions that build affective self-regulation skills in adolescents may decrease the risk of young adult substance use . . . Programs that teach goal-setting, self-monitoring, self-reinforcement and other skills to enhance self-regulation among early adolescents have been found to be significantly more effective in decreasing adolescent substance use than didactic programs that focus solely on the negative effects of substance use."[561] This longitudinal study also reported that there are significant interpersonal variations in self-regulation abilities. A study that compared self-management to goal-setting training found "self-management training superior to goal-setting training for improving maintenance of learned interpersonal skills."[562] *The Smart Way* teaches all of the things that improve long-term outcomes plus the new (and very helpful) definition of the purpose and use of emotions.

"Drinking [alcohol] to cope with negative emotions is the drinking motive most predictive of problematic drinking"[563] The tendency to focus on negative emotions is a "risk factor for the onset and maintenance of alcohol use disorders."[564] Both the absence of strategies for dealing with negative emotion and lack of skill at identifying emotions were highly correlated with drinking to cope.

The Smart Way Meta-cognitve Processes you learn in this book provide numerous ways to cope with negative emotions in constructive ways. Understanding that emotions are guidance and the Emotional Guidance Scale will help individual recognize how they are feeling so they can proactively manage their cognitive processes and experience more positive emotions.

In a study of men seeking treatment for alcohol addiction they found "that:
1. Abstinence is associated with a shift toward more adaptive emotion regulation patterns, and
2. Inefficient regulation strategies may lead to craving and the maintenance of alcohol use"[565]

An earlier study found, "enhancement of general emotion-regulation skills . . . is an important target in the treatment of alcohol dependence."[566] I would say it is better to prevent alcohol dependence by teaching children the skills before they become problem drinkers.

It is important that addiction recovery programs include stress management training because the problem is the result of poor or absent stress management skills. To prevent relapse, stress management skills are essential. Willpower is not enough to overcome the human need to feel better.

Eating disorders

A recent study found that negative emotional states increase cravings for specific foods.[567] Emotional Intelligence, "how people accommodate and adapt to intra- and interpersonal conditions by identifying emotions, incorporating emotions in thought processes, understanding emotional complexity, and manipulating emotions in self and others" has been positive correlated with lower levels of emotional eating.[568] The skills you learn in these pages increase Emotional Intelligence.

Smoking

The World Health Organization (WHO) estimates smoking causes over $500 billion in global economic damage each year. In the 1980's I could purchase a carton of cigarettes at the commissary on base for $3.23. Today, you pay three times that much for a single pack in Massachusetts, twice that in Colorado, and four times as much for a pack in New York City.[569] It's no wonder that 70% of smokers want to quit. My old habit would cost $11.80 a day, $354 a month, and a whopping $4,248 a year not counting higher premiums for life insurance, higher dry cleaning bills, window cleaning bills, or medical expenses for illness brought about or exacerbated by smoking. There is also the social cost. My husband would never have asked me on a date if I had still been a smoker when we met and none of my close friends or family smoke anymore. Smokers and non-smokers tend to be segregated during work breaks.

Individuals who still smoke nearly three decades after massive campaigns to educate people about the risks and a continuous stream of new techniques to help individuals kick the habit are more likely to belong to a low socioeconomic group and are more likely to suffer from a variety of mental health issues including anxiety, depression and a variety of personality disorders. While not all smokers fit this profile, these factors make it more difficult to quit. As those who are not affected by them successfully quit, more of the remaining smokers are those whose efforts may be hindered by these issues.[570]

In a Brazilian study, the negative factors associated with unsuccessful smoking cessation included stress/anxiety-relieving benefits, weight control, access/low cost of cigarettes, being around smokers and risk-exempting beliefs."[571] One study reported that 60% of those who still smoke suffer from anxiety.

Depression is also correlated to smoking, with those who have attempted to quit and failed are at the highest risk. "Some smokers who are trying to quit could be helped by concurrent treatment for depression."[572] Mood, anxiety, and personality and illicit substance use disorders were associated with persistent nicotine dependence and suggested that mental health treatment used in conjunction with smoking cessation might be a more effective way of helping such individuals quit smoking.[573]

Individuals who suffer from anxiety are two times more likely to smoke cigarettes and 30% more likely to be obese than individuals who have not been diagnosed with anxiety.[574]

Providing smokers with *The Smart Way* training so they can accurately interpret their Emotional Guidance and develop skills that help them manage their mood and/or anxiety could contribute to successful efforts to quit.

26: Violence

The most exciting phrase to hear in science, the one that heralds new discoveries, is not 'Eureka!' (I've found it!), but 'That's funny...'
Isaac Asimov

The introduction to a paper that was published in *Frontiers in Psychology* provides the most succinct explanation of why introducing *The Smart Way* is so critical to individuals and communities around the world. "Evidence has shown that children and adolescent exposure to abuse and violence are associated with homelessness, reduced capacity for attachment, increased vulnerability to repeated victimization, suboptimal physical and brain development, and persistent cognitive impairment. Studies have reported that children exposed to maltreatment are at higher risk of behavioral problems, learning and communication disabilities, internalizing and externalizing psychiatric disorders, and general clinical conditions, such as obesity and systemic inflammation later in life. In addition, a growing body of evidence points to the impact of maternal stress during pregnancy on neurodevelopmental disorders. Therefore, conditions during pregnancy and early-life can affect adult outcomes and health."[575] "Studies have linked maternal stressors including natural disasters, death of a family member, and reported levels of maternal anxiety or depression with an increased incidence of neurodevelopmental disorders including depression, anxiety, schizophrenia, and autism."[576]

Conversely, evidence shows that adequate social support is an important protective factor against child maltreatment."[577] *The Smart Way* provides tools that help individuals who experience adverse life events, in childhood or as adults, to bounce back with resilience, to manage stress to low levels, and thrive in spite of obstacles. "Research that demonstrated youth who reported that many, most, or all of the web sites they visited depicted real people fighting, shooting, or killing were 5 times more likely also to report seriously violent behavior, compared with those who reported that none of the web sites they visited had these depictions."[578]

This is what inspired the title of this book, Our Children Live in a War Zone. When you look at the experiences many of our children have, the environment is not different from a war zone. There may not be bombs dropping out of the sky, but there is gunfire, beatings, bullying, child abuse, and rage taken out on the children or those they care about. Many children live with fear for their safety and for their lives every day. It is a war zone and the price they and society is paying is high. Every ten seconds a report of child abuse is made with "more than 3 million reports of child abuse made in the United States involving more than 6 million children" each year and not all abuse is reported.[579] Add violent video games, television shows, movies, the 24/7 negative news that scours the globe to bring fear into your home, and terrorist attacks and the level of exposure to violence is far more than what was experienced by most children during the civil war.

"Exposure to violence by adolescents is associated with depression, hopelessness, and other psychological and emotional trauma."[580]

I've mentioned my crime prevention book previously. I wrote that book because the research shows me that we can stop most of the crime that occurs before it happens by building psychologically strong children. A program introduced in Minneapolis decreased violence and reduced homicides of youth by 77% in just three years.[581]

In Chicago, 70% of murders were the result of altercations in 2011.[582] The *Becoming a Man in Chicago* program delivered training to high-risk students who were doing poorly in school, providing cognitive behavior therapy (CBT) in conjunction with unusual sports, with the goal of encouraging the young men to question their automatic thoughts and biases before lashing out. After the training, crimes by the trained group were 44% lower than the control group and graduation rates moved from 13% to 23%.[583]

Arguments about violent video games have been going on since they were invented. I'm going to take a different track to discuss that aspect of the problem. I am addressing it because it is one of the simplest areas to address. Olympic athletes don't just train physically. Their coaches have them also visualize themselves succeeding at their events. Research has found that athletes who both practice (physically) and visually (mentally), outperform those who just practice physically. They've found that there is no difference in the mind's perception of whether you are actually doing something or if you are imagining doing it.

Physical practice is needed to develop the muscles and muscle memory. But the neurons that fire in the brain when someone is actually doing something and when the same person is visualizing doing something are the same. To the brain, it is as if you are doing what you're doing when you play the video game.

I would urge parents to consider this when you decide what your child is allowed to do. And yes, it is your choice. And yes, your child may have different rules than other children. That may be to their advantage. When my children would complain that one of their friends was allowed to do something I did not allow them to do my response was, "I'm sorry _____'s Mom does not love them as much as I love you." I didn't budge. No one is the same as someone else—not entirely—not even identical twins think exactly the same thoughts. Becoming comfortable with being different can serve your children well.

When my children were young I did not like what was on the television. Shows that depicted families who were demeaning to one another were common. I turned the TV off and my children weren't allowed to watch anything other than movies I'd approved for most of their formative years. They never went through that teenage phase where they were disrespectful or rebellious to me. As they matured I eased the restrictions and began allowing them to make more choices about what they watched. As a parent, you get to choose.

You may also want to inquire about what is on the television at friends' homes when they visit. A friend of mine's child was visiting a home where the man was openly watching porn in the family room when other children came to visit, exposing them to whatever was going on when they were in the room. As a parent you have the right to ask questions (or even visit) a home before you allow your children to go. I always spoke with parents before allowing my child to go to their home. I always inquired about whether they had weapons in the home and if they did, if they were secured. I'm not anti-gun, but I know not everyone takes care or considers visitors to their home. Their own children may know not to touch, but guests may not.

Research looking at 6th graders found, "The level of exposure to violence was the strongest correlate with a scale that measured their intent to use violence in hypothetical conflict situations. Also, frequency of marijuana, alcohol, cocaine, and cigarette use was associated with increased intentions to use violence. Adolescents who attended religious services more often were less likely to intend to use violence, regardless of their level of exposure to violence."[584]

The level of violence our children are exposed to is sickening. A national survey in 2009 found:[585]

- Sixty percent of American children were exposed to violence, crime, or abuse in their homes, schools, and communities
- Almost forty percent of American children were direct victims of two or more violent acts, and 1 in 10 were victims of violence five or more times.

- Children were more likely to be exposed to violence and crime than adults.
- Almost 1 in 10 American children saw one family member assault another family member, and more than 25% had been exposed to family violence during their lifetime.
- Exposure to one type of violence increased the likelihood that a child would be exposed to other types of violence and exposed multiple times.

Research that looked at children who were younger (around age 10) than most studies indicate prevention efforts need to begin at young ages and should address numerous factors including:[586]

- Substance use (best prevention is stress management and knowledge)
- Depression (best prevention is empowering stress management tools like *The Smart Way*)
- Health risk behaviors
- Sexual behavior and safety
- Physical activity
- Diet and nutrition (keep it fun)
- Violence (connection to one's humanity and positive emotions is best prevention)
- Developing connection to:
  - Family (supportive relationships, not demeaning, sarcastic, or intent on searching out and finding one's flaws)
  - Social skills that enable them to form healthy friendships
  - Perspectives about school that feel good
  - Religious or other positive group affiliations (i.e. Boy Scouts, Camp Fire, Girl Scouts, 4-H, athletics, hobbies, etc.)
- Cognitive skill development

I would add skills that build resilience, emotional intelligence, confidence, and self-esteem and that encouraging strong connections with other positively focused individuals. *The Smart Way Meta-cognitve Processes* combined with an understanding of Emotional Guidance goes a long way toward providing a strong foundation. If children are old enough to understand how to play a game where an object is hidden and they find it using clues of *you're getting warmer* or *you're getting colder*, they're old enough to understand their Emotional Guidance.

But before parents will trust their children to use their guidance, the parent has to experience it for themselves. We've been telling children not to listen to their guidance (although we didn't call it that) and to do what others tell them to do, even if it goes against their instincts for a very long time. It is how almost every parent alive was raised. Before we will allow our children to listen to their guidance above and beyond what we think they should do or not do, we have to learn how accurate and valuable guidance is. The only way to do that is to experience it in our own mind and body. To compare the thoughts we think to how they feel, adjust to better-feeling thoughts, and see how our lives improve.

It won't be that easy for the first generation. The second generation won't give it another thought—they'll already know everyone has guidance and that it is trustworthy. Get in the habit of asking your children what feels right to them.

I did not know much of this until my children were in high school. I raised them the best I could with what I knew, but I attempted to control far too much. Once I understood my guidance when they would ask me what they should do I would tell them, "I can't feel your guidance, but you can. What feels best to you?" When they told me, I'd then encourage them to follow through with it—even when I sometimes didn't think it was the right or wise course. I had to trust the process. It worked. Their lives have been enriched by the freedom to follow their guidance and yours will be, too.

I've known people who were incarcerated who began using their guidance and were able to find positive perspectives while they were living in prison. When they came out, their lives were nothing like the lives they left behind. They are different people, people who have better lives than they ever imagined they could have. Where someone lives today is not what matters, it's where they are going that matters.

27: Victimization

A wise woman wishes to be no one's enemy; a wise woman refuses to be anyone's victim.
Maya Angelou

An Australian study that evaluated abused children nine years afterwards found that "abuse is an independent risk factor for offending and delinquent behavior."[587] Research demonstrates that resilient characteristics provide protection against victims becoming offenders. *The Smart Way* is designed to enhance both resilience and positive emotions, both of which should decrease the likelihood that an abused child will become an abuser or delinquent.

> *Before you attempt to dismiss me as blaming the victim, remember that we can't solve a problem if we can't talk about it.*

People who become victims are not randomly selected. The selection process criminals use seems the opposite of fair. Previous victims are far more likely to be victims (again) than someone who has never been a victim. Some people want to attribute this to poverty or environment, insisting that it is environment that makes some people victims repeatedly while others escape harm. That view sounds logical, but it is not supported by the research.

Yes, some people who are repeatedly victimized such as drug addicts, but before they became drug addicts they were probably already a victim. Being a victim increases the risk that a person will be a drug addict. The odds that a woman who has been raped will be raped again is seven times greater than the odds that a woman who has never been raped will be raped the first time.[588]

The odds that a woman who was abused as a child will be raped are far greater than the odds that a woman who was never abused as a child will be raped. A boy or girl experiencing sexual harassment by 9th grade is a strong predictor that the child will experience "future victimization by peers and dating partners."[589]

Childhood sexual abuse, emotional abuse, psychological abuse and neglect are all predictive of rape and other forms of victimization as an adult. "Emotional abuse by itself is an important experience in relation to increased vulnerability for adult victimization, and family cohesion and emotional expressiveness increase the risk of adult rape only in relation to emotional abuse."[590] "Low levels of family cohesion predicted adult rape in the absence of childhood emotional abuse."[591]

It is not just re-victimization that is at issue. Victimization increases the risk of other adverse events. In the study that followed teenagers during their high school years, girls who were victims of sexual harassment had higher levels of numerous negative outcomes including:

- Suicidal thoughts
- Self-harm (i.e. cutting)
- Maladaptive dieting
- Early dating
- Substance use
- Physical peer violence

- Emotional distress
- Violent delinquency

Boys suffered many of the same negative outcomes and also peer relational victimization such as homosexual and homophobic slurs.[592]

To make the above statistics useful in preventing rape and victimization, we have to understand why. For many years, self-defense instructors have advised students that appearing confident and aware will reduce the likelihood that they will be targeted. But merely walking tall and looking around is not enough. As discussed in earlier chapters, communication occurs on many levels of our being, much of it below our conscious awareness. Attempting to look confident when you are frightened is not as good as being confident.

I was the victim of rape more than once and self-defense training did not prevent it from happening. Not only was I raped, I was also subjected to physical violence and emotional abuse by my partner. It was not until I became more confident that abusive situations ceased. When you are confident and sure, two things happen.

1. You become more aware of potential danger and take steps to mitigate the risk, and
2. You're able to exude your inner strength in a way that dissuades the potential victimizer that you're not worth the risk.

I was checking into a Hampton Inn while on a business trip. The room was supposed to have a refrigerator and did not have one. They sent a maintenance man to bring me a refrigerator and my floor-length hair caught his attention. I saw it come into his eyes the moment his thoughts turned evil. Instead of reacting with fear, I put thoughts in my mind that he'd be stupid to try and it would not be worth the cost to him and that it would be the last thing he did. We had a staring contest across the room, No words were spoken, but we both knew what was going on. I saw it in his eyes the moment he decided not to take the chance.

It takes a lot of inner strength for a woman who has been violated, perhaps for any woman—I can only speak from personal experience—to stand her ground and relay what I communicated with my eyes. But before we ever communicate with our eyes, we do the same with our bodies. Criminals do not choose their targets by selecting the ones that appear weakest. In an experiment where convicted criminals were asked to select who they would victimize from a recorded video, there was consistency in who they would select, but the people who would be targeted were not the ones who appeared to be the easiest targets. When their selections were analyzed and the more vulnerable have a less consistent gait.[593]

I can remember attempting to look confident as I was instructed in a self-defense class many years ago and feeling self-conscious and unsure if I looked confident enough. When I contrast that with feeling truly confident, the feel and posture are significantly different. In my own experience, and in a few of my students who had already made progress in increasing their inner strength before we met, incidents of victimization ceased when our confidence increased.

I had a friend who was the type of man who would aid a maiden in distress—not the sort who would hurt a woman who told the story of a woman he was in a relationship who had been abused by previous partners. One day they got in an argument and she cowered and he realized he had his hand up in the air as if he was going to strike her. He'd had no intention of striking her and did not do so. He was an old man when I knew him and he said he'd never again even come close to striking a woman. He'd ended the relationship immediately because he felt as if she was drawing behaviors out of him that were not who he was.

While it sounds strange, it sounds as if I am blaming the victim, it sounds as if I'm letting him off the hook, it sounds as if I'm saying she deserved or asked for the treatment. I'm not doing any of that—I'm looking at why something like that would happen and how to prevent it from occurring.

Earlier we talked about mirror neuros and how brains will sync to the most practiced thoughts on the same subject. In the example, the woman had been abused in prior relationships. She had developed a belief that men would mistreat her. While the man was not an abuser, neither had he spent time affirming that he treated women well. So when the two got together, her more practiced belief synced up with his obliviousness, leading to him almost striking her.

This lines up with my perspective about expectations and that we get what we expect from others. Now, let's go back and look at how this lines up with the research demonstrating that childhood sexual abuse significantly increases the risk of being raped as an adult. If the child develops a belief that others will sexually abuse her, she is practicing that belief, which in the case of date rape could be leading to the mirror neurons lining up. When she makes up her mind that she is no longer a victim, as I and some of my students do, her brain is on a different frequency—no longer sending the victim signal. This would lead to greater confidence, which would change the gait and make her less susceptible to stranger rape as well.

It would also show in her interpersonal encounters. If you're a vulnerable woman, a predator who is around you in a crowd may decide to come back when he knows you will be alone.

So, confidence is important, but it is not a false sense of bravado. Confidence that comes from inner strength is where your real power resides. Remember, we don't know everything yet. There is a lot of communication that is inexplicable. We don't know how people are truly connected. The nurse who got the headache when her brother was shot—how did that happen? We simply don't know. There is significant evidence that we are connected in ways we don't yet understand below the level of conscious awareness.

I use a homework assignment in my classes to demonstrate this. I have them imagine in the morning when they wake up that they have just been abandoned by their spouse who emptied the bank account and left a scathing letter reminding them of all their faults and adding some new ones to the list. Then I tell them to keep that in their mind and move through their morning feeling that way and see how the world responds to them.

Then I tell them to do the same thing on another day, only this time, imagine that you're a semi-famous actor (where people recognize you but might not know why they think they know you). Imagine that you have some wealth and a lot of people who love and respect you. Then, with that mindset, go move through your day and see how people treat you.

People will treat you very differently on the two days. On the second day, people will smile at you more, they'll hold the door open for you, they'll move out of your way when you're walking—giving way to the power. Try it, you'll see and feel the difference. Then remember that you have the ability to set your tone, to decide who you are every day. Who do you want to be?

Decide for yourself and practice the mindset.

For example, I noticed that while I was generally kind to other people, I could join in negative conversations that were not kind. I decided I didn't like it when I did that—especially afterwards. So I began affirming that I am a kind person. I decided I wanted to be kind—even when others were being unkind. Now when I am there and that is happening I don't automatically join in. I am aware that what they are doing is not consistent with who I am. It doesn't matter if they're only talking smack about a celebrity who has had their life blow up in the media. I don't want to partake of that brand of fun. It is not who I am or

who I want to be. I don't attempt to get them to stop. I simply don't join in and typically excuse myself when it happens.
- Who do you want to be?
- Practice being who you want to be.

Measures of Success

Traditional measures of success in school are grade point average, IQ, and ACT or SAT scores.

These scores are not correlated to actual success in life. We're taught to focus on them, we're measured and labeled by them, but in reality they don't make as much difference as other aspects of us.

One factor that contributes to success in school and life is Emotional Intelligence (EQ). Fortunately, EQ is flexible and individuals can increase their abilities, which will result in higher abilities to cope with demands and pressure without undue stress.

Emotional intelligence has been correlated with job performance and organizational outcomes.[594] Individuals with high emotional intelligence do better and people with low emotional intelligence do not do as well. There are four components to emotional intelligence ability:

- Experiential Emotional Intelligence
    - Identifying Emotions
    - Using Emotions
- Strategic Emotional Intelligence
    - Understanding Emotions
    - Managing Emotions (Self-Regulation)

Emotional Intelligence can also be viewed as a trait that characterizes how an individual copes with demands and pressure. *The Smart Way* is designed to increase both EQ ability and trait EQ.

Businesses and educators are being taught EI (EQ) in order "to improve individuals' evaluations and reactions to emotionally salient situations" because those who have this ability are better managers and make better decisions.[595] Other studies have found that low EQ may predict anxiety and depression in adolescents.[596]

The benefits of emotional intelligence show up in youth and extend throughout life. Researchers at Northcentral University in Prescott University looked at the emotional intelligence of 128 seniors (over age 65) and found that "for every 1-point increase in emotional intelligence, the risk of depression decreased by 6%."[597]

Emotional Guidance and the techniques offered in this book help you develop greater Emotional Intelligence and help you teach your children these skills. Emotional Guidance helps individuals at any level of their career, but for those who make it to the top, the ones who are quickly toppled lack emotional intelligence. It is an essential skill if you are a leader (or want to be). Emotional intelligence is also tied to clinical competency for nurses.[598]

In the schools where I have taught classes to increase happiness of the students, I have not seen the types of behaviors that increase intrinsic motivation being used. I assume the information has not transitioned from journal articles to training materials for teachers. When people are given a reason for doing the task that is meaningful to them, it increases the likelihood they will internalize their motivation.

Given the importance of autonomy to intrinsic motivation, "a meta-analysis of 128 laboratory experiments confirmed that, whereas positive feedback enhances intrinsic motivation, tangible rewards significantly undermine it,"[599] helping children develop an internal locus of control is an important contributor to their life-long success. "Negative feedback which decreased perceived competence was found to undermine both intrinsic and extrinsic motivation, leaving people amotivated."[600]

27: Victimization

28: Relationship Success

The only real security is not in owning or possessing, not in demanding or expecting, not in hoping, even. Security in a relationship lies neither in looking back to what it was, nor forward to what it might be, but living in the present and accepting it as it is now.
Anne Morrow Lindbergh

Social connections are important for many reasons, but the quality of friendships and the value it adds (or detracts) from one's life can vary significantly. Relationships that lean toward the negative can negatively impact happiness and goal achievement. Quality "friendships have important effects on adjustment and psychological well-being across the lifespan . . . providing perceived support, intimacy, reliable alliance, self-validation and emotional security."[601]

Supportive relationships are associated with better health and increased lifespan. A meta-analysis of 148 studies with over 300,000 participants revealed "a 50% increased likelihood of survival for participants with stronger social relationships. This finding remained consistent across age, sex, initial health status, cause of death, and follow-up period."[602] A study of 3,218 children in 5th grade revealed that children living with parents whose marital conflict was one standard deviation above average had a 20% greater risk of experiencing an injury that required medical assistance than their contemporaries with less volatile parental relationships.[603]

Social relationships, or the relative lack thereof, constitute a major risk factor for health—rivaling the effect of well-established health risk factors such as cigarette smoking, blood pressure, blood lipids, obesity and physical activity.
House, Landis, and Umberson; Science 1988

But relationships aren't easy to create or sustain when your emotional state is low or dipping into low states frequently. Research indicates happy people are more likely to marry[604] and more likely to remain married. It isn't just marriage relations that suffer when one or both people are in low emotional states. The filters in each of our brains lead us to interpret reality in ways that match our current and chronic emotional states, so when we're in a low emotional state we can mistake innocent comments as criticism. Someone who tends to be defensive can even interpret a compliment as criticism when he is interpreting reality through the filter created by a low emotional state. When neither person understands the connection between emotional state and thoughts, words, and actions, conversations that take place when one or both of them are in low emotional states can be as difficult as attempting to walk through landmine infested Sapper Hill in the Falkland Islands—you never know what will set off an explosion.

If one person understands the connection between emotional state and thoughts, words, and actions, the chances of maintaining a good relationship increase significantly. The one who understands the connection will be quick to forgive (sometimes instantaneously) when the other person responds in a negative way because he or she is in a bad mood. Simply knowing that the words say 95% - 100% about the emotional state of the person saying them and 0-5% about the person they're directed toward takes the sting out of harsh comments. They aren't personal and they know it.

If both people understand the connection between emotional state and words, they have a very good chance of a long and happy relationship. This is true for work relationships, friendships, and intimate relationships including partners, children and parents. This is truly a situation where knowledge is power.

Happy seniors in China receive significantly more visits from family than unhappy seniors receive according to research a friend of mine did that has not yet been published.

Several longitudinal studies indicate that the benefit of positivity adds about 10.7 years to the lifespan.[605-606] Good social connections add almost that much. We cannot, however add the two together and say happy people with good relationships live almost twenty years longer, because happiness contributes to good social relationships. What we can say is that learning how to use your Emotional Guidance and skills that help us improve our moods increase both our happiness and the quality of our relationships, both of which help our health and longevity.

Relationships can enhance or detract from healthy behaviors. There is "an accumulating body of evidence suggesting that engaging in health (or risk) behaviors mirrors the behavior choices of close social partners."[607]

Having a confidante has a positive effect on physical and mental health throughout the lifespan.

Perception vs. Reality

The perception of social support is more important than the reality. By this I mean that someone might have social support but have beliefs that others won't be there for them in times of need. In this situation, the perception that social support is absent has the same effect as if it did not exist. How strong an individual perceives the connection is matters more than the actual strength of the connection.[608] In *The Oxford Handbook of Happiness*, Lakey raises the implications of the fact that it is perception of support and not actual emotional support that confers the benefit of social support. My perspective on this is that the strong desire humans have for social support is based on innate knowledge that we should have it and that the vehicle through which it was always intended to come was, in fact, our Emotional Guidance. Emotional Guidance is not flakey like the people in our lives can be. Afterall they weren't born to see to our every need. Emotional Guidance is always constant. It does not get angry with us if we ignore its advice. It does not go away or die. It is always positively focused and it is easy (once you being using it) to feel the strength and depth of the support it provides.

Using Emotional Guidance equips us with skills and knowledge that enable us to develop and maintain better relationships with the people in our lives, but it also protects us from devastation when people disappoint us.

Home

Relationships in the home are some of the most critical for our success. But, being raised in a dysfunctional home or in an adverse environment does not condemn anyone to a life that remains bad. Partners who affirm and reinforce "one another's health promoting efforts and behaviors are positively associated with behavioral adherence."[609] But the way the topic is addressed makes a tremendous difference.

"I'm so glad you take good care of your health and I especially like it that you walk a few miles each day," is an example of affirming and reinforcing health promoting behaviors.

Contrast that with, "You haven't walked for over two weeks. You should take better care of your health," which is an attempt to control the other's behavior. "When partners attempt to exert control over one another's lapses in health behaviors, these efforts frequently are ineffective in bring about behavior change and sometimes fortify undesired behaviors."[610] Controlling efforts to help a partner adhere to a diet or exercise routine can cause lower intrinsic motivation.[611]

The underlying reason controlling attempts fail to have a beneficial effect is the basic human need for autonomy, which is discussed more fully in Chapter 18.

The best thing you can do for your relationships is work on your own happiness because when you're happy, you're easier to love and you find it easier to love others. Remember that happiness is associated with low stress. According to the American Psychological Association's annual *Stress in America* report, "41% of adults who are married or living with a partner say that they lost patience or yelled at their spouse or partner due to stress in the past month and 18% of those who are employed say they snapped at or were short with a coworker."[612]

Recipe for Falling in Love

I enjoy everything I teach, but one of the most fun things is when I teach how to fall in love with your spouse again. The class after I teach this lesson always arrives with more smiles and with a few stories they just have to share about the shift in a relationship they thought was past the passion they enjoyed in the beginning.

*Being **in love** is simply a form of unconditional love.*

To return to that state, find some quiet time (use the bathroom if you have to--sometimes necessary when there are several children running around) and make a list of things you appreciate about your spouse. While making the list focus on appreciating the things about your partner you like/love/appreciate the most. They can be fond memories or eager anticipation of future events. Spend a minimum of 10 minutes a day for five days making this list, but if you can find a half an hour, that's even better. Daily is more important at first than the difference between 10 or 30 minutes.

If you're artistic, you can draw or paint pictures of the things you appreciate about your spouse.

This is not a list of "You used to and I wish you would again." It's appreciating that your spouse is someone who does those things for you, even if its been a while.

You see,

Appreciation is a magic elixir

When you appreciate, you feel good.

When you feel appreciation and focus on the object of your appreciation, the object of your appreciation feels good. They can feel your appreciation at a visceral level and they respond in kind.

You don't have tell your spouse about the list you're making or share the list. You can. But it is not necessary. *The point is for you to fall in love again.* When you do, your spouse will respond to your renewed appreciation. When you appreciate someone unconditionally it's almost impossible for that person to not appreciate you in return--especially if that person has already committed to spend his or her life with you.

Added bonus: When you are in a state of appreciation, you're more attractive.

If you want to amp it up even more, after you have been writing your list for a few days, snuggle up to your spouse, look directly into his or her eyes, and begin calmly telling them what you appreciate about them. Let your feelings of appreciation shine forth from your eyes. Do this only once you're really feeling it. This must be authentic. If your relationship has been struggling, don't rush it. Make sure you feel it. There is a tremendous difference in the way it feels when you're really feeling appreciation vs. when you're forcing it.

Maintenance: Once a week, make a list of what you appreciate about your spouse.

Better yet: Make a habit to think about what you appreciate about your spouse every time you do something that you routinely do. When you do the dishes, take out the garbage, stop at a stoplight, in the shower, brush your teeth. Make appreciation a habit.

Enjoy a long and happy loving relationship.

PS – this works for children, parents, friends, and siblings, too

Dating

Reports of teen dating violence and abuse are common. Research indicates that 20 – 30% of teenagers who date experience verbal or psychological abuse in a given year.[613] A teenager with healthy self-esteem will not stay in a relationship with an abuser, if they find themselves in such a relationship. It is more likely that someone with low self-esteem will enter such a relationship and less likely that a person with low self-esteem will decide they deserve better and leave such an abusive relationship.

Rumination and Co-Rumination

> *Talking about our problems is our greatest addiction.*
> *Break the habit.*
> *Talk about your joys.*
> Rita Schiano

Government Advice: Share your stress.

Problem: It depends on how this is done. Co-rumination and complaining have both been associated with poor outcomes. Co-rumination is basically talking about your troubles with someone else, especially when the focus is on complaining and commiserating without the empowerment of problem solving.[614] Social contacts and close friendships are generally a protective factor against depression, but the protection disappears when the friendship involves excessive co-rumination.[615]

Co-rumination is defined as two or more people "extensively discussing and revisiting problems, speculating about problems, and focusing on negative feelings with peers."[616] Until recently, many therapy sessions bore a strong resemblance to co-rumination if you substitute "therapist" for "peers". Co-rumination increases the risk of depression so it's no wonder I meet people who have been *in therapy* for more than a decade who are still suffering from depression and other problems.

Community

Our brains also filter based on whether we consider something to be safe or a potential danger. As one's emotional state moves to higher zones, differences feel less threatening. The way people tend to see people they perceive as *like them* as **same** and people who differ from them as *other* lessens when experiencing positive emotions.[617] Our definition of self and the group(s) to which we belong affects how insiders and outsiders are viewed.

Some people narrowly define the in-group as family. Other define a broader in-group that may include members of their race, religion, socio-economic class, gender, sexual persuasion, nationality, sport affiliation, school affiliation, work, or other self-defined group. Our definition then determines who we consider as *same* and who is classified as *other*. We trust in-group members and are suspicious of non-members. The rules for who belongs to our group can become complicated. In the Black community it is not uncommon to exclude from the in-group individuals who have achieved financial success (regardless of their roots or race) and to exclude individuals who have different political preferences.

While conversing with a Black woman from Pittsburg, she commented that there were no successful Black female role models. I said, "What about Condoleezza Rice?" Her response was that Condi was born with a silver spoon in her mouth and had never lived the Black experience. Since then I was given a book about Condi's life and learned that she was born in a segregated South and her father taught high school. It's far from my definition of being born with a silver spoon in one's mouth, which I associate with trust funds and multi-generational money.

While I did not yet understand why she would distance herself from a woman I considered an example of what a woman could accomplish, I do now. It has to do with one's definition of self. In an earlier chapter I wrote about the experience that allowed me to believe that I could someday become a Vice President. Before that time I would not have been receptive to the idea that I could because it violated my definition of self. Once my definition of self expanded to encompass becoming a Vice President someday, I was able to conceive of the possibility for myself. Vice Presidents (of companies—not nations) became part of my concept of self—I could see the potential. Vice Presidents were no longer something different from what I was—they were no longer *other*. I began observing Vice Presidents to identify how they dressed, spoke, acted, and what sort of skills and education they achieved because I was going to be one. Until I adjusted my concept of self, Vice Presidents were *other*. I had them on a pedestal. I was nervous when I talked to them because they (in my mind) were superior to me. In the same way, when she looked at Condoleezza and denounced her having a Black experience, she was saying Condi was *other* from her perspective. It was not Condi's experience that made Condi *other* to this woman; it was the woman's self-perception that she was not like Condi.

Had she understood her Emotional Guidance, the negative emotion she felt when she thought of Condi as a role model would have encouraged her to find a better-feeling perspective. If she spent time contemplating her emotional reaction to the suggestion and trying new perspectives on to see how they felt, she would have eventually discovered that she could see Condi as a role model and that her own accomplishments could equal or even exceed those of Ms. Rice.

Her perspective was the result of cultural indoctrination—a process that created limiting beliefs about her own potential. This woman was not uneducated—she had a college degree—the first in her family to achieve a college education (just like me). But her education failed her. It failed to help her develop the psychological flexibility required to overcome beliefs that held her back.

In the same way that someone who believes they are good and that money is evil cannot accumulate wealth, a woman who believes she is a good Black woman and that good Black women do not have highly successful careers cannot achieve success. Her beliefs were in conflict with her desires and her beliefs won. They do every time. I have not spoken with this woman in a decade, but I remember our conversation frequently and hope that she has found a way to shift her beliefs.

Although I used Condoleezza Rice in my example with her, it was because we did not have a shared social circle and she would not have known any of the very accomplished Black women with whom I am friends or of other with whom I worked. Today I would handle it differently by inviting her to lunch and also inviting one of my accomplished Black friends in the hopes that someone who was not at the National Security Advisor level could help her believe in herself and her potential more.

Condi was a quantum leap for this particular woman, but if she had known how to use the right mental processes, Condi's example would have been able to benefit her. When I see a woman (or anyone, really) who has accomplished much more than I have and more than I believe I could, I realize they did not jump from being a child to being where they are—they followed a path. Even if I do not believe (or want) to achieve all that they have, there may be points along their path that I believe I can achieve that I would be interested in pursuing.

We often look at very successful people and act as if they just woke up one morning with that level of success. We talk about Facebook and PayPal and Instagram as if it was one idea that took off, when the truth is that they are all the result of thousands of ideas accumulating to form one complex thing. Our Emotional Guidance helps us know which ideas to embrace and which to discard. When we use our guidance, we can gather those ideas that become more than the sum of their parts—whether we are creating a business, a product, our family, or ourselves.

29: Educational Success

Not ignorance, but ignorance of ignorance, is the death of knowledge.
Alfred North Whitehead

The National Association of School Nurses published a position paper regarding the mental health of students that began:

It is the position of the National Association of School Nurses (NASN) that mental health is as critical to academic success as physical well-being.

A paper published by Portland State University points to the main reason some children fail to thrive at school. "We have found evidence . . . about the primacy of social goals. Among college- aged students, for example, the hope of achieving social goals (relating to friends, family, or romance) had a direct impact on positive mental health, whereas hope for achieving performance-oriented goals (relating to work or academics) did not. This and other research has convinced us that adolescents' social goals cannot be ignored if we expect them to pursue socially valued goals related to academic and career achievements."[618] This paper, about building hope, went on to tell us that, "the key characteristic of resilient children is that they find their own mentors in the community," and emphasized the importance of a secure base formed by emotional support and attachment.[619]

While good relationships with others is important, the secure base we all intuitively know we should have and sort of freak out if we can't find, is our Emotional Guidance. There is no more secure base. Even the best Mother's and Father's or doting grandparents do not and cannot be with us every moment of every day or respond to each of our thoughts by providing guidance that helps us move toward self-determined goals and avoid danger and undesired outcomes. Even if a parent should try, the parent's own goals and preferences could interfere with the ability to be objective about the child's preferences when they conflicted with the parent's preferences.

Emotional Guidance supports good relationships with others. Understanding the relationship between behavior and emotional state is of great benefit in not allowing petty problems to break apart a relationship that serves both parties well.

> *We have found evidence . . . about the primacy of social goals. Among college-aged students, for example, the hope of achieving social goals (relating to friends, family, or romance) had a direct impact on positive mental health, whereas hope for achieving performance-oriented goals (relating to work or academics) did not. This and other research has convinced us that adolescents' social goals cannot be ignored if we expect them to pursue socially valued goals related to academic and career achievements.*

Referring an individual to outside sources for confirmation of value and worth can lead to problems. If we encourage an adolescent to rely on a parent or mentor for emotional support and that person fails the child in some way, the child will turn elsewhere. Some groups equate scholastic achievement with *not being a good member of the group* or that cooperation with authorities is equal to defying the group needs.

Reliance on Emotional Guidance does not carry the potential pitfalls involved when, "strong identification with a group facilitates their motivation in accord with the group's goals."[620]

Researchers from the University of Florida stated, "For many years, our research team has worked with a variety of teachers and students with a wide range of behavioral needs and what we have seen over and over again is that when teachers use cognitive-behavioral strategies in their classroom, the effects on student behavior have been positive."[621] In 2013, a review in the *Journal of Child Psychology and Psychiatry* indicated, "nearly one third of papers made recommendations with respect to encouraging supportive school environments."[622] Unfortunately, none of the programs evaluated seemed to fit the recommendation that a solution "focus on the common determinates of health as a whole . . . rather than one specific or problems."[623]

I would add two other elements to education, one that should already be there. In fact, it is morally reprehensible that it is not.

There is extensive research that demonstrates teaching at-risk children how to increase their level of resilience significantly improves the trajectory of the outcomes they actually experience. Increased resilience brings about improved physical, mental, behavioral, relationship, and career outcomes. The studies include longitudinal studies that followed at-risk children through school and until they were out of their teens.

That this training is not being incorporated into elementary education on a widespread basis when it is clear it saves many children from the school to prison pipeline and from dropping out, addictions, teen pregnancy and other undesirable outcomes, violates what I consider to be a moral duty of adults and society.

A program that taught young men in Chicago cognitive behavioral therapy and intensive tutoring "had a profound effect on academic achievements. The impacts are large enough to raise the question of whether the field has given up prematurely on the possibility of improving academics outcomes for a youth."[624]

The second element of the research that I find reprehensible is that many of those that recommend implementation want to limit teaching resilience to only at risk children. Their arguments are misguided. One of them is that if we teach all children how to be more resilient, the *have's* may advance further and maintain or increase the gap. A society that does not want everyone to thrive as much as they can is shooting themselves in the foot. Also, there are many examples of giving tools to both those who have a strong desire to change their circumstances and those whose desire who is not as strong and those with the stronger desire grow more. Those who are in the worst situations will close the gap.

Another reason this approach is so misguided is that there is no way to know who is at-risk and in need of increased resilience. Poverty is not the only stressor for which resilience provides what some call a vaccination against poor outcomes. The outcome from abuse, which can happen in homes in any socioeconomic situation often depends on how resilient the abused child is. The difference between the resilient and non-resilient abused child can be as vast as one living under a bridge and the other attaining her doctorate degree and enjoying a good family life in adulthood. Resilience helps children dealing with any negative life event, from accidents, trauma, abuse, death of a loved one, financial hardship, loss of a job, racism, bullying, and more. Providing training to only some children is so misguided that it makes me wonder if the proponents of this approach have ever left their laboratories. Consider that if a program like this had been available in the 1970's, Jeffrey Dahmer would probably not have been given the training that could have prevented him from becoming a serial killer if the criteria being recommended had been applied to determine who receive training.

Resilience is a key factor in the difference between PTSD and posttraumatic growth. While PTSD is most often associated with veterans the situations that can cause it are numerous and include common things like giving birth and traffic accidents.

Resilience reduces stress, which is casually linked to many negative health outcomes. On the physical side, stress is linked to negative epigenetic changes, heart disease, obesity, diabetes, pre-term birth, and in the children of stressed mothers, increased behavioral and sleeping problems, and asthma.

Most mental health problems are linked back to chronic stress. Behavioral health is linked to stress as well. (i.e. crime, addictions, divorces, violence, and even bad behavior in traffic).

Why Mindset Should be a part of the Core Curriculum

A student's mindset has a significant impact on the results the student achieves. A 2015 paper by Rattan, Savani, Chugh and Dweck stated, without qualification, that, "the psychology of the student is key to academic achievement."[625] I concur. The paper referenced two categories where it has been demonstrated that the right mindset affects effort and results in substantial ways, including making the difference between graduating and dropping out. Mindset is important.

One is whether the student has a fixed or growth mindset and I've given that subject a separate heading in this chapter. The second question is one where the approach asks the wrong question. Research shows that when a student does not feel he or she belongs in the environment, for any number of reasons, achievement is lower and higher dropout rates are observed. They refer to the question, "Do I belong here?" that might be asked by a student because their gender, race, socioeconomic class, nationality or some other label is not generally associated with the school, course, or institution.

The true answer is that a person belongs anywhere his or her guidance leads them. If a student wants to take advanced calculus and happens to be female, what others think does not matter. The student's desire gives the student the answer. If being there is what you want to do (and that desire would be associated with positive emotion) then yes, you belong there. One has to be careful to find the pure thought of whether it is what the student wants, not one that considers what others think about it. If that pure thought receives positive emotion, then you belong there. Being there is on your path toward self-actualization.

The truth is also that someone who others believe belongs who feels bad about being there may not be in the best place for them. For example, someone who is trying to become more positively focused whose family is not taking the journey with them might feel bad when with the family. They may not be stable enough yet in their positive mindset to remain positive when surrounded by the negativity of others. It may make the situation feel confining or worse.

There is nothing wrong with a person absenting themselves until they are more stable in the desired emotional state. Being somewhere because you have to while resenting the necessity of being there is stressful. Either find a way to be there and feel good or don't go there. Attempting to get the rest of your family to change is not likely to work or to make your relationships with your family better. The best way to get others to take the journey is to go ahead and demonstrate with your own life that it's a great place to be.

What others think about whether you should be there is irrelevant to whether you should be there or not.

I'm not saying that others should not work to be inclusive, but as long as that is what is looked for, some people will not feel comfortable going where they want to go until the whole world agrees they should be there. That's not necessary. It's far from the best way for people to fulfil their potential and achieve their personal goals.

I don't mean to be critical of Carol Dweck and her associates work. Their conclusion is spot on—mindset should be part of core curriculums beginning at as young of an age as possible but no later than 3rd grade. They do advocate for testing and I am reserved on that subject. There is a controversy right now with articles in the NY Times by both Angela Duckworth and Jose Vilson about testing resiliency in schools. There is enough evidence that changing mindsets changes outcomes that programs designed to help students establish more productive mindsets could be tested indirectly by measuring the outcomes that we know mindsets positively impact such as graduation rates, grades, and discipline rates.

Self-efficacy Beliefs

Learning can be fun. Learning for the fun of learning can propel a student beyond the success attainable from simply meeting the requirements for graduation. A team of researchers who were looking at academic achievement through the lens of self-efficacy beliefs and self-regulated learning (beyond intelligence, personality traits, and self-esteem) found, "the beliefs students hold about their capacities to regulate their learning . . . was one of the most important predictors of success at school after previous academic achievement."[626]

At the time of the paper (2013), efforts to increase self-efficacy beliefs were being done are being approached by providing mastery experiences and modeling. Although there is nothing wrong with mastery experiences, a more direct approach might net quicker results (even from subsequent mastery experiences). Teaching children that their beliefs affect their thoughts and that if they didn't believe they could be successful at something or didn't believe they were smart when they did poorly with a task, the belief hindered their success. By changing the belief, past results are not representative of their potential once they change their belief about their ability. The information would have to come from a trusted individual who actually believes that beliefs affect outcome. If the child had learned *The Smart Way*, his Emotional Guidance would affirm the truth of the statement, even if it came from a source that was not fully trusted. Of course, if the teacher knew *The Smart Way*, he would believe the statement.

Positive Education

Positive Education, as discussed in *The Oxford Handbook of Happiness* "describes the purpose of focusing on positive education—to increase children's wellbeing—and defines *positive education* as education aiming to 'develop the skills of well-being, flourishing, and optimal functioning in children, teenagers, and students, as well as parents and educational institutions.'"[627]

The empirical evidence supporting positive education initiatives, which include learning skills that build resilience and emotional regulation skills, is more than compelling. When taken in its entirety it presents a clear picture of what ought to be done to provide children with the knowledge and skills they need to have the best possible lives. However, based on the information I've seen, it does not begin to reach the potential it could have if motivation theory (i.e. autonomy), meta-cognitve skills and Emotional Guidance were included in the structure. The structures I read about seemed highly structured with little room for autonomy—even as far as bathroom visits.

Contagious Stress

We all know stress can be contagious, transferring from one person to another.

If you see your boss walking through the office tense with pent up stress, you begin wondering what has her so stressed and hope it's not you. We are all able to sense stress around us, at a table of strangers silently eating lunch together, or even between two people who pass in the hall at work. Even when we don't know how we know, we KNOW.

Research has now shown that judgments about stressed people are generally lower than judgments about the same person (by others) when they aren't stressed. [628]

Let's take this to the low socioeconomic classroom where the students may all be stressed to some degree or another. The stressors a child living in poverty experiences are daily occurrences. If his competency is rated lower by a teacher who is unconsciously influenced by the stress and that teacher's beliefs about his potential are affected by the judgments, the Pygmalion Effect could come into play. Now look at it from the perspective of teachers who leave after only a year or two. If they don't know how to manage their own stress levels, to inoculate themselves against stress contagion that permeates their classrooms, the environment will be almost intolerable. Also, research has found that teachers can pass their anxiety on to students.[629]

A program that taught emotion regulation skills to 321 families of low income 8th graders show positive improvements in outcomes in numerous areas including reduced substance abuse, fewer conduct problems and school suspensions over a two-year follow-up period.[630] When a child misbehaves, it is a cry for help. They feel emotional pain and don't know how to make it feel better. This can be acted out as anger and aggression. Being defiant can give a child who feels powerless a sense of power. It is counterproductive, but at that moment in time, it felt better than continuing to feel powerless. Authoritarian discipline in homes and schools exacerbates the powerlessness many children feel. What the children really need is an adult who care about the whole child and who can help the child learn to manage emotions in a way that feels good.

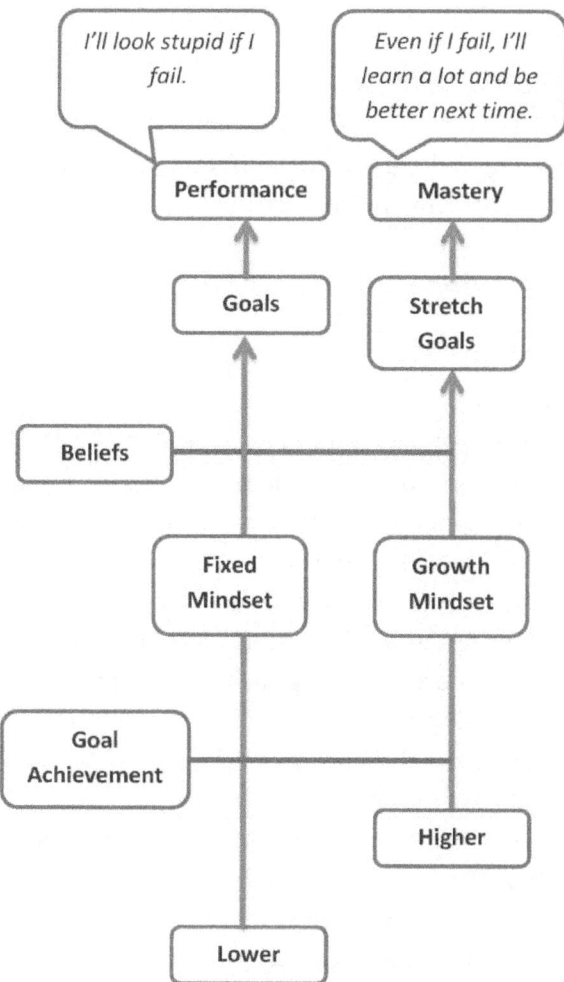

Fixed vs. Growth Mindset

There are two major types of mindsets. One is based on seeing oneself as a finished product with traits and abilities that are whatever they are, but with little ability of the individual to change them. That sort of belief is called a fixed mindset. An individual with a fixed mindset is at a decided disadvantage because there is no apparent reason to seek self-development and there is a high degree of motivation to *prove* the quality (or goodness) of what one is (because the idea of becoming more is not part of the person's worldview). Challenges to valued qualities can make a person with a fixed mindset feel vulnerable or anxious. They will focus on performance goals in an effort to prove their value and worth to others (and themselves).

On the other hand, an individual with a growth mindset perceives an ability to learn, grow, and adapt, and to become more along the way. The person with a growth mindset will seek new experiences for the knowledge to be gained from them. The growth mindset does not base self-esteem upon proving that he is smart enough, talented enough, pretty enough, or some other factor that is considered unchangeable. Students with a growth mindset are likely to enjoy studying and won't have test anxiety because the test is not determining the value of their personhood. Fortunately, like pessimism, a fixed mindset does not come with a life sentence. It can be changed to enhance the life experiences of the individual.

It makes sense to teach children the growth approach as early in life as possible and to reinforce that perspective throughout life.

> *Emotional Labor is a requirement that one display specific emotions during work, regardless of whether they are authentic, such as being cheerful while working with a patient you've come to like who is dying. Emotional labor is stressful. In the home, it is called Emotional Work. For example, a home with an authoritarian parent who demands you put a smile on your face requires emotional labor.*

Emotional Intelligence and Education

In one study of first year nursing students, 28% scored below average on using emotions to reason.[631] In light of the findings in psychology pointing to the purpose of emotions being to provide guidance and aid meta-cognitve processes, this absence of ability to use emotions as they were intended is extremely life-limiting. I agree that Emotional Intelligence training should be a part of the core curriculum for nurses and believe that it would help reduce the rapid burnout that is contributing to nursing shortages.

However, I would go further than making EI training a required part of nursing curriculum—a step I consider a stopgap measure. I would add training to all high schools on *The Smart Way*. I would begin with the basics in elementary school so students can begin using the skills. I strongly encourage this because it will improve:

- The trajectories of their lives, increasing the potential for life-long success
- Decrease stressful relationships that lead to undesired outcomes in homes and at school
- Lessen life-long chronic stress loads, which should go a long way to eliminating the mental and physical health disparate impact we're currently seeing for minorities and low socioeconomic groups

I would also strongly encourage retrofit work that teaches nurses who have already graduated Emotional Intelligence skills so they can:

- Reduce their daily stress load
- Potentially reduce or eliminate the high burnout rate
- Teach their children and potentially even share with patients ways to lessen stress

As far as patients stress levels are concerned, when you understand your Emotional Guidance and the meta-cognitve processes that create the level of stress it is easy to spot opportunities to change stress levels in others. It takes a level of Emotional Intelligence to know when to do so, but sometimes brief conversations can authentically reduce another's level of stress. For example, self-recriminations are often a significant contributor to stress. Just KNOWING that everyone always did the best they could in any given moment and that regret is felt because someone who has become more is looking back and regretting who they once were—that the person they are in this moment would make different choices and communicating that *KNOWing* can ease self-recriminations and the stress it creates in their bodies.

When you understand the Emotional Guidance Scale and have mastered tools that you can use to reduce stress and negative emotion, it is easy to find small openings where you can help others feel a little better, often in subtle ways. As I move through my days such opportunities present themselves frequently beyond my work with clients. Opportunities to help store clerks, people waiting in line next to me, family, friends, and business associates appear every day. Given the correlation between behavior and emotional state, with high stress associated with low emotional states, the more people who can offer even a little relief from stress to others could be of significant benefit on a cumulative basis. There is a ripple effect. Reducing the stress of one member of the family while they are picking up a few groceries translates into less stress in the home environment that evening. That can lead to better food decisions and better sleep that night. It can lead to better relationships in the home, which can help prevent development of illnesses and diseases.

The insight offered by the stranger at the grocery store may even be shared if the source of stress is shared by the family, providing even more direct relief from the stress burden. Recently, I read a Utopian view of developing Emotional Intelligence:

> *The best method to teach emotional intelligence to children is through elders leading by example or being a standing example of virtuous living. This is because young children emulate into their lives what their parents do or what their peer group does. If everyone of us are self-disciplined, self-controlled, generous, humble, modest, loving and caring, mutually respecting, noble and wise, benevolent and forgiving, cautious of our actions and activities, etc., this world would be a paradise for the growing children and their next generations. There must be a continuous quest in life for better living and evolution.*
> Prasanna Seshadri

I agree that in an ideal world, children could learn by example. But the world we live in is far from ideal. Many children are raised by parents who are far from the requirements that are required to organically develop high Emotional Intelligence. Relying on examples would ensure that the gap between children raised in supportive homes and the most vulnerable children widened. If we want all children to thrive, they must be given the tools to develop Emotional Intelligence in the more formal educational setting. Home schooled children should be offered classes on-line or at regional centers.

Appropriate Discipline

In my last book, *Is Punishment Ethical?*, I explored the scientific evidence questioning whether punishment deters undesired actions. My conclusion was that punishment as a response to undesired behaviors was based on false premises that the scientific literature now firmly refutes. Most people who look at the way we handle undesired behavior as parents and as a society don't evaluate the root. They tend to stay in the branches, evaluating whether the methods of punishment are appropriate or effective.

The reason my conclusion is that punishment is not ethical is because behavior and emotional state move in tandem—perhaps not in perfect harmony—but in the same direction at the same time. Good-feeling emotional states are associated with more kindness (even to strangers), better relationships with the people in our lives, better corporate citizenship, and better behaviors toward our self (pro-health behaviors). Bad-feeling emotional states are associated with worsening behaviors up to and including tragedies that make the national news. Punishments are designed to make the person who misbehaved feel worse, which increases the likelihood of worsening behaviors.

With that background about the effect of emotional state on behavior, the fact that "several studies demonstrate that African American students are suspended more harshly and for less serious and more subjective types of offenses compared to White students increases the risk of adverse behaviors. According to four individual studies, White students were referred much more frequently for offenses that are more easily identified objectively, such as smoking, vandalizing property, and leaving school grounds without permission, while African American students were more often referred for subjective behaviors, such as disrespect, excessive noise, and loitering."[632] Increased failures (i.e. drop-outs) would be supported by my conclusion about punishment not being ethical. The evidence bears this out, "Students who are suspended three or more times by the end of their sophomore year of high school are five times more likely to drop out than students who have not been suspended."[633] Some schools, termed *dropout factories* have graduate rates of less than 60%. These schools usually have high numbers of low socioeconomic student enrollment, fewer experienced teachers, and fewer Advanced Placement course offerings.

The Smart Way for children would go a long way in turning the *dropout factories* around. Students who come from low economic areas ravaged by crime will have a difficult time managing their behavior if they do not have strong self-regulatory skills. The evidence that increasing resilience changes the trajectories of their lives is compelling. If we want to stop the *cycle of violence* and poverty that ravages the lives of so many children, we must address the root cause and provide them with skills and knowledge they can use to overcome difficult beginnings. As I comment elsewhere, although those communities are a priority, the training is important for all because we don't know what children in fancy homes are living. Not all crimes and poor life outcomes originate in poor neighborhoods.

Labels

When children are labeled as disruptive or worse without recognizing that the child's behavior is the result of the emotional state and that the child may be experiencing significant stressors, everyone loses. The child is marginalized, labeled, and in many respects *given up upon*. There is a misguided belief that children who do not come to school and give it their best aren't worth the effort. But the fact of the matter is the children who are cast aside are probably doing their best under the circumstances they find themselves living in.

Marginalizing such children without digging deeper is a reflection of the current medical system that addresses symptoms without evaluating root causes that could be changed and eliminate the problem—including side effects. We have to remember that when we give up on a 3rd grader we are pretty much agreeing to bury him or her before they turn 18, or to house them in juvenile and adult detention facilities for most of their life. The cost of a little extra effort when a child is young will prevent a great deal of suffering and expense later. If we won't do it for the child, we should do it for ourselves. If we won't do it for the child or for ourselves, we should do it for our children or grandchildren because they will inhabit the same world, walk the same streets, and ride the same mass transit systems as the child we don't help. How their encounters play out depends on our actions now.

High School Dropout Rates

The economic impact of high school dropouts can be measured on the individual level, the community level and the national level.

On the personal level, a high school dropout is more likely to live in poverty and more likely to spend time in jail. In 2013 an adult who dropped out of high school earned an average income of $23,900 compared to $30,000 for those who graduated from high school.[634] "More than 1,200 high schools, serving more than 1.1 million students, still fail to graduate one-third or more of their students each year. These low-graduation-rate high schools primarily educate low-income students and students of color."[635]

According to the Alliance for Excellent Education, 2011 graduation rates varied significantly by race as follows:

	All Students	White	Black	Hispanic	Asian	American Indian
High School	79%	85%	67%	71%	87%	64%
College	56%	60%	38%	48%	68%	39%

I wish they would show statistics for bi-racial children because they often have a more difficult time because they do not feel they belong to any racial group. I've detailed my suggestions on approaching that problem elsewhere in the book, but until we know how many of the students in each category are actually bi-racial, we can't know what, if any, impact the ostracism some bi-racial children experience has on their outcomes. An educated guess is that it has a significant impact. In the 1960's Leonard Nimoy (Spock of the Star Ship Enterprise) responded to a letter from a bi-racial girl with wisdom and insight that is still applicable today. You can find the letter via a Google search for "Spock bi-racial letter." What I like most is he told the young girl to listen to her inner voice, essentially to listen to her guidance.

Increasing graduation rates can lead to double benefits. On the one hand, graduates will have higher lifetime earnings and contribute to the economy by paying taxes, buying houses, increasing the economy by spending their higher wages, and possible by beginning businesses. On the other hand, they will be less likely to be a drain on the economy by needing tax-support to survive. Over the long-term, they and their children will benefit from their lower levels of stress that will reduce the likelihood they will suffer from chronic diseases and their children may be raised in less stressful environments. Increasing graduation rates pays dividends across the lifespan.

Alliance for Excellent Education Fact Sheets reflect the following statistics relative to completion of high school:

- 75% of America's state prison inmates are high school dropouts
- 59% of America's federal prison inmates did not complete high school
- High school dropouts are 3.5 times more likely than high school graduates to be arrested in their lifetime
- A 1% increase in high school graduation rates would save approximately $1.4 billion in incarceration costs, or about $2,100 per each male high school graduate
- A one-year increase in average education levels would reduce arrest rates by 11%
- The cost to taxpayers of adult illiteracy is $224 billion per year
- U.S. companies lose nearly $40 billion annually because of illiteracy
- Teen girls in the bottom 20% of basic reading and math skills are five times more likely to become mothers over a two-year high school period than teen girls in the top 20%
- Students with low academic achievement are twice as likely to become parents by their senior year of high school, compared to students with high academic achievement
- The U.S. death rate for those with fewer than 12 years of education is 2.5 times higher than the rate of those with 13 or more years of education

College

If the ladder of educational opportunity rises high at the doors of some youth and scarcely rises at the doors of others, while at the same time formal education is made a prerequisite to occupational and social advance, then education may become the means, not of eliminating race and class distinctions, but of deepening and solidifying them.
Harry S. Truman

Angel B. Pérez, vice president of enrollment and student success at Trinity College, says the lack of minorities at leading Universities like Trinity with annual tuition of over $64,000 is an American higher education problem.[636] I disagree. The problem begins long before a student is ready for college. It begins in early elementary school when they are judged as possessing lower potential because of early home environment and/or poverty and (still) in some cases, race. In 2013, children "from families in the top family income quartile were over 8 times as likely to obtain a bachelor's degree by age 24 as those in the bottom family income quartile (77 percent compared with 9 percent)."[637] It may look like a higher education problem, but it does not begin when they are 17 or 18; it already has a strong track record by the time a child is deciding whether or not to go to college. This is not my area of expertise. I don't know why tuition costs so much at some Universities or how to change that current fact.

The Pygmalion Effect is alive and well in early childhood and does not stop exerting a deflating influence before a child goes to college. I've written elsewhere about how developing a stronger belief in self than the disbelief some others hold protects us from the Pygmalion Effect. That is a major step in the right direction because it leads to improved grades throughout school.

One of the recent arguments in a Supreme Court case was that taking students from schools in low income areas and putting them in competitive colleges was not fair because they were ill prepared for the challenges. This remark by Justice Scalia shortly before his death was met with outrage. I see both sides of the issue. There is the outrage that he would think minority and poor students don't belong in top colleges. I don't think that is what he meant. I think he was aware that our primary education system is flawed and that children in poor areas do not receive an equal education. There are many things I could cite to support this—they have fewer tenured teachers, more teachers with only a few years of experience, less money. The list is long. This is not a judgment about the **potential** of children who attend those schools.

Well, let me phrase that another way. The poor resources reflect a view that children raised in poverty are unlikely to put their educations to good use so why give them an equal education or that their parents aren't contributing as much so they don't deserve to have as many tax dollars to support their education. I strongly disagree with both these points of view, but they are at the root of the issue. Or, I hope, more accurately, they were at the root *in the beginning*. That it remains is another example of unexamined root causes. If we point to higher education outcomes and say it is a higher education problem, we continue ignoring the root.

Hopefully some of the readers of this book will find it is their passion to examine the roots of the education system in as much detail as I have examined what makes humans thrive and change a system that is broken at its roots.

A student who understands Emotional Guidance and how to manage his or her emotional state to good feeling states on a regular basis could attend a poorly funded school and be well prepared for the most competitive Ivy League college. But that requires personal initiative and intrinsic motivation, which will not be present if the child does not believe in the possibility of a better future. I know how to fix that, and by the time you finish this book, so will you.

Remember, cognitive abilities increase as emotional state increases. In the real world that translates into an ability to find a way to go to the college of choice regardless of obstacles, or to go to college regardless of obstacles. I've spoken to a number of low-income minority students who had narrow views about their possibilities. Some believed that a sports scholarship was the only way they'd ever go to college. Others had not considered alternatives and there are many. Here are a few alternatives:

- Consider a 2-year college for the first two years and then transfer to University (I did this, but it took me about six years to transfer—a subject for another book—I'll just say make sure you talk to a counselor and understand graduation requirements).
- Find an employer who reimburses college education expenses. There are many. (I did this.)
- Consider a good college in a less desirable location. A friend sent his children to a school in Northern Canada with very low tuition.
- Consider a college that has a work program.
- Consider a college in a less expensive country. My children considered some overseas Universities that were financially affordable.

- Consider getting a skill that will help you earn more than minimum wage as you work through college. I worked full-time throughout my college years and by the time I graduated I was ready for mid-management positions. The downside was I didn't have a life for the 13-years it took me to graduate. This is not my top recommendation but it is certainly a better alternative than not going to college for anyone who wants to do so.
- Consider trade or technical schools. Plumbers and electricians can make a good living, especially if they start their own business. One of my children's friends parent went to trade school and he has his own jet.
- Ask others how they did it.
- Get a merit scholarship.
- Invent something. The growing number of child entrepreneurs is exciting to see. Don't discount your age and inexperience—it means you're not looking at the world with limited beliefs about what can be.

The most important thing anyone can do is to believe they can find a way. Every time I believed I could, I was able to achieve what I set out to do, even when logic dictated that I shouldn't be able to do it.

If you want to go to college, work on believing in yourself as soon as possible and as much as possible and then figure out how. The Pew Research Center published a report on the growing discrepancies in income between those who go to college and those who don't and concluded that, "On virtually every measure of economic well-being and career attainment—from personal earnings to job satisfaction to the share employed full time—young college graduates are outperforming their peers with less education. And when today's young adults are compared with previous generations, the disparity in economic outcomes between college graduates and those with a high school diploma or less formal schooling has never been greater."[638]

Degree Creep

When I meet with educators, degree creep is a term that is often bandied about. My work demonstrates that the One Path our society has established to demonstrate knowledge and expertise is not the only path. There have been many influential autodidactic learners who have made significant contributions.

Every mind has a horizon in respect to its present intellectual capacity but not in respect to its future intellectual capacity.
Gottfried Leibniz

29: Educational Success

30: Career Success

Pleasure in the job puts perfection in the work.
Aristotle

Motivation is when your dreams put on work clothes
Benjamin Franklin

In Chapter 18, I touched on the importance of being able to align external motivators with intrinsic motivators because it reduces the stress of achieving the external goals and increases your likelihood of success. Recent research shows that "Career adaptability predicts subjective career success above and beyond personality traits and core self-evaluations."[639]

Career adaptability is "a psychosocial construct that reflects' employees resources for managing present and impending work and career challenges that may affect their integration in their social environment." Career adaptability is the result of self-regulatory capacities (i.e. meta-cognitve processes) that can change over time. [640] In other words, the self-regulatory capacities can be learned and developed.

In Zacher's article about career adaptability, he cited numerous benefits of career adaptability including: [641]

- Positively predicted team work skills
- Job search self-efficacy
- Tenacious goal pursuit
- Flexible goal adjustment
- Increase promotability and career satisfaction
- Predicted employees breadth of interests
- Predicted employee orientation to happiness
- Predicted general and professional well-being
- Predicted employee quality of life
- Predicted lower work stress
- Employee perceives fewer career barriers
- Predicted career commitment
- Predicted career identification
- Predicted career exploration
- Positively related to self-esteem
- Positively related to promotion focus
- Predicted engagement beyond the Big Five Traits
- Negatively related to general anxiety
- Negatively related to fear of failure

One critical factor to career success is being able to use the training one has spent time and money attaining. Some occupations, like nursing, require extensive schooling but have a high burnout rate—which means nurses are sometimes not using their education long enough to obtain the maximum benefits from it. When an individual from a lower socioeconomic background makes it through college to become an RN, they often have student loans. If they don't stay in the profession long enough to repay their loans, they would probably have been better off in another profession. There is no shortage of nursing jobs, in fact, we're seeing more frequent articles about nursing shortages. Job burnout is contributing to the shortage problem.

Burnout is an outcome of low resilience. Nursing can be emotional labor—work that takes a toll on one's psychological health. It can also be a physically demanding job, requiring long hours on one's feet. Even before a nurse graduates from college, some drop out of their course of study. In one study, 57% of Native American nurses dropped out before they completed their nursing training. This type of outcome means that the nurses paid for an education (or part of one) that they won't be able to use. It also means that there are not enough nurses who are Native American. There is a high demand for nurses who are the same ethnicity of the patients they serve. In some populations, the patient is more comfortable with someone from the same race.

The HeartMath method of increasing heart coherence was introduced and subsequent years had much lower drop-out rates in the nursing program for Native Americans, down to 37% from 57% and test scores on standardized tests increased by an average of 17 points.[642]

My desire is to see people who live in poverty rise to economic levels where they can enjoy the benefits of the American dream—regardless of what country they happen to live in. I want people to be able to aspire to become whoever they want to be and with effort, be able to achieve much of their dreams, goals, and desires. I am not suggesting everyone has to move to America, but that they have opportunities for economic advancement and autonomy wherever they happen to live.

We know career adaptability has a significant influence on career success. We know psychological skills contribute to career adaptability, yet we do not teach them in schools. This leaves me with two choices:

- Believe the system does not understand the importance of these skills because if they did, they would be included in the education system as a priority, or
- They know and there is some sort of grand conspiracy to keep the downtrodden down—as if their enjoying more would lessen what others have.

I'm not really one to buy into conspiracy theories and typically opt for other answers, when one is available. Thus, I am focusing my efforts at raising awareness so that our education systems will begin teaching children skills that will allow them to achieve the American Dream—a life that is better than that of their parents. And, this book is designed to provide individuals and parents the information they need to thrive, so even if it is a conspiracy, no one has to wait for schools to incorporate the life changing information provided herein—they can do it completely on their own. Everyone has the necessary elements—their own mind and their emotions. People can also establish groups to study together and share experiences.

The knowledge and skills presented in these pages increase Emotional Intelligence (EI) significantly. EI strengthens career adaptability.[643]

"In today's global economy, coping with the stress associated with career uncertainty and the unpredictability of ongoing changes requires frequent emotional and cognitive adjustments. To respond effective to career transitions, individuals must display both emotional intelligence and *career adaptability*.

Two factors that contribute to career adaptability are *concern* for the future that intrinsically motivates employees to prepare for upcoming tasks and challenges and *confidence*, the belief that they can achieve their career goals and solve problems that arise.[644] Understanding one's Emotional Guidance is the best way to develop confidence. Emotional Guidance will encourage self-development that prepares an individual for greater challenges in the future.

For example, when I learned I'd have an opportunity to speak when I earned my Fellowship in the Life Office Management Institute I joined Toastmaster's to prepare myself to take advantage of the opportunity. I did not understand that emotions were guidance in those days, but the message was clear that I should do that, despite being very afraid. In those days one-on-one conversations were stressful for me. Once I learned about Emotional Guidance I began wondering how much of the early encouragement to go to Toastmaster's was due to the impending opportunity and how much was related to developing comfort on the stage that was invaluable later in my career and is now a significant part of my second career. As a shy 18-year-old the concept of becoming a motivational and educational speaker was not in my self-concept of my most self-actualized self.

We see individuals who somehow, against seemingly stiff odds, rise up out of poverty and have a far better life than their parents. Today this is not a common event, but it could be—if children were given the psychological knowledge and skills that help them achieve their dreams.

Providing children with the opportunity to learn about their Emotional Guidance and develop meta-cognitve processes that empower them to be adaptable under a wide range of conditions will prepare them for educational and career success.

Unemployment

A meta-analysis of 237 cross-sectional and 87 longitudinal studies found psychological problems affected 34% of the unemployed compared to 16% of employed individuals.[645] Unemployment is not only correlated to mental distress, it causes it. Early researchers assumed that mental health problems led to unemployment and while that is also true in some instances, the negative mental impact of unemployment is significant absent pre-existing mental health issues.[646] "Intervention programs were found to have positive effects on mental health among continuously unemployed people. The effect was of medium size."[647] The risk of mental health problems rise during the first nine months of unemployment and affects male blue collar workers the most.[648] The study concluded, "The result is a clear and unequivocal warning that unemployment is a severe risk for public mental health that must be fought with all possible means."[649]

Employee Engagement

Employee engagement is significantly affected by the employee's emotional state, self-esteem, locus of control, and the ability of the role to elicit both a sense of autonomy and a bond with the organization. An article in the *Academy of Management Journal* recently reported that lunchbreak autonomy "plays a complex and pivotal role in conferring the potential energetic benefits of lunch break activities."[650] In other words, employees who are free to choose their lunchbreak activities find the breaks more restorative than those whose breaks are restricted, such as employees who are required to remain on the premises or whose breaks are so short that leaving the premises is not practical.

The Smart Way helps employees connect with the purpose of their company's mission in a way that is personally meaningful above and beyond the value of the paycheck and to feel closer and more connected to their co-workers.

When employees are unhappy or have low self-esteem it is unlikely they will be fully engaged.

31: Parenting

It is easier to build strong children than to repair broken men.
Frederick Douglass

Parents, whether they are struggling or thriving, want their children to be healthy, happy and successful in all areas of life. Resilient mindsets greatly increase the chances of positive outcomes. Even when you're thriving, you may not feel confident that your children will also thrive. Children of wealthy families can be depressed, slackers, experiment with or become addicted to drugs and/or alcohol, commit crimes, abuse their spouse or children, divorce, and experience other undesirable outcomes.

There are numerous parenting suggestions throughout this book that seem to belong more fully in the section about the topic the advice specifically addresses, whether it is poverty, building resilience, or developing healthy behaviors so the information in this area is not representative of all the parenting advice in these pages.

Parenting is the process of assisting a baby/child through childhood to adulthood with the intent to optimize the quality of life of the child without unnecessary detriment to one's own life experience.

Beyond the obvious, that infants are not equipped to survive without help during the first year or so of life, the quality of parenting can have a significant effect on a child's outcome. While parenting is not the only thing that matters because I've clearly seen one child follow an undesirable path while other children in the family did well, parents are in a great position to understand how to increase factors that can protect their children against adverse outcomes. One obstacles is that parents don't think their child will experience things that will lead to their needing resilience. But the life-events that can cause downward spirals are common. Large numbers of children experience some type of trauma, from a variety of circumstances including bullying, a car accident, an accident on the playing field, hearing the wrong words during a vulnerable moment, violence in the neighborhood, the unexpected loss of a loved one, or later while serving the country in the military.

A suggestion about father's involvement with their children encouraged developing the father's resilience early in the child's life, "Risk factors such as involvement in the criminal justice system, unemployment, and partner relationship challenges are highly relevant to these fathers who may struggle to stay involved with their children over time. Recent studies of fathers in fragile families have suggested that risk and resilience factors during the first few years following the birth of the child are critical for fathers' later involvement with the child and for child outcomes. For example, Fagan et al. found that fathers' cumulative risk during the first year following the birth of the child not only predicts father engagement when the child is an infant, but it also predicts father engagement when the child is 3 years old. The implication of these findings is that programs for fathers in fragile families should conduct early intervention both before and shortly following the birth of the child. Fathers who reduce their risk factors and increase their resilience factors during the first few years stand a better chance of being engaged with their children during the early preschool years, which are critical for children's early development. These findings would be further bolstered if early risk and resilience were also found to predict paternal engagement when the child is ready to enter school.[651] It would be better to develop that resilience before the child is conceived, which might make the family less fragile in the first place.

"There is also evidence that fathers with high levels of risk also experience more parenting stress, which tends to be negatively related to father engagement with children and . . . mothers also select out of relationships they perceive to be "unhealthy" because they view these fathers as having little to offer their children . . . mothers want their baby's father to be involved with the child, but only if the father does not have too many problems of his own and can provide for his children."[652]

A child can be considered part of a nested system of systems within systems. First, you have the child. If the child's mental and physical health is strong, the child is better able to survive and even eventually thrive even if the other systems are imperfect. Throughout history some people thrive even in the worst of times—they are the resilient ones. Throughout history, there are people who have suffered during the best of times—those are the ones whose thought processes are dysfunctional. Even if you want to blame their status as a repressed group (i.e. women, or a racial or religious minority group), if you look closely you will see that there were exceptions within those groups who did thrive whilst most with those *labels* did not. The more risk factors a person has to deal with, the more valuable psychological flexibility, resilience, optimism, and emotional intelligence become.

Risk factors can come from different areas of an individual's life, including family stressors and the environment and all of them have been shown to be associated with child engagement among fathers in fragile families in the United States: [653]

- Low income
- Low levels of education
- Escalating or persistent problems with drug and alcohol abuse
- Being convicted of a crime and subsequent incarceration
- Emotional health problems such as major depression and anxiety
- physical health problems
- Family risk factors include fathers' transitions to lower commitment relationships with the mother
- fathers' subsequent relationships are associated with decreased involvement with biological children from previous relationships
- Fathers who have children from other unions
- Children's risk factors include health problems and difficult temperament. the type of risk may be less important than the total number of risk factors

"Policy makers and social service professionals should strengthen programs that help couples negotiate each parent's role in rearing his or her children. In summary, the findings from this study further emphasize the need to detect risk and enhance resilience as early as possible to avoid long-term negative consequences from lack of father involvement. It also calls for more systematic research and development on risk and resilience."[654]

My children attended a small private school but three years in a row, classmates in their grade lost a parent to a car or motorcycle accident. One of them lost a parent and a sibling. We can't know what our children's lives will include. We can teach them to be more resilient, which will improve their outcomes if bad things do happen.

But it is not just adverse life events that involve death or physical trauma where resilience helps one bounce back. Setbacks in love or career can be traumatic for individuals who are not skilled in emotion regulation. Those who are more resilient recover faster and suffer less.

"Risky families characterized by chronic stress appear to generate immediate distress in children but also long-term sequelae for health . . . As a result of chronic stress, including family stress, dysregulation can occur in stress-regulation systems or the immune system, with lasting effects on health. There is growing concern about the long-term potential consequences of stress in early childhood . . . family stress can become biologically embedded in individual family . . . research on prenatal stress in mothers has been linked to lasting changes in the fetus"[655]

Researchers have linked poor maternal emotion regulation to maladaptive parenting and child behaviors.[656] Teaching individuals how to use *The Smart Way*, with its healthy emotion regulation techniques and Emotional Guidance should significantly reduce their use of maladaptive emotion regulation strategies that lead to problematic behaviors in their children.

As a parent, learning to understand self-regulation strategies and the purpose of emotions feels like someone has handed you the instruction book you looked for but could not find when your child was born. It suddenly becomes easier to make good decisions without angst across a wide variety of topics. It also becomes surprisingly easy to turn over age appropriate decision-making to your child once you understand that they have Emotional Guidance. How do you know what is age appropriate? Use your own guidance. Your children's well-being is one of your goals that your guidance considers. Although if you're like me, you may still be surprised at how well they use it.

Just the other day my youngest daughter (age 24 at this writing) went to run some errands and was going to stop at the post office to mail some orders (she makes jewelry). When she returned home she carried the packages she was going to mail back into the house and I asked her why she hadn't mailed them. She said she started feeling funny about going to the post office after closing (something she frequently does) so she turned around and came home. I commented, "I'm glad you listened to your guidance." She responded, "I usually do."

As a parent you can't always tell by observing that your child is using his or her guidance to make decisions. It is important for the family dynamic to allow members to ask one another what their guidance is telling them about which decision to make. The other day my hubby and I were going to have our annual mint milkshake date. He has the St. Patrick's shake at McDonalds for him and I enjoy a mint chocolate one from Arby's. I'd put my shoes on, but the eagerness I'd felt when we made the date wasn't present. I checked into my guidance which was telling me not to have a milkshake that night. We'd had leftover baked spaghetti for dinner and I was still full, but the feeling was more than being full. I told my husband that I no longer wanted the shake from Arby's and he said he was also feeling full and thought postponing our date night was a good idea.

It is best if both parents understand self-regulation and the purpose of emotions. Some research points to middle school children developing problems when their parents expectations about emotions differ significantly. Families that raised today's parents varied widely in how they acted toward and thought about emotion. In some families, emotions are a frequent topic of conversation and responsibility for how one feels is placed on an external source (i.e. "he embarrassed me or "she made me angry"). Some families avoid discussions that involve emotions at high cost. Other families might argue over whose emotions about a topic are right.

Although I recommend the scientifically (and religiously) supported *emotions as guidance*, it is important to note that consistency between parents who have a somewhat healthy style of dealing with emotions is better than inconsistency. When parents have conflicting styles the best course of action is to educate themselves about the style that leads to the best outcomes. Remember, our parents largely followed in their parents footsteps. The way they did what they did is unlikely to have been based on anything other than how their parents raised them and beliefs they formed (mostly by age six). The beliefs a parent has formed will make it seem as if the style they want to use is the best, but stepping back and looking at the impact of the style in light of what you know about what helps a child thrive can bring about the outcome you want.

Remember, having used an ineffective or even damaging style in the past is not something to feel guilty for. What you did in the past is the best you could do with what you knew at the time. But you have learned new information that enables you to make better decisions now. I completely changed much of the way I parented once I understood that my children had guidance and so did I. Our relationships improved, life became easier and none of the things I fought so hard to avoid using the old methods manifested after I stopped fighting against them.

I used my Emotional Guidance in the privacy of my own mind for a while before I trusted it enough to change my parenting style so don't feel pressured. When you begin trusting your guidance it will feel right to apply what you've learned to parenting. In the meantime, use any information you're ready to accept to improve the way you interact with others, including your children.

Overall, parental behavior toward a child and the parenting style do have an effect on the outcomes experienced by a child. Supportive, warm, and caring parenting styles which include an element of control, but also include communication and give and take (an opportunity for the child to express his views and desires) is associated with the best results. On the other hand, hostility, rejection, neglect and general coldness are associated with greater delinquency, as is control that is coercive, restrictive and does not allow the child to express her thoughts and desires. Given the evidence, it is important for parents to do a good job managing their own stress, "49% of parents surveyed say they lost patience with their children in the past month when they were feeling stressed."[657]

However, parenting style does not automatically lead to a desired or undesired outcome. Researchers reviewing a meta-analysis of 161 separate studies concluded that parenting style accounted for up to 11% of the variance in delinquency.[658] One of the best things a parent can do to prevent their child(ren) from becoming delinquent is to monitor their behavior. Awareness of their activities, both online and in person, makes a significant difference in outcomes.

The way the child processes information is, in my opinion, the factor that contributes the most to the outcome. A child who understands that a highly controlling parent is acting the way he acts because they care about the child's welfare—even if the behavior is frustrating and restrictive—can weather the storm far better than the child who believes the behavior is because there is something wrong with the child.

If parents would ask children to consider different perspectives on the same subject from an early age, training them to see that there are many possible accurate perspectives, the child's psychological flexibility would be significantly higher and the child would find the meta-cognitve process of reframing easy.

This can be incorporated in games, even before the child is able to talk. If you play a simple game of hide and seek with an object to entertain your baby, you can make the item reappear one way one time and another way another time, creating neuropathways that understand the cause of the same effect is not always the same.

As your child becomes conversant, ask your child why they think something happened and then ask them if there is another possible explanation. Create the concept that there are multiple answers that all feel logical from different perspectives. This will help your child find ones that feel better as you introduce

Emotional Guidance. When your child knows there may be more than one possible explanation, they will be ready to think about one possible answer and feel how that one feels and then compare that feeling to how another possible answer feels.

The goal is not to determine *one right* perspective. The goal is to determine which perspective feels the best and to find multiple perspectives.

For example, if your child tearfully tells you that their friend did not want to play with them at pre-school today, after you hug and assure your child of his or her lovability, ask if they ever feel like being alone. Then ask if their friend might have not felt like playing with anyone today or just been curious to learn something about an alternate playmate and wanted to know it now. This introduces the concept that others' rejection is not personal and helps them find different answers and then choose the one that feels best to them. Remember, it is the one that feels best to your child—not to you. Your child's guidance guides your child to your child's goals—which may not be identical to your goals.

For example, your child may really like another child but you know that child comes from a home that you will never allow your child to visit. You may actually be glad if their pre-school friendship seems to be on the rocks because you worry about the time when your child wants to visit the other child and you already know you're going to say no. But your child and this child may get along really well most of the time and it may be that they can be good friends at school even if you do not allow your child to visit the other child at home. Perhaps this child with the troubled home will find some much needed stability during visits to your home.

Help your child understand how the brain filters information between the subconscious and conscious mind and to consider whether their beliefs are contributing when they have a problem. As soon as your child is old enough to understand, teach him to use simple techniques like going more general when something feels bad. In the example above where a friend was not so friendly, going general might have including remembering how many other children there are to play with or that this one day was just one day but that most days are good days.

> *Teach your child to appreciate what they have—not by demanding they appreciate it—but because it feels good to appreciate what we have.*

Teach your child to appreciate what they have—not by demanding they appreciate it—but because it feels good to appreciate what we have. It can be the air we breathe, the food we eat, the dog we play with, the butterfly kisses we share, the feet that carry us from place to place, or anything that we can feel appreciation for.

"Poor family management practices such as failure to set clear expectations for children's behavior, poor monitoring and supervision, and severe and inconsistent discipline consistently predict later delinquency and substance abuse. In a sample followed up on after 20 years, the McCords found that parents' poor supervision and aggressive discipline predicted their children's convictions for person crimes well into their forties.

Wells and Rankin found that boys with very strict parents reported the most violence. Boys with very permissive parents reported the second highest level of violence. Boys with parents who were neither too strict nor too lax reported the least violence. Also, boys whose parents punished them inconsistently, sometimes punishing and sometimes ignoring the same behavior, were more likely to commit an offense against other persons than boys whose parents punished them more consistently. Parental punitiveness or harshness in discipline also predicted later violence."[659]

"Research indicates that parental attitudes favorable to behaviors such as alcohol use predict use of alcohol and drugs by youth."[660]

Although "adolescents whose parents are demanding, involved and supportive are at lower risk of engaging in problem behavior than adolescents whose parents are uninvolved and unsupportive"[661] it is possible to teach children how to establish their own demanding goals. Children do not want to fail. They fail because they do not know how to succeed. The **Setting Intentions** process is a great technique even young children can master. When small goals are achieved, one's sense of mastery increases, leading to self-determined larger goals.

Study skills are associated with greater success in school,[662] but also with avoiding delinquent behaviors. Intention setting can be used to develop study skills while increasing one's sense of autonomy through self-directed goal-setting. Children want to feel competent. When a child is struggling in school, the likelihood of them gravitating toward a self-determined identity where they can feel competent, even if that identity is socially undesirable, increases. "Adolescents whose parents are demanding, involved and supportive are at lower risk of engaging in problem behavior than adolescents hose parents are uninvolved and unsupportive."[663]

A child who is trained to understand her Emotional Guidance can use the ever-present guidance as a substitute for absent parental support and one who has healthy self-esteem and a believe that she can achieve her goals, can develop habits that demand the best of herself. Studies have repeatedly reported that one stable and supportive adult in a child's life is all that is required to shift the trajectory to a positive outcome, but the ability to provide that stable adult to all children is problematic. Beyond cost considerations, which are significant, parental issues such as drug and alcohol addiction, severe poverty, violence in the home and home environment, mental illness, physical illness, custody battles, and more are all factors that can undermine attempts to provide each child with a stable and reliable adult. Mentor programs that attempt to provide supportive adults are never able to meet the demand due to cost considerations and/or a lack of sufficient volunteers.

After using Emotional Guidance in my life for nearly a decade and seeing the difference it makes in the lives of those I have taught, I have reached the conclusion that the things we often seek from others, such as a stable and supportive adult, are sought because we intuitively know we should have stable support—we've just been led astray because we are taught to pay attention to what others want from us more than we do to how we feel and because we have nearly 90 years of misinformation about the purpose of emotions and the corrected information has reached a very limited number of individuals. If we rely more on our Emotional Guidance and cease demanding that other people be consistent in their reactions to and attention to us, we will all get along much better.

If our children are reliant on our response to find their emotional stability, we had better be really good at loving them unconditionally. The younger they are, the better we had better be. As difficult as it may be to admit it the first time, your child's Emotional Guidance is more reliable than you are can be a blow to one's ego. Emotional Guidance is *always* available, it is never too busy or distracted, it never has to leave to go grocery shopping or to go to work, it never needs time alone with its spouse. Those are sometimes guilt-producers for parents who are pulled in too many directions. When you accept that your child has guidance that is available 24/7, it can give you the ability to relax a little bit once your child knows how to interpret guidance accurately and knows that it is trustworthy.

That does not mean you can ignore your child's needs. You will actually be more capable of fulfilling the needs your child has because you are not solely responsible for maintaining his or her emotional well-being. Many parents try to keep their children happy, but that desire conflicts with the need to set appropriate boundaries. It is difficult to both discipline and soothe your child at the same time. If you're using your Emotional Guidance to help you regulate your own emotional state, you'll be a better parent.

There are numerous books and some children's games that focus on the ability to identify individual emotions. It is important to recognize how something makes us feel so we can use Emotional Guidance and also so we can talk about it, if we wish to do so. Help your children learn to communicate about how they feel and how to describe what they feel. Pay attention if they have strong emotional objections to something or someone. Many times parents assume a child is simply overreacting when they are actually providing strong clues that they are picking up on (or have already experienced) something uncomfortable about someone. Sometimes when that person is in a position of authority the parents have gone so far as to become angry at the child's reaction and verbally insisted that they obey the person who turns out to be someone who is being inappropriate with the child.

Yes, tired and hungry children will act out. But children don't usually act out without a reason. Take the time to recognize your child is upset and try to determine why. It may (hopefully) simply be fatigue, hunger, thirst, or the beginnings of a cold. But do take the time to be sure.

If your child is acting up and you can't figure out why, check in with your own emotions for clues. You have your child's welfare as one of your desires so your emotions will give you clues. If you have conflicting emotions, for example, you need your child to be happy with the sitter so you can go to something you really want or need to attend; your frustrating at your child's resistance may mask your own discomfort with some element of the situation. Take the time to sort out how you feel and why.

Researchers looking at adolescents distress related to poverty and illness found that about 28% of the stress adolescents experienced varied by the stress level their parents exhibited.[664]

Childhood abuse

Childhood abuse can take many forms and come from a variety of sources. Physical, sexual, and verbal abuse are fairly common. Research has shown that parenting classes that set appropriate expectations for children at specific ages are helpful with physically abusive parents. Emotional Guidance can become a parenting aid that provides moment-to-moment feedback about how you're looking at the situations you encounter with your child. Personally, before I understood the relationship between emotional state and behavior I was not able to discern patterns. It just seemed that sometimes my children were a major hassle to deal with and other times they could be a joy. It almost seemed as if they deliberately acted out when I was time-stressed. I probably didn't do worse than most parents before I knew what I know, but looking back there are many things I would do differently (better) if I were in the same situation again.

One reason is that I am now able to regulate my own emotional response. I don't have any more buttons for them to push. I understand where behaviors come from and how to help others self-regulate to better-feeling emotional states.

For a physically or verbally abusive parent, simply managing their own emotional state better will make them better parents. When they understand the power of their words to create self-fulfilling prophesies, they will stop calling their children derogatory names. That sort of behavior is both learned and the result of chronic low emotional states. When you feel good, calling someone else a name that makes them feel bad will make you feel bad. Only when you feel disempowered yourself does tearing someone else down feel good.

As the parent feels better, cognitive function improves, which leads to better decisions in other areas of life that ultimately reduce the stress in the home environment. Cognitive Behavior Therapy helps in the aftermath of child abuse for both the parent and the child, including non-offending Mothers.[665] Like other issues where Cognitive Behavioral Therapy is a helpful treatment, learning *The Smart Way* before (or after) an abusive situation will be beneficial. If implementation is as broad as it should be, it will be able to help many children whose abuse is not discovered or reported—something that CBT in the aftermath can't do.

Spankings are a symptom of lack of parenting skills and knowledge of how to raise children to be adults we will not just love, but like. When we limit the conversation to spankings we're addressing a symptom, not the root cause.

The animosity we so often see in teenagers is so commonplace that many parents think rebellion is to be expected from teens. It is not mandatory and when they feel confident and parents trust they have guidance, it's not difficult to avoid the angst and turmoil so many endures.

When your child comes out

LGBT adolescents are at greater risk in a society that is often less than supportive of their status. Being accepting when your child discloses their orientation to you can be of enormous benefit to both your child and your relationship, "experiences of family acceptance when adolescents disclose their sexual orientation as gay, lesbian, bisexual or transgendered are related to young adults self-reporting three times fewer high-risk behaviours such as drug use, HIV-related risky sexual behaviours, depression, and suicidal thoughts."[666]

Transitions out of Foster Care

Today, children who are transitioning out of foster care at age 18 have few available resources to help them move forward to college or in establishing themselves in a stable environment. While *The Smart Way* does not provide food or housing, it can reduce the stress a teenager feels when they find themselves on their own without family support at 18. Lower stress means increased cognitive ability which translates to the ability to see more solutions to one's problems.

I was on my own at 18 without family support and it was tough. I was fortunate to find a job that helped me pay for college and be able to put a roof over my head. I did okay, but I would have done much better if I had the stress management skills I have today. Sleepless nights filled with worries about the future interfere with one's ability to function at work the next day and I had my share of those. Many children are not as lucky as I was—they end up in homeless shelters or living on the street or team up with other children who are making less than desirable choices.

Understanding their Emotional Guidance would be invaluable to them. It would alleviate some of the feeling of being cast adrift in a cruel and harsh world. It is hard to perceive the world as completely awful when you have something that responds to your every thought with helpful and supportive guidance. Whether they consider the source a Higher Power or some as yet unexplained aspect that will someday be explained by quantum physics doesn't really matter. The fact is that the guidance is there in response to every thought and the guidance never tells you that you're stupid, worthless, or that you will never amount to anything. It is an ever-present cheerleader with insight that helps you make good decisions every step of the way.

10 Things Your Child Must Know to Stay out of Jail
1. Emotions are guidance
2. How to interpret emotions accurately
3. How to change thoughts to regulate emotion (Meta-cognitve Processes)
4. How to achieve a healthy level of self-worth and sustain it during changing circumstances
5. That his or her actions are the biggest factor in whether they achieve their dreams.
6. That what they think precedes what they do.
7. How to set their own standards and define who they want to be using Emotional Guidance
8. How to think positively.
9. They will always learn and grow—even after they are adults.

10. They are worthy of love and respect, but must first give it to their self.

Myth: The Absent Black Father
Research published by the CDC in 2013 showed that Black fathers are as involved in the daily activities of their children's lives as White and Latino fathers.[667] I don't know much about the current welfare laws, but when I was a child and young adult I knew people who were on welfare who had a man in their life but they had to hide his presence from the authorities and it was difficult for him to live in the family home because their benefits would be taken away if he was discovered living there. I do know it is less expensive for two adults and a child to live together than for the two adults to live apart with one taking care of the child. It costs more money to maintain two residences and the stress and strain on the relationship can undermine it, leading to worsening relationships.

When you look at the educational opportunities available to minorities at the time and the discrimination that kept many minorities from finding jobs equal to their potential contributions, the fact that a larger percentage needed public assistance does not say anything about the race other than members were doing the best they could in an often hostile environment. Take that a step further and look at the impact of those stressors on health, cognitive ability, and even hope and optimism and you'll see that it is not due to any racial qualities that so many Blacks did not do well.

Take that a step further and look at the situation through the lens of Learned Helplessness and you'll see that what people often perceive as laziness looks a lot like Learned Helplessness playing out. That's great news because Learned Helplessness can be unlearned.

31: Parenting

32: World Peace

Peace is not an absence of war, it is a virtue, a state of mind, a disposition for benevolence, confidence, justice.
Baruch Spinoza (1632 – 1677)

The following is an excerpt of a speech I wrote for a Martin Luther King, Jr. Day speech about the nature of peace and how to put peace in your heart. His works inspire me. He caught glimpses of how to achieve peace but as is so often the case, the world was not fully ready for his message. My speech was written in the hopes that we are more ready today than we were in the 1960's and if it is not, I hope that it will someday be ready for peace to pulsate in every heart.

Your world can be at peace by the end of the day.

Soldiers and politicians do not create peace. I appreciate those who serve. I include them in my prayers. But they are not creating peace. They do not have the power.

If there was no war, anywhere on Earth, would that mean there was peace?

No.

Peace is not the end of the fighting.

Peace is the end of the hating.

Politicians and soldiers cannot change your heart.

You can do that. Today, if you choose.

It is your choice.

Finding peace in your heart does not require the last weapon to be put down. It requires you not seeing the barriers others see.

Today, I will show you how to find the peace in your heart.

The world will only have peace when individuals make the choice to put peace in their own hearts.

No one has to wait for World Peace to enjoy a peaceful heart. In fact, as they wait, the world will never achieve peace.

To achieve World Peace we need to find the peace in our own hearts. Each of us can find peace within our own hearts at any time. We cannot make the world be at peace, but we can make our world at peace with a peaceful heart which leads to feelings of peace and love and unity with all.

Politicians and soldiers cannot put peace in individual hearts. Each of us has the power to do that in our own heart, now. Even when the governments declare peace, there is no peace unless and until peace resides in the hearts. Look at the US civil war . . . there are still those who do not have peace in their hearts over this yet I do not believe anyone remains alive in the body they inhabited during that conflict . . . because they have been taught not to be peaceful in their hearts regarding that.

As we move toward finding peace in our own heart, wonderful things happen in our lives.

No one can stop you from having peace in your heart now, except yourself.

It is your choice.

I chose peace as soon as I understood this and love living in peace with the world. Bless you.

Superficial happiness will not get you anywhere close but deep and stable happiness can and will bring you within reach of finding peace in your own heart because the path to both is the same. It is about understanding what you can and cannot control and not needing others to be different to validate your worth or value.

Once I chose peace, peace came to live in my heart.

My focus on peace brought me to words I had not seen before:

World peace must develop from inner peace. Peace is not just mere absence of violence. Peace is, I think, the manifestation of human compassion.
Dalai Lama XIV

And later still, I found this one:

Peace is not merely a distant goal that we seek, but a means by which we arrive at that goal.
Martin Luther King, Jr.

And then this one:

Each one has to find his peace from within. And peace to be real must be unaffected by outside circumstances.
Mahatma Gandhi

When you are proclaiming peace with your lips, be careful to have it even more fully in your heart.
St. Francis of Assisi

Education will help bring peace, but it must be the right kind of education.

Education that empowers individuals to believe in themselves, not only in their own worth and capabilities, but that as magnificent as they are, all others are magnificent beings as well. Our differences strengthen the whole.

Years ago, here in the South where I make my home, there was a blight on the American Chestnut trees which were once dominant in our forests. Other varieties of trees were not affected by the blight that eradicated vast areas of trees that once provided food and shelter to humans and animals. If only American Chestnut trees had existed, if we had not had the variety of trees… today there would be no trees.

Just like the trees, our variety provides great strength.

We need to look for the value of the differences we see in one another.

Does the Chestnut tree deride the Walnut tree for not making Chestnuts?

No, the Chestnut tree knew it was a Chestnut tree. It was a great tree.

Walnut trees are not diminished by the greatness of Chestnut trees, Walnut trees are great at being Walnut trees.

The only reason we want others to be like us is because we are insecure in who we are.

When we ask others to believe as we do, look as we do, act as we do, we are really asking them to validate our choices.

When we begin to understand that the blessings that come from the differences, the different perspectives, the different thought patterns, the different actions, and the different appearances are of far greater value than any value there is in sameness, we will be ready to embrace who we are fully. We will be free to express who and what we are.

Many believe that there is danger in someone being different.

They do not understand that the real danger lies in attempting to make everyone conform to a set mold.

We did not come into this life to be copycats.

We came to create ourselves anew and explore our potential.

At our very cores, we are all the same.

At our cores we are all benevolent and loving beings.

It is when we are constrained and held captive to expectations that limit us that we become less than loving.

When an individual is truly happy, they want others to share that happiness.

Science shows this again and again in their research.

It is the rules and constraints of society that create the behaviors we are attempting to prevent with the rules.

A circular malfeasance is being created and only deeper knowledge will release the masses from the ever tightening circle.

No one is trapped within that circle when they realize they control whether or not they will abide there, but most have been trained that they must remain in the circle that the pressure mounts within them creating stress and discord.

Look for the beauty and potential in all others.

It is always there, just as it is always within you.

Your inability to see your potential is your own self-created limitation.

Failure to see the beauty and potential in all others speaks about who you are Being in the moment; not about them.

Most self-created limitations are the acceptance of limiting beliefs and false premises that others teach us.

Examine your beliefs and their basis.

What must be true for your beliefs to be true?

We have to see the world as we want it to be, in order to inspire it to be that which we desire.

As we move toward finding peace in our own heart wonderful things happen in our lives.

No one can stop you from having peace in your heart now, except yourself.

It is your choice.

I am often very aware of the energetic differences in things and just that small change shifts the energy considerably.

Some time ago I made a decision that we live in a benevolent universe.

Einstein had a quote about this, "You can make conscious decisions to believe that you live in a benevolent universe or that you live in an evil place." He followed the quote with an explanation that the decision will determine your actions. If you live in a benevolent universe your actions will reflect that and if you live in an evil place you will do things like build bombs.

What do you believe about the world you live in?

I find that Henry Ford was exactly right "Whether you believe you can or you can't, you are right" meaning that your life reflects the truth of your own, personal beliefs back to you.

Since making the decision that I live in a benevolent universe (complete with a higher power that is not only very aware of each of us, but flowing the goodness we will allow to us) my life has become much better.

Since deciding that people are good at their core even people who are not always nice to others are nice to me. They sense on some level that I see the truth of them—the goodness that is the core of their Being—and that is the part of them that responds to me. There have even been times when I could see their own confusion as to why they were being so polite to me.

So, I am not saying that people are the same on the surface but there exists a part of all of us that desires peace and when we approach one another from that deep place we can find common ground from which progress may be made.

What, after all, is our goal?

Is it progress towards peace, or having everyone perceive the world the same as we do.

I submit it is the former and that the later becomes inconsequential when peace is achieved.

Reach for peace in your heart—in that innermost place where your most cherished dreams reside. Think of a moment when you felt at peace. Perhaps when you held an infant in your arms, when you were held by a loved one after making love, as you watched the sun rise or set over a pristine naturally beautiful place, or when you petted a beloved pet. Hold that feeling consciously and remind yourself that you are love—your essence is love. Your natural state is one of peace. Hold that feeling and tell yourself that it is possible to keep that peaceful feeling alive and vibrant in your heart.

Practice feeling the peace in your heart until all you have to do is reach gently for it. If you find yourself following old habits of thought that are not peaceful, allow yourself to return to the feeling of peace within you and feel it erase the discord you are feeling toward another.

The more you practice feeling peaceful toward others the easier it will become. You do not have to wait for them to reciprocate. The more stable peace becomes in your heart the more others will be aware of it. Even before you speak of it, many will feel the peaceful nature of your being. The way people respond to you will change. People will be more comfortable in your presence and will seek to spend time with you.

Relinquish hate.

Relinquish the need to control others.

Control yourself by practicing feeling the peace that is at the core of you, feel the peace that longs to be vivid in this world of ours.

Believe that the hearts of everyone has the same desire, even if the person has so many layers of negative emotion they cannot feel any peace—know that it is always there, eternal, and that it never dies. See it for them when they cannot. Know the goodness that resides at the core of everyone, including yourself. "At the interpersonal level… positive emotions increase people's sense of 'oneness' with close others." [668]

See peace as a living, breathing energy that wants to grow and fulfill its destiny.

Peace be upon you forevermore.

Part 4 — Toolkit

Provides processes that individuals can use to feel better from any emotional state.

33 : Processes (How to Think Positive)

Today, you have the opportunity to transcend from a disempowered mindset of existence to an empowered reality of purpose-driven living. Today is a new day that has been handed to you for shaping. You have the tools, now get out there and create a masterpiece.
Steve Maraboli

If all you're going to do is read this chapter, you might as well skip it and go do something you enjoy doing. The information in the earlier chapters was designed to help you be more open to new information and give you an understanding of how your thoughts, beliefs, emotional state, expectations, and focus work together to create the life you experience in each moment. The techniques and processes that follow are designed to help you implement the changes you want to make in the filters your brain uses that exert so much influence over your life.

Reading through them the first time through is fine. But if you want to make progress and thrive more in any area of your life, you have to do more than read them. You have to put them into action.

Not all processes designed to improve mood are created equally. I separate processes into three distinct categories. In reality, all you really need is to understand your Emotional Guidance and how to accurately interpret the meaning of your emotions. The processes help you use your Emotional Guidance, especially in the early days. The ideal outcome is consistent use until your automatic responses support your highest good. How long that takes will vary by individual.

Some people have lived a lot of trauma and drama, they've had repeated bouts of depression and maybe other physical, mental, or behavioral health issues. They can get to the point where their automatic processes support thriving. In fact, for some of them it is easier to achieve than for those whose lives have been more sedate—because they want it more.

Where you are is not what matters. What matters is using your Emotional Guidance until you become aware in the early stages when you've veered off the straightest path to where you want to go. When you make corrections early, you return to feeling good faster. The processes are very helpful in moving toward better-feeling states and reinforcing those states when you're there. There is even one process that can halt negative thoughts in their tracks even when you can't find anything good to think.

Read the processes, study them, understand which ones work best in different emotional states, then begin using them. The goal is not how many processes you do, the goal is feeling better. First you'll understand the processes intellectually. As you begin using them you will learn how it feels when you move to better-feeling emotional states on purpose. You'll feel your own power, perhaps for the first time, to decide for yourself how you want to feel instead of letting your circumstances or others dictate how you should feel.

Some processes provide immediate relief from negative emotions. Others assist in reprogramming neural pathways using beliefs you decide will serve your highest good. Some of the processes have little long-term effect; others have profound long-term effects.

At some point, you'll begin experiencing epiphanies. It may begin happening right away or it may take months before the first epiphany shows up. Typically they'll surprise you with a sudden leap in your understanding of something from your past or something that is going on now, or maybe a deeper understanding of a behavior pattern you've had for a long time. Any area of your life where you could understand at a deeper level has the potential to show up as an epiphany.

The important thing is what you do when it does. Typically, epiphanies represent a leap forward in your understanding that you were ready to take. As soon as you possibly can, stop and explore the information revealed to you in the epiphany. Journal about it or discuss it with a supportive friend. You want to assimilate the information into your personal knowledge base as much as possible and the best time to do that is when you're in the emotional state and mindset that brought the epiphany to you. If you can't stop right then, don't stress about it. One time I was in a meeting and I excused myself and just sent myself a brief text message to help me anchor the information.

In the days following an epiphany reinforce the new awareness by thinking about it at least daily. I've had students who had lived very traumatic pasts who reached a point where they were experiencing numerous epiphanies a day for a period of time.

Don't reach for epiphanies. They come easiest when you're just open to new information and in a calm, accepting state of mind. Some people were not trained to believe so many false premises. You may have an epiphany that seems huge to you and it is something someone else has always known. That's okay. This is your journey. Comparing your journey to that of someone else is not productive, regardless of whether the comparison makes you look good or bad. We all know things that others do not know and everyone else knows things we don't know. That's okay. It will never be otherwise.

Anyone can learn the skills and techniques but it is a learning process. I've met people who have been taught to ignore their emotions so much that developing the ability to feel how they feel is the hardest part of their journey. It's a really important first step because not feeling your emotions is suppression, which is associated with many negative outcomes in physical, mental, and behavioral health.

The three categories of processes are:

How to Think Positive (Root Cause Stress Relief)
- The best: provides unlimited beneficial long-term changes to your automatic responses to stressful situations
- Helps you become more optimistic
- Increases chronic emotional state
- Betwixt and Between Processes and Techniques
- The second best: consistent use leads to beneficial long-term changes
- Dose-dependent Stress Management Techniques
- Provide the least long-term benefit but are the fastest short-term solution: dose-dependent and does not change your baseline emotional set point or your automatic response.
- Use as needed until you've changed your automatic processes by using other techniques.

Conscious effort and repetition of the processes in this category is not required forever because your automatic responses will eventually become more supportive of your ability to thrive. It's sort of like learning to drive a car or even to walk—at first you must consciously think about every aspect, but eventually you'll automatically just feel better. The back story your mind creates to explain situations will feel better the first time so you'll spend less time reframing.

Once you become comfortable changing your perspective to shift your mood, it is easier to do it even when faced with a new stressful life event. Staying with the car analogy, if you know how to drive on the right side of the road (USA style) it is easier to learn a different way of driving, such as on the left side, than learning to drive from the beginning was.

Many of the processes that are automatic, such as turning on your blinker when you're going to make a turn, are still automatic.

The processes that change your neuropathways change the filters in your brain in ways that make your default setting more supportive of a life that feels good. In time, you won't have to think about using a technique to reduce your stress in situations you once found stressful, you will automatically have a perspective that is less stressful to you. As discussed in earlier chapters, your brain filters reality based on your beliefs, expectations, emotional stance, and focus. Your automatic response to things in your life will be consistent with your chronic emotional state and reinforce that emotional state. The back story your brain creates reinforces your emotional state. When you begin spending a lot of time in the Sweet Zone, your automatic response will help keep you there. Once you shift your chronic emotional stance and understand how much power you actually have to adjust your emotional response to a situation by changing your perspective, you will seldom have an automatic response below the Hopeful Zone.

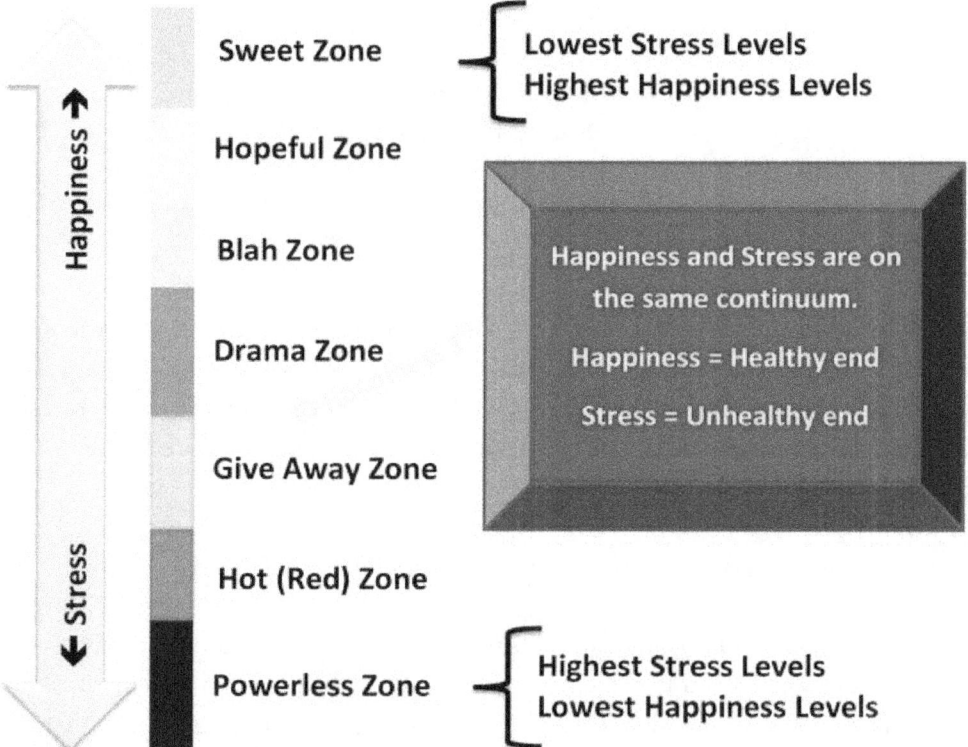

Some people object to an optimistic outlook or a Pollyannaish perspective. The research is clear that less stress is better for us in every area of life. It is helpful to realize that stress and happiness are essentially opposite ends of the same continuum.

This translates into real benefits. The happy person lives in a different world than the stressed person.

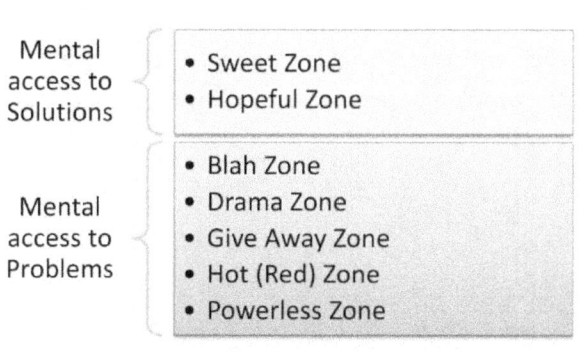

The way the brain of the same person interprets reality when the person is happy is very different from the way the person interprets reality when he is stressed. The happier the person is, the more her interpretation of reality differs from her interpretations when she is stressed.

Remember: Research demonstrates lower stress levels benefit you and everyone you interact with in many ways, including benefits that increase the potential for thriving and decrease the risk of unhealthy choices and negative life events.

Better:	Less likely to:
Immune system function in your body	Abuse drugs
Relationships	Abuse alcohol
Endocrine system function in your body	Commit a crime
Digestive function in your body	Commit suicide
Cognitive abilities	Bully others
Treatment of others, including strangers	Be bullied
Energy level	Develop eating disorders
Sleep habits	Smoke
Lifestyle habits	Develop chronic health issues
Long-term career success	Divorce
Resilience	Become depressed
Self-efficacy	Develop heart disease
Healthier Self-esteem	Have a pre-term delivery
Intrinsic motivation	Have a child who has asthma
Creativity	

When thinking about problems, it is not that the person with a positive mindset ignores the problem so much as it is that the positive mind has access to the solutions. A positively focused person may not see the problem—not because they don't understand the situation—but because they see it as an opportunity, not a problem. When something goes wrong, you'll see the silver-lining faster. You'll be more resilient.

One of Einstein's well-known quotes is:
We cannot solve our problems with the same thinking we used when we created them.

Our emotional state reflects the quality of our thinking (measured in terms of our ability to thrive). The same person will think different thoughts about the same situation when they are in different emotional zones. This is what Einstein is referencing in this quote. When your emotional state is higher, your mind will have thoughts that provide solutions. When you are in a lower emotional state, the thoughts you think will be focused on the problem and you may not be able to perceive a solution.

Training and experience can help you find solutions to problems but the confidence the training and/or experience provides increases your emotional state. If you have a history of successfully solving problems, you're more likely to be in the Hopeful Zone or higher when you become aware of a new problem.

One example that has helped many people realize the truth of this relationship between emotional state and problems is when they recognize that it was when they took a break—whether it was a vacation, a walk, a nap, or a shower that the solution suddenly occurred to them.

I hope that the above information has soothed any fears you may have developed about being positively focused. You will still see problems and you will still take the necessary steps to resolve them. What you won't do is catastrophize the problem, or allow it to derail your life. You won't ruminate about it and you are far less likely to lose sleep over it, which increases your ability to solve the problem because your brain is well-rested. The following processes directly address the root cause of stress, providing each individual who practices them a level of emotional agility that will make them more resilient, increase their emotional intelligence, and provide the other benefits listed above.

> *When you find yourself feeling negative emotion about somebody else, recognize it as a situation where a Right Response would serve you well.*

The Smart Way changes the filters your brain uses to process information before you are consciously aware of it. But you decide how to adjust the filters. Also remember, your filters are already programmed. For almost everyone, this means that your current default settings are based on your early life experience up to about age six. That is great news because it typically means deliberately shifting the filters will provide you with significant life enhancing results.

The following processes help you adjust the filters your mind uses and are effective methods of managing stress.

> *One important aspect not usually considered by most teachers is that the specific process that will be most effective varies due to the current emotional state. There are other variables, but this one always matters.*

In an earlier chapter, I mentioned that many commonly recommended happiness increasing/stress reducing techniques can be counter-productive. That's why, in the description for each process, I indicate what emotional state(s) the exercise is most suitable for. By now, you probably realize that in many cases the mental attitude is what determines whether the process is productive or counter-productive.

The purpose of the processes is to help you move up the EGSc and achieve the health, well-being, relationship, and success benefits that naturally occur when we are in higher zones. The EGSc is provided in Appendix I for reference.

Follow Your Guidance

If you learn how to follow your EGS, you can reach sustainable happiness without learning any other processes. The other processes are tools that can assist you in finding the better-feeling perspectives your guidance is leading you to, but they are not necessary if you simply learn to understand and follow your guidance.

1. The first step is awareness that we have guidance.
2. The second is setting an intention to hear its messages.
3. The third is listening to the messages—they are often subtle.
4. Correctly interpreting your guidance

In the beginning, we may only recognize that we received guidance in hindsight after we did not act upon it. The key here is not to beat ourselves up for failing to recognize it—that does not serve anyone. Recognizing we had guidance and did not heed it is a gift. It allows us to remember how it felt when we became aware of the guidance we overlooked, giving us a greater ability to realize the next time that those subtle messages are guidance.

Emotional Guidance works just like the child's game, *Hot* or *Cold*. While it does feel different to move from despair to anger than from anger to frustration, or from hope to passion, each of these steps is a step in the right direction; each is *getting warmer*.

The common element of any mental change in the right direction is that a feeling of relief (a releasing of tension or stress) is felt. The emotion that is in the *warmer* direction always feels better than emotions that are *getting colder*.

Emotions are responses to thoughts. Thinking about something pleasing (past, present, or future) will create *getting warmer* Emotional Guidance. Thinking about something unpleasant (past, present, or future) will create *getting colder* Emotional Guidance. Everyone has the ability to make the choice to think about someone or something and focus on an aspect that feels good or an aspect that feels bad. The Emotional Guidance system provides feedback to each thought.

Emotional Guidance leads to better feeling emotions, whether it is away from fear in a harmful environment or toward becoming the most we can imagine being.[669]

For many the hardest part of learning to follow the Emotional Guidance system is overcoming the conflicting instructions they received throughout life to use the opinions, expectations, and desires of others as guidance. The personal guidance provided by the Emotional Guidance sensory feedback system includes our goals in the order of importance the individual has assigned to them. On the surface it sounds very selfish, but an individual whose goals include being loving or respectful to others will be guided in a way that takes your goals about good relationships with others into consideration.

> *Adjusting your thoughts toward better-feeling perspectives will provide the most benefit to you.*

If you put your interests lower than those of others you become sacrificial and may become apathetic toward life because you won't be experiencing the joy of moving toward becoming who you want to become. When you do for others because it fulfills your personal goals (i.e. I take good care of my child because I want a good relationship with her or I am pleasant to my co-workers because it feels better to be nice than to be unkind) there is no sense of giving up what you want in order to please another so resentment does not build and keeping score about who has done more for the other makes no sense because you didn't do anything for someone else—you did it for yourself and it happened to benefit someone else.

You have to understand that being good and doing good feel really good when you are being good or doing good because it is what you want to do. Being good and doing good can lead to resentment when you feel forced, coerced, manipulated into, or other extrinsic motivations for your words or actions. Think about a time when you were forced to apologize to someone when you did not feel it. How would that have felt different if you had apologized simply because you want to live in peace and harmony with others?

It is able to guide you to situations that satisfy two views that seem opposing and irreconcilable when viewed rationally. In one case, a couple vehemently disagreed on where they wanted to live. The husband (Sam) wanted to live with less than a 15-minute commute and he worked in Los Angeles, California. The wife (Colette) wanted to live in an area surrounded by nature. They went to lunch one day and had yet another discussion about their seeming conflicting desires. They decided their relationship was more important than where they lived, but neither was willing to compromise. After lunch they went for a walk and when they passed a real estate office, both felt an urge to go in. They had not taken action on finding a new home because of their unresolved conflict about what they wanted.

They weren't sure why they were there because they did not want to fight about it again and neither was ready to compromise. A realtor (Sue), was getting off the phone with a client who had just agreed to list her property with her when Sam and Colette walked into the office. Sue invited the couple to sit down.

After introductions, Sue asked what she could do for them. Sam indicated Colette should go first. Colette explained their dilemma, including where Sam worked. Sue began laughing so hard she was clutching her belly. Sam and Colette looked at one another, thinking this was a sign that their problem could not be resolved. They began to stand when Sue uttered, "No. Please stay." as she brought her laughter under control.

Wiping tears from her eyes, Sue explained, "I'm sorry for my outburst. I've been in the real estate business for over twenty years in Los Angeles. I have not seen a property like that in more than a decade, until today. This morning I met with a woman whose house backs up to a nature preserve. The land is in a Nature Conservancy so it will never be developed." Looking at Sam, she continued, "I believe it is about 12 minutes from your office."

As Sam and Colette began grinning, she said, "I was on the phone with her when you came in. She just listed the house with me. If the house and price are agreeable, it looks like you have perfect timing." Your guidance can be like that, inclinations and urges that don't seem to make sense have led me to some of the best experiences of my life. They have also saved me from harm on more than one occasion. It has guided some of the best decisions I've ever made.

There also seems to be something at work that I cannot explain fully. Research supports my observations. I have seen many people use these techniques to improve their chronic emotional set point and their desire for others to be happy always seems to increase in tandem with their increases in happiness. Researchers have been able to show that happier people are kinder[670] to others, display less racism,[671] and are better corporate citizens. In general, they have better relationships with others. To anyone who is concerned about how this seems to have a selfish focus, I encourage you to trust the process.

Remember, that as Adam Smith said, "It is not from the benevolence of the butcher, the brewer, or the baker that we expect our dinner, but from their regard to their own interest."

I would also remind you that the commonly used Biblical saying is not "Love thy neighbor," it is "Love thy neighbor <u>as thyself.</u>" Many teachers throughout the ages have encouraged us to love and respect our self because most people will treat us no better than we treat ourselves. I have seen this in my own life. The more I respect myself the more I am respected. The more I treat myself kindly, the more others treat me kindly. This is true when you love yourself and it is true when you don't. Others treat you much the way you treat yourself.

The rational mind is not just filtered by beliefs. Expectations, emotional stance, and focus have a tremendous impact. That is one reason it is so hard for someone who has been in a chronic unhappy state to move to a better-feeling state using the rational mind. Habits of thought, like other habits, take time to change. Using the EGS as a guide to better-feeling thoughts, the rational mind is able to be reconditioned to support better-feeling emotional stances.

Our upbringing can have a significant effect on our ability to feel what emotion we are feeling. Some people were trained from young ages that being emotional was bad behavior. In many cases, emotions have been suppressed and these individuals may have a more difficult time labeling their emotions. However, this person will feel relief when a better-feeling thought is felt. Reaching for a feeling of relief will enable an individual with difficulty figuring out which zone he is in on the EGSc to use his guidance.

33 : Processes (How to Think Positive)

To love one's Self is not boastful
It is healthy to the core
All of our misery comes from
The fact we need to love more
Never too much love is possible
Can't happen, can never be true
Pour love into everything
In all we think, say and do
The healing elixir of every heart
Is the giving and being of Love
When we open ourselves to this Light
As below becomes as above.
Janine Jansma

Both affirmations and setting intentions can help the individual who has subdued emotions to become more aware of them. Even individuals who have not been conditioned to suppress their emotions become more aware of subtle differences as they gain experience using their EGS.

Some affirmations that could be helpful:

I will recognize my emotional response to my thoughts.
I will be aware as soon as my thoughts take my emotional state to a less comfortable one so that I can make adjustments early.
I am safe feeling my emotions because I have tools to help me find thoughts that will allow me to feel good.
My emotions affect my behavior. My job is to feel good so I'll be good.
I am strong. I am invincible. I am (fill in the blank with something that resonates with you)

It is important to only use affirmations that you believe are achievable. If you find your inner critic arguing with an affirmation, it will not help you. Try to affirm something that is less different from what you are already doing while you work on evicting the inner critic.

That critic is probably the result of someone who loved you but thought their job was to improve you. It may be a worse situation than that, although that is one of the most common sources of the inner critic that plagues so many people. It is not necessary to deride where you are before you can decide you want to be or do something different. It is perfectly acceptable to be good just as you are but want to become something better. There is no fault to be had in not yet having achieved the better you want to become. We are always in a state of becoming. As soon as humans reach a goal, we're planning our next one—sometimes we have more than one goal at a time. It's all okay. No matter how good someone becomes, they still find things they want to improve. It does not mean there is anything wrong with who they are—it only means they have the potential to be more.

It is critical that you allow yourself permission to feel whatever you feel. If you feel guilty about how you feel, guilt is low on the EGS. You can't move to great feeling zones if you feel guilty. You feel what you feel. What you feel is valid, from your current perspective. From your current perspective, what you feel is the appropriate response. From your current perspective, what you feel is what you can feel. You cannot change how you feel about the situation without changing your perspective. Doing so will make you sick.

Your current perspective is valid and right, from how you are perceiving the situation in this moment. That does not mean it is the only valid perspective about the topic. It does not mean it is the only perspective you can have bout the topic. It does not mean the perspective is true or right. It certainly does not mean it is the perspective that is best for your health, relationships, career, or overall well-being. In fact, if you feel anything less than excited expectation, joy, love, or appreciation, there is a perspective that is more supportive of your highest good.

That being said, do not beat yourself up for not being in that high emotional state. The path to feeling better does not include self-criticism or beating oneself about the head and shoulders with negativity. The path is one that supports you in becoming all you can become never requires condemnation of where you are, even if in your current perspective there are awful behaviors.

Step #1 only requires recognition that you have guidance.

It helps if you accept that you have a desire to feel better.

I'm seeing a lot of push back against what some are calling the Happiness Movement. When I read the details, it always seems to be someone who has come to believe they should be happy because they have a good life, but they aren't happy. They are *should-ing* themselves to lower emotional states. There is no *should* about how you feel. You could be married to a very attractive person who is very good to you, live in a house many dream about, have 2.5 perfect children, the exact pet you always wanted, perfect health, a great career or a fat bank account, and an attractive physic and be legitimately unhappy. If you're focused on something you don't have, or on those who do not yet have what you have, if you believe you have too much, or you believe the other shoe will drop any day, or you are focused on a tragedy that has happened to others you consider your in-group, or something that is happening to animals, or on someone who left you or died, or you did something you are beating yourself up over, or you feel guilty about something from your past, or you feel like you don't deserve what you have or that they'll figure out you're an imposter and not the person who they thought you were and on and on and on, you'll be unhappy. You're not focused on something that feels good. Of course you're unhappy. You could be happy. But you get to choose. Frequently, you're violating what Dr. Robert Holden calls your personal Happiness Contract. I refer to is as believing a false premise. Just believing you *should* be happy is a false premise. You could be happy—that's true. But don't *should* all over yourself.

It is also common for people to ask me, "How can I be happy when X is happening?" in reference to a tragedy somewhere in the world. First, using that analogy, no one ever could have been happy because our world has never had a time when there weren't awful things happening somewhere. Even if all the countries were at peace, how could we know whether the atrocities that occur in homes had stopped?

But an even more important point to consider is the research that demonstrates our cognitive abilities are better when we're in a better emotional state. So, if you really want to do something about bad things happening in the world, you'll get happy first so that you'll bring your best cognitive power to the table. The point that being happy first causes success[672] is so important, I named my company Happiness 1st Institute.

Beyond that, we live in a world where the resources we can apply to world problems seem limited. The research on optimism demonstrates that increasing optimism has significant potential to reduce many of the serious problems facing our time including most chronic diseases, crime, teen pregnancy, addictions, violence, and more. The cost of teaching children and adults the techniques outlines in this book is low. By moving ahead with that step, the problems that optimism provides protection against will decrease substantially, thus freeing resources to deal with the remaining issues.

33 : Processes (How to Think Positive)

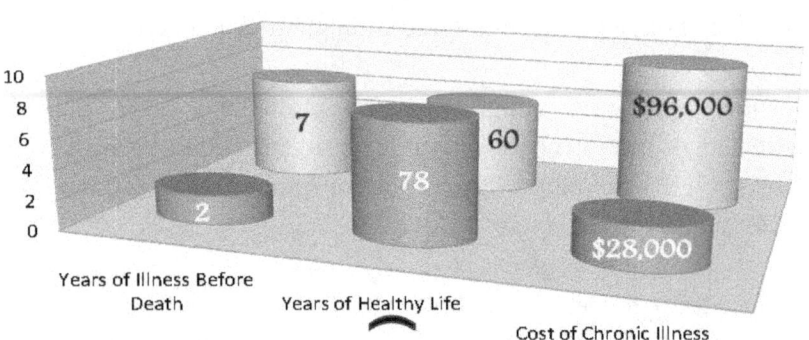

Optimists
2 years chronic & debilitating illness prior to death
78 healthy years of life
$28,000 cost of chronic illness care

Pessimists
7 years chronic & debilitating illness prior to death
60 years of healthy life
$96,000 cost of chronic illness care

We know optimism can be learned. Researchers have shown the old myths about personality being fixed traits were wrong. Personality traits are not fixed,[673, 674, 675, 676] "much of personality is a flexible and dynamic thing . . . it also includes the way one perceives self, others, and events."[677] Changes toward increasing negativity increases mortality in older men. A study of 1663 men showed that neuroticism (fear, anxiety, moodiness, worry, envy, frustration, loneliness, and jealousy) that increased with age significantly increased the risk of mortality (40% over a decade).[678] Recent research by Paulus, Vanwoerden, Norton and Sharp found that neuroticism was associated with psychological inflexibility, lack of emotion regulation strategies, and shame.[679] Participants in the same study that had goal-directed behavior, psychological flexibility, and emotion regulation strategies were able to reduce or avoid neuroticism tendencies. *The Smart Way* teaches individuals how to regulate emotion regardless of the emotional state they are currently experiencing. It also increases psychological flexibility by encouraging viewing circumstances from multiple perspectives. When Emotional Guidance is used to direct thoughts, it becomes clear that refuting shame is supported by one's Emotional Guidance.

Step # 2 is knowing you can move to perspectives that feel better. You can't jump from awful to terrific in one fell swoop. It takes baby steps. But it does not take long between first baby steps and running. A baby step, followed by a baby step, followed by a baby step, with your EGS supporting you every step of the way, saying, "Yes, come this way. That's right. Good." via emotional responses that feel better as you take those steps will help you build confidence.

> *How you feel will improve with every step along the way.*

When you have developed confidence, you can begin moving faster. You begin trusting that changing perspective has rewards—sometimes great rewards. You begin accepting the new perspectives faster because you're no longer doubting the process. Once that happens you're off and running. You're still not leaping tall buildings—you're still going one step at a time, but the time between steps can be so short that on a single subject you can move from very disempowered to empowered in under an hour. Don't beat yourself up if you're not at this speed yet. If you have trouble with this, compare yourself to your prior self, comparing how it used to take months to move as far as you can now shift in a day.

Even if you forget for a while on a subject and wallow in negativity, you still know the process, at any time you can decide to begin the process on a sore subject. It is not about beating yourself up if you do not immediately apply the process to every area of your life. In fact, don't start with your biggest issue. Start with small things and build your confidence. Then, when you tackle the bigger areas they will be far easier than you expected. What sort of big things can seem easy? With practice, the list is endless. It definitely includes facing an abuser and finding inner peace about the past, divorces that were devastating at the time, the loss of a child, unexpected heartbreak, loss of a job, overcoming long-term PTSD, beating chronic depression, reducing/eliminating fears that limit your life, and more.

You will also find that when you fix a problem in one area, it often helps in many other areas. A frustrating focus manifests in myriad ways throughout your day. It can include inept store clerks or waitresses, or inept driver's in front of you who fail to move when the light is green, it can involve teachers who seem to do things the hard way—whether it is letting you know the day before your child has to have something that you have to go to the store to buy or who mandate a field trip you have to take that conflicts with prior plans. It can include a manager at work who schedules you three weeks in advance on an important day you want off, but the policy does not allow you to request time-off more than two weeks in advance. It can involve someone putting the spaghetti back in the cupboard so when you pick it up, it all spills on the floor—the last box, now spread all over the floor instead of in the boiling pot on the stovetop—ten minutes before company is due to arrive.

When you move to a less frustrating zone, you will feel inspired actions that let you know the spaghetti is not in the cupboard correctly before it spills, you'll feel instincts to change lanes and not be behind the frustrating driver, you'll have a casual conversation with your manager where you mention the important date and she makes a note not to schedule you that day or allows you to go ahead and put in more than two weeks in advance. When you begin doing this deliberate work to shift your emotional state, it almost feels magical. I can talk about it for days—you will not really understand until you do the work yourself. When you experience the difference it makes, you'll feel more empowered.

Remember, the filters in our brain are designed as if we understand how they work. They literally hide information that is inconsistent with how they are programmed—whether it is in our best interest or not. They are not malicious or vindictive or determining our deservability (worthiness)—we do that. The filters only carry out their programming. Conscious programming is of enormous value.

Your Emotional Guidance provides reliable guidance and is appropriate when you are in any emotional state.

Subtle Differences

The way you experience every moment of your life is a result of many factors, but one of the factors you have more potential to control than you use is your emotional state. To demonstrate the difference, I'm going to write about the same experience twice and present them together. In one, your emotional state is the result of your observations about the situation and your emotional reaction to those perceptions about your situation. In the second experience, you take a few moments here and there to soothe yourself about disliked elements of your current situation. You've purchased new software for your computer and it's time to install it.

You're feeling a bit frustrated. You'd rather buy a new computer than upgrade this one but you don't feel you can justify a new computer right now.

You insert the CD into the drive to do the upgrade. You should be done in about five minutes and you're looking forward to using this new photo editing software.

The little bar appears that indicates the software is loading but then it seems to stop, stuck about ¼ of the way. The computer hums for a while, with no progress showing then a pop-up appears that says, "This software is not compatible with your operating system."

Your frustration spikes and you do that thing you do when you're beginning to feel a little anger. *Your emotional state is not pleasant but you don't do anything specific to change it. If your spouse or child shows up during this time the interaction will be less than you want it to be. You may say something that is unpleasant or give them less time than you want to. You may even be ugly to yourself in your own mind, "How could I not notice this software would not work with my operating system? I'm so dumb." If your relationship with your spouse is not supportive, your spouse may say this to you.*

You're feeling a bit frustrated. You'd rather buy a new computer than upgrade this one but you don't feel you can justify a new computer right now. *You tell yourself this is just a temporary situation and soon you'll be able to have a new computer. In the overall scheme of things, life is good. Your family is healthy and you have a lot of hopes and dreams you're looking forward to.*

You insert the CD into the drive to do the upgrade. You should be done in about five minutes and you're looking forward to using this new photo editing software.

The little bar appears that indicates the software is loading but then it seems to stop, stuck about ¼ of the way. The computer hums for a while, with no progress showing then a pop-up appears that says, "This software is not compatible with your operating system."

Your frustration spikes and you do that thing you do when you're beginning to feel a little anger. *You quickly recognize that you're not feeling how you want to feel and deliberately soothe yourself, "I'll figure this out." Or "I've solved other problems with my computer before. This is just going to take a little longer than I wanted it to." After you've soothed yourself, your interactions with family are pleasant because you're not blaming them or yourself for your frustration—it's just something you have to do in order to get what you want—photo editing software you are excited about.*

Your frustration and low level anger have already caused your cognitive processes to constrict. Your thinking is not as clear as you would like them to be. You decide to go back to the computer store and see if you can get photo editing software that will work with your operating system. *You forget that you had plans to go to the new restaurant your spouse wanted to try for lunch.*

You get in the car and begin driving to the computer store. *You're still feeling very frustrated. Traffic seems terrible and that makes you even more frustrated. When the big truck pulls in front of you without using his blinker, you feel a little angry.* You arrive at the computer store safely *but not in a good emotional state.*

The computer store employee who helps

Your emotional state is fluctuating between a little frustration and a feeling of confidence that you'll figure this out. While not where they would be if you were feeling passionate enthusiasm, your cognitive processes are not significantly constricted. You decide to go back to the computer store and see if you can get photo editing software that will work with your operating system. *You remember your plans to have lunch with your spouse and ask if you can go a little early so you can stop at the computer store before lunch. While your spouse gets ready to go, you use a search engine to find several software options that would work with your operating system. You look at the features and identify two that seem as good as the one that you're returning and one that is even better. The even better one is just a few dollars more than you paid for the one that does not work and you begin feeling this situation is not a problem, but a lucky accident.*

You and your spouse get in the car and begin driving to the computer store. You don't notice the traffic. You're enjoying telling your spouse about the better software you found and being happy that things always seem to work out well for you. When the big truck pulls in front of you without using his blinker you notice a bumper sticker on it that makes you laugh out loud and share an inside joke with your spouse. You arrive at the computer store safely *in an optimistic mood.*

you knows how to solve your problem, but he has also been having a frustrating morning, which has caused his cognitive processes to constrict and the information he needs to properly advise you is not available to him while he is focused on problems, which is all he can do in his current emotional state.

The sales clerk doesn't remember what product will solve your problem. He walks out onto the floor with you but every box he picks up is for a newer operating system than you have. He's getting frustrated and begins trying to get you to buy a new computer, which is not in your budget right now and you're already frustrated about that. The two of you walk around, both frustrated and neither accomplishing anything when you hear a text come into your phone. You check your phone and it's your spouse, asking if you forgot your plans to go to lunch together at a restaurant just a few minutes away from the computer store.

You know that if you don't have lunch at the agreed upon time it won't be a pleasant lunch so you tell the sales clerk you have to go and leave for home so you can have lunch with your spouse. Your trip was a waste of time. You still don't have working photo editing software.

You arrive at the restaurant with your spouse, who is not pleased you did not think about going to the computer store together. Your spouse is irritated that you're frustrated because lunch won't be much fun with you in your current mood. Your spouse does nothing to try to uplift you. Instead your spouse piles more reasons to feel bad on your already low emotional state.

Because you just want lunch to be over, you're hyper aware of how attentive the waitress is and she seems slow. The food does not taste as good as you both thought it would. (Food tastes better when you're in a good mood.)

Because neither of you enjoyed lunch very

The computer store employee who helps you knows how to solve your problem, but he has also been having a frustrating morning, which has caused his cognitive processes to constrict and the information he needs to properly advise you is not available to him while he is focused on problems, which is all he can do in his current emotional state.

Because your mood is significantly better, you recognize an opportunity to make him laugh, which improves his mood. The constriction of his cognitive processes eases and he suddenly remembers seeing that the exact product you're asking for, which usually has to be ordered because they don't carry it in the store, in the return area. He checks and someone had ordered it but returned it unopened because their hard drive crashed before it arrived and they bought a new computer instead.

This sales clerk is feeling friendly to you. He was feeling frustrated before you came in but you got him laughing and the two of you are having a good time. He decides to ask his manager if you can have a discount because it is already in the store and if you buy it, they don't have to return it. The manager agrees to give you a 20% discount on the price.

You leave the store with software you're pretty sure will work and you're excited about the additional features and feeling lucky about getting the good deal. With the 20% off the new software was actually less than the one that did not work.

You arrive at the restaurant with your spouse, who is pleased with the deal you got on the software. You're both ready to relax and enjoy a nice lunch together. You're focused on one another, catching up after a busy week. Because you're not in a hurry for lunch to be over and want to focus on your spouse, the waitress seems attentive enough. The food is even better than you both thought it would be. (Food tastes better when you're in a good mood.)

After lunch you leave an extra nice tip for the waitress because you're feeling flush from saving money on the software. Your spouse likes it when much, you leave a miserly tip and on your way out, complain to one another about how disappointed you are with the new restaurant you had been excited to try. You don't recognize you brought your own bad mood to lunch and if you'd changed your mood your lunch would have been much better.

When you get home you decide to give up for now and plop down in front of the TV for the rest of the afternoon.

you're nice to waitresses and squeezes your arm in appreciation of your generosity.

When you get home you install the software and begin learning to use the photo editing software.

This example was very detailed to demonstrate that just a little bit of deliberate tuning of perspective can make a tremendous difference in one's experiences. There was no long drawn out use of processes that took time. There were just deliberate shifts, mostly going more general about the subject.

The left column is a typical early 21st century experience where mood is derived by the current circumstances. When something that is not that big of a deal goes wrong, it adversely affects other things such as restricting cognitive processes. What was not evident in this example, but very important in the overall scheme of things is that immune function also decreased when frustration increased. Over time this has a significant bearing on quality of life. Also, it is not just that food does not taste as good when your mood is lower; the entire digestive function is at less than ideal levels when your mood is lower. Over time this increases the risk of both obesity and diabetes.

The individual on the right is not someone who was introduced to happiness increasing skills today. But within three months of remembering to use the skills by paying attention to how you feel and responding to discord with the process that feels best to you in your current circumstances, the column on the right could be representative of your experience. You've been living life much like the individual in Column 1 does for a long time. Three months is not a long time to wait for significant improvements.

In fact, you don't really have to wait three months. Three months is for the automated responses to begin feeling natural to you. You can have the emotional relief now by using the processes.

Happiness is a thing to be practiced...
...like the Violin.
John Lubbock

Don't be discouraged if the things Column 2 used to soothe frustration are not currently true for you. Life generally reflects the results of your chronic emotional states. As you feel increasingly better, other areas of life will improve, too.

33 : Processes (How to Think Positive)

Shift Your Focus

One of the most critical skills someone who is new to using his Emotional Guidance can develop is being able to deliberately change focus. It is the quickest path to relief in a distressing moment. Numerous techniques effectively help people change focus. In fact, most of the commonly taught *dose-dependent* techniques create a change of focus—that is why they work.[I]

There are two problems with dose-dependent techniques. The first is that they don't address the root cause of the distressing/stressful situation, which is why they are dose-dependent. The second is that research is clear that when people need it the most, they are less likely to use a dose-dependent technique, even when they know it works. In 2014, the American Psychological Association surveyed 2,968 individuals about their stress habits and 43% of the adults reported skipping exercise that they usually did to relieve stress "…because they were too stressed."[680]

Beyond that, the types of activities people reported using to manage stress were not stress relievers, but stress distractors. Ten percent of adults don't do anything to manage stress, 40% report watching two or more hours of television or movies a day to manage stress and 42% go online to manage stress and half that many play video games. Some people are using multiple methods, 43% reported using exercise, but as noted earlier, that same number reported not exercising when they felt too stressed.

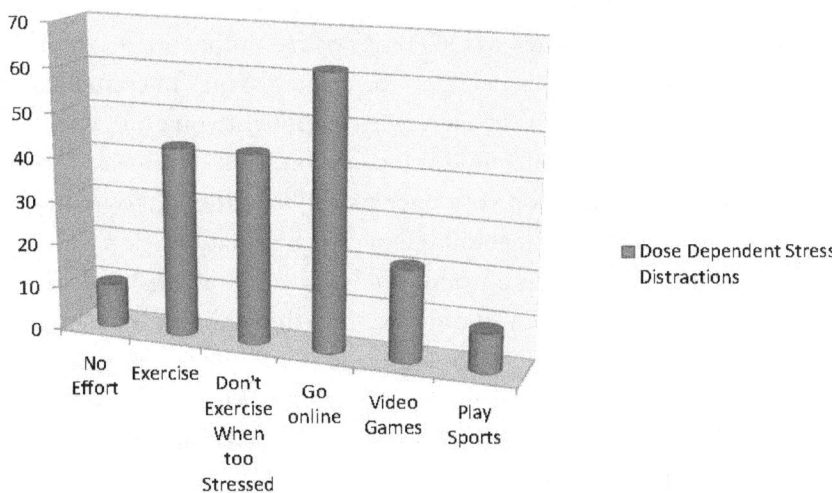

Even though focus change will not change your perception about the things you are stressed about, deliberately changing focus feels empowering. There is a significant difference between burying yourself in a book, watching movies or binging on your favorite show, or playing video games to distract yourself and deliberately choosing to do so with the knowledge that you're distracting yourself on purpose. Before I learned to use my mind to reduce stress using Right Responses, my main form of stress relief was reading. It was no unusual for me to escape into a book every day. I also used exercise at times, but reading was my escape. I used reading to escape both emotional and physical pain.

One time the only way I knew I needed to go to the hospital for the pain I was experiencing was because I could not read through it. I was so accustomed to escaping pain by reading that when I couldn't I knew something serious was wrong. It turns out a salmon bone I had swallowed had put a hole in my colon.

There is nothing wrong with using stress detractors on a temporary basis. To actually manage stress and improve your life, using techniques that change your neural pathways, following your guidance, and using Right Responses will reduce the stress you feel on a daily basis, which translates into more happiness, better health, and better relationships with yourself and others.

[I] Helping others, exercise, being in nature, listening to music, etc. are all methods of shifting focus.

33 : Processes (How to Think Positive)

Changing focus is appropriate for emotional zones on the EGSc below Hopeful. A change of focus creates a distraction from a stressful perspective about the current topic of thought. Changes of focus provide immediate relief from uncomfortable emotions. Unless repeated frequently and consistently, a change of focus does not shift the underlying mindset or emotional stance. For that reason, I recommend changes of focus for immediate relief, but used in combination with techniques that change perspective and/or reprogram your neural pathways to more supportive default settings.

Changing focus is the easiest to achieve. It is quickest and provides immediate emotional relief from high stress/low emotional states. Unless it becomes habitual, it is only an in-the-moment solution.

If an old topic that is just frequently in your mind because you keep remembering it is causing you stress, you may be better served by focusing your thoughts elsewhere as much as possible until you have more experience at this. If a topic with a distressing or less than optimal emotional stance associated with it is one that you encounter often, working your way up the EGSc is the preferred long-term solution. Although changing focus can provide fast relief, if a topic that does not feel good is encountered frequently, using other processes to move up the EGSc on that topic is well worth the effort.

As you learn, it is very helpful to remember that you have neurological pathways that will take you back to old thoughts and old ways of thinking. This is temporary. If you persist in focusing on the new way(s) of thinking your neural pathways will change. If you do not understand that finding yourself back in the old emotional place is a normal part of the growth process that will subside over time, it is easy to give up. This is the reason many people feel their low emotional state is hopeless.

Repetitive thoughts, whether they are assigned a label (such as OCD) or not are simply the result of a neural pathway that is easier to travel due to repetitive use. New paths can be created. You can consciously choose to think about something you want to think about each time a repetitive thought you don't want comes to mind. If you're persistent in changing the subject your mind is focused on, your automatic thoughts will eventually change. Be patient. You did not develop your current habits of thought overnight. There may also be an unconscious decision about what to think about happening but that decision can be made consciously. Our ability to develop automatic processes is a wonderful human characteristic.

Plan in advance what you will think about instead of what you don't want to think about. If necessary, write it down where you have access to it. Some people put post-it notes around their homes reminding them to think about the things they want to think about. Don't write a note that says, "Don't think about X." It will only make you think about it more. Don't write a note that says, "Think about what you want to think about." Be specific. If I were doing that I would write notes like this:

Think about the meadow by Antelope Lake.
Think about the warm sun caressing my body.
Think about floating on the water.
Think about (upcoming trip).

I can ride my bicycle without thinking about pedaling or how to turn the handlebars in the right direction. I can do all of the physical actions, and make decisions about those actions, below my level of conscious awareness while I carry on a conversation with someone riding with me or simply soak up spectacular mountain vistas. I can do it while my mind wanders and even while my mind plots out how to write a book.

But the fact that we can do things on autopilot does not mean we have to. If my leg cramps and pedaling in the usual way is painful, I have the ability to consciously decide to shift my foot on the pedal in a position that provides relief. In the same way, someone who has repetitive thoughts can decide to think about something differently or to think about the same thing in a different way.

If you lived in a house near the woods and took a walk each morning, initially you would probably travel the path with the least amount of brush and branches to move, etc. Perhaps you would follow a deer trail. After a while, walking that path every day would create a larger path that is even easier to walk. If you decided that you wanted to walk a different route it would be more difficult, you would have branches to move, perhaps logs to walk over, possibly thorns protruding into the path, etc. You can do it, but it is easier to walk the existing path. Also, sometimes, when you were not consciously focused on taking the new path you might automatically revert to the old path, and not realize it until you discover yourself quite a ways down the old path. It's not a big deal. Just turn around and walk the new path.

Many of my students relate to this analogy because they've done it at some point in their lives. After moving to a new home or job, they Or perhaps you have moved and found yourself, after a long day at work, automatically heading to your former home after a long day at work or to the old job on a morning when they are tired. It often happens a week or so into the new routine, when they are less conscious about the fact that they are going somewhere different. The new route has not become automated and the old neuropathways kick in. The old neuro circuits are still easier to use than the new route. Eventually your circuits all line up and even when you are on autopilot, you drive to your current residence or new job.

The biggest key is not to be upset when you find your thoughts on the old path. Just recognize where you are and move to where you want to be. Criticizing yourself for being on the old path is counter-productive. When we decide a thought-path no longer serves us we have to clear a little brush to walk a new path but it is worth the effort and it is only difficult at first. The second time is easier than the first and by the 10th; you cannot even recall how difficult it was the first time.

You cannot STOP thinking about something by trying to stop thinking about it because when you try to stop thinking about the thing you don't want to think about, you are thinking about it.

You can, however, decide to think about something else and every time you begin thinking about the topic you don't want to think about have something more pleasant to think about already planned as a diversion.

At first, you will still have the unwanted thoughts a bit, but you will spend less time with them and more time on the more pleasant thoughts.

KNOW that you can change your thoughts, even habitual thoughts. You have control. *You think them; they do not think you.* I would not label repetitive thoughts with a label that gives them more power than they deserve. With consistent effort, everyone can change their thought paths. The more power given to labels, the harder it is to believe in your ability to change and to find the hope that you can do it. Labels have power. Only use the ones you want to keep.

> *One reason developing skills in changing focus is critical is that it is the only type of process a new student can use to change a painful emotional state quickly. For someone who is considering self-harm, the ability to change focus quickly can be lifesaving. At low emotional states, finding a better feeling thought can seem impossible if you have not been taught skills to help you. It can feel as if you'll never feel better. The Focus Shift process empowers you with a way to shift your focus to a better feeling thought when you need it the most.*
>
> *I recommend this process for everyone. It is best prepared for when you are in the Hopeful or Sweet Zone, but the process is actually used when you are emotionally below*

the Hopeful Zone. This process is one of the few that provide quick relief when you are in the Powerless Zone.

Focus Shift—The List

I recommend everyone prepare to use this process in advance. When you are in a good mood, make a list of simple things that make you feel good when you think about them. The list should be things you can actually enjoy—not something you want (like winning the lottery). My list has things like sunrises, sunsets, flowers, babies, little red haired girls, doing something for someone else that makes me feel good when I remember it, and remembering overcoming obstacles in the past. On my list, I also have ice cream to remind myself of a specific time when I felt cared for. There is no right or wrong as long as it is something that makes you feel good when you think about it.

Keep your list in your wallet or purse. If you ever find yourself in an emotional state where you can't think of anything that feels better, all you have to do is remember you have the list. Take it out and look at it.

One time, many years ago, I was in that low place where I was unable to think a single good feeling thought. Remembering the list, but not anything that was on it, I found it in my purse. Reviewing it, there were no babies in the vicinity. It was midafternoon so no sunrises or sunsets were out. Then I saw flowers on the list. It was January, so even my yard lacked flowers. Then I remembered the grocery store has flowers.

I got in the car, drove to the grocery store, and spent about half an hour in the floral section. I admired the flowers, smelled the flowers, enjoyed the pretty colors, and the floral scents. By the time I left the store, my mood was greatly improved. I never again returned to such a low mood, because when my emotional state begins to decline, I take action sooner.

The list must be made when you feel good because that is when you can remember thoughts and memories that feel good to you.

My trip to the grocery store did not change any of the facts of the situation that had caused the low mood in the first place, but by shifting to a higher mood my mind was able to see the situation in a better light. Solutions that were not mentally accessible from the lower emotional state occurred to me once my emotional state felt better.

In the lowest emotional states, changing ones focus is the quickest path to feeling better in the moment. When the mood is that low, the most critical thing anyone can do is find a way to feel better. Sometimes that means sleeping.

Focus is the easiest aspect of our emotional stance to change quickly. Changing beliefs that do not serve us provides more progress, but changing a belief that is at the root of a low emotional state is very difficult when one is at a low emotional state. It is better to work on changing unsupportive beliefs when feeling hopeful or better.

A change of focus is a powerful tool. It is an easy one to practice and can be done under any circumstances.

I recommend this process below the Hopeful Zone and immediately when in the Powerless Zone.

If you are thinking that maybe you'd rather be dead or that those you care about would be better off if you were, call the toll-free, 24-hour hotline of the National Suicide Prevention Lifeline now at 1-800-273-TALK (1-800-273-8255); TTY: 1-800-799-4TTY (4889) to talk to a trained counselor.

Or, **call your doctor**

Dial 911

or go to an emergency room

For a free detailed booklet on depression and its treatment, go to: http://www.nimh.nih.gov/health/publications/depression/complete-index.shtml

International Emergency Numbers

Australia	000	Switzerland	112	UAE	112
New Zealand	111	India	102	Brazil	192
Fiji	000 or 911	Hong Kong	999	Costa Rica	911
United Kingdom	112 or 999	Israel	101 or 112	S. Africa	112, 10 177
Ireland	112 or 999	Japan	119	China	120
Turkey	112	Nepal	102	Philippines	117 or 112

If you are in this low emotional state and are thinking about harming yourself or someone else, **get help now. Call your local emergency number or go to an emergency room.**

Make Happiness a Priority

Everyone has acceptable levels of positive emotion that they will strive to manage their emotional state into, regardless of whether they have the skills to do so or not. Many people with low emotion regulation skills become comfortable in an uncomfortable Zone on the EGSc. If your comfort zone is not really comfortable, making happiness a priority will help you stay focused on learning and using the emotion regulation strategies you learn in these pages to achieve a more comfortable comfort zone.

Pay attention to how you feel. "people with different emotionality standards had equally intense emotions when self-focus was low, yet they differed significantly when self-awareness was high . . . People have intricate sets of standards concerning emotion. Like other standards, they only participate in self-regulation to the extent that attention is oriented internally."[681]

Deliberately Choose Happy Thoughts

These processes are very simple and are recommended for any emotional state below the Sweet Zone. When you're in the Sweet Zone, real life feels better than the process.

Basically, all you have to do is make a decision to deliberately focus on something that feels better. It can be something pleasing from your past, present, or future that creates a *getting warmer* feeling. With practice, the ability to focus oneself into a good feeling state regardless of circumstances can be developed.

Numerous enhancements can be used to give this process more power.

For example, I plan my life so that I always have something to look forward to. Then I intentionally give attention to the anticipated event and savor it now. I love to travel, so it is rare that I do not have a vacation to look forward to enjoying, but I can also enjoy vacations from my past by remembering the best parts of them. A year from now I'll be in Australia again, I'm already enjoying that journey now.

I've learned that planning a vacation further in advance increases my enjoyment of it. I savor the anticipation of it and then enjoy the actual trip. When I have a short planning horizon, the amount of enjoyment I receive from the trip is less.

It does not have to be a vacation. It can be anticipating a holiday with your family, a meal at a special restaurant, finishing a class or an education, reading a good book, an upcoming movie release, the meal on

33 : Processes (How to Think Positive)

the plate in front of you, a bottle of your favorite wine chilling in the refrigerator, a warm fire in the fireplace, a comfortable chair, a good friend, the feel of your body when you stretch, mastering these techniques and feeling in control of your emotional state, and more.

How many times have you eaten a good meal while thinking about something that diminished the experience?

This process is about being aware and deliberately choosing thoughts that feel good. The intention is what makes it a process. Most people simply allow whatever is top of their mind or in front of them to have their attention. We can do better than that—we can choose the object of our attention based on how it feels when we think about it.

Use your guidance to help you recognize when you're not feeling as good as you want to feel. Very few people on the planet today live their lives with as much happiness and joy as they could with just a little effort. I'm watching my youngest daughter employ some of the processes and philosophy I teach. She is catching herself sooner when she starts telling a story about what she does not like and deliberately switching the topic, sometimes mid-sentence, to one that feels better to talk about.

It is perfectly okay to change the subject or even withdraw from a conversation that is focused on something you do not want to think about. I'm not referring to things you may have to deal with at work or other necessary conversations. I'm referring to talking about things that do not have to be shared—the person who cut you off in traffic, the store clerk who was rude, the boss who did not give you time to express your view, the flat tire, the glass full of milk you dropped and broke when you were in a hurry, the sale item you went to purchase that was already sold out, and so many other things that happen to people every day.

If it does not feel good to tell the story or to listen to a story, don't do it. Talk about something that feels better. Redirect the conversation to a topic that will feel better for both of you. Being empathetic with someone who has a frustrating day does not help their frustration and it increases yours. It's far better to change the subject to something they will enjoy thinking about.

Be aware of how much time you give to subject that don't feel good and that aren't necessary to discuss. Even things that may be causing discord in your home life. For example, when my children hit middle school the fights about cleaning their room were becoming routine. It was not fun and our relationships were stressful because of tension. In my house, their rooms are upstairs and mine is downstairs. One of the best decisions I ever made was to withdraw from the fight. They could just close their door and I no longer had to try to control the uncontrollable.

I had been withholding allowing their friends over *until they cleaned their room*. Once I withdrew, I noticed that they would clean their room when they were expecting friends to come over. I did not have to manage their rooms.

It was a great lesson in choosing my battles. Are you focused on what matters?

As an aside, remember there is a saying that "You're never a prophet in your own land." if you're wondering why my daughter is not an expert in this already. I did not know what I know now when I was raising her. When I first began learning it, she saw me as I had always been. She *only* expressed an interest in learning these techniques after watching my life get infinitely better. As you learn, don't try to insist your family join you on this journey. If one or more members of your family are interested, that's great. But don't force or push the issue. It tends to backfire. It's better to let them see how much better you're doing and show an interest if they aren't as enthusiastic as you are when you begin this journey.

If you want to improve your relationships with them, you can do it even if they do not learn what you learn.

Positive Affirmations

Positive Affirmations are scientifically proven to reduce stress, when they are used correctly.[682] Used incorrectly, they are probably the most damaging commonly used technique. It is important to know how to use them correctly.

Positive Affirmations are recommended as long as the affirmation is for the current emotional stance reaching for no more than one zone higher than the current emotional stance.[J] Basically, you can do affirmations from any emotional stance as long as the affirmation is believable from your current position. Positive affirmations are one of the most widely taught techniques and they probably cause the most harm. They cause harm, not because the process is bad or defective, but because most teachers do not differentiate between when Positive Affirmations are beneficial and when they are inappropriate or counterproductive.

Positive affirmations have been scientifically shown to be counter-productive when the individual does not believe the affirmation.[683] The person can say the positive affirmation, but internally the mind refutes it, which makes the underlying negative belief stronger. Positive affirmations should only be used when they do not create this mental backlash. In other words, make adjustments that are not huge stretches from the existing belief on the specific topic. For example, affirming you love your job when you hate it just reinforces the aspects of the job you do not enjoy.

The researchers who found that Positive Affirmations were counterproductive for some associated it to low self-esteem. But the low self-esteem was not the root issue. The low self-esteem led to less favorable beliefs about the self (or was the result of less favorable beliefs about the self). It is not that individuals with low self-esteem can't benefit, they just can't begin with the same affirmations someone who has higher self-esteem can use. It does not mean that they can't get to those more affirming affirmations; it just means they can't do them today.

By affirming more positive beliefs that are only slightly better than what is already believed, new more positive beliefs are developed. Once that step is done, it can be repeated with new affirmations that are slightly better than the new beliefs. This can be done repeatedly. Life experience will improve each step of the way. It is not a situation where you have to reach the ultimate destination to benefit from the journey. If your mind refutes an affirmation, you're reaching too far. Take a smaller step. Using the process described in General to Specific can be very beneficial in identifying affirmations that move in the right direction.

Positive affirmations can be especially useful when involved in a situation where one faces a challenging message and has been shown to "release participants from concern over the evaluative threat posed by a challenging message."[684] For example, someone who has connected laziness with obesity in their own mind might feel shame if they gain weight. Obesity has more to do with stress and diet than with laziness. In fact, I've been forming a hypothesis that looks at laziness is a symptom, not an actual trait but that's a story for another time.

If the person with this belief goes to the doctor and is admonished for gaining weight, she could affirm important personal values and beliefs about herself to help her recover her self-esteem. She might reflect that a contributing factor to the weight gain was working long hours that have resulted in her receiving a nice promotion and salary increase, or looked at from another angle, made her better able to care for her family's needs and increased her skills so her employability is more stable, even if the economy takes a dive.

[J] Refer to the Emotional Guidance Scale (EGSc) in Appendix I for details on the Zones.

The key to using Positive Affirmations is to lean in direction of the desired emotion. This approach, applied consistently over time, results in amazing and delightful changes. If your emotional stance is in the Drama Zone, reach for another emotion in the same zone that feels slightly better or for one in the Blah Zone. If you attempt to affirm a thought that would be in the Hopeful Zone you're likely to have pushback in your own mind. Move to the Blah Zone and stabilize there by affirming thoughts you believe in the Blah Zone. Once you are stable, move to new thoughts that feel even better.

It is always the underlying mental attitude that determines whether something is counterproductive. For example, knowing that exercise makes one feel better is helpful when we actually exercise. When we feel bad and don't take the physical action of exercising, there is a tendency to add guilt for not exercising to the existing negative emotion—perhaps starting a downward spiral. When we understand how to adjust our perceptions to feel better, we can counter any guilt we begin to feel before it adds to our emotional burden.

Here is an example of trying to move too far, too quickly. The person is afraid of public speaking and shy about interacting with strangers.

Affirmation: *I am a charismatic public speaker.*

Internal dialogue: "*Who are you trying to fool? You couldn't talk your way out of a paper bag. If you get up on the stage they'll laugh you right off.*"

Affirmation: *I am a charismatic public speaker.*

Internal dialogue: "*Still trying to convince yourself of that? You can try forever; you don't have what it takes to be on stage.*"

Instead of leaping from the current belief (I am not even good at interpersonal communication. There is no way I can speak on stage in front of hundreds of people.) all the way to the desired belief, take a baby step.

Affirmation: *Today I will speak to a stranger, even if I am afraid. The worse that can happen is I'll look foolish.*

Internal dialogue: "*There is someone. Oh, this is scary.*"

Action: Walking toward the stranger.

Internal dialogue: "*Just say hello. Or ask him what time it is.*"

Internal dialogue: "*I can do this.*"

Action: "Hi, isn't it a pretty day?"

Internal dialogue: "*Wow. I got that out without tripping over my tongue. I can do this. What should I do next?*"

Internal dialogue: "*Tomorrow I'll speak to two strangers.*"

You can feel your progress as your belief shifts. Each shift, however slight, is positive motion forward. Affirming your progress serves two purposes. First, it is actually an affirmation of your personal power to change yourself. It reinforces an internal locus of control. Internal locus of control is associated with resilience and a healthy mental attitude. It also helps you stabilize yourself in the new place. This provides a firmer foundation for further progress. Affirming your progress helps maintain the better self-image and can increase your satisfaction with life.[685]

Positive affirmations that reach too far cement undesired beliefs more firmly in our minds. Remember, it is possible to feel hopeful that you will actually be able to have two conversations with strangers tomorrow and frightened about the idea of being on stage talking to a room full of strangers.

Pay attention to the internal dialogue. If your inner critic is responding, you have two choices. The easiest is to take a smaller step that your critic won't attack. The long-term solution is to kill your inner critic. You can also use your guidance, if saying the affirmation feels good, it's working. If it feels bad, you're taking too big of a step. Take a smaller step.

One common affirmation is *I am lovable.* A long time ago I tried this one and felt the backlash of negative emotion. It was way too much of a stretch from my beliefs at the time. I was blessed to have one friend who knew me very well, including the stuff I hated. I could not affirm that I was lovable but thinking about my friend who I was sure loved me in spite of knowing me well, I was able to affirm *Some people will love me even if they know me.* At the time, that was a big step for me.

What you affirm is not as important as how it feels. If it feels better it is helping. Once you believe the affirmation fully, which means you've thought about it long enough that it has become a belief; you're ready to take another step.

There are many uses for positive affirmations. You can use them to protect against the Pygmalion Effect and to be the more dominant belief in mirror neurons. You can use them to increase self-esteem. You can use them to improve competency at tasks. You can use them to make the group you identify with feel better, which leads to less negative feelings about groups you do not belong to.[686]

I have used them to affirm that the group I belong to is the human race. This has led to numerous changes in the way I think about myself and my relationship with the world. By making my dominant view about the group I belong to be human, national borders became less important and other man made labels (religion, national origin, etc.) became unimportant because everyone is part of the group I belong to. The broader you define the group you belong to, the more comfortable you become in different experiences.

Many groups define themselves narrowly, which leads to an us vs. them attitude about other groups. I find this unproductive.

Unlike most processes, the emotional zone this one works in depends on using it correctly (taking small steps toward better feeling thoughts) rather than the emotional stance the individual is in. That being said, in the lowest emotional states it can be difficult to find a better-feeling thought so other processes will be effective faster, especially in the Powerless Zone. Although, if you affirm very general things from the Powerless Zone, affirmations can still be productive. Examples could include *Life won't always be like this, The only way to go from here is up, This too shall pass, I know skills that can help me feel better, I have a focus list—it will help me feel better, I'll feel better after I get some sleep, Others have been in worse shape than I am and gone on to live a good life, Almost everyone who becomes successful fails first.* The choices are nearly endless.

Exercise:
One way to deliberately work on positive affirmations is to recognize where you currently stand, then create small steps between the two positions. This exercise can be done on very specific topics or very general topics. It is easier to begin with broader topics and then move on to more specific ones after you have experience with the process. Use statements that are positive—as if they are true now. "I am" statements are powerful when you do affirmations.

Where you are: _____
Where you want to be: _____
Realistic steps:
Then repeat and stabilize.

Example:

Where I am: *I am not happy with how often I exercise.*
Where I want to be: *I want to exercise more and feel satisfied with the amount of exercise I do.*
I'm not exercising enough because I have not made it enough of a priority.
I can make exercise a higher priority in my life.
It would be easier if I did exercise I like—it would make it easier for me to make it a priority.
I like to dance.
I can make a commitment to dance every day for twenty minutes.
I will dance every day for twenty minutes.
I will make play lists of music that makes me want to dance.
Moving my body more feels good.
I like moving my body.
I can do this.
I am capable of exercising as much as I desire.
My body is strong and will be stronger still because I am moving more.
I can live in a way where I am happier with how much I move.
I like understanding that I can change my habits more easily by first changing my thoughts.
I am getting the hang of this.
I feel good about how much I will exercise now.

Think Positive

> *Dwell on the beauty of life.*
> *Watch the stars, and see yourself running with them.*
> Marcus Aurelius

I include this as a process to attempt to provide some clarification and perhaps some emotional relief. *Be positive*, *Stay positive*, *Keep your chin up*, and *Don't let it get you down* are all forms of advice given frequently, without answering the question of how to actually achieve it.

First, if you've heard this advice and been unable to follow it—the reason is that without instructions, it is meaningless advice.

In a study of cancer patients and nurses about the definition of *being positive*, it was defined "as maintaining some sort of normality without letting cancer have a detrimental effect on daily living." Nurses identified hope, acceptance, fighting spirit and looking on the bright side as definitions of *being positive*. Nurses and patients identified environment and support of family, friends, and health professionals as factors that influence patient attitudes. Patients also identified other peoples' attitudes as important. It was concluded that *being positive* must be acknowledged as central to being able to cope with cancer and its treatment. The ability of nurses to care for patients with cancer and help them to remain positive will be improved if they develop a better understanding of the meaning of *being positive* for patients, and how other peoples' attitudes affect their state of mind.[687] This definition does not go nearly far enough and it may be one reason research into the benefit of positivity on health has not shown consistent results.

> *Someone who puts a smiling face forward who is screaming or deathly afraid on the inside is not in a positive frame of mind and the contradiction between their outward face and inward feelings is detrimental to their recovery and well-being.*

What does a beneficial positive focus look like? First, we have to look inside the mind to the thoughts. The outer face can be more or less positive but authenticity is another element that is beneficial to health, so I highly recommend consistency between the inner and outer mood. If you do not want people around you while you feel awful, retreat, but only if you are doing positive work on moving forward. Sometimes, from the worse perspectives, this is the best way. But do not retreat for long and if you are not making progress, ask for help from someone who understands how to change perspectives to ones that are more positive.

Perspective-taking, or Right Responses, are often the best method of improving emotional state. This is very true when you're ill. Do whatever you can that makes sense to take care of your health with the medical or Complimentary Alternative Medicine communities, but also work on your internal dialog.

The mind of the positively focused person has a belief that things can get better. The best way to cultivate this belief is to practice using one's Emotional Guidance and develop confidence in the process. Then apply processes appropriate to the current mood to shift perspective to a more positively focused one.

It also involves being less judgmental, angry, unforgiving, and just plain unloving toward others—whether strangers, family, friends, or enemies. When you judge another as lacking, your guidance is telling you there is a better perspective you can find about the person/situation. The negative emotion you feel is not telling you that the person/situation is awful—it is telling you that the perspective you are taking about the situation is not serving your highest good. The same is true when you are angry with someone else. When you refuse to forgive, you harm yourself, not the other person.

The perspective that your anger toward another punishes them is in error. It is possible for someone to feel anger toward me and I can be completely oblivious toward his or her feelings. Or, I can choose to think they are just living in the Hot Zone and they are the only one who can change that, the emotional zone they chose to live in—consciously or unconsciously—has nothing to do with me.

The perspective that refusing to forgive another punishes them in some way is also in error. Yes, it can be a catalyst for emotional pain—if they decide your forgiveness is important and necessary to their well-being. But whether or not to take that perspective is completely up to them—you do not have a say. I know people who are angry and unforgiving toward people who are no longer alive. If you are one of those people, imagine how it would feel if you weren't habitually angry. Imagine it, and feel it, and move toward that feeling. If you know someone who is habitually angry, the best thing you can do for them is to imagine them happy and to focus on your own happiness. It's contagious.

Reminiscence, when positive memories are chosen, is an effective method of thinking positive thoughts.[688] Recall past events with pleasant (or better) feelings.

Decisions

Decisions are powerful. When you make a decision, it changes your filters and primes you for success. It helps you stay on your path, even when you encounter obstacles. It clarifies the decision that is right for you when a choice must be made. For example, I had no idea how to get through college and worked full-time to put myself through. I knew I needed 60 units at community college to get my AA and transfer to the 4-year. After going to college nights from age 17 - 25, I finally had my 60 units but when I applied to graduate for my AA I learned that it was not just having 60 units—it was a specific mix of classes. So I studied the catalog, earned 32 more credits, transferred to University and graduated with honors--it would have been higher honors but I did not know that I had to re-take a class I failed within a year to keep it from affecting my GPA during a semester when I miscarried my first child. The second time I took it I aced it but the original F from when I was off following the miscarriage remains part of the average. It took me a total of 13 years going to college at night and basically not having a life outside of work or school during those years to graduate but I did it.

Why? Not because I'm special.

Not because my parents were able to guide me.

Not because I fit in socially. I never fit in and had some trouble with fellow students--largely because my determination made my grades mess up the class curve. I was not focused on playing, partying, or having fun. I was focused on getting an education so my future would be better. By the last few years of college the 1st day of class was predictable--kids would drop if the instructor was not willing to remove my grades from the curve.

I was not a lot smarter.

I was a lot more determined.

I had made up my mind that I was getting a college education and nothing would stop me. Nothing. It was my highest priority.

I made a decision. I decided I was someone who was going to have a college degree.

Anyone can make a decision. We all make them. We decide where our priorities lay. We decide what we are willing to give up to attain what we want. We decide if anything will stop us or if we will succeed no matter what happens along the way. We get to choose. What choices are you making? Do they support your highest good? Do they support your long-term goals? Are they going to help you be who you dream of being?

If not, you may want to think about them a little more often.
Believe you can. It matters.

Remember: Not making a decision is a decision. **Make Decisions** that feel good for long-term goals. Short-term goals can de-rail your long-term goals (i.e. drugs and alcohol).

Refute

Refuting is an especially powerful process for anyone who has never questioned his thoughts before. Thoughts do not equate to truth. It is common for someone to have a mistaken impression about someone—leaning too good or too bad.

When we realize that we can decide whether we want to go along with a thought or not, it is empowering. When combined with the feedback our EGS provides, we can determine whether a thought is leaning toward truth or not. When the thought feels bad, it is not our truth. When it feels good, it is our truth.

Use your EGS to identify thoughts that are not serving you. When you find one, refute it. Look for evidence of reasons it is wrong.

For example, many people have a belief that goes like this, "Life is hard." If you look at the lives of people with that belief, life is hard for them—but there are many people whose lives are not hard. The belief, "Life is hard" is refutable. Because life is not hard for everyone you know it is a belief and not destiny. Well, it is destiny(for you) if you keep the belief. Refuting it is one way to loosen the belief—sort of like wiggling a loose tooth. The best way to replace beliefs that do not serve you is to overwrite them with better beliefs that do.

If I had this belief (I don't because my life is not hard), I would begin by shifting to a belief along the lines of "Life is hard for some people but I'm learning new skills and it isn't going to be hard for me anymore." I would use this to refute the belief and reinforce the new, more desirable belief.

This would not be my final stop. After I had firmly shifted from "Life is hard" to "Life is hard for some people but I'm learning new skills and it isn't going to be hard for me anymore." I would use this to refute the belief and reinforce the new, more desirable belief.

This would not be my final stop. After I had firmly shifted from "Life is hard" to "Life is hard for some people but I'm learning new skills and it isn't going to be hard for me anymore," I would shift to an even better belief.

Eventually, I would move to the belief: "Life is easy and fun. I live a blessed life."

Remember, the negative emotion you feel when you think a thought that does not serve you means that thought is not the best perspective you can have on that subject. I like to call my thoughts like that "Bogus." It just feels good and lessens the power of those leftover beliefs that are not serving my highest good.

Exercise

What is true about your life that is not true of everyone else?
Think about things you feel jealous or envious about.

Jealousy and/or envy is seeing someone with something you want that you do not believe you can have.

Jealousy and envy are evidence that you do not believe you can have something. It is your guidance telling you that you're not finding a good perspective on that topic.

Take one subject at a time and find a thought that feels better about the topic. During the first step, just weaken the original thought. In subsequent steps, find a thought that feels a little better that you can believe. Keep moving toward thoughts that feel better. You can do this over a period of months, days, hours, or minutes. The more you practice, the faster you can shift your perspective and feel better.

Or, just call the original thought bogus. Sometimes you already know it is bogus on some level and it is just a habit of thought that is not serving you. If calling it bogus feels great, you know you were primed for changing it.

Setting Intentions

Setting intentions is a form of goal setting. When you set intentions to do certain things, it sensitizes the filters that decide which information will be sent to your conscious mind, highlighting information in alignment with your intentions. Identify the most personally meaningful values to guide your decisions and actions.

I used to work with a very quick-witted COO from New York who frequently responded while I was still formulating my response in our executive meetings. Often, this took the conversation in a new direction and my opportunity to add value passed without my input. I began setting the intention "The best answers I can think of will come to me quickly" as I walked to the boardroom for our meetings. My responses became faster. The COO was no longer always ahead of me in his responses. I still remember his face the first time I answered ahead of him—he was truly surprised that I spoke before he did.

Intentions can be set for one's life—much like a mission statement. They can be set for a year, a month, a day, a relationship, a journey, a conversation. Setting intentions is a very versatile form of goal setting.

Intentions can be general or specific. You can set a goal that your decisions will always lean toward your highest good. You can set an intention to be aware of situations where you can be of benefit to others.

What would you like to have more of in your life? What would you like to do better in your life?

I like goal setting. I had a 1, 2, 5, and 20-year plan when I was 21. I am convinced that many of my successes were the result of setting specific goals.

I like setting intentions because they do not require a lot of preparation or thought. They help one be in the flow more often when the intention is to be the best you can in the moment. Research shows that setting intentions reduces the energy required to complete the action[689] because it lowers the self-control required because it aligns what you want to do with what you need to do.

Setting intentions is good for any level on the EGSc. Much like with the Positive Affirmation process, the key is to set intentions you believe you can achieve. The difference between Setting Intentions and Positive Affirmations is that Setting Intentions is about something you are going to do and the outcome you desire from the activity.

Exercise:

Do you have an area of your life where you often feel just a little less than you want to be? Try setting an intention for what you would like better in those situations and see what happens. Make a decision to focus on setting intentions throughout a single day to set intentions for your activities and pay attention to how the day works out.

When you awaken, set an intention:
I will have the best day possible today.

When you go to have breakfast, set an intention that you will choose healthy food:
The healthiest foods will appeal to me the most.

Before you head out for the day set an intention:
My day will be productive and work out the best for me.

When you answer the phone:
I will have the right words to have the best outcome from this conversation.

When you travel:
My journey will be fun.[K]

Forgiving

> *The weak can never forgive. Forgiveness is the attribute of the strong.*
> Mahatma Gandhi

Based on the some of the feedback I have received from my students, I know that some of them use drugs and alcohol to feel better.

I'm not going to discourage anyone from wanting to feel better. It is natural to want to feel better.

We all know that both society and your body make the drug path to feeling better carry a heavy price.

What is offered in this book is a way to feel better that does not have the negative side effects of drugs or alcohol.

I am not going to tell you that you don't have reasons to feel bad. Some of you are living lives full of so many reason to feel bad those reasons could bring anyone to their knees in anguish. But those same

---

[K] I do not recommend reaching for a safe journey because it often contains the fear that it will not be safe. (See the discussion about the definition of peace for clarification.) Fun inherently implies safe and enjoyable.

circumstances can be perceived in multiple ways—some that feel better and some that feel worse. Finding the best possible perspective about your circumstances helps you feel better now and have a better future, greater resilience, and decreases your desire to use drugs and/or alcohol to dull the pain.

When you have a way to feel better without the risks drugs and alcohol involve you will choose the method with the lower risk.

The risks from drugs extend beyond the damage they can do to your body and mind. Because drugs are often illegal, their use results in increased exposure to criminals, risk of incarceration, risk of a criminal record for yourself, financial risk, relationship risks, and more.

> *Science, spiritual, and religious worldviews tend to agree about the importance and benefits of forgiveness.*

Trust me, if you experiment with using your guidance to feel better you will see that it works. Then, when you have a tool that will help you feel better without the high risks associated with drugs and alcohol that will be your choice. That choice will feel better to you. It will be your choice because your guidance will encourage it—not because it is what someone else wants you to.

The reason many turn to alcohol and drugs is that they want to feel better and they don't have the tools to do it another way. It may be to feel better from things that are happening in their lives or it may be because they have been taught to judge themselves through others eyes and peer pressure makes going along feel better than not doing along. It may be to dull the pain of memories that haunt them or survivor guilt. Perfectionism, self-criticism, critical parents, and low self-esteem contribute to feeling bad, but they can be overcome.

Whatever it is, the bottom line is the desire to feel better fuels the behavior. The desire to feel better is universal. It is not a bad thing. It is a natural and normal thing. It is an inescapable thing. Even those who live wonderful lives still have desires for more and better. It is inherent in our nature.

We have far more power over how we feel than most realize. If you experiment with how things feel and with finding better-feeling thoughts, you will quickly see how much power you can wield as far as how you feel in any given situation.

Let's look at some specific examples.

When someone feels anger, rage, or other negative emotions toward another they will often resist soothing the anger or forgiving the person by taking a stance that the other person does not deserve their forgiveness, their understanding, or their compassion.

Forgiveness is not about whether the other person deserves it or not. It is about the fact that you do deserve it. Your anger and rage hurt you. Whether your anger and rage hurt the person you are blaming is up to that person—<u>it's not up to you.</u>

The first step is seeing that you can hold onto anger against someone for a long time—years or decades. That anger does nothing to that other person. It does not diminish them in any way; it does not harm them in any way, unless they take a perspective where it does.

The other person has 100% control over whether your feelings of anger or rage harms them.

Someone could be angry at me, even someone I care about, and I could live with that anger from them for decades with no ill effects—if I take a stance that allows me to feel okay about their stance. It is the stance I take that makes the difference between whether their anger harms me or not. It has nothing to do with the stance they take. Well, their stance may make me work harder to find one of my own that feels good to me, but that is all the damage they have the power to do to me. They cannot make me suffer or continue to suffer by holding onto their anger if I am wise enough to find a stance that feels good to me.

Likewise, someone could refuse to forgive me and if I found a stance that felt good, the lack of forgiveness would not harm me in any way.

But, if I hold onto anger towards another, that anger harms me. Buddha said that holding on to anger is like holding a hot coal in one's hand that you want to throw at someone but you never throw it. The only one it burns is the one holding onto the anger.

Forgiveness is the same. It is not necessary to tell the person that you have forgiven them. Forgiveness is something you do in your own heart and mind. When you forgive, you let go of the anger and the harm the anger was causing you stops.

I have known people who held onto anger over things that happened to them when they were small children and never forgave the person they held responsible for their pain, even long after the person was dead. When one steps back from it, clearly the only one that can be harmed by that is the one holding onto the pain.

When you forgive, it is about finding a perspective that feels better to you. It makes your own personal mindscape a more pleasing place to live.

It is not about whether you are justified in your anger. We all have a great deal we could be angry about and all of it is justified. Justified anger hurts you as much as anger some would consider unjustified. Whether anger is justified or not does not matter. Don't beat up on yourself for feeling anger. Do let the anger go as soon as you can find a better-feeling perspective.

Letting go of anger is also not about taking down boundaries. If someone has done things that make you not want to be around them you can make that decision separate and apart from the decision to release yourself from the anger. Just because you have released the anger or forgiven someone does not mean you have to resume a relationship you do not want.

Unbundle your emotional stance from your actions.

I knew a man who would not tell a woman he loved her, even when he did because he had bundled love with a requirement to commit and to take care of her. He withheld his expression of love until he was ready to make a commitment. Loving someone and agreeing to spend a lifetime with them are two separate things. Unbundle them and your life will feel clearer. Do not assume others bundle the same things you bundle together.

Many of us have expectations. We will say,

"If he/she loved me they would _____."

What we really mean is, "When I love someone I _____ because I have bundled love and _____ together. I assume everyone else has bundled the same things I have bundled together."

We are all different. We all have different expectations. If you want to know what it means when someone else expresses an emotion, ask. Going deeper in your conversations and understanding is the only way you'll know what they intend.

Now, let's take it home. I know many of you are living with people who are hard to live with. Maybe they say disparaging things to you. Maybe they do not treat you well. Maybe they discourage you or nothing you do is ever good enough. Maybe they are downright mean to you.

You inherently know that this person, or these people, should love you and should treat you better. That is true. You deserve to be treated with love and respect.

But many of you mistakenly misinterpret that behavior to be reflecting something about your own value or worth. It has nothing to do with that.

Think for a minute about the last time you said something ugly to someone else. Even if it was just something you said in your own mind and did not speak out loud. When you did that, before you spoke or thought that ugly comment, were you feeling good or bad? Don't think about after because such comments often make someone who feels really bad feel a bit better and the feeling of relief one feels when they feel better does feel better than what was felt before.

Think about that and honestly answer the question, "Do I say ugly things to others (out loud or in my own mind) when I am unhappy? If I was happy, would I say the same thing?"

You'll realize that when you are happy you are much more likely to say nice things, perhaps to offer a compliment or words intended to uplift. When we are unhappy, what we say is not as nice.

They may be things deliberately crafted to be hurtful, or things that just end up that way due to our careless focus and thoughtlessness.

The same is true of those who interact with you. And yes, they can be unhappy for many years. There are children who grow up believing there is something wrong with them because they cannot please a parent they have tried to please. There is nothing wrong with the child—the parents' negative emotional state makes them unpleasable. Unless the parent learns how to deliberately shift his or her chronic negative perspective, the child will not please that parent. Others perceive the person as mean or spiteful, but the truth is that if the person felt emotionally better, he or she would behave in a nicer way.

It is not uncommon for individuals to spend an entire lifetime not really feeling good. Most individuals do not know how to change how they feel. They work to change the circumstances of their lives but until you change the inner landscape, the outer changes do not bring the emotional relief that is sought. How we feel is largely dependent upon our habits of thought and like any habit, they can be changed. The problem has been folks did not know how to change their habits of thought so they could feel better consistently. You have the tools that enable you to do that in this book.

Nasty comments reflect an unhappy emotional state. They are not speaking about your worth and value. I guarantee you, if that same person was happy, they would express themselves differently to you. Someone who is happy is likely to compliment not criticize.

Now, let' take it back to you.

If you'll really wrap your mind around the fact that those who are not nice to you are in an emotionally bad state and that their behavior is reflecting who they are; not who you are, you will be miles ahead of most of the world in your ability to be resilient and to find better-feeling stances of your own.

You will also see how important it is that you make feeling good a priority in your own life. You don't want to be that person that says hurtful things to those who expect your love—to your spouse, children, or friends. You really don't. But the only way to not become that person, and the more of the junk you've had in your life, the truer this is, is to care how you feel and do something about it.

Drugs and alcohol are a way to feel better and they can provide temporary relief but they can also cause problems that give even more reasons to seek relief. They do nothing about the chronic issues. Only by learning how to use your Emotional Guidance System can you develop the ability to feel good and be who you really want to be. You have the ability to be someone whose patterns of thought help them be happy instead of hindering them.

Remember, your emotions are there, responding to every thought you think. The thoughts that feel better are moving in the direction of your dreams and desires. The thoughts that feel worse are moving away from your dreams and desires. It is really that simple. The only way you can understand it fully is to use it. Ask yourself, does that thought feel good? Then ask yourself, "What thought would feel better?" No matter how good the thought is, there is always a better feeling one. There is no end to how good it can get.

Remember, if the thought feels bad, to find a better-feeling thought look for thoughts that are more general in nature.

Many people refuse to forgive someone who has hurt them not realizing that harboring ill will toward someone else harms their health, their enjoyment of life, and their potential for success.

Refusing to forgive is like walking through life with a leg shackle attached to your leg—it weighs you down, slows you down, and holds you back.

You've learned a lot about the connection between emotional state and behavior. Our best possible behavior when we are in the Powerless Zone is far less than the best behavior we can offer when we are in the Sweet Zone. The other thing is that none of us wake-up in the morning and decide to do less than the best we are able to do that day. Even when our behavior is far less than our best possible, or best ever, we are doing the best we can in the current emotional state.

Between knowing that forgiveness is the best choice for my personal well-being (and the best choice for your well-being as well) and that whatever happened, it was the best the person could do in that moment makes it easier to forgive. Research shows forgiveness is powerful medicine for the one who forgives.[690]

Another way to reach for forgiveness is attempting to see the situation from the other person's point of view. This can be an especially beneficial method when the unforgiven party has apologized[691] or if you are aware of a history that might have made the person more likely to do what they did.

The other piece is what I call unbundling. In many instances, we bundle forgiveness with allowing someone back into our lives. But the two things are not the same and can be unbundled. It is possible to forgive someone for something and make a decision not to have that person in your life. They are separate decisions and you get to decide how you want to handle any situation in your life.

It is also possible to love someone but choose not to have that person in your life. Loving and being involved do not have to be bundled. Many times the reason an individual does not want to forgive is because they do not want to risk a repeat of the event that felt so bad to them. By unbundling forgiveness from resuming a relationship, forgiveness may come more easily to you.

I recommend unbundled forgiveness for anyone who is holding onto hurt or anger, in any emotional stance.

Forgiveness Exercises
I want you to look yourself in the eyes in a mirror and say to yourself:

I have the power to love. I have the power to forgive.

Continue looking into your own eyes, willing yourself to believe your own words—to be the type of person who can forgive another because you deserve to live without the weight of negative emotion holding you down or holding you back from your dreams.

Think of someone you have held onto anger about. The person could be family, friend, foe, or even a stranger. Look inside yourself and try to find a perspective that feels better about the situation you've held onto anger about. **Write something down about how it would feel better to you to let go of the anger.** You can choose to tell the person or not, <u>this is for you</u>, not for anyone else.

Note: Do not begin with the person who is the most troubling to you. Begin with someone whose transgressions are not as sharp or painful. You're developing a pattern of behavior and patterns of thought. Your goal is to demonstrate to yourself how forgiving someone else makes you feel better.

Some of my students have struggled with finding it within themselves to forgive anyone. I'm always able to help them find a perspective that allows them with this healing. If you have a friend you trust, talk over your desire to forgive someone with your friend and maybe you'll find a way.

When you begin making a habit of forgiving small transgressions it becomes easier to revisit the bigger hurts and begin whittling away at them. If it is something that feels really big, for example, being abused as a child, you may have to chip away at it the way a sculptor chips away at the marble to find the beauty inside. Steps on that path may include:

1. Realizing that everyone does the best they can in any given moment, even when their best in that moment was awful—it was the best they could do at the time.
2. Recognize and begin seeing how emotional state affects behavior.
3. Recognize and begin seeing evidence that before anyone becomes someone who harms others, they were in pain.
4. Recognize that at the core of everyone there is someone good, even if that goodness is impossible to see because of all the layers of pain that hide the goodness.
5. Commit to feeling good and realize that you can't hold a grudge and feel good
6. Realize that in addition to emotional state, illness, lack of sleep, stress, and other factors can make someone's best in-the-moment be pretty awful.
7. If you were abused by someone, recognize that at the time they were doing the best they could—for whatever reasons. You don't have to know what happened to make them as they were. I can assure you that it's a never-ending story. Someone hurt them, but the person who hurt them was hurt by someone first and so on back through time. We cannot change the past, we can change the future and forgiveness stops the cycle.
8. Who are you because of what happened that you would not be if what happened had not happened?
- Would you be as strong as you are?
- Would you know you can endure as much as you can and still be a force for good in the world?
- Would you have as much compassion for others?
- What have you gained?
- What is the silver lining?

When you begin focusing on what you've gained, the way it looks changes. You may not wish anyone else to ever have to suffer as you did, but you may come to the point where you would not allow anyone to take the experience away from your life—even if that someday becomes possible because you realize that you would not have become all that you are if your past was easier.

Each step that feels better is good for you.

You may need a subtler approach. You may be attempting to bridge too much of a chasm between how you feel right now and forgiveness. If you think this might be what is hindering you look for a situation where you can find a different, slightly better feeling perspective. Use the processes to shift your focus and once you've stabilized your emotional set point on that topic, see if you can find a way to forgive. If you're still not there, repeat the step about finding a new perspective until you are.

> *Everything we hear is an opinion, not a fact.*
> *Everything we see is a perspective, not the truth.*
> Marcus Aurelius

Remember, the forgiveness is for you. Anger, rage, and even blame are blocked energy that is not good for your body or mind. Your body will not function as well when you hold onto these emotions as it will after they are released. You will perceive new relationships through a veil of distrust and even fear as long as you hold onto perspectives about past relationships that are painful. Your immune system will function better. Your cognitive abilities will be better. Your digestive function, endocrine system, and more will benefit.

It does not matter if what you're holding onto anger about is someone who abused you when you were a child or someone who cut you off in the parking lot yesterday; releasing the negative emotion helps you. I've had many students who have been able to release negative emotions about childhood issues who subsequently had very positive experiences. Two common ones have been weight loss and improvement in chronic health conditions. There has also been a trend of improved relationships with other people and new loves coming into their lives.

How might your life benefit from forgiveness?

Don't forget to forgive yourself. Guilt does not serve you either. When you release negative emotions, you've done good work. Celebrate. It may have felt like you did not do anything other than think, but forgiveness, releasing anger, blame, and guilt are action steps.

You may want to document the day. One way is to write a letter, taking the perspective of yourself in the future, and thank you for healing your hurt. Another way is to write a letter to the person you forgave—even if you'll never send it and even if they are deceased.

Remember, you are under no obligation to tell someone you have forgiven them but energetically it can provide additional healing to write the letter, even if you never intend to send it.

Write down things you can now feel about yourself that feel good, that you want to hold on to from this day.

When I first began my forgiveness journey, my list seemed impossibly long. It seemed as if it would take forever to find forgiveness about my past. It was not long until only the worst transgression was left and because I had practiced, that was far easier than I'd imagined it would be. Surprisingly, it was easier than the first one. Developing the habit of forgiveness makes it easier to do this work. Examples of affirmations that can make it easier to forgive more people for more things.

I have the power to love.
I have the power to forgive.
Forgiveness is a gift I give to myself.
I am stronger when I love than when I hate.
I can love fearlessly.
I can always find a better perspective about a situation and, in finding it, feel better now.
I am more powerful than I know.
I have great potential.
My emotions will give me immediate feedback any time I reach for better feeling thoughts.
Loving feels good even if I am not loved back - but only if I focus only on loving. Not if I look for what I am getting back and see lack.
If you are a person who believes in God: God will help me love and forgive.

If you are creative, you may choose to express the release of negative emotions in artwork.

Mirror Work

What you say to yourself when you look in the mirror is more powerful than what you say to yourself when you are not looking in a mirror. Many people have developed a habit of looking for flaws when they look in the mirror. If you look for what is wrong, begin praising yourself when you look in the mirror. You can praise your appearance, the intelligence of your body, the intelligence of your mind, your abilities, your resilience, or anything else that feels good when you say it.

If you're in the habit of saying negative things to yourself start telling yourself, "I am good. I deserve to have the good aspects of myself praised. I will focus on the aspects of myself that I appreciate."

As you give things you do not like less air time in your mind their importance will diminish. Your awareness of them will be less intense. You may even forget about them.

Changing the Past

Our back stories create the reality we experience much more than the facts of the situation. Every human, regardless of how rational they attempt to be, creates meaning via back stories which are filtered (biased) by existing beliefs, emotional state, expectations, past experiences (which are actually the back stories created in the past), and focus. We can literally change the past and any emotional carnage stemming from it, by changing the back story we attribute to our experiences.

Regret over the actions one took (or didn't take) often leads to self-recriminations that are unhealthy because of the stress they create in the body and because if they are severe, drugs and alcohol can be used as escape mechanisms. No one begins a day by saying they will be less than their best that day. In every moment, we do our best possible for that moment. Our best possible in a given moment is not the same as:

- Our potential best
- Our best ever

It is merely the best we can do in that moment with the knowledge and resources available to us. Levine, Lench and Safer concluded that, "Although memory bias is typically viewed as problematic, change in representations of emotional experience often promote goal-directed behavior and facilitate coping with challenging situations."[692] Finding a way to feel better about the past increases your current potential best which is what is important now. We can't change the past; we can only impact our best potential in this and future moments. Changing how we perceive the past, impacts our available resources in this moment.

Resources include factors such as adequate rest, nutrition, emotional state, as well as financial and social resources. Even making decisions can deplete your self-control. Researchers from four universities worked together to study the effect of decision-making on subsequent self-control and found that decision-making reduced individual's ability to exert self-control.[693] Their findings may point to the shift that both Johann von Goethe and Ralph Waldo Emerson alluded to, "These findings tentatively argue for something special about choice. Based on the Rubicon model, we have proposed that making a choice produces a lasting change in the person's mental apparatus by etching into the mind and brain the prescription for what to do. The change in mental programming is made at the time of choosing, regardless of whether the chosen action is to be implemented immediately or at some unspecified future time. Making this change requires energy and is depleting."[694]

Shift the available resources and the best potential behavior in that moment changes. It is completely unfair to judge your past actions as if your current resources were available when you said or did (or failed to do) what it is you now regret—no matter how egregious that thing is. As horrendous as it sounds, the new parent who forgets their child is in the backseat when they go to work is doing the best they can (in that moment). The parent is probably sleep deprived and stressed about the new level of responsibilities as well as the relationship changes that a baby can bring. When someone is overloaded mistakes happen—sometimes horrific ones. Holding on to crippling guilt about something you did in the past reduces your ability to do your potential best now.

They are not criminal acts. They are tragedies that reflect the lack of resources new parents believe are available to them and societal expectations that parents almost immediately resume their full-time jobs and other activities as if bringing new life into the world is not a life-changing event that can take some adjustment time. That parents in those situations are charged with a crime is a gross injustice. The punishment they will give themselves is far more than society can ever impose. They would never make the same mistake again because they would probably become paranoid about double and triple checking to avoid it.

If you are punishing yourself with regret, give yourself a break. You did the best you could at the time. The fact that you could do (or did do) better at another time does not mean you were capable of it in that moment. Your past actions will instruct your future actions. For example, I won't drive when I am overly tired. I have fallen asleep at the wheel, fortunately without tragic consequences. Having done so made me aware that it was possible for me to fall asleep so when I am tired I allow someone else to drive or I don't drive—not even to the grocery store.

I also stopped pushing myself to go to work when I was ill, because when I did I made mistakes and the fact that I was attempting to be a good corporate soldier by being there did not negate the errors. I was still responsible. I learned it was better not to work when the likelihood of making an error was high because I was ill.

Specifically Negative to Generally Negative Shift
When you are in low emotional states, you are being specific about something that does not feel good when you think about it. Shift your focus to more general thoughts and you will feel better. This example below explains the process.

Specifically negative > generally negative
Thought: *David does not like me.*
More general thought: *David does not like a lot of people, including me.*
Even more general thought: *Unhappy people are more likely to find reasons to not like someone. Unhappy people may not like me.*
Generally negative > Generally Positive
Not everyone in the world is unhappy. Happy people are more likely to like me.
More specific generally positive: *The happier I become the more other happy people will like me.*

Generally Positive > Specifically Positive
I am developing some skills and thought processes that will help me be happier in a sustainable way.
As I become happier those people who were annoyingly happy are no longer annoying.
I can see how my emotional state impacts my perception of others.
I can find more to appreciate about everyone in my life from my new, happier state.
It's fun to deliberately feel better.
Now that I know how to feel better on purpose, I won't freak out so much when I feel bad because I know how to get back to feeling-better.

I don't think I'll ever go back to feeling as bad as I once did because part of the reason I felt so bad was I did not know how to feel better and that was scary. It was like being lost but now I can find my way. I can feel happier anytime I want. It is up to me. I am in control. I like this. It feels really good. I am so glad that I can decide to be happier and then find the mindsets that allow me to feel better.

If you just remember that when you feel bad go more general and when you feel good if you want to feel even better you can get more specific.

When going specific, sometimes you can try to go more specific than what will feel good so just back up and be more general.

For example, if you have decided that you are going to college the thought of going to college can feel really good.

But if you don't yet know where you are going and someone is pushing you for answers about that it can feel bad not to know the answer yet. Just stay general. Say things like, "It is not yet time for me to make that decision. I will know when the time to decide is right. There is plenty of time. I don't have to decide today."

Likewise, if you know you are going it is fine to take a stance that you don't know how you'll pay for it, but just relish the belief that you are going. Your faith that it will work out serves you well. It allows the filters in your mind to remain open to ideas. If someone begins pressuring you about that, just stay general and not so specific that it begins feeling bad. "I don't know but that is OK. There are many people who went to college and finished college who did not know how they would do it when they were where I am. There are many ways to pay and I am open to all possibilities. I am not ready to close the doors on other possibilities by deciding on just one. There is plenty of time. I don't have to figure this out today. I am going and I know I will figure it out."

It is important that you decide how specific or general you can be on a subject in that moment. You are not required to go more specific than feels good. You could even say, "One thing I've learned is that things go better for me when I feel good and on this subject a general stance of faith serves me best right now. I understand your concern but trying to get more specific than I am ready for will not serve me well. It won't help me achieve this so I am going to stay general until something more specific feels as good. I'll be sure to let you know when I know more but for now maybe you can decide to feel good just knowing that I have confidence I will figure it out. I do. I am confident about that."

> When you have tools that help you feel better, it is not necessary to backslide.

This same conversation can be modified to deal with those pesky people (especially prevalent at reunions) who want to know things you don't yet know. You can modify these answers for questions about when you're going to get married, buy a home, have children, decide on a career, retire, or any number of other questions that inquiring minds seem to want to know about.

Then, there is always my favorite, "Why would you ask me that?" It is great way to diffuse a question (especially inappropriate ones) you do not want to address.

Let's bring this back around to drugs and alcohol for a moment. If those are paths you've been using to feel better, I encourage you to try the Emotional Guidance system. Once you master the Emotional Guidance system you'll be able to feel better without those risky and expensive crutches. If your body has become addicted, it only takes about three days to end the physical/chemical addiction. The reason so many backslide after going through withdrawal is not the chemical addiction—It is the untended desire to feel better.

Programs that convince you that you are bad for having wanted to feel better and using the only thing you knew that worked don't tend to the root cause—the desire to feel better. If that desire is not addressed and alternate solutions found, it is not likely that overcoming the physical addiction will lead to a permanent solution. Once the root cause—the desire to feel better—is addressed any method of overcoming the chemical dependence has a far greater chance of long-term success.

No one can be shamed into a happier life.

No one can be showered with guilt (for an addiction) and find a happier life.

See the Potential in Others and in Self

This is not the same as seeing the good in others. While that is a good practice, seeing the potential looks deeper. Seeing the good usually refers to seeing good that is manifesting in their experience. An example would be to see the kind heart of the failing student.

Seeing the potential in others, while not overlooking the kind heart of the aforementioned student, would also see within the student the potential to thrive in school instead of fail. I recommend this process for everyone to use to the best of their abilities.

Seeing the potential in others begins with an understanding that our best behavior in any moment is impacted by our emotional state in that moment. The current emotional state has significant impacts on all of the following:

Behavior	Intelligence	Relationships
Resilience	Well-Being	Emotional Intelligence (EQ)
Ability to think clearly	Health	

In addition, ES directly impacts decisions including involving diet, exercise, alcohol, drugs, and risky behavior. Our society has a tendency to judge individuals based on their current behavior. I will continue with the example of the student who is failing.

When a student is failing, there is a tendency to assume she will not succeed in school; that in fact, she is not capable of being successful in school. If we look below the surface and find that this student is being abused at home or bullied at school, we will realize that she is lower on the EGSc than she could be. Understanding that, we can see that given a better situation and knowledge of how to move to higher levels on the EGSc, she might become a successful student.

> *I know in my heart that man is good. That what is right will always eventually triumph. And there's purpose and worth to each and every life.*
> Ronald Reagan

This practice is important for both the person making the judgment and the student. For the person making the judgment, understand that our stress level rises and our emotional stance decreases when we judge another negatively.

For the student, in Chapter 9 I discussed mirror neurons and brain sync. Whoever has the more dominant belief about the student's potential for success will influence the other—without words having to be spoken. Researchers at USC and NYU have studied the consequences of affirming one's values and found that doing so creates cognitive

> *Technology is nothing. What's important is that you have a faith in people, that they're basically good and smart, and if you give them tools, they'll do wonderful things with them.*
> Steve Jobs

structure that results in an increased ability to see the big picture.[695] Students primed with a written self-affirming exercise before exams had lower stress on the day of their most stressful exam as measured by epinephrine and norepinephrine.[696]

In general, you can assume that someone behaving in undesirable ways has negative emotions that have not been responded to in of the three constructive methods. The best response to most negative emotion in modern society involves Right Responses (RRs).[697] This involves some action or a deliberate and conscious change in mindscape.

Emotions provide information to guide us. The other two appropriate responses are Fight (non-violent assertive resistance) or Flight.[698] Suppressing or denying emotions is dysfunctional and leads to many other problems.

If we judge ourselves based on our past actions without taking into consideration our emotional state when we made the choices we are judging, we significantly underestimate our potential.

Developing a habit of seeing others for their potential, rather than who they are being in the moment, makes us inspiring to them. By seeing what they cannot see in themselves, we help show them the way to become more of the potential within them.

Humanity has been operating in a way that hinders its ability to thrive. Much like attempting to run a marathon with a weight strapped to one leg would hinder progress, misinterpretation of our EGS has been impairing our ability to thrive. We now know enough to unlock the chains that have been holding us back.

Exercises:

Use your intention setting skills to set an intention to see the potential in yourself and others. I encourage you to reinforce this on a daily basis. You will love who you become.

Magnificence resides within all of us, and we need but tap into it and bring it forth.
Alan Cohen

The next time you think a negative thought about someone ask yourself if you are perceiving *who they are being* or *who they could be*. Then ask yourself, what is their potential? Who could this person become if she believed in herself? Who cold he become if others believed in him? Who could she become if she understood how to be happier? Who could he become if he knew how to forgive?

Pay attention to the difference in how you perceive the person after asking these questions. Take that new mental snapshot of the person and add detail to it, help to solidify that image as the person's potential in your own mind.

When you are going to interact with the person, imagine the person being their potential self. What does that look like? What does that feel like?

Do not use this potential self as a comparison to find fault with where the person is right now. Instead, use that image to encourage and uplift (even if just in the privacy of your own mind).

People will generally rise to your expectations. They'll also live down to your expectations if your expectations are low. If you doubt this, interact with someone you've decided is not trustworthy and see how the person treats you.

Wait. Oh, you don't think anyone is trustworthy. How does the world treat you? They are reflecting your opinion of them back to you. Try trusting someone for no reason whatsoever and see how they rise to your expectation as long as you trust them. Even someone who is generally not trustworthy behaves in a more trustworthy fashion when someone trusts them for no reason. Someone who is already trustworthy will become even more so when they are trusted for no apparent reason.

Children adjust their behavior to the expectations of the people they are with. Most people are aware that children act different with different adults. This is the reason. They are also very malleable. Researchers have shown that a teacher's high expectations positively impact the performance and can even turn a *slow* child into one who seems *gifted*.

Are you expecting what you want?

Go General

Anytime someone is in a low emotional state, he is focused on specifics. For example, if a health problem has him upset, he is focused on the specific aspect of his body that is not functioning the way he wants it to. As long as we are alive, more of our body is functioning well than not. He could have a kidney that is bad, but his mind, heart, lungs, arms, legs, eyes, nose, tongue, skin, and so much more are functioning perfectly. The narrow focus on the specific feels bad. As we deliberately think more generally about our entire body, we feel better.

When you have some quiet time, play with the concept of going general to feel better. If you are upset about a situation at work, mentally take a step back and identify how specifically you are focused. Are you focused on something that happened for only a few minutes out of an entire week? Are you focused on something one person out of 100 did? Are you focused on one day out of an entire year? If you feel negative emotion about it, you are focused specifically.

This is true even if you are looking at something you perceive as a global problem. If you focus on world hunger, you can bring yourself to your knees with the hit of negative emotion. From that position, you cannot be effective in resolving the problem. In that negative state, your cognitive abilities are severely restricted.

If you step back and think about how many people have adequate food, your emotional stance will improve. You may immediately think again of those who do not—it is your habit of thought if this issue is on your mind frequently. Deliberately think again of those who have enough to eat. While you are in that higher emotional state, ask yourself, "How can more people have enough to eat?" Give time a chance to bring solutions. When you find yourself thinking about the problem, begin telling yourself things like, "We'll figure it out soon" or "We're making technological advances all the time, a solution could be found any time now" or "There are a lot of smart people in the world who would like to solve this problem. I am not the only one who is concerned. The right idea will come to one of us."

Remember, it does not matter what the problem is, your ability to solve it is diminished when you feel negative emotion. That means the most you can do from that negative state is make yourself feel better. From that better-feeling state, you have more resources to help you find a solution.

Gabel and Harmon-Jones's research supports this process by demonstrating that high intensity emotion (positive and negative) narrow attention while low-intensity emotions broaden attention. When you're being very specific (about something that feels bad or something that feels good), you can lessen your emotional state by going more general, which will broaden your thought-action repertoire.[699]

This process is recommended for all zones below the Hopeful Zone. Increase your happiness first, then solve problems.

Exercise:

Let's try it now. Get a blank piece of paper. It can have lines or be completely blank. Write a sentence to describe something that has been bothering you. Think about the issue by asking yourself questions, such as "What is the opposite of this?" and "What does the big picture look like?" as well as "Will this matter tomorrow (or in 5 years)?"

Put the issue that is bothering you in a broader context. Then feel how your emotion about the topic shifts.

If your emotions become worse, you are going more specific, not more general. Be patient with yourself and try again. If you have been practicing the negative thoughts for a long time it can be a little bit like starting the lawn mower the first time in the spring, which means it requires a little more effort to get going but once you start, it is easier the next time.

General to Specific Exercise

When one's emotional stance is at the lower end of the EGSc, going more general will invoke better-feeling emotions. When you're on the high end of the EGSc, it is good to go more specific. You can actually bring yourself to a state akin to a natural high by going more specific while in the Sweet Zone. The key is to go as specific as you can while still feeling good.

Talking about doing it may seem difficult, but doing it is easy because your mind helps you when you are in the Sweet Zone. Before you begin this exercise, think about a topic where your emotional set point is in the Sweet Zone for a minute or two. This primes your mind to think of more thoughts in the Sweet Zone.

Before you go more specific with the topic you've chosen, I'm going to give you an example with something simple. The following is how I personally go more specific when I'm working and want to increase my cognitive abilities by increasing my emotional stance:

I love sitting here feeling the morning sun on my skin. Soaking in the warmth feels so wonderful I appreciate the sun, rising every morning without any effort at all on my part. I love the way the birds sing every morning, greeting the sun. I know the birds enjoy it too, that makes me feel more connected to nature and my world. Oh look, my hydrangeas are blooming! I love the big blue fluffy flowers. I always wanted big hydrangeas in my yard and now I have them. I am so blessed. Everything I ever dreamed of having is mine, and so much more than I ever imagined.

To be able to live and know that no matter what happens in life, I can find a perspective where I feel good is so amazing. I want everyone to have this freedom to live fully. Oh, look, the finches are on the birdfeeder. I love living where they come to feed. I love the big open area behind my house. I love watching the birds and the butterflies enjoy all the flowers I planted. I love how peaceful it is out here. My coffee tastes so good this morning.

:::stretching::: It feels so good to stretch. I love my body, its health, the way it helps me accomplish what I want to do and how wise it is. When I get a cut, it knows exactly what to do to heal. When I eat, my body knows how to take exactly what it needs and deliver it to the cells that need it. When I feel good, my body responds by feeling wonderful. It is awesome to live in such a smart body. I'm so glad I don't have to think about making sure my body does what it needs to in order to provide me with a wonderful home. It just knows what to do. I love that I can do things I've done many times, like riding a bicycle, driving a car, typing, or brushing my teeth and I don't have to think about the specifics. I just move into the motions and my body takes over. Isn't that wonderful? It is so much nicer than if I had to think about each little step in the process.

Life is so good and just becomes better all the time. Delightful little surprises, like the butterfly that is flitting around my flowers, showing up to surprise and delight me.

I love our planet. It is so beautiful. I love the way the plants know what to do, just like my body knows what to do. Plants begin growing at just the right time. I could tell the month and almost the day by when my peonies bloom, when the first rose of the season blooms, when the Daffodils, hyacinth, tulips, pansies, and grape hyacinths bloom. It is all so coordinated and all I had to do was plant them. Plants are so reliable, coming back year after year. I love the resilience of nature and how the way everything is interwoven. I love being outside and being able to begin my day this way. I love the way the rain comes and washes everything, the way the wind comes to dry it off, and how the rainbows appear when the sun shines while it is raining elsewhere. I love the absolute beauty of our planet, the stars in the sky at night and the way the moon seems so close when it lights up the night sky. I am so blessed to live on this magnificent planet with so much variety and beauty.

Can you feel how after writing out details of what you are appreciating you would feel very stable in the Sweet Zone? Do you feel the way it adds emphasis to things that I see every day, such as the flowers in my yard? By doing this, each time I see the flowers I am reminded of how good I can feel. By affirming the wisdom of my body[L] I increase my conscious trust in it. This reduces any concerns or worry I may have about a body declining because of age. By the way, research has shown that our expectations about aging are what we tend to experience. This exercise can be done verbally, orally, or simply in your head. Writing it is the most powerful when you are doing a general appreciation of life.

Remember, this exercise is best done when you are in the Sweet Zone on the EGSc. It can be done in the Hopeful Zone. Below the Hopeful Zone it can be counterproductive.

It is a good exercise for increasing your stability in the Sweet Zone. Whether you rarely feel the emotions in the Sweet Zone or you live most of your life there, the stabilizing influence of this exercise will increase your time in the Sweet Zone.

If you are in the Sweet Zone, try this exercise now.

Appreciation (not gratitude)

Appreciate everything, even the ordinary...Especially the ordinary.
Pema Chodron

*Mining the moment for something that feels good,
something to appreciate, something to savor, something to take in, that's what your moments are about.*
Abraham

It's amazing how beautiful the simple things are in life when we take time to notice them.
Kevin Hall

Many teachers teach gratitude as a way of increasing positive emotions. I prefer to teach appreciation. For about one third of people, there is no real difference, but for two thirds, appreciation is the more powerful practice. Research at Rutgers University published in 2012 supports my position that appreciation is more powerful.[700]

[L] By expecting my body to be smart and know what to do, there is coherence on the quantum level that is of great benefit to me.

The reason for this differentiation has to be explained on the quantum level. Despite all Webster's attempts, each of us have attached our own meanings to words and situations. On the quantum level, the words have vibrations that reflect the definition the person has for the word.

I'll provide an example using the word peace. To me it means a feeling I have been able to find inside my own heart where I feel love for everyone on the planet. I have learned that by placing peace in my own heart, I can feel at peace with the world—even while war rages somewhere on the planet. I am not intertwined with war, I am entwined with peace on the quantum level.

For many others, *peace* currently means something longed for but unattainable. That meaning has an entirely different vibration to it than the one I mean when I say or think the word peace.

I teach appreciation instead of gratitude because most people perceive appreciation in the same way. It is a feeling that is closely related to love.

I find that people seem to define gratitude in three distinct ways:
1. I am so grateful that someone bigger/better/more powerful than I am did for me something I could not do for myself,
2. I have to find a way to pay X back for doing this wonderful thing for me, I am indebted to X for the help I received in my time of need, and
3. A feeling of appreciation.

If you compare #1 and #2 to the emotional stances on the EGSc, you will notice that they are very different degrees of empowerment from appreciation. Appreciation is a completely empowered feeling. The other two definitions are at a much lower emotional state. Sometimes seemingly slight differences can make a difference. For this reason, I teach appreciation but I do not teach gratitude.

In the long run, each of us is better served seeing ourselves as able to help ourselves but appreciative of help that comes to us.

Research on the feeling of helplessness shows those who feel helpless give up and do not even try.[701] This is true of both animals and humans. The belief that our actions matter is critical to human thriving. Without the belief that success is a possibility, no effort will be put forth toward a desire.

Some people will say you do owe someone who has helped you. I disagree. Here is why: I teach human thriving for a living. While I charge for my programs and books, as I move through my day I often provide hints, tips, and a hand up to those I encounter. I do not do it so they will feel they owe me. I do not want them to feel they owe me. I do want them to appreciate but not so much appreciate me as the fact that we live in a world where help can come to us from a vast number of resources. I want them to feel the abundance that surrounds us in this way. I also do this for a very selfish reason, which is because it makes me feel good when I help others. My personal excitement, pleasure, and satisfaction from uplifting or inspiring another is the greatest gift I could receive. If they do not receive my gift, I don't get mine—the pleasure of knowing I was helpful to someone.

If someone receives my gift and feels gratitude using definition 1 or 2, she will need help again. How much have I truly helped her? She doesn't feel the sense of empowerment someone in a pure state of appreciation feels. She isn't receiving the health and well-being benefits that come from being empowered.

> *Appreciation is the recognition and enjoyment of the good qualities of someone or something. The something may be material, but it could also be an idea.*

So appreciate everything you can find to appreciate. Feel grateful if your definition of grateful is appreciation. If your definition of grateful is #1 or #2, reach for a feeling of appreciation instead. Feeling appreciation is a habit of thought you can develop.

Researchers tell us that humans become accustomed to what is normal for them and this tendency decreases their appreciation of the good things that are constant in their lives. But you have the ability to focus on those things and appreciate them. When you turn on the faucet, does clear water come into your home? When you get up on a cold winter's morning, do you have to go outside to relieve yourself or can you stay inside? Do you have shoes to wear when it is cold? Do you have sunglasses when it is bright outside? Do you have eyes to see? Do you have ears to hear? Do you have fingers that can touch? Does your heart beat without your constant attention to it? Obviously, I could fill this book with things to appreciate (and possibly sound crazy while I'm at it—but I would be a good-feeling crazy lady). What I've learned is that when I get on a roll about things to appreciate I begin feeling light and happy and a feeling of ease comes with the sense of deep appreciation. What is that experience worth to you? How much have you paid for experiences that you hoped would make you happy? How empowering is it to know that at any time and in any place you can wield the power of your own mind to navigate yourself to a high level of happiness?

I don't just appreciate the little things everyone takes for granted. My life is awesome. So far this year I've vacationed for nine weeks including two in Hawaii when the whales were there and the weather at home was cold and two weeks on a cruise ship in a suite with a butler at our beck and call. But notice how when I think of Hawaii my mind immediately goes to the whales? Because I savored their presence every day we were there. I was like a child with money in his pocket on the lookout for the ice cream man. Every whale I saw was celebrated. Every picture with a whale is treasured. Every story about that trip includes the whales. I can no longer think about Hawaii without thinking about how much I enjoyed the whales. My neuropathways about Hawaii include whales.

If you find enough to savor in your life, your mind won't have room for thoughts that don't feel good. I'll stop now but I could wax just as poetic about my shower, my kitchen, the people in my life, our dog, books I've read, modern technology, researchers, flowers, the mountains, the ocean, my mind, the human mind, my body, bodies in general, food, the Earth, the seasons, modern transportation, and more. I was not born this way. I was not this way in early adulthood. I trained myself to get this much enjoyment from life. There was a time when my marriage was so awful my parents stopped wanting to be around me because nothing nice was going to come out of my mouth. There have been times I was so depressed that I could not find a positive thought but all that was before I learned what it requires to be happy.

Pay attention to your words. Small differences make a difference. When I said that simple changes change your world I meant it. There is a tremendous difference between, "I think I can" and "I can" just as there's a difference between "I'm grateful" and "I appreciate your help." Use your EGS to feel for the differences, and become more attuned to them. It will change how you approach the situation and how you think about it.

Exercise appropriate for Hopeful Zone or above

Consciously look for something you can appreciate. Mentally (or by writing) think of as much about that person, place, event, or thing that you can appreciate. As your thoughts think of appreciating that, other things you appreciate will naturally come to your mind. Continue expressing appreciation for everything you can think of with appreciation. Practice this every morning and see how much more you find in your day to appreciate.

Family Exercise

Sometimes a family wants to shift to a more positive frame of reference together. Sometimes you have a child who is stuck in a negative mindset. This simple appreciate exercise has provided powerful, life changing results to many families.

Set aside a time of day, dinner is a good time for families that are able to eat together. Go around the table and have each person share three things they appreciated about their day. At first you may have to help. My eldest was in such a negative mindset as she began 1st grade that she would say "Nothing good ever happens." so I helped her by pointing out good things.

"Is there food on your plate?"

"Did we get home safely after school?"

"Do we have a table where we can eat?"

The things we appreciate do not have to be big, new, or exciting. We just need to feel appreciation. I had the same experience with a bank president during the midst of the economic downturn. He asked if he could begin with one a day because times were tough. He asked this moments after having spent almost five minutes telling me how wonderful and supportive his wife was about his long hours and reduced salary during the economic crisis his institution was experiencing. I asked him almost the same questions I had asked my daughter years before:

"When you sat down to dinner last night, was there food on your plate?"

"Did it taste good?"

"Did you have a table to put your plate on?"

Other things to appreciate surround us each day. The sun comes up every day. Air to breathe is freely available worldwide. The seasons come and go in their natural harmony without any effort from us. Our planet circles the sun at the perfect distance to support life.

> *Mining the moment for something that feels good,*
> *something to appreciate,*
> *something to savor,*
> *something to take in,*
> *that's what your moments are about.*
> Abraham

Relationship Appreciation Exercise

Appreciation is a powerful tool for building great relationships. If you spend a few minutes each day appreciating the people who are important in your life, your relationships will delight you. You don't have to tell them what you're doing. Begin general and go as specific as you can while still feeling good.

Phil:

I adore Phil. I love how he is so good to everyone. I love knowing he is trustworthy so I never have to think about whether he'll do the right thing. He'll be kind to others and to me. He'll respect anyone I bring home. I love how he always seems to be thinking about me and about how he can please me. I love that he does this even when I'm so involved with a book or designing a class that it may seem I'm ignoring him. He just loves me steadily and sure. I love how it so often seems he reads my mind. I love the way he has friendships that have lasted almost sixty years. I love how caring he is and the way he keeps track of people's birthdays and remembers them. I love his cooking and the way I never feel I have to nag him about anything. I love how trustworthy and reliable he is. I love the way he kisses me and the way he holds my hand, even when we're sleeping I can slide my hand into his and find a warm welcome.

Courtney:

I love Courtney's healers' heart. I love the way she is interested in so many different subjects that I am often surprised that someone I've known her entire life knows so much that I don't know. I love her adventurous spirit. She makes me wonder what she'll come up with next and I can't even imagine where she'll be or who she'll be in the years to come because she continues to grow and become more all the time. I love how she seems so free to be her unique self and the things she tries that I never would have done at her age. She has a sense of freedom about her that is refreshing and lovely. I love the way she is willing to clean up and how mature she has become while retaining that *Joie de Vivre* that is so inspiring. I love the way she sets goals and seems to effortlessly move toward them. I love that she has learned to drive and is able to enjoy life more than ever before.

Ashley:

I love Ashley's compassion for others and the way she cares so deeply for those in her life. I love how she has found something she enjoys and converted it into a business that is giving her more freedom than most her age (and most any age, really) enjoy. I love how she makes sure the quality of her products is always a good reflection of her. I love her creativity. I love that she found a way to combine that creativity with her business. I love how good she is at friendships and relationships. She has surprised and delighted me with her maturity in handling relationship troubles. I also love that she will actually ask my advice at times. I love her willingness to do what she believes is right even when others might disagree with her decisions. I love her willingness to sacrifice to do what she believes is right when that is necessary.

A boss:

I'm glad my boss was smart enough to know I would be good in this job. I love that he just lets me know the results he wants and leaves me to figure it out. I learn so much more and become so much more that way than I would if he told me what to do every step of the way. I love knowing I am supported if I have a problem. I love the opportunity to develop me because my job security is me—my knowledge and skills—not my company. The more I become, the more I will be and my boss is good at giving me opportunities to become more. I like working with my boss. I'm going to have fun today.

Try appreciating the main relationships in your life every day for a week and see what happens. Your connection will feel stronger. You'll enjoy them more and they'll enjoy you more.

It is easiest to begin in a general state of appreciation and then move to more and more specifics.

Body Appreciation

Researchers have discovered that sexual arousal, orgasm, and satisfaction in women increases as satisfaction with their own body increased and decreased as satisfaction with their body declined.[702] How the women actually felt about their body, not their size or age, was what had the biggest determination on their enjoyment. Appreciation of one's body has been shown to protect against the negative media exposure to ultra-thin idealized bodies that can have detrimental impacts on self-esteem, eating behaviors including the development of eating disorders.[703] I suspect men's ED may be more about how they feel and their beliefs about aging than about a physical malady.

Finding the Appreciable Aspects

Another exercise you could try is to take something you don't like and find the positive aspects about it. I saw the following saying framed in a gift shop in my travels and took a picture of it because I loved how it reframed something almost everyone can relate to:

Dirty Dishes
Thank heaven for dirty dishes
They have a tale to tell,
While other folks go hungry,
We're eating very well.
With home and health and happiness,
We shouldn't want to fuss,
By this stack of evidence
God's very good to us.

What aspects of daily life do you look at the negative aspects of while missing their positive side?

Amplify Positive Emotions

Just as going from specific to general can reduce negative emotions when your emotional state is below the Hopeful Zone, being more specific amplifies positive emotional states when you are in the Hopeful or Sweet Zones. The key is to not get so specific that your emotional state declines so it is important to pay attention to how you feel. When you are in the Sweet Zone it is possible to achieve emotional (natural) high's by doing this process. It can also be used as a type of foreplay when the focus of your thoughts is your lover's positive aspects. Verbalizing what you appreciate about your lover can strengthen your bond by focusing your attention on what you love about your partner and can enhance the appreciation your lover feels from you. The same strategy can be used with your children to strengthen your bond and enhance their self-esteem. Your appreciation, in all situations, must be authentic for it to be beneficial.

Find Joy

Look for things that are good in the world, even if they are happening to or for someone else and feel joy for the good fortune of another. If you want a good relationship, look for examples of good relationships in the world. This reinforces your belief that such relationships are possible. You don't have to take the whole relationship you witness, just find joy in the parts that feel good to you. Don't compare your situation (past or present) with the person you're observing—especially not negative comparison. Don't allow yourself to judge whether the person deserves what he or she is experiencing. Remind yourself that everyone, even you, deserve all the good they can find in life. Our uniqueness makes each of us very valuable to the world, regardless of whether we are a child or a king. Say to yourself, "I like seeing examples of what is possible in the world because if it is possible for another, it is possible for me."

Consider your Resources

This process is helpful in emotional stances below the Hopeful Zone. As you pay more attention to how you feel, subtle differences will be more apparent to you. As your chronic emotional stance moves up the EGSc, you will notice if you are below your normal level. When you are, don't panic. Be easy on yourself. Often your resources are depleted. Ask yourself some self-evaluative questions:
- Am I hungry?
- Am I overtired?
- Am I time-stressed?
- Am I in pain?
- Am I worried about something?

When your resources are depleted, you may revert to old habits. Don't worry that you are regressing. Identify what has depleted your resources and, if possible, do something about it. If it is a chronic issue, try to find a way to correct the problem.

When your resources are depleted, it can be difficult to maintain your resolve to attain certain goals. Perhaps you have committed to a new exercise routine but you're so tired that driving to the gym might be an unwise decision. Maybe you can have a salad with some protein for dinner instead of the larger meal you would have chosen. Mix and match things that continue to move you toward your goal. If you are just so exhausted that you can't seem to find the willpower to do anything toward your goal, focus on letting go of stress—which includes not beating yourself up for not doing anything that day. Remember, the self-induced stress from beating yourself up is worse for you than skipping a planned session at the gym.

When you set goals, plan for contingencies. Don't plan your goal as if every single day is going to be as smooth and perfect as you would wish it to be. We, our children, our spouses, and our parents can get sick. There are traffic jams, snow storms, and countless other events that we need to consider when setting goals. Find a balance that works for you. If you're a single parent with one child you might not need as much flexibility as the single parent with two kids. The adult with no children at home might be able to get by with less flexibility built into the plan, unless her parents have health issues or her grown children have grandbabies that might interrupt a plan.

If you find yourself in a conversation that is not going the way you want it to go, check your resources and that of the person you're interacting with. Very often conversations that destroy relationships occur when one or both people have depleted resources. It is better to withdraw from the conversation and resume it when the participants are in a better state.

Be flexible in your plans and easy on yourself when your plans stray from the original course. Becoming too stressed about sticking to an inflexible plan increases the stress level when the plan goes awry.

End Self-criticism

Man often becomes what he believes himself to be. If I keep on saying to myself that I cannot do a certain thing, it is possible that I may end by really becoming incapable of doing it. On the contrary, if I have the belief that I can do it, I shall surely acquire the capacity to do it even if I may not have it at the beginning.
Mahatma Gandhi

The first step to ending self-criticism is to give yourself permission and then set your intentions. For many of us, we have lived with that negative voice in our heads so long we mistake it for who we are. It isn't. It might be your mother, but it isn't your mother when she was in the Sweet Zone. (And yes, it is possible your mother was never in the Sweet Zone—the possibility of this is a common question in my programs.)

Think about what motivates you to exercise. If you exercise regularly, how do you explain your reason when asked? If you don't exercise regularly, do you tell yourself you should? Do you mentally beat yourself up for not exercising? Why do you tell yourself you should exercise more? If you are repeatedly telling yourself something like, "You don't exercise enough," or, "You're going to gain weight because you don't exercise enough," or, "If you don't start exercising you're going to die young," you are affirming the undesired. Affirming what you do not want leads to long term self-fulfilling prophesies.

The mechanics of negative self-talk are complex. First, self-criticism increases your level of stress. That causes biochemical changes in your body—including depressing your immune system, reducing your energy, and other stress responses. None of this is healthy for your body. Then, the mind, which is very malleable and obedient to repeated affirmations, forms beliefs that lead to the exact outcomes you are telling yourself you will experience by giving yourself the negative affirmations.

If you are in the habit of negative self-criticism, do everything you can to stop it. Refuting it is a good tool. You can begin by shifting a little bit. For example, "I am learning to reduce my stress level. When my level of stress is lower, I will naturally feel like exercising more. My body enjoys moving and soon I will move it more." This refuting statement may be more than you can believe right now. If that is so, find something you do believe that feels better than the negative self-talk. Take baby steps.

As you learn stress-decreasing skills and your energy level rises, kick it up a little: "I feel more energetic than I used to. I am enjoying adding exercise to my day. My body really enjoys moving. Now I enjoy it, too." Find affirmations that you can believe and that support what you want. If you can't believe anything close to what you want yet, just move in that direction a step at a time. With an unhealthy mindset about ourselves, or aspects of physical activity, we can harm our health by increasing stress:

1. Self-induced stress caused by making exercise about preventing illness.
2. Self-induced stress from negative self-criticism related to not exercising or not doing it well enough or often enough.
3. Stress from peer and parental pressure to act grown-up and forgo fun childish physical activities.

Research has shown the motivation behind physical activity affects the results.

If you do not make much progress eliminating the critic at first, put this intention aside and focus on building your trust in your guidance. Once you have experimented with your guidance and built trust in the answers you received from your guidance this task becomes easier. You can use your guidance to ask if what your critic is saying is true, if the self-criticism is beneficial, and other questions you may have about the inner critic.

When you are ready, refute the comments the inner critic is sharing. If the critic told me I couldn't do something, my response was "Watch me." If the critic told me I wasn't good enough, my response was to find evidence in the world that contradicted the critic. For example, if the critic told me I was unattractive, I would remember times when real people told me the opposite. If the critic told me I wasn't smart enough, I remembered how I have used my brain to solve problems.

If you feel ready to challenge your inner critic, try setting a timer on your phone to go off randomly several times a day during times when you may have a moment to think about what your inner voice is saying. When the alarm goes off, notice what your inner voice was saying and if it was negative use techniques in this section to challenge the premises of the negative words. You can refute it. You can go more general in what you're thinking about or you can look for facts that show the voice is wrong.

You can decide to change something about yourself without declaring your current state of being as bad or unworthy. You are like your life, a journey, not a destination. You are constantly changing and improvements can be part of that journey. There is not a requirement to declare that who you are is bad or wrong in order to grow. Does the crawling infant declare itself bad for not yet walking? No. The same holds true throughout life. You are where you are. Wherever that is can be improved.

33 : Processes (How to Think Positive)

Being kind to yourself matters. Do it.

The person in life that you will always be with the most, is yourself. Because even when you are with others, you are still with yourself, too! When you wake up in the morning, you are with yourself, lying in bed at night you are with yourself, walking down the street in the sunlight you are with yourself. What kind of person do you want to walk down the street with? What kind of person do you want to wake up in the morning with? What kind of person do you want to see at the end of the day before you fall asleep? Because that person is yourself, and it's your responsibility to be that person you want to be with. I know I want to spend my life with a person who knows how to let things go, who's not full of hate, who's able to smile and be carefree. So that's who I have to be.

C. Joy Bell

Low self-esteem usually has one of two roots. One is a habit of comparing oneself to others and looking for flaws. Remember, you are comparing your bloopers to someone else's highlight reel. Don't do that. It is not helpful to you. It does not make you more motivated.

If you're comparing your income to what someone else makes and finding fault with your results, you may also be hastening ill health and an early demise on yourself. There is significant research indicating it is the comparison you make and not the lower income that causes less desirable health outcomes.[704] You can adopt a different perspective. How about, "I'm smarter than he is. If he can make that much, so can I."

The other common root cause of low self-esteem is a parent or other significant influencer (sometimes a spouse) who repeatedly does and says things to make you feel less than you are. Remember what you have learned about the impact of ES on behavior. No one who was tearing you down was in a good emotional state. Someone in a good emotional state can find something to praise and love about anyone. Their comments, as hurtful as they felt at the time, only contain the power you gave them to hurt you. If you recognize that the comment reflects the person's ES at the time rather than a valid judgment of your worth, the pain lessens.

While teaching human thriving in high schools, I have had children ask me if it is possible their mom or dad has been angry their whole life. The relief on their face when I said yes let me know I mattered. I would also go on to explain that most people stay in their dominant ES for long periods—often for life—because society has not taught them how to change their ES. Even with the Think Positive movement, the concept was pushed but the how has been largely ignored.

Reframing prior experiences through a new lens that understands that adverse behavior from others was evidence of their low Emotional State, and not of your worth, can be very healing. It also increases compassion.

Imagine a rebellious teenage girl who has been frequently unkind to her chronically angry, or chronically frustrated, Mother, the epitome of a relationship on a downward spiral without a good ending. The angry Mom is literally training those around her to treat her in ways that make her angry. The daughter has learned this well. Even though she is a good person, without a deliberate intention to be otherwise, she is sucked into the Mom's current of anger. But now, armed with the information that her Mom's behavior is the result of not feeling emotionally good, she can set a new intention. She can decide who she is. For example, she can decide, "I am a kind person. I will do my best to be a positive force in this world." It will take practice because by this time the daughter has developed some neurological pathways that will work against her (just in beginning—later the new neurological pathways she deliberately cultivates will help her maintain who she has decided to be).

She can be conscious during her interactions with her mom and when her mom is not being supportive, rather than becoming defensive, she can recognize that her mom is feeling emotionally bad. Armed with that knowledge, she can look for ways to uplift mom—which is the only thing that is going to improve the undesired behavior. In saying this, recognize it is not the teenager's job to uplift her mom. It is not her responsibility. But, unless her mom understands the EGS, the other choices are not good ones. We can ignore mom; however, for a teenager living in her mom's home, this could lead to worsening behavior.

Without an understanding of the EGS, the teenager typically allows an inner critic to move into her mind and suffers low self-esteem that limits her life. With an understanding of the EGS, a much better outcome is possible.

My inner critic moved away a few years ago. You can encourage yours to move, too. Humor can help with the persistent inner critic. You can begin telling the critic how nice it is in some place far way, maybe Tahiti, and encouraging it to relocate and that you'll accept four critical postcards a year. Have fun with it. You give the critic its power by believing it. At any time, you have the ability to overthrow its reign.

Oh, and if it is your mom? Don't tell her. It won't help your relationship. It also does not mean she was a bad Mom. We live in an era when we have been trained to criticize those we love the most of all. The intention was good. Appreciate that you are learning a better way. Children tend to identify with their parents and therefore tend to internalize and self-inflict verbally abusive statements against themselves throughout their lives[705] as the result of a negatively focused or unhappy parent. The life sentence is optional. The skills in this book can provide release from the self-critical thought patterns.

Exercise

Pay attention to negative thoughts you think about yourself and make a note of them in a notebook. Spend some time each day, preferably when you're feeling hopeful or above but if you're seldom in hopeful, just try to catch yourself when you're feeling your best, and work on shifting the thought patterns.

Pull out the negative thought and find ways to lessen its hold.

Let's use age as an example.

Original thought: *I'm too old to get a good job. No one wants to hire someone in their 50's.*

Contrary thoughts:

50 isn't that old. 50 is the new 30. I'm still vibrant and alive. I just picked up some bogus beliefs about age during my life but now that I'm here I see they were really off the mark. I'm experienced and gaining some wisdom, but I'm nowhere near old. Employers would be lucky to hire me. I'm responsible. I am at a point in my life where I can really focus on my career without a lot of distractions. I'm mature and responsible. I don't look old. I don't feel old. All I have to do is go in there feeling energetic and bright and they'll be delighted to hire me. I'll make them believe they're having a lucky day.

Negative self-talk often lacks a basis in reality. It is most often a bogus belief you picked up somewhere that just isn't serving you. Refuting it and substituting a belief that serves you better enables you to form new beliefs. Remember, beliefs are just thoughts you've thought repeatedly until they became beliefs. Think new thoughts repeatedly for a while and you'll establish new beliefs.

Focus on Your Why

When you focus on why you want what you want, it helps propel you forward. For example, I left my old career to begin Happiness 1st Institute because I had learned the root cause of human thriving. Before I knew what I now know, I was happy doing a job where I helped people with their finances and helped the salespeople and the company do the right things—because I saw that as helping people. I helped the people who worked at the company by helping the company maintain its good reputation. I helped the salespeople by helping them understand the myriad rules they had to follow. I helped the public by ensuring there were ethical and honest experts they could talk to about their retirement and other financial planning goals. I loved what I did because I always framed my role as one where I was helping people.

But once I knew the keys to human thriving, helping people in the old way was not enough. I knew how to do so much more that would benefit them and not doing it felt awful. Many people have told me they would have been too afraid to leave a high salaried position to begin their own business in an entirely new field. But I focused on my why.

The best use of my time is helping others learn to thrive more.
Nothing I can do gives more value to the world than this.

That is my why. It is the reason I do what I do. It is the reason I don't want to do anything else. I could focus on the fact that this path has a much higher income potential than any job as an employee but that would not motivate me. Why? Because what would I want to do with the money? I'd want to use it to spread the knowledge I gained about human thriving. It gives me more freedom to travel, which is great, but what do I enjoy most when I travel? I enjoy teaching and learning new ways to help more people.

When you identify why you want what you want it, will motivate you and propel you toward your goals.

Reframe Failure
Our education system teaches most children that failing at something is bad. It also fails to teach us how to be resilient in the face of failure by depriving us of opportunities to lose.

Reframing what failure means is a worthwhile exercise for most people. In many instances, failure is a leg up, an elevator to quicker progress than would have ever been accomplished without the lessons learned from the experience. In some cases failure opens doors that would have remained closed without the knowledge and experience gained.

Failure can be a delay or a detour, but in hindsight,
it often turns out to be a shortcut.

Changing your perception of a situation from something that is threatening to one where the situation is a challenge—something you can achieve to bring yourself to a new level of competence helps you succeed. When you view a situation as threatening, your body goes into a stress reaction narrowing your perception and decreasing your immune, cognitive, and digestive functions. By reframing the situation as a challenge, your view broadens,[706] you'll be able to identify solutions with greater ease and you won't suffer the ill health effects from the stress response to a perceived threat.

Even if your work situation seems threatening, it is possible to do this. Instead of thinking thoughts along the lines of, "If I fail, I'll be out of work" think things more along the lines of, "This is helping me build my resume. Even if I fail, I will have experience in something new and that experience will prepare me for more opportunities." Depending on your current perception of self, you can take the positive reinforcement of the new (reframed) perspective further. One student told me his mantra, "Failure is not an option because I don't fail." This type of attitude is fine as long as you don't beat yourself up for it if you don't succeed. However, this type of attitude is associated with success, so if you can authentically feel this way, your chances of failure are very slim.

Use feedback from failures to inform your future actions. See failure, not as a desirable0 goal, but one that provides valuable information when it does occur—if that information is properly harvested and applied to future endeavors.

Exercise:

Write down a situation where you currently feel like you failed. Ask yourself some questions:
What did I learn from this situation?
What do I know now that would help me do better in the future if I encounter another situation like that one?
What would I do differently now?

It is pretty easy to see that you learn and grow as the result of every experience and that who you have become as a result of the experience knows more and is more prepared.

The truth is you can never go back and not know what you now know. That means that the person who "failed" no longer exists.

Sure, you could find a new way to fail and learn even more, but you cannot make the same mistake because you know too much.

Thomas Edison found 10,000 ways light bulbs didn't work before he found one that did. Did he fail 10,000 times or did he learn 10,000 times?

Researching successful individuals who failed at one point in time, like those in the list below, can help you realize that failure is just a part of success. Hint: Look for the failure(s) they experienced before success.

Michael Jordan	Oprah Winfrey	J. K. Rowling
Soichiro Honda	Tony Robbins	John Paul Mitchell
Sidney Poitier	Albert Einstein	Marilyn Monroe
Steve Jobs	Garth Brooks	Orville and Wilbur Wright
Akio Morita	Bill Gates	Harland David Sanders
Steven Spielberg	Stephen King	Winston Churchill
Abraham Lincoln	Charles Darwin	Ludwig van Beethoven
John Grisham	Dale Carnegie	Theodor Seuss Giesel
Elvis Presley	The Beatles	Louisa May Alcott
Charles Schultz	Jack London	Stephanie Meyer
Tom Landry	Joe Torres	Walt Disney
Thomas Edison	R.H. Macy	

Every adversity, every failure, every heartache
carries with it the seeds of an equal or greater benefit.
Napoleon Hill

Do not be embarrassed by your failures, learn from them and start again.
Richard Branson

I can accept failure, everyone fails at something. But I can't accept not trying.
<u>Michael Jordan</u>

Failure is simply the opportunity to begin again, this time more intelligently.
Henry Ford

Freedom is not worth having if it does not include the freedom to make mistakes.
Mahatma Gandhi

Improve Self-Esteem

High (healthy) self-esteem, Crocker and Park said, "The desire to believe that one is worthy or valuable drives behavior and shapes how people think about themselves, other people, and events in their lives."[707] Dr. Peter Kramer said, "Low self-worth and poor interpersonal skills—the usual causes of social awkwardness—are so deeply ingrained and difficult to influence that ordinarily change comes gradually, if ever."[708] This is one reason why learning about one's Emotional Guidance is so important. As soon as the guidance gains a person's trust, that person can begin using it to refute negative self-concepts and increase self-esteem. Trust in one's guidance can be built using other subjects that do not have as much practiced resistance to better-feeling thoughts.

It is important, maybe even critical, that self-esteem is built on a stable foundation. "Success at this pursuit [of self-esteem] leads to positive emotions, reduced anxiety, and a sense of safety and control over events and can be highly motivating. On the other hand, failure at the pursuit of self-esteem can lead to feelings of worthlessness, shame, sadness, and anger, leaving people feeling vulnerable to mortality or social rejection or feeling unable to cope with life events . . . there is little evidence that pursuing self-esteem by attempting to satisfy standards of value and worth actually increases social inclusion, competence, efficacy, relatedness, or immortality or leads to improved objective outcomes . . . when relationships with significant others are perceived to be highly conditional or critical, thoughts about those significant others trigger concerns about self-esteem and self-worth. . . Consistent with self-determination theory, we assume that relatedness, competence, autonomy, and self-regulation are always needs (but are not always adopted as goals)."[709]

"External contingencies of self-worth, which require validation from others, have greater costs . . . external contingencies of self-worth such as appearance, others' approval, competition, and academic competence are associated with more problems during the freshman year, whereas internal contingencies, such as virtue or religious faith, were associated with lower levels of these problems. Students who based their self-esteem on appearance partied more, used more alcohol and drugs, and were higher in symptoms of disordered eating, whereas students who based their self-esteem on virtue used less alcohol and drugs, had fewer symptoms of disordered eating, and even earned higher grades in college . . . Pursuing self-esteem by being virtuous, compassionate, generous, or altruistic would seem to have fewer costs, especially fewer costs for others."[710]

Numerous researchers recommended that developing non-contingent self-esteem would be a path to achieving self-esteem goals without the potential costs of many common methods, but Crocker and Wolfe, were not sure anyone with truly non-contingent self-esteem exists.[711] If non-contingent means not relying on one's Emotional Guidance, I would have to agree. However, it is possible to develop self-esteem using Emotional Guidance that is stable and secure and not reliant on external factors. My opinion is that self-esteem was designed to be based on our properly interpreted emotional responses.

"Self-worth that is completely non-contingent is not vulnerable to threat and therefore does not need to be protected or defended from threat. When self-esteem is truly non-contingent, it is simply a given and therefore becomes unnecessary to pursue."[712]

"The pursuit of self-esteem interferes with relatedness, learning, autonomy self-regulation, and mental and physical health. Pursuing self-esteem can be motivating, but other sources of motivation, such as goals that are good for the self and others, can provide the same motivation without the costs... Although chasing after self-esteem can motivate excellent performance, performance itself is not a fundamental human need, and it can be achieved through other less destructive sources of motivation. Recognition and acknowledgement are not the same as love and acceptance, and they do not create the safety and security people desire. People cannot protect themselves from dangers they experienced in childhood by proving that they are smart, strong, beautiful, rich, or admired or that they satisfy some other contingency of self-worth. In the words of Claire Nuer, a Holocaust survivor and leadership development trainer, "The only way to create love, safety, and acceptance is by giving them."" [713]

"Achieving a high level of self-esteem, or perhaps more important, avoiding low self-esteem, is important for health and well-being throughout the life span... Prospective studies conducted with children, adolescents, and young adults, for example, suggest that low self-esteem increases their susceptibility to a wide range of problematic outcomes and experiences such as depression, eating disorders, teenage pregnancy, victimization, difficulty sustaining and forming close relation-ships, involvement in antisocial behavior, substance use, and suicide ideation and attempts. Higher levels of self-esteem similarly have been found in other research to prospectively predict growth in socioemotional functioning among younger, preschool-age children and, at the other end of the developmental continuum, decreased likelihood of mortality among older adults. Several long-term longitudinal studies also have found that relatively high levels of self-esteem (or, alternatively, the relative absence of indications of low self-esteem) during childhood and adolescence predict more favorable psychological, social, and occupational outcomes during adulthood. Similarly, intervention research points toward the benefits of helping individuals to achieve a high level of self-esteem. In a recent meta-analysis of the effectiveness of esteem-enhancement programs for children and adolescents, program participants were found to experience gains not only in self-esteem but also in behavior, personality and emotional functioning, and academic performance. It is notable that the programs that produced the largest effects on the latter types of outcomes were those in which participants experienced the greatest increases in self-esteem. Improvements in self-esteem also appear to contribute to the effectiveness of a range of other types of interventions, such as cognitive–behavioral therapy, mentoring programs, and school reform initiatives. It is noteworthy that such interventions have the aim of not only strengthening self-esteem but also facilitating positive outcomes in a range of other areas (e.g., academic performance).[714]

It is useful to consider in this regard that high self-esteem has been included consistently among criteria used to define positive mental health. Yet an equally prominent theme in these conceptualizations is the interdependence of self-esteem with a range of other facets of positive mental health, such as a sense of mastery, autonomy, accurate perceptions of reality, a sense of optimism, interpersonal relatedness, and responsible behavior toward others. Only when self-esteem is pursued and attained in ways that promote these broad underpinnings of positive mental health does it seem reasonable to expect feelings of self-worth to be implicated consistently in overall health and well-being." [715]

"Self-protective/self-enhancing responses are oriented toward the goal of (1) forestalling the experience of self-devaluing judgments and consequent distressful self feelings (self-protective patterns) and (2) increasing the occasions rather than variable oriented (Bergman & Magnusson, 1997). A major implication of adopting this perspective is that the emphasis shifts from self-esteem and whether it is high or low in relative isolation from other factors (i.e., a variable-oriented approach) to a primary focus instead on the overall patterning of operating factors in the model that is characteristic of any given individual... These other operating factors include esteem formation and maintenance processes and whether they are adaptive or maladaptive. The model assumes, in particular, that it is the patterning of both the level of self-esteem (and its various facets) in combination with the strategies relied on to acquire and sustain self-esteem that will be most influential in shaping outcomes. . . The combination of high self-esteem and adaptive processes for acquiring and sustaining self-esteem then would be assumed to promote overall health and well-being, with positive functioning in different areas (e.g., behavioral) having a reciprocal influence on self-esteem and other model components in desirable directions. . . The theory and research that we have reviewed indicate that both the level and pursuit of self-esteem can be influential in shaping overall health and well-being. Accordingly, the investigation of how these relatively more static and dynamic facets of the self-esteem construct interrelate with one another to influence outcomes of interest should be a priority in future research. In doing so, attention should be given to clarifying the capacity for strategies that are relied on in the pursuit of self-esteem to be not only costly but also beneficial in terms of their implications for health and well-being."[716] Applying *The Smart Way* with Emotional Guidance to self-esteem development and maintenance is easy and effective.

". . . boosting self-esteem temporarily increases positive affect [mood] and decreases negative affect including anxiety. . . pursuing self-esteem has fewer costs when one attempts to satisfy relatively internal contingencies of self-worth rather than external contingencies."[717] One of the examples Crocker and Park use is when an advisor needs to provide a graduate student with negative feedback which may make the student angry, hurt or defensive—an outcome that could have negative self-esteem repercussions for the advisor and thus be avoided, despite the potential long-term consequences of the graduate student receiving needed negative feedback. If the student knows how to use his Emotional Guidance, he is unlikely to become angry, hurt or defensive for more than a few moments—even if that is the first reaction.

The chain result would be recognition of the negative emotion and almost immediate cognitive reappraisal to better-feeling emotional states. The end result, which an individual practiced in using meta-cognitve processes to feel better whom is aware that negative emotion is an internal feedback system advising him that the way he is perceiving the information is not the best-feeling perspective he could have about the subject, would be cognitive reappraisal to a better-feeling perspective.

One potential outcome would consider the advisor's intention to help the student and recognition that life is a journey where we always have the potential to improve who we show up as and that the advisor's guidance will help him achieve better outcomes faster. This stance recognizes that the advisor's purpose in providing the feedback is to help the student.

If the advisor is not intending to be helpful and the negative feedback is not accurate the student's Emotional Guidance will lead him to recognize that for some reason (known or unknown) the advisor is not acting in his best interests and the information can be safely ignored. He will not be hurt because he will recognize that the advisor's own negative emotional state led to the words.

There are millions of potential variations, but each has a path to thoughts that feel better, and all of them are in reach if the student has been practicing *The Smart Way*.

The advisor who has been practicing *The Smart Way* would have greater intuitive guidance about how to word the feedback and even if the student were not versed in cognitive reappraisal, could guide the conversation so that the student both took the advice seriously, but saw that it pointed to further growth and that knowing how to improve oneself is always of benefit.

Another example Crocker and Park used was inviting an unpopular child to a birthday party, where children who might not want the child to attend might be mean. First, unpopular children usually don't like themselves very much. If the child were taught *The Smart Way*, she would be more likely to find favorable self-images of herself and she would no longer be the unpopular child. But let's say she is the unpopular child but she has been learning how to apply *The Smart Way* and has really come to understand that one's emotional state and behavior are linked together. When one or more of the children teased her she would be less likely to take it personally and more likely to respond with compassion for the other child's low emotional state.

If the unpopular child did not know *The Smart Way* but the other children did, the likelihood of them teasing another child in a hurtful way is much lower because they would be maintaining their own emotional state in the Sweet Zone, which would lead to more inclusive and kinder behavior. If one child was mean to the unpopular girl, the others would be less likely to join in because being mean to someone would feel worse than they currently feel. Behavior is driven by a desire to feel better. In fact, they would be likely to stand up for the unpopular child because that would feel better than teasing her. There are many dynamics that could shift the actions. Everyone, including children, are individuals who are capable of responding in unique ways.

In Western societies, a backlash to high self-esteem sometimes occurs from multiple perspectives. High self-esteem can violate family or social group demands for being humble. High self-esteem can also be viewed as egotistical, or thinking you're better than others—especially when those around you have low self-esteem. A common saying is, "You're getting too big for your britches" is not referring to weight, but to expansive and ambitious ideas. Society is not well-served when people discount their value and worth.

I've found a way to have high self-esteem without it feeling egotistical to myself or others. I hold others in as high of regard as I do myself. That thinking oneself is really good is apparent when I tell my class, "I'm wonderful," followed by a long pause after which I say, "and so are you and you and you. Each and everyone one of you are wonderful in your beautifully unique way. Let yourself feel how wonderful you are."

The discomfort with my self-praise is always obvious. It is as if our society has a mandate that makes it forbidden to think well of ourself. Yet, high self-esteem is reported to be one of the strongest predictors of well-being . . . and it is so closely related to happiness that it could be considered a component of happiness."[718]

Find the Humor in Your Situation

Exaggerate the situation that you're finding stressful. Do you feel like you've been waiting in the doctor's office all day? Imagine spending years there, putting up holiday decorations, taking them down, having dinner parties in the waiting room with sick people sitting in chairs watching you entertain your friends, etc. Use your imagination to add humor to the situation. Laughter is very healthy. It literally provides our bodies with a good feeling chemical cocktail.

Exaggeration often makes a stressful situation seem humorous which lessens the stress.

Beat Depression

When I was doing some work in a high school the teenagers were allowed to give anonymous questions to me. Here is one of them:

Q. How do you overcome depression?
A. Depression is at the low end of the EGS.

You may want to ask for help, but even if you get professional help you can also help yourself.

Depression is accompanied by a feeling of powerlessness so taking steps on your own restores some of your feeling of personal power.

Understand, first that you are not going to jump from depression to joy in a couple of days but you can get from depression to better-feeling states in a day.

Society does not understand that anger and revenge are between depression and better-feeling emotions. When a depressed person becomes angry or vengeful society (parents, teachers, or friends) tend to push the person back down to depression. Depressed people are less trouble than angry ones and until they understand we have to travel through anger to feel better, they'll keep pushing us back into depression.

When you understand that anger and revenge are like cities you have to drive through just like you drive through Charlotte and Huntersville going from Rock Hill to Mooresville. You don't have to buy a house in Anger or Revenge to pass through. You don't even have to get off the freeway. You just need to take steps in your own mind to move through them.

Some belief structures tell us that we are bad to think bad thoughts. The root of this is that if we stay in those bad thoughts things don't work out well for us and we are likely to take actions that are not good for us and others. But it is the fastest and surest route to feeling better from a state of depression.

The first thing is to understand that you are thinking the thoughts for one purpose and one purpose only—to move to even better-feeling thoughts. If you have any doubt about your ability to move through angry and vengeful thoughts without acting on them then get help for this step.

When you think angry thoughts you are taking some of your power back and you can feel the relief as you move from depression to anger. The same is true when you move from anger to vengeful thoughts and from vengeful thoughts up to blame. Do not blame yourself or consider yourself bad for having those thoughts. Those thoughts will help you feel better.

Some of the theme places, Chuckie Cheese, for example, have this game where groundhogs pop-up and you bop them on the head. That is a good activity to do while you are in the stage of moving through vengeful thoughts. Pretend, just for the purpose of feeling better—not for practice—that your pummeling is getting your vengeance. You can do the same activity in your own mind.

You could go to a batting cage and hit baseballs. Real physical activity is better than a video game which tends to be addictive and you might find yourself going back to worse-feeling thoughts when you play the game again after you've done the work to move higher. Or just in your own mind. We did the college tour as a family a decade after the divorce and I will admit that during that trip I used mental acts of vengeance to move up the EGSc. On the surface the trip was not terribly unpleasant but if I had not had that tool it probably would have become very ugly.

I can't stress enough not to act on the thoughts you use to move through these two stages.

In the vengeful state I actually like to think of outlandish things that I know I could never do. Imagine me dragging a 6-foot-tall man up to the top of a hill inhabited by hungry animals. By choosing physically impossible thoughts it helps ensure that I won't act on the thoughts. One idea is taking the person in a spaceship to another planet and leaving the person on the planet. Get creative and have fun with it. You could even write a Bond screen play or become a Stephen King rival and make a novel out of it. Just don't act on it.

I actually do not suggest writing a novel like that because that keeps you in that mindset too long and what you really want is to move even higher on the EGS.

You also don't need to stay there a real long time. Let yourself get good and angry in your thoughts. 20 minutes may be plenty. When you are solidly angry (which feels better than depression) reach for vengeful thoughts that give the feeling of relief. Don't stay there long and any thoughts of acting on them should be immediately stopped. Then reach for blame. Blame is a lesser form of anger and seldom turns into actions society would frown on the way anger and vengeance do.

Spend more time in blame. Really get on a roll in your own mind blaming someone/something for the situation. Spend enough time there (at least 20 minutes) so that the next time you think about the situation that you were dealing with you go right to blame or if you end up back at a lower place you have a good enough sense of how it feels at blame and you can return to blame. You can use a fast-forward version of the your earlier visualization to move your emotional state quickly. It won't take as long to move back up the EGS once you have done it and created some stability at the higher emotional state.

When someone has been deliberately using this process for a few years they can develop enough skill and trust that they can move up, step-by-step, many steps in a single day. From depression to blame is great progress for someone who is new.

Understanding that you have patterns of thought that lead you back to an old emotional state and that you may find yourself back there again and again for a few months is very important. Many people give up when they find themselves back in depression. They are back just because depression has become a habit. By deliberately taking the steps you can change the habit. If you find yourself back in your old emotional state, just repeat the process to move up. I promise you, when you are consistent about this it won't be long until your mind automatically goes to a better-feeling emotional state automatically.

A strong habit of depression should stop returning to depression after consistent effort of about 3 months. In that time new neural pathways will develop. That does not mean you have to feel depressed for 3 more months before change happens. It means that the back-sliding will only last about that long but you'll spend more and more time in a better feeling state of mind during those months.

Moving beyond blame to higher levels can be done one step at a time. The important thing is to stabilize at the new level so you know how it feels there. It is easier to reach for the feeling when you are moving back up after old neuropathways guided you back to lower levels.

Measure your progress in feeling the relief; not in whether you are achieving joy.

If you are having any thoughts of harming yourself, ask or help. If you are having thoughts of harming others that you might act on I encourage the same. If you are unsure then err on the side of caution. Use your past behavior as a guide to what you are likely to do. If you just want help getting through this then ask for it. If you are dependent upon your parents and they aren't listening, talk to a school nurse, teacher, relative, or pick up the phone and call 911 if you're thinking about hurting yourself or someone else.

Psychotherapists focus on helping clients with mentally-based conditions listed in the DSM-V and are trained in assessment, diagnosis, and treatment of mental disorders,[719] usually considering a client cured when their emotional state reaches zero on a scale that ranges from -10 to +10. Learning about your Emotional Guidance can take you to +10 and beyond, with enough time. You're not alone either. If you are a teenager in an average high school class, the statistics on depression in young people indicate that there are probably half a dozen depressed individuals in your class. Adults also suffer from depression in high numbers. There is nothing wrong with you that can't be fixed—mostly depression is because you weren't taught how to use your emotions the way they were intended. Hardly anyone has been taught this because science had it wrong for 80 years.

The skills and knowledge I am providing, your EGS, and suggestions about other techniques to feel better, can provide individuals with a sort of immunization. I can't claim a guarantee against depression but your risk decreases greatly if you understand and use these tools designed to help you thrive.

Meditation is a great tool for everyone and especially for those who are depressed.

Affirmations should not be used until you get near the Hopeful Zone. Affirmations while someone is depressed result in the person arguing with it and digging themselves deeper. I recommend not using positive affirmations at the lower emotional states.

Affirmations that affirm the progress made in moving up are OK.

Decisions are a fantastic tool at this level. They will provide energy and shift the focus.

Here is an example, "I am done. I am not going to remain powerless any longer. I am going to learn how to understand the guidance my Emotional Guidance system is giving me and will move to better and better-feeling emotions over time. I will be easy with myself. It is OK for me to be happy and I am on my way. It may take a while but I have decided I am going to do all that I can to feel more empowered and move in that direction."

Come up with one that feels good to you. If some part of it feels off to you leave it out.

Oh, and hugs. Four to six hugs of 18 second durations daily if you have a willing source. If not go volunteer in an old folks home and you'll soon have a source.

Spend time in nature. Go for walks. Dance. Listen only to music that feels good. If the lyrics are negative and feel hopeless do not listen to it. Classical music in the background is also good.

The permanent fix is to learn how to master your thoughts and use your Emotional Guidance but other things can help.

If you have a tendency to see one problem as pervasive then refute that position and put the issue in perspective.

Refute negative self-talk.

Make a list of things that feel good and keep it with you. Pull it out to help you re-focus on better-feeling subjects when you can't find a positive thought.

Read about people who had a hard time and then thrived.

Be nice to yourself. Bubble baths with scented candles or bubbles and candlelight—yes, even for the men—can be soothing.

KNOW that there have been people where you are now (in depression) who have recovered and then thrived.

Are there things you want from life that you've convinced yourself you can't have? Use your EGS to change those beliefs.

Set small goals and reward yourself when you achieve them.

There was a time when taking a bath and brushing my hair was my goal for the day. Some days I did not accomplish that goal.

Be nice to yourself. You, as much as anyone else in the whole world, deserve your own love, respect, kindness and care.

Use Role Models

There is significant evidence that a single good role model can help an otherwise disadvantaged child thrive.

Why does a role model matter?

A role models help children believe in themselves. Because the role model demonstrates mindsets and thought processes that lead to beneficial outcomes.

This research has led to many programs that match underprivileged children with role models. Such programs are expensive, which means not every child who would benefit from a role model receives one. There is another way, one that is not limited by tight budgetary constraints.

Anyone can look for examples of role models to help expand his belief in his own potential. Highly successful people are not any better than you are. They have developed supportive patterns of thought. Even IQ is not static.[720]

Role models do not have to be alive and they can even be imaginary. Role models can be in books, movies, video games, or people we actually meet. Look for examples of role models to help you expand your belief in your potential. What do you want for yourself?

Do you want to love fearlessly? Look for examples of individuals who love in that way. It can be in a romantic relationship, familial relationship, or someone who loves others so much he gives his life serving them in some way.

> *I believe: that imagination is stronger than knowledge,*
> *myth is more potent than history,*
> *dreams are more powerful than facts,*
> *hope always triumphs over experience,*
> *laughter is the cure for grief,*
> *and Love is stronger than death.*
> Robert Fulghum

Do you want to maintain your good health into your 80's, 90's or beyond? There are many examples of individuals who are achieving that goal today. Find them and use their success to shore up your belief in your own ability to maintain your vitality beyond the average.

Do you want to go to college but you're poor? Look for examples of others who have done so despite having roots in poverty. One of the most inspiring examples of this in our time is Dr. Ben Carson. Do you want fame? Success? Creative genius? Your goal does not matter. Believing in your ability to achieve your goal does, and finding others who've achieved those goals gives you more trust in your own abilities. Your EGS will provide you with guidance, but role models of your own choosing will help you adjust your filters. Your EGS will always provide guidance along the shortest path to your goals, but your interpretation of the guidance is more likely to be on target when the programming of your filters is not creating crosswinds.

There is an Irish blessing that begins, *"May the road rise up to meet you. May the wind be always at your back..."* When your beliefs, expectations, emotional stance, and focus are aligned with your goals, following your guidance feels natural (and occurs intuitively). Life feels easier, as if the wind is at your back.

> *If we did all the things we are capable of doing, we would literally astound ourselves.*
> Ralph Waldo Emerson

Role models can be found in books about great people and great ideas. Quotes have probably formed more of a role model to me from a young age than any other source. I remember a field trip to San Francisco as a young teenager when I stood in a gift shop writing down wise sayings they had on plaques. There is something innate within us all that recognizes great truths even when we do not fully grasp their meaning. Many of the quotes I collected as a teen are still favorites today, although I see far deeper meaning in the words.

We do not have to wait for the world to place a wonderful role model into our lives before we can benefit from one. The words of the best role models throughout history have been captured in books and in quotes.

Do not wait for someone else to provide you with a role model. Find one that makes your heart sing and learn what you can of him or her. Think on the things they said that inspire you and ask yourself what they must have believed to have acted or said thus.

Books can also help us throw off shackles that hold us back. The one that is best for you will depend on where you are in your journey. Ask yourself, as you read anything, "What made this person good?" and then do those things, be those things for yourself. Your guidance will help you know what will serve your highest good.

When I let go of what I am, I become what I might be.
Lao Tzu

What a man thinks of himself, that is which determines, or rather indicates, his fate.
Henry David Thoreau

I have about concluded that wealth is a state of mind, and that anyone can acquire a wealthy state of mind by thinking rich thoughts.
Andrew Young

If constructive thoughts are planted positive outcomes will be the result. Plant the seeds of failure and failure will follow.
Sidney Madwed

Passion is energy. Feel the power that comes from focusing on what excites you.
Oprah Winfrey

We are what we think. All that we are arises with our thoughts. With our thoughts, we make the world.
Buddha

A man is but the product of his thoughts. What he thinks, he becomes.
Mahatma Gandhi

Finally, brethren, whatever is true, whatever is honorable, whatever is right, whatever is pure, whatever is lovely, whatever is of good repute, if there is any excellence and if anything worthy of praise, dwell on these things.
Philippians 4:8

A pessimist sees the difficult in every opportunity; an optimist sees the opportunity in every difficulty.
Winston Churchill

What you're thinking is what you're becoming.
Muhammad Ali

Darkness cannot drive out darkness;
only light can do that.
Hate cannot drive out hate;
only love can do that.
Martin Luther King, Jr.

34 : Betwixt and Between Processes and Techniques

We are a continuum. Just as we reach back to our ancestors for our fundamental values, so we, as guardians of that legacy, must reach ahead to our children and their children. And we do so with a sense of sacredness in that reaching.
Paul Tsongas

The techniques in this category can help you shift your chronic emotional stance upward when you consistently use them over time. However, they do not directly address the root cause of stress, so the upside is limited. Habits of thought that tend to drag you down will continue to derail your progress until you change your habits of thought. The processes in this chapter have better long-term outcomes than dose-dependent processes alone, but do not provide the long-term potential that is achievable with techniques that address the root cause of stress—your mindset and habits of thought.

Don't remind the world that it is sick and troubled.
Remind it that it is beautiful and free.
Mooji

Techniques in this chapter provide temporary relief in ways that can provide some lasting benefits—not as great as the benefits that can be obtained by changing meta-cognitve processes and beliefs that do not serve your highest good—but more than dose-dependent methods, which are commonly recommended. The following processes fall somewhere in between the ones that change the neuropathways and the dose-dependent processes.

Some of these activities have been studied and proven effective at improving mood and health that are, in my opinion, not 100% dose-dependent but they are also not directly taking control of the thought process in the way that provides the most immediate (and long-term) empowerment.

Also, if you engage in dysfunctional thought processes while you are engaged in these activities they can actually be counter-productive. For example, if you co-ruminate with your massage therapist while you receive a massage the stress from co-ruminating counterbalances much of the benefit of the massage. Likewise, if you spend the time you're getting a massage ruminating about your problems, it will offset the benefits of massage.

That being said, I highly recommend these processes, to those to whom they appeal. A longer discussion of the research was included in my earlier book, *Prevent Suicide: The Smart Way*. The long-term health and wellness benefits they provide are well documented.

Massage Therapy
The 2009 NHS Health and Well-Being report[721] stated: "Stress reduction is the primary reason many people access complementary massage and its value should not be underestimated. With all the benefits of lymphatic movement, muscle pain reduction, scar tissue break-up, and other good things it should be

understood just how very important the simple reduction of stress is to the human body." Americans make 75 million visits to more than 120,000 practitioners each year.[722] The list of benefits from massage is long.

Yoga

Yoga helps you improve strength, flexibility, and balance. Some types improve the body's stress response and relaxation and others help with weight loss and provide a vigorous cardio workout. Some people reject yoga as a religious practice. It can be part of a religious practice but the intent and way yoga is done determines whether the practice of yoga is a religious practice. Yoga can be compatible with any religious worldview and has been scientifically proven to provide significant benefits.

Studies on Yoga provide convincing evidence for its effectiveness over autonomic nervous system. Bagchi and Wenger reported that yogic meditation induces inner relaxation of ANS without inducing sleep as well as raising immune levels in the body without exaggerating physiological manifestation against external stimuli, thereby providing a balance between body and outside world."[723]

There are numerous types of yoga. Even individuals with physical impairments are able to participate in variations that have been designed with physical limitations in mind.

Tai Chi

Tai chi is a mind-body practice that originated in China as a martial art. Today it is considered a complimentary or alternative form of medicine because of the documented health benefits.

Tai chi is sometimes referred to as "moving meditation"—practitioners move their bodies slowly, gently, and with awareness, while breathing deeply. It is purported that focusing the mind solely on the movements of the form helps to bring about a state of mental calm and clarity.[724] Tai Chi involves slow, relaxed, and graceful movements that flow into one another. The body is in constant motion, and posture is important. Individuals practicing tai chi must also concentrate, which means they have to ignore distracting thoughts; and they must breathe in a deep and relaxed, but focused manner.

A significant amount of research demonstrates Tai Chi provides a wide variety of mind and body benefits. Based on the research, Tai Chi is very beneficial and especially so for older adults. *The Journal of American Geriatric Society* published research showing that Tai Chi provides protection against the shingles equivalent to that provided by the varicella vaccine. The Tai Chi group in this study also showed significant improvements for physical functioning, bodily pain, vitality, and mental health.[725]

Aromatherapy

Aromatherapy has been used for centuries for various forms of stress relief, including calming during childbirth. Inhaling clary sage essential oil reduces stress.[726] Lavender is effective in alleviating agitated behaviors in patients with dementia. For individuals who are vulnerable to side effects from medications, aromatherapy with lavender may offer an alternative option.[727] Aromatherapy massage is a viable complementary therapy that significantly reduces anxiety in breast cancer patients.[728]

Energy Healing

Energy healing stimulates the body's natural healing process. Practitioners are trained by master practitioners who have completed three levels of training and a supervised mentorship. A growing body of evidence indicates this Alternative Treatment is beneficial.

- **Reiki**
- **Therapeutic Touch**[729]
- **Healing Touch**

Relax

Our society does not understand relaxation or stress relief very well. Even the American Psychological Association perpetuates the myth that things like playing video games, watching television, surfing the internet, exercising, having a glass of wine, eating or smoking are methods of stress relief. They are distractions, they change your focus, but they do not change where you left the topic(s) that are causing you stress. Even hobbies, which many people use to relax do not change where you left your stressors. In fact, if you don't know how to use your mind, the time you spend on your hobbies can be counterproductive.

If you spend time on an activity, make sure the time you spend is enjoyable. If you watch television, don't listen to the commercials—especially the ones that plant seeds in your mind about the body being fragile and that age makes us weak or incapable of basic functions. If you can choose a way of watching that eliminates commercials, choose it. Avoid the news and even the previews of coming updates—they spew violence and hatred into your mind without warning.

Meditation

Some people reject meditation as a religious practice. It can be part of a religious practice, but the intent and way meditation is done determines whether the practice of meditation is a religious practice. Meditation can be compatible with any religious worldview. It has been scientifically proven to provide significant benefits.

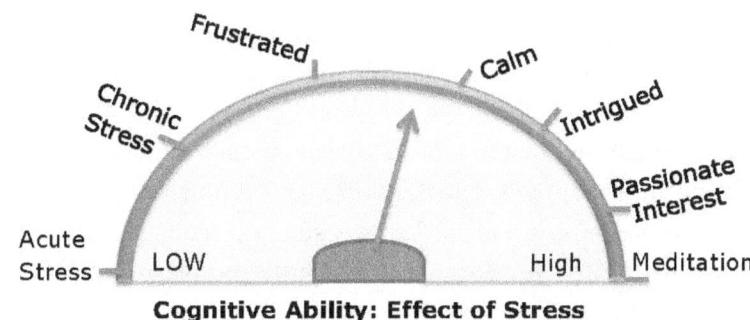

On the stress scale, meditation is above passion, indicating higher cognitive ability and lower stress. This is because meditation is a process that clears the mind of habitual thought, clearing the way for insight. Emotions respond to thought. Meditation provides a respite from thought and therefore from emotion. Meditation is the most researched of the recommended processes. The documented results indicate that meditation enhances every area of life.

If you choose to meditate, I recommend fifteen minutes per day. If you find yourself in a distressing situation you cannot fully control (i.e. hospital or prison), meditating longer may be of benefit. As with all things, let your Emotional Guidance guide your decision. Meditating at the beginning of the day often produces the best results, but if your schedule makes this stressful, fit it in when you can. I also recommend meditation as a tool at other times to regain one's center if the day's events have taken them off-kilter.

Traditional Therapy

There is a wide variety of traditional psychotherapies. They can be helpful, especially if you are dealing with difficult issues while you learn how to use your Emotional Guidance. I strongly encourage you to use your guidance in choosing your therapist and in choosing to stay with a specific therapist. I have used traditional therapy and had some wonderful help along the way. I've also had therapists who were taking me in the wrong direction and my emotions were letting me know they were not helping. If you feel a therapist will be beneficial to you, but the one you've found doesn't feel good, find another. Research has demonstrated that the quality of the therapeutic relationship reported by patients early in treatment contributed significantly to the outcome.[730]

Therapists are great for things where the person needs guidance, but most people can do this better on their own with the right training if their goals are increased happiness and stress reduction. On a happiness/stress (unhappiness) scale of -10 to +10, therapy is designed to take people to zero. The cognitive and health benefits come at 8+.

Self-hypnosis

Both self-hypnosis and hypnosis conducted by a therapist can help shift underlying beliefs that are not serving one's highest good. It can also be helpful in alleviating fears and increasing self-esteem.

If you've developed affirmations that you believe are true (or can be true) within your current belief structure, you can record a CD with a combination of relaxing suggestions followed by affirmations.

Never operate machinery, including automobiles, while listening to relaxing or hypnosis media.

Bio-feedback

Bio-feedback is a type of training that teaches an individual how to have greater control over bodily processes (bio) that are typically controlled below the level of conscious thought. It can take between 8 to 50 one-hour sessions to create a level of control that helps with the specific issue(s) being addressed. The research shows it can be helpful with many health concerns.

However, bio-feedback is still dose-dependent. It is an indirect method when compared to emotion regulation using cognitive reappraisal. Imagine a person in a boat in calm waters. Nearly everyone can manage to stay in the boat (not fall or be tossed overboard) in calm waters. But when the waves begin to toss the boat about, people can begin to fall out. In this case, it is the people who lack resilience and the ability to cope who fall out of the safety of the boat. It may increase their ability to stay in the boat, but at some point, biofeedback will not be enough to keep them in the boat. On the other hand, cognitive/psychological/emotional flexibility allows the individual to repeatedly adjust their mindset until intrinsic habits of thought automatically include positive reappraisal, which will calm even the most turbulent waters. In this scenario, it is the equivalent of donning a life jacket, wet suit and scuba gear.

The main benefit of bio-feedback that I see is that it demonstrates clearly the mind-body connection and awareness of the results people are able to achieve can heighten belief in our ability to mentally affect our physical body. This increased belief can help us form beliefs that support our highest good and allow us to use positive affirmations that move further in the direction we wish to shift.

Optimism Exercise

If used repeatedly and in a variety of life domains, this process could result in long-term changes. If used only once or not often, it will result in good-feelings on a short-term basis, but not long-term changes in one's habits of thought. It's up to you and how you use it. I would only use this exercise when you are in a Hopeful or Better emotional state because the likelihood of mental pushback increases as emotional state declines.

Visualize and/or write about your best possible self, seeing yourself being the best you can currently imagine being. Do not beat yourself up for not yet being your best possible self—no matter how good one becomes there will always be room for growth. It is the nature of humans we are ever-evolving beings. You can focus on one area of life, a narrow subject (i.e. you making the best ribs in town), or you can focus more broadly (i.e. being a winner at something you want to do well at). You can use the same one every time or you can mix it up. As long as it feels good while you do it, you are helping yourself. If it does not feel good, stop or use a different subject. If you can't find a way to make it feel good, stop and use it when you're in a better-feeling emotional state.

Neuro Linguistic Programming (NLP)

I had never heard of NLP before I began teaching what I teach. When people began telling me my program was similar to NLP I decided to check into NLP. There seem to be similarities although without taking a course I have limited knowledge. The most important difference I see is Emotional Guidance (which is missing from the NLP literature I've found) and without understanding your guidance, you're doing it blindfolded. Emotional Guidance pulls it all together and provides you with a compass with your personal due North.

Emotional Disclosure

In an experiment where individuals received a wound from a punch biopsy was monitored for rate of healing, the study group's wound healed 11% faster than the control group's wound. [731] The intervention the study group received was writing about personal emotional experiences. The emotional disclosure apparently improved emotional state, which is known to improve immune system function.

EFT (Emotional Freedom Technique)

I was not able to find any scientific evidence supporting EFT as a therapy. I have seen a documentary where it provided significant benefits for pain relief. I have a number of friends who use it and strongly believe in its benefits. One such friend has used it to discard her reading glasses after using it to improve her vision. She is old enough to collect social security and I found this particular benefit rather convincing. How much of the benefit is from changing energy along the body's meridians and how much is from the affirmations used in conjunction with the tapping is impossible to tell.

Jeanine Joy

35 : Dose-dependent Stress Management Techniques

Every great and deep difficulty bears in itself its own solution. It forces us to change our thinking in order to find it.
Niels Bohr

Dose-dependent processes or techniques change mood but do not generally have a long-term effect that makes life feel better naturally. These types of activities are dose-dependent because, like medicines that treat symptoms instead of the root cause, the effect is contingent on whether the prescription is followed. Dose-dependent techniques are like drugs that you must take for life. They work, but you're dependent upon the technique to feel better and its effectiveness may decline over time, making it necessary to increase the dosage.

I'll give you an example. By age 10 my eyesight was very limited. When I got my first pair of glasses I felt like I was being too nosey about people at stop lights because I could actually see the faces of passengers in cars next to me. Before that time I did not realize that passengers could see into other vehicles because I couldn't. I had to get annual eye exams and when I graduated from Junior High my graduation present was contact lenses. I continued wearing contacts most of the time until 2001. During the cold war when I worried about a nuclear attack from Russia one of my biggest concerns was how I would get contacts so I could see if the worse happened. I always thought I'd survive (I had a plan), but that plan included finding a way to secure enough contact lenses to last me forever on my way out of town.

When I would swim in the ocean I couldn't wear my contacts and I worried I'd get turned around and not know where the shore was. On a business trip to Cedar Rapids, Iowa my contacts got too dry on the plane and I had to remove them to avoid damage to my eyes, but my glasses were in my checked bag because I didn't think I'd need them. My connecting flight in Chicago O'Hare airport was cancelled and I was re-directed from American to United, which required me to navigate to a different terminal with very limited sight. After reaching the other terminal, the flight was again re-scheduled and I was routed back to another terminal in the American section. The added stress of not being able to see the signs until I was right up on them took this from a frustrating experience to a frightening one.

It was the final impetus for me to have my eyesight fixed using modern techniques. A few months later I had the surgery and have had perfect vision ever since. I don't have to buy contacts, carry solution with me, carry my glasses *in case* I need them, or any of the other irritating things that poor eyesight demanded of me. My eyesight is perfect. I no longer have to give thought to what I need to do so I can see. I just see—perfectly.

Contact lenses and glasses are dose-dependent techniques for improving vision. The surgery I had to fix my eyes fixed the root cause.

Dose-dependent stress management techniques are like glasses and contacts . . . you have to use them to get the benefit. And, just like my experience in O'Hare, sometimes dose-dependent stress management techniques fail when you really need them. The American Psychological Association reported that 43% of people who use exercise as a stress management took don't use it when they are highly stressed because they are *too stressed*. Just like my contact lenses failed me when I needed to navigate O'Hare airport, dose-dependent stress management techniques can fail you when you need the relief the most.

Early research concentrated on dose-dependent techniques so you'll find more research for them but don't mistake a greater quantity of empirical data but that is not a statement about the veracity of the techniques that are not dose-dependent. It is only indicative of what has been studied so far. This is partially because research on processes that change automatic responses would need a longitudinal design, which means the research is more expensive. As far as I'm concerned, the sooner robust research is done on techniques that are not dose-dependent , the faster more people will be helped.

Because they have been researched, many teachers primarily recommend and teach dose-dependent techniques to their students. You may be familiar with them. I only recommend their use while learning techniques that address the root cause of stress directly.

Dose-dependent techniques include:

Exercise	Being in Nature	Spending time with a friend
Gratitude	Helping others	Deep Breathing
Pet Your Pet	18 second hugs	Being Creative
Sleeping	Journaling	Confiding in a friend

The most commonly recommended and, unfortunately, the most studied methods of stress relief are dose-dependent methods that derive their efficacy primarily from changing one's focus. They are included here for two reasons. First, it is helpful to have tools that reduce your in-the-moment stress level. Secondly, it is important to understand the inherent weakness in these commonly recommended strategies—their dose-dependent nature.

Studies of these methods have recorded positive results because they do provide in-the-moment stress relief. However, the dose-dependent nature means the relief is only available when someone actually uses them.

The nature of depression and other low moods is that it decreases intrinsic motivation and desire to do some of the very things that would provide the temporary relief these dose-dependent methods can provide.

There is nothing wrong with using dose-dependent techniques. They benefit many people every day. But using only dose-dependent techniques is sort of like having a broken leg that you can't have set today—taking pain meds to reduce the pain you're in makes sense until the leg can be properly set and heal. But choosing to just take the pain medicine for the rest of your life instead of having the leg set does not make sense.

Processes that change neuropathways and meta-cognitve habits create better automatic responses to stimulus, so the first reaction is less stressful. Todd Kashdan and Jonathan Rottenberg reported that, "Well-practiced behaviors easily become automated wherein conscious intentions are no longer a prerequisite to perform an act. That is, by repetition, a person can act without conscious thought to guide and monitor every behavior."[732] Annually more than 10% of the world's population experience episodes of depression. The prevalence of chronic stress is even greater. 1.5% of the population suffers from anxiety issues every year. UC Davis says 20% of the population have trouble with anger issues.[733] Teaching *The Smart Way*, which help reverse the harm done by the former misunderstanding of how to interpret emotions, is so important to increasing public health and promoting long-term well-being.

Exercise

Exercise is often recommended as a way to reduce stress, and if used correctly, it is effective. There is a lot of research supporting the benefits of exercise. I have not seen any research that compared a group who exercised as usual compared to a group that received stress management classes and exercised. I would like to see that research.

My Make Play OK™ campaign makes exercise fun instead of something likely to invoke guilt and add to the stress load.

- I recommend exercise, but not as an isolated solution. Forty-three of people who usually engage in physical activity and know exercise helps their stress level do not exercise when they are stressed.[734]

At a minimum, ones EGS should be used in conjunction with exercise to help adjust thought patterns to less stressful perspectives.

Exercisers are cautioned:
- Not to be self-critical of their exercise achievements.
- Not to feel guilty if they miss a day;
- Not to dwell on things that bring up negative emotion while exercising
- Exercising while highly stressed increases the risk of injury

Someone who has a habit of self-criticism who takes up an otherwise healthy exercise routine may use exercise as another reason to be self-critical. The negative emotion from the self-criticism sabotages their efforts and reduces their emotional stance. The negative emotions the person feels in response to the self-criticism diminishes benefits they may gain from the exercise.

Helping Others

Providing service to others is often recommended as a way to improve mood.

It is effective some of the time because:
- It changes the person's focus
- If the person has a habit of comparing his or her situation to others, it often provides someone in a worse situation to compare to, which makes the comparison of self to others feel better.
- It can also increase guilt in those who are unable to help others due to physical or time limitations.

If you help strangers because you've been guilted into doing it, you will eventually feel resentment that you have to spend your time in that way. The same actions done because it makes you happy to do something for someone else will not create resentment.

Breathe

For most of us, breathing is something we do without thought. But breathing consciously can be very comforting. Place a note somewhere you will see it often. Write *Breathe*[735] on the note. When you see the note, consciously take a deep slow breathe in and then release. Repeat as necessary until you feel calmer. If you know you are going to have a stressful day, you can set reminders to pop-up on your computer or smart phone reminding you to breathe.

Develop a habit of using wait time to breathe deeply and mindfully. Use it when you're stopped at a traffic light, waiting your turn in line, waiting for something to finish cooking, or waiting for the kids to join you in the car.

Jeanine Joy

This process is recommended for any zone below the Hopeful Zone. It can provide immediate releasing of stress. Long-term benefits are possible if deeper, more conscious breathing becomes a habit.

Pet Your Pet

Our pets are wonderful stress relievers. Petting your cat or dog relieves your level of stress. A dog also encourages physical activity because of the need to walk the dog. Physical activity and being outside are both dose-dependent stress relievers. A dog can ensure you do both multiple times a day. A dog can be enough—it's not the same as treating the root cause, but consistent use of dose-dependent stress relievers do help millions maintain a lower level of stress that improves their lives in countless ways.

Bathe

Both baths and showers can help you change your mood. With either a bath or a shower you can add candlelight. With a bath you can add relaxing music. With a shower you can add energetic music that vibrates the air around you. Use your power of focus to think about future, present or past things that feel good. Use what feels good as the criteria for what you chose to think about. If your thoughts drift to less pleasant ones, simply redirect your thoughts back to something more pleasant.

Pamper your body

Sometimes you need to feel cared for and it's not happening through the method you want it to happen. Perhaps you've had surgery, which can be traumatizing to both your body and your mind, but your family does not understand that you need to feel cared for more during your recovery. Or, perhaps you are alone. Pampering your body can help you feel cared for. Use some nice scented lotion (or oil if you prefer) and massage it gently into your skin wherever you can comfortably reach. Take your time. For example, when you rub the fingers of one hand with the other, don't just rub it in as if it is a job. Take your time and feel the muscles and tendons that enable your hands to do all the things they do for you. If there are sore spots and rubbing them feels good, pause and gently massage the muscles. Care for your body with the lotion as if your body were that of your lover's body.

You can amp this technique up by thinking about the miracle your body is. How it began with a single cell and multiplied, with each cell knowing what to become (eyes, nose, toes, fingernails, heart, lungs, etc.). You can think about how that miracle continues every day. How your body can take oxygen from the air and deliver it to cells throughout your body without your having to think about it or understand the process. Or how it can take the nutrients from food and deliver them to where they need to go, separating out and discarding the waste without you having to think about it. You can think about how it is healing anything that is wrong, how it knows what to do and does it easily.

Confide in a friend

This is a risky one. Spending time with a friend while you lament about your problems won't be beneficial. Spending time with a friend doing something you both enjoy will be helpful. If you must confide and discuss your problems, do it from the perspective that you can find solutions and look for the most empowered perspective you can find about the troubling situation.

Sleep

Lack of adequate sleep impairs our cognitive abilities and can make us moody or depressed so yes, get enough sleep. "When they do not get enough sleep, 21 percent of adults report feeling more stressed. Adults with higher reported stress levels (8, 9 or 10 on a 10-point scale) fare even worse — 45 percent feel even more stressed if they do not get enough sleep."[736]

Knitting

Knitting has been found to be an effective dose-dependent stress reliever. I believe it is because the repetitive actions are a form of meditation. I caution against focusing on your problems while you knit.

Choosing Food

Go to a place where you are going to order a meal. On your way there and before you go in to the business, think about your body emphasizing how smart it is and what it is able to do. Your body knows how to separate the nutrients from the food you eat and route them to the cells in your body that need them. It separates waste from valued resources. Your body knows more about how to do this than the smartest scientists on the planet. It is one way that your body displays its intelligence.

When you receive the menu briefly close your eyes and ask your inner self for guidance, "What do I want to eat?" Then make a quick decision, noting how the decision you make feels good to you. Pay attention to how you feel about the food you've chosen to order. Do you see how your emotions played a role in your choice?

Note: Do not assume because your body chose a particular food today that the same food is always the best choice. Under different circumstances you will be guided to different foods that fit the needs of your body at the time.

Journal

Journaling is like confiding in a friend. If you journal about everything you perceive as bad or wrong in your life, or the world, it won't help you. If you journal about things that feel good when you focus on them, it will.

Be creative

Being creative can bring us to flow moments that help us feel better. Paint, craft, draw, color, scrapbooking, jewelry making, quilting, and other creative pursuits can engage your attention and shift your focus away from topics that do not feel good.

18-second hug

Physical contact, with humans or animals, releases chemicals in our bodies that promote good moods. Hugs that last 18 seconds or longer (this is a very long hug in western society) release those chemicals. Snuggling and/or cuddling is even better.

Pause

When you feel a sudden drop in your emotional state, pause before you respond. If someone you care about says something that makes you feel a sudden drop like that, it is very unlikely they mean it the way you perceive it. If they are angry, they may mean it that way in that moment, but if you take the time to pause and think of the bigger picture, you won't make matters worse. Deciding in advance who you want to be (see **Setting Intentions**) will help you re-center. If you're able to take a walk, do so. If you're at work and your area does not provide privacy or space to calm down, the restroom or stairwell may be useful. Just taking a deep breath can help you enough that you can find a different perspective.

Happy Place

A Happy Place can be of enormous benefit to you. You have to create it in advance. Your Happy Place resides in your imagination and it can be anything and everything you want it to be. You can have multiple Happy Places. What is it? It is a pleasing situation (place, people, food and drink, activities, scenery) that you enjoy thinking about being. It can be from your past (as long as you enjoy your time thinking about it, not if you are yearning for what once was), a potential future, or completely made up. I love to fish, the feel of the sun on my skin, the feel of a boat rocking beneath me, and virgin strawberry daiquiri's. In one of my Happy Places I have a yacht and I am sailing around the world, going to the best place to fish at any given time. A crew is in charge of the boat, so all I have to do is relax, fish, and enjoy the occasional visitor I bring on board with me. I created my first Happy Place by thinking about it for twenty minutes twice a week while I was on a massaging table at the chiropractor's office.

What is a Happy Place good for? How about enjoying spending two hours in the dentist chair while you are getting a root canal but your mind is in your happy place catching fish? How about enjoying waiting at the DMV in those hard plastic chairs? I have a few other Happy Places. One is time alone with my husband, the venue changes, but we're always alone with no television in comfortable surroundings. When I am planning a vacation, the destination becomes a Happy Place that I enjoy in advance of the actual trip. Yesterday a friend told me this was her "Bucket List Year." While I wouldn't restrict myself to one year, it makes me think how much more anyone can enjoy their "Bucket List" if they create Happy Places out of the things on the list.

There are times to be realistic. But getting a root canal isn't one of them. It's better to go to your Happy Place. Have fun with your imagination.

Sing

Listen to uplifting music or classic music

Here, too, music can take your mood up or down. If you're feeling down about the end of a relationship wallowing in sad songs won't make you feel better.

Take Care of Your Body

If you've been putting off health related care—take care of it.

One of the most common health issues I see being ignored is urinary incontinence. This is a very common issue for women who have given birth to children but it is not discussed because they are ashamed. They don't tell their friends or their doctors. Urinary incontinence makes a woman feel old, makes her limit physical activities, and can lead to depression. There are very effective procedures that can fix the problem. Don't put off this or any other medical care you need to feel your best. You have to live in your body and you deserve to live in the best feeling body possible.

> *Love*
> *Think of 10 things you Love.*
> *Write them down.*
> *Now....don't you feel better.*
> *You're welcome.*
> Pam Morgan

> *Love is the bridge between you and everything.*
> Rumi

Nature

Research points to the happiness increasing benefits of being in nature. Being outside has a positive influence on mood. Spending time in nature is recommended as a way to temporarily reduce stress at every zone on the EGSc. Time in nature is a temporary mood improvement tool that works when the mindset accompanying the time in nature is positive. The benefits may extend past the time spent in nature, but it does not create lasting changes unless the time is used to adjust ones mindset to more positive perspectives.

36: Religious and Spiritual Views

The World is my country, all mankind are my brethren, and to do good is my religion.
Thomas Paine

This chapter is for individuals who may be asking how Emotional Guidance and an increased focus on being happy fits with their religious or spiritual worldview. Although religion is not necessary to use or benefit from *The Smart Way* because it is taught from a scientific platform, it is consistent with the religious texts of six major religions—a fact that may be important to many of the 86% of the world's population who have a worldview that includes a Higher Power.

It is important because 86% of the world's population believes God exists and religious or spiritual beliefs are part of their worldview. Soon after I began teaching how Emotional Guidance works, I began receiving the question, "Is this consistent with my religious worldview?" It was clear that many people had to be confident that using Emotional Guidance did not conflict with their existing worldview before they would consider using it—regardless of how much it might benefit them.

It is possible and consistent with religious texts to view the guidance as coming from God. Guidance is promised in Holy books and no other explanation comes close to fulfilling those promises.

I looked for evidence in the texts as opposed to the teachings. There are many interpretations of the teachings of each Holy book. I knew from my early experience with Christianity that the way the passages were interpreted was not consistent with the way I am interpreting them. In fact, the same passage was responsible for my exodus from the church when I was a 14-year-old seeker. I had set a goal to read the Bible cover-to-cover and when I found passages in proverbs that sounded great to me, but which I did not understand, I asked the Minister at the church I was attending.

The passages were:

Proverbs 3:5 states, "Trust in the LORD with all your heart; do not depend on your own understanding."

Proverbs 16:9 states, "A man's heart plans his way, but the Lord directs his steps."

The answer I was given was the passages meant that when I was confused or needed guidance I should talk to my minister or read the Bible. I immediately knew the answer was wrong because when the words were written most people were illiterate, only the very wealthy had Bibles and churches were not readily available. I left the church because I felt the minister was either lying to me or didn't know himself and was unwilling to admit that to me. At 14, I expected a minister to know all the answers. That was the beginning of my journey into learning about other belief structures—a journey which has been invaluable.

My personal beliefs are the product of that search.

My point is not to sabotage any religious beliefs. I now understand that not all clergy have the same amount of religious education. Some have limited their studies to one sect of one religion while others have explored many worldviews. If you want to talk with your Rabbi, Imam, Minister, Yogi, Reverend, Guru, Priest, Monk, Dalai Lama, or other member of the clergy about Emotional Guidance I encourage you to ask him or her to read the scientific explanations of Emotional Guidance before you ask about the passages. If your clergy is not familiar with the concept of Emotional Guidance it is unlikely he will agree that the interpretation fits. Once Emotional Guidance is understood and used so that one has experience with it, it is difficult to interpret the passages any other way.

The passages from other worldviews that support using Emotional Guidance are:

From The Koran (Al-Qur'an), "By this the reader will observe that the Mohammedans are no strangers to Quietism. Others, however, understand the words of the soul, which, having attained the knowledge of the truth, rests satisfied, and relies securely thereon, undisturbed by doubts; or of the soul which is secure of its salvation, and free from fear or sorrow."

If you have not been consciously using your Emotional Guidance, this passage may not make sense. But when you have been aware of its messages, you discover the ability to feel satisfied and secure, undisturbed by doubts and free from fear or sorrow.

From Śrīmad-Bhāgavatam, "The Lord's mercy is therefore available both in the form of the instructing spiritual masters and the Supersoul within the heart."

In this passage, I interpret "the Supersoul within the heart" as the source of Emotional Guidance. The wisdom guidance provides feels like soul-wisdom, it is beyond what man knows or is able to discern even with the most advanced technology.

From The Tâo Te Ching, "1. Without going outside his door, one understands (all that takes place) under the sky; without looking out from his window, one sees the Tâo of Heaven. The farther that one goes out (from himself), the less he knows."

This passage refers to the wisdom that comes from within. When you tune yourself to listen to your Emotional Guidance, you are tuned to your highest and best inner self—a steady presence that can be obscured when one is too busy with the distractions of the outside world. The best life is one lived not in quiet solitude and contemplation, but out in the world while staying tuned to the inner wisdom. Of course, that is my opinion which is ultimately only applicable to me. For some the life of quiet contemplation may be what their Emotional Guidance leads them to.

From Buddhist teachings on the path of virtue, "Wisdom is born of meditation deep, but lost by mind's distraction; knowing these Two paths of loss and gain, so let him live, Let him so direct his life that wisdom may increase."

This is similar to my notes about the Tâo Te Ching so I won't repeat myself.

From Confucius, "By three methods we may learn wisdom: first, by reflection, which is noblest; second, by imitation, which is easiest; and third, by experience, which is the most bitter."

Reflection refers to what I defined as meta-cognition in chapter. When you reflect upon your thoughts and how you feel when you think a thought, you're directed to make better choices (wise choices). When we imitate others we may appear to be doing or saying the right things, but our reasons (back story) may vary significantly from the back story of the person we're imitating. Experiences tend to be repeated until we reflect upon them. How many people have you known who seem to be caught in a negative circle. They have relationships with someone who has a different name and face, yet the relationship is very much a copy of a prior failed relationship? It does not matter if the relationship is with a person, a job, money, or home. The story remains on repeat (often much like a movie remade or an elongated Groundhog Day) until, by reflection, the pattern is interrupted and changes.

Spiritual beliefs are much more difficult to quantify.

One spiritual community that supports Emotional Guidance is the Law of Attraction community as taught by Abraham-Hicks. I specify the teacher because other teachers of the Law of Attraction, such as

Mike Dooley, do not support the concept of all emotions as guidance. He credits only strong emotions with creative power.[737]

I have not felt the need to explore and document my findings in spiritual communities because I find that many spiritual people take bits and pieces of various teachings and cobble them together to form a belief structure that works for them. The concept of not adopting something because it does not fit within their worldview applies only to not adopting hard and fast rules (dogma). Many in the spiritual communities, like me, see some truth in many (or all) religious and spiritual teachings. They take what feels right to them and leave the rest, which is essentially following their Emotional Guidance even if they don't know they have it.

The Smart Way does not require belief in any specific religion or spiritual practice, but its key tenets are supported by six major religions and evidence-based science. Emotional Guidance and that happiness leads to desirable behaviors is strongly supported by science. Improved outcomes, even for those living in circumstances where poor outcomes are anticipated, are achieved when skills that increase resilience are learned.

For some, Emotional Guidance will reinforce their faith. Whether it does so or not will be an individual outcome. A belief in God is not required to receive Emotional Guidance or to benefit from guidance. None of the religious passages that support Emotional Guidance say:

- God guides your steps if you have established a relationship with God in your own life.
- God guides your steps if you have opened communication channels between yourself and God.
- God guides your steps if you are worthy of guidance.
- God guides your steps after you've done sufficient good works to earn guidance from God.
- God guides your steps if you believe in God.

Years ago, a friend and I were having dinner with the former Ambassador to Afghanistan whom my friend knew well and I had just met. The Ambassador asked my friend to describe me in one word. The word he chose was overachiever. What I did when confronted with students who wanted assurance that what I was teaching was consistent with their worldview was to begin researching the world's religions to see if Emotional Guidance was consistent. Even though I live in what is commonly referred to as the Bible-Belt in the United States, I did not limit my research to Christianity. I wanted to help everyone, not just Christians. Ergo, my friend's description of me as an overachiever was right once again.

But the research paid off. I found evidence in the texts of six major religions supporting the use of Emotional Guidance. The language varied, but there is no other experience that matches the words better than using Emotional Guidance. The first book I was published in was a joint effort peer-reviewed textbook about resilience and my chapter was about using Emotional Guidance to increase resilience and its consistency with religious worldviews. One of my peer-reviewers was an Atheist and I was still able to keep the religious aspects in the chapter for the same reason this chapter is being included here.

The saying, "You can lead a horse to water, but you can't make him drink" is very applicable here. For many people, unless they are sure that using Emotional Guidance is consistent with their religious worldview, they won't use it—regardless of how thirsty they are.

Jeanine Joy

Faith and Death

Emotional Guidance can be scientifically attributed to something we do not yet understand fully on the quantum plane, or it can be attributed to God, Source, the Creator, Jehovah, Allah, or whatever name you use to refer to the Great Spirit. The two are not mutually exclusive.

If Emotional Guidance is coming from the Creator that means the Creator is aware of our every thought. Our Creator is always aware of us and of what we want and is always guiding us toward our desire.

This ever present guidance can enhance the belief that our Creator loves and cares about us. It can also enhance the sense that death is not an ending to be mourned, which to me means that it is not the end. Because when you apply the concept of a Right Response to grief you see that your guidance is directing you to better feeling thoughts about the passing of a loved one. How an individual responds to the guidance during a time of great sorrow depends on how much experience the person has using Emotional Guidance.

Starting during a time of great sorrow or with the biggest issue is a mistake. It is best to begin with smaller things, even if you are currently experiencing tremendous adversity. If one has not built up faith in the process and seen how beneficial Emotional Guidance can be in every moment of every day, it would be almost impossible to accept views about something like death that are contrary to the expectations of society.

On the other hand, society's expectations about death often contradict themselves. The 86% with religious or spiritual beliefs generally believe that death is not the end and that there is something that follows death. Many worldviews believe the new experience is better than the one in the physical body here on Earth, yet when someone dies they encourage grieving, as if the person is completely gone or in a bad place.

Energy cannot be created or destroyed, it can only be changed from one form to another.
Albert Einstein

Our society is confused about death. We don't like to spend time thinking about death so the discord between our beliefs is not resolved. For example, in this Tweet by Michael Reagan, he says Nancy Reagan is once again with President Ronald Reagan but he refers to him as "the man she loved" in the past tense. So she is now with him in present tense, but not capable of loving now.

"She is once again with the man she loves," would reflect a consistency of beliefs.

Michael Reagan @ReaganWorld · 25m
I am saddened by the passing of my step mother **Nancy Reagan**...She is once again with the man she loved.God Bless...

The part of us that survives the death of our body is the part that loves. If there is a part of her that is with President Reagan, that part of her loves him still.

I've met many people during my journey who do not feel grief when someone dies, yet they admit they fake sorrow because it is expected by others. I've noticed that those who grieve the most seem to be those who regret what they did not do while the person was alive. Someone who uses Emotional Guidance will be able to soothe herself out of deep grief, if that is the initial reaction to the loss of a loved one.

Today many people have come to believe that God has forsaken us because of the awful things that happen in our world. When you begin understanding that everyone is receiving guidance, even if they never listen to it, the concept of being forsaken cannot take root. In my studies I learned that there are two basic forms of prayer. One is beseeching and begging in nature. By its very nature, when you're beseeching and begging you're feeling negative emotion and asking someone to change the circumstances so you'll feel better. You're not following your Emotional Guidance. That type of prayer rarely works. But you are receiving guidance. The negative emotion that leads some to beg and plead is guidance that would lead them to the answers they seek if they listened. The things that happen when they don't listen aren't punishments, the guidance continues being provided. God is not like your angry parent who might have said, "I told you once and I'm not going to tell you again." God is consistent and always calls you toward the light, toward, peace, toward love.

If you compare this type of prayer to the information about Coherence in Chapter 14, you'll see that this type of prayer would have to defy the laws of quantum physics in order to manifest.

Misinterpreting emotions, believing that negative emotion validates your current thought, is the main reason for suffering.

The other type of prayer is one that demonstrates strong faith and trust that help is on the way. Can you see how such prayers would feel better and receive better emotional responses? Prayers of appreciation express confidence (faith/trust) that God is there for us and is helping us. Just by structuring our prayers as appreciation we feel better. If you compare this type of prayer to Coherence in Chapter 14 you'll see that it creates Constructive Coherence, which increases the likelihood your prayer will be answered.

37: Recommendations and Running the Numbers

Be not astonished at new ideas; for it is well known to you that a thing does not therefore cease to be true because it is not accepted by many.
Baruch Spinoza

No sensible decision can be made any longer without taking into account not only the world as it is, but the world as it will be.
Isaac Asimov

My final recommendation is global introduction of *The Smart Way*. Some will claim that global implementation is too costly—much as I was told, "What makes humans thrive" was too ambitious of a question. I see it the opposite, not implementing it bears the highest cost, both in terms of human suffering and also in hard dollar costs. Ask yourself what world you want your grandchildren to live in.

Today our world struggles with many expensive social problems that, in addition to the human toll, have a very high financial cost:

- Poverty
    - Adult
    - Child ($500 Billion annually)[738]
- Escalating chronic disease expenses
    - Heart disease ($320 Billion annually)
    - Suicide[739]
        - Attempts (4.7 Billion in 2005)
        - Completed ($16 Billion in 2005)
    - Childhood Depression (unknown)[740]
    - Adult Depression ($210.5 billion in 2010)[741]
    - Diabetes ($245 Billion in 2013)[742]
- Crime ($261 billion/yearly)[743]
    - 1 out of every 45 adults in the U.S. was under some form of community correctional supervision (Pew, 2009)[744]

In 2012, a paper published in *Health Policy* recognized that health promotion interventions seeking, "to improve individual' ability to make informed decisions and control their personal life. To achieve such empowerment, individuals have to undergo a personal development process which may include consciousness raising and the acquisition of problem solving skills."[745] The paper spoke of the difficulty in quantifying the improved outcomes beyond their impact on health. I'm not saying that all of the above problems will be completely resolved using widespread training of *The Smart Way*, but when you follow the pathways from stress to outcomes, it becomes clear that each problem should experience a significant decline. The way I think of it is that if we significantly decrease even just some of these areas, the funds we would no longer have to spend on that problem could increase our ability to find solutions to the other problems.

To a greater or lesser degree, all the above problems are correlated with stress and *The Smart Way* is the most powerful stress reduction tool available. In addition, *The Smart Way* improves competence in a number of areas that are strong predictors of adolescent mental health and long-term well-being including:
- Emotional Intelligence
- Resilience
- Positivity
- Internal Locus of Control
- Relationships (social skills)
- Self-esteem

A study in Los Angeles found that 31% of the 879 students screened reported clinical PTSD and/or depression symptoms. Despite being given referrals to community mental health agencies, few of the 46 children in the waitlist control group followed up on the referrals.[746] You've read enough by now to understand the long-term consequences of not seeking help. A better way has to be used. A culture of mental health supported by knowledge, skills and Emotional Guidance has the potential to make our world unrecognizably better in a single generation.

Lately there has been movement toward expanding the definition of "a good society" to one where the citizens "can trust one another, have a sense of freedom, and have close social relationships."[747] Several years ago, Dr. Ed Diener shared the draft of a report he prepared for the United Nations[748] contemplation of recommending subjective well-being be included in evaluating the health of nations. Training as many children and adults as possible how to use meta-cognitve emotion regulation and Emotional Guidance would go a long way toward improving subjective well-being around the world.

It's difficult to provide details of the benefits succinctly because they are so many. It sounds unbelievable that one solution would affect so many areas of life. That is why I've included so many citations to support my statements. Even if this book just gets people talking and asking, "What if she is right?" it will be worth all the effort because once the possibility is considered we're on our way to the better future for all.

"Schools are one of the most important developmental contexts in young peoples' lives, and can be a key source of the skills and competencies that support their capacity for successful adaptation. Furthermore, schools provide accessible and relative stable sites within which to locate interventions to promote wellbeing and represent a common setting for children and adolescents, thus facilitating universal promotion-based interventions. Thus, schools are uniquely placed to promote the wellbeing of young people and of school communities more broadly."[749] It is not enough to teach schoolchildren, although that would go a long way toward improving life for many. According to the US Department of Education, 3.4% of children are homeschooled. It would be wise to provide education sessions for parents, not only because this information overturns information they were taught, but because *The Smart Way* improves outcomes regardless of what point in one's life they learn it. One of my earliest clients was a Vietnam veteran who had suffered from severe life-limiting PTSD until he learned *The Smart Way*.

Step I: Train the trainers
    Teach teachers, clergy, psychologists, social workers, youth group leaders, & others to provide training to large groups) in *The Smart Way Meta-cognitve Processes & Emotional Guidance*

Step 2: Implement training programs in schools, prisons, work, religious institutions, and parent groups.

Create televised shows to reach more.

Step 3: Encourage communities to form support groups to help one another master the techniques, sharing success stories and encouragement.

Step 4: Lapel pins that individuals can wear to indicate they've been trained and are willing to help others

Step 5: Document results and share.

The time it takes to add *The Smart Way* to the curriculum will be more than made up for by the benefits. Higher emotional states are associated with more pro-social behavior, increased cognitive abilities, higher test scores, improved immune function and more pro-health behaviors, fewer adverse health behaviors such as drugs and alcohol, and a focus on fulfilling potential.

Because *The Smart Way* is essentially teaching people how to use their minds to think in healthier ways and how to use their Emotional Guidance as it was intended, it provides vast benefits in every aspect of life. One of those areas is the broad category of resilience, another is physical health via multiple conduits including more pro-health decisions when happy and another is better immune function when happy (low stress), both of which contribute to better physical health. In 2014, Khanlou and Wray conducted a review of the existing literature on resilience from a public health perspective. They stated, "Resilience is seen as an important element to maintaining and promoting child and youth mental health, and as a life-long buffer to potential threats to wellbeing over time and transition."[750]

When we run the numbers, one of the most important things to consider is that this is a one-generation major event, unlike the problems that will be avoided in the future, which are currently chronic and spreading rapidly. Families that develop adaptive ways of existing in the world will "nurture adaptive systems that lay the foundation for future resilience in their children and pass on accumulated cultural wisdom and practices that also build capacity for adaptation."[751] Even if the first wave only eliminated half the problems, a world with half the problems we currently have would have stopped the growth of those problems (experts currently expect the problems to grow which would free up resources to solve the remaining problems and develop even better ways to prevent young lives from traveling paths that are destructive to themselves or others.

Other programs that have a Cognitive Behavior Therapy (CBT) component have experienced significant success both at reducing crime and improving academic success. "The bulk of the research evidence clearly indicates that the programs most likely to produce robust results in reducing criminal recidivism have cognitive-behavioral foundations that target behaviors related to offending and amenable to change, and that use social learning strategies."[752] The problem with those programs is Cognitive Behavioral Therapy is expensive and typically done one-on-one. CBT is like having an expert marksman standing beside you while you draw the bow and attempt to shoot the arrow into the bulls-eye while you're blindfolded. Teaching individuals *The Smart Way* takes the blindfold off so they can see the target and increase their skill at any time, not in a weekly 50-minute session. Therapists are still valuable in the area they were trained for—to help those with diagnosed mental illnesses. Using *The Smart Way* in conjunction with therapy has been beneficial to my students who have done both.

An article in the *Canadian Journal of Psychiatry* concluded, "Everyone could benefit from investment in improved mental health in the workplace. However, because the benefits associated with improved worker mental health are often distributed among several stakeholders, the incentives for any single stakeholder to pay for additional services for workers may be diluted. As a consequence, no one invests. Nevertheless, there is a role for all stakeholders, just as there are potential benefits for all. Along with government, employers, employees, and the health care system must invest in promoting good workplace health."[753] I submit that addressing good mental health in adolescence has the same stakeholders and the potential to prevent more problems and to be more effective because the younger we begin, the fewer dysfunctional cognitive habits will have to be corrected.

The Smart Way can be taught to large groups, which will reduce the cost of implementation.

Conclusion

In a recent article in the Charlotte Observer, Kay McSpadden who teaches high school in York, South Carolina ended her article with "If we valued children, we'd focus on the big picture instead of insisting that he bottom line is the only view. We would ensure our own children's future safety and happiness by addressing the very real needs of other people's children now—the children who will grow up to be our children's citizen companions."[754]

Imagine

Imagine a world where parents do not worry about their children being bullied or becoming depressed or worse. Imagine a world where marriages are deeper relationships because neither partner is afraid of rejection if they reveal their innermost thoughts and feelings. Imagine a world where couples take responsibility for their own happiness. Imagine a world where people enjoy being kinder to one another, a world without hate and fear. Imagine a world full of confident people who know their own value and worth and also see the same high value and worth in those with whom they share this beautiful planet. Imagine a world where people are able to align their passion with their work and feel more fulfilled. Imagine a world where more than ten percent of the population is not depressed each year. Imagine a world where adults who were abused as children finally feel safe, where they no longer use food and weight as a shield to protect them from the world. Imagine a world where people don't spend many years suffering with chronic illnesses before they die because they live longer and only begin to lose their vitality as death nears.

The state-of-the-art in formal psychological circles has been limited by a variety of factors as evinced by "it is accurate to conceptualize that common processes underlie the maintenance, and relief from all forms of psychopathology."[755] If you review the information later in this chapter, you will see that psychopathology is associated with feeling disempowered and mental health is associated with feeling empowered. It's not rocket science.

I am not beating up on therapists. Many of the ones I know have their hearts in the right place and have studied the training they've been given. Few (if any) subscribe to scientific journals across disciplines once they finish their training. They attend continuing education classes, but those are not state-of-the-art either. Psychological health is too important to wait for a generation of therapists to retire and for University programs to find a way to teach better methods. If you're going to spend 50 minutes with the goal of helping someone with psychological challenges, you might as well use the best possible methods. It's going to take the same amount of time.

I'm reminded of my experience when I was going to have Lasik eye surgery and I went to the most popular eye doctor in Charlotte. After my examination they gave me a piece of paper with three treatment options. Option #1 would improve my vision, but I'd probably still need glasses. Option #2 had a better chance of eliminating my need for glasses, but the potential outcome was not as good as option #3. Of course, the price tag increased as the anticipated success of the procedure improved. I left and never returned. From my point of view, a doctor of any sort offering a treatment option that delivered less than the best possible result was unethical. It seemed like they'd bought new equipment, but since they'd invested in the now outdated equipment and training on it, they were willing to use it for someone who was willing to have an inferior result with their eyesight.

The need to remain current in one's own discipline leaves almost no time to explore what other scientific disciplines say about human thriving, which leads to significant empirical data being unknown by psychologists until long after empirical evidence is published in journal articles.

In some states, universities cannot allow someone who does not have a Ph.D. in a subject to teach graduate level courses and maintain their accreditation. This leaves autodidactic learners on the sidelines—even when Deans become aware of and value the knowledge the autodidactic learner could bring to the classroom. In earlier times, autodidactic learners include notable inventors such as Thomas Edison, Benjamin Franklin, Jimi Hendrix, Johann Wolfgang von Goethe, Ernest Hemingway, Louis L'Amour (my favorite childhood writer), J.A. Rogers, Ray Bradbury, Christopher Hughes, Frank Lloyd Wright, Louis Sullivan (creator of the modern skyscraper), Leonardo da Vinci (for his science-he was trained in art), the Wright Brothers, and Henry Ford. The requirement to have a degree one level higher than those being taught will obtain means Frank Lloyd Wright and Louis Sullivan could not teach architecture and Ernest Hemingway, Ray Bradbury and Louis L'Amour would not be able to teach Creative Writing.

We have brilliant autodidactic learners, but barriers prevent them from having a seat at the table. We value the piece of paper more than the knowledge. This prevents students from learning from some of the best. It makes education a closed system. For example, T. Harv Eker dropped out of college and through a series of failures learned how to succeed. He provides world-class training in business, marketing, public speaking and more. I've attended his public speaking and marketing training. They are intense and provide valuable information. My youngest daughter who was a freshly minted college graduate attended Eker's marketing program with me and agreed that the knowledge gained over a few days in his program was more applicable to real life and valuable than several semesters of marketing at college. It was a common sentiment from the hundreds of people attending.

Researchers don't ask big questions. Most have to produce papers within a time-frame that fits their education criteria. It takes longer than that to research big questions and perhaps more importantly, big questions are outside the paradigm of silo'd disciplines. I spent more than a decade doing Primary Research and forming hypothesis. The first hypothesis I tested was four years after I began. If I was in a University program and took that long I'd flunk out. I didn't have a timeframe. I simply had insatiable curiosity to figure out the answer—curiosity that created a frame for my perspective in all my daily interactions. In *The Structure of Scientific Revolutions*, Thomas Kuhn wrote:

> *One of the things a scientific community acquires with a paradigm is a criterion for choosing problems that, while the paradigm is taken for granted, can be assumed to have solutions . . . A paradigm can, for that matter, even insulate the community from those socially important problems that are not reducible to puzzle form, because they cannot be stated in terms of the conceptual and instrumental tools the paradigm supplies.*

Is this person thriving? What area of life is he/she thriving in? If not, what characteristics does this person share with other people I've known who didn't thrive? If yes, what does this person do? How does she act? How does he speak? What does she believe? How does he treat others? How does she think about herself? Is he educated? Does she use proper English? Does he work hard? Who does she know? What experiences have made this person into who he is today? What goals does she have?

Jeanine Joy

I was off-track in the early days because I had beliefs that working hard and speaking and writing well were the keys to success. They definitely help. But they aren't the difference makers.

My second hypothesis was about expectation. I had a belief that you had to earn what you received. I had become aware of someone who always seemed to get what she wanted and she was definitely not earning what she was receiving. I began watching her and paying attention to what she was doing. I decided she simply expected the things she was receiving, as if they were her due. I didn't like it. It went against what I believed. But I saw her successfully receive things I'd never received despite years of hard work, just by expecting them to be given to her.

I began experimenting with expectation. I changed my expectations at work and realized that I had always believed that through hard work I would get what I wanted, but there was no way to measure when I'd done enough hard work and then deserved to receive what I thought I had earned. I didn't have a barometer that said, "There, now you've earned it. You should now expect to receive it."

I looked around at others and decided that I deserved to be a Vice President based on my responsibilities. I asked my boss, "Why aren't I a Vice President" and he said, "I don't know. You should be." Wow.

That was an eye-opener. I should be. I wanted to be. But until I expected it, it didn't happen. When I expected it, it came quickly.

Hmmm, I have to believe I deserve it before others will believe I deserve it? I played with that a lot over the next few years and helped friends begin expecting better outcomes—all of our lives improved. Not just in our financial lives, but in the respect we were shown, in our relationships, in how the school treated me as a parent and more.

38: PS

Education is not a tool for development - individual, community and the nation. It is the foundation for our future. It is empowerment to make choices and emboldens the youth to chase their dreams.
Nita Ambani

Understanding how to accurately interpret one's Emotional Guidance is enough to change the trajectory of millions of lives. For the children who are taught about their guidance and encouraged to use it from a young age it is all they need to achieve far more of their potential than they ever could without understanding of the meaning of their emotions.

Adults who have established habits of thought that do not serve them can use their guidance to improve the trajectory of their lives, but the process would be slower if that was the only tool they had available. I've spent the last seven years finding and developing practical methods to help adults shift more quickly. Those methods are described in any of my books that have *The Smart Way* in the title or inside the front cover. For any adult who chooses to use only Emotional Guidance, it is important to understand that you have neurological pathways that make your current way of thinking easiest. I encourage my students to be very patient and expect that the old habits of thought will continue to be common on any subject where you have spent much time for up to 3 months. It could be less or more, depending on how ingrained the beliefs are and how diligent you are in using your guidance.

Be easy on yourself. You did not learn your current habits of thought in a day and you won't create new habits in a day.

Anytime you are feeling less than you want to feel, take your thoughts less specific (more general). You can also use a change of focus to change your mood but changing focus, the easiest and fastest way to change mood, does little toward automating better thought patterns in the future. Finding new perspectives that feel better creates immediate and long term change.

I wish you the best in this adventure we call life. You deserve it.

If you found any aspect of this book beneficial to you, please consider leaving a review.
My goal is to help as many people as possible thrive more. In today's competitive publishing marketplace, reviews often make the difference between whether your book reaches the audience you want to help or not.

Honest reviews and feedback, positive or negative, are always welcome.

The most helpful review sites are Amazon.com or Goodreads.com
Reviews may be anonymous.

Jeanine Joy

Appendix I
Appendix I - Emotional Guidance Scale (EGSc)

In general, emotional states can be defined (broadly) with the following feelings:

Sweet Zone
- Joy
- Empowered
- Passion
- Happy
- Inspired
- Optimism
- Fulfilled
- Appreciation
- Love
- Enthusiasm
- Positive Expectation
- Trust
- Serene
- Secure
- Freedom
- Awe
- Eagerness
- Belief
- Faith
- Satisfied
- At ease

Hopeful Zone
- Hopefulness
- Gratitude
- Upbeat

Blah Zone
- Contentment
- Apathy
- Boredom
- Dispirited
- Pessimism
- Empty

Drama Zone
- Frustration
- Overwhelmed
- Irritation
- Disappointment
- Impatience
- Indignant

Give Away Zone
- Doubt
- Guilt
- Worry
- Discouragement
- Blame
- Offended

Hot (Red) Zone
- Anger
- Outraged
- Revenge
- Provoked
- Rage
- Furious

Powerless Zone
- Hatred
- Insecurity
- Grief
- Powerless
- Hopeless
- Suicidal
- Bullied
- Fear
- Depression
- Learned Helplessness
- Melancholy
- Unimportant
- Jealousy
- Unworthiness
- Despair
- Guarded
- Unwanted
- Exploited

Appendix II

Future research should consider individual thought processes (i.e. coping skills, cognitive reappraisal, etc.) when determining long-term health outcomes of adverse events. Unless and until research is done on actual thought processes, the strong link between reappraisals that lower stress levels and positive outcomes will not have the empirical documentation that will allow them to be widely implemented and supported with the funding they deserve.

Jeanine Joy

Appendix III - Self-Test[756]

	1	2	3	4	5	6	7	8	9	10

Mark the line below to indicate where you are now.
Example: Use a "E" to mark how you feel now (at the end of the book)
Tired frequently_____E ___ Well-rested
The location of this E indicates you feel rested more than you feel too tired
Sad frequently_____Rarely Sad
Fuzzy thinking_____Clear headed
Not sleeping well_____Sleeping well
Hopeless_____Hopeful
Exhausted_____Energized
Scattered_____Focused
Overwhelmed_____Capable
Stuck_____Letting go
Resentful_____Forgiving
Close-hearted_____Open-hearted
Frustrated_____Appreciative
Broken_____Whole
Depressed_____Happy
Anxious_____Calm
Unbalanced_____Balanced
Uncomfortable_____Comfortable
Defined by my illness/problem/or past _____Self-defined
Low self-esteem_____High self-esteem
Complete_____Evolving
No energy_____Vital and alive
Angry_____Accepting
Vengeful_____Understanding
Old_____Wise
My body does not recover quickly _____My body is strong
Isolated_____Connected
Bored_____Interested
Boring_____Fun
Life is hard_____Life is easy

Sources of More Information

I have several websites with information that will be helpful.
www.Happiness1st.com
www.HouseofPeaceandLove.org
www.JeanineJoy.US
www.AchieveAffinity.org

I am available to teach *The Smart Way Program* and for motivational speeches that include an educational component.

The focus of each is on increasing Human Thriving.
- Happiness 1st Institute offers classes to individuals and companies that teach skills that increase resilience, happiness, employee engagement, lower stress, and provide other significant benefits.
- The House of Peace and Love for All is my ministry where I work on some of the projects that are closest to my heart, such as increasing peace in the world and increasing human thriving in a way that is open to members of all religious affiliations. I seek to increase faith not convert.
- JeanineJoy.US is my author website where you can learn more about my books.
- Achieve Affinity is a non-profit organization I co-founded with my husband to bring the information provided by Happiness 1st Institute to schools and others who cannot afford the services of Happiness 1st Institute

I blog on all four sites and on LinkedIn.
You can follow me on Twitter: @JeanineJoyJOY
You can also follow me on Goodreads.com
Radio shows I've been on are archived on Happiness1st and I will soon be broadcasting a weekly radio show for The House of Peace and Love for All
Facebook: https://www.facebook.com/Happiness1st

Please remember to review the book on Amazon and Goodreads to let me know how it helped you. Thanks!

Jeanine Joy

Special Offer

I occasionally hold Introductory Sessions to introduce individuals, businesses, physicians and clergy *The Smart Way*. Please come to one of the sessions as my guest. If the Introductory Session is not serving a meal, you may attend as my guest free of charge. If a meal is being served, I ask that you cover the cost of your meal.

If you are interested in a program for your school, business or other organization, please contact me at Thrive More Now Publishing, P.O. Box 6888, Concord NC 28078 (704) 251-5150.

If you are interested in having me speak at your event, please contact me via LinkedIn (preferred), Twitter (JeanineJoyJOY), my publisher or my website, Happiness1st.com

Glossary

This is not intended to be an extensive glossary, but to explain some terms that may be new to the reader and may not be explained exactly as they are here in the dictionary. In some cases, the term is one I have created to refer to a concept.

Also, since attempting to alternate between he and she, or to use the gender neutral one can make the writing cumbersome, or, in the case of he or she, make the reader wonder whom I am speaking about, I am transitioning to greater use of the singular they.

Anthropic mechanism is the concept that "everything about human beings can be completely explained in mechanical terms, as surely as can everything about clocks or the internal combustion engine."[757]

Cognitive Dissonance Individuals whose beliefs, opinions, or behaviors are inconsistent with one another are experiencing cognitive dissonance. Cognitive Dissonance is uncomfortable and something will need to change to reconcile the dissonance.

HPA axis The hypothalamic–pituitary–adrenal axis (HPA axis or HTPA axis), also known as the limbic–hypothalamic–pituitary–adrenal axis (LHPA axis) and, occasionally, as the hypothalamic–pituitary–adrenal–gonadotropic axis, is a complex set of direct influences and feedback interactions among three endocrine glands: the hypothalamus, the pituitary gland (a pea-shaped structure located below the hypothalamus), and the adrenal (also called "suprarenal") glands (small, conical organs on top of the kidneys).

The interactions among these organs constitute the HPA axis, a major part of the neuroendocrine system that controls reactions to stress and regulates many body processes, including digestion, the immune system, mood and emotions, sexuality, and energy storage and expenditure. It is the common mechanism for interactions among glands, hormones, and parts of the midbrain that mediate the general adaptation syndrome (GAS).[1] While steroid hormones are produced mainly in vertebrates, the physiological role of the HPA axis and corticosteroids in stress response is so fundamental that analogous systems can be found in invertebrates and monocellular organisms as well. (Wiki, 2/2016)

Meta-cognitve Processes- thinking about thinking and techniques that allow a person to adjust their thoughts so they feel better.

The Galileo Effect is the human tendency to cling to existing beliefs despite overwhelming evidence that the new idea better explains what happens. It is a common human behavior because our minds interpret new information through the lens of our current paradigm. Understanding how our mind filters information before we become consciously aware of it can help us retain a more open mindset that will see and benefit from new information faster.

Positive affect is basically another way to say happiness

Index

A. Rogers, 425
Abraham, 382
Abraham Lincoln, 191, 259, 393
ACE Pyramid, 246
Addiction, 151
addictions, 136
Adverse Childhood Experiences ACE, 10
Affirmation, 362
Akio Morita, 393
Albert Einstein, 131, 393
Alcohol abuse, 342
Alison Beard, 189
Alliance for Excellent Education, 314
Andrew Young, 402
Angel B. Pérez, 315
Angela Duckworth, 310
Anger, 42, 370
Anthropic mechanism, 54
Anxiety, 38, 180, 262
Apartheid, 191
Appreciation, 74, 382
Aromatherapy, 404
Automatic response, 340
Back stories, 82
Back story, 164
Barbara L. Fredrickson, 180
Behavior, 378
Being positive, 364
Belief, 81, 132, 134, 135, 152
Beliefs, 132, 143, 188
Ben Carson, 401
Benjamin Franklin, 241, 425
Benjamin I. Goldstein, 259
Bias, 122
Biases, 75
Bill Gates, 393
Biofield, 118
Bipolar Disorder, 190
Blah Zone, 358, 362
Body dysmorphic disorder, 41
Boiled frog analogy, 112
Born to be Good, 121
Brain, 131, 132, 144
Brian Tracy, 109
Bright side, 364
Buddha, 402
Buddhist, 69, 125
Bullying, 342
C. Joy Bell, 390
Capgras Delusion, 72
Career Adaptability, 320
Carol Dweck, 143, 144, 310
Cathy Spatz Widom, 223

Cellular communication, 125
Change/shift filter, 85
Changes of focus, 356
Charles Darwin, 393
Charles S. Carver, 93
Charles Schultz, 393
Chemical addiction, 378
Christianity, 125
Christopher Hughes, 425
Chronic Emotional Stance, 403
Chronic Emotional States, 155
Chronic Fatigue Syndrome, 43
Chronic health issues, 341
chronic psychosocial stress. *See* Chronic Stress
Chronic stress, 70, 176
Cindy Lightner, 121
Clarity, 136
Classic Physics, 165
Clinical trials, 80
Cognitive Dissonance, 273
Cognitive function, 378
Complementary and Alternative Medicines (CAM), 79
Confabulation, 82
Conflicting emotions, 123
Confucius, 125
Conor Friedersdorf, 280
Conscientiousness, 18
Conscious mind, 132
Consciousness, 131
Consider Resources, 387
Constructive Interference, 166
Contingencies, 388
Coronary Heart Disease (CHD), 42
Co-rumination, 261, 304
creep alert, 99, 103, 104
Crime, 342
Cuckoo bird, 77
Cultural anthropologists, 78
Cultural indoctrination, 72
Dacher Keltner, 121
Dale Carnegie, 393
Dan Siegel, 98
Darrell Weismann, 120
David Benhayon, 39
David Bohm, 190
David Lindley, 194
David Schwartz, 144
Daymond John, 150
Decisions, 365
Default setting, 341
Defensiveness, 119
Degree Creep, 317

Deliberately shift, 371
Depressed, 342
Depression, 18, 38, 158, 160, 259, 260, 261, 290, 293, 397, 421, 428
Desires, 123
Destructive Interference, 168
Digestive System function, 342
Divorce, 342
Donald Trump, 171
Dose Dependent, 340
Dose-dependent processes, 409
Dr. Darrell Weismann, 120
Dr. Joy Degruy, 14
Dr. Larry Dossey, 194
Dr. Robert Holden, 188
Drama Zone, 155, 156, 159, 358, 362, 428
Drop Out Factories, 314
Drugs and alcohol, 369
Dustin Hoffman, 143
Eating disorders, 342
Eating Disorders, 41
Ed Diener, 175, 422
Edward Deci, 200
EFT (Emotional Freedom Tapping), 407
Elvis Presley, 393
Emotion: A Self-regulatory Sense, 116
Emotional agility, 180
Emotional guidance, 344
Emotional Guidance, 86, 119, 150, 176
Emotional Guidance Scale, 114
Emotional Guidance Sensory Feedback System (EGS), 85
Emotional Guidance System, 93, 102, 110, 114, 116, 121, 136, 226
Emotional Guidance System (EGS), 93, 110, 371, 377
Emotional Intelligence, 8, 290, 299, 312, 378
Emotional Intelligence (EQ), 378
Emotional response, 122, 136, 151
Emotional Set Point, 161
Emotional stance, 132, 161
Emotional Stance, 137, 155
Emotional stances, 122
Emotional states, 159
Empower, 383
Empowered, 158, 176
Empowerment, 159
Endocrine System function, 342
Energy healing, 404

Ernest Hemingway, 210, 425
Eva Szigethy, 39
Evil, 121
Expectation, 148, 379
Expectations, 132, 151
Experienced emotionally, 122
External Locus of Control, 214
Failure, 392, 393
False premises, 162
False Premises, 188
Fatigue, 387
Fear, 121, 160, 187
Filter, 131, 132, 137, 157
Filtering process, 71, 139
Filtering system, 124
Filters, 82, 110, 131, 134, 143
Flourish, 121
Flow, 187
Focus, 122, 132, 134, 163, 355, 358
Forgiving, 369
Frank Lloyd Wright, 425
Galileo Effect, 80, 88, 165
Gambling, 40
Garth Brooks, 393
General Wellbeing (GWB), 180
Generally negative, 376
Generally Positive, 376
Give Away Zone, 358
Go general, 380
Go specific, 381
Goals, 134, 388, 401
Gratitude, 382
Habits of thought, 403
Happiness, 175
Happiness Contract, 188
Harland David Sanders, 393
Healing Touch, 404
Heart (cardiovascular) disease, 342
Heart disease. *See* Cardiovascular
Henry Ford, 100, 101, 167, 335, 393, 425
Herbert Fröhlich, 168
Hindu, 125
Holly Mosier, 123
Hopeful Zone, 155, 156, 160, 341, 342, 358, 362, 380, 382, 384, 387, 399, 411, 428
Hopeless, 151
Hopelessness, 136
Hot (red) Zone, 358
Hot Zone, 156, 160, 365
Howard Thurman, 138
HPA axis. *See* Glossary

Human Needs, 197, 303
Human thriving, 124
Humor, 391
Hunger, 387
Hypertension, 41
Ignaz Semmelweis, 78
Immune system function, 80
Immune System function, 342
implicit theories. *See* Back Story
Inner critic, 389
Insomnia, 41
Instinct, 78
Intelligence, 378
Interference, 166
Internal dialogue, 362
Internal Locus Of Control, 214
Interpret reality, 70
Interpretations of reality, 73
Intrinsic motivation, 178
Irritable Bowel Syndrome IBS, 42
Isaac Asimov, 421
Islam, 125
J. K. Rowling, 393
Jack London, 393
Jerry Rice, 148
Jimi Hendrix, 425
Joe Torres, 393
Johann von Goethe, 167
Johann Wolfgang von Goethe, 425
John Grisham, 393
John Lennon, 175
John Paul Mitchell, 393
Jonathan Haidt, 82
Jonathan Rottenberg, 72, 410
Jose Vilson, 310
KAHLIL GIBRAN, 93
Karen Kaplan, 190
Karl Menninger, 211
Kay McSpadden, 424
Kevin Hall, 382
Kim Innes, 251
Lao Tzu, 402
Law enforcement officer, 117
Learned Helplessness, 211, 428
Leonardo da Vinci, 425
Lifestyle habits, 342
Limiting belief, 136
Lloyd Alexander, 191
Long-term outcomes, 403
Louis Sullivan, 425
Louisa May Alcott, 393
Low self-esteem, 390

Ludwig van Beethoven, 393
Lyubomirsky, Sonja, 175, 179
MADD, 121
Mahatma Gandhi, 368, 388, 402
Marilyn Monroe, 393
Mark Walker, 178
Martin E. P. Seligman, 65, 121, 260
Martin Seligman, 82
Maslow's Hierarchy of Needs, 181
Massage Therapy, 403
Matthew D. Della Porta, 175
Matthieu Ricard, 86, 139
Meaning, 111, 122
Meditation, 405
Mental attitude, 343
Michael Jordan, 133, 393
Milton Hershey, 149
Mind-body connection, 80
Mindy Kaling, 121
Miscommunication, 118
Monarch butterflies, 77
Mood Disorders, 40
Motivation, 133
Muhammad Ali, 402
Napoleon Hill, 167, 187, 393
Negative Life Event. *See* Negative Life Events
Negative life events, 125
Negative news, 122
Negative self-talk, 124
Neural pathways, 339
Niels Bohr, 409
Nocebo, 80
Nomanono Isaacs, 191
Non-Suicidal Self-Injury, 197
Non-Suicidal Self-Injury (NSSI), 197
Oberlin College, 280
Obsessive Compulsive Disorder OCD, 41
Opinions, 73, 115
Opportunity, 342
Oprah Winfrey, 393, 402
Optical illusions, 73
Optimism, 114
Optimistic, 187
Optimists, 181
Orville & Wilbur Wright, 393
Orville and Wilbur Wright, 393
Pain
    Physical or Emotional, 387
Parenting, 177
Parsimony Principle, 77
Paul Tsongas, 403

Index

Peace, 131, 191
Pema Chodron, 382
Perception, 85, 124, 131, 132, 133, 164
Personal interpretation., 136
Perspective, 72, 138, 163, 180, 346
Pessimism, 113
Phobias, 41
Placebo, 80
Positive Affirmations, 361
Positive Education, 310
Positive expectation, 181
Positive mindset, 342
Positively focused, 365
Positivity, 180
Posttraumatic Stress Disorder PTSD, 41
Potential, 152, 378
Powerless Zone, 358, 363
Practiced expectations, 151
Premenstrual Syndrome PMS, 43
President Reagan, 418
Primary Prevention, 140
Programmed, 138, 143
Programming, 132, 134
PTSD, 34, 38, 41, 205, 208, 209, 210, 212, 224, 250, 309, 349, 422
Puget Sound, 99
Pursuit of happiness, 176
Pygmalion, 153, 363
Quantum physics, 125, 178
Quantum Physics, 105, 165
Quotes, 136
R. H. Macy, 393
R.H. Macy, 393
Ralph Waldo Emerson, 89, 167, 401
Rational brain, 119
Rational mind, 111
Ray Bradbury, 425
Reality, 70, 131, 132, 133
Reframing, 390
Refute, 366
Reiki, 404
Relief, 136
Repetitive thoughts, 356
Resilience, 124, 125, 342, 378
Rheumatoid Arthritis, 43
Richard Branson, 393
Richard Ryan, 200
Right Response (RR), 121, 123, 379
Right Responses (RRs), 116
Risky behavior, 378
Robert Biswas-Diener, 175
Role Model, 400
Ronald Reagan, 378
Root cause, 114, 123
Root Cause Stress Relief, 340
Roy F. Baumeister, 96, 220
Rumination, 261, 304
Schizophrenia, 40
Self-affirming exercise. *See* Positive Affirmations
Self-control. *See* Self-Regulation
Self-criticism, 82, 187, 388
self-esteem, 54
Self-esteem, 152
Self-Esteem, 54, 394
Self-fulfilling prophesies, 388
Self-induced stress, 389
Selfish, 344
Self-realization, 95
Sensory Guidance, 161
Sensory systems, 85
Setting intentions, 367
Shades of Joy, 99
Shame, 378
Shawn Achor, 175, 263
Sidney Madwed, 402
Sidney Poitier, 393
Simona Bujoreanu, 39
Sleep habits, 342
Smoker, 342
Smoking Cessation, 40
Social Anxiety Disorder SAD, 262
Soichiro Honda, 393
Solutions, 342
Specifically negative, 376
Stephanie Meyer, 393
Stephen King, 393
Steve Jobs, 393
Steven Spielberg, 393
Stress, 111, 125, 160, 343
Stress Management Techniques, 340
Stressed, 387
Substance Use Disorders. See Alcohol and Drug Abuse
Success, 393
Suicide, 159, 342
Surface thinking, 74
Sustainable happiness, 343
Sweet Zone, 155, 156, 161, 357, 359, 372, 381, 382, 388, 428
Synchronicities, 93
T. Harv Eker, 150, 425
Tai chi, 404
Tal Ben-Shahar, 175
Taste, 75
The Beatles, 393
The Galileo Effect. *See* Glossary
The HeartMath Institute, 80, 244, 246
The Institute of Noetic Science, 80
The List, 358
The Smart Way, iii, 4, 13, 14, 33, 54, 113, 159, 178, 180, 190, 193, 222, 230, 261, 286, 289, 293, 343, 410, 417, 421, 422, 423, 424, 427
Theodor Seuss Giesel, 393
Therapeutic Touch, 404
Think Positive, 364
Think positively, 113
Thomas Edison, 393, 425
Thomas Kuhn, 425
Thoughts, 86, 123, 161
Thoughts,, 357
Tiger Woods, 171
Todd Kashdan, 72, 410
Tom Landry, 393
Tony Robbins, 187, 393
Topic, 161, 356
Traditional psychotherapies, 405
Trinity College, 315
True Happiness, 32, 177, 189, 228, 251
Unbundle, 370
Unique perspectives, 74
Unworthy, 187
Validation, 119
Viktor Frankl, 123
Vivid Senses, 169
Walt Disney, 393
Wavelengths, 74, 75, 76
Well-Being, 378
Werner Heisenberg, 69
Winston Churchill, 393, 402
Worried, 387
Wright Brothers, 149, 425
Yoga, 404

Bibliography

"Visualizing Eleven Dimensions" (2010). [Motion Picture]. Retrieved from http://einsteinsintuition.com/2013/thad-meets-ted/

Abravanel, B. T., & Sinha, R. (2015, February). Emotion Dysregulation Mediates the Relationship between Lifetime Cumulative Adversity and Depressive Symptomatology. *Journal of Psychiatric Research, 61*, 89-96. doi:doi:10.1016/j.jpsychires.2014.11.012.

Achor, S. (2010). *The Happiness Advantage: Seven Principles of Positive Psychology That Fuel Success and Performance at Work.* Random House.

Achor, S., & Gielan, M. (2015, September 2). Make Yourself Immune to secondhand Stress. *Harvard Business Review*, p. Epub.

Acierno, R. K. (1999). 7 x more likely to be victimized ??? TITLE. *Jnl. of Anxiety Disorders*. Retrieved from http://www2.ucsc.edu/rape-prevention/statistics.html

Ager, A. (2013). Annual Research Review: Resilience and child well-being--public policy implications. *The Journal of Child Psychology and Psychiatry, 54*(4), 488-500.

Agnew, R. (1992). Foundation for a general strain theory of crime and delinquency. *Criminology, 30*, 47-87.

Ali, M. M., Dwyer, D. S., Vanner, E. A., & Lopex, A. (2010). Adolescent Propensity to Engage in Health Risky Behaviors: The Role of Individual Resilience. *International Jouranl of Environmental Research and Public Health, 7*, 2161-2176.

Allen, J. (2007). *As A Man Thinketh.* Wilder Publications.

Alliance for Excellent Education. (2013). *Cliimate Change: Implementing School Discipline Practice That Create a Positive School Climate.* All4ED.org: Alliance for Excellent Education.

Allison, S. T., Uhles, A. N., Asuncion, A. G., Beggan, J. K., & Mackie, D. M. (2006, July 28). Self-serving outcome-biases in trait judgments about the self. *Current Research in Social Psychology*, 202-214.

American Academy of Pediatrics. (2012, October 22). *Children with Mental Health Disorders More Often Identified as Bullies.* Retrieved from aap.org: https://www.aap.org/en-us/about-the-aap/aap-press-room/pages/Children-with-Mental-Health-Disorders-More-Often-Identified-as-Bullies.aspx?nfstatus=401&nftoken=00000000-0000-0000-0000-000000000000&nfstatusdescription=ERROR%3a+No+local+token

American Public Health Association (APHA). (2015). Racism and Its Effect on Children's Health. doi:https://www.linkedin.com/pulse/racism-its-impact-childrens-health-jeanine?trk=mp-reader-card

Anderson, J. G., & Taylor, A. G. (2011). The Metabolic Syndrome and Mind-Body Therapies: A Systematic Review. *Journal of Nutrition and Metabolism*, 8. doi:10.1155/2011/276419

Andrews, R. A., Lowe, R., & Clair, A. (2011). The relationship between basic need satisfaction and emotional eating in obesity. *Australian Journal of Psychology*, 207-213.

APA. (2013). *Stress in America: Missing the Health Care Connection .*

APA. (2014). *Stress in America: Are Teens Adopting Adults' Stress Habits?* American Psychological Association. American Psychological Association. Retrieved from http://www.apa.org/news/press/releases/stress/2013/stress-report.pdf

APA. (2015). *Stress in America: Paying with our Health.* American Psychological Association.

APA. (2016). *Stress in America: The Impact of Discrimination.* American Psychological Association.

Appleton, A. A., Buka, S. L., Loucks, E. B., Gilman, S. E., & Kubzansky, L. D. (2013). Divergent Associations of Adaptive and Maladaptive Emotion Regulation. (APA, Ed.) *Health Psychology*, 748-756. doi:DOI: 10.1037/a0030068

Armeli, S., O'Hare, R. E., Covault, J., Scott, D. M., & Tennen, H. (2016, January 29). Episode-specific drinking-to-cope motivation and next-day stress reactivity. *Anxiety Stress Coping*, 1-12.

Armstrong, A. R., Galligan, R. F., & Critchley, C. R. (2011). Emotional Intelligence and psychological resilience to negative life events. *Personalit and Individual Differences, 51*, 331-336.

Arnow, B. (2004). Relationships between childhood maltreatment, adult health and psychiatric outcomes, and medical utilization. *Journal of clinical Psychiatry, 65*(Suppl 12:10-5).

Aronson, J. &. (2005). Stereotypes and the Fragility of Academic Competence, Motivation, and Self-Concept. In A. E. (Eds.) (Ed.), *The handbook of competence and motivation. .* New York: Guilford.

Aronson, J. F. (2002). *Reducing the effects of stereotype threat on African American College students by shaping theories of intelligence.* Journal of Experimental Social Psychology.

Aronson, J. (n.d.). *Fixed versus malleable ability instructions affect the MCAT scores of minority students.* (New York University ed.). Unpublished data.

Ashby, F. G. (1999). A neuropsychological theory of positive affect and its influence on cognition. *Psychological Review*, 106, No. 3: 529-50.

Asher, M. S., & Levounis, P. (Eds.). (2014). *The Behavioral Addictions.* Arlington: American Psychiatric Publishing.

Ashkanasy, N. M. (2011). International Happiness: A Multilevel Perspective . *The Academy of Management Perspectives*, 23-29.

Assagioli, R. (1965). *Psychosynthesis: A Collection of Basic Writings.* New York: The Viking Press.

VI | Bibliography

Association, A. P. (2013). *DSM V (Diagnostic and statistical manual of mental disorders)* (5th ed.). APA.

Badr, H. E., & Moody, P. M. (2005). Self-Efficacy: A Predictor for Smoking Cessation Contemplators in Kuwaiti Adults. *International Journal of Behaviorial Medicine*, 273-277.

Bale, T. L. (2011). Sex differences in prenatal spigenetic programing of stress pathways. *Informa Healthcare*, 348-356.

Bandura, A. (1986). *Social Foundations of Thought and Action*. Prentice-Hall.

Banik, G., & Gajdošová, B. (2014). Positive changes following cancer: posttraumatic growth in context of other factors in patients with cancer. *Support Care Cancer, 22*, 2023-2029. doi:DOI 10.1007/s00520-014-2217-0

Banks, A. (2011, March). The Mythic Reality of the Autonomous Individual. *Zygon, 46*(1).

Barasch, M. I., & Hirshberg, C. (1995). *Remarkable Recovery: What Extraordinary Healings Tell Us About Getting Well and Staying Well.*

Baratta, M. V., Rozeske, R. R., & Maier, S. F. (2013). Understanding Stress Resilience. *Frontiers in Behavioral Neuroscience*, 1-112. doi:DOI 10.3389/978-2-88919-185-7

Bardwell, W. A. (1999). Psychological correlates of sleep apnea. *Journal of Psychosomatic Research*, 47: 583-96.

Barn, R., & Tan, J.-P. (2012). Foster youth and crime: Employing general strain theory to promote understanding. *Journal of Criminal Justice, 40*, 212-220.

Barnica, B. (2014, April 18). *How Biophotons Show that we are made of light*. Retrieved from thespiritscience.net: http://thespiritscience.net/2014/04/18/biophotons-demonstrate-were-al-made-of-light/

Bar-On, R., & Parker, J. D. (Eds.). (2000). *The Handbook of Emotional Intelligence: Theory, Development, Assessment, and applications at Home, School, and in the Workplace.* San Francisco, CA: Jossey-Bass, A Wiley Company.

Barron, K. E., & Harackiewicz, J. M. (2001). Achievement Goals and Optimal Motivation:Testing Multiple Goal Models. *Journal of Personality and Social Psychology, 80*(5), 706-722. doi:DOI: 10.1037//0022-3514.80.5.706

Barry, C. T., Grafeman, S. J., Adler, K. K., & Pickard, J. D. (2007). The relations among narcissism, self-esteem, and delinquency in a sample of at-risk adolescents. *Journal of Adolescence*, 933-942.

Batmanghelidj, D. F. (2003). *Your Body's Many Cries for Water.* Global Health Solutions, Inc.

Bauer, M. E., Jeckel, C. M., & Luz, C. (2009). The role of stress factors during aging of the immune system. *Annals of the New York Academy of Sciences*, 139-52. doi:doi: 10.1111/j.1749-6632.2008.03966.x

Baumann, N., Kashel, R., & Kuhl, J. (2005). Striving for Unwated Goals: Stress-Dependent Discrepancies Between Explicit and Implicit Achievement Motives Reduce Subjective Well-Being. *Journal of Personality and Social Psychology, 89*(5), 781-799.

Baumeister, R. F. (2012). Human Evil: The myth of pure evil and the true causes of violence. In A. P. Association, M. Mikulincer, & P. R. Shaver (Eds.), *The social psychology of morality: Exploring the causes of good and evil* (pp. 367-380). Washington D.C., USA.

Baumeister, R. F. (2015). Success. *Journal of Personality, 72*, 271-322. Retrieved 2015

Baumeister, R. F., & Beck, A. (1999). *Evil: Inside Human Violence and Cruelty.* New York: Henry Holt and Company, LLC.

Baumeister, R. F., Gailliot, M., DeWall, C. N., & Oaten, M. (2006). Self-Regulation and Personality: How Interventions Increase Regulatory Success, and How Depletion Moderates the Effects of Traits on Behavior. *Journal of Personality, 74*(6), 1773 - 1802. doi:DOI: 10.1111/j.1467-6494.2006.00428.x

Baumeister, R. F., Vohs, K. D., DeWall, C. N., & Zhang, L. (2007, May 16). How Emotion Shapes Behavior: Feedback, Anticipation, and Reflection, Rather Than Direct Causation. *Personality and Social Psychology Review, 11*(2), 167-203. Retrieved September 23, 2015, from <file:///C:/Users/Jeanine/Documents/baumeister%20how%20emotion%20shapes%20behavior.pdf>

Baumeister, R. F., Vohs, K. D., DeWall, N., & Zhang, L. (2007, May). How Emotion Shapes Behavior: Feedback, Anticipation, and Reflection, Rather Than Direct Causation. *Personality and Social Psychology Review, 11*(2), 167-203. doi:DOI: 10.1177/1088868307301033

Baumesiter, R. F., Vohs, K. D., & Tice, D. M. (2007). The Strength Model of Self-Control. *Current Directions in Psychological Science*, 351-355.

Baumrind, D. (1960). Effects of Authoritative Parental Control on Child Behavior. *University of Berkeley*.

Beard, A. (2015, July - August). The Happiness Backlash. *Harvard Business Review*, p. Psychology.

Bebner, G. G. (1980). The "Mainstreaming" of America: Violence Profile No. 11. *Journal of Communication, Vol. 30*, No. 3: 10 - 29.

Beck, M. (2009, March 17). Stress so bad it hurts—Really . *Wall Street Journal*, p. Health Journal.

Beck, R., & Fernandez, E. (1998). Cognitive-Behavioral Therapy in the Treatment of Anger: A Meta-Analysis. *Cognitive Therapy and Research, 22*(1), 63-74.

Beevers, C. G., & Carver, C. S. (2003). Attentional Bias and Mood Persistence as Prospective Predictors of Dysphoria. *Cognitive Therapy and Research*, 619-637.

Beihl, D. A., Liese, A. D., & Haffner, S. M. (2008). Sleep Duration as a Risk Factor for Incident Type 2 Diabetes. *Ann Epidemiology*. doi:doi:10.1016/j.annepidem.2008.12.001

Bender, K. (2010). Why do some maltreated youth become juvenile offenders? A call for further investigation and adaptation of youth services. *Children and Youth Services Review 32, 32*, 466-473. doi:10.1016/j.childyouth.2009.10.022

Benedetti, F., Pollo, A., Lopiano, L., Lanotte, M., Vighetti, S., & Rainero, I. (2003, May 15). Conscious Expectation and Unconscious Conditioning in Analgesic, Motor, and Hormonal Placebo/Nocebo Responses. *The Journal of Neuroscience, 23*(10), 4315-4323.

Benjamin, G. K. (1986). The Role of legal education in producing psychological distress among law students and lawyers. *American Bar Foundation Research Journal*, 225-252.

Bennett, T., Holloway, K., & Farrington, D. (2008). The statistical association between drug misuse and crime: A meta-analysis. *Aggression and Violent Behavior, 13*, 107-118.

Benoit, A. K., Meller, S., Tan, P. Z., Ladouceur, C. D., Sheeber, L. B., Forbes, E. E., . . . Ryan, N. D. (2015, November 9). Parental autonomy granting and child perceived control: effects on the everyday emotional experience of anxious youth. *Journal of Child Psychology and Psychiatry*, Epub.

Ben-Shahar, T. (2007). *Happier*. New York: McGraw Hill.

Ben-Shahar, T. (Writer). (2009). *Happiness 101* [Motion Picture]. Retrieved 12 2009

Bergen, H. A. (2004). Sexual abuse, antisocial behaviour and substance use: Gender differences in young community adolescents. *Australian and New Zealand Journal of Psychiatry, 38*, 34-41.

Berk, L. T. (1989). Neuroendocrine and stress hormone changes during mirthful laughter. *American Journal of the Medical Sciences*, 298: 390-96.

Berking, M., Margraf, M., Ebert, D., Wupperman, P., Hofmann, S. G., & Junghanns, K. (2011, June). Deficits in Emotion-Regulation Skills Predict Alcohol Use During and After Cognitive Behavioral Therapy for Alcohol Dependence. *Journal of Consulting and Clinical Psychology, 79*(3), 307-318. doi:http://dx.doi.org/10.1037/a0023421

Bernard, B. (1996). Fostering resiliency in children and youth: promoting protective. In B. Bernard, *The Strengths perspective in social work practice* (pp. 167-182). New York: Longman.

Berry, M. E., Chapple, I. T., Ginsberg, J. P., Gleichauf, K. J., Meyer, J. A., & Nagpal, M. L. (2014, March). Non-pharmacological Interention for Chronic Pain in Veterans: A Pilot Study of Heart Rate Vriability Biofeedback. *Global Advances in Health and Medicine, 3*(2), 28-33.

Besharat, M. A., & Forushani, N. Z. (2011). Relationship between emotional intelligence and perceived stress among female students. *Social and Behavioral Sciences 30*, 1109-1112.

Beth Israel Deaconess Medical Center. (1989 era). *Stress Management with the Relaxation Response*. Boston: Mind/Body Medical Institute.

Bhatia, V., & Tandon, R. K. (2005, March). Stress and the gastrointestinal tract. *Journal of Gastroenterology and Hepatology, 20*(3), 332-339. doi:DOI: 10.1111/j.1440-1746.2004.03508.x

Birnbaum, H. G., Kessler, R. C., Kelley, D., Ben-Hamadi, R., Joish, V. N., & Greenberg, P. E. (2010). Employer burden of mild, moderate, and severe major depressive disorder: mental health services utilization and costs, and work performance. *Depression and Anxiety, 27*(1), 78-89. doi:DOI: 10.1002/da.20580

Black, P. H. (2003). The inflammatory response is an integral part of the stress response:Implications for atherosclerosis, insulin resistance, type II diabetes and metabolic syndrome X . *Brain, Behavior, and Immunity*, 350-364.

Blackborow, M., Tuck, C., Lambert, P., Disney, J., Porter, J., & Jordan, A. (2013). Position Statement: Mental Health of Students. Silver Springs, Maryland, USA: National Association of School Nurses (NASN).

Blackwell, L. S. (2007). Implicit theories of intelligence predict achievement across an adolescent transition: A longitudinal study and an intervention. *Child Development*, 78(1): 246-263.

Blackwell, L. T. (2007). Implicit Theories of Intelligence Predict Achievement Across an Adolescent Transition: A Longitudinal Study and an Intervention. *Child Development*, 78, 246-263.

Blatt, S. J., Sanislow III, C. A., Zuroff, D. C., & Pilkonis, P. A. (1996). Characteristics of Effective Therapists Further Analyses of Data from the National Institute of Mental Health Treatment of Depression Collaborative Research Program. *Journal of Consulting and Clinical Psychology, 64*(6), 1276-1284.

Blechert, J., Goltsche, J. E., Herbert, B. M., & Wilhelm, F. H. (2014). Eat your troubles away: Electrocortical and experiential correlates of food image processing are related to emotional eating style and emotional state. *Biological Psychology, 96*, 94-101.

Boardman, J. D., & Alexander, K. B. (2011). Stress trajectoriese, health behaviors, and the mental health of black and white young adults. *Social Science and Medicine*, 1659-1666.

VIII | Bibliography

Boehm, J. K. (2012, July). The heart's content: The association between positive psychological well-being and cardiovascular health. *Psychological Bulletin, Epub April 2012*, 138(4):655-91 . doi:DOI: 10.1037/a0027448.

Bolton, L. R., Becker, L. K., & Barber, L. K. (2010). Big Five trait predictors of differential counterproductive work behavior dimensions. *Personality and Individual Differences*, 537-541. doi:doi:10.1016/j.paid.2010.03.047

Bomyea, J., Amir, N., & Lang, A. J. (2012). The relationship between cognitive control and posttraumatic. *J Behav Ther Exp Psychiatry, 43*(2), 844-848. doi:doi:10.1016/j.jbtep.2011.12.001

Bomyea, J., Ritsbrough, V., & Lang, A. J. (2012, November). A consideration of select pre-trauma factors as key vulnerabilities in PTSD. *Clinical Psychological Revue, 32*(7), 630-641. doi:doi:10.1016/j.cpr.2012.06.008

Bonanno, G. (2004). Loss, trauma, and human resilience: Have we underestimated the human capacity to thrive after extremely aversive events? *American Psychologist*, 59: 20-28.

Bonanno, G. A., & Diminich, E. D. (2013). Annual Research Review: Positive adjustment to adversity--trajectories of minimal-impact resilience and emergent resilience. *Journal of Child Psychology and Psychiatry, 54*(4), 378-401. doi:doi:10.1111/jcpp.12021

Borders, A., & Liang, C. T. (2011). Rumination partially mediates the association between perceived ethnic discrimination, emotional distress, and aggression. *Cultural Diversity and Ethnic Minority Psychology, 17*(2), 125-133.

Bornemann, B., Winkielman, P., & van der Meer, E. (2012). Can you feel what you do not see? Using internal feedback to detect briefly presented emotional stimuli. *International Journal of Psychophysiology*, 116-124. doi:doi:10.1016/j.ijpsycho.2011.04.007

Bos, P. A., Brummelman, E., & Terburg, D. (2015, January). Cgnition as the tip of the emotional iceberg: A nero-evolutionary perspective. *Behavioral Brain Siencce*, e72.

Bouchard, S. M., & Hook, M. A. (2014). Psychological Stress as a Modulator of Functional Recovery Following Spinal Cord Injury. *Frontiers in Neurology*. Retrieved from http://www.ncbi.nlm.nih.gov/pmc/articles/PMC3988397/

Boyce, C. J., Wood, A. M., Daly, M., & Sedikides, C. (2015, February 9). Personality Change Following Unemployment. *Journal of Applied Psychology*. doi:http://dx.doi.org/10.1037/a0038647

Brach, C., & Fraserirector, I. (2000, November). Can Cultural Competency Reduce Racial and Ethnic Health Disparities? A Revew and Conceptual Model. *Medical Care Research and Review, 57 Supplement*, 181-217.

Brandt, M. J., & Reyna, C. (2011, September). The Chain of Being: A Hierarchy of Morality. *Perspectives on Psychological Science, 6*(5), 428-446. doi:doi: 10.1177/1745691611414587

Bray, I. (2009). *Healthy Employees, Healthy Business.* NOLO.

Breaking the Silence: Suicide Prevention in Law Enforcement (n.d.). [Motion Picture]. Retrieved 2014, from https://www.youtube.com/watch?v=u-mDvJIU9RI#t=378

Brissette, I., Scheier, M., & Carver, C. S. (2002). The Role of Optimism in Social Network Development, Coping, and Psychological Adjustment During a Life Transition. *Journal of Personality and Social Pscyhology, 82*(1), 102-111. doi:DOI: 10.1037//0022-3514.82.1.102

Brito, C. C., & Oliveira, M. T. (2013). Bullying and self-esteem in adolescents from public schools. *Jornal de Pediatria, 89*(6), 601-607. doi:http://dx.doi.org/10.1016/j.jped.2013.04.001

Broderick, J. (2012). Presentation at PPIA 2012. *Positive Psychology in Action, Inc. Positive Health Promotion Forum.* Houston, Tx.

Broderick, J. (2013). Trusting One's Emotional Guidance Builds Resilience. In Venkat Pulla, Shane Warren and Andrew Shatte (Ed.), *Perspectives on Coping and Resilience* (pp. 254-279). Laxmi Nagar, Delhi: Authors Press.

Brodish, A. B., Cogburn, C. D., Fuller-Rowell, T. E., Peck, S., Malanchuk, O., & Eccles, J. S. (2011, October 1). Perceived Racial Discrimination as a Predictor of Health Behaviors: the Moderating Role of Gender. *Race and Social Problems, 3*(3), 160–169. doi:10.1007/s12552-011-9050-6

Brooks, R., & Goldstein, S. (2004). *The Power of Resilience: Achieving Balance, Confidence, and Personal Strength in Your Life .* McGraw Hill.

Brown, A. (2012, October 30). With Poverty Comes Depression, More Than Other Illnesses. *Gallup*.

Brown, J. D., & Taylor, S. E. (1986). Affect and the Processing of Personal Information: Evidence for Mood-Activated Self-Schemata. *Journal of Experimental Social Psychology, 22*, 436-452.

Brown, S. F. (2009). Social closeness increases salivary progesterone in humans. *Hormones and Behavior*, 56:108-111.

Brown, W. S. (1993). Endocrine correlates of sadness and elation. *Psychosomatic Medicine*, 55: 458-67.

Browne, S. (2001). *The Nature of Good and Evil.* Carlsbad, California: Hay House.

Browne-Yung, K., Ziersch, A., & Baum, F. (2013). 'Faking til you make it': Social capital accumulation of individuals on low incomes living in contrasting socio-economic neighbourhoods and its implications for health and wellbeing. *Social Science & Medicine*, 9-17. doi:doi.org/10.1016/j.socscimed.2013.02.026

Bruce, A. (2005). *Beyond the Bleep: The definitive unauthorized guide to What the Bleep Do We Know?!* St Paul: Disinformation.

Bruzzese, J.-M., Carcone, A. I., Lam, P., Ellis, A. D., & Naar-King, S. (2014). Adherence to Asthma Medication Regimes in Urban African American Adolescents: Application of Self-Determination Theory. *Health Psychology, 33*(5), 461-464. doi:http://dx.doi.org/10.1037/a0033510

Bryan, T. a. (1991). Positive mood and math performance. *Journal of Learning Disabilities*, 24:490-94.

BTO.org. (n.d.). Retrieved 2014, from http://www.bto.org/science/migration/tracking-studies/cuckoo-tracking/what-have-we-learnt

Bujoreanu, PhD, S., Benhayon, M.D., PhD, D., & Szigethy, M.D., PhD, E. (2011 November). *Treatment of Depression in Children and Adolescents*. Retrieved from Pediatric Super Site: PediatricSuperSite.com

Burnette, J. L., O'Boyle, E. O., VanEpps, E. M., Pollack, J. M., & Finkel, E. J. (2012 (in press), May 9). Mindsets Matter: A Meta-Analytic Review of Implicit Theories and Self-Regulation. *Psychological Bulletin*, 1-63.

Burns, A. B. (2008). Upward spirals of positive emotion and coping: Replication, extension, and initial exploration of neurochemical substrates. *Personality and Individual Differences*, 44: 360-70.

Bush, D. E., Ziegelstein, R. C., Patel, U. V., Thombs, B. D., Ford, D. E., Fauerbach, J. A., . . . Bass, E. B. (2005). *Post-Myocardial Infarction Depression*. Agency for Healthcare Research and Quality.

Butler, A. C., Chapman, J. E., Forman, E. M., & Beck, A. T. (2006). The empirical status of cognitive-behavioral therapy: A review of meta-analyses. *Clinical Psyhology Review, 26*, 17-31. doi:doi:10.1016/j.cpr.2005.07.003

Buzinski, S. G., & Price, A. (2015, July - September). Don't Tell Me What to Do: Highly Restrictive Goals Promote Temptation Indulgence. *Sage OPEN*, 1-11.

BY BRANDEL FRANCE DE BRAVO, M., SARAH MILLER, R., & BECKER, A. J. (n.d.). *Are E-Cigarettes Safer Than Regular Cigarettes?* Retrieved from Cancer Treatment and Prevention Fund: http://www.stopcancerfund.org/uncategorized/are-e-cigarettes-safer-than-regular-cigarettes/

Cabral, C. (2010). Psychological functioning Following Violence: An examination of Posttraumatic Growth, Distress and Hope Among Interpersonal Violence Survivors. Retrieved from http://hdl.handle.net/1807/24544

Calhoun, L. G. (1989-1990). Positive aspects of critical life problems: recollections of grief. *Omega*, 29: 265-272.

Campbell, D. T. (1975). On the conflicts between biological and social evolution and between psychology and moral tradition. *American Psychologist, 30*, pp. 1103-1126.

Campbell, J., & Ehlert, U. (2012). Acute psychological stress: Does the emotional stress response correspond with psysiological responses? *Psychoneuroendocrinology*, 1111-1134.

Cardichon, J., & Lovell, P. (2015). *Below the Surface: Solving the Hidden Graduation Rate Crisis*. Alliance for Excellent Education. all4ed.org. Retrieved from http://all4ed.org/reports-factsheets/belowthesurface/

Carinci, J. P. (2005). *The Power of Being Different*. Bloomington: AuthorsHouse.

Carrico, A. W., & Moskowitz, J. T. (2014). Positive Affect Promotes Engagement in Care After HIV Diagnosis. *Health Psychology, 33*(7), 686-689. doi:http://dx.doi.org/10.1037/hea0000011

Carroll, R., Metcalfe, C., & Gunnell, D. (2014). Hospital Presenting Self-Harm and Risk of Fatal and Non-Fatal Repetition: Systematic Review and Meta-Analysis. (C. U. Lise Lotte Gluud, Ed.) doi:doi:10.1371/journal.pone.0089944

Carucci, R. (2016, January 16). Three Ways Your Brain is Hazardous to Great Decision Making. *Forbes*, p. 9:30 a.m. Retrieved 2016

Carvalho, J., & Nobre, P. (2012). Dynamic Factors of Sexual Aggression: The Role of Affect and Impulsiveness. *Criminal Justice and Behavior*, 376-387.

Carver, C. S. (2015, July 9). Control Processes, Priority Management, and Affective Dynamics. *Emotion Review, 7*(4), 301-307.

Cascio, C. N., O'Donnell, M. B., Tinney, F. J., Lieberman, M. D., Taylor, S. E., Strecher, V. J., & Falk, E. B. (2015). Self-affirmation activates brain systems associated iwth self-related processing and reward and is reinforced by future orientation. *Social Cognitive and Affective Neuroscience*, Epub.

Catalino, L. I., & Fredrickson, B. L. (2011). A Tuesday in the Life of a Flourisher: The Role of Positive Emotional Reactivity in Optimal Mental Health. *Emotion, 11*(4), 938-950. doi:DOI: 10.1037/a0024889

Cauffman, E. F. (1998). Posttraumatic stress disorder among female juvenile offenders. *Journal of the American Academy of Child & Adolescent Psychiatry, 37*, 1209-1216.

Caunt, B. S., Fanklin, J., Brodaty, N. E., & Brodaty, H. (2013). Exploring the Causes of Subjective Well-Being A Content Analysis of Peoples' Recipes for Long-Term Happiness. *Journal of Happiness Studies*, 475-499. doi:DOI 10.1007/s10902-012-9339-1

CDC. (2016). *CDC.gov*. Retrieved from violence prevention: http://www.cdc.gov/violenceprevention/pdf/youth-violence-accomplishments-a.pdf

Chan, C. W. (1996). The Philosopher. *Good and Evil in Chinese Philosophy, Volume LXXXIV*. Retrieved September 25, 2015, from http://www.the-philosopher.co.uk/good&evil.htm

Chang, J. (2011). A Case Study of the "Pygmalion Effect""Teacher Expectations and Student Achievement. *International Education Studies, 4*(1), 198-201. Retrieved 2015

Chapman, D. P. (2004). Epidemiology of adverse childhood experiences and depressive disorders in a large health maintenance organization population. *Journal of Affective Disorders, 82*(2), 217-225.

Chapman, R. L., Buckley, L., Sheehan, M. C., Shochet, I. M., & Romaniuk, M. (2011). The impact of school connectedness on violent behavior, transport risk-taking behavior, and associated injuries in adolescence. *Journal of School Psychology, 49*, 399-410.

Charil, A., Laplante, D. P., Vaillancourt, C., & King, S. (2010). Prenatal stress and brain development. *Brain Research Reviews, 65*, 56-79. doi:doi:10.1016/j.brainresrev.2010.06.002

Chen, E. M. (2012, March 1). 'Shift-and-Persist' Strategies: Why Being Low in Socioeconomic Status isn't Always Bad for Health. *Perspectives on Psychological Science: A Journal of the Association for Psychological Science, 7*(2): 135-158.

Cheng, H., & Furnham, A. (2003). Personality, self-esteem, and demographic predictions of Happiness and Depression. *Personality and Individual Differences, 34*, 921-942.

Cherkin, D. C., Eisenberg, D., Sherman, K. J., Barlow, W., Kaptchuk, T. J., Street, J., & Deyo, R. A. (2001, April 23). Randomized Trial Comparing Traditional Chinese Medical Acupuncture, Therapeutic Massage, and Self-care Education for Chronic Low Back Pain. *JAMA Internal Medicine (formerly Archieves of Internal Medicine), 161*(8), 1081-1088. doi:doi:10.1001/archinte.161.8.1081

Chicago Police Department. (2011). *Analysis of 2011 Murders*. Chicago. Retrieved 8 21, 2015, from http://home.chicagopolice.org/wp-content/uploads/2014/12/2011-Murder-Report.pdf

Childhelp. (2015). *Child Abuse Statistics and Facts*. Retrieved from www.childhelp.com.

Chiodo, D., Wolfe, D. A., Crooks, C., Hughes, R., & Jaffe, P. (2009). Impact of Sexual Harassment Victimization by Peers on Subsequent Adolescent Victimization and Adjustment: A Longitudinal Study. *Jouranl of Adolescent Health, 45*, 246-252.

Christian, L. M. (2012). Physiological reactivity to psychological stress in human pregnancy: Current knowledge and future directions. *Progress in Neurobiology, 99*, 106-116. doi:http://dx.doi.org/10.1016/j.pneurobio.2012.07.003

Christian, L. M. (2012). Psychoneuroimmunology in pregnancy: Immune pathways linking stress with maternal health, adverse birth outcomes, and fetal development. *Neuroscience and Biobehavioral Reviews, 36*, 350-361. doi:doi:10.1016/j.neubiorev.2011.07.005

Cimpian, A. A.-M. (2007). Subtle linguistic cues impact children's motivation. *Psychological Science, 18*, 314-316.

Cisler, J. M., & Olatunji, B. O. (2012). Emotion Regulation and Anxiety Disorders. *Current Psychiatry Reports, 14*(3), 182-187.

Ciucci, E., Baroncelli, A., Grazzani, I., Ornaghi, V., & Caprin, C. (2016, March). Emotional Arousal and Regulation: Further Evidence of the Validity of the "How I Feel" Questionnaire for Use With School-Age Children. *Journal of School Health, 86*(3), 195-203. doi:DOI: 10.1111/josh.12370

Clark, P. (2010, April). Preventing Future Crime With Cognitive Behavioral Therapy. *National Institute of Justice Journal No. 265*, 22-24.

Clarke, M., Lewchuk, W., de Wolff, A., & King, A. (2007). 'This just isn't sustainable': Precarious employment, stress and workers' health. *International Journal of Law and Psychiatry*, 311-326. doi:doi:10.1016/j.ijlp.2007.06.005

Clinic, M. (n.d.). *E-cigarette safety concerns*. Retrieved from Mayo Clinic: http://www.mayoclinic.org/healthy-living/quit-smoking/expert-answers/electronic-cigarettes/faq-20057776

Clore, G. L., & Palmer, J. (2009). Affective guidance of intelligent agents: How emotion controls cognition. (J. Gratch, Ed.) *Cognitive Systems Research, 10*, pp. 21-30. doi:doi:10.1016/j.cogsys.2008.03.002

Clow, A. (2010). The iceberg of social disadvantage and chronic stress: Implications for Public Health. *Neuroscience and Biobehavioral Reviews 35*.

Cobb, S. (1976). Social Support as a Moderator of Life Stress (Presidential Address). *Sections of Community Health and Psychiatry of teh Programs in medicine at Brown University.*

Codier, E., & Odell, E. (2013 (In Press)). Measured emotional inteligence ability and grade point average in nursing students. *Nurse Education Today*. Retrieved 2015

Coetzee, M., & Harry, N. (2014). Emotional intelligence as a predictor of employees' career adaptability. *Journal of Vacational Behavior, 84*, 90-97.

Cohen, S. D. (2003). Emotional style and susceptibility to the common cold. *Psychosomatic Medicine.*

Cohen, S., Tyrrell, D. A., & Smith, A. P. (1991). Psychological Stress and Susceptibility To the Common Cold. *New England Journal of Medicine.*

Cohn, M. A. (2009). Happiness unpacked: Positive emotions increase life satisfaction by building resilience. *Emotion*, 9: 361-368.

Cohn, M. A., & Fredrickson, B. L. (2010, Sept). In search of durable positive psychology interventions: Predictors and consequences of long-term positive behavior change. *The Journal of Positive Psychology, 5*(5), 355-366. doi:DOI: 10.1080/17439760.2010.508883

Colby, D. A., & Shifren, K. (2013, January). Optimism, mental health, and quality of life: A study among breast. *Health & Medicine Psychology, 18*(1), 10-20. doi:http://dx.doi.org/10.1080/13548506.2012.686619

Colt, G. H. (n.d.). *The Healing Power of Touch*. Retrieved from www.toddlertime.com: http://www.toddlertime.com/mh/terms/healing-touch.htm

Compare, A., Zarbo, C., Shonin, E., Van Gordon, W., & Marconi, C. (2014). Emotional Regulation and Depression: A Potential Mediator between Heart and Mind. *Cardiovascular Psychiatry and Neurology*, 10. doi:http://dx.doi.org/10.1155/2014/324374

Conley, J. (2007). *Peak: How Great Companies Get Their Mojo from Maslow*. New York: Jossey-Bass.

Connor, K. M., & Davidson, J. R. (2003). DEVELOPMENT OF A NEW RESILIENCE SCALE: THE CONNOR-DAVIDSON RESILIENCE SCALE (CD-RISC). *Depression and Anxiety, 18*, 76-82. doi:DOI: 10.1002/da.10113

Conwell, R. H. (2009). *Acres of Diamonds: Our everyday opportunities*. Kindle: Public Domain books.

Coren, S. A., & Luthar, S. S. (2014, November). Pursuing Perfection: Distress and Interpersonal Functioning Among Adolescent Boys in single-Sex and Co-Educational Independent Schools. *Psychology in the Schools, 51*(9), 931-946. doi:DOI: 10.1002/pits.21795

Correll, J., Spencer, S. J., & Zanna, M. P. (2004). An affirmed self and an open mind: Self-affirmation and sensitivity to argument strength. *Journal of Experimental Social Psychology, 40*, 350-356. doi:doi:10.1016/j.jesp.2003.07.001

Corso, P. S. (2008). Health-related quality of life among adults who experienced maltreatment during childhood. *American Journal of Public Health, 98* (6), 1094-1100.

Costa, P. T., & McCrae, R. R. (1988). Personality in Adulthood: A Six-Year Longitudinal Study of Self-Reports and Spouse Ratings on the NEO Personality Inventory. *Journal of Personality and Social Psychology, 54*(5), 853-863.

Cotman, C. W. (2007). Exercise builds brain health: Key roles of growth factor cascades and inflammation. *Trends in Neurosciences*, 30: 464-72.

Council, A. B. (2013). *Clary Sage Essential Oil, but Not Lavender Essential Oil, Reduces Stress during Urodynamic Examinations*.

Counsellor, D. (1955). *The Uratia Book*. Open Source.

Cozier, Y. C., Wise, L. A., Palmer, J. R., & Rosenberg, L. (2009). Perceived Racism in Relation to Weight Change in the Black Women's Health Study. *Annals of Epidemiology*, 19:379–387.

Craig, W. M. (1998). The Relationship among bullying, victimization, depression, anxiety, and aggression in elementary school children. *Peraonality Individual Differences, 24*(1), 123-130.

Crandall, A., Ghazarian, S. R., Day, R. D., & Riley, A. W. (2015, December 24). Maternal Emotion Regulation and Adolescent Behaviors: The Mediating Role of Family functioning and Parenting. *Journal Youth Adolescents*, Epub.

Craven, I. L. (1989). Meditation and psychotherapy. *Canadian Journal of Psychiatry, 142*, 1-8.

Creswell, J. D., Welch, W. T., Taylor, S. E., Sherman, D. K., Gruenewax, T. L., Gruenewald, T. L., & Mann, T. (2005). Affirmation of Personal Values Buffers Neuroendocrine and Psychological Stress Responses. *Psychological Science, 16*(11), 847-851.

Crittenden, C. N., Pressman, S. D., Cohen, S., Janicki-Deverts, D., Smith , B. W., & Seeman, T. E. (2014). Social Integration and Pulmonary Function in the Elderly. *Health Psychology, 33*(4). doi:http://dx.doi.org/10.1037/hea0000029

Crocker, J. (1999). Social Stigma and Self-Esteem: Situations Construction of Self-Worth. *Journal of Experimental Social Psychology, 35*, 89-107.

Crocker, J., & Park, L. E. (2004). Reaping the Benefits of Pursuing Self-Esteem Without the Costs? Reply to DuBois and Flay (2004), SHeldon (2004), and Pyszczynski and Cos (2004). *Psychological Bulletin*, 430-434. Retrieved 2016

Crocker, J., & Park, L. E. (2004). The Costly Pursuit of Self-Esteem. *Psychological Bulletin, 130*(3), 392-414. doi:DOI: 10.1037/0033-2909.130.3.392

Crosby, A. E., Han, B., Ortega, L. A., Parks, S. E., & Gfroerer, J. (2011). *Suicidal Thoughts and Behaviors Among Adults Aged >18 Years --- USA, 2008-2009*. Centers for Disease Control and Prevention, Division of violence Prevention, National Center for Injury Prevention and Control. Mobidity and Mortality Weekly Report (MMWR). Retrieved 2014, from http://www.cdc.gov/mmwr/preview/mmwrhtml/ss6013a1.htm?s_cid=ss6013a1_e

Crowley, C. a. (2004). *Younger Next Year: A Guide to Living Like 50 Until You're 80 and Beyond*. New York: Workman.

Cubic, B., Neumann, C., Kearney, L., McGrath, R., Ruddy, N., Rybarczyk, B., & Zamudio, A. (2012). *Report of the Primary Care Training Task Force to the APA Board of Educational Affairs*.

Cure Violence. (2015). *Cure Violence*. Retrieved from http://cureviolence.org/: http://cureviolence.org/

Cutrona, C. E., Abraham, W. T., Russell, D. W., Beach, S. R., Gibbons, F. X., Gerrard, M., . . . Philibert, R. (2015). Financial strain, inflammatory factors, and haemoglobin A I c levels in African American women. *British Journal of Health Psychology, 20*, 662-679.

XII | Bibliography

Cutuli, D. (2014, September 19). Cognitive reappraisal and expressive suppressive strategies role in the emoiton regulation: An overview of their modulatory effects and neural Correlates. *Frontiers in Systems Neuroscience, 8*. doi:doi: 10.3389/fnsys.2014.00175

Daily, S. (2001, July 13). *Keeping up your overall health may keep dementia away, study suggests.* Retrieved 2011

Daily, S. (2012). A healthy teenager is a happy teenager. *Economic and Social Research Council (ESRC).*

Dalton, P., Mauté, C., Jaén , C., & Wilson, T. (2013, October 9). Chemosignals of Stress Influence Social Judgments. *PLOS One*, Epub. Retrieved from http://journals.plos.org/plosone/article?id=10.1371/journal.pone.0077144

Dan-Glauser, E. S., & Gross, J. J. (2013). Emotion Regulation and Emotion Coherence: Evidence for Strategy-Specific Effects. *Emotion*, 832-842.

Danner, D. D. (2001). "Positive Emotions in Early Life and Longevity: Findings from the Nun Study." . *Journal of Personality and Social Psychology.*, 804-13.

Danner, D. D. (2001). Positive Emotions in Early Life and Longevity. Findings from the Nun Study. *Journal of Personality and Social Psychology, 80*, No. 5.804-813. doi:10.1039//0022-3514.80.5.804

DANNER-VLAARDINGERBROEK, G., KLUWER, E., VAN STEENBERGEN, E. F., & VAN DER LIPP, T. (2013). Knock, knock, anybody home? Psychological availability as link between work and relationship. *Personal Relationships, 20*, 52-68. doi:DOI: 10.1111/j.1475-6811.2012.01396.x

Darley, J. M., & Batson, C. D. (1973). From Jerusalem to Jericho: A Study of Situational and Dispositional Variables in Helping Behavior. *JPSP, 27*, 100-108.

Darley, J. M., & Batson, C. D. (1973). From Jerusalem to Jericho: A Study of Situational and Dispositional Variables in Helping Behavior. *JPSP, 27*, 100-108.

Davidson, R. J. (2000). Emotion, plasticity, context, and regulation: Perspective from affective neuroscience. *Psychological Bulletin*, 126: 890-909.

Davis, A. (2005). *Seeing with our Brains.* Retrieved from http://serendip.brynmawr.edu/bb/neuro/neuro05/web2/adavis.html

Davis, R. C., & Smith, B. (1994). Teaching Victims Crime Prevention Skills: Can Individuals Lower their Risk of Crime? *Criminal Justice Review*, 56.

Davis, S. K., & Humphrey, N. (2012). Emotional intelligence predicts adolescent mental health beyond personality and cognitive ability. *Personality and Individual Differences*, 144-149.

Day, L., Hanson, K., Maltby, J., Proctor, C., & Wood, A. (2010). Hope uniquely predicts objective academic achievement above intelligence and personality, and previous academic achievement. *Journal of Research in Personality, 44*, 550-553. doi:doi:10.1016/j.jrp.2010.05.009

de Araujo, P., & Lagos, S. (2013). Self-esteem, education, and wages revisited. *Journal of Economic Psychology, 34*, 120-132.

De Lissnyder, E., Koster, E. H., Goubert, L., Onraedt, T., & Vanderhasselt, M.-A. (2012). Cognitive control moderates the association between stress and rumination. *Journal of Behavior Therapy and Experimental Psychiatry*, 519-525.

De Neve, J.-E., Diener, E., Tay, L., & Xuereb, C. (2013). The Objective Benefits of Subjective Well-Being. In J. Helliwell, R. Layard, & J. Sachs (Ed.). (pp. 1-35). New York: United Nations. Retrieved 2015

De Vriendt, T., Moreno, L. A., & De Henauw, S. (2009). Chronic stress and obesity in adolescents: Scientific evidence and methodological issues for epidemiological research. *Nutrition, metabolism, & Cardiovascular Disease, 19*, 511-519.

de Wit, L., Luppino, F., van Straten, A., Penninx, B., Zitman, F., & Cuijpers, P. (2010). Depression and obesity: A meta-analysis of community-based studies. *psychatry Research, 178*, 230-235.

Deci, E. L. (1996). *Why we do what we do.* New York: Penguin.

Deci, E. L., & Ryan, R. M. (2000). The "What" and "Why" of Goal Pursuits: Human Needs and the Self-Determination of Behavior. *Psychological Inquiry, 11*(4), 227-268. doi:doi:10.1207/S15327965PLI1104_01

Deechakawan, PhD, RN, W., Cain, PhD, K. C., Jarrett, PhD, RN, M. E., Burr, MSEE, PhD, R. L., & Heitkemper, PhD, RN, FAAN, M. M. (2012, November 20). Effect of Self-Management Intervention on Cortisol and Daily Stress Levels in Irritable Bowel Syndrome. *Biological Research for Nursing*, 26-36. doi:10.1177/1099800411414047

Dennison, B. (2004). Touch the pain away: new research on therapeutic touch and persons with fibromyalgia syndrome. *Holistic Nursing Practice, 18*(3), 142-151.

DeSteno, DeSteno, D., Gross, J. J., & Kubzansky, L. (2013). Affective Science and Health: The Importance of Emotion and Emotion Regulation. *Health Psychology, 32*(5), 474-486. doi:http://dx.doi.org/10.1037/a0030259

Dewa, C. S., McDaid, D., & Ettner, S. L. (2007). An International perspective on worker mental health problems: who bears the burden and how are costs addressed? *Canadian Journal of Psychiatry, 52*(6), 346-56.

Dewar, A. J. (2012). *Achievement Goals and Emotions in Competitive Sport.* Thesis, University of Birmingham, School of Sport and Exercise Sciences.

Dewar, A. J., & Kavussanu, M. (2011). Achievement goals and emotions in golf: The mediating and moderating role of perceived performance. *Psychology of Sport and Exercise, 12*, 525-532. doi:doi:10.1016/j.psychsport.2011.05.005

Dhabhar, F. S. (2013). Psychological stress and immunoprotection versus immunopathology in the skin. *Clinical Dermatology, 31*(1), 18-30. doi:doi: 10.1016/j.clindermatol.2011.11.003.

Dhayanandhan, B., & Bohr, Y. (2016, January). The role of identity development in moderating stress and promoting dydic sensitivity in adolescent mothers. *Canadian Journal of Behavioural Science, 48*(1), 39-48.

Diabetes.org. (2016). *Diabetes.org*. Retrieved from Diabetes.org: http://www.diabetes.org/diabetes-basics/statistics/?referrer=https://www.google.com/

Diamond, A. B. (2007). Preschool program improves cognitive control. *Science*, 318, 1387-1388.

Diener, E. N. (2002). Dispositional affect and job outcomes. *Social Indicators Research*, 229-259.

Diener, E., & Biswas-Diener, R. (2008). *Happiness: Unlocking the Mysteries of Psychological Wealth.* Blackwell Publishing.

Diener, E., & Chan, M. Y. (2011). Happy People Live Longer: Subjective Well-Being Contributes to Health and Longevity. *The International Association of Applied Psychology: Health and Well-Being*, 1-43. doi:10.1111/j.1758-0854.2010.01045.x

Diener, E., & Tay, L. (2012 (draft)). *A Scientific Review of the Remarkable Benefits of Happiness for Successful and Healthy Living.* United Nations, Report of the Well-Being Working Group, Royal Governmentof Bhutan Report to the united Nations General Assembly, Well-being and Happiness: A New Deveopment Paradigm. New York: UN. Retrieved 2012

Dietze, P., Jenkinson, R., Aitken, C., Stoove, M., Jolley, D., Hickman, M., & Kerr, T. (2013). The Relationship between alcohol use and injecting drug use: Impacts on Health, crime, and wellbeing. *Drug and Alcohol Dependence, 128*, 111-115.

DiFulvio, G. T. (2011). Sexual minority youth, social connection and resilience: From personal struggle to collective identity. *Social Science & Medicine, 72*, 1611e1617.

Dillon, S. (2009, January 22). Study sees an Obama effect as lifting black test-takers. *New York Times*.

Dissanayake, R. K., & Bertouch, J. V. (2010, October). Psychosocial interventions as adjunct therapy for patients with rheumatoid arthritis: a systematic review. *International Journal of Rheumatic Diseases, 13*(4), 324-334. doi:DOI: 10.1111/j.1756-185X.2010.01563.x

Dockray, S., & Steptoe, A. (2010). Positive Affect and psychobiological processes. *Neuroscience and Biobehavioral Reviews*, 69-75.

Dodge, N. (2007). *The Brain That Changes Itself.* New York: Penguin.

Doerrfeld, A. S. (2012, July). Expecting to lift a box together makes the load look lighter. *Psychological Research*(December 9, 2011 online), 76(4): 467-475. doi:10.1007/s00426-001-0387-4

Dolezsar, C. M., McGrath, J. J., Herzig, A. J., & Miller, S. B. (2014,Vol 33, No 1). Perceived Racial Discrimination and Hypertension: A Comprehensive Systematic Review. *Health Psychology*, 20-34. doi:http://dx.doi.org/10.1037/a0033718

Dooley, M. (2009). *Infinite Possibilities: The Art of Living Your Dreams.* NY: Atria Books.

Dossey, M.D., L. (2013). Unbroken Wholeness. *Explore, 9*(1), 1 - 8.

Drago, F. (2011). Self-esteem and earnings. *Journal of Economic Psychology, 32*, 480-488. doi:doi:10.1016/j.joep.2011.03.015

Dretsch, M. N., Thiel, K. J., Athy, J. R., Irvin, C. R., Sirmon-Fjordbak, B., & Salvatore, A. (2012). Mood symptoms contribute to working memory decrement in active-duty soldiers being treated for posttraumatic stress disorder. *Brain and Behavior*, 357-364. doi:doi: 10.1002/brb3.53

Driessen, E., & Hollon, S. D. (2010). Cognitive Behavioral Therapy for Mood Disorders: Efficacy, Moderators, and Mediators. *Psychiatric Clinics of North America, 33*(3), 537-555. doi:10.1016/j.psc.2010.04.005

D'Silva, S., & et al. (2012). Mind-Body Medicine Therapies for a Range of Depression Severity: A Systematic Review. *The Academy of Psychosomatic medicine*, 407-423.

Dube, S. R. (2003). Childhood abuse, neglect and household dysfunctino and the risk of illicit drug use: The Adverse Childhood Experience Study. *Pediatrics, 111*(3), 564-572.

DuBois, D. L., & Flay, B. R. (2004). The Healthy Pursuit of Self-Esteem: Comment on and Alternative to the Crocker and Park (2004) Formulation. *Psychological Bulletin, 130*(3), 415-420. doi:DOI: 10.1037/0033-2909.130.3.415

Dudding, J. (2003). Photographs of Maori as Cultural Artefacts and their Positioning within the Museum. *Papers Originating from MEG Conference 2002: Power and Collecting. 15*, pp. 8-18. Edinburgh, Scotland: Museum Ethnographers Group. Retrieved 2015, from Stable URL: http://www.jstor.org/stable/40793707

Dudovitz, R. N., Li, N., & Chung, P. J. (2013). Behavioral Self-Concept as Predictor of Teen Drinking Behaviors. *Academic Pediatrics, 13*(4).

Dukudraw. 5 Blind men and elephant. *TRUE Prevention*. Custom drawing--Fiverr, Malaysia.

Dunn, Gilman, Willett, Slopen, & Molnar. (2012). Abuse Prevalence Rates for women in the United States are Staggering. UPDATE.

Dupont, A., Bower, J. E., Stanton, A. L., & Ganz, P. A. (2014). Cancer-Related Intrusive thoughts Predict Behavioral Symptoms Following Breast Cancer Treatment. *Health Psychology, 33*(2), 155-163. doi:http://dx.doi.org/10.1037/a0031131

Bibliography

DuRant, R. H., Altman, D., Wolfson, M., Barkin, S., Kreiter, S., & Krowchuk, D. (2000). Exposure to violence and victimization, depression, substance use, and the use of violence by young adolescents. *The Journal of Pediatrics*, 707-713.

Durmer, J. S., & Dinges, D. F. (2005). Neurocognitive Consequences of Sleep Deprivation. *Seminars in Neurology, 25*(1), 117-129. doi:DOI: 10.1055/s-2005-867080

Dweck, C. &. (1988). A social-cognitive approach to motivation and personality. *Psychological Review*, 95, 256-273.

Dweck, C. (2007). The secret to raising smart kids. *Scientific American: Mind, December/January*, 36-43.

Dweck, C. S. (2008). Can Personality Be Changed? The Role of Beliefs in Personality and Change. *Current Directions in Psychological Science, 17*(6).

Dweck, C. S. (2008). *Mindset: The New Psychology of Success.* New York: Ballantine Books.

Dweck, C. S. (n.d.). Forward. In R. S. F.D. Horowitz (Ed.), *The Development of Giftedness and Talent Across the Life-Span* (p. Forward). Washington, DC: American Psychological Association.

Dyer, D. W. (2008). *Change Your Thoughts--Change Your Life* . Carlsbad.

Dylan, B. (Performer). (1963). Blowin' In The Wind. On *The Freewheelin' Bob Dylan* [CD]. New York.

Eddy, M. B. (1875). *Science and Health with Key to the Scriptures.* Washington.

Edward T. Creagan, M. (2014). *Mayoclinic.org.* Retrieved 8 28, 2014

Edwards, V. J. (2003). Adverse childhood experiences and health-related quality of life as an adult. (K. Kendall-Tackett, Ed.) *Victimization and Health.*

Ein-Dor, T., Hirschberger, G., Perry, A., Levin, N., Cohen, R., Horesh, H., & Rothschild, E. (2014). Implicit Death Primes Increase alcohol Consumption. *Health Psychology, 33*, 748-751. doi:http://dx.doi.org/10.1037/a0033880

Eiser, J. R., & Pahl, S. (2001). Optimism, Pessimism, and the Direction of Self-Other Comparisons. *Journal of Experimental Social Psychology, 37*, 77-84. doi:doi:10.1006/jesp.2000.1438

Ekmund, P. (1992). An argument for basic emotions. *Cognition and Emotion, 6*, 169-200.

Elkins, R. S. (2014). *My Bright Shining Star: A Mother's True Story of Brilliance, Love & Suicide.* Cambridge, UK: Perfect Publishers Limited.

Emery, A. A., Heath, N. L., & Mills, D. J. (2015, December 19). Basic Psychological Need Satisfaction, Emotion Dysregulation, and Non-suicidal Self-Injury Engagement in Young Adults: An Application of Self-Determination Theory. *Journal Youth Adolescents*, Epub.

Epel, E. D. (n.d.). Can meditation slow rate of cellular aging? Cognitive stress, mindfulness, and telemeres? *NY Academy of Science.* doi:NIHMS221333

Erbes, C. E. (2005, December). Posttraumatic Growth among American Former Prisoners of War. *Traumatology, Vol. 11*, pp. 285-295.

Ericsson, K. C. (Ed.). (2006). *The Cambridge Handbook of Expertise and Expert Performance.* New York: Cambridge University Press.

Eskine, K. J. (n.d.). Organic Foods Reduce Prosocial Behavior and Harshen Moral Judgments. *Dept of Psychological Sciences.*

Estrada, C. I. (1997). Positive affect facilitates integration of information and decreases anchoring in reasoning among physicians. *Organizational Behavior and Human Decision Processes*, 72: 117-135.

Extremera, N., & Rey, L. (2015). The moderator role of emotion regulation ability in the link between stress and well-being. *Frontiers in Psychology: Emotion Science*, Epub.

Fagan, J., & Lee, Y. (2012). Effects of Fathers' Early Risk and Resilience on Paternal Engagement With 5-Year-Olds. *Family Relations: Interdisciplinary Journal of Applied Family Studies, 61*, 878-892. doi:DOI:10.1111/j.1741-3729.2012.00741.x

Fagley, N. S. (2012). Appreciation uniquely predicts life satisfaction above demographics, the Big 5 personality factors, and gratitude. *Personality and Individual Differences, 53*, 59-63. doi:doi:10.1016/j.paid.2012.02.019

Fan, A. Z., Strine, T. W., Jiles, R., & Mokdad, A. H. (2008). Depression and anxiety associated with cardiovascular disease among persons aged 45 years and older in 38 states of the United States, 2006. *Preventive Medicine, 46*, 445-450. Retrieved 2015

Fazio, R. H. (2004). Attitude formation through exploration: valence asymmetries. *Journal of Personality and Social Psychology*, 87: 293-311.

Federal Interagency Forum on Child and Family Statistics. (2015). *America's Children: Key National Indicators of Well-Being, 2015.* Washington D.C: Government Printing Office.

Feldman, B. L., Tarr, M. J., & Lebrecht, S. (2012). 'Micro-Valences: Perceiving Affective Valence in Everyday Objects'. *Frontiers in Psychology.* doi:10.3389/fpsyg.2012.00107

Felitti, V. J. (1998). Relationship of childhood abuse and household dysfunction to many of the leading causes of death in adults: The adverse childhood experiences (ACE) study. *American Journal of Preventive Medicine, 14*, 245-258.

Ferdinand, k. C., Orenstein, D., Hong, Y., Journigan, J. G., Trogdon, J., Bowman, J., . . . Vaccarino, V. (2011). Health economics of cardiovascular disease: Defining the researchagenda. *CVD Prevention and Control*, 91-100.

Figner, B., & Weber, E. U. (2011). Who Takes Risks and Why? Determinants of Risk Taking. *Current Directions in Psychological Science, 20*(4), 211-216. doi:doi: 10.1177/0963721411415790

Findley, K. A., & O'Brien, B. (n.d.). *Psychological perspectives: Cognition and Decision Making.* Wisconsin University Law School. Retrieved 5 6, 2014, from http://ssrn.com/abstract=2438869

Flett, G. L., & Hewitt, P. L. (2014, November). A PROPOSED FRAMEWORK FOR PREVENTING PERFECTIONISM AND PROMOTING RESILIENCE AND MENTAL HEALTH AMONG VULNERABLE CHILDREN AND ADOLESCENTS. *Psychology in the Schools, 51*(9), 899-912. doi:DOI: 10.1002/pits.21792

Flett, G. L., Blankstein, K. R., Hewitt, P. L., & Koledin, S. (1992). Components of Perfectionism and Procrastination in College Students. *Social Behavior and Personality, 20*(2), 85-94.

Flett, G. L., Hewitt, P. L., & Heisel, M. J. (2014). The destructiveness of perfectionism revisited: Implications for the assessment of suicide risk and the prevention of suicide. *Review of General Psychology, 18*(3), 156-172.

Ford, B. Q., Mauss, I. B., & Gruber, J. (2015). Valuing happiness is associated with bipolar disorder. *Emotion*, 211-222.

Förster, J., Liberman, N., & Kuschel, S. (2008). The Effect of Global Versus Local Processing Styles on Assimilation Versus Contrast in Social Judgment. *Journal of Personality and Social Psychology, 94*(4), 579-599. doi:DOI: 10.1037/0022-3514.94.4.579

Fortin, A. H. (2002). Communication Skills to Improve Patient Satisfaction and Quality of Care. *Ethnicity & Disease*, 53-58.

Foss, B., & Dyrstad, S. M. (2011). Stress in obesity: Cause or consequence? *Medical Hypotheses, 77*, 7-10. doi:doi:10.1016/j.mehy.2011.03.011

Frankl, V. (1946). *Man's Search for Meaning.* Beacon Press.

Fredrickson, B. a. (2002). Positive emotions trigger upward spirals toward emotional well-being. *Psychological Science*, 13:172-75.

Fredrickson, B. L. (1998). What good are positive emotions? *Review of General Psychology*, 2: 300-319.

Fredrickson, B. L. (2001). The role of positive emotions in positive psychology: The broaden-and-build theory. *American Psychologist*, 56: 218-26.

Fredrickson, B. L. (2003). What good are positive emotions in crises?: A Prospective study of resilience and emotions following the terrorist attacks on the United States on September 11, 2001. *Journal of Personality and Social Psychology*, 84: 365-76.

Fredrickson, B. L. (2005). Positive affect and the complex dynamics of human flourishing. *American Psychologist*, 60(7): 678-686.

Fredrickson, B. L. (2005). Positive Emotions broaden the scope of attention and though-action repertoires. *Cognition and Emotion*, 19: 313-332.

Fredrickson, B. L. (2009, May). The Science of Happiness. (A. Winter, Interviewer) The Sun Magazine.

Fredrickson, B. L. (2010). *Positivity.* Three Rivers Press.

Fredrickson, B. L., & Branigan, C. (2005). Positive Emotions broaden the scope of attention and thought-action repertoires. *Cognition and Emotion*, 19: 313-332.

Fredrickson, B.L., et al. (2008).

Friborg, O., Hjemdal, O., Rosenvinge, J. H., Martinussen, M., Aslaksen, P. M., & Flaten, M. A. (2006). Resilience is a moderator of pain and stress. *Journal of Psychosomatic Research, 61*, 213-219. Retrieved 2015

Friedersdorf, C. (2015, 9 11). *The Rise of Victimhood Culture.* Retrieved 2 2016, from The Atlantic: http://www.theatlantic.com/politics/archive/2015/09/the-rise-of-victimhood-culture/404794/

Frye, J., & Sarter, B. (2013). Experience With the "Banerji Protocols" in Treatment of Chronic Disease. *Global Advances in Health and Medicine, 2*(Suppl):13B. doi:10.7453/gahmj.2013.097CP.S13B

Gaarder, E. &. (2002). Tenuous borders: Girls transferred to adult court. *Criminology, 40*, 481-517.

Gabbidon, S. I., & Boisvert, D. (2012). Public opinion on crime causation: An exploratory study of Philadelphia area residents. *Journal of Criminal Justice, 40*, 50-59.

Gable, P., & Harmon-Jones, E. (2010). The Blues Broaden, but the Nasty Narrows: Attentional Consequences of Negative Affects Low and High in Motivational Intensity. (A. f. Science, Ed.) *Psychological Science*, 211-215.

Gable, S. a. (2004). What do you do when things go right? The intrapersonal and interpresonal benefits of sharing positive events. *Journal of Personality and Social Psychology*, 87: 2: 228-45.

Gagné, M., & Deci, E. L. (2005). Self-determination theory and work motivation. *Journal of Organizational Behavior, 26*, 331-362.

Gallagher, W. (2009). *Rapt.* New York: Penguin.

Garland, E. L., Fredrickson, B., Kring, A. M., Johnson, D. P., Meyer, P. S., & Penn, D. L. (2010). Upward spirals of positive emotions counter downward spirals of negativity: Insights. *Clinical Psychology Review*, 849-864. doi:doi:10.1016/j.cpr.2010.03.002

Gaynes, B. N., Gavin, N., Meltzer-Brody, S., Lohr, K. N., Swinson, T., Gartlehner, G., . . . Miller, W. C. (2005). *Perinatal Depression: Prevalence, Screening, Accuracy, and Screening Outcomes.* Agency for Healthcare Research and Quality.

Gerend, M. A., & Pai, M. (n.d.). Social determinants of Black-White disparities in breast cancer mortality: a review. *Cancer Epidemiol Biomarkers & Prevention*, 2913-23. doi:doi: 10.1158/1055-9965

XVI | Bibliography

Gervais, M. W. (2005). the evolution and functions of laughter and humor: A synthetic approach. *Quarterly Review of Biology*, 80: 395-430.

Gianini, L. M., White, M. A., & Masheb, R. M. (2013, August). Eating Pathology, Emotion Regulation, and Emotional. *Eating Behaviors, 14*(3), 309-313. doi: doi:10.1016/j.eatbeh.2013.05.008

Gibbons, F. X., Kingsbury, J. H., Weng, C.-Y., Gerrard, M., Cutrona, C., Wills, T. A., & Stock, M. (2014). Effects of Perceived Racial Discrimination on Health Status and Health Behavior: A Differential Mediation Hypothesis. *Health Psychology, Vol. 33, No. 1*, 11-19. doi:http://dx.doi.org/10.1037/a0033857

Gil, K. M. (2004). Daily mood and stress predict pain, health care use, and work activity in African American adults with sickle cell disease. *Health Psychology*, 23: 67-74.

Gillie, B. L., & Thayer, J. F. (2014, July). Individual differences in resting heart rate variability. *Frontiers in Psychology, 5*. doi:doi: 10.3389/fpsyg.2014.00758

Gist, M. (1997). Training Design and Pedagogy: Implications for Skill Acquisition, Maintenance, and Generalization. In M. Gist, M. A. Quiñones, & A. Ehrenstein (Eds.), *Training for a rapidly changing workplace: Applications of psychological research* (pp. 201-222). Washington DC, US: American Psychological Association.

Glashouwer, K. A., de Jong, P. J., & Penninx, B. W. (2012). Prognostic value of implicit and explicit self-associations for the course of depressive and anxiety disorders. *Behaviour Research and Therapy, 50*, 479-486. Retrieved 2015

Godard, N. (1949). *Out of this World.*

Goebbels, A. F., Lakerveld, J., Ament, A. J., Bot, S. D., & Severens, J. L. (2012). Exploring non-health outcomes of health promotion: The pespective of participants in a lifestyle behaviour change interention. *Health Policy, 106*, 177-186.

Goethe, G. p. (n.d.). Quote about the power of decisions.

Goldberg, B. (2002). *Bias: A CBS Insider Exposes How the Media Distort the News.* Washington DC: Regnery Publishing, Inc.

Goldstein, E. (1704). *Sensation and Perception.* Belmont, CA: Wadsworth.

Goldstein, MD, PhD, B. I. (2015, February). Reducing the Cost and Burden of Depression: Incorporate Heart and Get an Early Start. *Journal of Clinical Psychiatry*(76).

Goldstein, R. Z., Craig, A., Bechara, A., Garavan, H., Childress, A. R., Paulus, M. P., & Volkow, N. D. (2009). The Neurocircuitry of Imparied Insight in Drug Addiction. *Cell Press*, 372-380.

Goleman, D. (1995). *Emotional Intelligence: Why It Can Matter More Than IQ.* New York: Bantam Dell.

Goleman, D. (2006). *Social Intelligence.* Bantam Books.

Gonzalez, H. M., Tarraf, W., Whitfield, K. E., & Vega, W. A. (2010). The epidemiology of major depression and ethnicity in the United States. *Journal of Psychiatric Research, 44*, 1043-1051.

Good, A., Harris, P. R., Jessop, D., & Abraham, C. (2015). Open-mindedness can decrease persuasion amongst adolescents: The role of self-affirmation. *British Journal of Health Psychology, 20*, 228-242. doi:DOI:10.1111/bjhp.12090

Good, C. A. (2003). Improving adolescents' standardized test performance: An Intervention to reduce the effects of stereotype threat. . *Journal of Applied Developmental Psychology,*, 24, 645-662.

Good, C. R. (2007a). Theories of intelligence influence females' sense of belonging, intent to continue, and achievement in math. *Unpublished data, Columbia University.*

Good, C. R. (2007b). Adults' theories of intelligence affects feedback to males and females in math. *Unpublished data, Columbia University.*

Good, C. R. (2007c). Genius portrayed as inborn versus acquired influences students' theories of intelligence, motivation, and performance in math. *Unpublished data, Columbia University.*

Goodin, B. R., Pham, Q. T., Glover, T. L., Sotolongo, A., King, C. D., Sibille, K. T., . . . Fillingim, R. B. (2013). A Perceived Racial Discrimination, but Not Mistrust of Medical Researchers, Predicts the Heat Pain Tolerance of African Americans With Symptomatic Knee Osteoarthritis. *Health Psychology, 32*(11), 1117-1126. Retrieved from http://dx.doi.org/10.1037/a0031592

Goodwin, R. D., Pagura, J., Spiwak, R., Lemeshow, A. R., & Sareen, J. (2011). Predictors of persistent nicotine dependence among adults in the United States. *Drug and Alcohol Dependence, 118*, 127-133. Retrieved 2016

Gorelick, D. E.-R. (2014). Depression, Stress, Hostility All Linked to Increased Stroke. *Stroke.*

Gorin, A. A., Powers, T. A., Koestner, R., Wing, R. R., & Raynor, H. A. (2014). Autonomy support, Self-Regulation, and Weight Loss. *Health Psychology, 33*(4), 332-339.

Gouin, J.-P., Hantsoo, L., & Kiecolt-Glaser, J. K. (2008). Immune Dysregulation and Chronic Stress Among Older Adults: A Review. *Neuroimmunomodulation, 15*, 251-259. doi:doi:10.1159/000156468

Gould, M., Jamieson, P., & Romer, D. (2003, May). Media Contagion and Suicide Among the Young. *American Behavioral Scientist, 46*(9), 1269-1284. doi:DOI: 10.1177/0002764202250670

Gould, R. L. (1978). *Transformations.* New York: Simon and Schuster.

Graber, R., Turner, R., & Madill, A. (2015). Best friends and better coping: Facilitating psychological resilience through boys' and girls' closest friendships. *British Journal of Psychology*, epub.

GradDipClinNsg, J. O., Wilkes BSc PhD RN CM MHPEd GradDipEd(Nur, L. M., Luke RN BN DipNsg, S., & George MPH, A. (2003). 'Being positive': perceptions of patients with cancer and their nurses. *Journal of Advanced, ISSUES AND INNOVATIONS IN NURSING PRACTICE*, 262-270.

Graham, J. R., Calloway, A., & Roemer, L. (2015). The Buffering Effects of Emotion Regulation in the Relationship Between Experiences of Racism and Anxiety in a Black American Sample. *Cognitive Therapy and Research, 39*(5), 553-563.

Grana R, B. N. (2014). E-cigarettes: a scientific review. *Circulation*, 129:1972-1986.

Grant, H. &. (2003). Clarifying achievement goals and their impact. *Journal of Personality and Social Psychology*, 85, 541-553.

Greenberg, M. H. (2007). Optimistic managers and their influence on productivity and employee engagement in a technology organization. *Gallup Management Journal, Vol. 2, No. 1*.

Greenberg, P. E., Fournier, A.-A., Sisitsky, T., Pike, C. T., & Kessler, R. C. (2015). The Economic Burden of Adults with Major Depressive Disorder in the United States 2005 and 2010). *The Journal of Clinical Psychiatry*(76), 155-162. doi:doi:10.4088/JCP.14m09298)

Greenberg, P. E., Fournier, A.-A., Sisitsky, T., Pike, C., & Kessler, R. C. (2015). The Economic Burden of Adults with Major Depressive Disorcer in the United States (2005 and 2010). *The Journal of Clinical Psychiatry*, 155-162. Retrieved from http://www.psychiatrist.com/jcp/article/Pages/2015/v76n02/v76n0204.aspx

Greenspon, T. S. (2014, November). Is There an Antidote to Perfectionism? *Psychology in the Schools*, 986-998. doi:DOI: 10.1002/pits.21797

Greer, T. M., Brondolo, E., & Brown, P. (2013). Systemic Racism Moderates Effects of Provider Racial Biases on Adherence to Hypertension Treatment for African Americans. *Health Psychology, 33*(1), 35-42. doi:http://dx.doi.org/10.1037/a0032777

Grierson, B. (2014, October 22). What if Age Is Nothing but a Mind-Set? *NY Times*. Retrieved from http://www.nytimes.com/2014/10/26/magazine/whatifageisnothingbutamindset.

Griffin, K. W., Lowe, S. R., Acevedo, B. P., & Botwin, G. J. (2015). Affective Self-Regulation Trajectories During Secondary School Predict Substance Use Among Urban Minority Young Adults. *Journal Child and Adolescent Substance Abuse, 24*(4), 228-234.

Gromet, D. M., & Darley, J. M. (2009, March). Retributive and restorative justice: Importance of crime severity and shared identity in people's justice responses. *Australian Journal of Psychology, 61*(1), 50*57.

Guarneri, M.D., M. (2014). The Science of connection. *Global Advances in Health and Medicine - editorial, 3*(1).

Gunzenhauser, C., Fäsche, A., Friedlmeier, W., & von Suchodoletz, A. (2014, January 3). Face it or hide it: parental socialization of reappraisal and response suppression. *Frontiers in Psychology*. doi:doi: 10.3389/fpsyg.2013.00992

Gurhan, N., Ozbas, A. A., Ugurlu, N., Dogan, H., & Kabatas, E. (2012). Self-esteem and psychological symptoms for the students of vocational high school of health services. *Social and Behavioral Sciences, 47*, 2237-2242.

Gwen Latendresse, C. P. (2009). The Interaction Between Chronic Stress and Pregnancy: Preterm Birth from a Biobehavioral Perspective. *Journal of Midwifery Womens health, 54*(1), 8-17. doi:doi:10.1016/j.jmwh.2008.08.001

Gyamfi, C., Gyamfi, M. M., & Berkowitz, R. L. (2003, July 1). Ethical and Medicolegal Considerations in the care of a Jehovah's Witness. *OBSTETRICS & GYNECOLOGY, 102*. doi:doi:10.1016/S0029-7844(03)00236-9

Haddock, G., & Gebauer, J. E. (2011). Defensive self-esteem impacts attention, attitude strength, and self-affirmation processes. *Journal of Experimental Social Psychology, 47*, 1276–1284. doi:doi:10.1016/j.jesp.2011.05.020

Hagerty, B. B. (2015, 1 10). Prayer May Reshape Your Brain...and Your Reality. *NPR*. Retrieved from http://www.npr.org/templates/story/story.php?storyId=104310443

Haidt, J. (1992). MORAL JUDGMENT, AFFECT, AND CULTURE, or Is It Wrong to Eat Your Dog? Retrieved from http://people.stern.nyu.edu/jhaidt/articles/haidt.1992.dissertation.pub001b.pdf

Haidt, J. (2006). *The Happiness Hypothesis: Finding Modern Truth in Ancient Wisdom. Why the Meaningful Life Is Closer Than You Think.* New York: Basic Books.

Halliwell, E. (2013). The impact of thin idealized media immages on body satisfaction: Does body appreciation protect women from negative effects? *Body Image, 10*, 509-514.

Hameoff, S. R. (1998, April). 'Funda-Mentality': is the conscious mind subtly linked to a basic level of the universe? *Trends in Cognitive Scienes, 2*(4).

Hanh, T. N. (2009). *Happiness: Essential Mindfulness Practices.* Berkeley: Parallalax.

Harman, W. (1998). *Global Mind Change.* Barrett-Koehler Publishers, Inc.

Harris, P. F. (2008). *Jesus Taught It, Too!: The Early Roots of The Law of Attraction.* USA: All Things That Matter Press.

Bibliography

Harris, R., Cormack, D., Tobias, M., Yeh, L.-C., Talamaivao, N., Minister, J., & Timutimu, R. (2012). The pervasive effects of racism: Experiences of racial discrimination in New Zealand over time and associations with multiple health domains. *Social Science & Medicine*, 408-415.

Harter, J., & Agrawal, S. (2014). *Actively Disengaged Workers and Jobless in Equally Poor Health.* Gallup.

Harvard, M. S. (n.d.). *www.health.harvard.edu.* Retrieved 2014, from Harvard Health Publications: http://www.health.harvard.edu/newsletters/Harvard_Womens_Health_Watch/2006/November/Recognizing_the_mind-skin_connection?print=1

Harvey, J., & Delfabbro, P. H. (2004). Psychological resilience in disadvantaged youth: A critical overview. *Australian Psychologist, 39*(1), 3-13.

Haslam, S. S. (2008, March 4). How stereotyping yourself contributes to your success (or failure). *Scientific American Mind.*

Hastie, R., Landsman, R., & Loftus, E. F. (1978-1979). Eyewitness Testimony: The Dangers of Guessing. *Jurimetrics Journal*(19).

Hawkins, D. R. (1995). *Power vs. Force.* Sedona: Hay House.

Hawkins, J. D., Herrenkohl, T. I., Farrington, D. P., Brewer, D., Caalano, R. F., Harachi, T. W., & Cothern, L. (2000). *Predictors of Youth Violence.* Office of Justice Programs, Office of Juvenile Justice and Delinquency Prevention. U.S. Department of Justice.

Hay, L. (1989). Healer, Heal Thyself. In L. Andrews, N. Cousins, R. Dass, L. Dossey, S. Gawain, J. Halifax, . . . O. C. Simonton, R. P. Carlson, & B. Shield (Eds.), *Healers on Healing* (pp. 22-25). Los Angeles, CA: Jeremy P. Tarcher, Inc.

Hayes, S. C. (2004). Acceptance and commitment therapy, relational frame theory, and the third wave of behavioral and cognitive therapies. . *Behavioral Therapy*, 639-665.

Hayes, S. C., Strosahl, K., Wilson, K. G., Bissett, R. T., Pistorello, J., & Toarmino, D. (2004). Measuring experiential avoidance: A preliminary test of a working model. *Pychological Record, 54*(4), 553-578.

Health and Human Services. (2011). *Costs and Consequences - Million Hearts.* HHS, HHS. Retrieved from http://millionhearts.hhs.gov/learn-prevent/cost-consequences.html

HeartMath Institute. (2010, May 5). *Resilience Picks You Up, Keeps You Going.* Retrieved September 4, 2015, from heartmath.org: http://www.heartmath.org

Helm, C. A. (2013, July). Relationship Between Racial Microaggression and Psychological Wellbeing of African Americn College Students. *A Dissertation Submitted to the Faculty of University of Minnesota.* Minnesota.

Helson, R., & Kwan, V. S. (2002, September). Personality change over 40 years of adulthood: hierarchical linear modeling analyses of two longitudinal samples. *Journal of Personality and Social Psychology, 83*(3), 752-66.

Henry, J. D., Castellini, J., Moses, E., & Scott, J. G. (2016, Feb-Mar). Emotion regulation in adolescents with mental health problems. *Journal Clinical and Experimental Neuropsychology, 38*(2).

Hidaka, B. H. (2012, January 12). Depression as a disease of modernity: Explanations for increasing prevalence. *Journal of Affective Disorders*(140), 205-214. doi:10.1016/j.jad.2011.12.036

Higginson, S., & Mansell, W. (2008). What is the mechanism of psychological change? A qualatative analysis of six individuals who experienced personal change and recovery. *Psychology and Psychotherapy: Theory, Research, and Practice*, 309-328. Retrieved 2015

Hill, N. (1994). *Keys to Success.* New York: Penguin Group.

Hill, N. (1997). *Napoleon Hill's Keys to Success: The 17 Principles of Personal Achievement.*

Hill, P. I., & Lapsley, D. K. (2009). The ups and downs of the moral eprsonality: Why it's not so black and white. *Journal of Research in Personality, 43*, 520-523.

Hill, P. I., & Lapsley, D. K. (2009). The ups and downs of the moral personality: Why it's not so black and white. *Journal of Research in Personality, 43*, 520-523.

Hill, T. E. (2010). How clinicians make (or avoid) moral judgments of patients: implications of the evidence for relationships and research. *Philosophy Ethics Humanities Medicine, 5.*

Hilmert, C. J., Dominguez, T. P., Schetter, C. D., Srinivas, S. K., Glynn, L. M., Hobel, C. J., & Sandman, C. A. (2014). Lifetime Racism and Blood Pressure Changes During Pregnancy: Implications for Fetal Growth. *Health Psychology, Vol. 33, No. 1*, 43-51. doi:DOI: 10.1037/a0031160

Hiroto, D. S. (1974). Locus of control and learned helplessness. *Journal of Experimental Psychology*, 102: 187-193.

Hirsch, J. K., & Sirois, F. M. (2014, March). Hope and Fatigue in Chronic Illness: The role of perceived stress. *Journal of Health Psychology.*

Hitsman, B., Borrelli, B., McChargue, D. E., Spring, B., & Niaura, R. (2003). History of Depression and Smoking Cessation Outcome: a Meta-Analysis. *Journal of Consulting and Clinical Psychology, 71*(4), 657-663. doi:DOI: 10.1037/0022-006X.71.4.657

Ho, S., Rajandram, R. K., Chan, N., Summan, N., McGrath, C., & Zwahlen, R. (2011). The roles of hope and optimism on posttraumatic growth in oral cavity cancer patients. *Oral Oncology, 47*, 121-124.

Hoersting, R. C., & Jenkins, S. R. (2011). No place to call home: Cultural homelessness, self-esteem and cross-cultural identitites. *International Journal of Intercultural Relations, 35*, 17-30.

Hoeve, M., Dubas, J. S., Eichelsheim, V. I., van der Laan, P. H., Smeenk, W., & Gerris, J. R. (2009). The Relationship Between Parenting and Delinquency: A Meta-Analysis. *Journal of Abnormal Child Psychology, 37*, 749-775.

Hoffman, B. (2010). "I think I can, but I'm afraid to try": The role of self-efficacy beliefs and mathematics anxiety in mathematics problem-solving efficiency. *Learning and Individual Differences, 20*, 276-283. doi:doi:10.1016/j.lindif.2010.02.001

Hofmann, S. G., Asnaani, A., Vonk, I. J., Sawyer, A. T., & Fang, A. (2012, October 1). The Efficacy of Cognitive Behavioral Therapy: A Review of Meta-analyses. *Cognitive Therapy and Research, 36*(5), 427-440. doi:10.1007/s10608-012-9476-1

Hogan, Ph.D., M. F., Adams, J., Arredondo, Jr., R., Godbole, A. G., Harbin, H. T., Huang, L. N., . . . Yates, D. F. (2003). *President's New Freedom Commission on Mental Health* .

Holden, D. R. (2008). *Success Intelligence.* Hay House.

Holden, R. (2007). *Happiness Now: Timeless Wisdom for Feeling Good FAST*. Hay House.

Holden, R. (2009). *BE Happy: Release the Power of Happiness in you.* Carlsbad: Hay House.

Holmes, E. S. (1923). *Creative Mind: A Series of Talks on Mental and Spiritual Law and Creative Mind and Success.* Forgotten Books.

Holt-Lunstad, J., Smith, T. B., & Layton, J. B. (2010). Social Relationships and Mortality Risk: A Meta-analytic Review. (C. Brayne, Ed.) *PLoS Med, 7*. doi:doi:10.1371/journal.pmed.1000316

Holzer, H. J., Schanzenbach, D. W., Duncan, G. J., & Ludwig, J. (2007). *The Economic Costs of Poverty in the United States: Subsequent Effects of Children Growing up Poor.* National Poverty Center, National Poverty Center Working Paper Series. Retrieved from http://www.npc.umich.edu/publications/u/working_paper07-04.pdf

Hong, Y. Y. (n.d.). Implicit theories, attributions, and coping: A meaning system approach. *Journal of Personality and Social Psychology*.

Hopp, H., Troy, A. S., & Mauss, I. B. (2011). The unconscious pursuit of emotion regulation: Implications for psychological health. *Cognitive Emoiton*, 532-545.

Hossain, J. L., & Shapiro, C. M. (2002, June). The prevalence, cost implications, and management of sleep disorders: an overview. *Journal of sleep research, 6*(2), 85-102. doi:10.1055/s-2002-32322

Hounkpatin, H. O., Wood, A. M., Boyce, C. J., & Dunn, G. (2015). An Existential-Humanistic View of Personality Change: Co-Occurring Changes with Psyhological Well-Being in a 10 Year Cohort Study. *Social Indicators Research*, 455-470. Retrieved 2015

House, J. S., Landis, K. R., & Umberson, D. (1988, July 29). Social relationships and health. *Science, 241*(4865), 540-545. doi:DOI: 10.1126/science.3399889

Howell, W. L. (2014, Spring). Addiction Science: Unraveling clues to addictive behaviors. *Research: Carolina Arts & Sciences*, pp. 29-30.

Hryhorczuk, C., Sharma, S., & Fulton, S. E. (2013, October). metabolic disturbances connecting obesity and depression. *Frontiers in Neuroscience*, 177.

http://www.theawl.com/2014/08/how-much-a-pack-of-cigarettes-costs-state-by-state. (2014). Retrieved from The Awl: http://www.theawl.com/2014/08/how-much-a-pack-of-cigarettes-costs-state-by-state

Hu, T., Zhang, D., Wang, J.-L., Mistry, R., Ran, G., & Wang, X. (2014, April). Relation between emotion regulation and mental health: A meta-analysis-review. *Psychological Reports, 114*(2), 341-362. doi: DOI: 10.2466/03.20.PR0.114k22w4

Hubbard, D. J. (2002). A meta-analysis of the predictors of deliquency among girls. *Journal of Offender Rehabilitation, 34*, 1-13.

Hudson, D. I., Puterman, E., Bibbins-Domingo, K., Matthews, K. A., & Adler, N. E. (2013). Race, life course socioeconomic position, racial discrimination, depressive symptoms and self-rated health. *Social Science & Medicine, 97*, 7-14. Retrieved PDF - printed

Huntjens, R. J., Rijkeboer, M. M., Krakau, A., & de Jong, P. J. (2014). Implicit versus explicit measures of self-concept of self-control and their differential predictive power for spontaneous trait-relevant behaviors. *Journal of Behavior Therapy and Experimental Psychiatry, 45*, 1 - 7.

Hutchins, M. (n.d.). *Chapter 9: Chemical Senses: Olfaction and Gustation.* Retrieved from University of Texas Health: http://neuroscience.uth.tmc.edu/s2/chapter09.html

Huynh, V. W. (2012, July). Ethnic Microaggressions and the Depressive and Somatic Symptoms of Latino and Asian American Adolescents. *Journal of Youth and Adolescence*, 831-846.

Hwang, B., Moser, D. K., & Dracup, K. (2013). Knowledge Is Insufficient for Self-Care Among Heart Failure Patients With Psychological Distress. *Health Psychology, 33*(7), 588-596.

Jeanine Joy

XX | Bibliography

Hwang, B., Moser, D. K., & Dracup, K. (2014). Knowledge Is Insufficient for Self-Care Among Heart Failure Patients with Psychological Distress. *Health Psychology, 33*(7), 588-596. doi:http://dx.doi.org/10.1037/a0033419

Ibrahim, A. K., Kelly, S. J., Adams, C. E., & Glazebrook, C. (2013). A systematic review of studies of depression prevaalence in university students. *Journal of Psychiatric Research, 47*, 391-400.

Ikuenobe, P. (2010). Conceptualizing Racism and Its Subtle Forms. *Journal for the Theory of Social Behaviour*, 41:2.

Imanishi, J., Kuriyama, H., Shigemori, I., Watanabe, S., Aihara, Y., Kita, M., . . . Fukui, K. (2007). Anxiolytic Effect of Aromatherapy Massage in Patients with Breast Cancer. *eCAM*. doi:doi:10.1093/ecam/nem073

Infurna, F. J., & Gerstorf, D. (2014). Perceived Control Relates to Better Functional Health and Lower Cardiac-Metabolic Risk: The Mediating Role of Physical Activity. *Health Psychology, 33*(1). doi:DOI: 10.1037/a0030208

Innes, K. E., Vincent, H. K., & Taylor, A. G. (2007, July-August). Chronic stress and insulin resistance-related indices of cardiovascular disease risk, Part 1: neurophysiological responses and pathological sequelae. *Alternative Therapies Health Medicine, 13*(4), 46-52.

Inouye, S., Takizawa, T., & Yamaguchi, H. (2001). Antibacterial activity of essential oils and their major constituents against respiratory tract pathogens by gaseous contact. *Journal of Antimicrobial Chemotherapy, 47*(5), 565-573. doi:doi:10.1093/jac/47.5.565

Institute of Educational Sciences. (2013). *Fast Facts: Income of Young Adults*. National Center for Educational Statistics.

Inzlicht, M., & Gutsell, J. N. (2007). Running on empty: neural signals for self-control failure. *Psychological Science*, 993-997.

Ioannis Sotiropoulos, C. C. (2001, May 25). Stress Acts Cumulatively to Precipitate Alzheimer's Disease-Like Tau Pathology and Cognitive Deficits. *Journal of Neuroscience*, 31(21):7840-7847. doi:10.1523/JNEUROSCI.0730-11.2011

Irwin, M. R., Olmstead, R., & Oxman, M. N. (2007). Augmenting immune responses to varicella zoster virus in older adults: a randomized, control trial of Tai Chi. *Journal American Geriatric Society, 4*, 511-517. Retrieved from http://www.ncbi.nlm.nih.gov/pubmed/17397428?ordinalpos=3&itool=EntrezSystem2.PEntrez.Pubmed.Pubmed_Results Panel.Pubmed_DefaultReportPanel.Pubmed_RVDocSum

Isen, A. M. (1972). Effect of feeling good on helping: Cookies and kindness. *Journal of Personality and Social Psychology*, 21: 384-88.

Isen, A. M. (1976). Duration of the effect of good mood on helping: Footprints in the sands of time. *Journal of Personality and Social Psychology*, 34: 385-93.

Isen, A. M. (1987). Positive affect, cognitive processes, and social behavior. *Advances in Experimental Social Psychology*, 20: 203-53.

Isen, A. M. (1991). The influence of positive affect on clinical problem solving. *Medical Decision Making*, 11:221-27.

Ito, T. A., & Cacioppo, J. T. (1999). The Psychophysiology of Utility Appraisals. In D. Kahneman, E. Diener, & N. Schwarz (Eds.), *Well-Being: The Foundations of Hedonic Psychology* (pp. 470-488). USA: Russell Sage Foundation.

Ito, T., & Urland, G. R. (2003). Race and gender on the brain: Electro-cortical measures of attention to the race and gender of multiple categorizable individuals. *Journal of Personality and Social Psychology*, 616-26.

Jahn, R. G. (2007). Sensors, filters, and the source of realitly. *Explore(NY)*, 3(3): 326-37, 345.

James, I., Andershed, B., Gustavsson, B., & Ternestedt, B.-M. (2010). Emotional knowing in nursing practice: In the encounter between life and death. *2*.

James, W. (1890 (2007)). *The Principles of Psychology, Vol 1*. New York: Cosimo.

Jauch-Chara, K. a. (2014). Obesity--A neuropsychological disease? Systematic review and neuropsychological model. *Progress in Neurobiology, In Press*, xxx. Retrieved January 2014

Jauch-Chara, K., & Oltmanns, K. M. (2014). Obesity - A neuropsychological disease? Systematic review and neuropsychological model. *Progress in Neurobiology*, xxx-xxx (In Press).

Jeffers, S. (1987). *Feel the Fear...and Do It Anyway*. New York : Ballantine Books.

Jennifer O'Neill, H. T. (2014). Applying an equity lens to interventions: using PROGRESS ensures consideration of socially stratifying factors to illuminate inequities in health. *Journal of Clinical Epidemiology 67* , 56-64.

Jensen, S. E., Pereira, D. B., Whitehead, N., Buscher, I., McCalla, J., Andrasik, M., . . . Antoni, M. H. (2013). Cognitive-Behavioral Stress Management and Psychological Well-Being HIV + Racial/Ethnic Minority Women with Human Papillomavirus. *Heatlh Psychology, 32*(2), 227-230. doi:DOI: 10.1037/a0028160

Jobin, J., Wrosch, C., & Scheier, M. F. (2014). Associations Between Dispositional Optimism and Diurnal Cortisol in a Community Sample: When Stress Is Perceived as Higher Than Normal. *Health Psychology, 33*(4), 382-391. doi:http://dx.doi.org/10.1037/a0032736

Johnson, K. J. (2010). Smile to see the forest: Facially expressed positive emotions broaden cognition. *COGNITION AND EMOTION*, 24(2): 299-321.

Johnson, M. B., Bertrand, S. W., Fermon, B., & Foley, J. (2014). Pathways to Healing: Person-centered Responses to Complimentary Services. *Global Advances in Health and Medicine, 3*(1), 8-16.

Joiner, F. a. (2002).

Jones, J., & Mosher, W. D. (2013). *Fathers' Involvement with their children: United States, 2006-2010*. Center for Disease Control CDC, National Health Statistics Report. CDC.

Jordan, M., & Livingstone, J. B. (2013). Coaching vs Psychotherapy in Health and Wellness: Oerlap, Dissimilarities, and the Potential for Collaboration. *Global Advances in Health and Wellness, 2*(4), 20-27.

Joseph, M. M., McIntosh, M. S., & Joseph, C. M. (2014). The Effects of Various Comfort Food on Heart Coherence in Adults. *Scientific Absracts on Health and Organizational Outcomes in Healthcare*, Suppl1.

Joy, J. (2013). *Shades of Joy.* Unpublished Manuscript.

Joy, J. (2014). *True Prevention--Optimum Health: Remember Galileo Wellness at the Root Cause for the 21st Century.* Charlotte, NC, USA: Thrive More, Now.

Judge, T. A., & Bono, J. E. (2001). Relationship of Core Self-Evaluations Traits—Self-Esteem, Generalized Self-Efficacy, Locus of Control, and Emotional Stability—With Job Satisfaction and Job Performance: A Meta-Analysis. *Journal of Applied Psychology, 86*(1), 80-92. doi:DOI: 10.1037//0021-9010.86.1.80

Jung, Y.-H., Kang, D.-H., Jang, J. H., Park, H. Y., Byun, M. S., Kwon, S. J., . . . Kwon, J. S. (2010). The effects of mind-body training on stress reduction, positive affect, and plasma catecholamines. *Neuroscience Letters, 479*, 138-142.

Junior, G. C., Neves, L. M., Cipriano, G. F., Chiappa, G. R., & Borghi-Silva, A. (2014 In Press). Cardiovascuolar Disease Prevention and Implications for Worksite Health Promotion Progams in Brazil. *ScienceDirect*, xxx-xxx.

Justin M. Hill, P. M. (2011 (September). The Development of a Brief Acceptance and Mindfulness-Based Program Aimed at Reducing Sexual Revictimization Among College Women With a History of Childhood Sexual Abuse. *Journal of Clinical Psychology Vol. 67(9)*, 969--980.

KALTIALA-HEINO, R., RIMPELA¨, M., RANTANEN, P., & RIMPELA¨, A. (2000). Bullying at school—an indicator of adolescents. *Journal of Adolescence, 23*, 661-674. doi:doi:10.1006/jado.2000.0351

Kalynchuk, L. (2010). Preface: Behavioral and neurobiological consequences of stress. *Progress in Neuro-Psychopharmacology & Biological Psychiatry*, 731-732.

Kane, J. (2007). An examination of a Two-Factor Model of Ruminating and its Impact on the Relationship between Posttraumatic Growth and Posttraumatic Stress Disorder (PTSD). *Dissertation, George Mason University.* Retrieved from http://hdl.handle.net/1920/5635

Kashdan, T. B., & Jonathan, R. (2010). Psychological flexibility as a fundamental aspect of health. *Clinical Psychology Review*, xxx-xxx (In Press). doi:doi:10.1016/j.cpr.2010.03.001

Kayman, S., Bruvold, W., & Stern, J. S. (1990). Maintenance and relapse after weight loss in Women: behavioral aspects. *The American Journal of Clinical Nutrition, 52*, 800-807.

Kellam, S. G., Mackenzie, A. C., & Brown, C. H. (2011). The good behavior game and the future of prevention and treatment. *Addiction Science Clinical Practice, 6*(1), 73-84.

Keller, M. C. (2005). A warm heart and a clear head: The contingent effects of mood and weather on cognition. *Psychological Science*, 16: 724-731.

Keltner, D. (2009). *Born to be Good.* New York: W. W. Norton & Company Limited.

Khanlou, N., & Wray, R. (2014). A Whole Community Approach toward Child and Youth Resilience Promotion: A Review of Resilience Literature. *International Journal of Mental Health Addiction, 12*, 64-79. doi:DOI 10.1007/s11469-013-9470-1

Kiecolt-Glaser. (1999). Stress, Personal Relationships, and Immune Function: Health Implications. *Brain, Behavior, and Immunity 13*, 61-72. Retrieved 10 8, 2014

Kikue Sakaguchi, a. T. (2006). Person Perception through Gait Information and Target Person Perception through Gait Information and Target Comparison of likely Targets in Experiments and Real Life. *J Nonverbal Behav 30:63–85*, 63-85. doi:DOI 10.1007/s10919-006-0006-2

Kilmer, R. P., Gil-Rivas, V., Tedeschi, R. G., Cann, A., Calhoun, L. G., Buchanan, T., & Taku, K. (2009). Use of the Revised Posttraumatic Growth Inventory. *Journal of Traumatic Stress, 22*(3), 248-253. doi:DOI: 10.1002/jts.20410

Kilpatrick, D. G., Resnick, H. S., Milanak, M. E., Miller, M. W., Keyes, K. M., & Friedman, M. J. (2013, October). National Estimates of Exposure to Traumatic Events and PTSD Prevalence Using DSM-IV and DSM-5 Criteria. *Journal of Trauma and Stress, 26*(5), 537-547. doi:doi:10.1002/jts.21848

Kim, E. S., Park, N., & Peterson, C. (2011). Health and Retirement Study. *Stroke.* doi:DOI:10.1161/STROKEAHA.111.613448

Kim, H. J., & Agrusa, J. (2011). Hospitality service employees' coping styles: The role of emotional intelligence, two basic personality traits, and socio-demographic factors. *International Journal of Hospitality Management, 30*, 588-598. doi:doi:10.1016/j.ijhm.2010.11.003

Kim, M.-H., Gorouhi, F., Ramirez, S., Granick, J. L., Byrne, B. A., Soulika, A., . . . Isseroff, R. R. (2014, March). Catecholamine stress alters neutrophil trafficking and impairs wound healing by β adrenergic receptor mediated upregulation of IL-6. *J Invest Dermatol*, 809-817.

Kim, S. H., & Hamann, S. (2007, May). Neural correlates of positive and negative emotion regulation. *Journal of Cognitive Neuroscience, 19*(5), 776-98.

Kimhi, S., & Eshel, Y. (2009). Individual and Public Resilience and Coping with Long-Term Outcomes of War. *Journal of Applied Biobehavioral Research, 14*(2), 70-89.

King, Jr., M. L. (Performer). (1964). Acceptance Speech, Martin Luther King Jr.'s Nobel Peace Prize. Oslo, Norway. Retrieved from http://www.nobelprize.org/nobel_prizes/peace/laureates/1964/king-acceptance.html

King, R. B., McInerney, D. M., & Watkins, D. A. (2012). How you think about your intelligence determines how you feel in school: The role of theories of intelligence on academic emotions. *Learning and Individual Differences*(22), 814-819.

Kingshott, R., Cowan, J., Jones, D., Flannery, E., Smith, A., Herbison, G., & Taylor, D. (2004). The role of sleep-disordered breathing, daytime sleepiness, and impaired performance in motor vehicle crashes--a case control study. *Sleep and Breathing*.

Kivetz, Y., & Tyler, T. R. (2006). Tomorrow I'll be me: The effect of time perspective on the activation of idealistic versus pragmatic selves. *Organizational Behavior and Human Decision Process*, 193-211. doi:doi:10.1016/j.obhdp.2006.07.002

Kjerulf, A. (n.d.). *Happy Hour is 9 to 5*. 2006: Lulu Publishing.

Kliewer, W. (2015, December 16). Victimization and Biological Stress Responses in Urban Adolescents: Emotion Regulation as a Moderator. *Journal Youth Adolescents*, Epub.

Knudsen, H. K., Ducharme, L. J., & Roman, P. M. (2007). Job stress and poor sleep quality: Data from an American sample of full-time workers. *Social Science & medicine, 64*, 1997-2007. doi:doi:10.1016/j.socscimed.2007.02.020

Kobylinska, D., & Karwowska, D. (2015, October 27). How automatic activation of emotion regulation influences experiencing negative emotins. (P. Kusev, Ed.) *Frontiers in psychology*, 1-4.

Koerner, N., Antony, M. M., Young, L., & McCabe, R. E. (2013, April). Changes in Beliefs about the Social Competence of Self and Others Following Group Cognitive Behavioral Therapy. *Cognitive Therapy Research, 37*(2), 256-265.

Kohlberg, L., & Hersh, R. H. (1977). Moral Development: A Review of the Theory. *Theory into Practice*, 53-59.

Kok, B. E., Coffey, K. A., cohn, M. A., Catalino, L. I., Vacharkulksemsuk, T., Algoe, S. B., . . . Fredrickson, B. L. (2012). How Positive Emotions Build Physical Health: perceived Positive Social Connections Account for the Upward spiral Between Positive Emotions and Vagal Tone. *Psychological Science, 24*(7), 1123-1132. doi:DOI: 10.1177/0956797612470827

Koob, G. F., Buck, C. L., Cohen, A., Edwards, S., Park, P. E., Schlosburg, J. E., . . . George, O. (2014, Jan). Addiction as a stress surfeit disorder. *Neuropharmacology, 76*, 370-382. doi:doi: 10.1016/j.neuropharm.2013.05.024

Kopelman, S. R. (2006). The three faces of Eve: Strategic displays of positive, negative, and neutral emotions in negotiations. *Organizational Behavior and Human Decision Processes*, 99:81-101.

Kotter. (2014). *Kotter International*. Retrieved from (http://www.kotterinternational.com/our-principles/urgency)

Kottwitz, M. U., Grebner, S., Semmer, N. K., Tschan, F., & Elfering, A. (2014). Social Stress at Work and Change in Women's . *Industrial Health*, 163-171.

Kowalenko, T., Cunningham, R., Sachs, C. J., Gore, R., Barata, I. A., Gates, D., . . . McClain, A. (2012). Violence: Recognition, Management, and Prevention. *The Journal of Emergency Medicine, 43*(3), 523-531.

Kraag, G., Zeegers, M. P., Kok, G., Hosman, C., & Abu-Saad, H. H. (2006). School programs targeting stress management in children and adolescents: A meta-analysis. *Journal of School Psychology*, 449-472. doi:doi:10.1016/j.jsp.2006.07.001

Kramer, P. D. (2012, June 20). *The Transformation of Personality*. Retrieved from psychologytoday.com: www.psychologytoday.com/articles

Krieger, N., Chen, J. T., Waterman, P. D., Hartman, C., Stoddard, A. M., Quinn, M. M., . . . Barbeau, E. M. (2008). The inverse hazard law: Blood pressure, sexual harassment, racial discrimination, workplace abuse and occupational exposures in US low-income black, white and Latino workers. *Social Science & Medicine , 67*, 1970-1981.

Krieger, N., Smith, K., Naishadhamb, D., Hartman, C., & Barbeau, E. M. (2005). Experiences of discrimination: Validity and reliability of a self-report measure for population health research on. *Social Science and Medicine 61*, 1576-1596.

Kudinova, A. Y., Owens, M., Burkhouse, K. L., Barretto, K. M., Bonanno, G. A., & Gibb, B. E. (2015, May). Differences in emotion modulation using cognitive reappraisal in individuals with and without suicidal ideation: An ERP study. *Cognitive Emotion, 15*, 1-9.

Kudinova, A. Y., Owens, M., Burkhouse, K. L., Barretto, K. M., Bonanno, G. A., & Gibb, B. E. (2015, May). Differences in emotion modulation using cognitive reappraisal in individuasl with and without suicidal ideation: An ERP study. *Cognitive Emotion*, 1-9 (Epub).

Kutz, I., Burysenko, J. K., & Benson, H. (1985a). Meditation and psychotherapy: a rationale for the integration of dynamic psychotherapy, the relaxation response and mindfulness meditation. *American Journal of Psychiatry, 142*, 1-8.

Kutz, I., Leserman, J., Dorrington, C., Morrison, C. H., Borysenko, J., & Benson, H. (1985b). Meditation as an adjunct to psychotherapy, an outcome study. *Psychotherapy Psychosomatics, 43*, 209-218.

Kwong, J. Y., Wong, K. F., & Tang, S. K. (2013). Comparing predicted and actual affective responses to process versus outcome: An Emotion-as-feedback perspective. *Cognition, 129*, 42-50. doi:http://dx.doi.org/10.1016/j.cognition.2013.05.012

Kyckelhahn, T., & Martin, T. (2013). *Justice Expenditures and Employment Extracts, 2010 - Preliminary Table 1*. (O. o. Bureau of Justice Statistics, Producer, & US Departement of Justice) Retrieved from Kyckelhahn, Tracey, and Tara Martin. 2013. "Justice Expenditures

Ladhani, S. (2014, 11 7). Research: Child Development Starts Before Conception. *Panther Power (The Science of Human Potential(c))*.

Lai JC, E. P. (2005). Optimism, positive affectivity, and salivary cortisol. *British Journal of Health Psychology*, 4:467-84.

Laitinen, J., Ek, E., & Sovio, U. (2002). Stress Related Eating and Drinking Behavior and BMI and Predictors of this Behavior. *Preventive Medicine*, 29-39.

Laloyaux, J., Dessart, G., Van der Linden, M., Lernaire, M., & Laroi, F. (2016, February 1). Maladaptive emotion regulation strategies and stress sensitivity mediate the relation between adverse life events and attenuated positive psychotic symptoms. *Cognitive Neuropsychiatry*, 1-14 (Epub).

Lampe, A., Doering, S., Rumpold, G., Solder, E., Krismer, M., Kantner-Rumplmair, W., . . . Söllner, W. (2003). Chronic Pain Syndromes and their relation to childhood abuse and stressful life events. *Journal Psychosomatic Research, 54*(4), 361-7. Retrieved 2014

Lan, C., Lai, J. S., & Chen, S. Y. (2002). Tai Chi Chuan: an ancient wisdom on exercise and health promotion. *Sports Medicine, 32*(4), 217-24.

Langer, Ph.D., E. (2009). *Counterclockwise*. New York: Ballantine.

Lansford, J. E. (2002). A 12-year prospective study of the long-term effects of early child physical maltreatment on psychological, behavioral and academic problems in adolescence. *Archives of Pediatric Medicine, 156*, 824-830.

Lansing, A. H., & Bert, C. A. (2014). Topical Review: Adolescent Self-Regulation as a Foundation for Chronic Illness Self-Management. *Journal of Pediatric Psychology, 39*(10), 1091-1096. Retrieved 2016

Larry Dossey, M. (1993). *Healing Words: The Power of Prayer and The Practice of Medicine.* New York: Harper One.

Larson, N.-H. &. (1998). Coping with Loss.

Latendresse, CNM, PhD, G. (2009). The Interaction Between Chronic Stress and Pregnancy: Preterm Birth from a Biobehavioral Perspective. *Journal of Midwifery Womens health, 54*(1), 8-17. doi:doi:10.1016/j.jmwh.2008.08.001

Latendresse, G. (2009). The Interaction Between Chronic Stress and Pregnancy: Preterm Birth from A Biobehavioral Perspective. *Journal Midwifery Womens Health.* doi:doi:10.1016/j.jmwh.2008.08.001

Laury, J. R. (1990). *Ho for California!: Women's Overland Diaries from the Huntington Library.* California.

Lazarus. (1991). *Cognition and Emotion.*

Lazarus, R. S. (1993). From Psychological Stress to the Emotions: A History of Changing Outlooks. *Annual Review Psychology*, 1-21.

Leary, M. R., Schreindorfer, L. S., & Haupt, A. L. (1995, September). The Role of Low Self-Esteem in Emotional and Behavioral Problems: Why is Low Self-Esteem Dysfunctional? *Journal of Social and Clinical Psychology, 14*(3), 297-314.

Lee, E.-J., & Jang, J.-w. (2010). Profiling good Samaritans in online knowledge forums: Effects of affiliative tendency, self-esteem, and public individuation on knowledge sharing. *Computers in Human Behavior, 26*, 1336-1344. doi:doi:10.1016/j.chb.2010.04.007

Lee, P. C., & Stewart, D. E. (2013). Does a Socio-Ecological School Model Promote Resilience in Primary Schools? *Journal of School Health, 83*(11), 795-804.

Lee, T. Y., Cheung, C. K., & Kwong, W. M. (2012). Resilience as a Positive Youth Development Construct: A Conceptual Review. *The Scientific World Journal, Article ID 390450*, 1-9. doi:doi:10.1100/2012/390450

Leith, K., & Baumeister, R. F. (1996, December). Why do bad moods increase self-defeating behavior? Emotion, risk tasking, and self-regulation. *Journal of Personality and Social Psychology, 71*(6), 1250-1267.

Leon, A., Levin, E. C., & Koo, J. Y. (2013). Psychodermatology: An Overview. *Seminars in Cutaneous Medicine and Surgery* (pp. 64-67). Frontline Medical Communications.

Lépine, J.-P., & Briley, M. (2011). The increasing burden of depression. *Neuropsychiatric Disorder Treatment, 7*(Suppl 1), 3-7. doi: 10.2147/NDT.S19617

Lerner, J. S., & Keltner, D. (2000). Beyond valence: Toward a model of emotion-specific influences on judgement and choice. *Cognition and Emotion, 14*(4), 473-493. Retrieved 10 8, 2014, from http://www.tandf.co.uk/journals/pp/02699931.html

Levenson, M. R., Aldwin, C. M., & Yancura, L. (2006, November/December). Positive Emotional Change: Mediating Effects of Forgiveness and Spirituality. *EXPLORE, 2*(6). doi:doi:10.1016/j.explore.2006.08.002

Levine, L. J., Schmidt, S., Kang, H. S., & Tinti, C. (2012). Remembering the silver lining: reappraisal and positive bias in memory for emotion. *Cognitive Emotion, 26*(5), 871-84.

Levine, Linda J.; Lench, Heather C.; Safer, Martin A;. (2009). Functions of Remembering and Misremebering Emotion. *Applied Cognitive Psychology, 23*, 1059-1075.

Levy, N., & Bayne, T. (2004). A will of one's own: Consciousness, control, and character. *International Journal of Law and Psychiatry, 27*, 459-470.

Lewis, S. (2011). *Positive Psychology at Work: How Positive Leadership and Appreciative Inquiry Create Inspiring Organizations.* Wiley-Blackwell.

Li, W.-D., Arvey, R. D., & Song, Z. (2011). The influence of general mental ability, self-esteem and family socioeconomic status on leadership role occupancy and leader advancement: The moderating role of gender. *The Leadership Quarterly, 22*, 520-534. doi:doi:10.1016/j.leaqua.2011.04.009

Liberman, V., Anderson, N. R., & Ross, L. (2010). Achieving difficult agreements: Effects of Positive Expectations on negotiation processes and outcomes. *Journal of Experimental Social Psychology, 46*, 494-504. doi:doi:10.1016/j.jesp.2009.12.010

Lieberman, M. D. (n.d. 2015). The Brain's Braking System (and how to 'use your words' to tap into it). *Neuroleadership (IN PRESS).*

Lieberman, R., & Cowan, K. C. (2011, October). Bullying and Youth Suicide: Breaking the Connection. *Principal Leadership.* NASSP.org. Retrieved from http://www.nassp.org/Content/158/PLOct11_schoolpsych.pdf

Light, K. C. (2005). More frequent partner hugs and higher oxytocin levels are linked to lower blood pressure and heart rate in premenopausal women. *Biological Psychology*, 69: 5-21.

Liju, V. B., Jeena, K., & Kuttan, R. (2011). An evaluation of antioxidant, anti-inflammatory, and antinociceptive activities of essential oil from Curcuma longa. L. *Indian Journal Pharmacology, 43*(5), 526-531. doi:doi: 10.4103/0253-7613.84961

Limar, I. V. (2011). C.G. Jung's Schronicity and Quantum Enganglement: Schrodinger's Cat 'Wanders' Between Chromosomes. *NeuroQuantology*(9), 313-321.

Lin, P. W.-k., Chan, W.-c., Ng, B. F., & Lam, L. C.-w. (2007). Efficacy of aromatherapy (Lavandula angustifolia) as an intervention for agitated behaviors in Chinese older persons with dementia: a cross-over randomized trial. *International Journal Geriatric Psychiatry, 22*, 405-410.

Lindstrom, B., & Eriksson, M. (2006). Contextualizing salutogenesis and Antonovsky in public health development. *Public Health & Epidemiology, 21*(3), 238-244.

Linley, P. A. (2004, February). Positive Change Following Trauma and Adversity: A Review. *Journal of Traumatic Stress, Vol. 17, No. 1*, pp. 11 - 21.

Lipton, B. H., & Bhaerman, S. (2009). *Spontaneous Evolution: Our Positive Future (and a way to get there from here).* Carlsbad: Hay House.

Litt, D. M., Stock, M. L., & Gibbons, F. X. (2015). Adolescent alcohol use: Social comparison orientation moderates the impact of friend and sibling behavior. *Brittish ournal of Health Psychology, 20*, 514-533. Retrieved 2015

Liu, Y., Wheaton, A. G., Chapman, D. P., & Croft, J. B. (2013). *Sleep Duration and Chronic Diseases among US Adults Age 45 Years and Older: Evidence from the 2010 Behavioral Risk Factor Surveillance Survey.* CDC, Division of Population Health, Centers for Disease Control and Prevention, Atlanta. doi:http://dx.doi.org/10.5665/sleep.302

Lloyd, C., Smith, J., & Weinger, K. (2005). Stress and Diabetes: A Review of the Links. *Diabetes Spectrum, 18*(2).

Lloyd, Ph.D., C., Smith, J., & Weinger, K. (2005, April). Stress and Diabetes: A Review of the Links. *Diabetes Spectrum, vol. 18*(No. 2), 121-127. doi:doi: 10.2337/diaspect.18.2.121

Lloyd, S. J., Malek-Ahmadi, M., Barclay, K., Fernandez, M. R., & Chartrand, M. S. (2012). Emotional intelligence (EI) is a predictor of depression status in older adults. *Archives of Gerontology and Geriatrics, 55*, 570-573.

Lockwood, P. L., Seara-Cardoso, A., & Vidingn, E. (2014). Emotion Regulation Moderates the Association between. *PLOS one.*

Lohmann, MS, LPC, R. C. (2013, June 27). *Teen Bullying: A CBT Approach to Addressing the Issue.* Retrieved from Psychology Today: https://www.psychologytoday.com/blog/teen-angst/201306/teen-bullying-cbt-approach-addressing-the-issue

Lopresti, A. L., Hood, S. D., & Drumond, P. D. (2013). A review of lifestyle factors that contribute to important pathways associated with major depression: Diet, sleep, and exercise. *Journal of Affective Disorders, 148*, 12-27.

Lorenzet, S. J. (2005). Benefiting from mistakes. The impact of guided errors on learning, performance, and self-efficiacy. *Human Resource Development quarterly*, 16:301-322.

Lowery, B. S., Hardin, C. D., & Sinclair, S. (2001). Social Influence Effects on Automatic Racial Prejudice. *Journal of Personality and Social Psychology, 81*(5), 842-855. doi:DOI: 1O.1O37//O022-35I4.8I.5.842

Luoma, J. B., & Villatte, J. L. (2012). Mindfulness in the Treatment of Suicidal Individuals. *Cognitive and Behavioral Practice, 19*, 265-276.

Luthans, F., & Youssef, C. M. (2007). *Emerging Positive Organizational Behavior.* Leadership Institute. Leadership Institute Faculty Publications.

Ly, T., Guard, A., & Black, S. (2012). *CalMHSA Suicide Prevention Social Marketing Project-Baseline Media Analysis.* Educational Development Center, Inc., CalMHSA California Mental Health Services Authority. Retrieved from http://www.sprc.org/sites/sprc.org/files/library/Media%20Analysis%20Report%20FinalAug2012.pdf

Lyles, A., Cohen, L., & Brown, M. (2009). *Transforming Communities to Prevent Child Sexual Abuse and Exploitation: A Primary Prevention Approach.* Oakland: Prevention Institute.

Lynch, F. L., & Clarke, G. N. (2006). Estimating the Economic Burden of Depression in Children and Adolescents. *American Journal of Preventative Medicine, 31*, 143-151. Retrieved PDF - printed

Lyubomirsky, s. (n.d.). Retrieved from http://www.faculty.ucr.edu/~Sonja/papers/LKD2005.pdf

Lyubomirsky, S. (2007). *The How of Happiness.* New York: Penguin.

Lyubomirsky, S. (2008). *The How of Happiness: A Scientific Approach to Getting the Life You Want.* New York: The Penguin Press.

Lyubomirsky, S. S. (2005). Pursuring Happiness: The architecture of sustainable change. *Review of General Psychology*, 9: 111-31.

Lyubomirsky, S., & Porta, M. D. ((in press)). Boosting Happiness and Buttressing Resilience: Results from Cognitive and Behavioral Interventions. In J. W. Reich, A. J. Zautra, & J. Hall (Eds.), *Handbook of adult resilience: Concepts, methods, and application.* New York, NY, USA: Guilford Press. Retrieved 2015

Lyubomirsky, S., King, L., & Diener, E. (2005). The benefits of frequent positive affect: Does happiness lead to success? *Psychological Bulletin, 131*(6), 803-55.

Lyubomirsky, S., King, L., & Diener, E. (2005). The Benefits of Frequent Positive Affect: Does Happiness Lead to Success? *Psychological Bulletin, 131*(6), 803-855. doi:DOI: 10.1037/0033-2909.131.6.803

Maguire, E. G. (2000). Navigation-related structural change in the hippocampi of taxi drivers. *Proceedings of the National Academy of Sciences, USA, 97*(8): 4398-4403.

Maier, S. U., Makwana, A. B., & Hare, T. A. (2015, 8 5). Acute Stress Impairs Self-Control in Goal-Directed Choice by Altering Multiple Functional Connections within the Brain's Decision Circuits. *Neuron, 87*, 621-631.

Malta, L. A., McDonald, S. W., Hegadoren, K. M., Weller, C. A., & Tough, S. C. (2012, December 15). Influence of interpersonal violence on maternal anxiety, depression, stress and parenting morale in the early postpartum: a community based pregnancy cohort study. *BMC Pregnancy and Childbirth*, 153.

Mani, A., Mullainathan, S., Shafir, E., & Zhao, J. (2013). Poverty Impedes Cognitive Function. *Science*, 976-980.

Mansor, A., Kirmani, S., Tat, H. H., & Azzman, M. (2012). Harnessing Positivity at Workplace from Perception to Action. *Social and Behavioral Sciences, 40*, 557-564.

Marinier III, R. P., & Laird, J. E. (2008). A Cognitive Architecture Theory of Comprehension and Appraisal. *Journal of Cognitive Systems Research*, Epub.

Marques, A. H., Oliveira, P. A., Scomparini, L. B., Rêgo e Silva,1, U. M., Silva, A. C., Doretto, V., . . . Scivoletto, S. (2015). Community-Based Global Health Program for Maltreated Children and Adolescents in Brazil: The Equilibrium Program. *Frontiers in Psychiatry, 6*, Epub. doi:10.3389/fpsyt.2015.00102

Martin, R. C., & Dahlen, E. R. (2005). Cognitive emotion regulation in the prediction of depression, anxiety, stress, and anger. *Personality and Individual Differences*, 1249-1260. doi:doi:10.1016/j.paid.2005.06.004

Martins, A., Ramalho, N., & Morin, E. (2010). A Comprehensive meta-analysis of the relationship between Emotional Intelligence and health. *Personality and Individual Differences*, 554-564.

Martire, L. M., & Franks, M. M. (2014). The Role of Social Networks in Adult Health: Introduction to the Special Issue. *Healthy Psychology, 33*(6), 501-504. Retrieved 2016

Marx, D. M., Ko, S. J., & Friedman, R. A. (2009). The "Obama Effect": How a salient role model reduces race-based performance differences. *Journal of Experimental Social Psychology*, 953–956. doi:doi:10.1016/j.jesp.2009.03.012

Maslow, G. R., Dunlap, K., & Chung, R. J. (2015). Depression and Suicide in Children and Adolescents. *Pediatrics in Review, 36*(7).

Mason, D. (2011). *The H Factor: how Happiness Will Improve Your Bottom Line and Healp Your Organization Thrive.* Alpharetta: Dyer Publishing.

Mason, F., & Lodrick, Z. (2013). Psychological consequences of sexual assault. *Best Practices & Research clinical Obstetrics and Gynaecology 27*, 27-37.

Mason, W. A., Fleming, C. B., Ringle, J. L., Thompson, R. W., Haggerty, K. P., & Synyer, J. J. (2015). Reducing Risks for Problem Behaviors During the High School Transition: Proximal Outcomes in the Common Sense Parenting Trial. *Journal Child and Family Studies*, 2568-2578.

Mason, W. A., January, S. A., Fleming, C. B., Thompson, R. W., Parra, G. R., Haggerty, K. P., & Snyder, J. J. (2016, February). Parent Training to Reduce Problem Behaviors over the Transition to High School: Tests of Indirect Effects through Improved Emotion Regulation Skills. *Child Youth Services Review*, 176-183.

Massad, C. M. (1979). Selective perception of events. *Journal of Experimental Social Psychology*, 15(6): 513-532.

Masten, A. S., & Monn, A. R. (2015). Child and Family Resileince: A Call for Integrated Science, Practice, and Professional Training. *Family Rlations: Interdisciplinary Journal of Applied Family Studies, 64*, 5-21.

Master, J. C. (1979). Affective states, expressive behavior, and learning in children. *Journal of Personality and Social Psychology, 37*: 380-90.

Masters, D. P. (1975). *Ministers/Bachelors Degree Course Study Lessons*. California: International Metaphysical Ministry.

Masters, P. L. (1989 (revised 2012)). *Master's Degree Curriculum* (Vol. Volume 1). University of Metaphysics.

Masters, P. L. (1989). *Bachelor's Degree Curriculum* (Vol. 3). University of Metaphysics.

Masters, P. L. (1989). Bachelor's Degree Curriculum. University of Metaphysics.

Maston, A. S. (2001). Ordinary magic: Resilience processes in development. *American Psychologist, 56*: 27-38.

Matthews, E. E., & Cook, P. F. (2009). Relationships among optimism, well-being, self-transdence, coping, adn social support in women during treatment for breast cancer. *Psycho-Oncology, 18*. doi:DOI: 10.1002/pon.1461

Matthews, P. S. (Producer). (2016). *Epigenetics of Post Traumatic Slave Syndrome (PTSS) with Dr. Joy DeGruy (Part 1)* [Motion Picture]. Retrieved 2016 - associated with film Out of Darkness, from https://www.youtube.com/watch?v=l0-oKl_WIn4

Mawe, S. M. (n.d.). *Dandelion: The Extraordinary Life of a Misfit*.

Maxfield, M. G. (1996). The cycle of violence revisited 6 years later. *Archives of Pediatrics and Adolescent Medicine, 150*, 390-395.

Mayer, E. A. (2000). The neurobiology of stress and gastrointestinal disease. *Gut, 47*, 861-869. doi:doi:10.1136/gut.47.6.861

McCarthy, B. a. (2011). Get Happy! Positive Emotion, Depression and Juvenile Crime. *American Sociological Association Annual Meeting*. Las Vegas.

McCarthy, B., & Casey, T. (2011). Get Happy! Positive Emotion, Depression and Juvenile Crime. *American Sociological Associaion Annual Meeting*. Las Vegas: UC Davis.

McClave, A. K., Dube, S. R., Strine, T. W., Kroenke, K., Caraballo, R., & Mokdad, A. H. (2009). Associations between smoking cessation and anxiety and depression. *Addictive Behaviors*, 491-497.

McClellan, D. S. (1997). Early victimization, drug use, and criminality: A comparison of male and female prisoners. *Criminal Justice and Behavior, 24*, 455-476.

McClusky, M. (2014). Science Has Finally Figured Out How Elite Athletes Best Each Other. Pay Attention. *LinkedIn Pulse*.

McCracken, L. M., Gutierrez-Martinez, O., & Smyth, C. (2013). "Decentering" reflects psychological flexibility in people with chronic pain and correlates with their quality of functioning. *Health Psychology*, 820-3. Retrieved 2014

McCraty, R., & Atkinson, M. (2014). Electrophysiology of Intuition: Pre-stimulus Responses in Group and Individual Participants Using a Roulette Paradigm. *Global Advances in Health and Medicine, 3*(2), 16-27. doi:DOI:10.7453/gahmj.2014.014

McCraty, R., & Zayas, M. (2014). Intuitive Intelligence, Self-regulation, and Lifting Consciousness. *Global Advances in Health and Medicine, 3*(2), 56-65. doi:DOI: 10.7453/gahmj.2014.013

McCraty, R., Atkinson, M., & Bradley, R. T. (2004). Electrophysiological Evidence of Intuition. Part 1: The Surprising Role of the Heart," 10(1) (2004), pp. 133 - 143. *Journal of Alternative and Complementary Medicine, 10*(1), 133*143.

McDonald, G., Jackson, D., Wilkes, L., & Vickers, M. H. (2012). A work-based educational intervention to support the development of personal resilience in nurses and midwives. *Nurse Education Today, 32*, 378-384. doi:doi:10.1016/j.nedt.2011.04.012

McEwen, B. S. (1998). Protective and damaging effects of stress mediators. *New England Journal of Medicine*, 338: 171-79.

McEwen, B. S., & Stellar, E. (1993). Stress and the individual. Mechanisms leading to disease. *Archives of Internal Medicine, 153*(18), 2091-101.

McGee, R., & Williams, S. (2000). Does low self-esteem predict health compromising behaviours among adolescents? *Journal of Adolescense, 23*, 569-582.

McGregor, B. A., Antoni, M. H., Boyers, A., Alfen, S. M., Blomberg, B. B., & Carver, C. S. (2004, January). Cognitive-Behavioral stress management increases benefit finding and immune function among women with early-stage breast cancer. *ournal of Psychosomatic Research, 56*(1), 1-8.

McGregor, I., Haji, R., & Kang, S.-J. (2008). Can ingroup affirmation relieve outgroup derogation? *Journal of Experimental Social Psychology, 44*, 1395-1401. doi:doi:10.1016/j.jesp.2008.06.001

McGregor, J. (2006, July 10). Business Week. *How Failure Breeds Success*.

McHugh, R. K., Hearon, B. A., & Otto, M. W. (2010, September). Cognitive-Behavioral Therapy for Substance Use Disorders. *Psychiatric Clinics of North America, 33*(3), 511-525. doi:10.1016/j.psc.2010.04.012

McIlveen, P., Beccaria, G., & Burton, L. J. (2013). Beyond conscientiousness: Career optimism and satisfaction with academic major. *Journal of Vocational Behavior, 83*, 229-236. doi:http://dx.doi.org/10.1016/j.jvb.2013.05.005

McMillen, J. C. (1997). Perceived benefit and mental health after three types of disaster. *Journal of Consulting and Clinical Psychology*, 65: 733-739.

McSpadden, K. (2016, January last week). What we would do if we valued all children? *The Charlotte Observer*.

Meissner, C., & Brigham, J. (2001). Thirty years of investigating the own-race bias in memory for faces. *Psychology, Public Policy, and Law 7*, 3 - 35.

Merrifield, C., Balk, D., & Moscovitch, D. A. (2013). Self-portrayal concerns mediate the relationship between recalled teasing and social anxiety symptoms in adults with anxiety disorders. *Journal of Anxiety Disorders, 27*, 456-460.

Messman, T. L., & Long, P. J. (1996). Child Sexual Abuse and its Relationship to Revictimization in Adult Woman: A Review. *Clinical Psychology Review, 16*(5), 397-420.

Messman-Moore, T. L., & Brown, A. L. (2004). Child maltreatment and perceived family environment as risk factors for adult rape: is child sexual abuse the most salient experience? *Child Abuse & Neglect 28*, 1019–1034.

Miller, L. R., & Cano, A. (2009). Comorbid Chronic Pain and Depression: Who Is at Risk? *The journal of Pain*, 619-627.

Millings, A., Buck, R., Montgomery, A., Spears, M., & Stallard, P. (2012). School connectedness, peer attachment, and self-esteem as predictors. *Journal of Adolescence, 35*, 1061–1067.

Min, J. A., Yu, J. J., Lee, C. U., & Chae, J. H. (2013, November). Cognitive emotion regulation strategies contributing to resilience in patients with depression and/or anxiety disorders. *Comprehensive Psychiatry, 54*(8), 1190-7.

Min, J.-A., Lee, C.-U., & Lee, C. (2013). Mental Health Promotion and Illness Prevention: A Challenge for Psychiatrists. *Psychiatric Investigations*, Epub.

Mitsikostas, D. D., Mantonakis, L. I., & Charlarakis, N. G. (2010). Nocebo is the enemy, not placebo. A meta-analysis of reported side effects after placebo treatment in headaches. (I. H. Society, Ed.) *Cephalalgia, 0*(0), 1-12. doi:DOI: 10.1177/0333102410391485

Moffitt, T. E. (2001). Childhood predictors differentiate life-coursepersistent and adolescence-limited antisocial pathways among males and females. *Development and Psychopathology, 13*, 355-375.

Mohd, R. S. (2008, October). Life Event, Stress and Illness. *The Malaysian Journal of Medical Sciences, 15*(4), 9-18.

Moksnes, U. K., Moljord, I. E., Espnes, G. A., & Byrne, D. G. (2010). The association between stress and emotional states in adolescents: The role of gender and self-esteem. *Personality and Individual Differences, 49*, 430-435. doi:doi:10.1016/j.paid.2010.04.012

Monarch-butterfly.com. (n.d.). Retrieved from http://www.monarch-butterfly.com/

Montgomery, J. (2012, May). *Cafe Mom*, Cancer Might be the best thing that ever happened to me. Retrieved 2012, from http://wwwthestir.cafemom.com/healthy_living/136851/cancer_might_be_the_best

Morales, J. R., & Guerra, N. G. (2006, July/August). Effects of Multiple Context and Cumulative Stress on urban Children's Adjustment in Elementary School. *Child Development, 77*(4), 907-923.

Morley, S., Eccleston, C., & Williams, A. (1999). Systematic review and meta-analysis of randomized controlled trials of cognitive behaviour therapy and behaviour therapy for chronic pain in adults, excluding headache. (I. A. Pain, Ed.) *Pain, 80*, 1-13.

Moroz, S. E. (2015 , September). Discrimination is in the Eye of the Beholder: Perception of Discrimination and Microaggressions. *A thesis submitted in partial fulfillment of the requirements for the degree in Master of Science, Graduate Program in Psychology*. Ontario.

Moullec, L. K., & Blais, L. (2011). The efficacy of brief motivational interviewing to improve medication adherence in poorly controlled nonadherent asthmatics: results from a randomized controlled pilot study. *Program and abstrcts of the Chest 2011 Annual Meeting*, (p. Abstract 4). Honolulu.

Mroczek, D. K., & Spiro III, A. (2007, May). Personality Change Influences Mortality in Older Men. *Association for Psychological Science, 18*(5), 371-376. doi:doi:10.1111/j.1467-9280.2007.01907.x.

Muehsam, D., & Ventura, C. (2014, March). Life Rhythm as a Symphony of Oscillatory Patterns: Electromagnetic Energy and Sound Vibration Modulaes Gene Expression for Biological Signaling and Healing. *Global Advances in Health and Medicine, 3*(2), 40-55.

Mulford, C., & Giordano, P. (2008, October). Teen Dating Violence: A Closer Look at Adolescent Romantic Relationships. *National Institute of Justice*, NCJ 224089.

Munro, E. (2013). "People just need to feel important, like someone is listening": Recognising museums' community engagement programmes as spaces of care. *Geoforum, 48*, 54-62. doi:http://dx.doi.org/10.1016/j.geoforum.2013.04.008

Murphy, D.D., Ph.D., J. (1968). *The Cosmic Power Within You*. West Nyack.

Murphy, E. R., Barch, D. M., Pagliaccio, D., Luby, J. L., & Belden, A. C. (2015 (in press)). Functional connectivity of the amygdala and subgenual cingulate during cognitive reappraisal of emotions in children with MDD history is associated with rumination. *Developmental Cognitive Neuroscience*.

Murphy, J. (1964SA). *The Miracle of Mind Dynamics*. Reward Books.

Murphy, R., Straebler, S., Cooper, Z., & Fairburn, C. G. (2010, September). Cognitive Behavioral Therapy for Eating Disorders. *The Psychiatric Clinics of North America*, 611-627. doi:10.1016/j.psc.2010.04.004

Nadal, K. L., Wong, Y., Issa, M.-A., Meterko, V., Leon, J., & Wideman, M. (2011). Sexual Orientation Microaggressions: Processes and Coping for Lesbian, Gay, and Bisexual Individuals. *Journal of LGBT Issues in Counseling, 5*(1), 21-46.

Nadler, R. S. (2011). *Leading with emotional Intelligence: Hands-on strategies for building confident and collaborative star performers.* New York: McGraw Hill.

name, a. (2014, 3 3). ACA stinks. *WSJ.*

NAMI - National Alliance for Mental Illness. (2013). *Fact Sheet.* Arlington: NAMI.

Namrata. (2011). Teachers' beliefs and expectations towards marginalized children in a classroom setting: a qualitative analysis. *Procedia Social and Behavioral Sciences, 15,* 850-853. doi:doi:10.1016/j.sbspro.2011.03.197

Nancy S. Wu, L. C. (2010). Childhood trauma and health outcomes in adults with comorbid substance abuse mental health disorders. *Addictive Behaviors, 35,* 68-71.

National Alliance on Mental Illness. (2016). *Famous People with Mental Illness.* Retrieved from NAMI.org: http://namivirginia.org/assets/pdfs/Famous%20People%20with%20Mental%20Illness%20Powerpoint%20Presentation.pdf

National Center for Chronic Disease Prevention and Health Promotion. (2009). *Adverse Childhood Experiences Reported by Adults--Five States.* National Center for Chronic Disease Prevention and Health Promotion, Division of Adult and Community Health. Retrieved 2016

National Institute of Justice. (2012). Findings from the Comprehensive National Survey on Children's Exposure to Violence. *National Institute of Justice,* Epub.

Nearchou, F. A., Stogiannidou, A., & Kiosseoglou, G. (2014). Adaptation and Psychometric Evaluation of a Resilience Measure in Greek Elementary School Students. *Psychology in the Schools, 51*(1), 58-95. Retrieved 2015

Neff, K. D. (2003). The Development and Validation of a Scale to Measure Self-Compassoin. *Self and Identity, 2,* 223-250. doi:DOI: 10.1080/15298860390209035

Nelson, S. K., Fuller, J. A., Choi, I., & Lyubomirsky, S. (2014, April 29). Beyond Self-Protection: Self-Affirmation Benefits Hedonic and Eudaimonic Well-Being. *Personality and Social Psychology Bulletin, 40*(8), 998-1011.

Nettles, R., & Balter, R. (Eds.). (2011). *Multiple Minority Identities.* New York, NY, USA: Springer Publishing Company.

Newall, N. E., Chipperfield, J. G., Bailis, D. S., & Stewart, T. L. (2013). Consequences of Loneliness on Physical Activity and Mortality in Older Adults and the Power of Positive Emotions. *Health Psychology, 32*(8), 921-924. doi:http://dx.doi.org/10.1037/a0029413

Newell, B. R., & Shanks, D. R. (2014). Unconscious influences on decision making: A Critical Review. *Behavioral and Brain Sciences, 37,* 1-61.

Newman, M. L., Holden, G. W., & Delville, Y. (2005). Isolation and the stress of being bullied. *Journal of Adolescence, 28,* 343-357.

Ng, J. Y., Ntoumanis, N., & Thorgersen-Ntoumani, C. (2014). Autonomy support and control in weight management: What important others do and say matters. *British Journal of Health Psychology, 19,* 540-552.

NHS. (2009). *2009 NHS Health and Well-Being report.*

NHS. (2009). *Airedale Case Study.* NHS Trust. Retrieved 8 29, 2014, from http://www.nhshealthandwellbeing.org/pdfs/Staff%20H&WB%20Case%20Studies%20VFinal%2023-11-09.pdf

Nietzel, M. T., & Himelein, M. J. (1987, Spring). Crime Prevention Through Social and Physical Environmental Change. *The Behavior Analyst, 10*(1), 69-74.

NIH. (n.d.). *National Institute of Health.* Retrieved 2014, from http://www.nlm.nih.gov/medlineplus/magazine/issues/winter08/articles/winter08pg6b.html

Nisbett, R. E. (2003). *The Geography of Thought: How Asians and Westerners Think Differently...and Why.* New York: The Free Press.

Nolen-Hoekosema, S. G. (1986). Learned helplessness in children: A longitudinal study depression, achievement, and explanatory style. *Journal of Personality and Social Psychology,* 51: 435-442.

Norrish, J. M., Williams, P., O'Connor, M., & Robinson, J. (2013). An applied framework for Positive Education. *International Journal of Wellbeing, 3*(2), 147-.

Nudo, R. J. (1996). Use dependent alterations of movement representations in primary motor cortex of adult squirrel monkeys. *Journal of Neuroscience,* 16: 785-807.

O'Doherty, F. (1991). Is drug use a response to stress? *Drug and Alcohol Dependence, 29,* 97-106.

Oishi, S., & Schimmack, U. (2010, July). Culture and Well-Being: A New Inquiry Into the Psychological Wealth of Nations. *Pespectives on Psychological Science, 5*(4), 463-471.

O'keefe, V. M., Wingate, L. R., Cole, A. B., Hollingsworth, D. W., & Tucker, R. P. (2015). Seemingly Harmless Racial Communications Are Not So Harmless: Racial Microaggressoins Lead to Suicidal Ideation by Way of Depressive Symptoms. *Suicide and Life-Threatening Behavior, 45*(5), 567-676. doi:DOI: 10.1111/sltb.12150

Okon-Singer, H., Hendler, T., Pessoa, L., & Shackman, A. J. (2015, February). The neurobiology of emotion-cognition interactions: fundamental questions and strategies for future research. *Frontiers in Human Neuroscience, 9,* 1-14. doi:doi: 10.3389/fnhum.2015.00058

Okunda, M., Balán, I., Petry, N. M., Oquendo, M., & Blanco, C. (2009, December). Cognitive Behavioral Therapy for Pathological Gambling: Cultural Considerations. *American Journal of Psychiatry, 166*(12), 1325-1330. doi:doi:10.1176/appi.ajp.2009.08081235.

Ong, A. D., Bergeman, C. S., Bisconti, T. L., & Wallace, K. A. (2006). Psychological Resilience, Postive Emotions, and Successful Adaptation to Stress in Later Life. *Journal of Personaltiy and Social Psychology 91*, 730-49.

Ong, A. D., Burrow, A. L., & Fuller-Rowell, T. E. (2012, October). Positive emotions and the social broadening effects of Barack Obama. *Cultural Diversity and Ethnic Minority Psychology, 18*(4), 424-428.

Ong, A. D., Mroczek, D. K., & Riffin, C. (2011, August 1). The Health Significance of Positive Emotions in Adulthood and Later Life. *Social and Personality Psychology Compass, 5*(8), 538-551. doi:doi: 10.1111/j.1751-9004.2011.00370.x

Ornstein, R. E. (1977). *The Psychology of Consciousness.* Harcourt Brace Jovanovich, Inc.

Ostir, G. V. (2001). The association between emotional well-being and teh incidence of stroke in older adults. *Psychosomatic Medicine,* 63: 210-15.

Ostir, G. V., Markides, K. S., Black, S. A., & Goodwin, J. S. (2000). Emotional well-being predicts subsequent functional independence and survival. *Jouranl American Geriatric Society,* 473-478.

Ou, S.-R., & Reynolds, A. J. (2010). Childhood predictors of young adult male crime. *Children and Youth Services Review, 32,* 1097-1107. doi:doi:10.1016/j.childyouth.2010.02.009

Outcomes, C. o. (2007). *Preterm Birth: Causes, Consequences, and Prevention.* (R. E. Behrman, & A. S. Butler, Eds.) National Academies Press. Retrieved from http://www.nap.edu/catalog/11622.html

Ozier, A. D., Kendrick, O. W., Leeper, J. D., Knol, L. L., Perko, M., & Burnham, J. (2008). Overweight and Obesity Are Associated with Emotion-and Stress-Related Eating as Measured by the Eating and Appraisal Due to Emotions and Stress Questionnaire. *Journal of the AMERICAN DIETETIC ASSOCIATION.* doi:doi: 10.1016/j.jada.2007.10.011

Padgett, D. A., & Glaser, R. (2003). How stress influences the immune response. *TRENDS in Immunology, 24*(8). doi:doi:10.1016/S1471-4906(03)00173-X

Pahl, J. R. (2001). Optimism, Pessimism, and the Direction of Self-Other Comparisons. *Journal of Experimental Social Psychology 37,* 77-84.

Parashar, F. (2015). *Optimism and Pessimism.* Retrieved from www.positivepsychology.org: www.positivepsychology.org

Parton, S. (2016, March 12). Complaining is Terrible for You, According to Science. (J. Stillman, Interviewer)

Patchell, B. (2014). Coherent Learning: Creating High-leel Performance and Cultural Empathy from Student to Expert. *Scientific Abstracts on Health and Organizational Outcomes in Healthcare, 3*(1), 20.

Paul, K. I., & Moser, K. (2009). Unemployment impairs mental health: Meta-Analysis. *Journal of Vocational Behavior, 74,* 264-282.

Paulson, T. L. (2010). *The Optimism Advantage: 50 Simple Truths to transform Your Attitudes and Actions into Results.* Hoboken: Wiley.

Paulus, D. J., Vanwoerden, S., Norton, P. J., & Sharp, C. (2016, January 15). Emotion dysregulation, psychological inflexibility, and shame as explanatory factors between neuroticism and depression. *Journal of Affective Disorders, 190,* 376-385. doi:http://dx.doi.org/10.1016/j.jad.2015.10.014

Pedersen, A., Zachariae, R., & Boybjerg, D. H. (2010, October). Influence of psychological stress on upper respiratory infection--a metaanalysis. *Psychosomatic Medicine, 72*(8), 823-32. doi:doi: 10.1097/PSY.0b013e3181f1d003.

Peeters, C. F., Klaassen, C. A., & van de Wiel, M. A. (15). *Evaluating the Scientific Veracity of Publications by dr. Jens Förster.* University of Amsterdam.

Peil, K. T. (2014). Emotion: A Self-regulatory Sense.

Perez-De-Albeniz, A., & Holmes, J. (2000). Meditation: concepts, effects and uses in therapy. *International Journal of Psychotherapy, 5,* 49-59.

Perrewe, P. L., & Zellars, K. I. (1999). An examination of attributions and emotions in the transational approach to the organizational stress process. *Journal of Organizational Behavior, 20,* 739-752.

Petersen, G. L., Finnerup, N. B., Colloca, L., Amanzio, M., Price, D. D., Jensen, T. S., & Vase, L. (2014). The magnitude of nocebo effects in pain: A meta-analysis. *Pain, 155*(8), 1426-1434. doi:doi:10.1016/j.pain.2014.04.016.

Peterson, C. &. (1987). Explanatory style and academic performance among university freshmen. *Journal of Personality and Social Psychology,* 53: 603-607.

Peterson, J. L., & DeHart, T. (2013). Regulating connection: Implicit self-esteem predicts positive non-verbal behavior. *Journal of Experimental Social Psychology,* 99-105.

Peterson, T. D. (2009). Yale Journal of Health Policy, Law, and Ethics. 9:357-434.

Bibliography

Petit, G., Luminet, O., Maurage, F., Tecco, J., Lechantre, S., Ferauge, M., . . . de Timary, P. (2015, December). Emotion Regulation in Alcohol dependence. *ALCOHOLISM: CLINICAL AND EXPERIMENTAL RESEARCH, 39*(12). doi:10.1111/acer.12914

Petronella Croisant, S. A., Laz, T. H., Rahman, M., & Berenson, A. B. (2013). Gender Differences in Risk Behaviors Among High School Youth. *Global Advances in Health and Medicine, 2*(5), 16-22.

Pew Research Center Social & Demographic Trends. (2014). *The Rising Cost of Not Going to College.* Washington D.C.: Pew Research Center.

Phillips, L. J., McGorry, P. D., Garner, B., Thompson, K. N., Pantelis, C., Wood, S. J., & Berger, G. (2006). Stress, the hippocampus and the hypothalamic-pituitary-adrenal axis: implications for the development of psychotic disorders. *Australian/New Zealand Journal of Psychiatry, 40*(9), 724-741.

Piaget, J. (1932). *The Moral Judgment of the Child.* Rouledge, Trench, Trubner & Co., Ltd.

Pietrzak, R. H., & Southwick, S. M. (2011). Psychological resilience in OEF–OIF Veterans: Application of a novel classification approach and examination of demographic and psychosocial correlates. *Journal of Affective Disorders, 133*, 560-568.

Pinquart, M. (2009). Moderating effects of dispositional resilience on associations between hassles and psychological distress. *Journal of Applied Developmental Psychology, 30*, 53-60.

Plank, M. (1936, January). New Ideas. *Surving the Swastika: Scientific Research in Nazi Germany.*

Plant, E. A., Peruche, M., & Butz, D. A. (2005). Eliminating automatic racial bias: Making race non-diagnostic for responses to criminal suspects. *Journal of Experimental Social Psychology, 41*, 141-156.

Polley, R. B. (1998). The SYMLOG Practitioner: Applications of small group research (New York: Praeger). In D. Goleman, *Working with Emotional Intelligence* (p. p. 188). New York: Bantam.

Polman, E., & Kim, S. H. (2013, December). Effects of Anger, Disgust, and Sadness on Sharing with Others. *Personality and Social Psychology Bulletin, 39*(12), 1683-1692. doi:doi: 10.1177/0146167213500998

Polman, E., & Ruttan, R. L. (2011, September 14). Effects of Anger, Guilt, and Envy on Moral Hypocrisy. *Personality and Social Psychology Bulletin*, 129-139. doi: doi: 10.1177/0146167211422365

Pool, G. J., Wood, W., & Leck, K. (1998). The Self-Esteem Motive in Social Influence: Agreement With Valued Majorities and Disagreement with Derogated Minorities. *Journal of Personality and Social Psychology, 75*(4), 967-975. doi:0022-3514/98/$3.00

Pool, L. D., & Qualter, P. (2012). Improving emotional intelligence and emotional self-efficacy through a teaching intervention for university students. *Learning and Individual Differences, 22*, 306-312.

Popp, F., Nagl, W., Wolf, R., Li, K. H., Scholz, W., & Weingartner, O. (1984). New evidence for Coherence and DNA as Source. *Cell Biophysics*, 33-52.

Post, S. G. (2005). Altruism, happiness, and health: It's good to be good. *International Journal of Behavioral Medicine, 12*: 66-77.

Postmes, L., Sno, H. N., Goedhart, S., van der Stel, J., Heering, H. D., & de Haan, L. (2014). Schizophrenia as a self-disorder due to perceptual incoherence. *Schizophrenia Research, 152*, 41-50. doi:http://dx.doi.org/10.1016/j.schres.2013.07.027

Poulin, i. J. (2014). Volunteering Predicts Health Among Those Who Value Others: Two National Studies. *Health Psychology, 33*(2), 120-129. doi:http://dx.doi.org/10.1037/a0031620

Powell, S. R. (2003). Posttraumatic growth after war: A study with former refugees and displaced people in Sarajevo. *Journal of Clinical Psychology, 59*: 71-83.

Press, A. (June 18, 2008). *Gallup-Healthways Well-Being Index.* Poll: Unhappy workers take more sick days.

Pressman, S. D. (2005). Does positive affect influence health? *Psychological Bulletin*, 131: 925-71.

Prevention Institute. (n.d.). *Fact Sheet: Vilence and Chronic Illness.*

Prevention, A. F. (n.d.). *After a Suicidie: A Toolkit for Schools.* Retrieved 2014, from Suicide Prevention Resource Center: http://www.sprc.org/sites/sprc.org/files/library/AfteraSuicideToolkitforSchools.pdf?sid=38034

Priest, N., Paradies, Y., Trenerry, B., Truong, M., Karlsen, S., & Kelly, Y. (2012). A Systematic review of studies examining the relationship between reported racism and health and wellbeing for children and young people. *Social Science & Medicine*, 408-415.

Promising Practices Network. (2003). *Cognitive Behavioral Intervention for Trauma in Schools (CBITS).*

Pryce-Jones, J. (2010). *Happiness at Work: maximizing your Psychological Capital for Success.* Wiley-Blackwell.

Puhl, R., Luedicke, J., & Peterson, J. L. (2013). Public Reactions to Obesity-Related Health Campaigns: A Randomized Controlled Trial. *American Journal of Preventive Medicine, 45*(1): 36-48.

Pyszczynski, T., Greenberg, J., Solomon, S., Arndt, J., & Schimel, J. (2004). Why Do People Need Self-Esteem? A Theoretical and Empirical Review. *Psychological Bulletin, 130*, 435-468. doi:DOI: 10.1037/0033-2909.130.3.435

Quigley, K. S., & Barrett, L. F. (2014 (in press)). Is there consistency and specificity of autonomic changes during emotional episodes? Guidance from the conceptual act theory and psychophysiology. *Biological Psychology*, xxx-xxx. Retrieved 2014

Quon, E. C., & McGrath, J. J. (2013). Subjective Socioeconomic Status and Adolescent Health: A Meta-Analysis. *Heatlh Psychology, 33*(5), 433-447. doi:http://dx.doi.org/10.1037/a0033716

Raedt, R. D. (2012). Cognitive Control moderates the association between stress and rumination. *Journal of Behavior Therapy and Experimental Psychiatry*, 519-525.

Räikkönen K., M. K. (1999). Effects of optimism, pessimism, and trait anxiety on ambulatory blood pressure and mood during everyday life. *Journal of Personality and Social Psychology*, 76(1): 104-13.

Ramsey , D. X. (2013, May 26). *Black woman rises to leadership in Daughters of the American Revolution*. Retrieved from TheGrio.com: http://thegrio.com/2013/05/26/black-woman-rises-to-leadership-in-daughters-of-the-american-revolution/2/#allen-craft_right_with_gloria_williams

Raposa, E. B., Hammen, C. L., Brennan, P. A., Najman, J. M., & O'Callaghan, F. (2014). Early Adversity and Heatlh Outcomes in Young Adults: The Role of Ongoing Stress. *Health Psychology, Vol. 33, No. 5*, 410-418.

Rattan, A., Savani, K., Chugh, D., & Dweck, C. S. (2015). Leveraging Mindsets to Promote Academic Achievement: Policy Recommendations. *Perspectives on Psychological Science, 10*(6), 721-726.

Rebekah E. Gunns, L. J. (2002 Fall). Victim Selection and Kinematics: A Point-Light investigation of vulnerability to attack. *JOURNAL OF NONVERBAL BEHAVIOR 26(3),*.

Reckenwald, A., Mancini, C., & Beauregard, E. (2013). The Cycle of Violence: Examining the Impact of Maltreatment Early in Life on Adult Offending. *Violence and Victims, 28*(3), p. 466-482(17). doi:http://dx.doi.org/10.1891/0886-6708.VV-D-12-00054

Reeve, C. (2002). *Nothing is Imposible: Reflections on a New Life*. Random House.

Regional Research Institute for Human Services. (2005, Summer). Building Hope for Adolescents: The Importance of A Secure Social Base. *FOCAL POINT Research, Policy, and Practice in Children's Mental Health*, p. 1.

Rhodes, G. S., Brake, & et al. (1989). Expertise and configural coding in race recognition. *British Journal of Psychology*, 313-31.

Rhodes, G., Brake, S., & et al. (1989). Expertise and configural coding in face recognition. *British Journal of Psychology 80*, 313-31.

Ricard, M. (2003). *Happiness: A Guide to Developing Life's Most Important Skill*. Little, Brown and Company.

Riccomini, P. J., Bost, L. W., Katsiyannis, A., & Zhang, D. (2005). *Cognitive Behavioral Interventions: An Effective Approach to Help Students wtih Disabilities Stay in School*. National Dropout Prevention Center for Students with Disabilities (NDPC-SD) , College of Health, Education, and Human Development - Clemson University. Clemson: Office of Special Education Programs of the U.S. Department of Education. Retrieved from http://www.ndpc-sd.org/documents/Practice_Guides/CBI_Practice_Brief.pdf

Rice. (n.d.). *Biography.com*. Retrieved July 16, 2014, from http://www.biography.com/people/condoleezza-rice-9456857

Richard G. Wilkinson, K. E. (2006). Income inequality and population health: A review and explanation of the evidence. *Social Science & Medicine 62* , 1768–1784. Retrieved from www.elsevier.com/locate/socscimed

Richard W. Voss, D. M. (1997, Summer). Beyond the Telescope of Gender-polemics: Need for a Wide Angle Lens in Pastoral Vision. *The Journal of Pastoral Care, 51*(2).

Ritter, N. (2013, February). Predicting Recidivism Risk: New Tool in Philadelphia Shows Great Promise. *National Institute of Justice, 271*, NCJ 240696.

Riva, P., Wirth, J. H., & Williams, K. D. (2011). The Consequence of Pain: The social and psysical pain overlap on psychological responses. *European Journal of Social Psychology, 41*, 681-687. Retrieved 2015

Rivera, B. &. (1990). Childhood victimization and violent offending. *Violence and Victims, 5*, 19-35.

Robbins, A. (1991). *Awaken the Giant Within*. New York: Free Press.

Robbins, S. P. (2016). From the Editor--Sticks and Stones: Trigger Warnings, Microaggressions, and Political Correctness. *Journal of Social Work Education, 52*(1), 1-5.

Roberson, D., Davidoff, J., Davies, I. R., & Shapiro, L. R. (2004). The Development of Color Categories in Two Languages: A Longitudinal Study. *Journal of Experimental Psychology, 133*(4), 554-571. doi:http://dx.doi.org/10.1037/0096-3445.133.4.554

Robert A. Rissman, M. A. (2012). Corticotropin-releasing factor receptor-dependent effects of repeated stress on tau phosphorylation, solubility, and aggregation. *Proceedings of the National Academy of Sciences*. doi:10.1073/pnas.1203140109

Robert Assagioli, M. (1965). *Psychosynthesis: A collection of basic writings*. New York: The Viking Press.

Robert Wood Johnson Foundation. (2015). *How Children's Social Competenece Impacts Their Well-Being in Adulthood: Findings from a 20-Year Study on the Outcomes of Children Screened in Kindergarten*. RWJF. Robert Wood Johnson Foundation. doi:http://www.rwjf.org/en/library/research/2015/07/how-children-s-social-competence-impacts-their-well-being-in-adu.html

Robertson, S. M., Stanley, M. A., Cully, J. A., & Naik, A. D. (2012). Positive Emotional Health and Diasbetes Care: Concepts, Measurement, and Clinical Implications. *Psychosomatics, 53*, 1-12.

Robins, J. L., McCain, N. L., Gray, D. P., Elswick, R. K., Walter, J. M., & McDade, E. (2006). Research on psychoneuroimmunology tai chi as a stress management approach for individuals with HIV disease. *Applied Nursing Research, 19*(1), 2-9. Retrieved from http://www.ncbi.nlm.nih.gov/pmc/articles/PMC2211366/

Robins, J. W., McCain, N. L., Gray, D. P., Elswick, R. K., Walter, J. M., & McDade, E. (2006). Research on psychoneuroimmunology: Tai Chi as a stress management approach for individuals with HIV disease. *Applied Nursing Research, 19*(1), 2-9. Retrieved from http://www.ncbi.nlm.nih.gov/pmc/articles/PMC2211366/pdf/nihms37158.pdf

Robinson-Whelen S, K. C.-G. (1997). Distinguishing optimism from pessimism in older adults: is it more important to be optimistic or not to be pessimistic? *Journal Personality and Social Psychology, 73*(6): 1345-53.

Robinson-Wood, T., Balogun-Mwangi, O., Boadi, N., Fernandes, C., Matsumoto, A., Popat-Jain, A., & Zhang, Z. (2015). Worse Than Blatant Racism: Phenomenological Investigation of Microaggressions among Black Women. *Journal of Ethnographic & Qualitative Research, 9*, 221-236.

Rodriguez-Cerdeira, C., Pera-Grasa, J. T., Molares, A., Isa-Isa, R., & Arenas-Guzmán, R. (2011, September). Psychodermatology: Past, Present and Future. *The Open Dermatology Journal, 5*, 21-27.

Roger VL, G. A.-J. (n.d.). *Heart disease and stroke statistics--2012 update: a report from the American Heart Association.* American Heart Association Statistics Committee and Stroke.

Rollin, M., Bradley, R. T., & Atkinson, M. (2004). Electropsyciological Evidence of Intuition. Part 1: The Surprising Role of the Heart. *Journal of alternative and Complementary Medicine*, 10(1) pp. 133-143.

Ronit Peled, D. C.-S.-V. (2008). Breast cancer, psychological distress and life events among young women. *BMC Cancer*, 8:245. doi:doi:10.1186/1471-2407-8-245

Rose, A. J., Carlson, W., & Waller, E. M. (2007). Prospective Associations of Co-Rumination with Friendship and Emotional Adjustment: Considering the Socioemotional Trade--Offs of Co-Rumination. *Developmental Psychology, 43*(4), 1019-1031.

Rosenberg, T. (2015, January 15). For Better Crime Prevention, a Dose of Science. *The New York Times*, p. The Opinion Pages.

Rosenthal, R., & Jacobson, L. (1966). Teachers' Expectancies: Determinants of Pupils' IQ Gains. *Psychological Reports*, 115-118.

Rosenthal, R., & Lawson, R. (1963). A Longitudinal Study of the Effects of Experimenter Bias on the Operant Learning of Laboratory Rats. *Journal Psychiatric Research*, 61-72.

Ross-Sheriff, F. (n.d.). Microaggression, Women, and Social Work. *Journal of Women and Social Work, 27*(3), 233-236. doi:DOI: 10.1177/0886109912454366

Roth, T. L., Lubin, F. D., Funk, A. J., & Sweatt, J. D. (2009). Lasting Epigenetic Influence of Early-Life Adversity on the BDNF Gene. *Society of Biophysical Psychiatry*, 65:760–769.

Rowe, G. H. (2007). Positive affect increase the breath of attentional selection. *Proceedings of the National Academy of Sciences of the United States of America*, 104: 383-88.

Rubenstein, E. (1999). *An Awakening from the Trances of Everyday Life: A Journey to Empowerment.* Sages Way Press.

Rubie-Davies, C., Hattie, J., & Hamilton, R. (2003). Great Expectations: Implications for New Zealand Students. *NZARE Conference 2003*, (pp. 1-14). Auckland.

Rubik, B., Muehsam, D., Hammerschlag, R., & Jain, S. (2015). Biofield Science and Healing: History, Terminology, and Concepts. *Global Advances in Health and Medicine*, suppl 8-14.

Rubin, A. (n.d.). Psychological Stress and Immune Function.

Rudy, B. M., David III, T. E., & Matthews, R. A. (2012). The Relationship Among Self-efficacy, Negative Self-referent Cognitions, and Social Anxiety in Children: A Multiple Mediator Model. *Behavior Therapy, 43*, 19-628.

Russell, D. E. (1986). *The Secret Trauma: Incest in the Live of Girls and Women.* New York: Basic Books.

Rutter, M. (1987). Psychosocial resilience and protective mechanisms. *American Journal of Orthopsychiatry*, 316-331.

Ryan, J. G. (2009). Cost and Policy Implications From the Increasing Prevalence of Obesity and Diabetes Mellitus. *Gender Medicine, 6*(Theme Issue).

Ryan, R. M., & Deci, E. L. (2008). A Self-Determination Theory Approach to Psychotherapy: The Motivational Basis for Effective Change. *Canadian Psychology, 49*(3), 186-193.

Ryan, R. M., & Deci, L. E. (2001). On Happiness and Human Potentials: A Review of Research on Hedonic and Eudaimonic Well-Being. *Annual Review Psychology, 52*, 141-66.

Ryff, C. D., Singer, B. H., & Dienberg Love, G. (2004). Positive health: connecting well-being with biology. *Philos Trans R Soc Lond B Biol Sci.*, 1383-94.

Sachs-Ericsson, N., Blazer, D., & Arnow, B. (n.d.). Childhood sexual and physical abuse and the 1-year prevalence of medical problems in the National Comorbidity Survey. *Health Psychology*, 32-40.

Sachs-Ericsson, N., Cromer, K., Hernandez, A., & Kendall-Tackett, K. (n.d.). A Review of childhood Abuse, Health, and Pain-Related Problems: The Role of Psychiatric Disorders and Current Life Stress. 170-188. doi:10.1080/15299730802624585

Sachs-Ericsson, N., Kendall-Tackett, K., & Hernandez, A. (2007). Childhood abuse, chronic pain, and depression in the National Comorbidity Survey. *Child Abuse & Neglect, 31*, 531-547.

Sachs-Ericsson, Natalie, Verona, E., Joiner, T., & Preacher, K. J. (2006, July). Parental verbal abuse and the mediating role of self-criticism in adult internalizing disorders. *Journal of affective disorders, 93*, 71-78.

Salami, S. O. (2007). Management of Stress among Trainee-Teachers Through Cognitive-Behavioural Therapy. *Pakistan Journal of Social Sciences, 4*(2), 299-307.

Saleminka, E., van den Houta, M., & Kind, M. (2007). Trained interpretive bias: Validity and effects on anxiety. *Journal of Behavior Therapy and Experimental Psychiatry 34*, 45–63.

Salwen, J. K., Hymowitz, G. F., Vivian, D., & O'Leary, K. D. (2014 (in press)). Childhood abuse, adult interpersonal abuse, and depression in individuals with extreme obesity. *Child Abuse & Neglect*, xxx-xxx. Retrieved 2014, from http://dx.doi.org/10.1016/j.chiabu.2013.12.005

Salwen, J. K., Hymowitz, G. F., Vivian, D., & O'Leary, K. D. (2014). Childhood abuse, adult interpersonal abuse, and depression in individuals with extreme obesity. *Child Abuse & Neglect*, xxx-xxx (In Press).

Sandberg, J. (2000). Understanding Human Competence at Work: An Interpretative Approach. *Academy of Management Journal, 43*(1), 9 - 25.

Sani, F., Herrera, M., Wakefield, J. R., Boroch, O., & Gulyas, C. (2012). Comparing social contact and group identification as predictors of mental health. *The British Psychological Society, 51*, 781-790. doi:DOI:10.1111/j.2044-8309.2012.02101.x

Sani, F., Madhok, V., Norbury, M., Dugard, P., & Wakefield, J. R. (2015). Greater number of group identification is associated with healthier behavior: Evidence from a Scottish community sample. *British ournal of Health Psychology, 20*, 466-481.

Sarah Wheeler, A. B. (2009). Psychopathic Traits and Perceptions of Victim Vulnerability. *Criminal Justice and Behavior*. doi:DOI: 10.1177/0093854809333958

Sarma, K. (2008). *Mental Resilience: The Power of Clarity: how to develop the focus of a warrior and the peace of a monk*. Novato: New World Library.

Sarno, J. (1991). *Healing Back Pain: The Mind-Body Connection*. New York: Warner.

Satinsky, S., Reece, M., Dennis, B., Sanders, S., & Sardzell, S. (2012). An assessment of body appreciation and its relationship to sexual function in women. *Body Image, 9*, 137-144.

Saxbe, D. E., Margolin, G., Shapiro, L. S., Ramos, M., Rodriguez, A., & Iturralde, E. (2014). Relative Influences: Patterns of HPA Axis Concordance During Triadic Family Interaction. *Health Psychology, 33*(3), 73-281. doi:http://dx.doi.org/10.1037/a0033509

Sbarra, , D. A., Smith, H. L., & Mehl, M. R. (2001, September 21). Advice to divorcees: Go easy on yourself. *Association for Psychological Science*.

Schafer, M. H., Wilkinson, L. R., & Ferraro, K. F. (2013, March). Childhood (Mis)fortune, Educational Attainment, and Adult Health: Contingent Benefits of a College Degree? *College completion and Adult Health, 91*(3), 1007-1034. doi:doi: 10.1093/sf/sos192

Scheier, M. F. (1989). Dispositional optimism and recovery from coronary artery bypass surgery. The beneficial effects on physical and psychological well-being. *Journal of Personality and Social Psychology*, 57: 1024-1040.

Schleider, J. L., Velex, C. E., Krause, E. D., & Gillham, J. (2014). Perceived Psychological Control and Anxiety in Early Adolescents: The Mediating Role of Attributional Style. *Cognitive Therapy Research*, 38: 71-81.

Schmitz, T. W. (2009). Opposing influence of affective state valence on visual cortical-encoding. *Journal of Neuroscience*, 29: 7199-7207.

Schnall, S., & Roper, J. (2010). Elevation Puts Moral Values Into Action. *Dept of Social and Developmental Psychology, University of Cambridge, School of Psychology*.

Schnall, S., Roper, J., & Fessler, D. M. (2010). Elevation Leads to Altruistic Behavior. *Psychological Science*. doi:DOI: 10.1177/0956797609359882

Schnall, S., Roper, J., & Fessler, D. M. (2010, February 3). Pay It Forward: Elevation Leads to Altruistic Behavior. *Psychological Science*.

Schneider, K. L., Appelhans, B. M., Whited , M. C., Oleski, J., & Pagoto, S. L. (2010, December). Trait anxiety, but not trait anger, predisposes obese individuals to emotional eating. *Appetite*, 701-706. doi:doi: 10.1016/j.appet.2010.10.006

Schneider, T. R. (2004). The role of neuroticism on psychological and physiological stress responses. *Journal of Experimental Social Psychology*, 795-804.

Schoemaker, P. J. (2006, June). Wisdom of deliberate mistakes. *Harvard Business Review*.

Schubert, C. (2012, May). Pursuing Happiness. *KYKLOS, 65*(2), 2445-261.

Schwartz, D. J. (1965). *The Magic of Thinking Big*. New York: Prentice-Hall.

Schwartz, et al. (2003). Altruistic social interest behaviors are associated with better mental health. *Psychosomatic Medicine*, 65: 778-785.

Schwartz, J. M. (2003). *The Mind and The Brain: Neuroplasticity and the Power of Mental Force*. New York: Harper Perennial.

Schwartz, M. (2013, July). Low Self-Esteem: A Missed Diagnosis. *Psychology Today*.

Schwarz, D. J. (1959 (2007)). *The Magic of Thinking BIG*. New York: Simon & Schuster.

Scoglio, A. A., Rudat, D. A., Garvert, D., Jarmolowski, M., Jackson, C., & Herman, J. L. (2015, December 16). Self-Compassion and Responses to Trauma: The Role of Emotion Regulation. *Journal Interpersonal Violence*, Epub. Retrieved 2016

Scwebel, D. C., Roth, D. L., Elliott, M. N., Chien, A. T., Mrug, S., Shipp, E., . . . Schuster, M. A. (2012). Marital conflict and fifth-greaters' risk for injury. *Accident Analysis and Prevention, 47*, 30-35.

Seery, M. D. (2011). Traumatic experiences may make you tough. *Association for Psychological Science*.

Segerstrom, S. C. (2005). Optimism and Immunity: Do Positive thoughts always lead to positive effects? *Brain, Behavior, and Immunity, 19*, 195-200. doi:doi:10.1016/j.bbi.2004.08.003

Seligman, M. &. (1986). Explanatory style as a predictor of productivity and quitting among life insurance sales agents. *Journal of Personality and Social Psychology*, 50: 832-838.

Seligman, M. (2011). *Flourish: A Visionary New Understanding of Happiness and Well-Being*. New York: Free Press.

Seligman, M. (n.d.). Berkeley-Oakland Study (ongoing). *Reported by Seligman in Flourish*.

Seligman, M. E. (1992). Power and powerlessness: Comments on "Cognates of personal control". *Applied & Preventive Psychology*, 119-120.

Seligman, M. E. (1992). Power and powerlessness: Comments on "Cognates of Personal Control". *Applied and Presentive Psychology*, 119-120.

Seligman, M. E. (2002). *Authentic Happiness: Using the new positive psychology to realize your potential for lasting fulfillment*. New York: Free Press.

Seligman, M. E. (n.d.). *The Optimistic Child*.

Seligman, M. E., Ernst, R. M., Gillham, J., Reivich, K., & Linkins, M. (2009). Positive education: positive psycyology and classroom interventions. *Oxford Review of Education, 35*(3), 293-311. doi:DOI: 10.1080/03054980902934563

Seligman, M. N.-H. (1990). Explanatory style as a mechanism of disappointing athletic performance. *Psychological Science*, 1:143-146.

Seligman,, M. (2006). *Learned Optimism* (Originally published 1991 ed.). New York: Simon & Schuster.

Shahar, T. B. (2007). *Happier*. New York: McGraw Hill.

Shahba, S. a. (2013). Comparative Study of Problem-solving and Emotional Intelligence on Decreasing of third Grade Girl Students' Aggression of the Rajaee Guidance School of Tehran. *Procedia--Social and Behavioral Sciences, 84*, 778-780. Retrieved 2014

Shahba, S., & Allahvirdiyani , K. (2013). Comparative Study of Problem-solving and Emotional Intelligence on Decreasing of third Grade Girl Students' Aggression of the Rajaee Guidance School of Tehran. *Procedia--Social and Behavioral Sciences, 84*, 778-780. Retrieved 2014

Shalvi, S., Eldar, O., & Bereby-Meyer, Y. (2012). Honesty Requires time (and Lack of Justifications). *psychological Science, 23*(10), 1264-1270. doi:doi: 10.1177/0956797612443835

Shapiro, D. H. (1982). Overview: clinical and psysiological comparison of meditation with other self-control strategies. *American Journal of Psychiatry, 139*, 267-274.

Shapiro, D. H. (1992). Adverse effects of meditation: a preliminary investigation of long-term mediators. *International Journal of Psychosomatics, 39*, 62-67.

Shapiro, M. (2012). *Transforming the Nature of Health: A Holistic Vision of Healthing That Honors Our Connection to the Earth, Others, and Ourselves*. Berkeley: North Atlantic Books.

Shapiro, S. L. (2005). Meditation and positive psychology. In C. R. Snyder (Ed.), *Handbook of Positive Psychology* (pp. pp. 632-645). New York: Oxford University Press.

Sharif, A. (n.d.). *Islamic Thinking Miracle of Positive*. Retrieved from http://alhajsharif.blogspot.com/2013/06/islamic-thinking-miracle-of-positive.html

Sharon, I. (2015, May 24). *Civil servant commits suicide after Facebook accusations of racism*. Retrieved from Times of Israel: http://www.timesofisrael.com/civil-servant-commits-suicide-after-facebook-accusations-of-racism/

Shayan, N., & AhmadiGaab, T. (2012). The effectiveness of social skills training on students' level of happiness. *Procedia - Social and Behavioral Scienes, 46*, 2693-2696.

Shelter, L. (2013, May/June). The Toll of TRAUMA: Addressing Mental Health in Law Enforcement. *National Academy Associate: The Magazine of the FBI National Academy Associates, 15*(3).

Shenk, D. (2010). *The Genius in All of Us*. Doubleday.

Shenk, J. W. (2009, June 1). Writing about the Grant Study. *The Atlantic*. Writing in September 1938 [Arlie] Brock declared that medical research paid too much attention to sick people; that dividing the body up into symptoms and diseases--and viewing it through the lenses of a hundred micro-specialities--could never shed light: on the urgent quesion of how, on the whole, to live well.

Sherman, D. K., Bunyan, D. P., Creswell, J. D., & Jaremka, L. M. (2009). Psychological Vulnerability and Stress: The Effects of Self-Affirmation on. *Health Psychology, 28*(5), 554-562. doi:DOI: 10.1037/a0014663

Sherman, K. J., Cherkin, D. C., Wellman, R. D., Cook, A. J., Hawkes, R. J., Delaney, K., & Deyo, R. A. (2011, December 12). A Randomized Trial Comparing Yoga, Stretching, and a Self-care book for Chronic Low Back Pain. *JAMA Internal Medicine (Formerly Archives of Internal Medicine), 171*(22), 2019-2026. doi:doi:10.1001/archinternmed.2011.524

SHERRILL, B. C. (Composer). (n.d.). Blowin' In The Wind.

Shifrer, D., & Langenkamp, A. (2012). A Mixed methods Study of How Socioeconomic Status is Associated with Adolescents' Sense of Control. *Unbundling Youth, Family, and Community involvement in College Access*, (pp. 0-8). Austin.

Shih, M. P. (1999). Stereotype susceptibility: Identity salience and shifts in quantitative performance. *Psychological Science*, 10: 80-83.

Shinn, F. S. (1941). *The Game of Life and How to Play it*.

Shmotkin, D., & Shrira, A. (2011). Happiness and Suffering in the Life Story: An Inquiry into Conflicting Expectations Concerning the Association of Perceived Past with Present Subjective Well-Being in Old Age. *Journal of Happiness Studies*. doi:DOI 10.1007/s10902-011-9270-x

Siebert, A. (2005). *The Resiliency Advantage: Master Change, Thrive under Pressure, and Bounce Back from Setbacks*. San Francisco: Berrett-Koehler Publishers, Inc.

Siebold, S. (2010). *177 Mental Toughness Secrets of the World Class*. London House.

Siegel, D. (2016, 1 23). *Science Says: Listen to Your Gut*. Retrieved from DrDanSiegel.com: http://www.drdansiegel.com/blog/2016/01/23/sciencesayslistentoyourgut/

Silva, P. J. (2002). Self-Awareness and the Regulation of Emotion Intensity. *Self and Identity, 1*, 3-10.

Simmons, A., & Yoder, L. (2013, January - March). Military Resilience: A Concept Analysis. *Nursing Forum, 48*(1), 17-25.

Simons, D. J. (1999). Gorillas in our midst: Sustained inattentional blindness for dynamic events. *Perception*, 28: 1059-1074.

Simons-Morton, B. G., Crump, A. D., Haynie, D. L., & Saylor, K. E. (1999). Student-school bonding and adolescent problem behavior. *Health Education Research: Theory & Practice*, 99-107.

Simonton, O. C., Simonton, S., & Creighton, J. L. (1978). *Getting well again : a step-by-step, self-help guide to overcoming cancer for patients and their families*. New York: St Martin's Press.

Sinetar, M. (1986). *Ordinary People as Monks and Mystics: Lifestyles for Self-discovery*. Mahwah: Paulist Press. Retrieved 2014

Singh, V. P., Khandelwal, B., & Sherpa, N. T. (2015). Psycho-neuro-endocrine-immune mechanisms of action of yoga in type II diabetes. *Ancient Science of Life, 35*(1), 12-17. doi:10.4103/0257-7941.165623

Sire, J. W. (2009). *The Universe Next Door: A Basic Worldview*.

Skenazy, L. (2014, 5 19). Land of the free, home of the scared: An interview with Lenore Skenazy. (B. Frezza, Interviewer) Forbes.

Slater, M., Rovira, A., Southern, R., Swapp, D., Zhang, J. J., Campbell, C., & Levine, M. (2013). Bystander Responses to a Violent Incident in an Immersive Virtual Environment. *PLoS ONE, 8*(1), EPub.

Slopen, N., Koenen, K. C., & Kubzansky, L. D. (2014). Cumulative Adversity in Childhood and Emergent Risk Factors for Long-Term Health. *The Journal of Pediatrics*, Epub.

Smith, A. (2011, October 25). *Considering the "Cycle of Violence"*. Retrieved November 29, 2015, from Criminology on the Streets: criminologyonthestreets.com

Smith, C. &. (1995). The relationship between childhood maltreatment and adolescent involvement in delinquency. *Criminology, 33(4)*, 451-481.

Smith, R. L., & Rose, A. J. (2011, November). The "Cost of Caring" in Youths' Friendships: Considering Associations Among Social Perspective-Taking, Co-Rumination, and Empathetic Distress. *Developmental Psychology*, 1792-1803.

Snape, M. C. (1997, October). Reactions to a traumatic event: The good, the bad and the ugly? *Psychology, Health & Medicine, Vol. 2(3)*, 237-242.

Sobhi-Gharamaleki, N., & Rajabi, S. (2010). Efficacy of life skills training on increase of mental health and self-esteem of students. *Procedia Social and Behavioral Sciences, 5*, 1818-1822. doi:doi:10.1016/j.sbspro.2010.07.370

Solomon, C. R., & Serres, F. (1999). Effects of Parental Verbal Aggression on Children's Self-esteem and School Marks. *Child Abuse & Neglect, 23*(4), 339-351.

Sood, P., Priyadarshini, S., & Aich, P. (2013). Estimation of Psychological Stress in Humans: A Combination of Theory and Practice. *PLOS One*.

Southwick, S. M., Bonanno, G. A., Masten, A. S., Panter-Brick, C., & Yehuda, R. (2014, July). Resilience definitions, theory, and challenges: interdisciplinary perspectives. *European Journal of Psychotraumatology*, Epub 1-14.

Springer, K. W., Sheridan, J., Kuo, D., & Carnes, M. (2003). The Long-term Health Outcomes of Childhood Abuse: An overview and a Call to Action. *J. Gen Intern Med*, 18(10: 864-870.

St. Augustine (Augustine of Hippo). (MCMLV). *Confessions & Enchiridion*. (A. C. Outler, Trans.) Hippo Regius (now Algeria): Holiness Data Ministry. Retrieved September 24, 2015

Stagman, S., & Cooper, J. L. (2010). *Children's Mental Health: What Every Policymaker Should Know*. Mailman School of Public Health, National Center for Children in Poverty. New York: Columbia University.

Stangier, U. (2016, March). New Developments in Cognitive-Behavioral Therapy for Social Anxiety Disorder. *Current Psychiatry Reports, 18*(3), Epub.

Stathis, P., Smpiliris, M., Konitsiotis, S., & itsikostas, D. D. (2013, November 12). Nocebo as a potential confounding factor in clinical trials for Parkinson's disease treatment: a meta-analysis. *European Journal of Neurology, 20*(3), 527-533. doi:doi: 10.1111/ene.12014

Statistics, C. P.-C. (2012, January). *CDC.gov*. Retrieved 2014, from http://www.cdc.gov/mmwr/preview/mmwrhtml/mm6051a7.htm?s_cid=mm6051a7_w

Staw, B. a. (1993). Affect and managerial performance: A test of teh sadder-but-wiser vs. happier-and-smarter hypothesis. *Administrative Science Quarterly*, 38: 304-31.

Staw, B. S. (1994). Employee positive emotion and favorable outcomes at the workplace. *Organizational Science*, 5: 51-71.

Stefanucci, J. P. (2006). Skating down a steeper slope: Fear influences the perception of geographical slant. *Perception*, 37: 321-323.

Stein, B. G. (1981 (winter)). Attracting Assault: Victims nonverbal cues. *Journal of Communication*.

Steptoe, A. W. (2005). Positive affect and health-related neuroendocrine, cardiovascular, and inflammatory responses. *Proceedings of the National Academy of Sciences*. doi:102:6508-12

Steven R. Gold, B. B. (1999). RISK OF Sexual revictimization: A Theoretical Model. *Aggression and Violent Behavior, Vol. 4, No. 4*, pp. 457–470.

Stickgold, R. M. (2000). Replaying the game: Hypnagogic images in normal and amnesiacs. *Science*, 290: 350-353.

Stock, M. L., Gibbons, F. X., Peterson, L. M., & Gerrard, M. (2013). The Effects of Racial Discrimination on the HIV-Risk Cognitions and Behaviors of Black Adolescents and Young Adults. *Health Psychology, 32*(5), 543-550. doi:DOI: 10.1037/a0028815

Stoeber, J., & Janssen, D. P. (2011). Perfectionism and coping with daily failures: positive framing helps achieve satisfaction at the end of the day. *Anxiety, Stress & Coping*.

Strine, T. W., Mokdad, A. H., Dube, S. R., Balluz, L. S., Gonzalez, O., Berry, J. T., . . . Kroenke, K. (2008). The association of depression and anxiety with obesity and unhealthy behaviors among community-dwelling US Adults. *General Hospital Psychiatry, 30*, 127-137.

Stutzer, A., & Frey, B. S. (2006, April). Does marriage make people happy, or do happy people get married? *The Journal of Socio-Economics, 35*(2), 326-347. doi:doi:10.1016/j.socec.2005.11.043

Suicide Info.CA. (2010). *The Cost of Suicide*. Centre for Suicide Prevention, Calgary. Retrieved from https://suicideinfo.ca/LinkClick.aspx?fileticket=Jz_OfDJ9HUc%3D&tabid=538

suicide, w. o. (n.d.). *Perfectionism + depression = loaded gun quote*. Retrieved from http://www.jhnewsandguide.com/news/top_stories/suicide-numbers-troubling/article_887ec4af-9c9e-550a-acba-3ff69bceb51d.html

Sultan, S., Epel, E., Sachon, C., Vaillant, G., & Hartemann-Heurtier, A. (2008). A longitudinal study of coping, anxiety and glycemic control in adults with type 1 diabetes. *Psychology and Health, 23*(1), 73-89. doi:DOI: 10.1080/14768320701205218

Summerville, A. (2011, November). Counterfactual Seeking: The scenic overlook of the road not taken. *Peraonality and Social Psychological Bulletin, 37*(11), 1522-33. doi:doi: 10.1177/0146167211413295

Sun, R. C., & Shek, D. T. (2012). Beliefs in the Future as a Positive Youth Development Construct: A Conceptual Review. *The Scientific WorldJournal*, Epub, 1 - 8.

Suttie, J. (2008). Minfulness and Meditation in Schools: Mindful Kids, Peaceful Schools. *Greater Good Magazine*.

Swanston, H. Y. (2003). Juvenile crime ,aggression and delinquency after sexual abuse: A longitudinal study. *British Journal of Criminology, 43*, 729-749.

Swanston, H. Y., Swanston, H. Y., Parkinson, P. N., O'Toole, B. I., Plunkett, A. M., Shrimpton, S., & Oates, R. K. (2003). Juvenile crime ,aggression and delinquency after sexual abuse: A longitudinal study. *British Journal of Criminology, 43*, 729-749.

Swencionis, C., Wylie-Rosett, J., Lent, M. R., Ginsberg, M., Cimino, C., Wassertheil-Smoller, S., . . . Segal-Isaacson, C.-J. (2013). Weight Change, Psychological Well-being and vitality in Adults Participating in a Cognitive-Behavioral Weight Loss Program. *Health Psychology, 32*(4), 439-446.

Swencionis, C., Wylie-Rosett, J., Lent, M. R., Ginsberg, M., Cimino, C., Wassertheil-Smoller, S., . . . Segal-Isaacson, C.-J. (2013). Weight Change, Psychological Well-Being, and Vitality in Adults Participating in a Cognitive-Behavioral Weight Loss Program. *Health Psychology, 32*(4), 439-446. doi:DOI: 10.1037/a0029186

Swenson, C. C., & Chaffin, M. (2006). Beyond psychotherapy: Treating abused children by changing their social ecology. *Aggression and Violent Behavior, 11*, 120-137.

Sy, T. C. (2005). The contagious leader: Impact of the leader's mood on the mood of group members, group affective tone, and group process. *Journal of Applied Psychology*, 90:295-305.

T. Bryan Karasu, M. (2012, April 11). *The Mystery of Happiness*. Retrieved 2012, from http://www.psychologytoday.com/blog/the-mystery-happiness/201204/dont-be-afraid-dying

Talbot, M. (1991). *The Holographic Universe.* New York: Harper Collins.

Tammemagi, C. M., Nerenz, D., Neslund-Dudas, C., Feldkamp, C., & Nathanson, D. (2005). Comorbidity and survival disparities among black and white patients with breast cancer. *Journal American Medical Association (JAMA), 294*(14), 1765-72.

Tams, L. (2016, January 8). *Dispelling myths about stress.* Retrieved from Michigan State University Extension: www.msu.edu/news/dispelling_myths_about_stress

Tartakovsky, M. (n.d.). Depression and Anxiety Among College Students. *Psych Central.* Retrieved December 8, 2011, from http://psychcentral.com/llib/2008/depression-and-anxiety-among-college-students/

Taut, D., Renner, B., & Baban, A. (2012). Reappraise the Situation but Express Your Emotions: Impact of Emotion Regulation Strategies on ad libitum Food Intake. *Frontiers in Psychology.*

Tavakoli, M. (2010). A Positive approach to stress, resistance, and organizational Change. *Social and Behavioral Sciences, 5*, 1794-1798. doi:doi:10.1016/j.sbspro.2010.07.366

Team, F. S. (2015, September 24). *Firstsun.com.* Retrieved from http://www.firstsun.com/2015/09/23/leadership-7-inspiring-leadership-lessons-that-shaped-pope-francis-jorge-bergoglio-obtained-some-of-his-greatest-leadership-skills-before-he-became-pope/

Tedeschi, R. G. (2007). Evaluating resource gain: Understanding and misunderstanding posttraumatic growth. *Applied Psychology: An International Reivew,* 56(3): 396-406.

Tedeschi, R. G. (n.d.). *Posttraumatic Growth -- Positive Changes in the Aftermath of Crisis.*

TEDx (Producer). (Dec 18, 2012). *Is there scientific proof we can heal ourselves? Lissa Rankin, MD at TEDxAmericanRiviera* [Motion Picture]. Retrieved from https://www.youtube.com/watch?v=LWQfe__fNbs#t=14

Teo, S. T., Yeung, M., & Chang, E. (2012). Administrative stressors and nursing job outcomes in Australian public and non-profit health care organisations. *Journal of Clinical Nursing,* 1443-1452. doi: doi: 10.1111/j.1365-2702.2011.03871.

Tepper, B. J., Carr, J. C., Breaux, D. M., Geider, S., Hu, C., & Hua, W. (2009). Abusive supervision, intentions to quit, and employees' workplace deviance:A power/dependence analysis. *Organizational Behavior and Human Decision Processes, 109*, 156-167. doi:doi:10.1016/j.obhdp.2009.03.004

Thagard, P., & Aubie, B. (2008). Emotional consciousness: A neural model of how cognitive appraisal and somatic perception interact to produce qualitative experience. *Consciousness and Cognition,* 811-834. doi:doi:10.1016/j.concog.2007.05.014

The American Institute for Cognitive Therapy. (2016). *Warning Signs of Too Much Stress.* Retrieved from cognitivetherapy.com: www.cognitivetherapy.com

(1960). The Dog in the Manger. In A. Fables, *Happy Hours in Storyland* (Vol. II, p. p. 16). New York: The University Society, Inc.

The HeartMath Institute. (2012, November 11). *Coherence.* Retrieved from www.heartmath.com: www.heartmath.com

The Pell Institute for the Study of Opportunity in HIgher Education and PennAHEAD Alliance for Higher Education and Democracy. (2015 Revised Edition). *Indicators of Higher Education Equity in the United States - 45-year Trend Report.* The Pell Instittue.

The term Kobayashi Maru - . (n.d.). Describes a no-win scenario, or, as in this case, a situation where the obvious (and only) solution requries that the problem be redefined. *Star Trek II: The Wrath of Kahn.*

Thomas, W. I., & Thomas, D. S. (1928). *The Child in America: Behavior Problems and Programs.* New York, NY: Plimpton Press.

Thompson, R. D., Delaney, P., Flores, I., & Szigethy, E. (2011, April). Cognitive-Behavioral Therapy for Children with Comorbid Physical Illiness. *Child and Adolescent Psychiatric Clinics of North America, 20*(2), 329-348. doi:doi:10.1016/j.chc.2011.01.013

Thomson, E., & McLanahan, S. S. (2012, September). Reflections on "Family Structure and Child Well-Being: Economic Resources vs. Parental Socialization". *Social Forces, 91*(1), 45–53. doi:doi: 10.1093/sf/sos119

Thurston, R. C., Rewak, M., & Kubzansky, L. D. (2013). An Anxious Heart: Anxiety and the Onset of Cardiovascular Diseases. *Progress in Cardiovascular Diseases,* 524-537.

Timmons, M. (2002). *Moral Theory: An Introduction*. lanham * Boulder * New York * Oxford: Rowman & Littlefield Publishers, Inc.

Torche, F., Warren, J. R., Halpern-Manners, A., & Valenzuela, E. (2012). Panel Conditioning in a Longitudinal Study of Adolescents' Substance Use: Evidence from an Experiment. *Social Forces, 90*(3), 891-918. Retrieved 2014, from http://sf.oxfordjournals.org

Tornblom, A. W., Werbart, A., & Rydelius, P. A. (2013). Shame behind the masks: the parents' perspective on their sons' suicide. *Archieves of Suicide Research, 17*(3), 242-61. doi: doi: 10.1080/13811118.2013.805644

Torrey, M.D., E. F., Zdanowicz, Esq., M. T., Kennard, M.P.A., S. A., Lamb, H. R., Eslinger, D. F., Biasotti, M. C., & Fuller, D. A. (2014). *The Treatment of Persons with Mental Illness in Prisons and Jails: A State Survey*. TACReports.org/greatment-behind-bars: Research from the Treatment Advocacy Center.

Trine, R. W. (1897). *In Tune With The Infinite*. Retrieved from http://newtohoughtlibrary.com/trineRalphWaldo/inTune/#1

Trougakos, J. P., Hideg, I., Cheng, B. H., & Beal, D. J. (2013, March 25). Lunch Breaks Unpacked: The Role of Autonomy as a Moderator of Recovery during Lunch. *Academy of Management Journal, 57*(2), 405-421.

Troy, A. S., Shallcross, A. J., Davis, T. S., & Mauss, I. B. (2013, September 1). History of Mindfulness-Based Cognitive Therapy is Associated with Increased Cognitive Reappraisal Ability. *Mindfulness, 4*(3), 213-222.

Trudel-Fitzgerald, C., Boehm, J. K., Kivimaki, M., & Kubzansky, L. (2014). TAKING THE TENSION OUT OF HYPERTENSION: A PROSPECTIVE STUDY OF PSYCHOLOGICAL WELL BEING AND HYPERTENSION. *Journal of Hypertension*. Retrieved from http://positivehealthresearch.org/research/taking-tension-out-hypertension-prospective-study-psychological-well-being-and-hypertension#sthash.ibuHrQoQ.dpuf

Trunzo, J. J., & Pinto, B. M. (2003). Social Support as a Mediator of Optimism and Distress in Breast Cancer Survivors. *Journal of consulting and Clinical Psychology, 71*(4), 805-811. doi:DOI: 10.1037/0022-006X.71.4.805

Tsuchiya, M., Horn, S., & Ingham, R. (2013, January). Positive changes in Japanese breast cancer survivors: A qualitative study. *Psychology, Health & Medicine*, 107-116. doi:http://dx.doi.org/10.1080/13548506.2012.686620

Tugade, M. M. (2004). Resilient Individuals use positive emotions to bounce back from negative emotional experiences. *Journal of Personality and Social Psychology*, Journal of Personaltiy and Social Psychology.

Turiano, N. A., Pitzer, L., Armour, C., Arlamangla, A., Ryff, C. D., & Mroczek, D. K. (2012). Personality Trait Level and Change as Predictors of Health Outcomes: Findings From a National Study of.). *The Journals of Gerontology, Series B: Psychological Sciences and Social Sciences, 67*, 4-12. doi: doi:10.1093/geronb/gbr072.

Uchino, B. N., Cacioppo, J. T., & Kiecolt-Glaser, J. K. (1996). The Relationship Between Social Support and Physiological Processes: A Review With Emphasis on Underlying mechanisms and Implications for Health. *Psychological Bulletin, 119*, 488-531.

Ullan, A. M., Beler, M. H., Fernandez, E., Lorente, F., Badia, M., & Fernandez, B. (2012). The Effect of a Program to Promote Play to Reduce Children's Post Surgical Pain: With Plush Toys, It Hurts Less. *American Society for Pain Management Nursing, 15*(1), 273-282.

Ullman, H. H. (2006). Child Sexual Abuse, Coping Responses, Self-Blame, Posttraumatic Stress Disorder, and Adult Sexual Revictimization. *Journal of Interpersonal Violence 21: 652*. doi:DOI: 10.1177/0886260506286879

Ungar, M., Ghazinour, M., & Richter, J. (2013). Annual Research Review: What is resilience within the social ecology of human development? *The Journal of Child Psychology and Psychiatry*(54), 348-366.

University of California at Davis. (2016). *Anger_Management.pdf*. Retrieved from http://www.ucdmc.ucdavis.edu/hr/hrdepts/asap/Documents/Anger_Management.pdf

University of Florida Educator's Blog:Behavior Management Resource Guide. (2014, July 14). *Cognitive-behavioral Strategies in the Classroom*. Retrieved from ufl.edu: Cognitive-behavioral Strategies in the Classroom

University, O. S. (2012, May 23). Wearing two different hats. Moral decisions may depend on the situation.

Urban Networks to Increase Thriving Unity through Violence Prevention. (Prevention Institute). *Making the case Fact Sheet: Violence and Health Equity*. Oakland.

Vaillant, G. E. (2012). *Triumphs of Experience: The Men of the Harvard Grant Study*.

Val, E. B. (2006). Posttraumatic growth, positive changes, and negative changes in Madrid residents following the March 11, 2004, Madrid train bombings. *Journal of Loss and Trauma*, 11: 409-424.

van Breda, A. D. (2015). A comparison of youth resilience across seven South African sites. *Child and Family Social Work*, Epub.

van der Werff, S. J., van den Berg, S. M., Pannekoek, J. N., Elzinga, B. M., & van der Wee, N. J. (2013, May). Neuroimaging resilience to stress: a review. (R. Rozeske, Ed.) *frontiers in Behavioral Neuroscience, 7*.

Van Liew, J. R., Christensen, A. J., Howren, M., Bryant, H., Karnell, L., & Funk, G. F. (2014, April). Fear of recurrence impacts health-related quality of life and continued tobacco use in head and neck cancer survivors. *Health Psychology, 33*(4), 373-381.

Vanderhasselt, M.-A., Koster, E. H., Onraedt, T., Bruyneel, L., Goubert, L., & De Raedt, R. (2014). Adaptive cognitive emotion regulation moderates the relationship between dysfunctional attitudes and depressive symptoms during a stressful life period: A prospective study. *Journal of Behavior Therapy and Experimental Psychiatry, 45*, 291-296. doi:http://dx.doi.org/10.1016/j.jbtep.2014.01.003

Vannucci, A., Shomaker, L. B., Field, S. E., Sbrocco, T., Stephens, M., Kozlosky, M., . . . Tanofsky-Kraff, M. (2014). History of Weight Control attempts Among Adolescent Girls with Loss of Control Eating. *Health Psychology, 33*(5), 419-423.

Varker, T., & Devilly, G. J. (2012). An analogue trial of inoculation/resilience training for emergency services personnel: Proof of concept. *Journal of Anxiety Disorders*, pp. 696-701. doi:doi:10.1016/j.janxdis.2012.01.009

Vartanian, L. R., Wharton, C. M., & Green, E. B. (2012). Appearance vs. health motives for exercise and for weight loss. *Psychology of Sport and Exercise, 13*, 251-256.

Vedhara, K., Morris, R. M., Booth, R., Horgan, M., Lawrence, M., & Birchall, N. (2007). Changes in mood predict disease activity and quality of life in patients with psoriasis following emotional disclosure. *Journal of Psychosomatic Research, 62*, 611-619. Retrieved 2015

Veilleux, J. C., Skinner, K. D., Reese, E. D., & Shaver, J. A. (n.d.). *Negative affect intensity influences drinking to cope through facets of emotion dysregulation,*. University of Arkansas.

Virginia Hill Rice, P. R. (2012). Theories of Stress and its Relationship to Health. In *Handbook of Stress, Coping, and Health, Implications for Nursing Research, Theory, and Practice* (Second Edition ed., p. Chapter 2). Save Publication, Inc.

Visser, C. (n.d.). *Coert Visser's Blog*. Retrieved from http://www.solworld.org/: http://www.solworld.org/

Vo, D. X., & Park, M. J. (2008). Stress and Stress Management Among Youth and Young Men. *American Journal of Men's Health, 2*, 352-366.

Voellmin, A., Entringer, S., Moog, N., Wadhwa, P. D., & Buss, C. (2013). Maternal positive affect over the course of pregnancy is associated with the length of gestation and reduced risk of preterm delivery. *Journal of Psychosomatic Research, 75*, 336-340. doi:http://dx.doi.org/10.1016/j.jpsychores.2013.06.031

Vohs, K. (2013). The Poor's Poor Mental Power. *Science*, 969-970.

Vohs, K. D., Schmeichel, B. J., Nelson, N. M., Baumeister, R. F., Twenge, J. M., & Tice, D. M. (2008). Making Choices Impairs Subsequent Self-Control: A Limited-Resource Account of Decision Making, Self-Regulation, and Active Initiative. *Personality Processes and Individual Differences, 94*(5), 883-898.

Von Ah, D., Kang, D.-H., & Carpenter, J. S. (2007). Stress, Optimism,and Social Support: Impact on Immune Responses in Breast Cancer. *Research in Nursing & Health*, 72-83. doi:DOI: 10.1002/nur.20164

Vona-Davis, L., & Rose, D. P. (2009). The influence of socioeconomic disparities on breast cancer tumor biology and prognosis: a review. *Journal of Women's Health*, 883-93. doi:doi: 10.1089/jwh.2008.1127

Voss, R. W. (1997, Summer). Beyond the Telescope of Gender-polemics: Need for a Wide Angle Lens in Pastoral Vision. *The Journal of Pastoral Care, 51*(2).

Vulpe, A., & Dafinoiu, I. (2011). Positive emotions' influence on attitude toward change, creative thinking and their relationship with irrational thinking in Romaian adolescents. *Social and Behavioral Sciences, 30*, 1935-1941.

Wager, T. D. (2007). Placebo effects on human u-opioid activity during pain. *Proceeding of the National Academy of Sciences of the United States of America*, 104: 11056-61.

Wagner, E. F., Myers, M. G., & McIninch, J. L. (1999). STRESS-COPING AND TEMPTATION-COPING As Predictors of Adolescent Substance Use. *Addictive behaviors, 24*(6), 769-779.

Wakslak, C. J., & Trope, Y. (2009). Cognitive consequences of affirming the self: The relationship between. *Journal of Experimental Social Psychology, 45*, 927-932. doi:doi:10.1016/j.jesp.2009.05.002

Walcott-McQuigg, J. A. (2000, January). Psychological factors influencing cardiovascular risk reduction behavior in low and middle income African-American women. *Journal of National Black Nurses Association, 11*(1), 27-35.

Walker, C., & Papadopoulos, L. (Eds.). (2005). *Psychodermatology: The Psychological Impact of Skin Disorders*. Cambridge, UK: Cambridge University Press.

Wallace, T. A., Martin, D. N., & Ambs, S. (2011). Interactions among genes, tumor biology and the environment in cancer health disparities: examining the evidence on a national and global scale. *Carcinogenesis*, 1107-1121. Retrieved from http://www.ncbi.nlm.nih.gov/pmc/articles/PMC3149201/?report=reader#__ffn_sectitle

Walsh, F. (2002). Bouncing forward: Resilience in the aftermath of September 11. *Family Processes*, 41: 34-36.

Walsh, N. D. (2005). *The Complete Conversations with God: an uncommon dialogue*. Charlottesville: Hampton Roads Publishing Company, Inc. and G.P. Putman's Sons by The Penguin Group.

Wang, C., Collet, J. P., & Lau, J. (2004). The effect of Tai Chi on health outcomes in patients with chronic conditions: a systematic review. *Archives of Internal Medicine, 164*(5), 493-501. Retrieved from http://www.ncbi.nlm.nih.gov/pubmedhealth/PMH0021031/

Wang, P. S., Beck, A. L., Berglund, P., McKenas, D. K., Pronk, N. P., Simon, G. E., & Kessler, R. C. (2004, October). Effects of Major Depression. *American Journal of Psychiatry, 161*, 1885-1891.

Wang, Y., Yang, L., & Wang, Y. (2014). Suppression (but not reappraisal) impairs subsequent error detection: an ERP study of emotion regulation's resource-depleting effect. *PLOS One*. doi:doi:10.1371/journal.pone.0096339

Waugh, A., McNay, L., Bewar, B., & McCaig, M. (2013). Supporting the development of interpersonal skills in nursing, in an undergraduate mental health curriculum: Reaching the parts other strategies do not reach through action learning. *Nurse Education Today*, (In Press). Retrieved from http://dx.doi.org/10.1016/j.nedt.2013.10.002

Waugh, A., McNay, L., Dewar, B., & McCaig, M. (2013). Supporting the develop of interpersonal skills in nursing, in an undergraduate mental health curriculum: Reaching the parts other strategies do not reach through action learning. *Nurse Education Today*, xxx-xxx. Retrieved 2014

Waugh, C. E. (2008). Adapting to life's slings and arrows: Individual differences in resilience when recovering from an unanticipated threat. *Journal of Research in Personality*, 42: 1031-46.

Waugh, C. E. (2008). The neural correlatees of trait resilience when anticipating recovery from threat. *Social Cognitive and Affect Neuroscience*, 3: 322-332.

WCVB.com. (n.d.). *50 Famous People who Suffered from Mental Illness*. Retrieved from http://www.wcvb.com/health/14414700: http://www.wcvb.com/health/14414700

Webb, T. L., & Sheeran, P. (2003). Can implementation intentions help to overcome ego-depletion? *Journal of Experimental Social Psychology, 39*, 279-286. doi:doi:10.1016/S0022-1031(02)00527-9

Weijers, D., Jarden, A., Angner, E., Burns, G., Chadwick, E., Jose, P. E., . . . Thin, N. (2013). Review of The Oxford handbook of happiness. (S. A. David, I. Boniwell, & A. C. Ayers, Eds.) *International Journal of Wellbeing, 3*(2), 1097. doi:10.5502/ijw.v3.i2.8

Weil, A. (1983). *Health and Healing: The Philosophy of Integrative Medicine*. Houghton Mifflin Company.

Weinman, J., Ebrecht, M., Scott, S., Walburn, J., & Dyson, M. (2008). Enhanced wound healing after emotional disclosure intervention. *British Journal of Health Psychology, 13*, 95-102. doi:DOI:10.1348/135910707X251207

Weiss, T. (2002). Posttraumatic growth in women with breast cancer and their husbands: An intersubjective validation study. *Journal of Psychosocial Oncology*, Vol. 20(2), 65-80.

Weissman, D. D. (2005). *The Power of Infinite Love & Gratitude: An Evolutionary Journey to Awakening Your Spirit*. Hay House.

Wells, J. (2011). The impact of stress amongst health professionals. *Journal of Mental Health, 20*(2), 111-114. doi:DOI: 10.3109/09638237.2011.556161

West, D. S., DiLillo, V., Bursac, Z., Gore, S. A., & Greene, P. G. (2007). Motivatoinal interviewing improves weight loss in women with type 2 diabetes. *Diabetes Care*, 1081-1087.

West, L. M., Graham, J. R., & Roemer, L. (2013). Functioning in the face of racism: Preliminary findings on the buffering role of values clarification in a Black American sample. *ournal of Contextual Behavioral Science, 2*(1-2), 1-8.

Wethington, E., & Kessler, R. C. (1986). Perceived Support, Received Support, and Adjustment to Stressful Life Events. *Journal of Health and Social Behavior, 27*, 78-89.

White, J. B. (2008). Fail or Flourish? Cognitive appraisal moderates the effect of solo status on performance. *Personalityand Social Psychology Bulletin*.

WHO. (n.d.). Retrieved from World Health Organization: http://www.who.int/mediacentre/factsheets/fs317/en/

Wible, D. P. (2014). Physician Suicide 101 Secrets, Lies, Solutions. Retrieved from http://www.consultantlive.com/articles/physician-suicide-101-secrets-lies-solutions?GUID=&rememberme=1&ts=01112014

Widom, C. S. (1989). The cycle of violence. *Science*, 160-166.

Widom, C. S. (2000). Childhood victimization and the derailment of girls and women to the criminal justice system. (D. M. J. Reno, Ed.) *Research on women and girls in the justice system*, 27-36.

Widows, M. R.-J. (2005). Predictors of Posttraumatic Growth Following Bone Marrow Transplantation. *Cancer Health Psychology*, Vol. 24, No. 3, 266-273.

Wiering, B. M., Albada, A., Bensing, J. M., Ausems, M., & van Dulmen, A. (2013). The influence of dispositional optimism on post-visit anxiety. *Psycho-Oncology, 22*, 2419-2427. doi:DOI: 10.1002/pon.3292

Wiki. (2016). *Jerry Rice*. Retrieved from www.wikipedia.com/jerry_rice: www.wikipedia.com/jerry_rice

Wiki. (2016). *Stanford Marshmallow Experiments*. Retrieved from Wikipedia: https://en.wikipedia.org/wiki/Stanford_marshmallow_experiment

Wiki. (n.d.). *Donner Party*. Retrieved 2015, from https://en.wikipedia.org/wiki/Donner_Party

Wiki. (n.d.). *https://en.wikipedia.org/wiki/Mechanism_(philosophy)*.

Wikipedia. (2016). *Executive Function*. Retrieved from Wikipedia: www.wikipedia.com/Executive_Function

Wikipedia. (2016). *www.Wikipedia.com/co-rumination*.

Wikström, P.-O. H., Tseloni, A., & Karlis, D. (2011, September). Do people comply with the law because they fear getting caught? *European Journal of Criminology, 8*(5), 401-420. doi:10.1177/1477370811416415

Wilkinson, K. (2008). *The Happiness Factor: How to be Happy No Matter What!* Austin: Ovation Books.

Willen, L. (2016, January 11). *Fixing a higher education "caste system" that screams inequality: Help us find answers.* Retrieved from http://hechingerreport.org/: http://hechingerreport.org/

Wilson, J. A., & Zozula, C. (2011). Reconsidering the Project Greenlight Intervention: Why Thinking About Risk Matters. *National Institute of Justice*, Epub.

Wilson, P. A., Stadler, G., Boone, M. R., & Bolger, N. (2014). Fluctuations in depression and well-being are associated with sexual risk episodes among HIV-positive men. *Health Psychology*, 681-5. doi:doi: 10.1037/a0035405

Wimberly, S. R., Carver, C. S., & Antoni, M. H. (2008). Effect of optimism, interpersonal relationships, and distress on psychosexual well-being among women with early stage breast cancer. *Psychology and Health, 23*(1), 57-72. doi:DOI: 10.1080/14768320701204211

Wingo, A. P., Ressler, K. J., & Bradley, B. (2014). Resilience characteristics mitigate tendency for harmful alcohol and illicit drug use in adults wiht a history of childhood abuse: A Cross-sectional study of 2024 inner-city men and women. *Journal of Psychiatric Research*. doi:doi: 10.1016/j.jpsychires.2014.01.007

Winseman, A. L., Clifton, D. O., & Liesveld, C. (2003). *Living Your Strengths.* New York: Gallup Press.

Winter, D. A. (2007). Construing the Construction Processes of Serial Killers and Other Violent Offenders: The Limits of Credulity. *Journal of Constructivist Psychology, 20*, 247-275. doi:DOI: 10.1080/10720530701347902

Wiseman, R. (2003). *The Luck Factor.* New York: Miramax.

Wittayanukorn, S., Qian, J., & Hansen, R. A. (2014). Prevalence of depressive symptoms and predictors of treatment among US adults from 2005 to 2010. *General Hospital Psychiatry*, xxx-xxx (In Press).

Witthöft, M. &. (2013, March). Are media warnings about the adverse health effects of modern life self-fulfilling? An experimental study on idiopathic environmental intolerance attributed to electromagnetic fields (IEI-EMF). *Journal of Psychosomatic Research, Volume 74, Issue 3*, 206-212.

Witthöft, M., & Rubin, J. (2013). Are media warnings about the adverse health effects of modern life self-fulfilling? An experimental study on idiopathic environmental intolerance attributed to electromagnetic fields (IEI-EMF). *Journal of Psychosomatic Research, 74*(3), 206. doi:DOI: 10.1016/j.jpsychores.2012.12.002

Wong, E., Tschan, F., Messerli, L., & Semmer, N. K. (2013). Expressing and Amplifying Positive Emotions Facilitate Goal Attainment in Workplace Interactions. *Frontiers in Psychology*, 188. doi:doi: 10.3389/fpsyg.2013.00188

Wood, J. (2013, 7 14). *Study Finds Gang Members Suffer High Levels of Mental Illness.* Retrieved 7 14, 2013, from Psych Central: Wood, J. (2013). Study Finds Gang Mem bers Suffer High Levels of Mental Illness. Psych Central. Retrieved on July 14, 2013, from

Wood, J. (2013, 7 14). *Study Finds Gang Members Suffer High Levels of Mental Illness.* Retrieved 7 14, 2013, from Psych Central: Wood, J. (2013). Study Finds Gang Members Suffer High Levels of Mental Illness. Psych Central. Retrieved on July 14, 2013, from

Wood, J. V., Perunovic, W. E., & Lee, J. W. (2009). Positive Self-Statements Power for Some, Peril for Others. *Psychological Science, 20*, 860-866. doi:doi: 10.1111/j.1467-9280.2009.02370.x

Worden, J. K., Flynn, B. S., Merrill, D. G., Waller, J. A., & Haugh, L. D. (1989). Preventing Alcohol-imparied driving through community self-regulation. *American Journal of Public Health, 79*(3), 287-290.

World Health Organization (WHO). (2000). *The World Health Organizaation's Information Series on School Health: Skills for Health: Skills-based health education including life skills: An important component of a Child-Friendly/Health-Promoting School.* WHO.

Wrzesniewskji, A. (2003). Finding Positive Meaning in Work. *Positive Organizational Scholarship*.

Wrzesniewskji, A. M. (1997). Jobs, Careers, and Calllings: People's relations to their work. *Journal of Research in Personality*, 31: 21-33.

Wu, G., Feder, A., Cohen, H., Kim, J. J., Calderon, S., Chamey, D. S., & Mathe, A. A. (2013). Understanding Resilience. *Frontiers in Behavioral Neuroscience*, 10. doi:doi: 10.3389/fnbeh.2013.00010

Wu, G., Feder, A., Cohen, H., Kim, J. J., Calderon, S., Chamey, D. S., & Mathe, A. A. (2013). Understanding Resilience. *Frontiers in Behavioral Neuroscience*, 10. doi:doi: 10.3389/fnbeh.2013.00010

Wu, N. S., Schaire, L. C., Dellor, E., & Grella, C. (2010). Childhood trauma and health outcomes in adults with comorbid substance abuse mental health disorders. *Addictive Behaviors, 35*, 68-71.

Yeh, G. Y., Wang, C., Wayne, P. M., & Phillips, R. S. (2008). The effect of tai chi exercise on blood pressure: a systemic review. *Preventative Cardiology, 11*(2).

Zacher, H. (2014). Career adaptability predicts subjective career success above and beyond personality traits and core self-evaluations. *Journal of Vocational Behavior, 84*, 21-30.

Zapf, D. (2002). Emotion work and psychological well-being A review of the literature and some conceptual considerations. *Human Resource Management Review, 12*, 237-268. doi:PII: S1 0 5 3 - 4 8 2 2 (0 2) 0 0048-7

Zawadzki, M. J., Graham, J. E., & Gerin, W. (2013). Ruminatin and Anxiety Mediate the Effect of Loneliness on Mood and sleep Quality in College Students. *Health Psychology, 32*(2), 212-222. doi:DOI: 10.1037/a0029007

Zhuo, X., Zhang, P., & Hoerger, T. J. (2013). Lifetime Direct Medical Costs of Treating Type 2 Diabetes and Diabetic Complications. *American journal of Preventive Medicine*, 253-261.

Zimmer-Gembeck, M. J., & Skinner, E. A. (2014). The Development of Coping: Implications for Psychopathology and Resilience. In D. Cicchetti (Ed.), *Developmental Psychopathology* (Vol. Resubmission #2, pp. 1-117). Oxford, England: Wiley & Sons. Retrieved January 2016

Zuffiano, A., Alessandri, G., Gerbino, M., Kanacri, B. P., Di , Giunta, L., . . . Caprara, G. V. (2013). Academic achievement: The unique contribution of self-efficacy beliefs in self-regulated learning beyond intelligence, personality traits, and self-esteem. *Learning and Individual Differences, 23*, 158-162. doi:doi:10.1016/j.lindif.2012.07.010

Zukav, G. (1989). *The Seat of the Soul.* New York: Fireside.

Zyromski, B., & Joseph, A. E. (n.d.). *Utilizing Cognitive Behavioral Interventions to Positively Impact Achievement in Middle School Students.* Retrieved from http://files.eric.ed.gov/fulltext/EJ894786.pdf

Zysberg, L., & Rubanov, A. (2010). Emotional Intelligence and Emotional Eating Patterns: A New Insight into the Antecedents of Eating Disorders? *Journal of nutrition Education and Behavior, 42*, 345-348.

Citations

[1] (McCraty & Zayas, Intuitive Intelligence, Self-regulation, and Lifting Consciousness, 2014)
[2] (Wu, et al., 2013)
[3] (Hogan, Ph.D., et al., 2003)
[4] (Quigley & Barrett, 2014 (in press))
[5] (Laloyaux, Dessart, Van der Linden, Lernaire, & Laroi, 2016)
[6] (National Center for Chronic Disease Prevention and Health Promotion, 2009)
[7] (Harvey & Delfabbro, 2004)
[8] (Simons-Morton, Crump, Haynie, & Saylor, 1999)
[9] (Harvey & Delfabbro, 2004)
[10] (Harvey & Delfabbro, 2004)
[11] (Ciucci, Baroncelli, Grazzani, Ornaghi, & Caprin, 2016)
[12] (Harvey & Delfabbro, 2004)
[13] (Harvey & Delfabbro, 2004)
[14] (Robert Wood Johnson Foundation, 2015)
[15] (Matthews, 2016)
[16] (Baumeister R. F., Success, 2015)
[17] (Martin & Dahlen, 2005)
[18] (Baumeister R. F., Success, 2015)
[19] (Baumeister R. F., Success, 2015)
[20] (Harvey & Delfabbro, 2004)
[21] (Litt, Stock, & Gibbons, 2015)
[22] (Hounkpatin, Wood, Boyce, & Dunn, 2015)
[23] (Pool & Qualter, 2012)
[24] (Levine, Schmidt, Kang, & Tinti, 2012)
[25] (Compare, Zarbo, Shonin, Van Gordon, & Marconi, 2014)
[26] (Compare, Zarbo, Shonin, Van Gordon, & Marconi, 2014)
[27] (Vaillant, 2012)
[28] (Hopp, Troy, & Mauss, 2011)
[29] (Hopp, Troy, & Mauss, 2011)
[30] (Hopp, Troy, & Mauss, 2011)
[31] (Hu, et al., 2014)
[32] (Troy, Shallcross, Davis, & Mauss, 2013)
[33] (Scoglio, et al., 2015)
[34] (Sbarra, , Smith, & Mehl, 2001)
[35] (Kivetz & Tyler, 2006)
[36] (Cisler & Olatunji, 2012)
[37] (Armstrong, Galligan, & Critchley, Emotional Intelligence and psychological resilience to negative life events, 2011)
[38] (Kobylinska & Karwowska, 2015)
[39] (APA, 2014)
[40] (Murphy, Barch, Pagliaccio, Luby, & Belden, 2015 (in press))
[41] (Kudinova, et al., Differences in emotion modulation using cognitive reappraisal in individuals with and without suicidal ideation: An ERP study, 2015)
[42] (Zyromski & Joseph)
[43] (Ryan & Deci, A Self-Determination Theory Approach to Psychotherapy: The Motivational Basis for Effective Change, 2008)

[44] (Butler, Chapman, Forman, & Beck, 2006)
[45] (Strine, et al., 2008)
[46] (ADAA, 2016)
[47] (Stangier, 2016)
[48] (Koerner, Antony, Young, & McCabe, 2013)
[49] (Hofmann, Asnaani, Vonk, Sawyer, & Fang, 2012)
[50] (Brown A. , 2012)
[51] (Greenberg, Fournier, Sisitsky, Pike, & Kessler, The Economic Burden of Adults with Major Depressive Disorcer in the United States (2005 and 2010), 2015)
[52] (Driessen & Hollon, 2010)
[53] (Bujoreanu, PhD, Benhayon, M.D., PhD, & Szigethy, M.D., PhD, 2011 November)
[54] (Butler, Chapman, Forman, & Beck, 2006)
[55] (Driessen & Hollon, 2010)
[56] (Hofmann, Asnaani, Vonk, Sawyer, & Fang, 2012)
[57] (Rosenberg, 2015)
[58] (Hofmann, Asnaani, Vonk, Sawyer, & Fang, 2012)
[59] (Clark, 2010)
[60] (Riccomini, Bost, Katsiyannis, & Zhang, 2005)
[61] (Rosenberg, 2015)
[62] (Morley, Eccleston, & Williams, 1999)
[63] (Hofmann, Asnaani, Vonk, Sawyer, & Fang, 2012)
[64] (Butler, Chapman, Forman, & Beck, 2006)
[65] (Rosenberg, 2015)
[66] (Lohmann, MS, LPC, 2013)
[67] (American Academy of Pediatrics, 2012)
[68] (Hofmann, Asnaani, Vonk, Sawyer, & Fang, 2012)
[69] (Butler, Chapman, Forman, & Beck, 2006)
[70] (Rosenberg, 2015)
[71] (Driessen & Hollon, 2010)
[72] (McHugh, Hearon, & Otto, 2010)
[73] (McHugh, Hearon, & Otto, 2010)
[74] (Hofmann, Asnaani, Vonk, Sawyer, & Fang, 2012)
[75] (Okunda, Balán , Petry, Oquendo, & Blanco, 2009)
[76] (Okunda, Balán , Petry, Oquendo, & Blanco, 2009)
[77] (Hofmann, Asnaani, Vonk, Sawyer, & Fang, 2012)
[78] (Okunda, Balán , Petry, Oquendo, & Blanco, 2009)
[79] (Hofmann, Asnaani, Vonk, Sawyer, & Fang, 2012)
[80] **(Phillips, et al., 2006)**
[81] (Hofmann, Asnaani, Vonk, Sawyer, & Fang, 2012)
[82] (Butler, Chapman, Forman, & Beck, 2006)
[83] (Hofmann, Asnaani, Vonk, Sawyer, & Fang, 2012)
[84] (Hofmann, Asnaani, Vonk, Sawyer, & Fang, 2012)
[85] (Hofmann, Asnaani, Vonk, Sawyer, & Fang, 2012)
[86] (Murphy, Straebler, Cooper, & Fairburn, 2010)
[87] (Hossain & Shapiro, 2002)
[88] (Hofmann, Asnaani, Vonk, Sawyer, & Fang, 2012)
[89] (Mohd, 2008)
[90] (Mohd, 2008)
[91] (Boehm, 2012)

[92] (Hofmann, Asnaani, Vonk, Sawyer, & Fang, 2012)
[93] (Beck & Fernandez, 1998)
[94] (Hofmann, Asnaani, Vonk, Sawyer, & Fang, 2012)
[95] (Hofmann, Asnaani, Vonk, Sawyer, & Fang, 2012)
[96] (Hofmann, Asnaani, Vonk, Sawyer, & Fang, 2012)
[97] (Salami, 2007)
[98] (Anderson & Taylor, 2011)
[99] (Lansing & Bert, 2014)
[100] (McGregor, et al., 2004)
[101] (Hofmann, Asnaani, Vonk, Sawyer, & Fang, 2012)
[102] (Deechakawan, PhD, RN, Cain, PhD, Jarrett, PhD, RN, Burr, MSEE, PhD, & Heitkemper, PhD, RN, FAAN, 2012)
[103] (Hofmann, Asnaani, Vonk, Sawyer, & Fang, 2012)
[104] (Dissanayake & Bertouch, 2010)
[105] (Hofmann, Asnaani, Vonk, Sawyer, & Fang, 2012)
[106] (Nettles & Balter, 2011)
[107] (Nettles & Balter, 2011)
[108] (Nettles & Balter, 2011)
[109] (Nettles & Balter, 2011)
[110] (Nettles & Balter, 2011)
[111] (Nettles & Balter, 2011)
[112] (Nettles & Balter, 2011)
[113] (Nettles & Balter, 2011)
[114] (Nettles & Balter, 2011)
[115] (Nettles & Balter, 2011)
[116] (Nettles & Balter, 2011)
[117] (Baumeister R. F., Vohs, DeWall, & Zhang, 2007)
[118] (Clore & Palmer, 2009)
[119] (King, McInerney, & Watkins, 2012) (Perez-De-Albeniz & Holmes, 2000)
[120] (Dan-Glauser & Gross, 2013)
[121] (Kwong, Wong, & Tang, 2013)
[122] (Wong, Tschan, Messerli, & Semmer, 2013)
[123] (Peil, 2014)
[124] (Burnette, O'Boyle, VanEpps, Pollack, & Finkel, 2012 (in press))
[125] (Johnson, Bertrand, Fermon, & Foley, 2014)
[126] (Cure Violence, 2015)
[127] (Thomas & Thomas, 1928)
[128] (Visser)
[129] I'm not sure what to call this, perhaps sense of taste. Although I was taught that taste buds are on the tongue, more recent research has demonstrated that taste is a combination of senses, some in the nasal passages, some on the tongue, and some in the intestines, which are combined with other things before our conscious brain recognizes the taste of something.
[130] (Chicago Police Department, 2011)
[131] (Kashdan & Jonathan, 2010) (slight change due to communication/clarification with Dr. Kashdan)
[132] (Hastie, Landsman, & Loftus, 1978-1979)

Jeanine Joy

[133] (Hutchins)
[134] (Davis A., 2005)
[135] (BTO.org)
[136] (Monarch-butterfly.com)
[137] (BTO.org)
[138] (Harman, 1998)
[139] (Frye & Sarter, 2013)
[140] (Marinier III & Laird, 2008)
[141] (Boehm, 2012)
[142] (Benedetti, et al., 2003)
[143] (Petersen, et al., 2014)
[144] (Mitsikostas, Mantonakis, & Charlarakis, 2010)
[145] (Goldstein)
[146] (Goldstein, 1704)
[147] (Haidt, The Happiness Hypothesis: Finding Modern Truth in Ancient Wisdom. Why the Meaningful Life Is Closer Than You Think, 2006)
[148] (Seligman,, 2006)
[149] (Bos, Brummelman, & Terburg, 2015)
[150] (Carucci, 2016)
[151] (Lebrecht, Bar, Feldman, Barrett, & Tarr, 2012)
[152] (Schneider T. R., 2004)
[153] (Lewis, 2011)
[154] (Wikipedia, 2016)
[155] (Shenk D., 2010)
[156] (Maguire, 2000)
[157] (Ricard, 2003)
[158] (Carver, 2015)
[159] (Carver, 2015)
[160] (Peil, 2014)
[161] (Siegel, 2016)
[162] Unpublished manuscript (*Shades of Joy*)
[163] (Baumeister R. F., Vohs, DeWall, & Zhang, 2007)
[164] (Simonton, Simonton, & Creighton, 1978)
[165] This link was referenced in another report citing (Matthews and Glass, 1981). I have been unable to find this research despite several hours of searching. If anyone has access to it, or information about it, I would be most appreciative of receiving an update.
[166] (Barasch & Hirshberg, 1995)
[167] (Tams, 2016)
[168] (Virginia Hill Rice, 2012)
[169] The EGSc is a compilation of similar scales used by a variety of teachers including David Hawkins, L. Ron Hubbard, and Abraham-Hicks. The zones are my addition. The science supporting the Emotional Guidance scale, or that emotions provide guidance, did not exist when the earlier scales were created. All emotions could be placed on the scale. It is simplified to reflect emotions that are similar in degrees of empowerment in each zone.
[170] (Peil, 2014)
[171] (Campbell D. T., 1975)
[172] (Fredrickson, B.L., et al., 2008)
[173] (Lazarus, 1991)
[174] (Fredrickson B. L., The Science of Happiness, 2009)
[175] (Baumeister R. F., Vohs, DeWall, & Zhang, 2007)

[176] (Rubik, Muehsam, Hammerschlag, & Jain, 2015)
[177] (Muehsam & Ventura, 2014)
[178] (Haidt, The Happiness Hypothesis: Finding Modern Truth in Ancient Wisdom. Why the Meaningful Life Is Closer Than You Think, 2006)
[179] (Goldberg, 2002)
[180] (Seligman M. , 2011)
[181] (Rubenstein, 1999)
[182] (Fredrickson B. L., Positivity, 2010)
[183] (Ekmund, 1992)
[184] (Rubenstein, 1999)
[185] (Talbot, 1991)
[186] (Ricard, 2003)
[187] (Eiser & Pahl, 2001)
[188] (Oregon State University , 2012)
[189] (Montgomery, 2012)
[190] (Feldman, Tarr, & Lebrecht, 2012)
[191] (Sbarra, , Smith, & Mehl, 2001)
[192] (Rudy, David III, & Matthews, 2012)
[193] (Allison, Uhles, Asuncion, Beggan, & Mackie, 2006)
[194] (Fredrickson B. L., The Science of Happiness, 2009) (Seligman,, 2006) (Seligman M. , 2011) (Fredrickson, B.L., et al., 2008)
(Achor, 2010)
[195] (Peil, 2012)
[196] (Seligman, 2006)
[197] (Barnica, 2014)
[198] (Barnica, 2014)
[199] (Barnica, 2014)
[200] (Nisbett, 2003)
[201] (Nisbett, 2003)
[202] (Ornstein, 1977)
[203] (Lipton & Bhaerman, 2009)
[204] (Peil, 2014)
[205] (Baumeister R. F., Vohs, DeWall, & Zhang, 2007)
[206] (Ryan & Deci, 2001)
[207] (Ryan & Deci, 2001)
[208] (Correll, Spencer, & Zanna, 2004)
[209] (Schwarz, 1959 (2007))
[210] (Burnette, O'Boyle, VanEpps, Pollack, & Finkel, 2012 (in press))
[211] (Newell & Shanks, 2014)
[212] (King, McInerney, & Watkins, 2012)
[213] (Dhayanandhan & Bohr, 2016)
[214] (APA, 2015)
[215] (Baumesiter, Vohs, & Tice, 2007)
[216] (Hopp, Troy, & Mauss, 2011)
[217] (Baumeister R. F., Success, 2015)

Jeanine Joy

[218] (Wiki, 2016)
[219] (Langer, Ph.D., 2009)
[220] (Diener & Biswas-Diener, 2008)
[221] (Grierson, 2014)
[222] (Langer, Ph.D., 2009)
[223] (Rollin & Atkinson, 2004)
[224] (Nadler, 2011)
[225] (Nadler, 2011)
[226] (Bruce, 2005)
[227] (Goleman, Social Intelligence, 2006)
[228] (Rosenthal & Jacobson, Teachers' Expectancies: Determinants of Pupils' IQ Gains, 1966)
[229] (Chang, 2011)
[230] (Rubie-Davies, Hattie, & Hamilton, 2003)
[231] (Rubie-Davies, Hattie, & Hamilton, 2003)
[232] (Mani, Mullainathan, Shafir, & Zhao, 2013)
[233] (Perrewe & Zellars, 1999)
[234] (Lerner & Keltner, 2000)
[235] (Lazarus R. S., 1993)
[236] (Boehm, 2012)
[237] (Fredrickson B. L., Positivity, 2010)
[238] (Lyubomirsky, King, & Diener, The benefits of frequent positive affect: Does happiness lead to success?, 2005)
[239] (Sharon, 2015)
[240] (Brown & Taylor, 1986)
[241] (Baumeister & Beck, Evil: Inside Human Violence and Cruelty, 1999)
[242] (Morley, Eccleston, & Williams, 1999)
[243] (Beevers & Carver, 2003)
[244] (Lindstrom & Eriksson, 2006)
[245] (Diener & Chan, Happy People Live Longer: Subjective Well-Being Contributes to Health and Longevity, 2011)
[246] (Vaillant, 2012)
[247] (Berry, et al., 2014)
[248] (Berry, et al., 2014)
[249] (Limar, 2011)
[250] (Dossey, M.D., 2013)
[251] (Dossey, M.D., 2013)
[252] (Boehm, 2012)
[253] (Parton, 2016)
[254] (Popp, et al., 1984)
[255] (The HeartMath Institute, 2012)
[256] (Diener & Biswas-Diener, 2008)
[257] (Achor, 2010)
[258] (Ben-Shahar, Happiness 101, 2009)
[259] (Ben-Shahar, Happier, 2007)
[260] (Ashkanasy, 2011)
[261] (Lyubomirsky & Porta, Boosting Happiness and Buttressing Resilience: Results from Cognitive and Behavioral Interventions, (in press))
[262] (Boehm, 2012)
[263] (Boehm, 2012)

[264] (McCarthy & Casey, 2011)
[265] (Lyubomirsky, King, & Diener, The Benefits of Frequent Positive Affect: Does Happiness Lead to Success?, 2005)
[266] (Achor, 2010)
[267] (Christian, Psychoneuroimmunology in pregnancy: Immune pathways linking stress with maternal health, adverse birth outcomes, and fetal development, 2012)
[268] (Latendresse, CNM, PhD, 2009)
[269] (Voellmin, Entringer, Moog, Wadhwa, & Buss, 2013)
[270] Although research has reported this link, they have not been able to explain it. I believe the answer will be found in the connections we form on the quantum level.
[271] (Ozier, et al., 2008)
[272] (Lyubomirsky & Porta, Boosting Happiness and Buttressing Resilience: Results from Cognitive and Behavioral Interventions, (in press))
[273] (Turiano, et al., 2012)
[274] (Dweck C. S., Can Personality Be Changed? The Role of Beliefs in Personality and Change, 2008)
[275] (Boyce, Wood, Daly, & Sedikides, 2015)
[276] (Helson & Kwan, 2002)
[277] (Hounkpatin, Wood, Boyce, & Dunn, 2015)
[278] (Turiano, et al., 2012)
[279] (Weijers, et al., 2013)
[280] (Fredrickson B. L., Positivity, 2010)
[281] (Bandura, 1986)
[282] (Snyder, Hope Theory: Rainbows in the mind, 2002)
[283] (Regional Research Institute for Human Services, 2005)
[284] (Regional Research Institute for Human Services, 2005)
[285] (Regional Research Institute for Human Services, 2005)
[286] (Regional Research Institute for Human Services, 2005)
[287] (Maston, 2001)
[288] (Regional Research Institute for Human Services, 2005)
[289] (Regional Research Institute for Human Services, 2005)
[290] (Weijers, et al., 2013)
[291] (Diener & Biswas-Diener, 2008)
[292] (Achor, 2010)
[293] (Lyubomirsky, King, & Diener, The Benefits of Frequent Positive Affect: Does Happiness Lead to Success?, 2005)
[294] (Fredrickson B. L., 2005)
[295] (Holden R. , BE Happy: Release the Power of Happiness in you, 2009)
[296] (Holden R. , BE Happy: Release the Power of Happiness in you, 2009)
[297] (Beard, 2015)
[298] (Ford, Mauss, & Gruber, 2015)
[299] (Luthans & Youssef, 2007)
[300] (Barry, Grafeman, Adler, & Pickard, 2007)
[301] (Masten & Monn, 2015)
[302] (Emery, Heath, & Mills, 2015)
[303] (Emery, Heath, & Mills, 2015)

[304] (Gist, 1997)
[305] (Hoffman, 2010)
[306] (Mason, et al., 2015)
[307] (van Breda, 2015)
[308] (Sani, Herrera, Wakefield, Boroch, & Gulyas, 2012)
[309] (Deci & Ryan, 2000)
[310] (Deci & Ryan, 2000)
[311] (Infurna & Gerstorf, 2014)
[312] (Buzinski & Price, 2015)
[313] (Buzinski & Price, 2015)
[314] (Buzinski & Price, 2015)
[315] (van Breda, 2015)
[316] (van der Werff, van den Berg, Pannekoek, Elzinga, & van der Wee, 2013)
[317] (van der Werff, van den Berg, Pannekoek, Elzinga, & van der Wee, 2013)
[318] (Wingo, Ressler, & Bradley, 2014)
[319] (Simmons & Yoder, 2013)
[320] (Wingo, Ressler, & Bradley, 2014)
[321] (Wingo, Ressler, & Bradley, 2014)
[322] (Kimhi & Eshel, 2009)
[323] (Kimhi & Eshel, 2009)
[324] (Lyubomirsky & Porta, Boosting Happiness and Buttressing Resilience: Results from Cognitive and Behavioral Interventions, (in press))
[325] (Southwick, Bonanno, Masten, Panter-Brick, & Yehuda, 2014)
[326] (Min, Yu, Lee, & Chae, 2013)
[327] (Wingo, Ressler, & Bradley, 2014)
[328] (Ali, Dwyer, Vanner, & Lopex, 2010)
[329] (Khanlou & Wray, 2014)
[330] (Nearchou, Stogiannidou, & Kiosseoglou, 2014)
[331] (Lee & Stewart, 2013)
[332] (Baratta, Rozeske, & Maier, 2013)
[333] (Kim & Agrusa, 2011)
[334] (Kudinova, et al., 2015)
[335] (Zimmer-Gembeck & Skinner, 2014)
[336] (Kilpatrick, et al., 2013)
[337] (Kilpatrick, et al., 2013)
[338] (Bonanno & Diminich, 2013)
[339] (Fredrickson B. L., Positivity, 2010)
[340] (Shifrer & Langenkamp, 2012)
[341] (Lee, Cheung, & Kwong, 2012)
[342] (van der Werff, van den Berg, Pannekoek, Elzinga, & van der Wee, 2013)
[343] (Wu, et al., 2013)
[344] (Federal Interagency Forum on Child and Family Statistics, 2015)
[345] (Regional Research Institute for Human Services, 2005)
[346] (Wu, et al., 2013)
[347] (Wu, et al., 2013)
[348] (Khanlou & Wray, 2014)
[349] (Benoit, et al., 2015)
[350] (Parashar, 2015)
[351] (Parashar, 2015)

[352] (Dudovitz, Li, & Chung, 2013)
[353] (Dweck C. S., Can Personality Be Changed? The Role of Beliefs in Personality and Change, 2008)
[354] (Sandberg, 2000)
[355] (Leith & Baumeister, 1996)
[356] (Lyubomirsky, King, & Diener, The Benefits of Frequent Positive Affect: Does Happiness Lead to Success?, 2005)
[357] (Fredrickson B. L., Positivity, 2010)
[358] (Carvalho & Nobre, 2012)
[359] (Wiki, 2016)
[360] (Huntjens, Rijkeboer, Krakau, & de Jong, 2014)
[361] (Baumeister R. F., Vohs, DeWall, & Zhang, 2007)
[362] (Wikström, Tseloni, & Karlis, 2011)
[363] (Dan-Glauser & Gross, 2013)
[364] (McCraty & Zayas, Intuitive Intelligence, Self-regulation, and Lifting Consciousness, 2014)
[365] (Baumeister, Gailliot, DeWall, & Oaten, 2006)
[366] (Ou & Reynolds, 2010)
[367] (Allen, 2007)
[368] (McCraty & Zayas, Intuitive Intelligence, Self-regulation, and Lifting Consciousness, 2014)
[369] (Winter, 2007)
[370] (Lyubomirsky, King, & Diener, The Benefits of Frequent Positive Affect: Does Happiness Lead to Success?, 2005)
[371] (Darley & Batson, 1973)
[372] (McCarthy B. a., 2011)
[373] (Wu, et al., Understanding Resilience, 2013)
[374] (Dietze, et al., 2013)
[375] (Bennett, Holloway, & Farrington, 2008)
[376] (Okon-Singer, Hendler, Pessoa, & Shackman, 2015)
[377] (Swanston, et al., 2003)
[378] (Hill & Lapsley, The ups and downs of the moral personality: Why it's not so black and white, 2009)
[379] (Winter, 2007)
[380] (Widom C. S., 1989)
[381] (Smith A., 2011)
[382] (Kliewer, 2015)
[383] (Barn & Tan, 2012)
[384] (Pietrzak & Southwick, 2011)
[385] (Lerner & Keltner, 2000)
[386] (Voss, 1997)
[387] (Pietrzak & Southwick, 2011)
[388] (Haidt, The Happiness Hypothesis: Finding Modern Truth in Ancient Wisdom. Why the Meaningful Life Is Closer Than You Think, 2006)
[389] (Wood J., Study Finds Gang Members Suffer High Levels of Mental Illness, 2013)
[390] (Torrey, M.D., et al., 2014)
[391] (Barn & Tan, 2012)
[392] (Agnew, 1992)
[393] (Garland, et al., 2010)

Jeanine Joy

[394] (Reckenwald, Mancini, & Beauregard, 2013)
[395] (Shahba S. a., 2013)
[396] (Wu, et al., Understanding Resilience, 2013)
[397] (Assagioli, 1965)
[398] (Mansor, Kirmani, Tat, & Azzman, 2012)
[399] (Sun & Shek, 2012)
[400] (Nietzel & Himelein, 1987)
[401] (Gabbidon & Boisvert, 2012)
[402] (Federal Interagency Forum on Child and Family Statistics, 2015)
[403] (de Araujo & Lagos, 2013)
[404] (Krieger, et al., 2008)
[405] (Baumrind, 1960)
[406] (Cheng & Furnham, 2003)
[407] (Baumrind, 1960)
[408] (Baumrind, 1960)
[409] (de Araujo & Lagos, 2013)
[410] (Drago, 2011)
[411] (Thompson, Delaney, Flores, & Szigethy, 2011)
[412] (Mohd, 2008)
[413] (Mohd, 2008)
[414] (Extremera & Rey, 2015)
[415] (Pinquart, 2009)
[416] (Blackborow, et al., 2013)
[417] (Extremera & Rey, 2015)
[418] (Abravanel & Sinha, 2015)
[419] (HeartMath Institute, 2010)
[420] (National Center for Chronic Disease Prevention and Health Promotion, 2009)
[421] (The American Institute for Cognitive Therapy, 2016)
[422] (Beth Israel Deaconess Medical Center, 1989 era)
[423] (Vo & Park, 2008)
[424] (Min, Lee, & Lee, 2013)
[425] (Prevention Institute)
[426] (Riva, Wirth, & Williams, 2011)
[427] (Mohd, 2008)
[428] (McEwen & Stellar, Stress and the individual. Mechanisms leading to disease, 1993)
[429] (McEwen & Stellar, Stress and the individual. Mechanisms leading to disease, 1993)
[430] (Wu, et al., 2013)
[431] (Dockray & Steptoe, 2010)
[432] (Boehm, 2012)
[433] (Junior, Neves, Cipriano, Chiappa, & Borghi-Silva, 2014 In Press)
[434] (Junior, Neves, Cipriano, Chiappa, & Borghi-Silva, 2014 In Press)
[435] (Boehm, 2012)
[436] (Junior, Neves, Cipriano, Chiappa, & Borghi-Silva, 2014 In Press)
[437] (De Neve, Diener, Tay, & Xuereb, 2013)
[438] (Boehm, 2012)
[439] (Cascio, et al., 2015)
[440] (Walcott-McQuigg, 2000)
[441] (Anderson & Taylor, 2011)
[442] (Lloyd, Ph.D., Smith, & Weinger, 2005)

[443] (Cutrona, et al., 2015)
[444] (Lloyd, Ph.D., Smith, & Weinger, 2005)
[445] (de Wit, et al., 2010)
[446] (Strine, et al., 2008)
[447] (de Wit, et al., 2010)
[448] (APA, 2014)
[449] (Salwen J. K., Hymowitz, Vivian, & O'Leary, 2014 (in press))
[450] (Slopen, Koenen, & Kubzansky, 2014)
[451] (de Wit, et al., 2010)
[452] (Andrews, Lowe, & Clair, 2011)
[453] (Laitinen, Ek, & Sovio, 2002)
[454] (Andrews, Lowe, & Clair, 2011)
[455] (Hudson, Puterman, Bibbins-Domingo, Matthews, & Adler, 2013)
[456] (Friborg, et al., 2006)
[457] (Ullan, et al., 2012)
[458] (Vedhara, et al., 2007)
[459] (Fan, Strine, Jiles, & Mokdad, 2008)
[460] (Jung, et al., 2010)
[461] (Kalynchuk, 2010)
[462] (Boardman & Alexander, 2011)
[463] (NAMI - National Alliance for Mental Illness, 2013)
[464] (Stagman & Cooper, 2010)
[465] (Blackborow, et al., 2013)
[466] (Henry, Castellini, Moses, & Scott, 2016)
[467] (Baumann, Kashel, & Kuhl, 2005)
[468] (Cubic, et al., 2012)
[469] (Cohn & Fredrickson, 2010)
[470] (WCVB.com)
[471] (WCVB.com)
[472] (WCVB.com)
[473] (WCVB.com)
[474] (WCVB.com)
[475] (WCVB.com)
[476] (WCVB.com)
[477] (WCVB.com)
[478] (WCVB.com)
[479] (WCVB.com)
[480] (National Alliance on Mental Illness, 2016)
[481] (National Alliance on Mental Illness, 2016)
[482] (National Alliance on Mental Illness, 2016)
[483] (National Alliance on Mental Illness, 2016)
[484] (Goldstein, MD, PhD, 2015)
[485] (Maslow, Dunlap, & Chung, 2015)
[486] (Paulus, Vanwoerden, Norton, & Sharp, 2016)
[487] (Abravanel & Sinha, 2015)

[488] (Seligman M. E., Power and powerlessness: Comments on "Cognates of personal control", 1992)
[489] (Brown A., 2012)
[490] (Gonzalez, Tarraf, Whitfield, & Vega, 2010)
[491] (Ibrahim, Kelly, Adams, & Glazebrook, 2013)
[492] (Ibrahim, Kelly, Adams, & Glazebrook, 2013)
[493] (Strine, et al., 2008)
[494] (De Lissnyder, Koster, Goubert, Onraedt, & Vanderhasselt, 2012)
[495] (De Lissnyder, Koster, Goubert, Onraedt, & Vanderhasselt, 2012)
[496] (Martin & Dahlen, 2005)
[497] (Dweck C. S., Can Personality Be Changed? The Role of Beliefs in Personality and Change, 2008)
[498] (Lopresti, Hood, & Drumond, 2013)
[499] (Greenberg, Fournier, Sisitsky, Pike, & Kessler, The Economic Burden of Adults with Major Depressive Disorcer in the United States (2005 and 2010), 2015)
[500] (Birnbaum, et al., 2010)
[501] (Lépine & Briley, 2011)
[502] (Wang, et al., 2004)
[503] (Lépine & Briley, 2011)
[504] (Strine, et al., 2008)
[505] (ADAA, 2016)
[506] (ADAA, 2016)
[507] (Stangier, 2016)
[508] (Glashouwer, de Jong, & Penninx, 2012)
[509] (Merrifield, Balk, & Moscovitch, 2013)
[510] (Leary, Schreindorfer, & Haupt, 1995)
[511] (Achor & Gielan, Make Yourself Immune to secondhand Stress, 2015)
[512] (Pyszczynski, Greenberg, Solomon, Arndt, & Schimel, 2004)
[513] (Pyszczynski, Greenberg, Solomon, Arndt, & Schimel, 2004)
[514] (Schubert, 2012)
[515] (Malta, McDonald, Hegadoren, Weller, & Tough, 2012)
[516] (APA, 2016)
[517] (Crocker, Social Stigma and Self-Esteem: Situations Construction of Self-Worth, 1999)
[518] (Lowery, Hardin, & Sinclair, 2001)
[519] (Bhatia & Tandon, 2005)
[520] (Ong, Burrow, & Fuller-Rowell, Positive emotions and the social broadening effects of Barack Obama, 2012)
[521] (American Public Health Association (APHA), 2015)
[522] (Slater, et al., 2013)
[523] (Sani, Madhok, Norbury, Dugard, & Wakefield, 2015)
[524] (Sani, Herrera, Wakefield, Boroch, & Gulyas, 2012)
[525] (Sani, Herrera, Wakefield, Boroch, & Gulyas, 2012)
[526] (Sani, Herrera, Wakefield, Boroch, & Gulyas, 2012)
[527] (Lowery, Hardin, & Sinclair, 2001)
[528] (Graham, Calloway, & Roemer, 2015)
[529] (Pool, Wood, & Leck, 1998)
[530] (Pool, Wood, & Leck, 1998)
[531] (Nettles & Balter, 2011)
[532] (Nettles & Balter, 2011)
[533] (Nettles & Balter, 2011)
[534] (Nadal, et al., 2011)
[535] (Graham, Calloway, & Roemer, 2015)

536 (Helm, 2013)
537 (Moroz, 2015)
538 (O'keefe, Wingate, Cole, Hollingsworth , & Tucker , 2015)
539 (Huynh, 2012)
540 (Borders & Liang, 2011)
541 (West, Graham, & Roemer, 2013)
542 (Fortin, 2002)
543 (Robinson-Wood, et al., 2015)
544 (Robinson-Wood, et al., 2015)
545 (Petronella Croisant, Laz, Rahman, & Berenson, 2013)
546 (Leith & Baumeister, 1996)
547 (Hwang, Moser, & Dracup, Knowledge Is Insufficient for Self-Care Among Heart Failure Patients with Psychological Distress, 2014)
548 (Huntjens, Rijkeboer, Krakau, & de Jong, 2014)
549 (Huntjens, Rijkeboer, Krakau, & de Jong, 2014)
550 (Baumeister R. F., Vohs, DeWall, & Zhang, 2007)
551 (Baumesiter, Vohs, & Tice, 2007)
552 (Vohs K. , 2013)
553 (Mani, Mullainathan, Shafir, & Zhao, 2013)
554 (Mani, Mullainathan, Shafir, & Zhao, 2013)
555 (De Lissnyder, Koster, Goubert, Onraedt, & Vanderhasselt, 2012)
556 (World Health Organization (WHO), 2000)
557 (World Health Organization (WHO), 2000)
558 (Asher & Levounis, 2014)
559 (Wingo, Ressler, & Bradley, 2014)
560 (Armeli, O'Hare, Covault, Scott, & Tennen, 2016)
561 (Griffin, Lowe, Acevedo, & Botwin, 2015)
562 (Gist, 1997)
563 (Veilleux, Skinner, Reese, & Shaver)
564 (Veilleux, Skinner, Reese, & Shaver)
565 (Petit, et al., 2015)
566 (Berking, et al., 2011)
567 (Blechert, Goltsche, Herbert, & Wilhelm, 2014)
568 (Zysberg & Rubanov, 2010)
569 (http://www.theawl.com/2014/08/how-much-a-pack-of-cigarettes-costs-state-by-state, 2014)
570 (Goodwin, Pagura, Spiwak, Lemeshow, & Sareen, 2011)
571 (Junior, Neves, Cipriano, Chiappa, & Borghi-Silva, 2014 In Press)
572 (McClave, et al., 2009)
573 (Goodwin, Pagura, Spiwak, Lemeshow, & Sareen, 2011)
574 (Strine, et al., 2008)
575 (Extremera & Rey, 2015)
576 (Bale, 2011)
577 (Marques, et al., 2015)
578 (CDC, 2016)
579 (Childhelp, 2015)

Jeanine Joy

[580] (DuRant, et al., 2000)
[581] (Urban Networks to Increase Thriving Unity through Violence Prevention, Prevention Institute)
[582] (Rosenberg, 2015)
[583] (Rosenberg, 2015)
[584] (DuRant, et al., 2000)
[585] (National Institute of Justice, 2012)
[586] (DuRant, et al., 2000)
[587] (Swanston, et al., 2003)
[588] (Acierno, 1999)
[589] (Chiodo, Wolfe, Crooks, Hughes, & Jaffe, 2009)
[590] (Messman-Moore & Brown, 2004)
[591] (Messman-Moore & Brown, 2004)
[592] (Chiodo, Wolfe, Crooks, Hughes, & Jaffe, 2009)
[593] (Kikue Sakaguchi, 2006)
[594] (Codier & Odell, 2013 (In Press))
[595] (Lloyd, Malek-Ahmadi, Barclay, Fernandez, & Chartrand, 2012)
[596] (Lloyd, Malek-Ahmadi, Barclay, Fernandez, & Chartrand, 2012)
[597] (Lloyd, Malek-Ahmadi, Barclay, Fernandez, & Chartrand, 2012)
[598] (Codier & Odell, 2013 (In Press))
[599] (Gagné & Deci, 2005)
[600] (Gagné & Deci, 2005)
[601] (Graber, Turner, & Madill, 2015)
[602] (Holt-Lunstad, Smith, & Layton, 2010)
[603] (Scwebel, et al., 2012)
[604] (Stutzer & Frey, 2006)
[605] (Vaillant, 2012)
[606] (Danner D. D., 2001)
[607] (Martire & Franks, 2014)
[608] (Sani, Herrera, Wakefield, Boroch, & Gulyas, 2012)
[609] (Martire & Franks, 2014)
[610] (Martire & Franks, 2014)
[611] (Ng, Ntoumanis, & Thorgersen-Ntoumani, 2014)
[612] (APA, 2015)
[613] (Mulford & Giordano, 2008)
[614] (Smith & Rose, 2011)
[615] (Rose, Carlson, & Waller, 2007)
[616] (Wikipedia, 2016)

[618] (Regional Research Institute for Human Services, 2005)
[619] (Regional Research Institute for Human Services, 2005)
[620] (Gagné & Deci, 2005)
[621] (University of Florida Educator's Blog:Behavior Management Resource Guide, 2014)
[622] (Ager, 2013)
[623] (Min, Lee, & Lee, 2013)
[624] (Rosenberg, 2015)
[625] (Rattan, Savani, Chugh, & Dweck, 2015)
[626] (Zuffiano, et al., 2013)
[627] (Weijers, et al., 2013)
[628] (Dalton, Mauté, Jaén, & Wilson, 2013)

[629] (Hoffman, 2010)
[630] (Mason, et al., 2016)
[631] (Codier & Odell, 2013 (In Press))
[632] (Alliance for Excellent Education, 2013)
[633] (Alliance for Excellent Education, 2013)
[634] (Institute of Educational Sciences, 2013)
[635] (Cardichon & Lovell, 2015)
[636] (Willen, 2016)
[637] (The Pell Institute for the Study of Opportunity in HIgher Education and PennAHEAD Alliance for Higher Education and Democracy, 2015 Revised Edition)
[638] (Pew Research Center Social & Demographic Trends, 2014)
[639] (Zacher, 2014)
[640] (Zacher, 2014)
[641] (Zacher, 2014)
[642] (Patchell, 2014)
[643] (Coetzee & Harry, 2014)
[644] (Zacher, 2014)
[645] (Paul & Moser, 2009)
[646] (Paul & Moser, 2009)
[647] (Paul & Moser, 2009)
[648] (Paul & Moser, 2009)
[649] (Paul & Moser, 2009)
[650] (Trougakos, Hideg, Cheng, & Beal, 2013)
[651] (Fagan & Lee, 2012)
[652] (Fagan & Lee, 2012)
[653] (Fagan & Lee, 2012)
[654] (Fagan & Lee, 2012)
[655] (Masten & Monn, 2015)
[656] (Crandall, Ghazarian, Day, & Riley, 2015)
[657] (APA, 2015)
[658] (Hoeve, et al., 2009)
[659] (Hawkins, et al., 2000)
[660] (Hawkins, et al., 2000)
[661] (Simons-Morton, Crump, Haynie, & Saylor, 1999)
[662] (Simons-Morton, Crump, Haynie, & Saylor, 1999)
[663] (Simons-Morton, Crump, Haynie, & Saylor, 1999)
[664] (Ungar, Ghazinour, & Richter, 2013)
[665] (Swenson & Chaffin, 2006)
[666] (Ungar, Ghazinour, & Richter, 2013)
[667] (Jones & Mosher, 2013)
[668] (Garland, et al., 2010)
[669] (Broderick, Trusting One's Emotional Guidance Builds Resilience, 2013)
[670] (Schnall, Roper, & Fessler, Pay It Forward: Elevation Leads to Altruistic Behavior, 2010)
[671] (Ito & Urland, 2003)
[672] (Lyubomirsky, King, & Diener, The benefits of frequent positive affect: Does happiness lead to success?, 2005)

[673] (Boyce, Wood, Daly, & Sedikides, 2015)
[674] (Costa & McCrae, 1988)
[675] (Mroczek & Spiro III, 2007)
[676] (Helson & Kwan, 2002)
[677] (Dweck C. S., Can Personality Be Changed? The Role of Beliefs in Personality and Change, 2008)
[678] (Mroczek & Spiro III, 2007)
[679] (Paulus, Vanwoerden, Norton, & Sharp, 2016)
[680] (APA, 2014)
[681] (Silva, 2002)
[682] (Creswell, et al., 2005)
[683] (Wood, Perunovic, & Lee, 2009)
[684] (Correll, Spencer, & Zanna, 2004)
[685] (Nelson, Fuller, Choi, & Lyubomirsky, 2014)
[686] (McGregor, Haji, & Kang, 2008)
[687] (GradDipClinNsg, Wilkes BSc PhD RN CM MHPEd GradDipEd(Nur, Luke RN BN DipNsg, & George MPH, 2003)
[688] (Hofmann, Asnaani, Vonk, Sawyer, & Fang, 2012)
[689] (Webb & Sheeran, 2003)
[690] (Wilkinson, 2008)
[691] (Winseman, Clifton, & Liesveld, 2003)
[692] (Levine, Linda J.; Lench, Heather C.; Safer, Martin A;, 2009)
[693] (Vohs, et al., 2008)
[694] (Vohs, et al., 2008)
[695] (Wakslak & Trope, 2009)
[696] (Sherman, Bunyan, Creswell, & Jaremka, 2009)
[697] (Peil, 2014)
[698] (Peil, 2014)
[699] (Gable & Harmon-Jones, 2010)
[700] (Fagley, 2012)
[701] (Seligman,, 2006)
[702] (Satinsky, Reece, Dennis, Sanders, & Sardzell, 2012)
[703] (Halliwell, 2013)
[704] I've seen this increase income in < 1 year by 60%. It has to do with both expectation and belief in our self and worthiness.
[705] Childhood Verbal Abuse and Risk for Personality Disorders During Adolescence and Early Adulthood
[706] (Fredrickson B. L., 2005)
[707] (Crocker & Park, 2004)
[708] (Kramer, 2012)
[709] (Crocker & Park, 2004)
[710] (Crocker & Park, 2004)
[711] (Crocker & Park, 2004)
[712] (Crocker & Park, 2004)
[713] (Crocker & Park, 2004)
[714] (DuBois & Flay, 2004)
[715] (DuBois & Flay, 2004)
[716] (DuBois & Flay, 2004)
[717] (Crocker & Park, Reaping the Benefits of Pursuing Self-Esteem Without the Costs? Reply to DuBois and Flay (2004), SHeldon (2004), and Pyszczynski and Cos (2004), 2004)

[718] (Cheng & Furnham, 2003)
[719] (Jordan & Livingstone, 2013)
[720] (Shenk D. , 2010)
[721] (Carroll, Metcalfe, & Gunnell, 2014)
[722] (Colt)
[723] (Singh, Khandelwal, & Sherpa, 2015)
[724] (Robins J. W., et al., 2006)
[725] (Irwin, Olmstead, & Oxman, 2007)
[726] (Council, 2013)
[727] (Lin, Chan, Ng, & Lam, 2007)
[728] (Imanishi, et al., 2007)
[729] (Dennison, 2004)
[730] (Blatt, Sanislow III, Zuroff, & Pilkonis, 1996)
[731] (Weinman, Ebrecht, Scott, Walburn, & Dyson, 2008)
[732] (Kashdan & Jonathan, 2010)
[733] (University of California at Davis, 2016)
[734] (APA, 2013)
[735] (Siebert, 2005)
[736] (APA, 2014)
[737] (Dooley, 2009)
[738] (Holzer, Schanzenbach, Duncan, & Ludwig, 2007)
[739] (Suicide Info.CA, 2010)
[740] (Lynch & Clarke, 2006)
[741] (Greenberg, Fournier, Sisitsky, Pike, & Kessler, 2, 2015)
[742] (Diabetes.org, 2016)
[743] (Kyckelhahn & Martin, 2013)
[744] (Ritter, 2013)
[745] (Goebbels, Lakerveld, Ament, Bot, & Severens, 2012)
[746] (Promising Practices Network, 2003)
[747] (Oishi & Schimmack, 2010)
[748] (Diener & Tay, A Scientific Review of the Remarkable Benefits of Happiness for Successful and Healthy Living, 2012 (draft))
[749] (Norrish, Williams, O'Connor, & Robinson, 2013)
[750] (Khanlou & Wray, 2014)
[751] (Masten & Monn, 2015)
[752] (Wilson & Zozula, 2011)
[753] (Dewa, McDaid, & Ettner, 2007)
[754] (McSpadden, 2016)
[755] (Higginson & Mansell, 2008)
[756] (Johnson, Bertrand, Fermon, & Foley, 2014)
[757] (Wiki)

Jeanine Joy

Notes

Notes: